The SPIRIT®

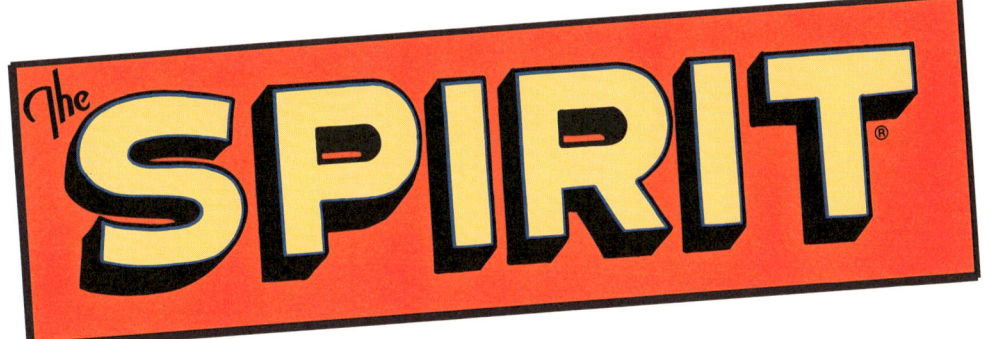

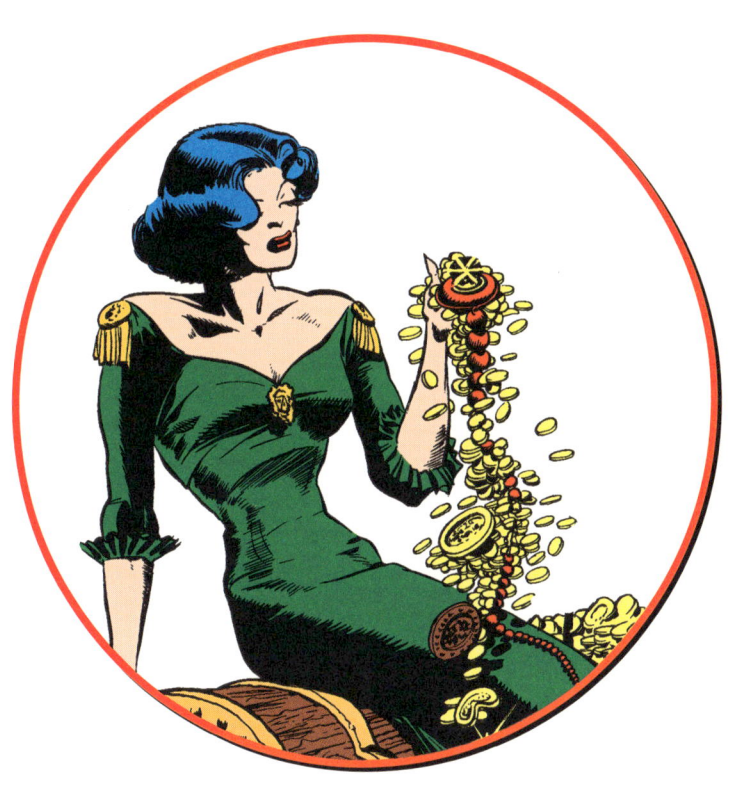

VOLUME -15-

JULY 6 1947 to DECEMBER 28 1947

Denny Colt, a young criminologist,
believed to have lost his life in a fight against crime,
was buried in a state of suspended animation.
He awoke one day in Wildwood Cemetery
to carry on his struggle...his true identity
known only to Police Commissioner Dolan.

**He is feared by criminals
of all stripes as the SPIRIT!**

DC COMICS

New York, New York

WILL EISNER'S

The SPIRIT®

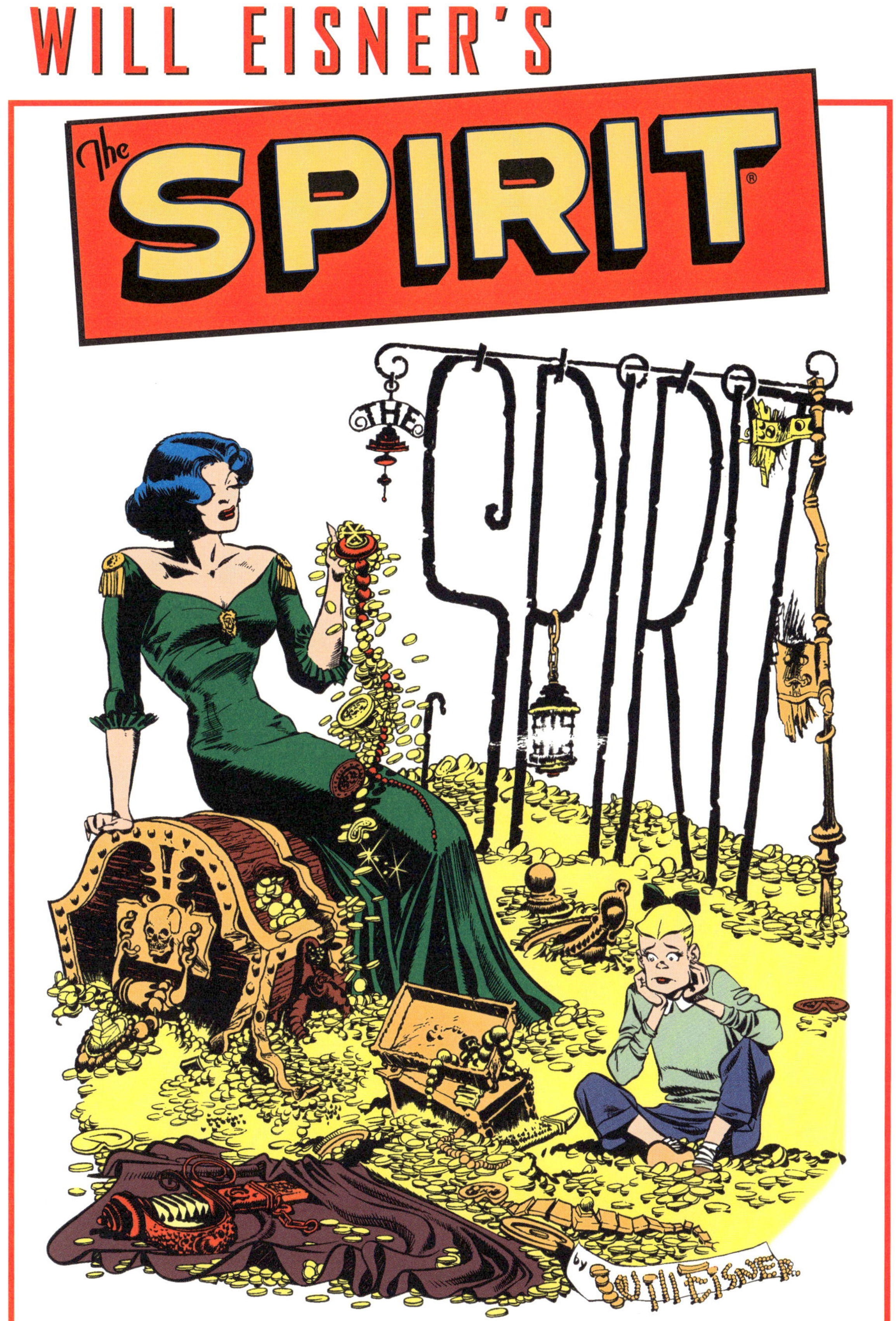
THE
SPIRIT
by
WILL EISNER

ARCHIVES

DC COMICS

DAN DIDIO
VP-Editorial

DALE CRAIN
Senior Editor-Collected Editions

AMIE BROCKWAY-METCALF
Art Director

PAUL LEVITZ
President & Publisher

GEORG BREWER
VP-Design & Retail Product Development

RICHARD BRUNING
Senior VP-Creative Director

PATRICK CALDON
Senior VP-Finance & Operations

CHRIS CARAMALIS
VP-Finance

TERRI CUNNINGHAM
VP-Managing Editor

ALISON GILL
VP-Manufacturing

RICH JOHNSON
VP-Book Trade Sales

HANK KANALZ
VP-General Manager, WildStorm

LILLIAN LASERSON
Senior VP & General Counsel

JIM LEE
Editorial Director-WildStorm

DAVID MCKILLIPS
VP-Advertising & Custom Publishing

JOHN NEE
VP-Business Development

GREGORY NOVECK
Senior VP-Creative Affairs

CHERYL RUBIN
Senior VP-Brand Management

BOB WAYNE
VP-Sales & Marketing

Cover illustration by
WILL EISNER

Cover color by
JAMISON

Special thanks to
BILL BLACKBEARD, *Director of the San Francisco Academy of Comic Art and* **DIAMOND INTERNATIONAL GALLERIES** *for loan of source material, and* **DENIS KITCHEN.**

Throughout the run of The Spirit, Will Eisner was assisted by many talented individuals, among them John Belfi, Phillip (Tex) Blaisdell, Chris Christiansen, Jack Cole, Martin DeMuth, Jim Dixon, Jules Feiffer, Dick French, Lou Fine, Jerry Grandenetti, Abe Kaenegson, Jack Keller, Robin King, Alex Kotzky, Joe Kubert, Andre LeBlanc, Marilyn Mercer, Klaus Nordling, Ben Oda, Bob Palmer, Don Perlin, Bob Powell, Sam Rosen, Aldo Rubano, Sam Schwartz, John Spranger, Manny Stallman, Manly Wade Wellman, Al Wenzel, Wallace Wood, *and* Bill Woolfolk. *The Author and Publisher wish to thank them for their vital contributions.*

WILL EISNER'S THE SPIRIT ARCHIVES VOLUME 15.
Published by DC Comics. Cover, introduction and compilation copyright © 2004 Will Eisner.
Originally published as individual weekly comic sections, Copyright 1947 by Will Eisner. All Rights Reserved.

The SPIRIT, images of Denny Colt, Commissioner Dolan, and Ebony are registered trademarks owned by Will Eisner. The stories, characters and incidents featured in this publication are entirely fictional.
DC Comics does not read or accept unsolicited submissions of ideas, stories or artwork.
DC Comics, 1700 Broadway, New York, NY 10019.
A Warner Bros. Entertainment Company
Printed and bound in China.
ISBN 1-4012-0162-8. First Printing.

WILL EISNER'S THE SPIRIT ARCHIVES
volume fifteen

INTRODUCTION *by N. C. Christopher Couch* 7

Strip #	Title	Page Number
371	**WANTED**	11
	Original publication date: July 6 1947	
372	**THE SPIRIT'S FAVORITE FAIRY TALES FOR JUVENILE DELINQUENTS: HANZEL UND GRETEL**	18
	Original publication date: July 13 1947	
373	**LI'L ADAM**	25
	Original publication date: July 20 1947	
374	**THE LAMP**	32
	Original publication date: July 27 1947	
375	**COMPETITION**	39
	Original publication date: August 3 1947	
376	**SIGN OF THE OCTOPUS**	46
	Original publication date: August 10 1947	
377	**THE PICNIC**	53
	Original publication date: August 17 1947	
378	**SHOWDOWN WITH THE OCTOPUS**	60
	Original publication date: August 24 1947	
379	**BLIND**	67
	Original publication date: August 31 1947	
380	**A KILLER AT LARGE**	74
	Original publication date: September 7 1947	
381	**INTO THE LIGHT**	81
	Original publication date: September 14 1947	
382	**END OF THE S.S. RAVEN**	88
	Original publication date: September 21 1947	
383	**U.F.O.**	95
	Original publication date: September 28 1947	
384	**THE SPIRIT'S FAVORITE FAIRY TALES FOR JUVENILE DELINQUENTS: CINDERELLA**	102
	Original publication date: October 5 1947	
385	**MR. McDOOL**	109
	Original publication date: October 12 1947	

386 **DOPPELGANGER** **116**
Original publication date: October 19 1947

387 **THE HALLOWE'EN SPIRIT OF 1947:**
THE BURNING OF P.S. 43 .... **123**
Original publication date: October 26 1947

388 **THE CRIMINAL** **130**
Original publication date: November 2 1947

389 **MR. BOWSER'S ELECTION** **137**
Original publication date: November 9 1947

390 **THE FIGHTING MACHINE** **144**
Original publication date: November 16 1947

391 **MONEY, MONEY** **151**
Original publication date: November 23 1947

392 **SLIPPERY EALL** **158**
Original publication date: November 30 1947

393 **DEATH OF HUGO** **165**
Original publication date: December 7 1947

394 **SNOW** **172**
Original publication date: December 14 1947

395 **THE CHRISTMAS SPIRIT OF 1947: JOY** **179**
Original publication date: December 21 1947

396 **UMBRELLA HANDLES** **186**
Original publication date: December 28 1947

INTRODUCTION

"HE WAS MEANT TO BE A PERMANENT VILLAIN, LIKE HOLMES'S MORIARTY, A VILLAIN WHO WOULD RETURN AGAIN AND AGAIN."
—WILL EISNER, DESCRIBING THE OCTOPUS

Humor and sadness. Violence and tranquility. Darkness and light. Artist and businessman. There's never been a creator in comics who has embraced and embodied opposites in his work and his career with as much vigor and gusto as Eisner. Like the paired masks of comedy and tragedy that symbolize the theater, or the pairing of opposites that underlies structuralist paradigms, Eisner is a creator who effortlessly moves from one artistic pole to another.

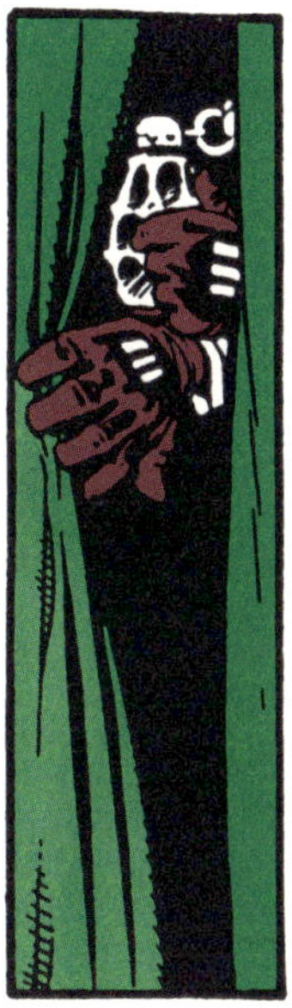

In the latter half of 1947, according to Spirit historian Dave Schreiner, Eisner was in the middle of a "home run barrage" of innovative and diverse Spirit tales when he created the stories in this volume. During the war, THE SPIRIT had become a rather repetitive detective adventure strip in the hands of Eisner's appointed caretakers. When Eisner returned, one of his tasks was to expand the strip to encompass multiple genres again. Eisner's inaugural story on his return was a "Christmas Spirit," the first seasonal tale in THE SPIRIT since he had been drafted.

Although superheroes dominated American comic books from the birth of Superman in 1938, one of the riches of the medium in this country was its diversity of genres. Comic books were the cousins of the pulp magazines — those sprawling, oversized anthologies of short stories, novelettes and serialized novels printed on the cheapest grades of paper that would hold ink—which were the cradle of modern mystery, horror, science-fiction and detective literature. These same types of stories were found in the comics pages of the newspapers that included the SPIRIT section, but only Eisner brought all the genres of comics and pulps into a *single* strip. This is one of the most innovative characteristics of Eisner's postwar SPIRIT, a high-water mark of American comics.

Eisner was a voracious reader of all types of literature, including pulps and novels and short stories by popular and literary authors. Although he would later create one of the most aesthetically successful science-fiction

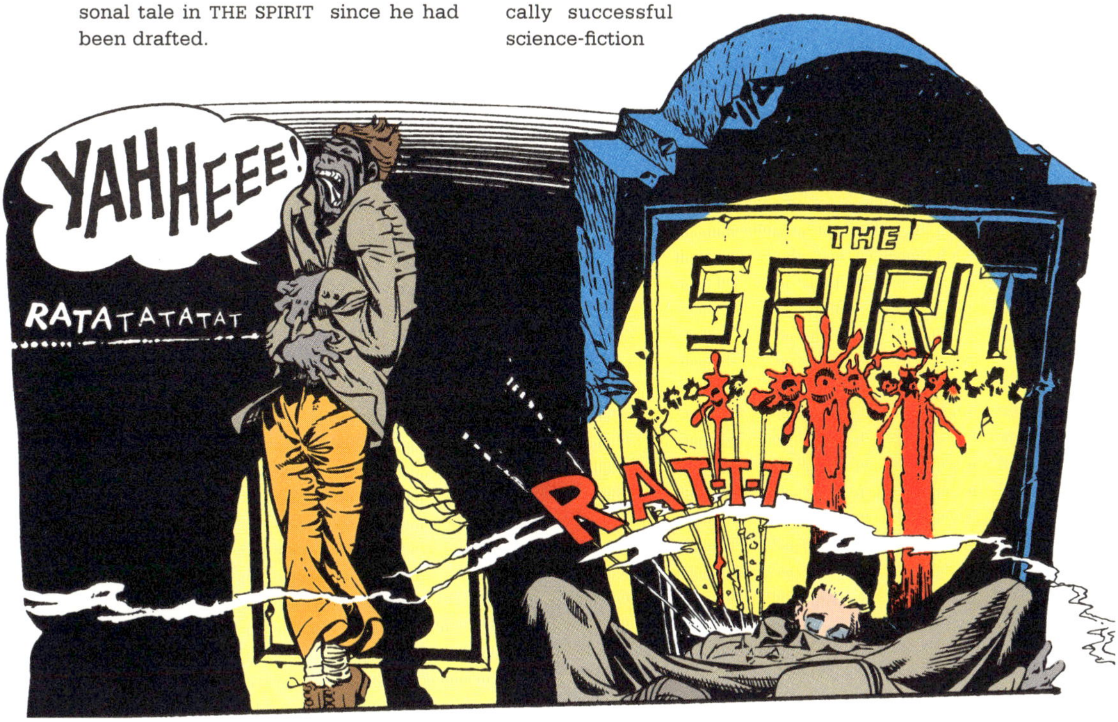
YAHHEEE!
RATATATATAT
THE SPIRIT
RAT-T-T

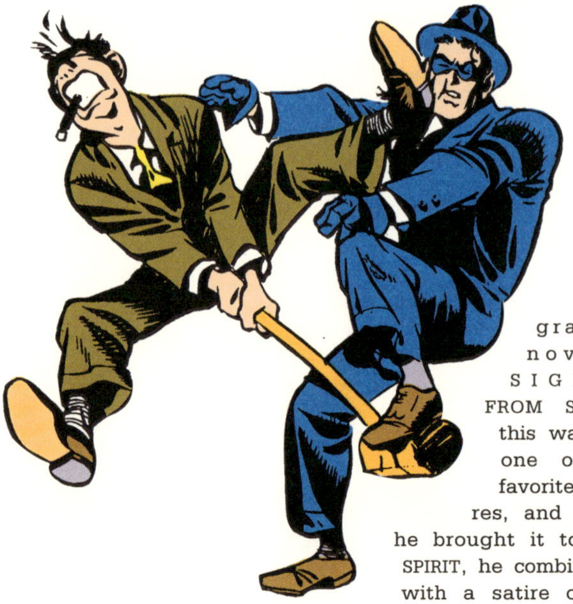

graphic novels, SIGNAL FROM SPACE, this was not one of his favorite genres, and when he brought it to THE SPIRIT, he combined it with a satire of the actor and auteur Orson Welles. Taking off from Welles's famous Mercury Theater radio drama of a Martian invasion, Eisner created Awsome Bells, a corpulent actor so egomaniacal that a Martian is unable to take him prisoner. He simply won't believe the invader is for real. Eisner added one more element to the complicated mix of this story (which already combined media satire and SF): an event from current headlines, appropriate for a comic book in the newspaper. In July 1947, reports of a crashed flying saucer in Roswell, New Mexico, had added UFO to popular language.

One of Eisner's best-known media satires focused solely on the world of comic strips, and involved some skillful manipulation by the creator of Li'l Abner, Al Capp. Lauded in its day by luminaries like John Steinbeck, Abner is today perhaps best remembered for spawning Sadie Hawkins Day, when the gals can ask out the guys, and the movie version of the Broadway play. But Abner was as big as strips got in the 1940s, its hillbilly characters and storylines widely appreciated as some of the best political satire of the day. Capp was a media celebrity. That didn't stop him from exploiting his connections to get even more publicity, using Eisner as his pawn. In spring 1947, Capp called Eisner to suggest they have a fake feud, each satirizing the other's creations in their strips. Eisner leaped at the chance, and was working on the section that roasted "Li'l Adam, the Stupid Mountain Boy" when Newsweek called, asking to do an article on him. Naturally, the Capp satire was featured in the article. But no satire of the *Spirit* ever showed up in *Abner*. "He had euchered me into doing a parody of *Li'l Abner* which *Newsweek* picked up, and he had been given a run of publicity. I was being used as a tool," Eisner explained to Schreiner when Kitchen Sink Press reprinted *Li'l Adam*.

Capp had nothing to do with the story, which skewers not only *Abner*, but *Little Orphan Annie* and *Dick Tracy* as well. "That was all mine," notes Eisner. One of the suspects in the murder of *Adam* creator Al Slapp is the cartoonist of *Nick Stacy,* angered by *Fearful Fooznick,* a strip-within-a-strip satire of his detective. This references Capp's real *Tracy* satire, *Fearless Fosdick,* Li'l Abner's favorite strip. Movie and comic satires in the SPIRIT certainly paved the way for the later success of similar stories in MAD Magazine, but Eisner refuses to take credit for leading the way. "Harvey Kurtzman and I both read the same humor magazines. They were excellent and had huge circulations, magazines like *Judge, Life* and *Ballyhoo*. Their satires inspired both of us."

Light satires on the popular arts of the day were balanced in the postwar SPIRIT by darker crime stories, especially those featuring Eisner's new

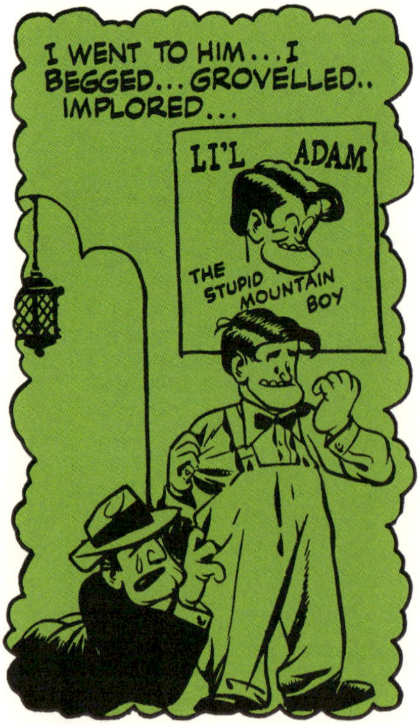
I WENT TO HIM...I BEGGED...GROVELLED.. IMPLORED...
LI'L ADAM
THE STUPID MOUNTAIN BOY

villain, the Octopus. In the postwar SPIRIT, Eisner worked hard to flesh out an ensemble cast of characters, including newcomers like eager patrolman Sam Klink, the Scots insurance inspector, Mr. McDool, and the evil Octopus. He did this in part to help create continuity, a necessary ingredient for a newspaper strip, where last week's comics sell this week's paper. Eisner as businessman always had an eye on the newspaper editors, who wanted continuity, while as artist he envisioned possibilities.

Continuity? He'll show you continuity. Eisner created two linked three-story arcs, each one alternating dark, light and dark again in tone and design, a symphony in comics (8/10 to 9/14). In the stunning opening sequence, the Spirit is brutally beaten by the Octopus and his psychopathic thug. In the second story, the Spirit's gang goes on a picnic in the country, while in the third an explosion apparently kills the Octopus and injures the Spirit. In the second three-story movement, the Spirit discovers he's blind, solves a comic-relief shaggy-dog story of a crime, and then regains his sight with Dr. Silken Floss's help. At its climax, the story-arc symphony returns to the dark dominant note of the opening violence, but the darkness lifts, moving "into the light" seen through the Spirit's recovering eyes.

The Octopus is one of the most elegant and symbolically resonant of Eisner's postwar characters. Never seen except for his purple gloves, the Octopus is not an ex-Nazi, but an international criminal mastermind who flourished in the brutal and evil societies created in Europe under the Nazis. Popular fiction after World War II featured many ex-SS officers or Nazi officials as villains. Eisner's Octopus was spawned by a pervasive but little-recognized Nazi evil, corruption of entire societies, and symbolizes the persistence of that corruption after the war.

By showing only his gloves, Eisner set himself an aesthetic challenge that he met with spectacular chiaroscuro fight scenes. Eisner's hero also wears gloves, and hides his face as well, behind a mask. It's well known that Eisner never wanted the mask, but it was there, and it plays a role in this pairing of opposites. When Eisner created a villain who also hides his face, the two antagonists are linked in a way that shows that good and evil are hard to separate in a complex world.

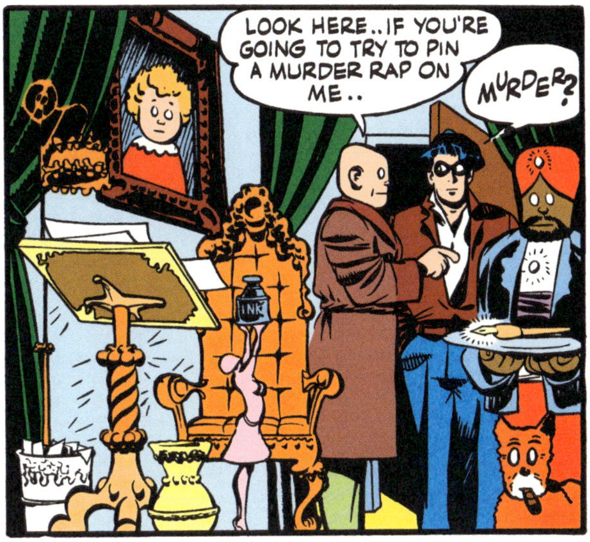
LOOK HERE..IF YOU'RE GOING TO TRY TO PIN A MURDER RAP ON ME..
MURDER?
INK

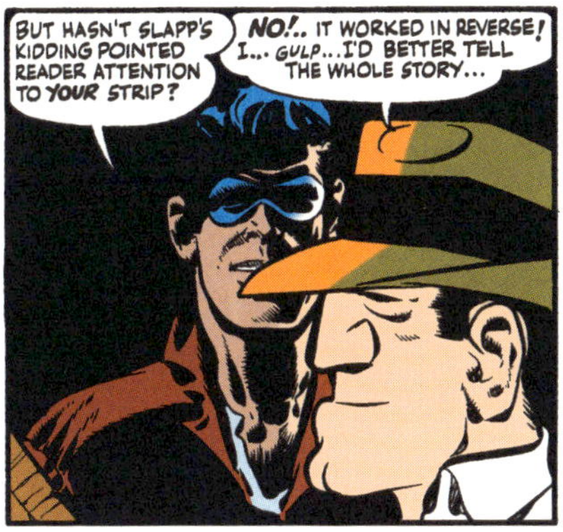
BUT HASN'T SLAPP'S KIDDING POINTED READER ATTENTION TO YOUR STRIP?
NO!.. IT WORKED IN REVERSE! I... GULP...I'D BETTER TELL THE WHOLE STORY...

— N. C. Christopher Couch

Couch is the author of The Will Eisner Companion, *with Stephen Weiner, published by DC Comics. He holds a Ph.D. in art history from Columbia University, and has published many articles and books on Latin American art and comics. He was senior editor at Kitchen Sink Press, and teaches the history of comics at the University of Massachusetts at Amherst and the School of Visual Arts, New York.*

COMIC BOOK SECTION

WANTED

July 6 1947

ACTION Mystery ADVENTURE

WANTED

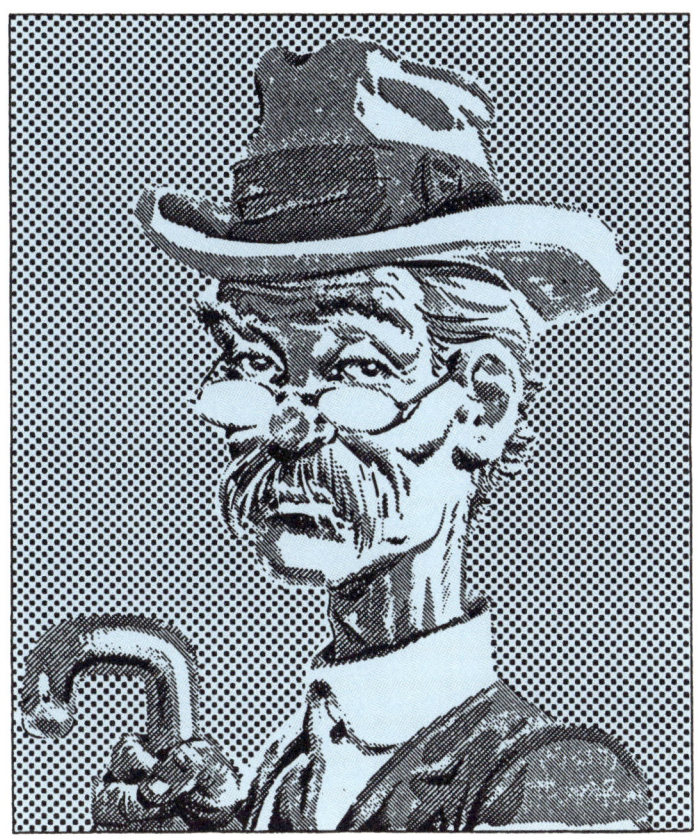

(MORTIMER J. TITMOUSE, 5 FT. 5½ INCHES TALL, OF SLIGHT BUILD, LIGHT HAIR, NEARSIGHTED, NERVOUS TWITCH OF RIGHT EYE (BOTH EYES ARE GREY)

WE ARE EMPLOYING OUR SPACE THIS WEEK FOR THE BENEFIT OF THIS CIVILIZATION WHICH, IN OUR OWN OPINION, IS CERTAINLY *DOOMED* UNLESS THIS MAN IS FOUND AT ONCE!

(ANY INFORMATION LEADING TO THE ARREST OF MR. TITMOUSE SHOULD BE COMMUNICATED AT ONCE TO COMMISSIONER DOLAN. POLICE HEADQUARTERS, CENTRAL CITY, OR THE SPIRIT

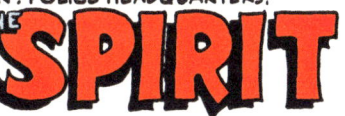

By Will Eisner

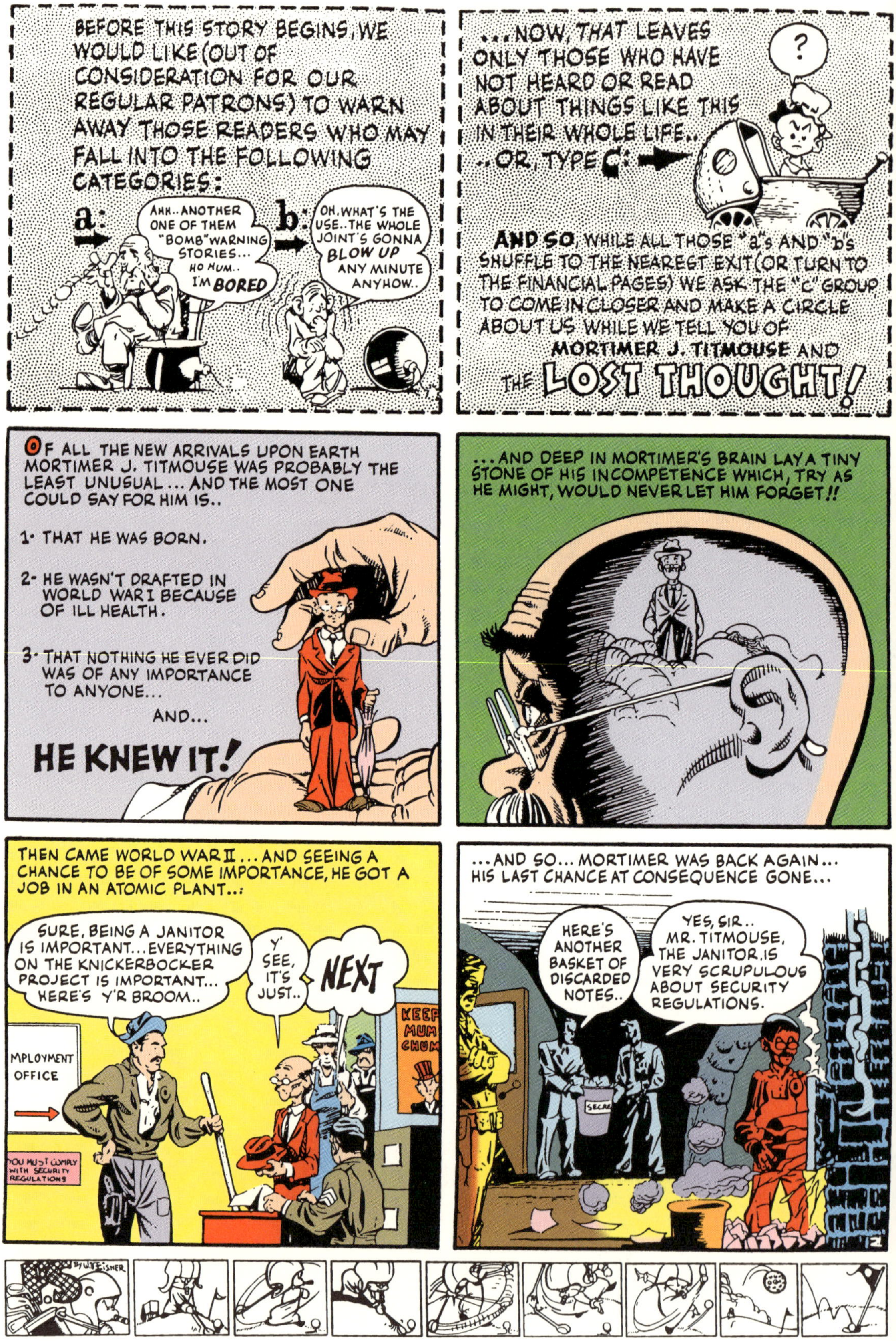

BEFORE THIS STORY BEGINS, WE WOULD LIKE (OUT OF CONSIDERATION FOR OUR REGULAR PATRONS) TO WARN AWAY THOSE READERS WHO MAY FALL INTO THE FOLLOWING CATEGORIES:
a:
AHH.. ANOTHER ONE OF THEM "BOMB" WARNING STORIES... HO HUM.. I'M BORED
b:
OH, WHAT'S THE USE.. THE WHOLE JOINT'S GONNA BLOW UP ANY MINUTE ANYHOW..
...NOW, THAT LEAVES ONLY THOSE WHO HAVE NOT HEARD OR READ ABOUT THINGS LIKE THIS IN THEIR WHOLE LIFE.. ..OR, TYPE C:
?
AND SO, WHILE ALL THOSE "a"s AND "b"s SHUFFLE TO THE NEAREST EXIT (OR TURN TO THE FINANCIAL PAGES) WE ASK THE "c" GROUP TO COME IN CLOSER AND MAKE A CIRCLE ABOUT US WHILE WE TELL YOU OF
MORTIMER J. TITMOUSE AND
THE LOST THOUGHT!
OF ALL THE NEW ARRIVALS UPON EARTH MORTIMER J. TITMOUSE WAS PROBABLY THE LEAST UNUSUAL... AND THE MOST ONE COULD SAY FOR HIM IS..
1- THAT HE WAS BORN.
2- HE WASN'T DRAFTED IN WORLD WAR I BECAUSE OF ILL HEALTH.
3- THAT NOTHING HE EVER DID WAS OF ANY IMPORTANCE TO ANYONE...
AND...
HE KNEW IT!
...AND DEEP IN MORTIMER'S BRAIN LAY A TINY STONE OF HIS INCOMPETENCE WHICH, TRY AS HE MIGHT, WOULD NEVER LET HIM FORGET!!
THEN CAME WORLD WAR II... AND SEEING A CHANCE TO BE OF SOME IMPORTANCE, HE GOT A JOB IN AN ATOMIC PLANT..:
SURE, BEING A JANITOR IS IMPORTANT... EVERYTHING ON THE KNICKERBOCKER PROJECT IS IMPORTANT... HERE'S Y'R BROOM..
Y' SEE, IT'S JUST..
NEXT
MPLOYMENT OFFICE
OU MUST COMPLY WITH SECURITY REGULATIONS
KEEP MUM CHUM
...AND SO... MORTIMER WAS BACK AGAIN... HIS LAST CHANCE AT CONSEQUENCE GONE...
HERE'S ANOTHER BASKET OF DISCARDED NOTES..
YES, SIR.. MR. TITMOUSE, THE JANITOR, IS VERY SCRUPULOUS ABOUT SECURITY REGULATIONS.
SECRE
2

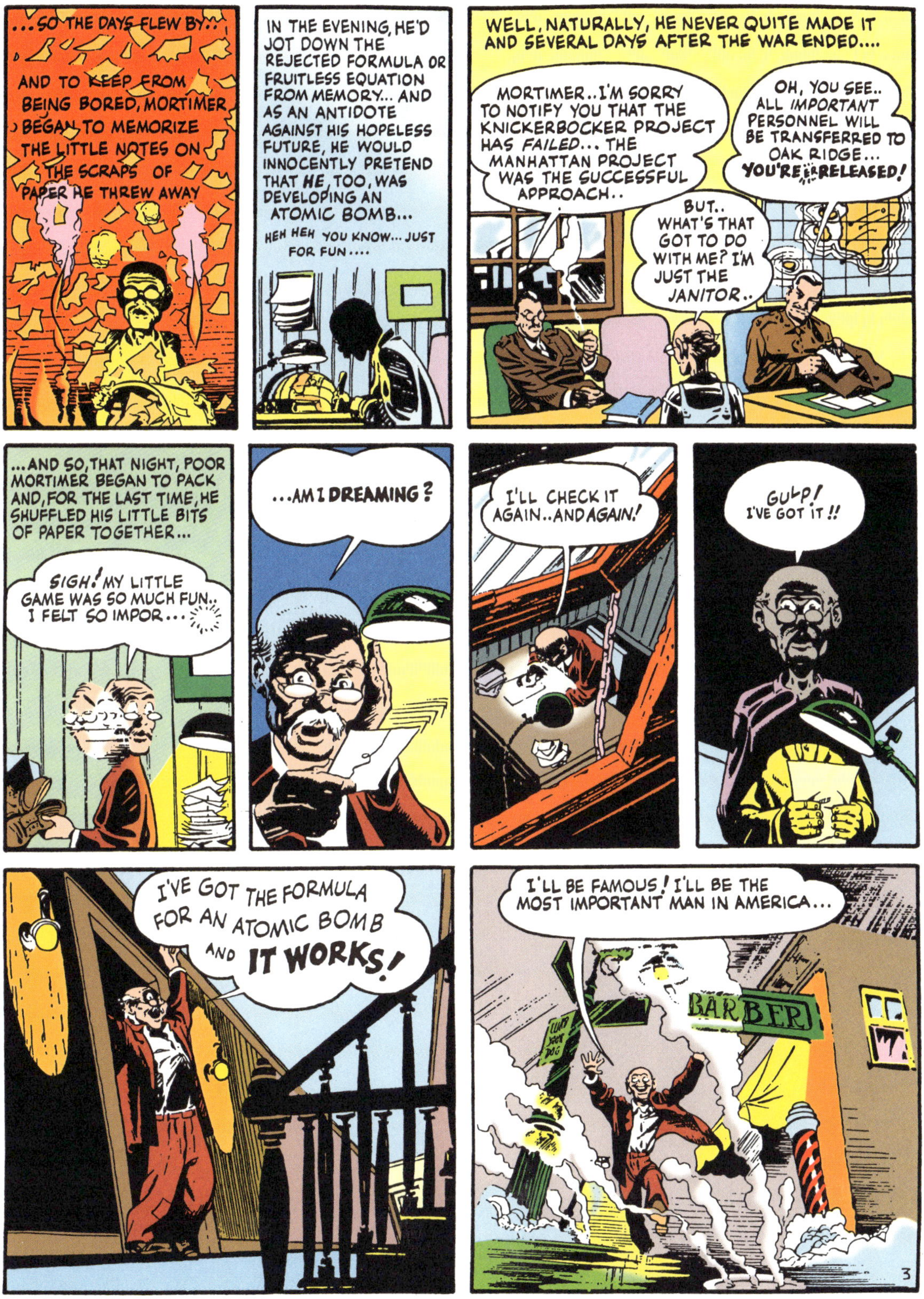
...SO THE DAYS FLEW BY...
AND TO KEEP FROM BEING BORED, MORTIMER BEGAN TO MEMORIZE THE LITTLE NOTES ON THE SCRAPS OF PAPER HE THREW AWAY
IN THE EVENING, HE'D JOT DOWN THE REJECTED FORMULA OR FRUITLESS EQUATION FROM MEMORY... AND AS AN ANTIDOTE AGAINST HIS HOPELESS FUTURE, HE WOULD INNOCENTLY PRETEND THAT HE, TOO, WAS DEVELOPING AN ATOMIC BOMB...
HEH HEH YOU KNOW... JUST FOR FUN....
WELL, NATURALLY, HE NEVER QUITE MADE IT AND SEVERAL DAYS AFTER THE WAR ENDED....
MORTIMER..I'M SORRY TO NOTIFY YOU THAT THE KNICKERBOCKER PROJECT HAS FAILED... THE MANHATTAN PROJECT WAS THE SUCCESSFUL APPROACH..
BUT.. WHAT'S THAT GOT TO DO WITH ME? I'M JUST THE JANITOR..
OH, YOU SEE.. ALL IMPORTANT PERSONNEL WILL BE TRANSFERRED TO OAK RIDGE... YOU'RE RELEASED!
...AND SO, THAT NIGHT, POOR MORTIMER BEGAN TO PACK AND, FOR THE LAST TIME, HE SHUFFLED HIS LITTLE BITS OF PAPER TOGETHER...
SIGH! MY LITTLE GAME WAS SO MUCH FUN.. I FELT SO IMPOR...
...AM I DREAMING?
I'LL CHECK IT AGAIN..AND AGAIN!
GULP! I'VE GOT IT!!
I'VE GOT THE FORMULA FOR AN ATOMIC BOMB AND IT WORKS!
I'LL BE FAMOUS! I'LL BE THE MOST IMPORTANT MAN IN AMERICA...
BARBER
3

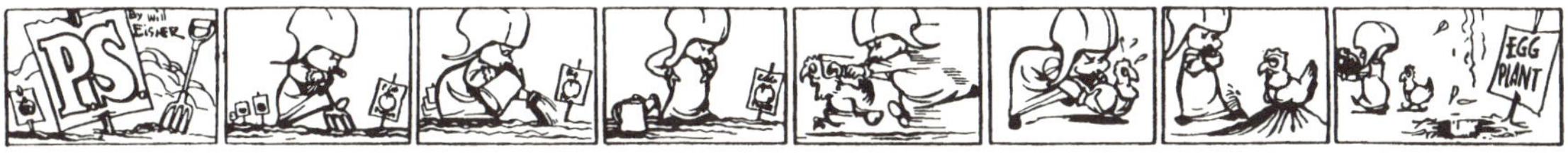
P.S.
By Will Eisner
EGG PLANT

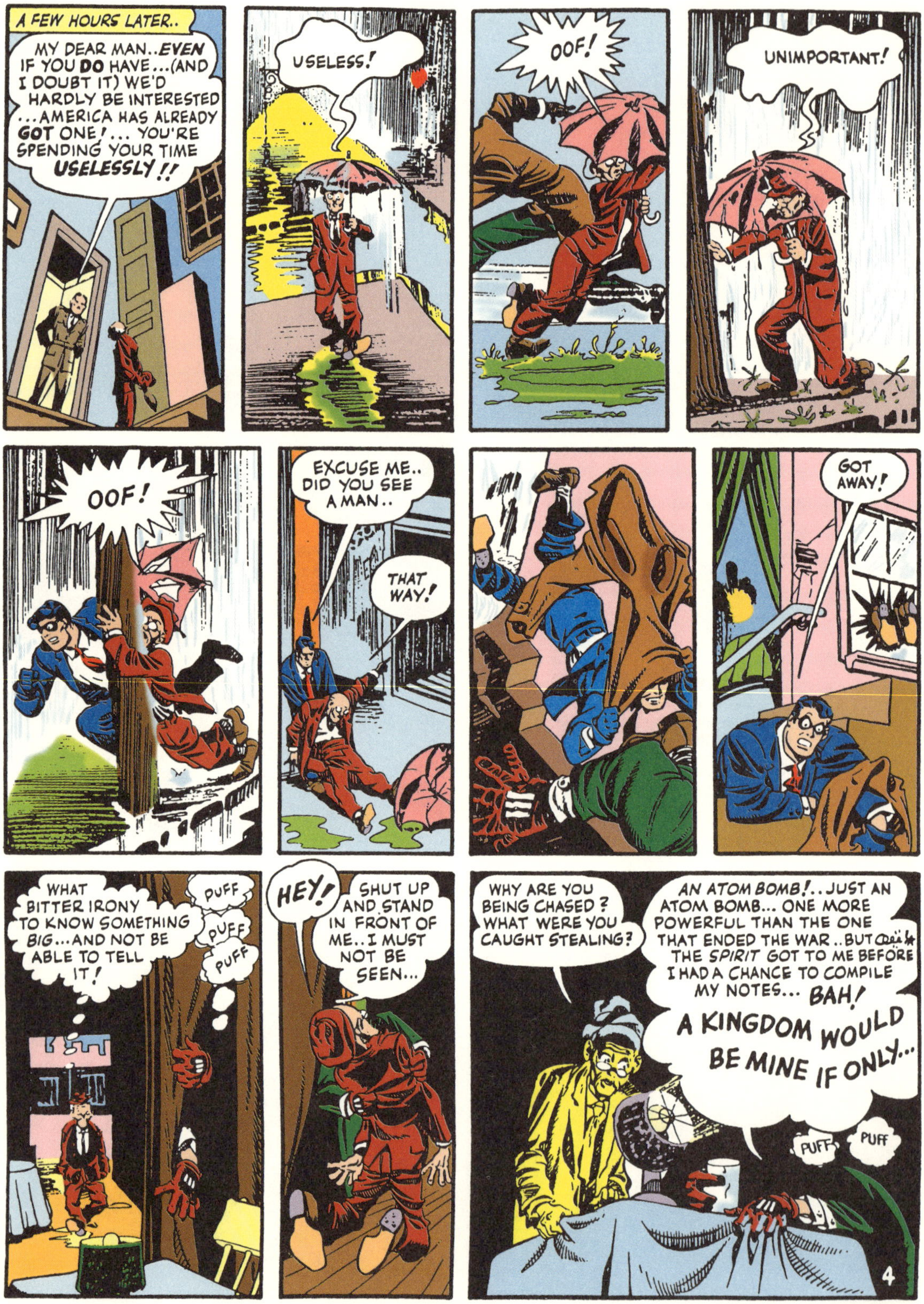
A FEW HOURS LATER..
MY DEAR MAN..EVEN IF YOU DO HAVE...(AND I DOUBT IT) WE'D HARDLY BE INTERESTED ...AMERICA HAS ALREADY GOT ONE!... YOU'RE SPENDING YOUR TIME USELESSLY!!
USELESS!
OOF!
UNIMPORTANT!
OOF!
EXCUSE ME.. DID YOU SEE A MAN..
THAT WAY!
GOT AWAY!
WHAT BITTER IRONY TO KNOW SOMETHING BIG...AND NOT BE ABLE TO TELL IT!
PUFF
PUFF
PUFF
HEY!
SHUT UP AND STAND IN FRONT OF ME..I MUST NOT BE SEEN...
WHY ARE YOU BEING CHASED? WHAT WERE YOU CAUGHT STEALING?
AN ATOM BOMB!..JUST AN ATOM BOMB... ONE MORE POWERFUL THAN THE ONE THAT ENDED THE WAR..BUT THE SPIRIT GOT TO ME BEFORE I HAD A CHANCE TO COMPILE MY NOTES... BAH!
A KINGDOM WOULD BE MINE IF ONLY...
PUFF
PUFF
4

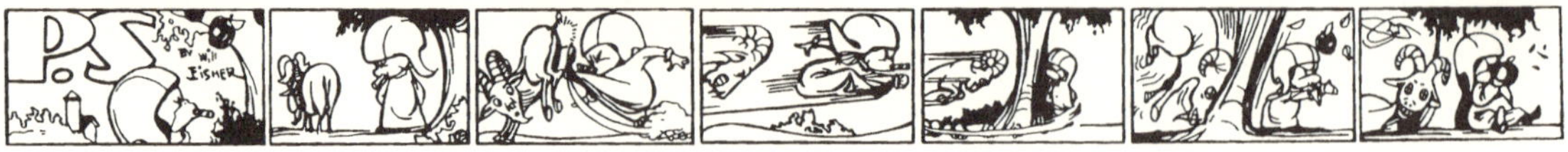
P.S.
BY WILL EISNER

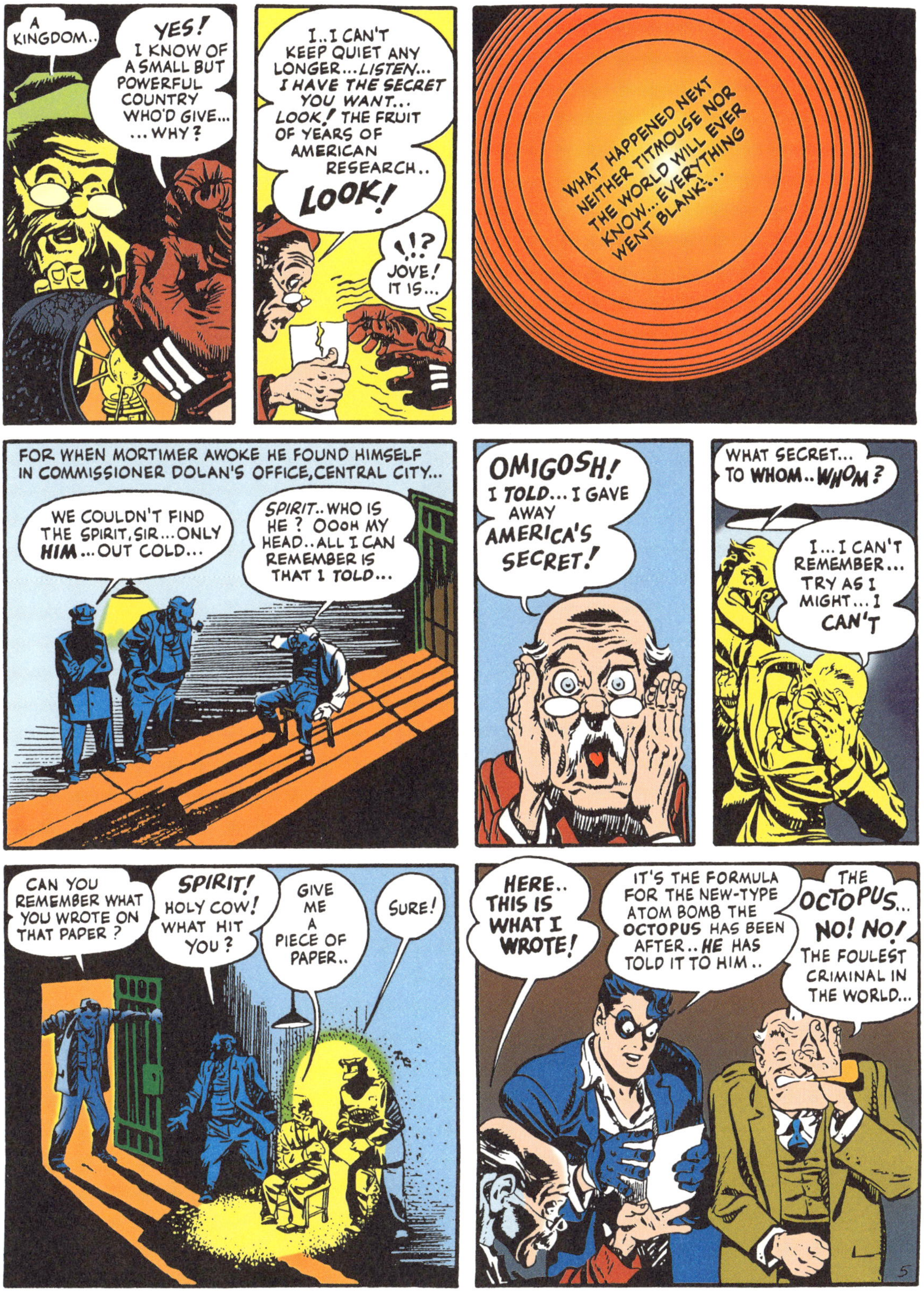
A KINGDOM..
YES! I KNOW OF A SMALL BUT POWERFUL COUNTRY WHO'D GIVE... ...WHY?
I..I CAN'T KEEP QUIET ANY LONGER...LISTEN... I HAVE THE SECRET YOU WANT... LOOK! THE FRUIT OF YEARS OF AMERICAN RESEARCH..
LOOK!
!!? JOVE! IT IS...
WHAT HAPPENED NEXT NEITHER TITMOUSE NOR THE WORLD WILL EVER KNOW...EVERYTHING WENT BLANK...
FOR WHEN MORTIMER AWOKE HE FOUND HIMSELF IN COMMISSIONER DOLAN'S OFFICE, CENTRAL CITY...
WE COULDN'T FIND THE SPIRIT, SIR...ONLY HIM...OUT COLD...
SPIRIT..WHO IS HE? OOOH MY HEAD..ALL I CAN REMEMBER IS THAT I TOLD...
OMIGOSH! I TOLD...I GAVE AWAY AMERICA'S SECRET!
WHAT SECRET... TO WHOM..WHOM?
I...I CAN'T REMEMBER... TRY AS I MIGHT...I CAN'T
CAN YOU REMEMBER WHAT YOU WROTE ON THAT PAPER?
SPIRIT! HOLY COW! WHAT HIT YOU?
GIVE ME A PIECE OF PAPER..
SURE!
HERE.. THIS IS WHAT I WROTE!
IT'S THE FORMULA FOR THE NEW-TYPE ATOM BOMB THE OCTOPUS HAS BEEN AFTER..HE HAS TOLD IT TO HIM..
THE OCTOPUS... NO! NO! THE FOULEST CRIMINAL IN THE WORLD...
5

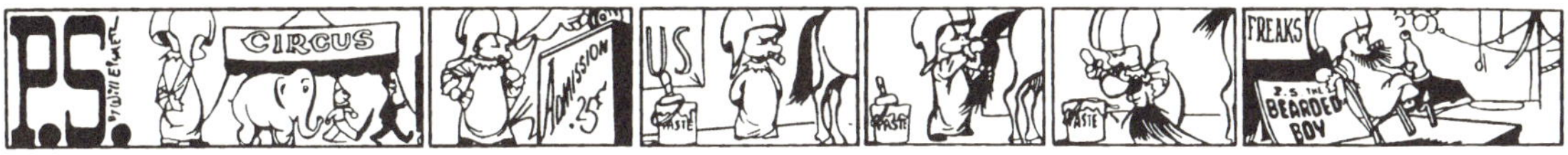
P.S.
CIRCUS
ADMISSION 25¢
FREAKS
BEARDED BOY

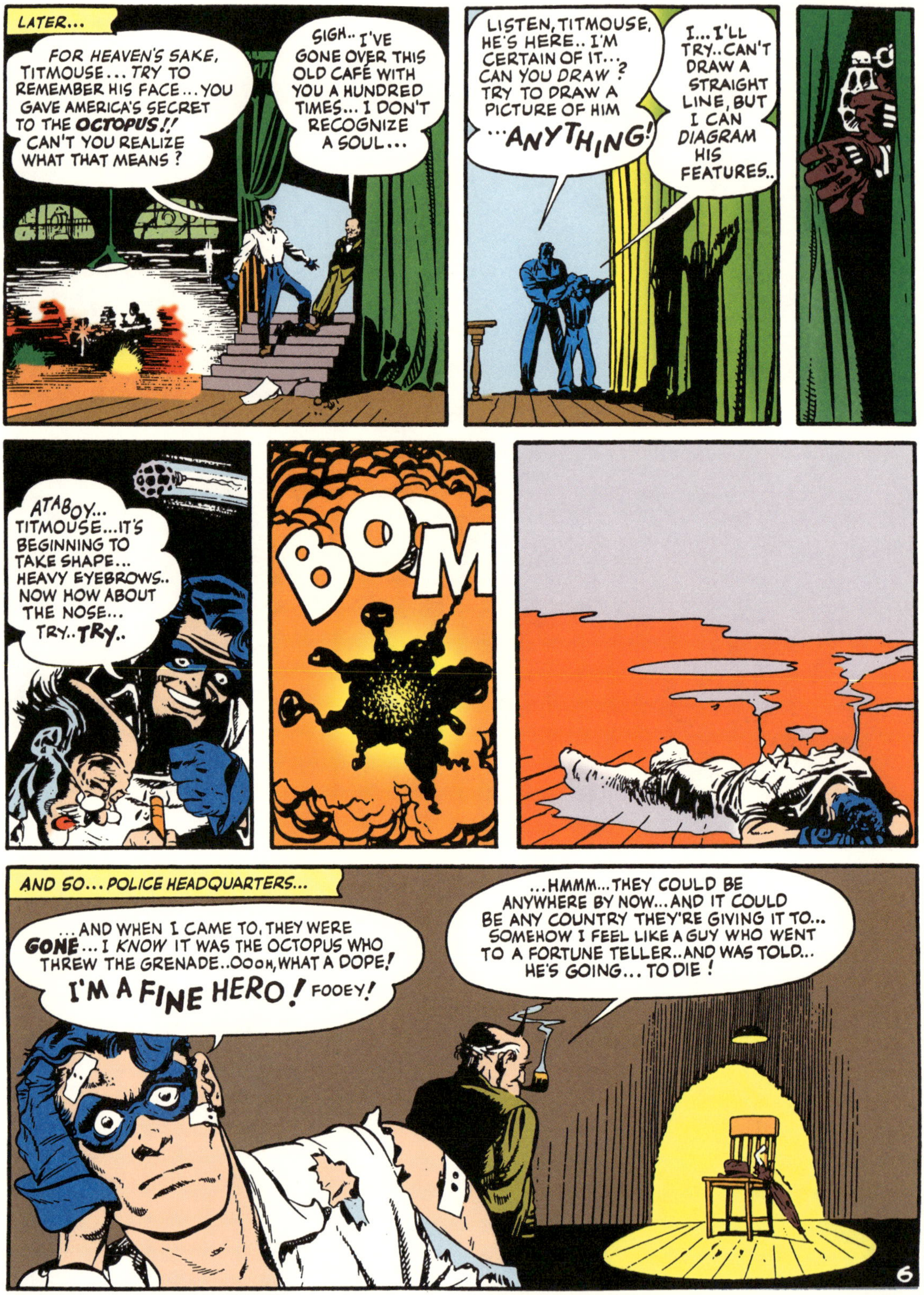
LATER...
FOR HEAVEN'S SAKE, TITMOUSE... TRY TO REMEMBER HIS FACE... YOU GAVE AMERICA'S SECRET TO THE OCTOPUS!! CAN'T YOU REALIZE WHAT THAT MEANS ?
SIGH.. I'VE GONE OVER THIS OLD CAFÉ WITH YOU A HUNDRED TIMES... I DON'T RECOGNIZE A SOUL...
LISTEN, TITMOUSE, HE'S HERE.. I'M CERTAIN OF IT... CAN YOU DRAW ? TRY TO DRAW A PICTURE OF HIM ...ANYTHING!
I... I'LL TRY.. CAN'T DRAW A STRAIGHT LINE, BUT I CAN DIAGRAM HIS FEATURES..
ATABOY... TITMOUSE...IT'S BEGINNING TO TAKE SHAPE... HEAVY EYEBROWS.. NOW HOW ABOUT THE NOSE... TRY.. TRY..
BOOM
AND SO... POLICE HEADQUARTERS...
...AND WHEN I CAME TO, THEY WERE GONE... I KNOW IT WAS THE OCTOPUS WHO THREW THE GRENADE..OOOH, WHAT A DOPE! I'M A FINE HERO! FOOEY!
...HMMM...THEY COULD BE ANYWHERE BY NOW...AND IT COULD BE ANY COUNTRY THEY'RE GIVING IT TO... SOMEHOW I FEEL LIKE A GUY WHO WENT TO A FORTUNE TELLER..AND WAS TOLD... HE'S GOING... TO DIE !
6

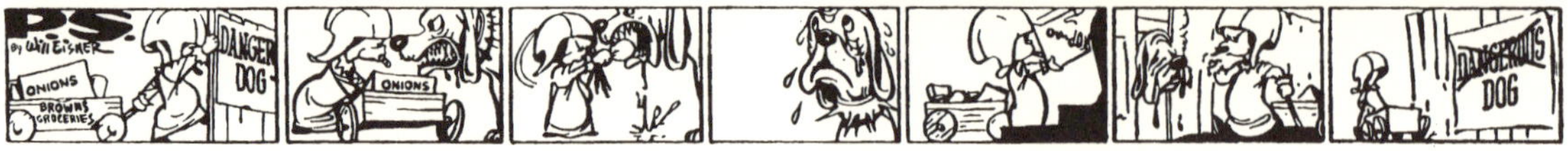
P.S.
BY WILL EISNER
DANGER DOG
ONIONS
BROWNS GROCERIES
ONIONS
DANGEROUS DOG

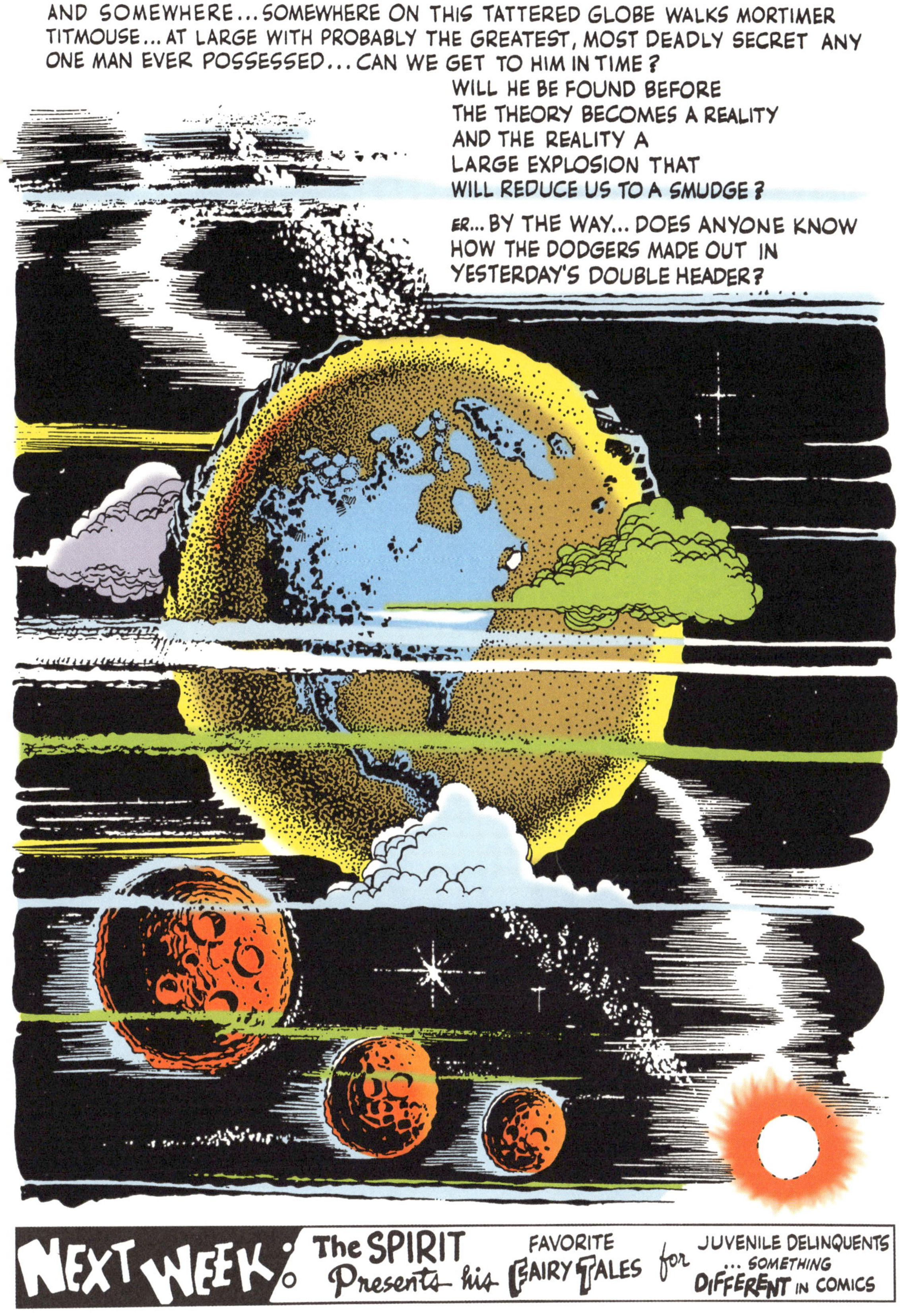
AND SOMEWHERE... SOMEWHERE ON THIS TATTERED GLOBE WALKS MORTIMER TITMOUSE... AT LARGE WITH PROBABLY THE GREATEST, MOST DEADLY SECRET ANY ONE MAN EVER POSSESSED... CAN WE GET TO HIM IN TIME?
WILL HE BE FOUND BEFORE THE THEORY BECOMES A REALITY AND THE REALITY A LARGE EXPLOSION THAT WILL REDUCE US TO A SMUDGE?
ER... BY THE WAY... DOES ANYONE KNOW HOW THE DODGERS MADE OUT IN YESTERDAY'S DOUBLE HEADER?
NEXT WEEK: The SPIRIT Presents his FAVORITE FAIRY TALES for JUVENILE DELINQUENTS ... SOMETHING DIFFERENT IN COMICS

COMIC BOOK SECTION

THE SPIRIT'S FAVORITE FAIRY TALES FOR JUVENILE DELINQUENTS: HANZEL UND GRETEL

July 13 1947

ACTION Mystery ADVENTURE

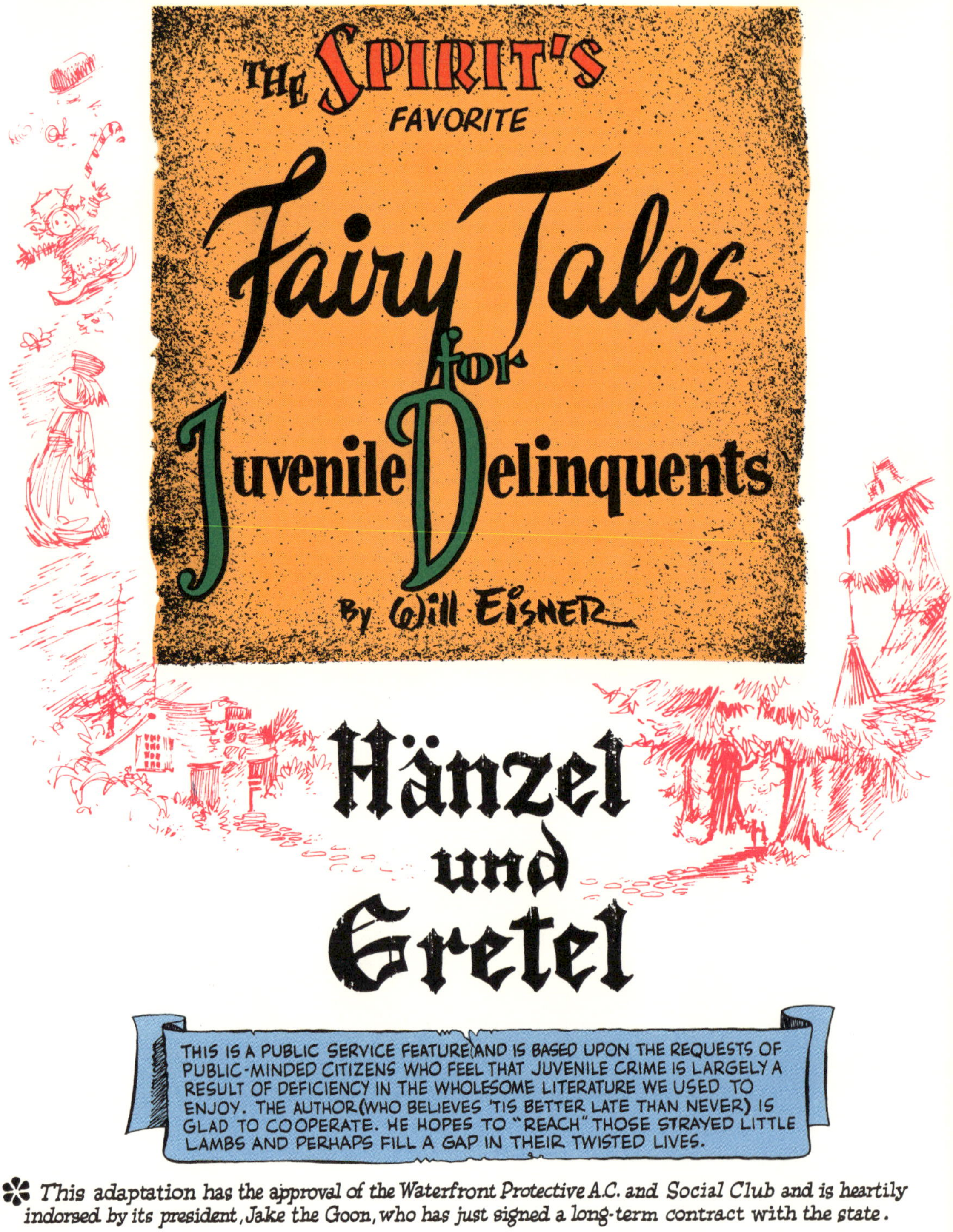
THE SPIRIT'S FAVORITE
Fairy Tales for Juvenile Delinquents
By Will Eisner
Hänzel und Gretel
THIS IS A PUBLIC SERVICE FEATURE AND IS BASED UPON THE REQUESTS OF PUBLIC-MINDED CITIZENS WHO FEEL THAT JUVENILE CRIME IS LARGELY A RESULT OF DEFICIENCY IN THE WHOLESOME LITERATURE WE USED TO ENJOY. THE AUTHOR (WHO BELIEVES 'TIS BETTER LATE THAN NEVER) IS GLAD TO COOPERATE. HE HOPES TO "REACH" THOSE STRAYED LITTLE LAMBS AND PERHAPS FILL A GAP IN THEIR TWISTED LIVES.
This adaptation has the approval of the Waterfront Protective A.C. and Social Club and is heartily indorsed by its president, Jake the Goon, who has just signed a long-term contract with the state.

Once upon a time there lived, in Central City, a poor hijacker named FOSGNOV SLASH... he had come upon hard times and so lived in abject poverty with his two children and their stepmother, a former première danseuse at the Gaiety, named MINNIE the MINK.

Father	Hänzel	Gretel	Stepmother

Papa Fosgnov loved his little family and tried to provide as best he could...

But a temporary recession had set in...

and things were mighty tough.

"WHAT! THE *SPIRIT* OUTSMARTED YA AGAIN? ⚡☆✱#! DIS IS DE *FOURTH* JOB YA SNAFFED UP IN 6 WEEKS... YOU BETTER LAY LOW ...Y'R HOTTER'N A SIDEWALK IN LIMBO!"

"...BUT MINNIE.. WHO'S GONNA SCROUNGE OUR GRUB AND MOVIE MONEY?"

"WHO DO YA *THINK*, BRAT? *YOU!* NOW GET OUT AND GATHER SOME LETTUCE OR I'LL POUND Y'R CUTE LITTLE HEADS TO A ROTTEN *PULP!*"

"...AW MINNIE LAY OFFA 'EM, CAN'TCHA?"

"AAAH Y'FODDER'S MOUSTACHE!"

SLAP

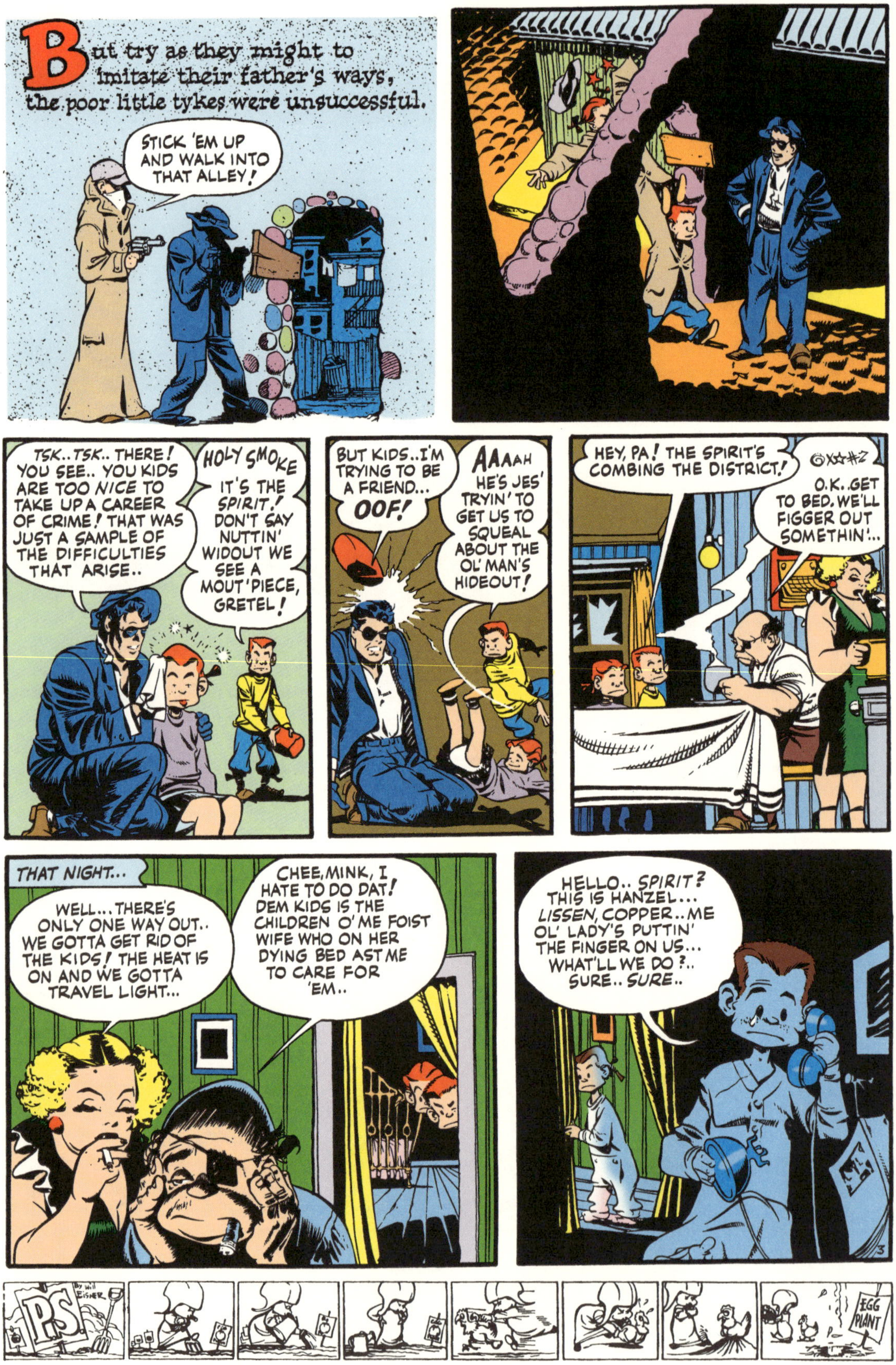
But try as they might to imitate their father's ways, the poor little tykes were unsuccessful.
STICK 'EM UP AND WALK INTO THAT ALLEY!
TSK..TSK.. THERE! YOU SEE.. YOU KIDS ARE TOO NICE TO TAKE UP A CAREER OF CRIME! THAT WAS JUST A SAMPLE OF THE DIFFICULTIES THAT ARISE..
HOLY SMOKE IT'S THE SPIRIT! DON'T SAY NUTTIN' WIDOUT WE SEE A MOUT'PIECE, GRETEL!
BUT KIDS..I'M TRYING TO BE A FRIEND... OOF!
AAAAH HE'S JES' TRYIN' TO GET US TO SQUEAL ABOUT THE OL' MAN'S HIDEOUT!
HEY, PA! THE SPIRIT'S COMBING THE DISTRICT!
O.K..GET TO BED. WE'LL FIGGER OUT SOMETHIN'...
THAT NIGHT...
WELL... THERE'S ONLY ONE WAY OUT.. WE GOTTA GET RID OF THE KIDS! THE HEAT IS ON AND WE GOTTA TRAVEL LIGHT...
CHEE, MINK, I HATE TO DO DAT! DEM KIDS IS THE CHILDREN O' ME FOIST WIFE WHO ON HER DYING BED AST ME TO CARE FOR 'EM..
HELLO.. SPIRIT? THIS IS HANZEL... LISSEN, COPPER..ME OL' LADY'S PUTTIN' THE FINGER ON US... WHAT'LL WE DO ?.. SURE.. SURE..
3
P.S.
By Will Eisner
EGG PLANT

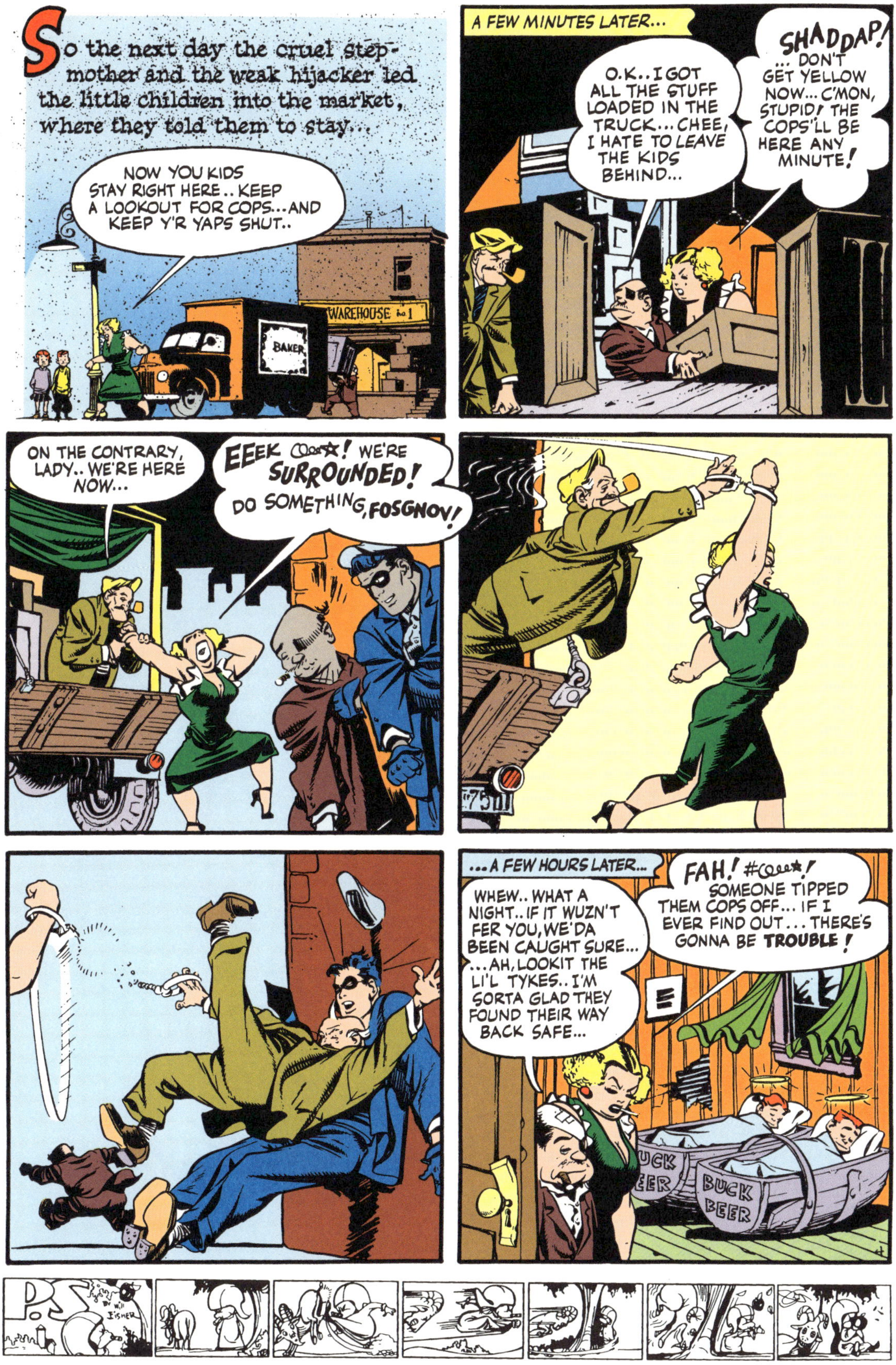
So the next day the cruel step-mother and the weak hijacker led the little children into the market, where they told them to stay...
NOW YOU KIDS STAY RIGHT HERE.. KEEP A LOOKOUT FOR COPS...AND KEEP Y'R YAPS SHUT..
WAREHOUSE no 1
BAKER
A FEW MINUTES LATER...
O.K..I GOT ALL THE STUFF LOADED IN THE TRUCK...CHEE, I HATE TO LEAVE THE KIDS BEHIND...
SHADDAP! ... DON'T GET YELLOW NOW... C'MON, STUPID! THE COPS'LL BE HERE ANY MINUTE!
ON THE CONTRARY, LADY.. WE'RE HERE NOW...
EEEK #@*! WE'RE SURROUNDED! DO SOMETHING, FOSGNOV!
...A FEW HOURS LATER...
WHEW.. WHAT A NIGHT.. IF IT WUZN'T FER YOU, WE'DA BEEN CAUGHT SURE... ...AH, LOOKIT THE LI'L TYKES.. I'M SORTA GLAD THEY FOUND THEIR WAY BACK SAFE...
FAH! #@*! SOMEONE TIPPED THEM COPS OFF... IF I EVER FIND OUT... THERE'S GONNA BE TROUBLE!
BUCK BEER
P.S. BY WILL EISNER

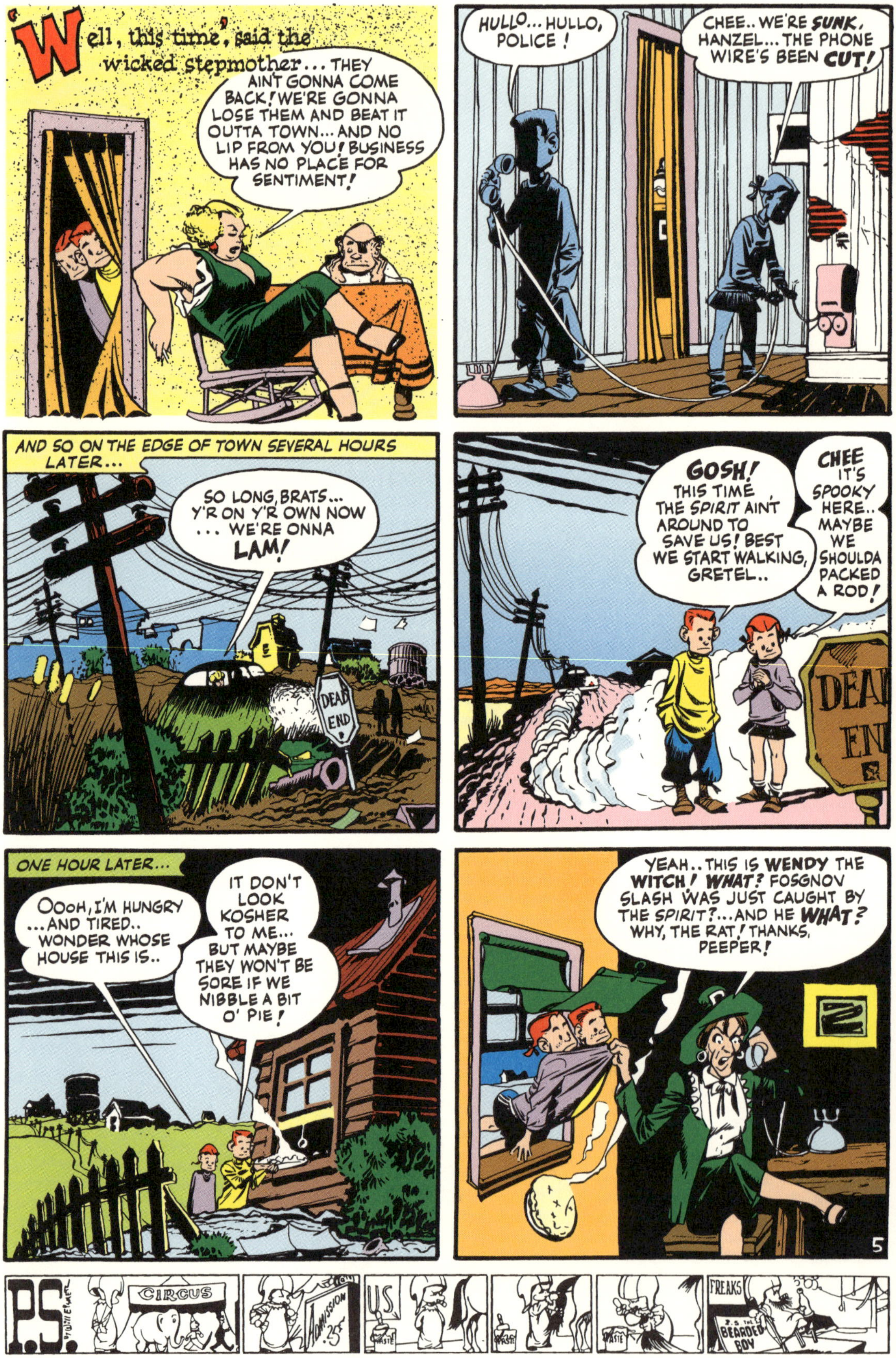
Well, this time, said the wicked stepmother... THEY AIN'T GONNA COME BACK! WE'RE GONNA LOSE THEM AND BEAT IT OUTTA TOWN... AND NO LIP FROM YOU! BUSINESS HAS NO PLACE FOR SENTIMENT!
HULLO... HULLO, POLICE!
CHEE.. WE'RE SUNK, HANZEL... THE PHONE WIRE'S BEEN CUT!
AND SO ON THE EDGE OF TOWN SEVERAL HOURS LATER...
SO LONG, BRATS... Y'R ON Y'R OWN NOW ... WE'RE ONNA LAM!
DEAD END
GOSH! THIS TIME THE SPIRIT AIN'T AROUND TO SAVE US! BEST WE START WALKING, GRETEL..
CHEE IT'S SPOOKY HERE.. MAYBE WE SHOULDA PACKED A ROD!
ONE HOUR LATER...
OOOH, I'M HUNGRY ...AND TIRED.. WONDER WHOSE HOUSE THIS IS..
IT DON'T LOOK KOSHER TO ME... BUT MAYBE THEY WON'T BE SORE IF WE NIBBLE A BIT O' PIE!
YEAH.. THIS IS WENDY THE WITCH! WHAT? FOSGNOV SLASH WAS JUST CAUGHT BY THE SPIRIT?...AND HE WHAT? WHY, THE RAT! THANKS, PEEPER!
5
P.S.
CIRCUS
ADMISSION 25¢
FREAKS
P.S. THE BEARDED BOY

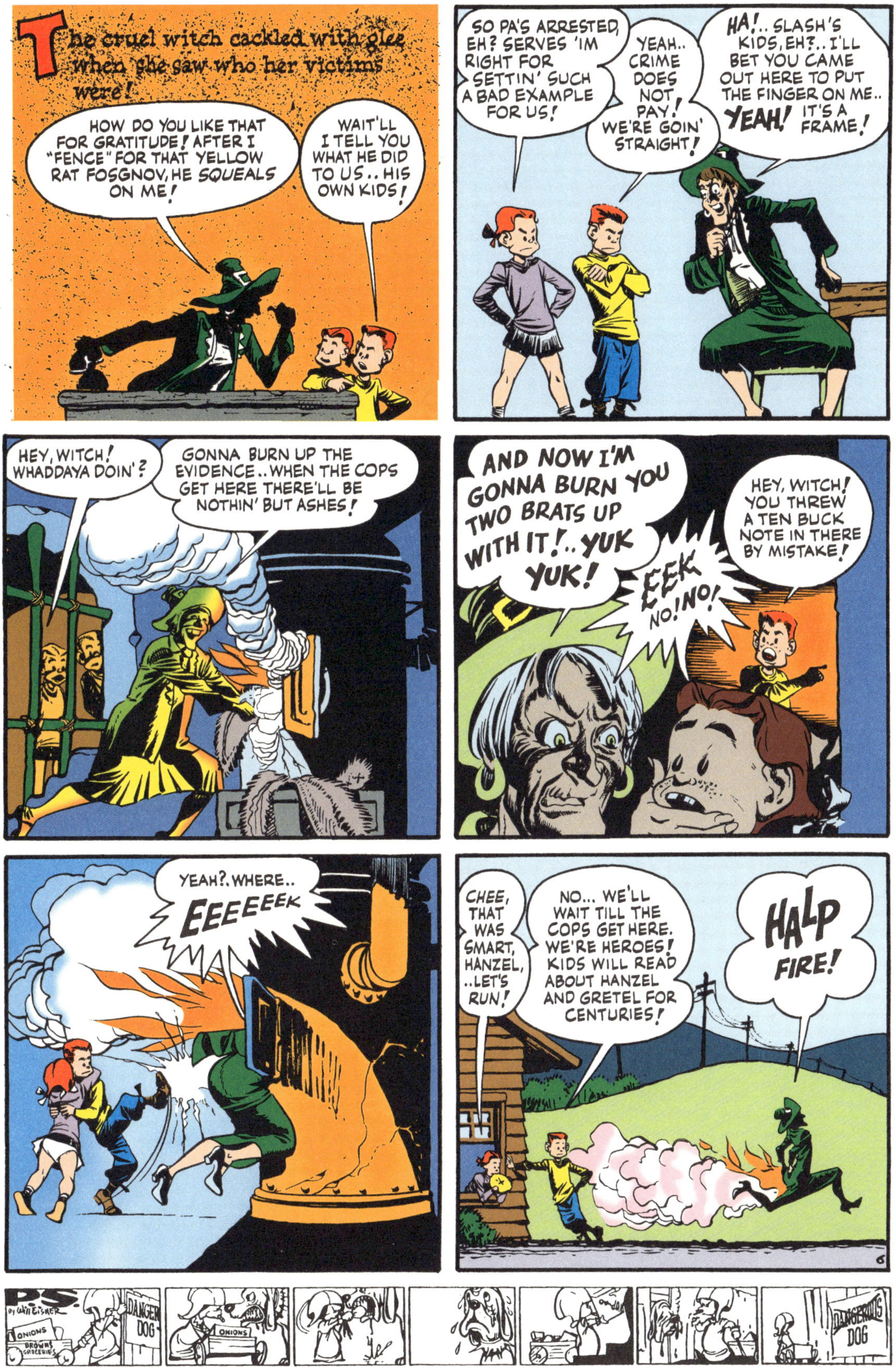
The cruel witch cackled with glee when she saw who her victims were!
HOW DO YOU LIKE THAT FOR GRATITUDE! AFTER I "FENCE" FOR THAT YELLOW RAT FOSGNOV, HE SQUEALS ON ME!
WAIT'LL I TELL YOU WHAT HE DID TO US.. HIS OWN KIDS!
SO PA'S ARRESTED, EH? SERVES 'IM RIGHT FOR SETTIN' SUCH A BAD EXAMPLE FOR US!
YEAH.. CRIME DOES NOT PAY! WE'RE GOIN' STRAIGHT!
HA!.. SLASH'S KIDS, EH?.. I'LL BET YOU CAME OUT HERE TO PUT THE FINGER ON ME.. YEAH! IT'S A FRAME!
HEY, WITCH! WHADDAYA DOIN'?
GONNA BURN UP THE EVIDENCE..WHEN THE COPS GET HERE THERE'LL BE NOTHIN' BUT ASHES!
AND NOW I'M GONNA BURN YOU TWO BRATS UP WITH IT!.. YUK YUK!
EEK NO! NO!
HEY, WITCH! YOU THREW A TEN BUCK NOTE IN THERE BY MISTAKE!
YEAH?. WHERE.. EEEEEEK
CHEE, THAT WAS SMART, HANZEL, ..LET'S RUN!
NO... WE'LL WAIT TILL THE COPS GET HERE. WE'RE HEROES! KIDS WILL READ ABOUT HANZEL AND GRETEL FOR CENTURIES!
HALP FIRE!
6
P.S. BY Will Eisner
DANGER DOG
ONIONS
BROWN'S GROCERIES
DANGEROUS DOG

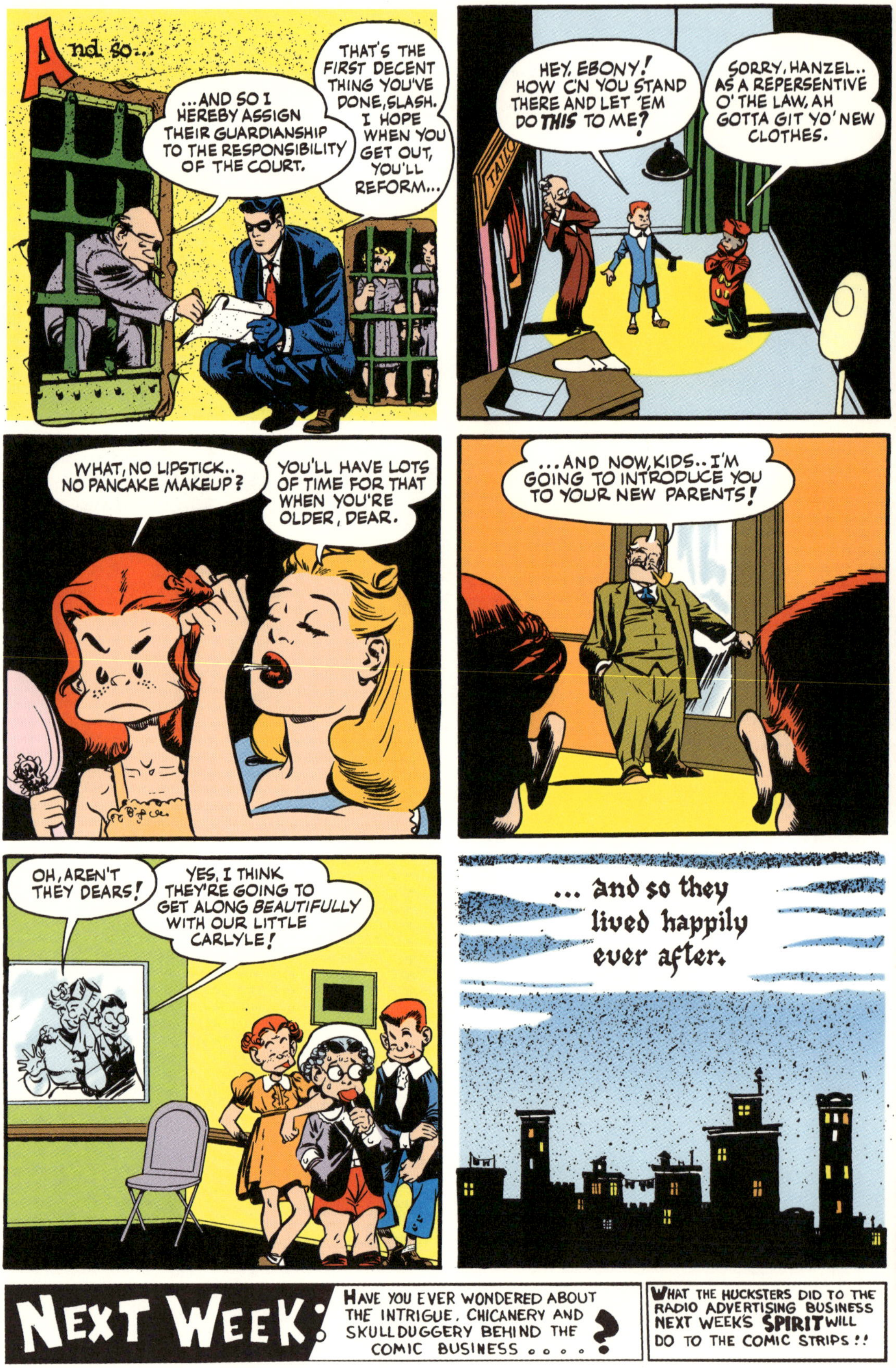
And so...
...AND SO I HEREBY ASSIGN THEIR GUARDIANSHIP TO THE RESPONSIBILITY OF THE COURT.
THAT'S THE FIRST DECENT THING YOU'VE DONE, SLASH. I HOPE WHEN YOU GET OUT, YOU'LL REFORM...
HEY, EBONY! HOW C'N YOU STAND THERE AND LET 'EM DO THIS TO ME?
SORRY, HANZEL.. AS A REPERSENTIVE O' THE LAW, AH GOTTA GIT YO' NEW CLOTHES.
WHAT, NO LIPSTICK.. NO PANCAKE MAKEUP?
YOU'LL HAVE LOTS OF TIME FOR THAT WHEN YOU'RE OLDER, DEAR.
...AND NOW, KIDS.. I'M GOING TO INTRODUCE YOU TO YOUR NEW PARENTS!
OH, AREN'T THEY DEARS!
YES, I THINK THEY'RE GOING TO GET ALONG BEAUTIFULLY WITH OUR LITTLE CARLYLE!
... and so they lived happily ever after.
NEXT WEEK:
HAVE YOU EVER WONDERED ABOUT THE INTRIGUE, CHICANERY AND SKULLDUGGERY BEHIND THE COMIC BUSINESS ....?
WHAT THE HUCKSTERS DID TO THE RADIO ADVERTISING BUSINESS NEXT WEEK'S SPIRIT WILL DO TO THE COMIC STRIPS!!

COMIC BOOK SECTION

LI'L ADAM

July 20 1947

ACTION Mystery ADVENTURE

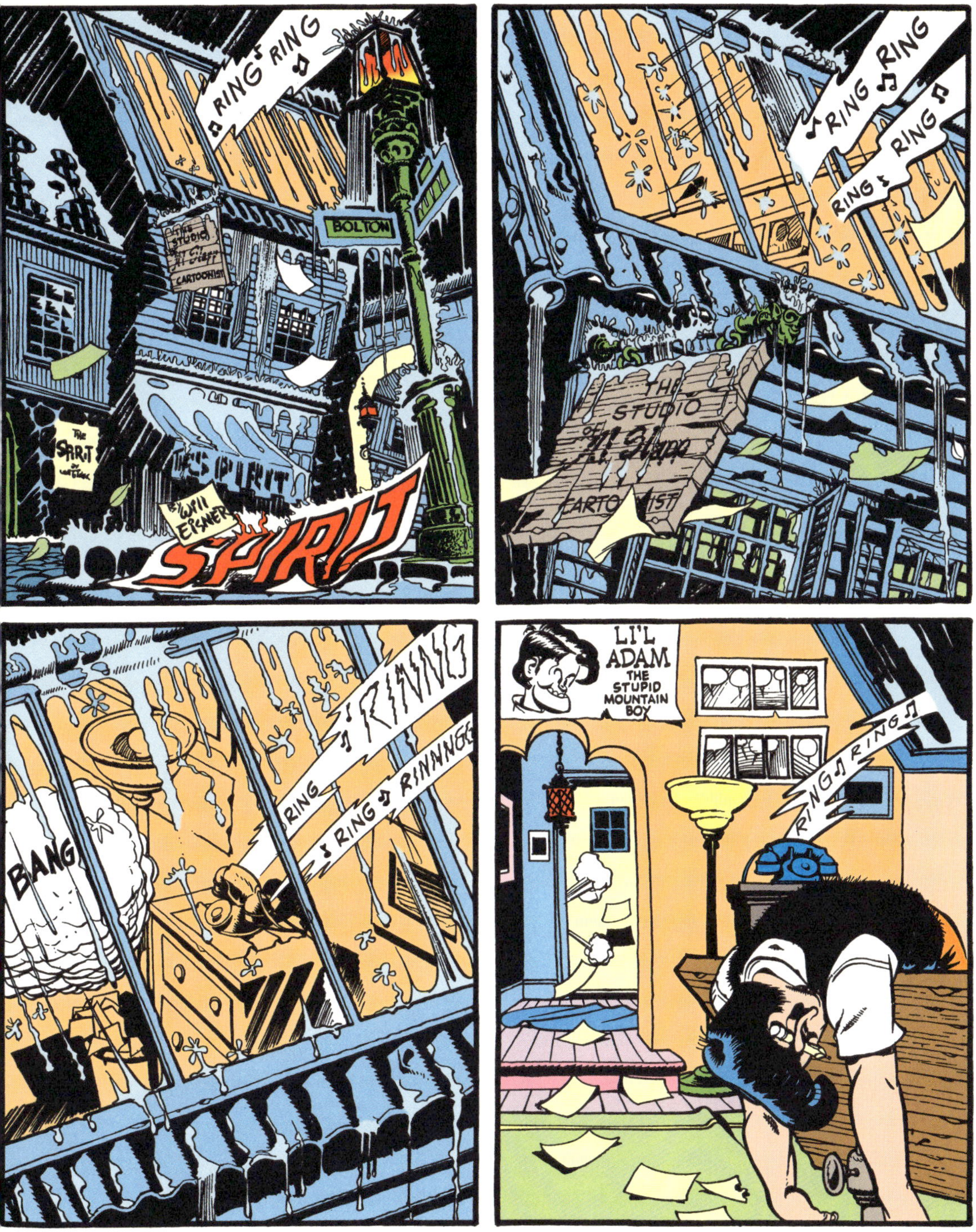

RING RING
BOLTON
CARTOONIST
By Will Eisner
SPIRIT
RING RING
RING RING
THE STUDIO
BANG
RING RINNNG
RING RINNNGG
LI'L ADAM
THE STUPID MOUNTAIN BOY
RING RING

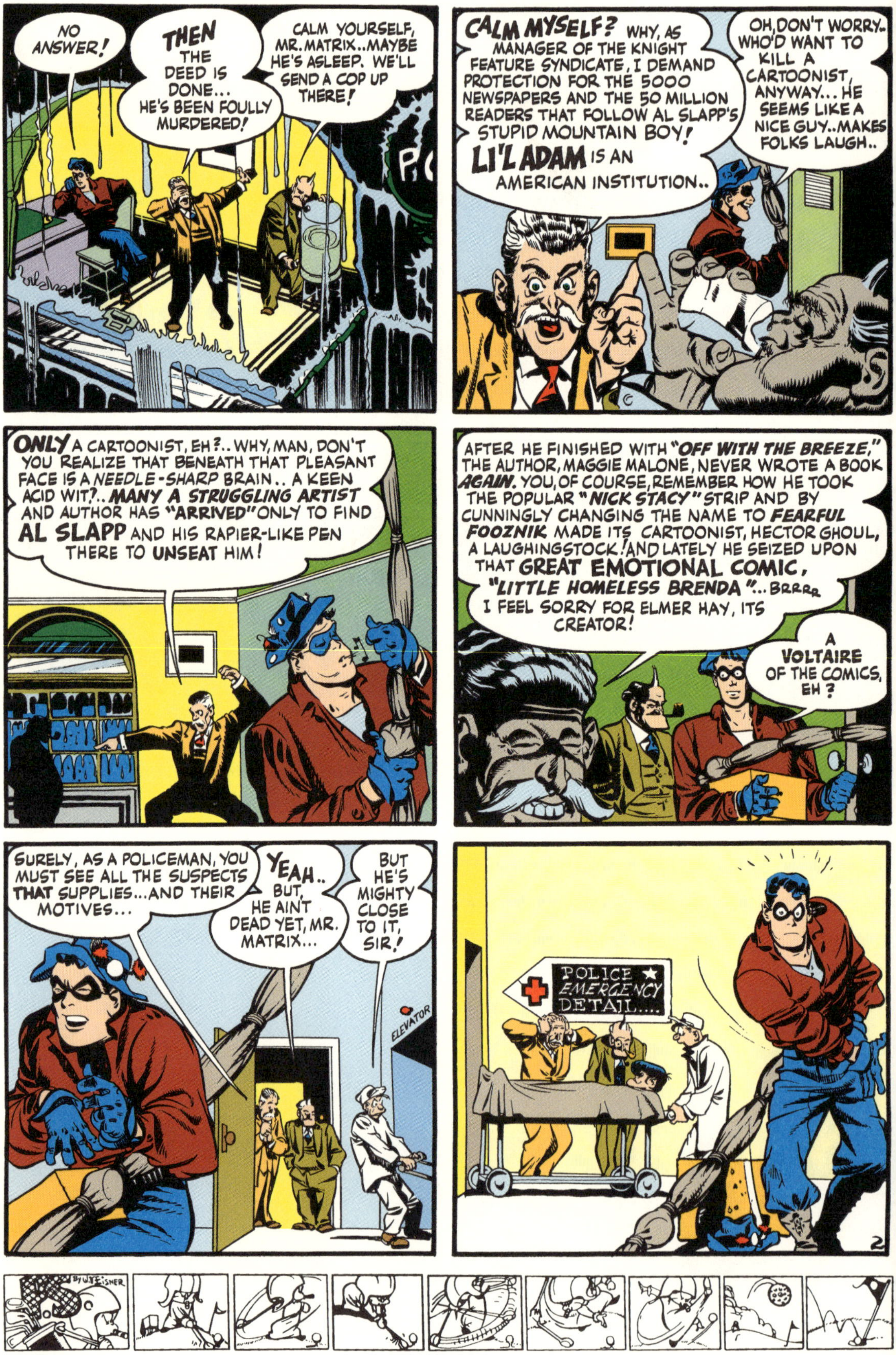
NO ANSWER!
THEN THE DEED IS DONE... HE'S BEEN FOULLY MURDERED!
CALM YOURSELF, MR. MATRIX..MAYBE HE'S ASLEEP. WE'LL SEND A COP UP THERE!
CALM MYSELF? WHY, AS MANAGER OF THE KNIGHT FEATURE SYNDICATE, I DEMAND PROTECTION FOR THE 5000 NEWSPAPERS AND THE 50 MILLION READERS THAT FOLLOW AL SLAPP'S STUPID MOUNTAIN BOY! LI'L ADAM IS AN AMERICAN INSTITUTION..
OH, DON'T WORRY.. WHO'D WANT TO KILL A CARTOONIST, ANYWAY... HE SEEMS LIKE A NICE GUY..MAKES FOLKS LAUGH..
ONLY A CARTOONIST, EH?.. WHY, MAN, DON'T YOU REALIZE THAT BENEATH THAT PLEASANT FACE IS A NEEDLE-SHARP BRAIN.. A KEEN ACID WIT?.. MANY A STRUGGLING ARTIST AND AUTHOR HAS "ARRIVED" ONLY TO FIND AL SLAPP AND HIS RAPIER-LIKE PEN THERE TO UNSEAT HIM!
AFTER HE FINISHED WITH "OFF WITH THE BREEZE," THE AUTHOR, MAGGIE MALONE, NEVER WROTE A BOOK AGAIN. YOU, OF COURSE, REMEMBER HOW HE TOOK THE POPULAR "NICK STACY" STRIP AND BY CUNNINGLY CHANGING THE NAME TO FEARFUL FOOZNIK MADE ITS CARTOONIST, HECTOR GHOUL, A LAUGHINGSTOCK! AND LATELY HE SEIZED UPON THAT GREAT EMOTIONAL COMIC, "LITTLE HOMELESS BRENDA"... BRRRR I FEEL SORRY FOR ELMER HAY, ITS CREATOR!
A VOLTAIRE OF THE COMICS, EH?
SURELY, AS A POLICEMAN, YOU MUST SEE ALL THE SUSPECTS THAT SUPPLIES...AND THEIR MOTIVES...
YEAH.. BUT, HE AIN'T DEAD YET, MR. MATRIX...
BUT HE'S MIGHTY CLOSE TO IT, SIR!
ELEVATOR
POLICE ★ EMERGENCY DETAIL....
2
BY W.E. EISNER

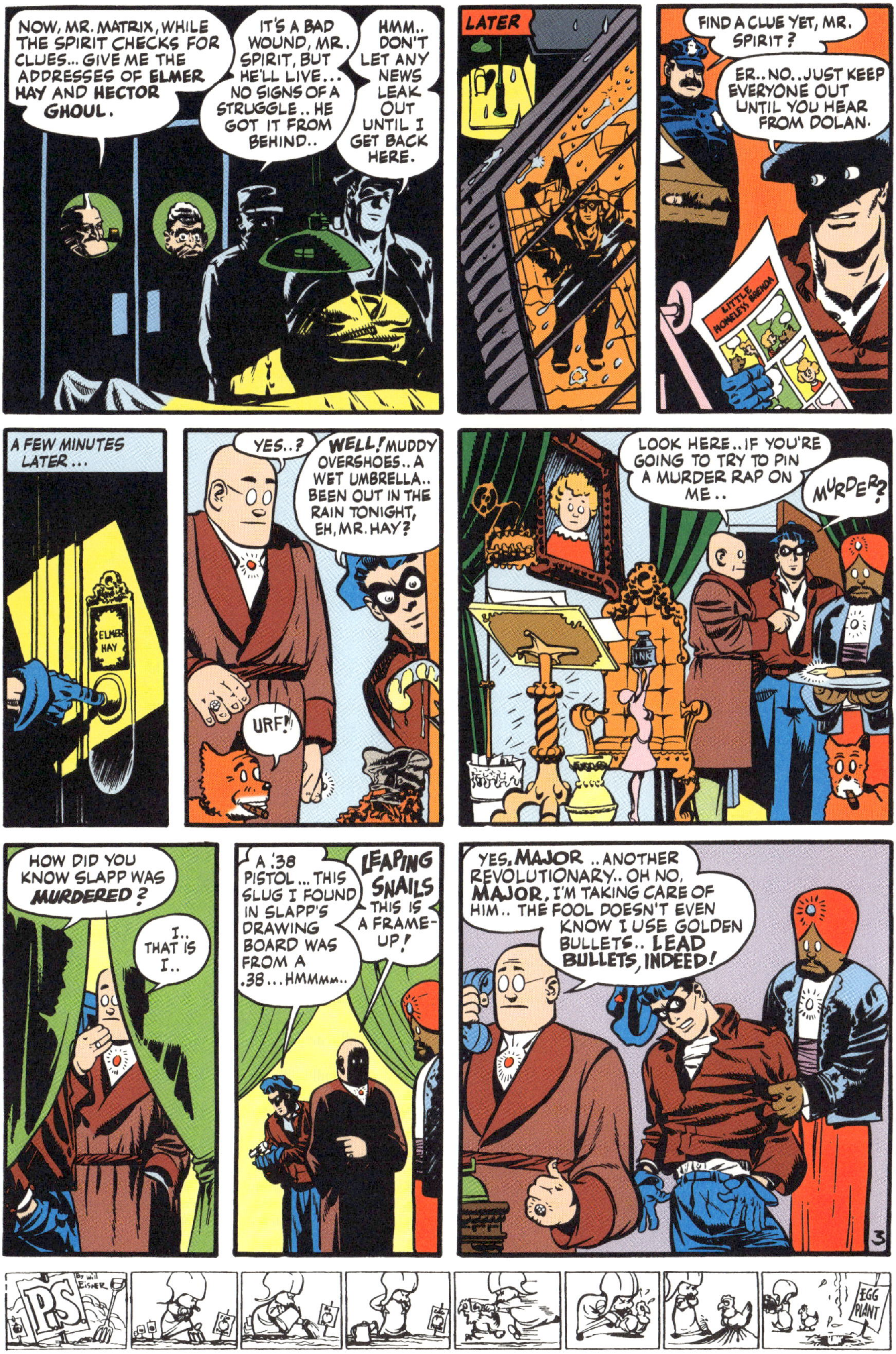
NOW, MR. MATRIX, WHILE THE SPIRIT CHECKS FOR CLUES... GIVE ME THE ADDRESSES OF ELMER HAY AND HECTOR GHOUL.
IT'S A BAD WOUND, MR. SPIRIT, BUT HE'LL LIVE... NO SIGNS OF A STRUGGLE.. HE GOT IT FROM BEHIND..
HMM.. DON'T LET ANY NEWS LEAK OUT UNTIL I GET BACK HERE.
LATER
FIND A CLUE YET, MR. SPIRIT?
ER.. NO.. JUST KEEP EVERYONE OUT UNTIL YOU HEAR FROM DOLAN.
LITTLE HOMELESS BRENDA
A FEW MINUTES LATER...
ELMER HAY
YES..?
WELL! MUDDY OVERSHOES.. A WET UMBRELLA.. BEEN OUT IN THE RAIN TONIGHT, EH, MR. HAY?
URF!
LOOK HERE.. IF YOU'RE GOING TO TRY TO PIN A MURDER RAP ON ME..
MURDER?
INK
HOW DID YOU KNOW SLAPP WAS MURDERED?
I.. THAT IS I..
A .38 PISTOL... THIS SLUG I FOUND IN SLAPP'S DRAWING BOARD WAS FROM A .38... HMMMM...
LEAPING SNAILS THIS IS A FRAME-UP!
YES, MAJOR.. ANOTHER REVOLUTIONARY.. OH NO, MAJOR, I'M TAKING CARE OF HIM.. THE FOOL DOESN'T EVEN KNOW I USE GOLDEN BULLETS.. LEAD BULLETS, INDEED!
3
P.S.
EGG PLANT

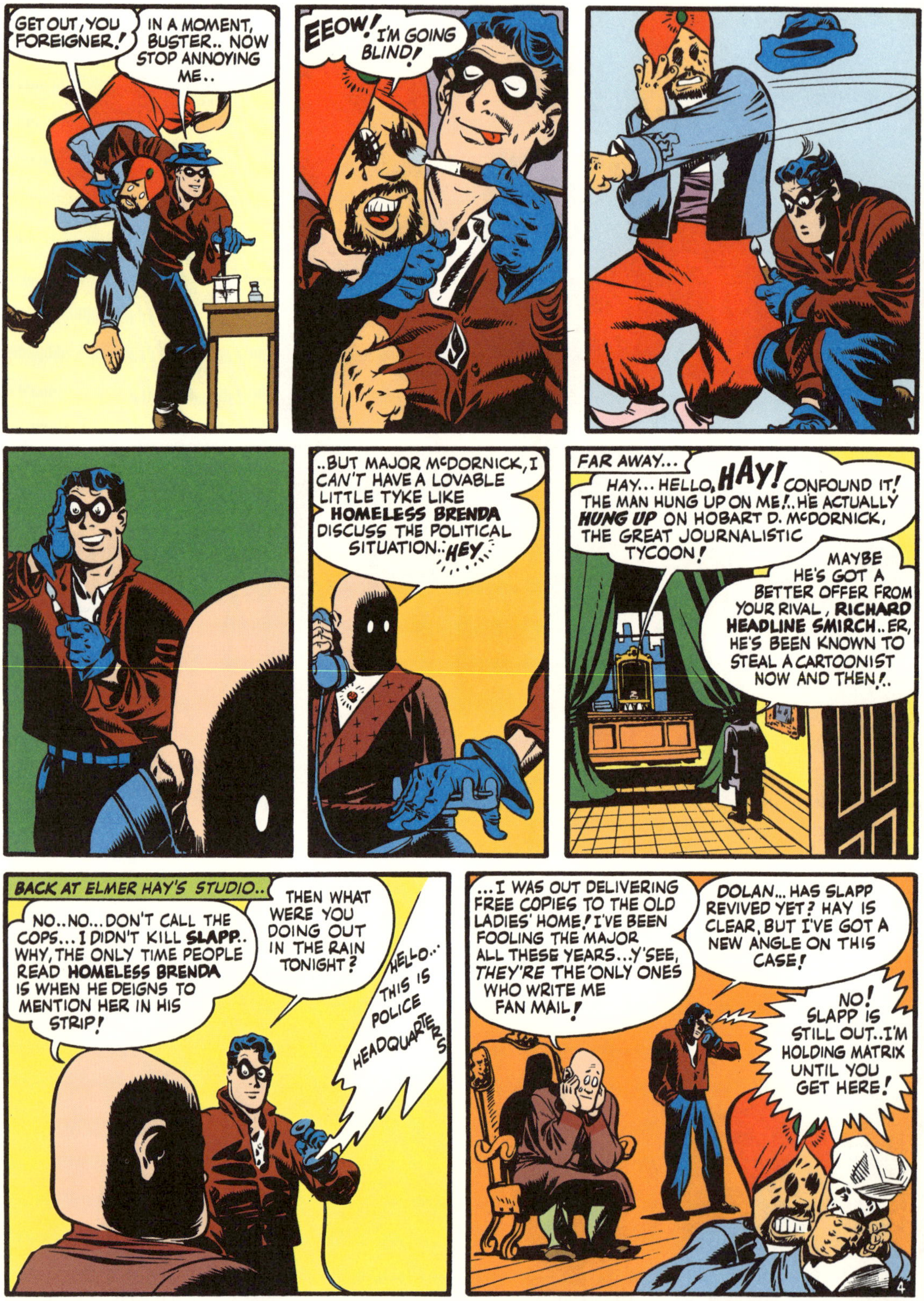
GET OUT, YOU FOREIGNER!
IN A MOMENT, BUSTER.. NOW STOP ANNOYING ME..
EEOW! I'M GOING BLIND!
..BUT MAJOR McDORNICK, I CAN'T HAVE A LOVABLE LITTLE TYKE LIKE **HOMELESS BRENDA** DISCUSS THE POLITICAL SITUATION.. HEY
FAR AWAY...
HAY... HELLO, HAY! CONFOUND IT! THE MAN HUNG UP ON ME!..HE ACTUALLY **HUNG UP** ON HOBART D. McDORNICK, THE GREAT JOURNALISTIC TYCOON!
MAYBE HE'S GOT A BETTER OFFER FROM YOUR RIVAL, **RICHARD HEADLINE SMIRCH**..ER, HE'S BEEN KNOWN TO STEAL A CARTOONIST NOW AND THEN!..
BACK AT ELMER HAY'S STUDIO..
THEN WHAT WERE YOU DOING OUT IN THE RAIN TONIGHT?
NO..NO...DON'T CALL THE COPS...I DIDN'T KILL **SLAPP**.. WHY, THE ONLY TIME PEOPLE READ **HOMELESS BRENDA** IS WHEN HE DEIGNS TO MENTION HER IN HIS STRIP!
HELLO.. THIS IS POLICE HEADQUARTERS
...I WAS OUT DELIVERING FREE COPIES TO THE OLD LADIES' HOME! I'VE BEEN FOOLING THE MAJOR ALL THESE YEARS...Y'SEE, THEY'RE THE ONLY ONES WHO WRITE ME FAN MAIL!
DOLAN... HAS SLAPP REVIVED YET? HAY IS CLEAR, BUT I'VE GOT A NEW ANGLE ON THIS CASE!
NO! SLAPP IS STILL OUT..I'M HOLDING MATRIX UNTIL YOU GET HERE!
4

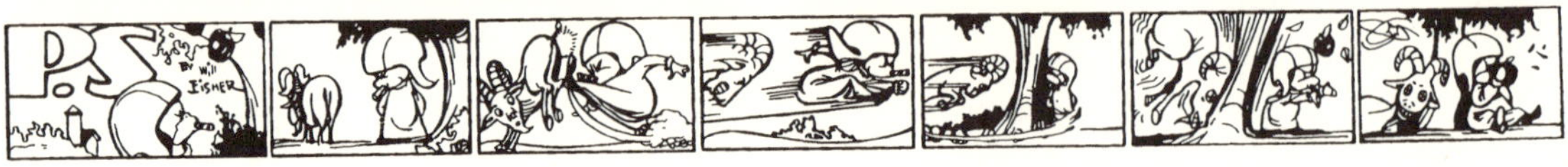

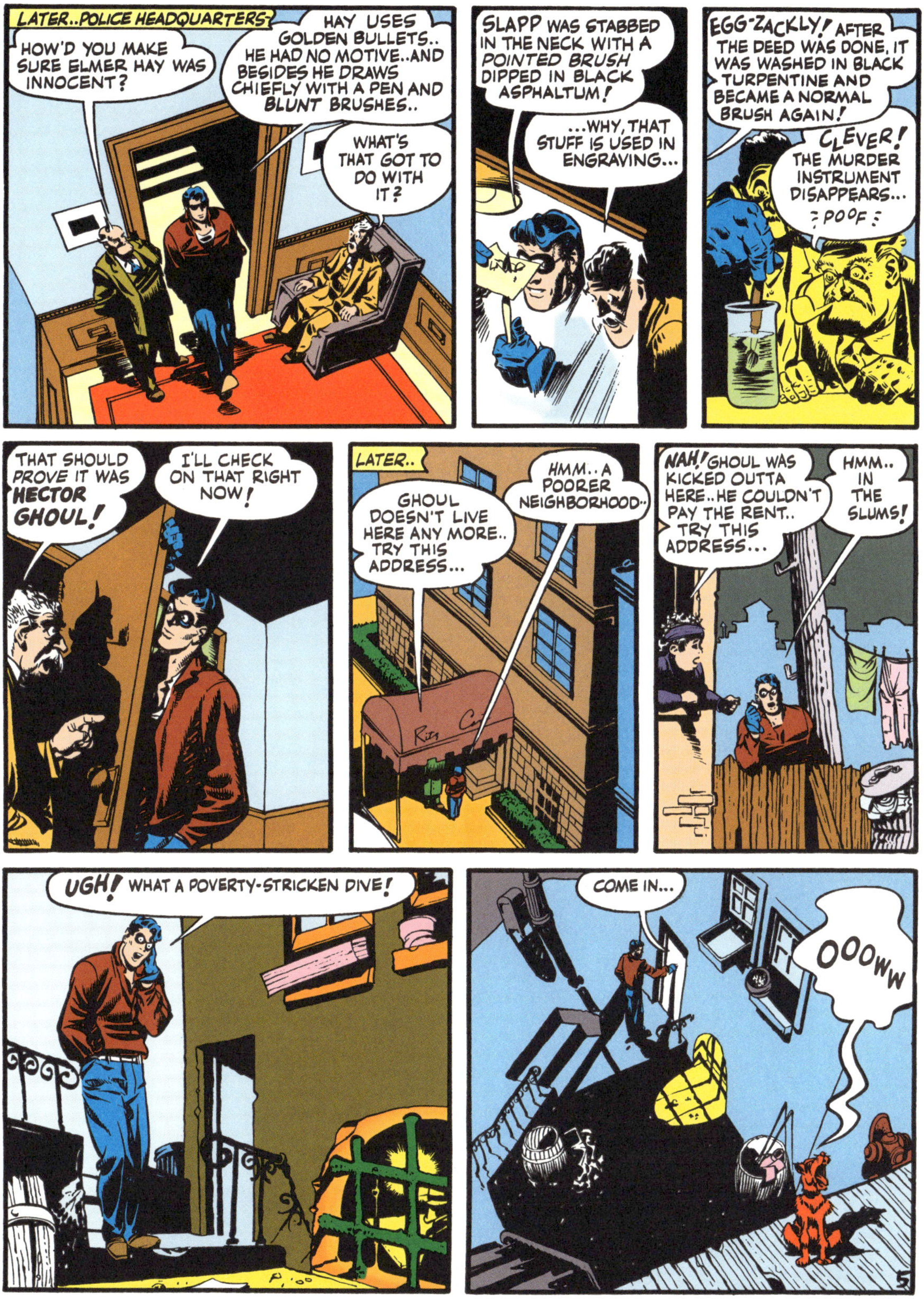
LATER..POLICE HEADQUARTERS:
HOW'D YOU MAKE SURE ELMER HAY WAS INNOCENT?
HAY USES GOLDEN BULLETS.. HE HAD NO MOTIVE..AND BESIDES HE DRAWS CHIEFLY WITH A PEN AND BLUNT BRUSHES..
WHAT'S THAT GOT TO DO WITH IT?
SLAPP WAS STABBED IN THE NECK WITH A POINTED BRUSH DIPPED IN BLACK ASPHALTUM!
...WHY, THAT STUFF IS USED IN ENGRAVING...
EGG-ZACKLY! AFTER THE DEED WAS DONE, IT WAS WASHED IN BLACK TURPENTINE AND BECAME A NORMAL BRUSH AGAIN!
CLEVER! THE MURDER INSTRUMENT DISAPPEARS... POOF
THAT SHOULD PROVE IT WAS HECTOR GHOUL!
I'LL CHECK ON THAT RIGHT NOW!
LATER..
GHOUL DOESN'T LIVE HERE ANY MORE.. TRY THIS ADDRESS...
HMM..A POORER NEIGHBORHOOD..
NAH! GHOUL WAS KICKED OUTTA HERE..HE COULDN'T PAY THE RENT.. TRY THIS ADDRESS...
HMM.. IN THE SLUMS!
UGH! WHAT A POVERTY-STRICKEN DIVE!
COME IN...
OOOWW
5

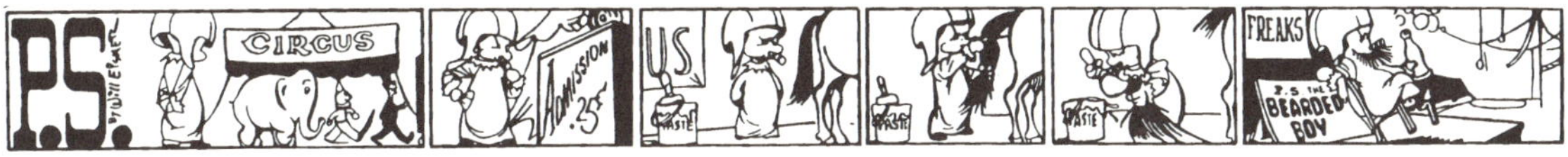
P.S.
CIRCUS
ADMISSION 25¢
FREAKS
P.S. THE BEARDED BOY

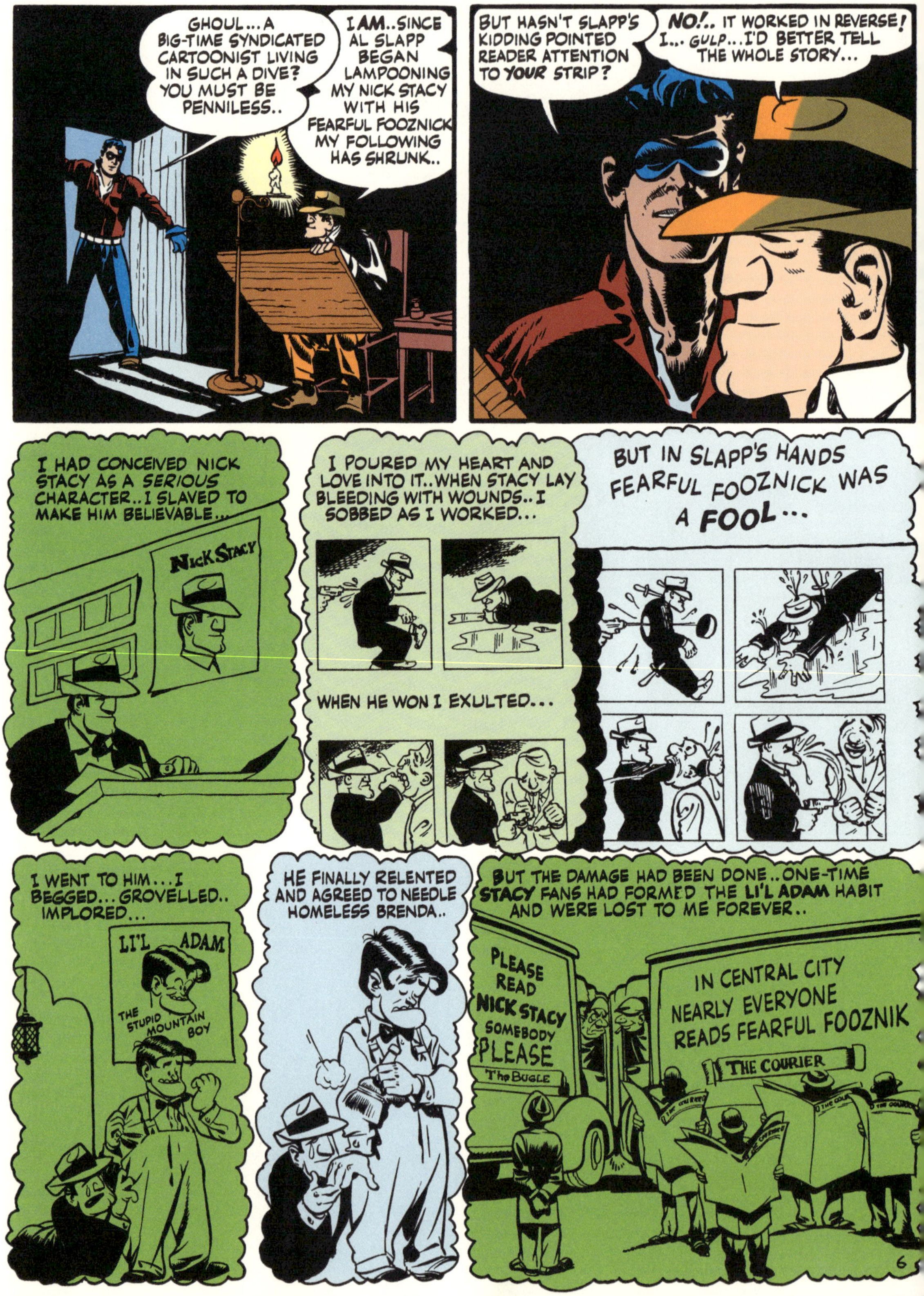
GHOUL... A BIG-TIME SYNDICATED CARTOONIST LIVING IN SUCH A DIVE? YOU MUST BE PENNILESS..
I AM..SINCE AL SLAPP BEGAN LAMPOONING MY NICK STACY WITH HIS FEARFUL FOOZNICK MY FOLLOWING HAS SHRUNK..
BUT HASN'T SLAPP'S KIDDING POINTED READER ATTENTION TO YOUR STRIP?
NO!.. IT WORKED IN REVERSE! I... GULP...I'D BETTER TELL THE WHOLE STORY...
I HAD CONCEIVED NICK STACY AS A SERIOUS CHARACTER..I SLAVED TO MAKE HIM BELIEVABLE...
NICK STACY
I POURED MY HEART AND LOVE INTO IT..WHEN STACY LAY BLEEDING WITH WOUNDS..I SOBBED AS I WORKED...
WHEN HE WON I EXULTED...
BUT IN SLAPP'S HANDS FEARFUL FOOZNICK WAS A FOOL...
I WENT TO HIM...I BEGGED... GROVELLED.. IMPLORED...
LI'L ADAM
THE STUPID MOUNTAIN BOY
HE FINALLY RELENTED AND AGREED TO NEEDLE HOMELESS BRENDA..
BUT THE DAMAGE HAD BEEN DONE..ONE-TIME STACY FANS HAD FORMED THE LI'L ADAM HABIT AND WERE LOST TO ME FOREVER..
PLEASE READ NICK STACY SOMEBODY PLEASE
The BUGLE
IN CENTRAL CITY NEARLY EVERYONE READS FEARFUL FOOZNIK
THE COURIER
6

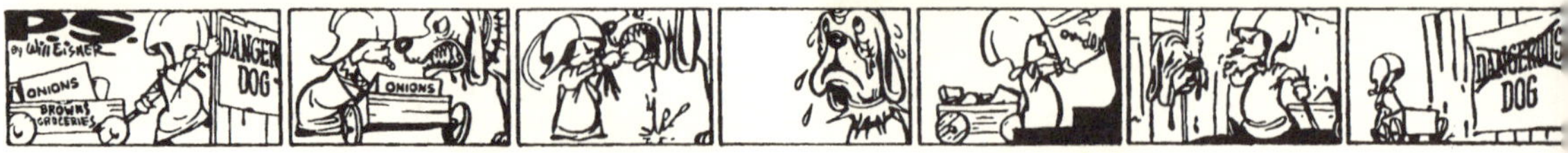
P.S.
By Will Eisner
ONIONS
DANGER DOG
ONIONS
DANGEROUS DOG

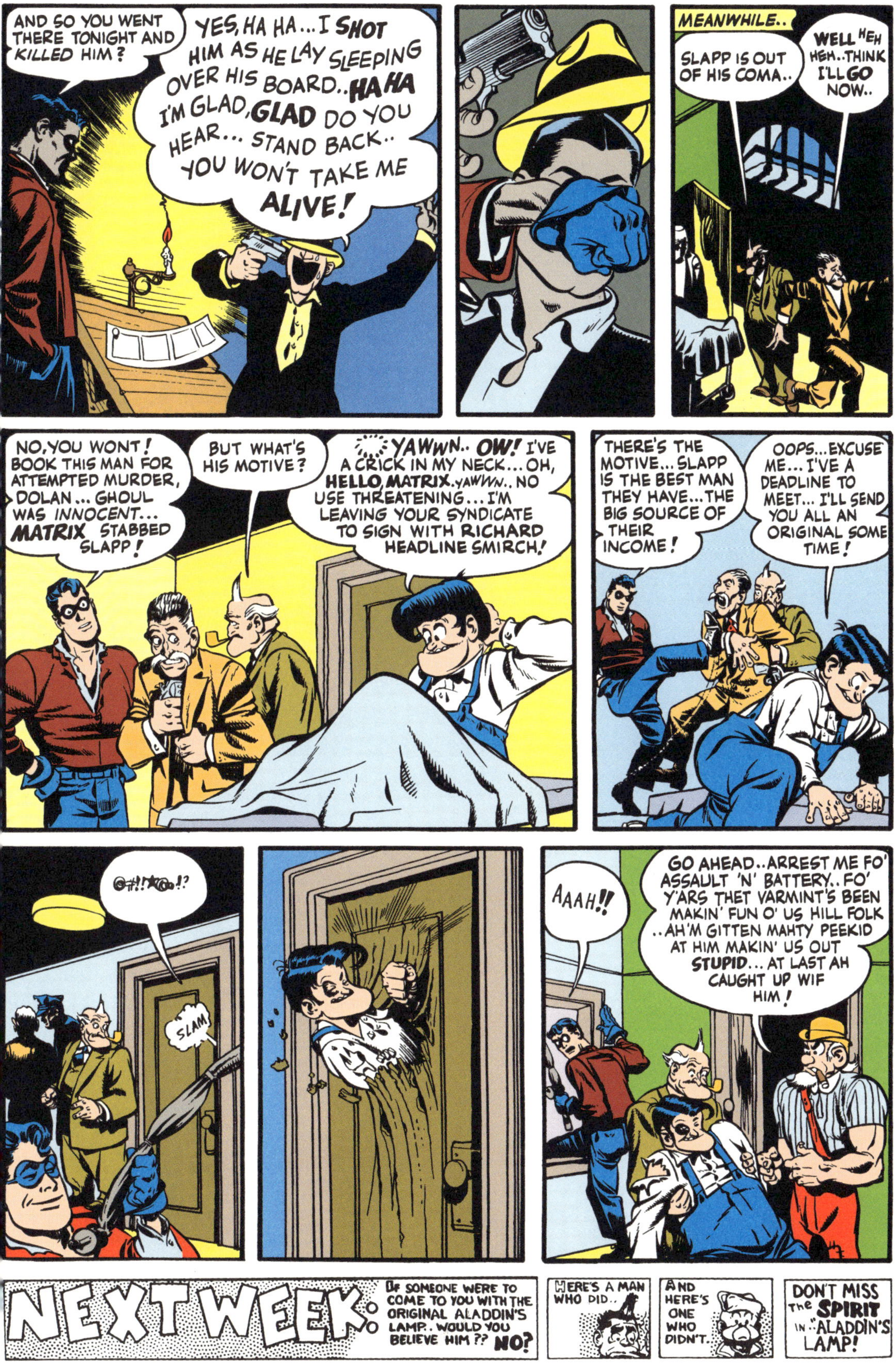
AND SO YOU WENT THERE TONIGHT AND KILLED HIM?
YES, HA HA... I SHOT HIM AS HE LAY SLEEPING OVER HIS BOARD.. HA HA I'M GLAD, GLAD DO YOU HEAR... STAND BACK.. YOU WON'T TAKE ME ALIVE!
MEANWHILE..
SLAPP IS OUT OF HIS COMA..
WELL HEH HEH..THINK I'LL GO NOW..
NO, YOU WONT! BOOK THIS MAN FOR ATTEMPTED MURDER, DOLAN... GHOUL WAS INNOCENT... MATRIX STABBED SLAPP!
BUT WHAT'S HIS MOTIVE?
YAWWN.. OW! I'VE A CRICK IN MY NECK... OH, HELLO, MATRIX.. YAWWN.. NO USE THREATENING... I'M LEAVING YOUR SYNDICATE TO SIGN WITH RICHARD HEADLINE SMIRCH!
THERE'S THE MOTIVE... SLAPP IS THE BEST MAN THEY HAVE... THE BIG SOURCE OF THEIR INCOME!
OOPS... EXCUSE ME... I'VE A DEADLINE TO MEET... I'LL SEND YOU ALL AN ORIGINAL SOME TIME!
@#!*@..!?
SLAM
AAAH!!
GO AHEAD.. ARREST ME FO' ASSAULT 'N' BATTERY.. FO' Y'ARS THET VARMINT'S BEEN MAKIN' FUN O' US HILL FOLK ..AH'M GITTEN MAHTY PEEKID AT HIM MAKIN' US OUT STUPID... AT LAST AH CAUGHT UP WIF HIM!
NEXT WEEK:
IF SOMEONE WERE TO COME TO YOU WITH THE ORIGINAL ALADDIN'S LAMP.. WOULD YOU BELIEVE HIM?? NO?
HERE'S A MAN WHO DID..
AND HERE'S ONE WHO DIDN'T.
DON'T MISS The SPIRIT IN "ALADDIN'S LAMP!"

COMIC BOOK SECTION

ACTION Mystery ADVENTURE

THE LAMP

July 27 1947

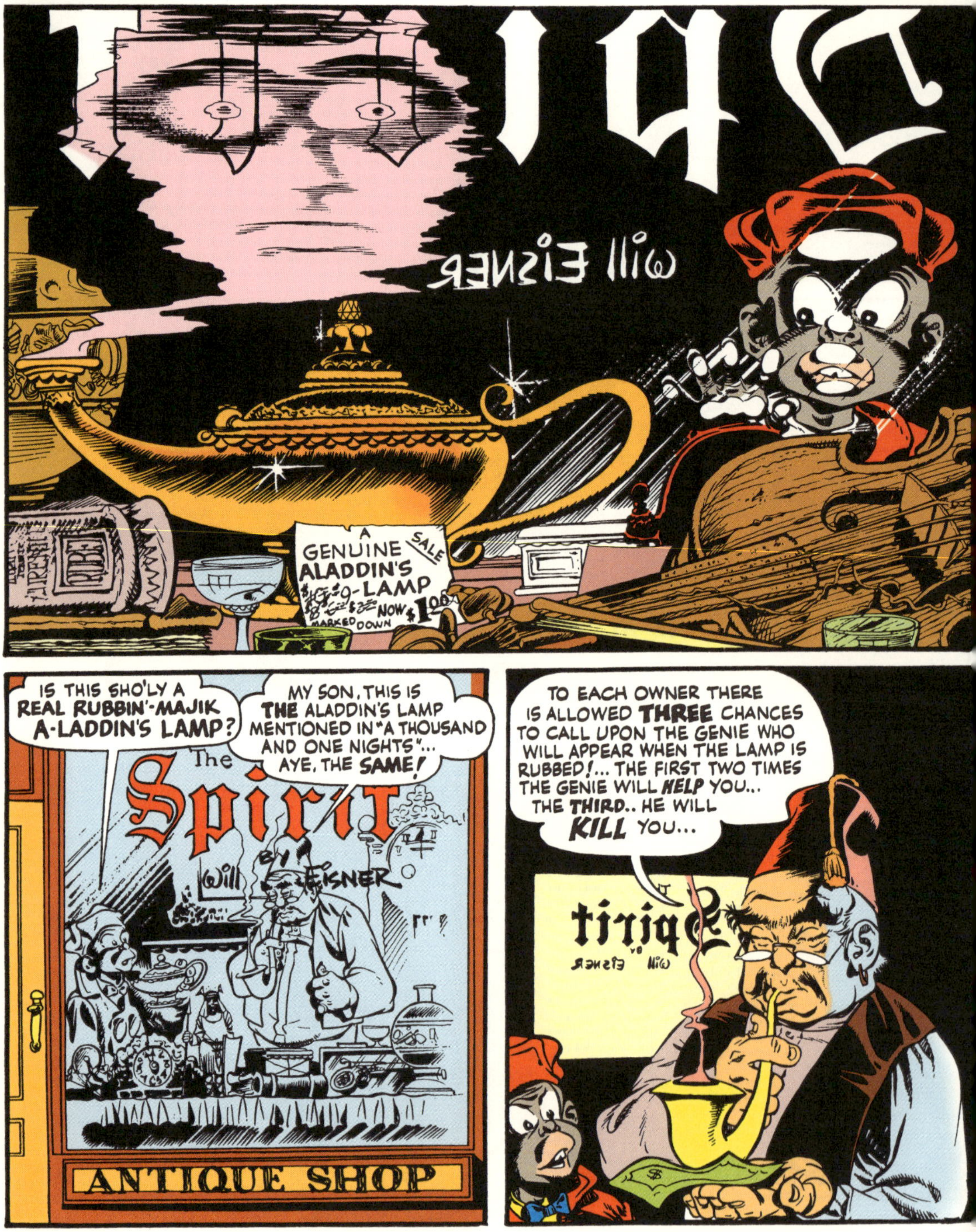

A GENUINE ALADDIN'S LAMP
SALE
NOW $1.00
MARKED DOWN
IS THIS SHO'LY A REAL RUBBIN'-MAJIK A-LADDIN'S LAMP?
MY SON, THIS IS THE ALADDIN'S LAMP MENTIONED IN "A THOUSAND AND ONE NIGHTS"... AYE, THE SAME!
The Spirit
BY Will EISNER
ANTIQUE SHOP
TO EACH OWNER THERE IS ALLOWED THREE CHANCES TO CALL UPON THE GENIE WHO WILL APPEAR WHEN THE LAMP IS RUBBED!... THE FIRST TWO TIMES THE GENIE WILL HELP YOU... THE THIRD.. HE WILL KILL YOU...

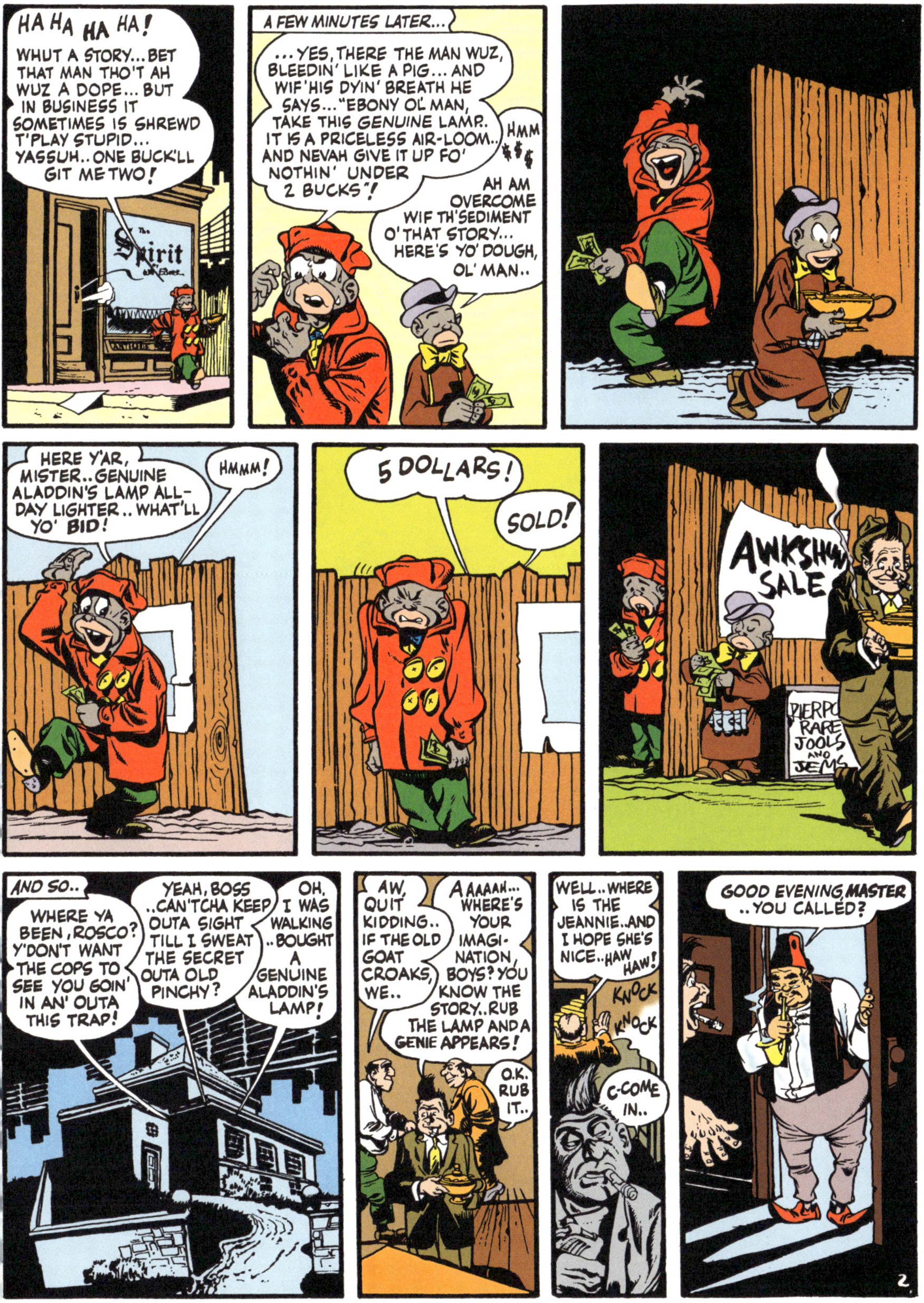
HA HA HA HA!
WHUT A STORY... BET THAT MAN THO'T AH WUZ A DOPE... BUT IN BUSINESS IT SOMETIMES IS SHREWD T'PLAY STUPID... YASSUH.. ONE BUCK'LL GIT ME TWO!
The Spirit
A FEW MINUTES LATER...
...YES, THERE THE MAN WUZ, BLEEDIN' LIKE A PIG... AND WIF HIS DYIN' BREATH HE SAYS..."EBONY OL' MAN, TAKE THIS GENUINE LAMP. IT IS A PRICELESS AIR-LOOM.. AND NEVAH GIVE IT UP FO' NOTHIN' UNDER 2 BUCKS"!
HMM $$$
AH AM OVERCOME WIF TH'SEDIMENT O'THAT STORY... HERE'S YO' DOUGH, OL' MAN..
HERE Y'AR, MISTER.. GENUINE ALADDIN'S LAMP ALL-DAY LIGHTER.. WHAT'LL YO' BID!
HMMM!
5 DOLLARS!
SOLD!
AWKSHUN SALE
PIERPO RARE JOOLS AND JEMS
AND SO..
WHERE YA BEEN, ROSCO? Y'DON'T WANT THE COPS TO SEE YOU GOIN' IN AN' OUTA THIS TRAP!
YEAH, BOSS ..CAN'TCHA KEEP OUTA SIGHT TILL I SWEAT THE SECRET OUTA OLD PINCHY?
OH, I WAS WALKING ..BOUGHT A GENUINE ALADDIN'S LAMP!
AW, QUIT KIDDING.. IF THE OLD GOAT CROAKS, WE..
AAAAAH... WHERE'S YOUR IMAGI-NATION, BOYS? YOU KNOW THE STORY..RUB THE LAMP AND A GENIE APPEARS!
O.K. RUB IT..
WELL.. WHERE IS THE JEANNIE..AND I HOPE SHE'S NICE..HAW HAW!
KNOCK KNOCK
C-COME IN..
GOOD EVENING, MASTER ..YOU CALLED?
2

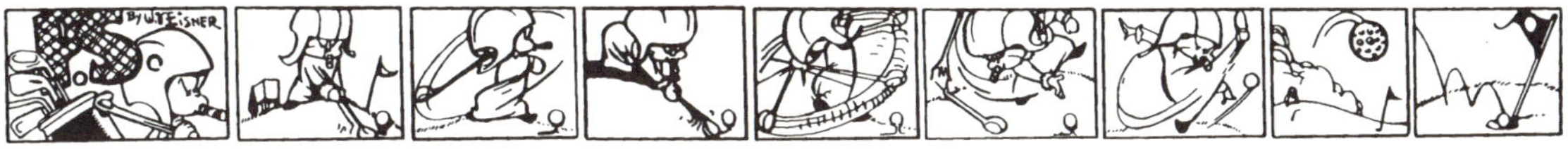
BY W. EISNER

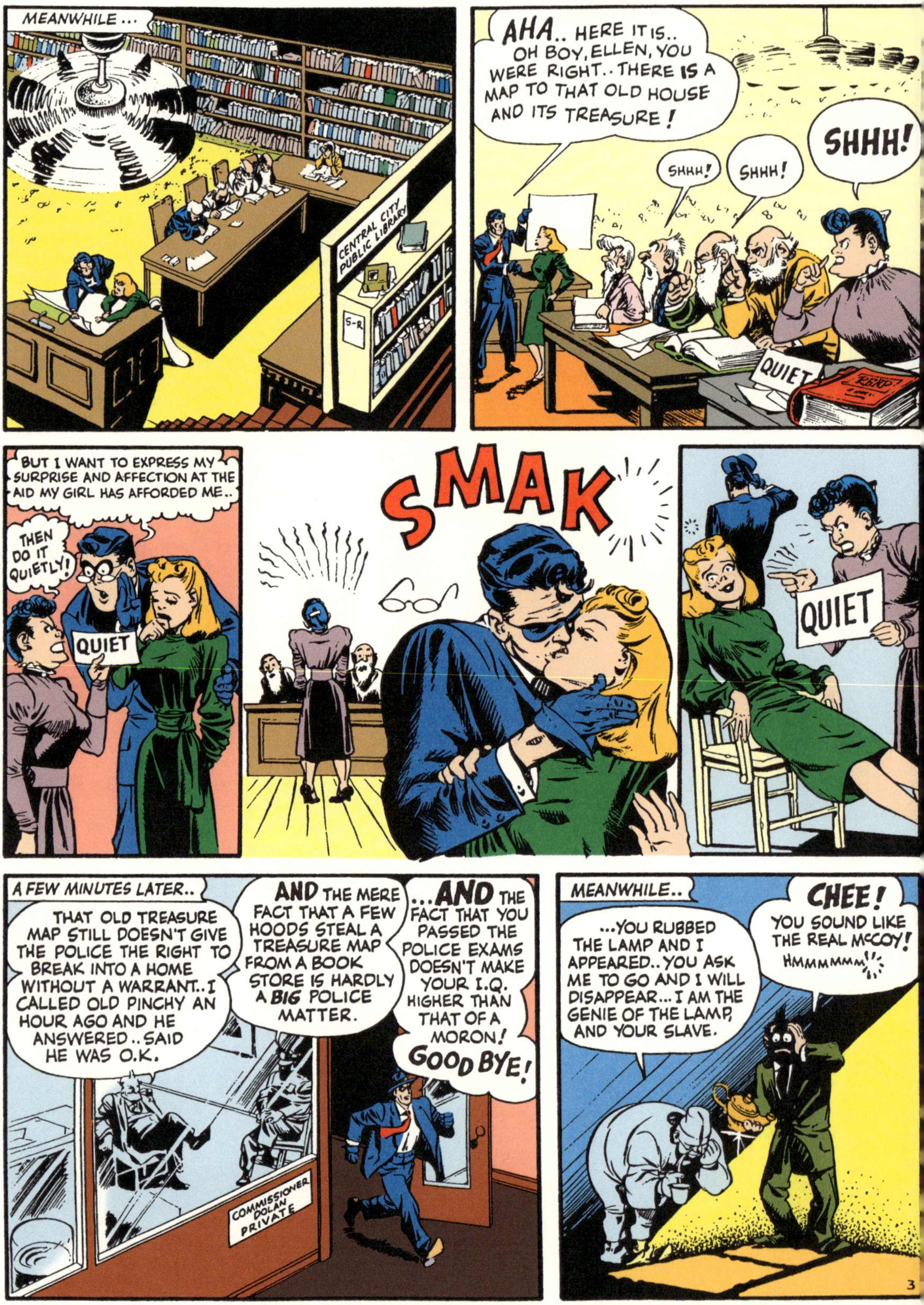
MEANWHILE ...
CENTRAL CITY PUBLIC LIBRARY
S-R
AHA.. HERE IT IS.. OH BOY, ELLEN, YOU WERE RIGHT.. THERE IS A MAP TO THAT OLD HOUSE AND ITS TREASURE!
SHHH!
SHHH!
SHHH!
QUIET
BUT I WANT TO EXPRESS MY SURPRISE AND AFFECTION AT THE AID MY GIRL HAS AFFORDED ME..
THEN DO IT QUIETLY!
QUIET
SMAK
QUIET
A FEW MINUTES LATER..
THAT OLD TREASURE MAP STILL DOESN'T GIVE THE POLICE THE RIGHT TO BREAK INTO A HOME WITHOUT A WARRANT.. I CALLED OLD PINCHY AN HOUR AGO AND HE ANSWERED .. SAID HE WAS O.K.
AND THE MERE FACT THAT A FEW HOODS STEAL A TREASURE MAP FROM A BOOK STORE IS HARDLY A BIG POLICE MATTER.
...AND THE FACT THAT YOU PASSED THE POLICE EXAMS DOESN'T MAKE YOUR I.Q. HIGHER THAN THAT OF A MORON! GOOD BYE!
COMMISSIONER DOLAN PRIVATE
MEANWHILE..
...YOU RUBBED THE LAMP AND I APPEARED.. YOU ASK ME TO GO AND I WILL DISAPPEAR... I AM THE GENIE OF THE LAMP, AND YOUR SLAVE.
CHEE! YOU SOUND LIKE THE REAL McCOY! HMMMMMM!

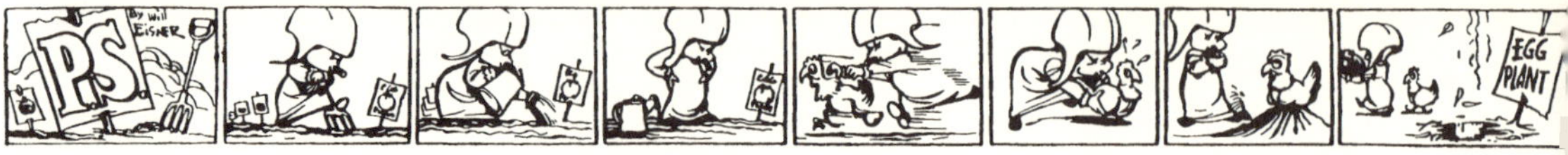
P.S.
By Will Eisner
EGG PLANT

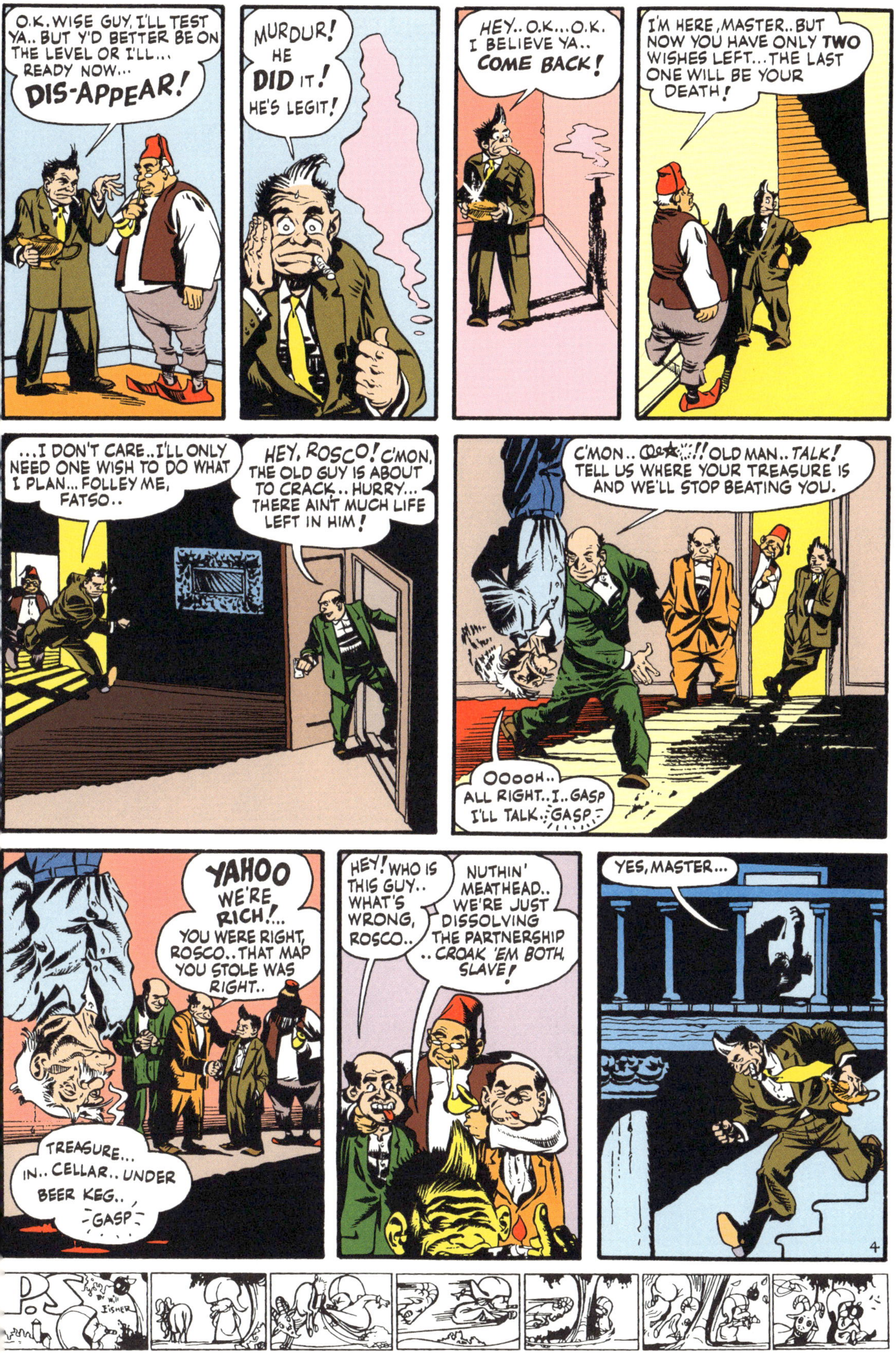

O.K. WISE GUY, I'LL TEST YA.. BUT Y'D BETTER BE ON THE LEVEL OR I'LL... READY NOW... DIS-APPEAR!
MURDUR! HE DID IT! HE'S LEGIT!
HEY.. O.K... O.K. I BELIEVE YA.. COME BACK!
I'M HERE, MASTER.. BUT NOW YOU HAVE ONLY TWO WISHES LEFT... THE LAST ONE WILL BE YOUR DEATH!
...I DON'T CARE.. I'LL ONLY NEED ONE WISH TO DO WHAT I PLAN... FOLLEY ME, FATSO..
HEY, ROSCO! C'MON, THE OLD GUY IS ABOUT TO CRACK.. HURRY... THERE AIN'T MUCH LIFE LEFT IN HIM!
C'MON.. !! OLD MAN.. TALK! TELL US WHERE YOUR TREASURE IS AND WE'LL STOP BEATING YOU.
OOOOH.. ALL RIGHT.. I.. GASP I'LL TALK.. GASP
YAHOO WE'RE RICH!... YOU WERE RIGHT, ROSCO.. THAT MAP YOU STOLE WAS RIGHT..
TREASURE... IN.. CELLAR.. UNDER BEER KEG.. GASP
HEY! WHO IS THIS GUY.. WHAT'S WRONG, ROSCO..
NUTHIN' MEATHEAD.. WE'RE JUST DISSOLVING THE PARTNERSHIP.. CROAK 'EM BOTH, SLAVE!
YES, MASTER...
4
P.S. BY WILL EISNER

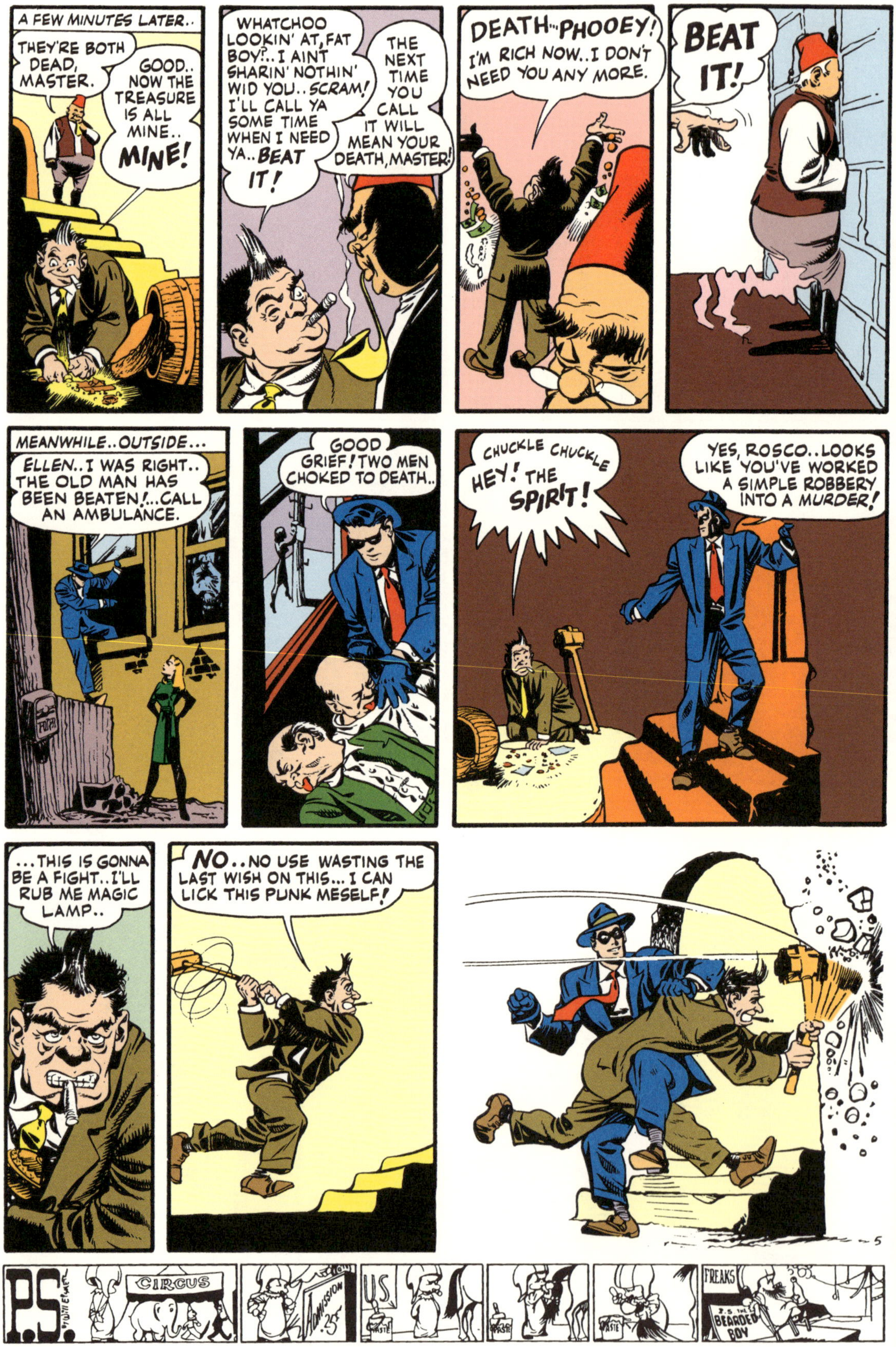
A FEW MINUTES LATER..
THEY'RE BOTH DEAD, MASTER.
GOOD.. NOW THE TREASURE IS ALL MINE.. MINE!
WHATCHOO LOOKIN' AT, FAT BOY?.. I AIN'T SHARIN' NOTHIN' WID YOU.. SCRAM! I'LL CALL YA SOME TIME WHEN I NEED YA.. BEAT IT!
THE NEXT TIME YOU CALL IT WILL MEAN YOUR DEATH, MASTER!
DEATH... PHOOEY! I'M RICH NOW.. I DON'T NEED YOU ANY MORE.
BEAT IT!
MEANWHILE.. OUTSIDE...
ELLEN.. I WAS RIGHT.. THE OLD MAN HAS BEEN BEATEN!...CALL AN AMBULANCE.
GOOD GRIEF! TWO MEN CHOKED TO DEATH..
CHUCKLE CHUCKLE
HEY! THE SPIRIT!
YES, ROSCO.. LOOKS LIKE YOU'VE WORKED A SIMPLE ROBBERY INTO A MURDER!
...THIS IS GONNA BE A FIGHT.. I'LL RUB ME MAGIC LAMP..
NO.. NO USE WASTING THE LAST WISH ON THIS... I CAN LICK THIS PUNK MESELF!
P.S.
CIRCUS
ADMISSION 25¢
FREAKS
P.S. THE BEARDED BOY

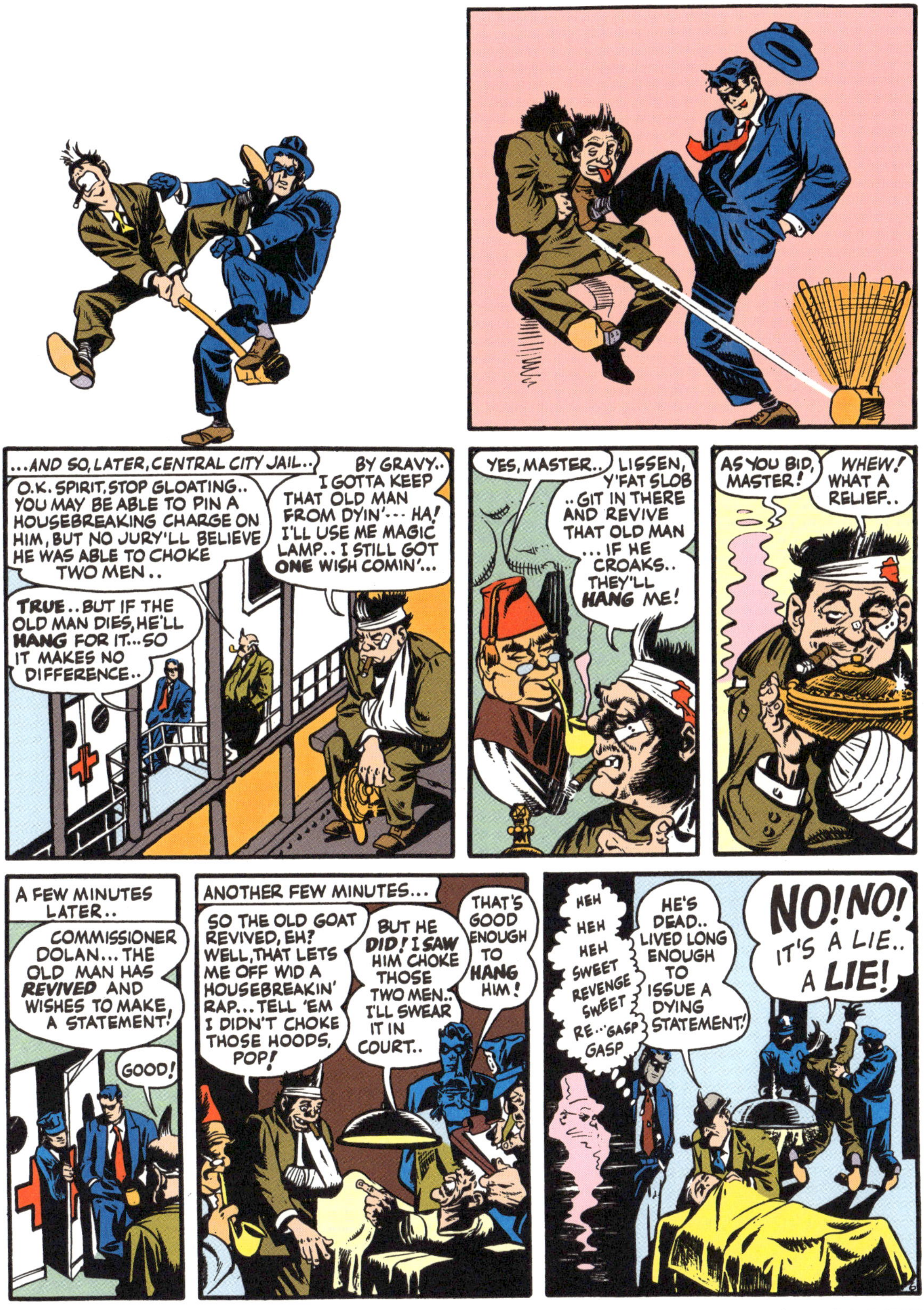
...AND SO, LATER, CENTRAL CITY JAIL..
O.K. SPIRIT, STOP GLOATING.. YOU MAY BE ABLE TO PIN A HOUSEBREAKING CHARGE ON HIM, BUT NO JURY'LL BELIEVE HE WAS ABLE TO CHOKE TWO MEN..
TRUE..BUT IF THE OLD MAN DIES, HE'LL HANG FOR IT...SO IT MAKES NO DIFFERENCE..
BY GRAVY.. I GOTTA KEEP THAT OLD MAN FROM DYIN'--- HA! I'LL USE ME MAGIC LAMP.. I STILL GOT ONE WISH COMIN'...
YES, MASTER..
LISSEN, Y'FAT SLOB ..GIT IN THERE AND REVIVE THAT OLD MAN ... IF HE CROAKS.. THEY'LL HANG ME!
AS YOU BID, MASTER!
WHEW! WHAT A RELIEF..
A FEW MINUTES LATER..
COMMISSIONER DOLAN... THE OLD MAN HAS REVIVED AND WISHES TO MAKE A STATEMENT!
GOOD!
ANOTHER FEW MINUTES...
SO THE OLD GOAT REVIVED, EH? WELL, THAT LETS ME OFF WID A HOUSEBREAKIN' RAP... TELL 'EM I DIDN'T CHOKE THOSE HOODS, POP!
BUT HE DID! I SAW HIM CHOKE THOSE TWO MEN.. I'LL SWEAR IT IN COURT..
THAT'S GOOD ENOUGH TO HANG HIM!
HEH HEH HEH SWEET REVENGE SWEET RE...GASP GASP
HE'S DEAD.. LIVED LONG ENOUGH TO ISSUE A DYING STATEMENT!
NO! NO! IT'S A LIE.. A LIE!

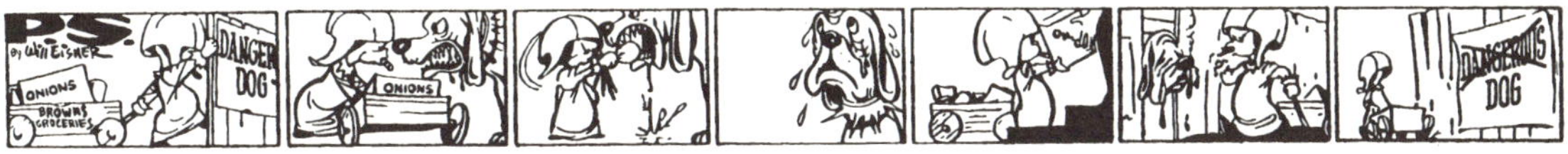
P.S.
BY Will Eisner
DANGER DOG
ONIONS
ONIONS
DANGEROUS DOG

SOME WEEKS LATER..
WELL THAT'S THAT... LET'S GO HOME, EBONY... I DON'T LIKE THIS PART OF CRIME-FIGHTING...
HEY LOOKIT... THE ALADDIN'S LAMP I SOLD TO PIERPONT..
ROSCO DIES IN CHAIR FOR MURDER!
5467X
I WONDER IF IT REALLY IS A WISHIN' LAMP LIKE THE MAN SAID...
I'LL RUB IT..
AH MIGHT HAVE KNOWN IT WUZ A PHONEY!
EBONY...COME ALONG...
YASSUH, MIST' SPIRIT...
TSK TSK ... I COULD HAVE SWORN I WAS SUMMONED..
The Spirit
By Will Eisner
ANTIQUE SHOP
Spiri
By Will Eisner
FOR SALE GENUINE ALADDIN'S LAMP $5.00
ANTIQUE S
Next Week:
LET US LEAF THROUGH SOME OF THE SKETCHES FOR NEXT WEEK'S SPIRIT
HMM... A NEW CHARACTER... OFFICER SAM KLINK..
SAREE..
AND..
EEEK! P'GELL
GULP

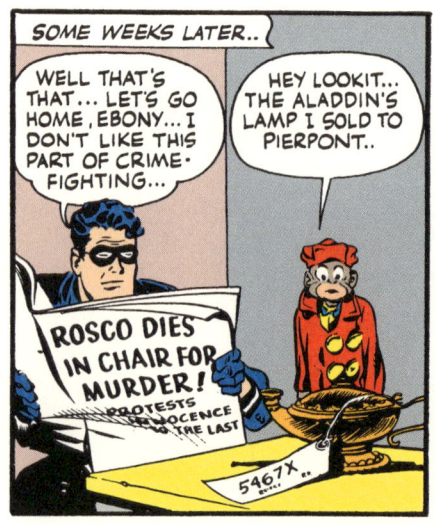

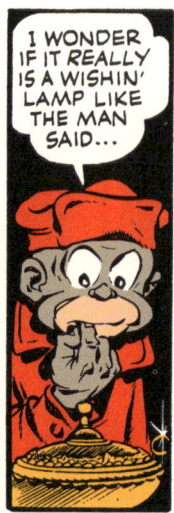

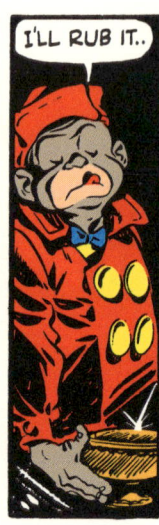

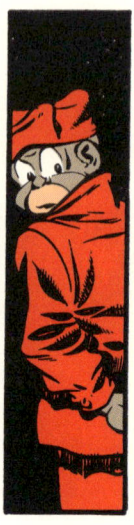

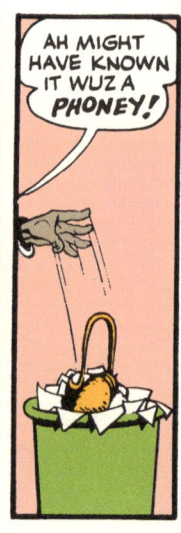

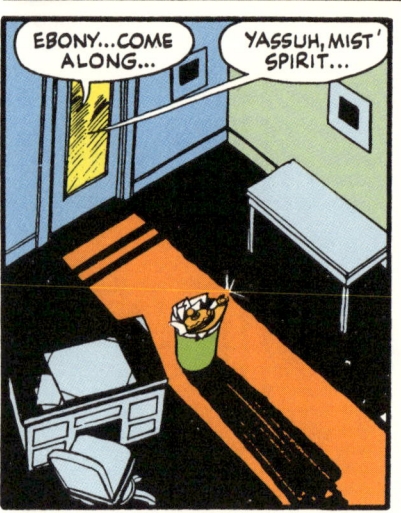

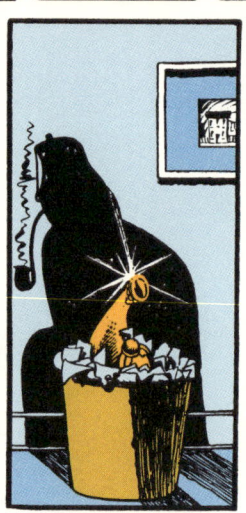

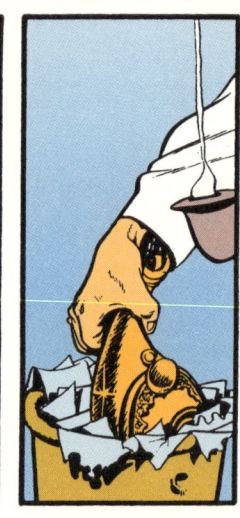

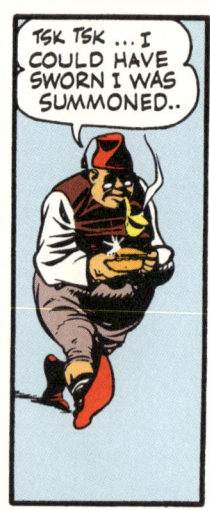

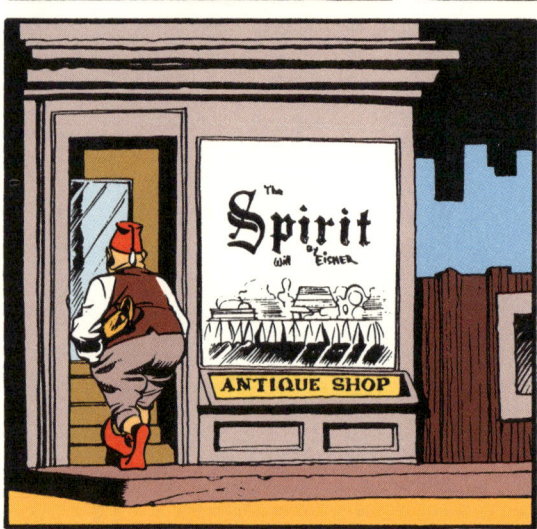

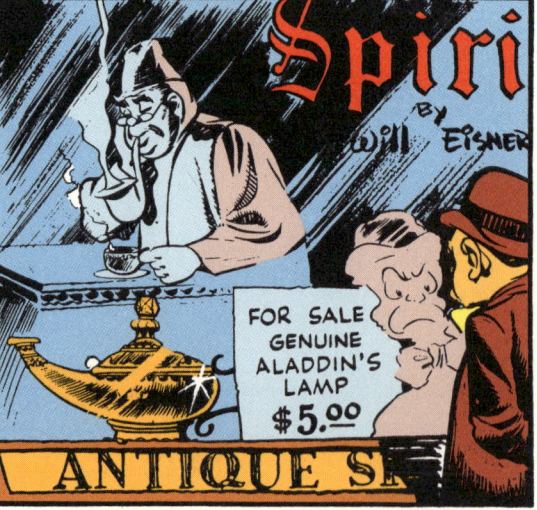

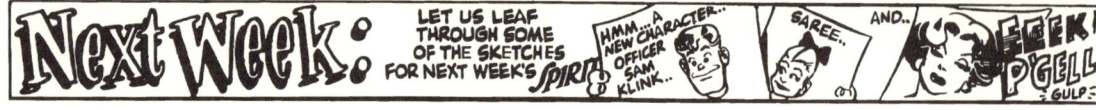

COMIC BOOK SECTION

COMPETITION

August 3 1947

ACTION Mystery ADVENTURE

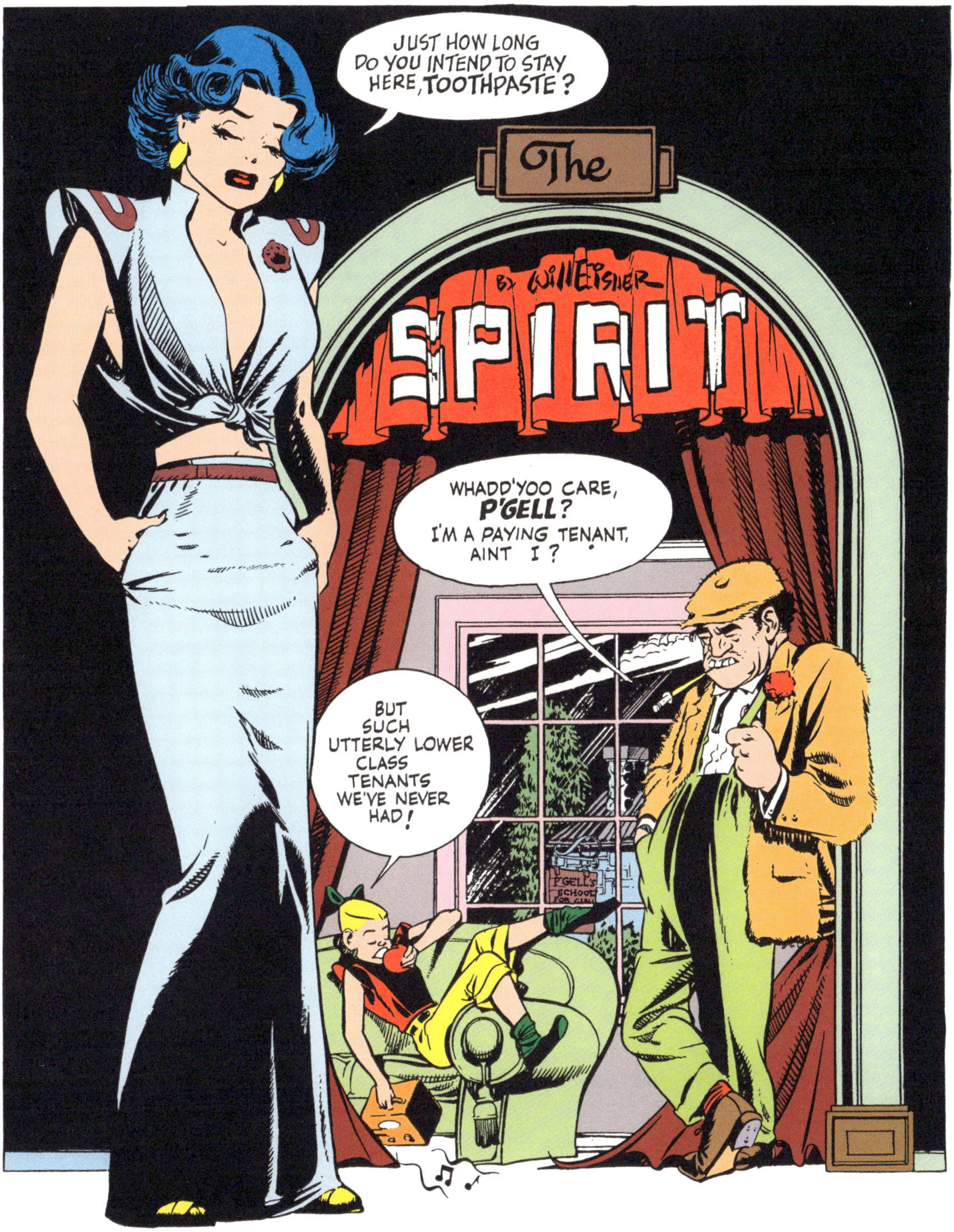

JUST HOW LONG DO YOU INTEND TO STAY HERE, TOOTHPASTE?
The
BY WILL EISNER
SPIRIT
WHADD'YOO CARE, P'GELL? I'M A PAYING TENANT, AINT I?
BUT SUCH UTTERLY LOWER CLASS TENANTS WE'VE NEVER HAD!

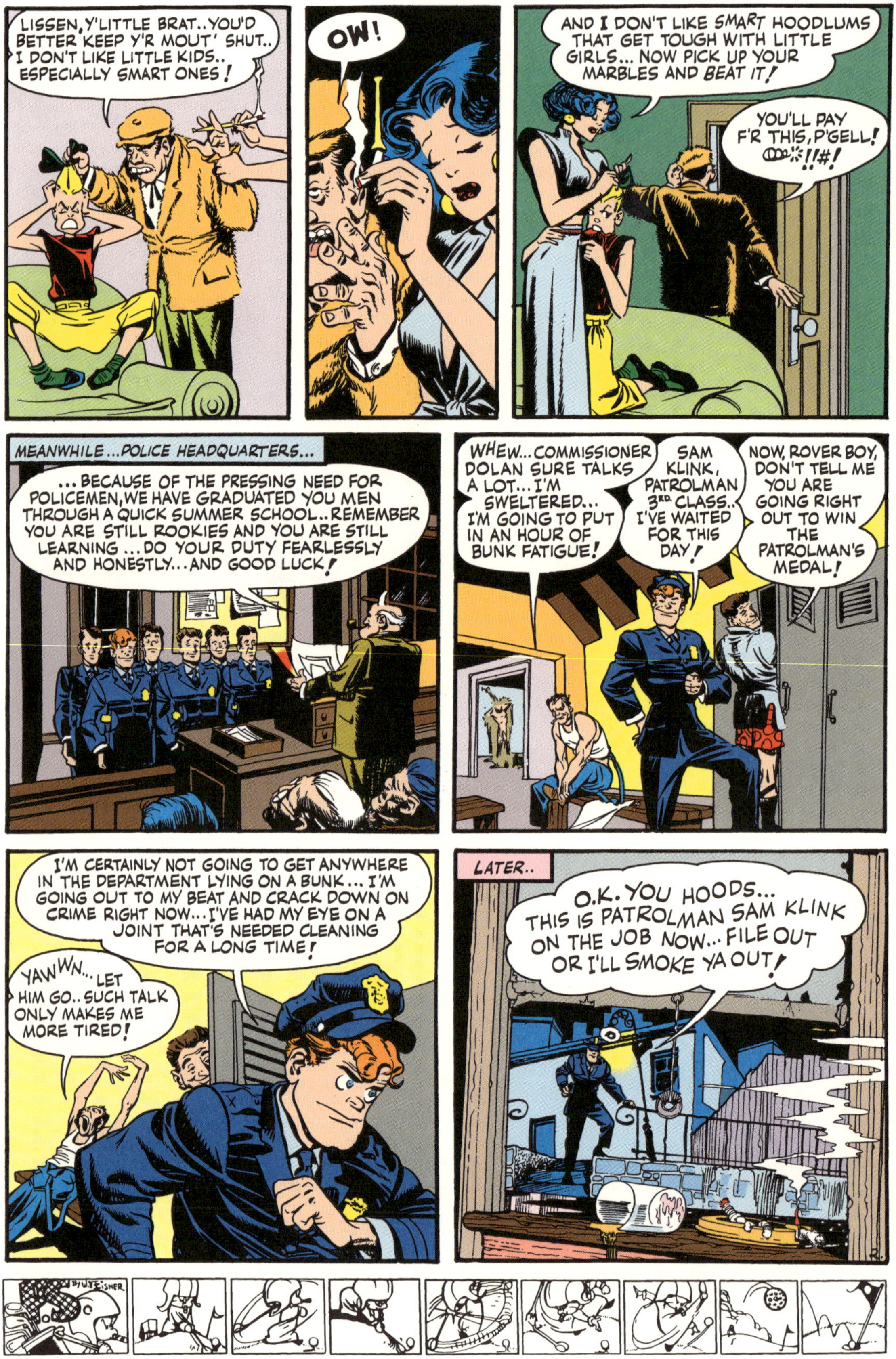

LISSEN, Y'LITTLE BRAT.. YOU'D BETTER KEEP Y'R MOUT' SHUT.. I DON'T LIKE LITTLE KIDS.. ESPECIALLY SMART ONES!
OW!
AND I DON'T LIKE SMART HOODLUMS THAT GET TOUGH WITH LITTLE GIRLS... NOW PICK UP YOUR MARBLES AND BEAT IT!
YOU'LL PAY F'R THIS, P'GELL! !!#!
MEANWHILE ...POLICE HEADQUARTERS...
... BECAUSE OF THE PRESSING NEED FOR POLICEMEN, WE HAVE GRADUATED YOU MEN THROUGH A QUICK SUMMER SCHOOL.. REMEMBER YOU ARE STILL ROOKIES AND YOU ARE STILL LEARNING ... DO YOUR DUTY FEARLESSLY AND HONESTLY... AND GOOD LUCK!
WHEW... COMMISSIONER DOLAN SURE TALKS A LOT... I'M SWELTERED... I'M GOING TO PUT IN AN HOUR OF BUNK FATIGUE!
SAM KLINK, PATROLMAN 3RD. CLASS.. I'VE WAITED FOR THIS DAY!
NOW, ROVER BOY, DON'T TELL ME YOU ARE GOING RIGHT OUT TO WIN THE PATROLMAN'S MEDAL!
I'M CERTAINLY NOT GOING TO GET ANYWHERE IN THE DEPARTMENT LYING ON A BUNK... I'M GOING OUT TO MY BEAT AND CRACK DOWN ON CRIME RIGHT NOW... I'VE HAD MY EYE ON A JOINT THAT'S NEEDED CLEANING FOR A LONG TIME!
YAWWN... LET HIM GO.. SUCH TALK ONLY MAKES ME MORE TIRED!
LATER..
O.K. YOU HOODS... THIS IS PATROLMAN SAM KLINK ON THE JOB NOW... FILE OUT OR I'LL SMOKE YA OUT!

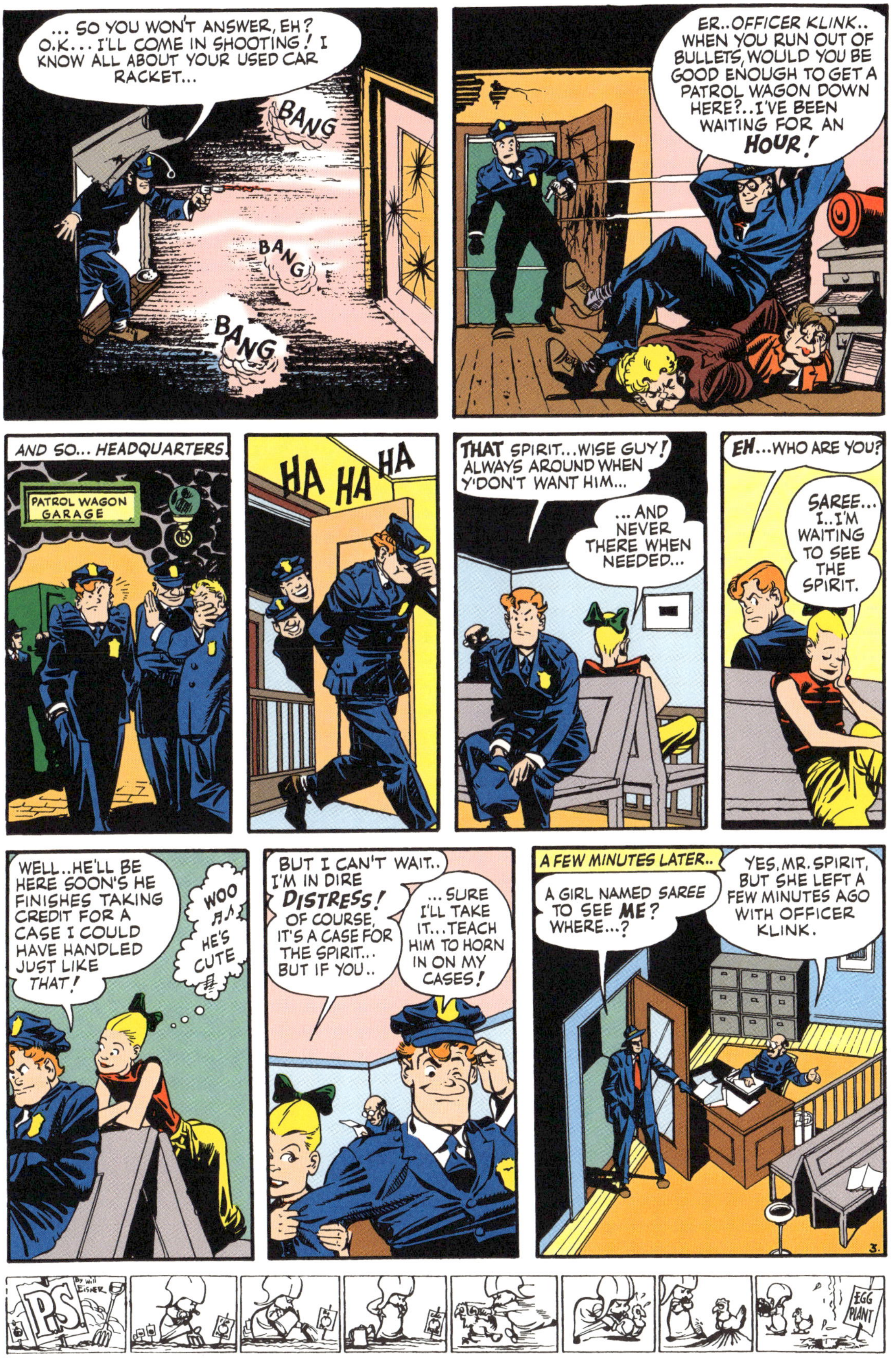
... SO YOU WON'T ANSWER, EH? O.K... I'LL COME IN SHOOTING! I KNOW ALL ABOUT YOUR USED CAR RACKET...
BANG
BANG
BANG
ER..OFFICER KLINK.. WHEN YOU RUN OUT OF BULLETS, WOULD YOU BE GOOD ENOUGH TO GET A PATROL WAGON DOWN HERE?..I'VE BEEN WAITING FOR AN HOUR!
AND SO... HEADQUARTERS!
PATROL WAGON GARAGE
HA HA HA
THAT SPIRIT...WISE GUY! ALWAYS AROUND WHEN Y'DON'T WANT HIM...
...AND NEVER THERE WHEN NEEDED...
EH...WHO ARE YOU?
SAREE... I..I'M WAITING TO SEE THE SPIRIT.
WELL..HE'LL BE HERE SOON'S HE FINISHES TAKING CREDIT FOR A CASE I COULD HAVE HANDLED JUST LIKE THAT!
WOO HE'S CUTE
BUT I CAN'T WAIT.. I'M IN DIRE DISTRESS! OF COURSE, IT'S A CASE FOR THE SPIRIT.. BUT IF YOU..
...SURE I'LL TAKE IT...TEACH HIM TO HORN IN ON MY CASES!
A FEW MINUTES LATER..
A GIRL NAMED SAREE TO SEE ME? WHERE...?
YES, MR. SPIRIT, BUT SHE LEFT A FEW MINUTES AGO WITH OFFICER KLINK.
3.
P.S.
By Will Eisner
EGG PLANT

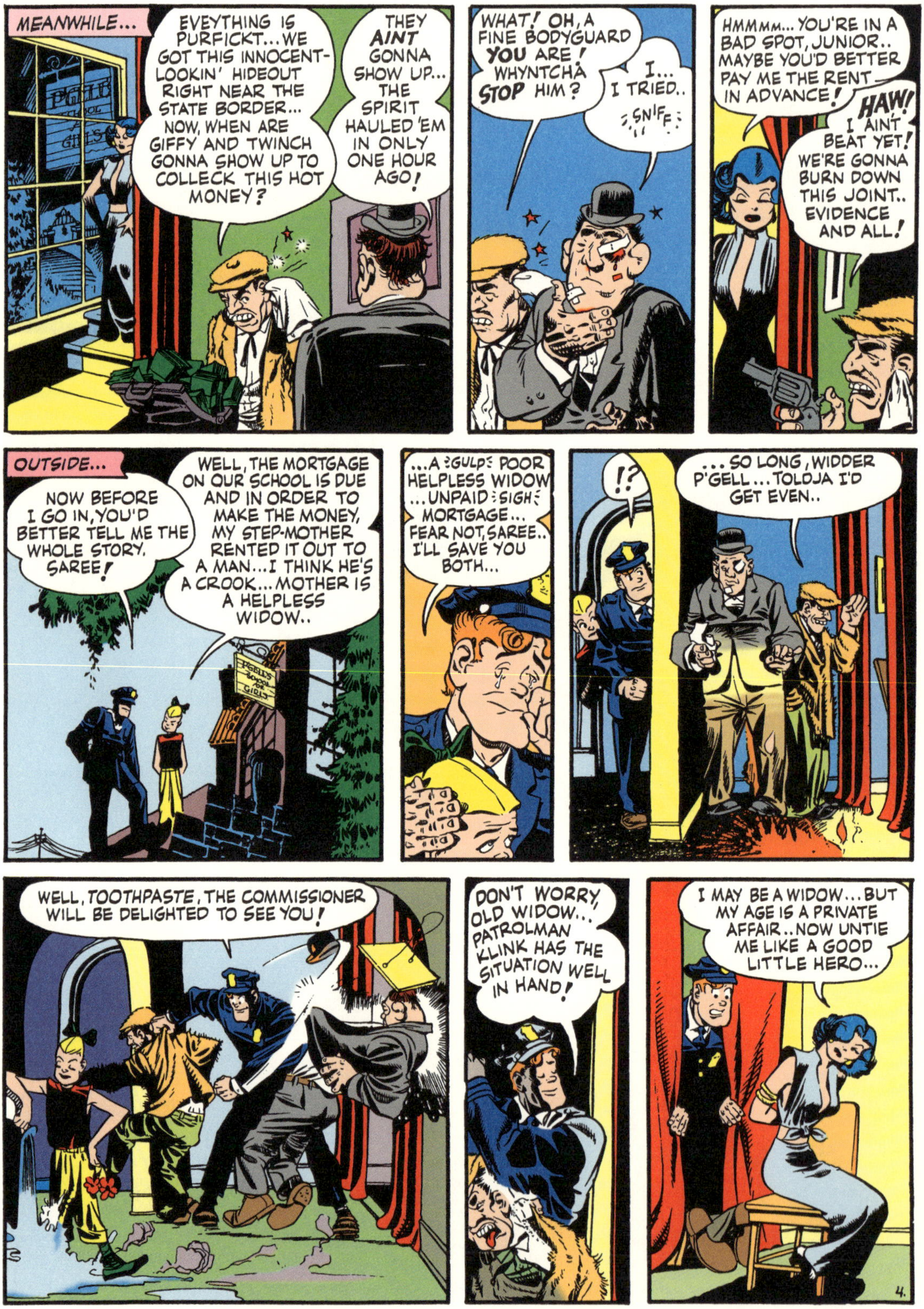
MEANWHILE...
EVEYTHING IS PURFICKT...WE GOT THIS INNOCENT-LOOKIN' HIDEOUT RIGHT NEAR THE STATE BORDER... NOW, WHEN ARE GIFFY AND TWINCH GONNA SHOW UP TO COLLECK THIS HOT MONEY?
THEY AINT GONNA SHOW UP... THE SPIRIT HAULED 'EM IN ONLY ONE HOUR AGO!
WHAT! OH, A FINE BODYGUARD YOU ARE! WHYNTCHA STOP HIM?
I... I TRIED.. SNIFF
HMMMM... YOU'RE IN A BAD SPOT, JUNIOR.. MAYBE YOU'D BETTER PAY ME THE RENT IN ADVANCE!
HAW! I AIN'T BEAT YET! WE'RE GONNA BURN DOWN THIS JOINT.. EVIDENCE AND ALL!
OUTSIDE...
NOW BEFORE I GO IN, YOU'D BETTER TELL ME THE WHOLE STORY, SAREE!
WELL, THE MORTGAGE ON OUR SCHOOL IS DUE AND IN ORDER TO MAKE THE MONEY, MY STEP-MOTHER RENTED IT OUT TO A MAN... I THINK HE'S A CROOK... MOTHER IS A HELPLESS WIDOW..
...A GULP POOR HELPLESS WIDOW ...UNPAID SIGH MORTGAGE... FEAR NOT, SAREE.. I'LL SAVE YOU BOTH...
!?
...SO LONG, WIDDER P'GELL... TOLDJA I'D GET EVEN..
WELL, TOOTHPASTE, THE COMMISSIONER WILL BE DELIGHTED TO SEE YOU!
DON'T WORRY, OLD WIDOW... PATROLMAN KLINK HAS THE SITUATION WELL IN HAND!
I MAY BE A WIDOW... BUT MY AGE IS A PRIVATE AFFAIR.. NOW UNTIE ME LIKE A GOOD LITTLE HERO...
4.

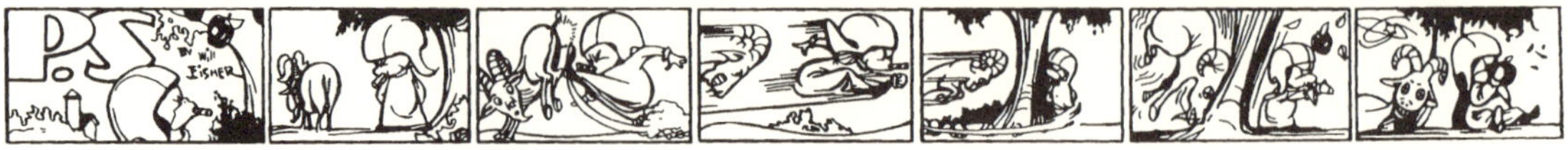
P.S.

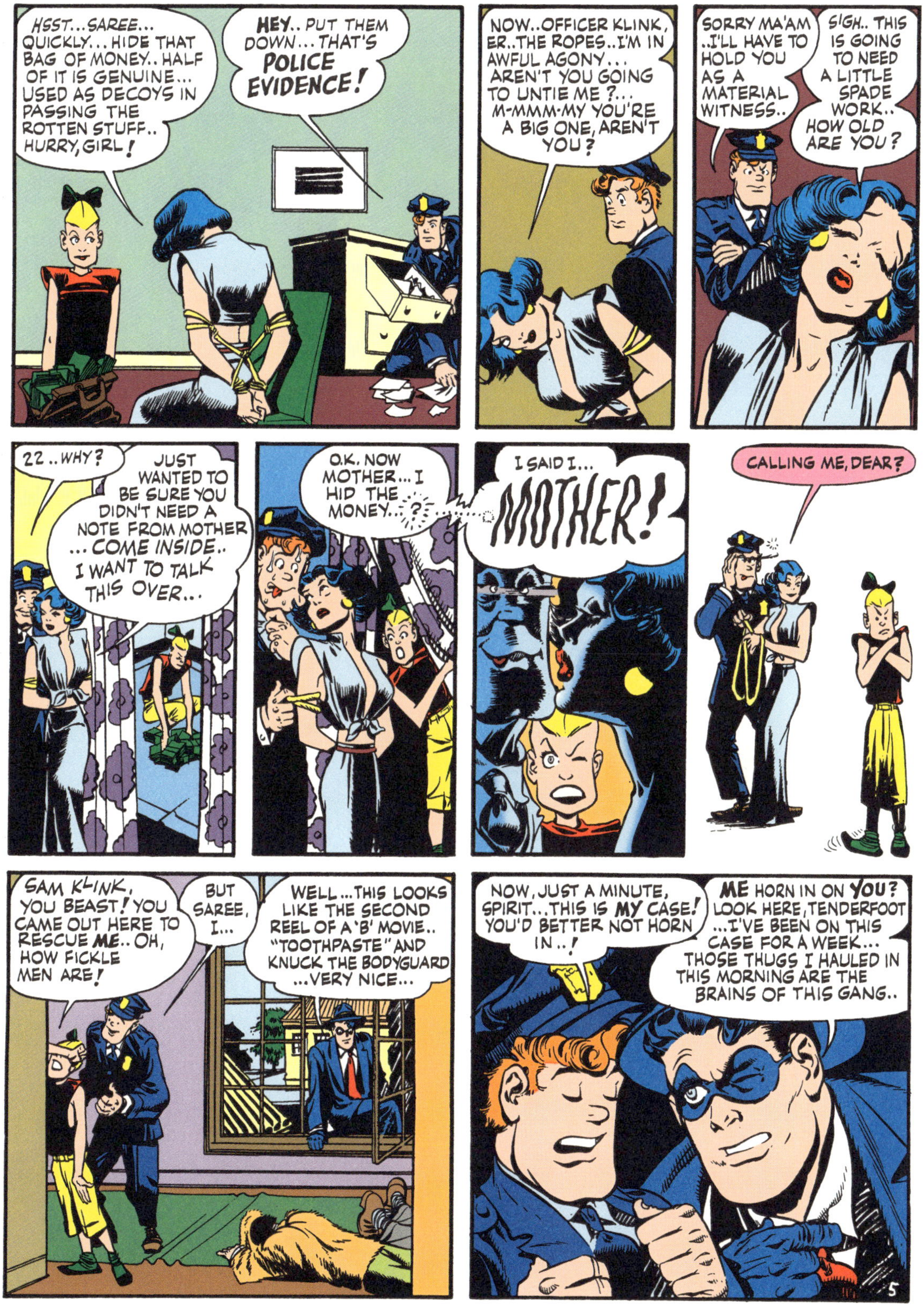
HSST...SAREE... QUICKLY... HIDE THAT BAG OF MONEY.. HALF OF IT IS GENUINE... USED AS DECOYS IN PASSING THE ROTTEN STUFF.. HURRY, GIRL!
HEY.. PUT THEM DOWN... THAT'S POLICE EVIDENCE!
NOW..OFFICER KLINK, ER..THE ROPES..I'M IN AWFUL AGONY... AREN'T YOU GOING TO UNTIE ME ?... M-MMM-MY YOU'RE A BIG ONE, AREN'T YOU?
SORRY MA'AM ..I'LL HAVE TO HOLD YOU AS A MATERIAL WITNESS..
SIGH.. THIS IS GOING TO NEED A LITTLE SPADE WORK.. HOW OLD ARE YOU?
22.. WHY?
JUST WANTED TO BE SURE YOU DIDN'T NEED A NOTE FROM MOTHER ... COME INSIDE.. I WANT TO TALK THIS OVER...
O.K. NOW MOTHER... I HID THE MONEY..?
I SAID I... MOTHER!
CALLING ME, DEAR?
SAM KLINK, YOU BEAST! YOU CAME OUT HERE TO RESCUE ME.. OH, HOW FICKLE MEN ARE!
BUT SAREE, I...
WELL...THIS LOOKS LIKE THE SECOND REEL OF A 'B' MOVIE.. "TOOTHPASTE" AND KNUCK THE BODYGUARD ...VERY NICE...
NOW, JUST A MINUTE, SPIRIT...THIS IS MY CASE! YOU'D BETTER NOT HORN IN..!
ME HORN IN ON YOU? LOOK HERE, TENDERFOOT ...I'VE BEEN ON THIS CASE FOR A WEEK... THOSE THUGS I HAULED IN THIS MORNING ARE THE BRAINS OF THIS GANG..
5

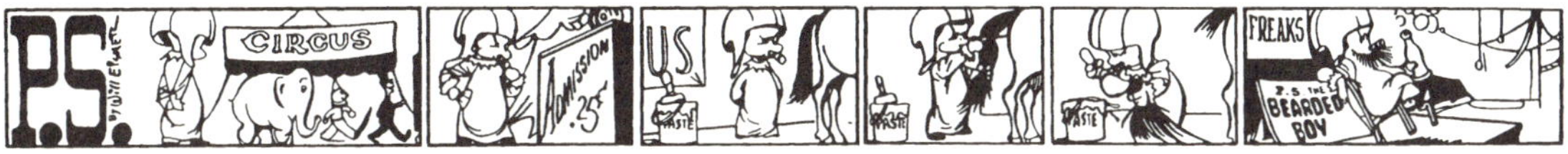
P.S.
CIRCUS
ADMISSION 25¢
FREAKS
P.S. THE BEARDED BOY

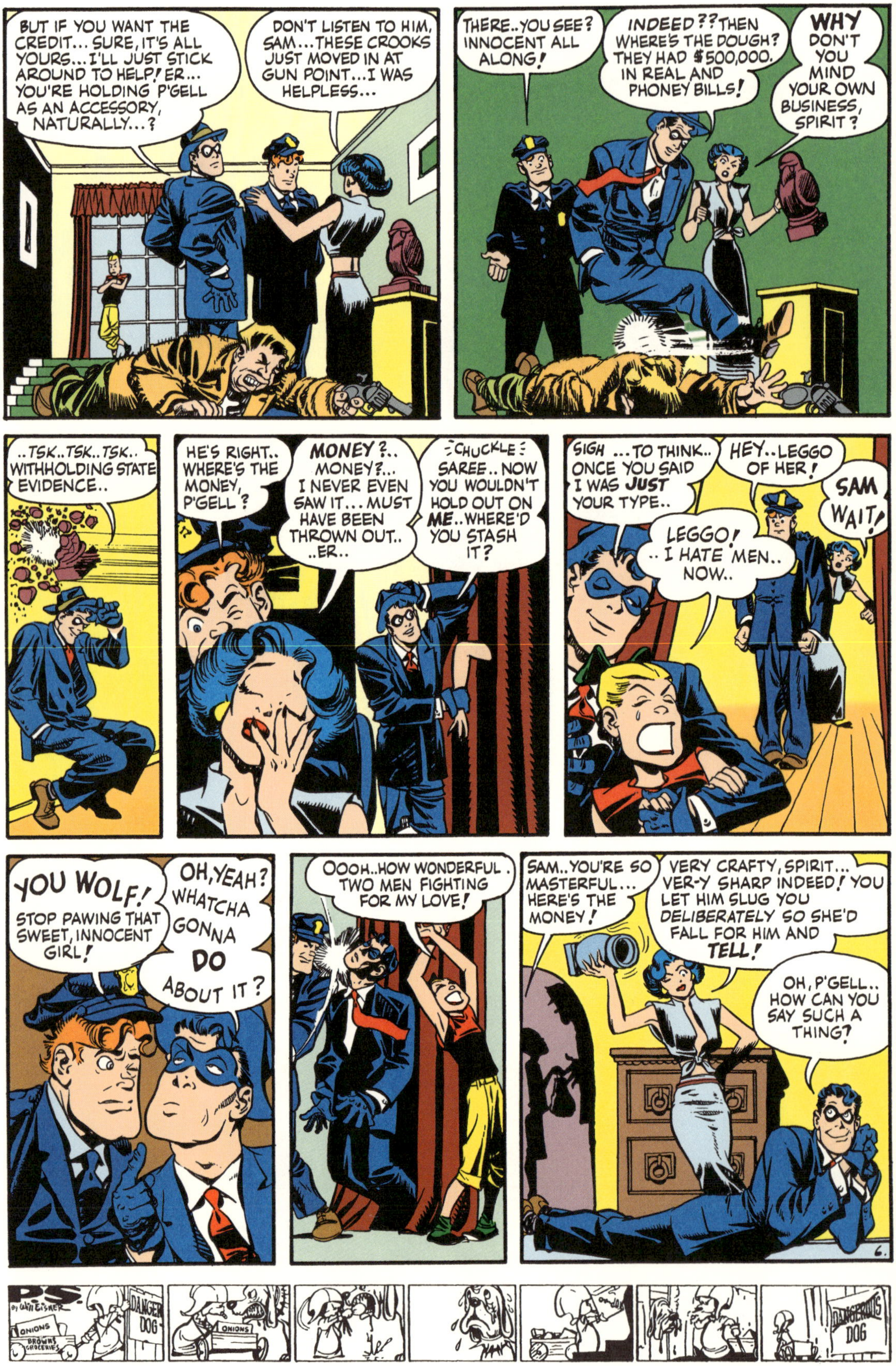

BUT IF YOU WANT THE CREDIT... SURE, IT'S ALL YOURS... I'LL JUST STICK AROUND TO HELP! ER... YOU'RE HOLDING P'GELL AS AN ACCESSORY, NATURALLY...?
DON'T LISTEN TO HIM, SAM... THESE CROOKS JUST MOVED IN AT GUN POINT... I WAS HELPLESS...
THERE..YOU SEE? INNOCENT ALL ALONG!
INDEED?? THEN WHERE'S THE DOUGH? THEY HAD $500,000. IN REAL AND PHONEY BILLS!
WHY DON'T YOU MIND YOUR OWN BUSINESS, SPIRIT?
..TSK..TSK..TSK.. WITHHOLDING STATE EVIDENCE..
HE'S RIGHT.. WHERE'S THE MONEY, P'GELL?
MONEY?.. MONEY?... I NEVER EVEN SAW IT... MUST HAVE BEEN THROWN OUT.. ..ER..
CHUCKLE SAREE.. NOW YOU WOULDN'T HOLD OUT ON ME..WHERE'D YOU STASH IT?
SIGH ...TO THINK.. ONCE YOU SAID I WAS JUST YOUR TYPE..
HEY..LEGGO OF HER!
SAM WAIT!
LEGGO! .. I HATE MEN.. NOW..
YOU WOLF! STOP PAWING THAT SWEET, INNOCENT GIRL!
OH, YEAH? WHATCHA GONNA DO ABOUT IT?
OOOH..HOW WONDERFUL. TWO MEN FIGHTING FOR MY LOVE!
SAM..YOU'RE SO MASTERFUL... HERE'S THE MONEY!
VERY CRAFTY, SPIRIT... VER-Y SHARP INDEED! YOU LET HIM SLUG YOU DELIBERATELY SO SHE'D FALL FOR HIM AND TELL!
OH, P'GELL.. HOW CAN YOU SAY SUCH A THING?
6.
P.S.
DANGER DOG
ONIONS
DANGEROUS DOG

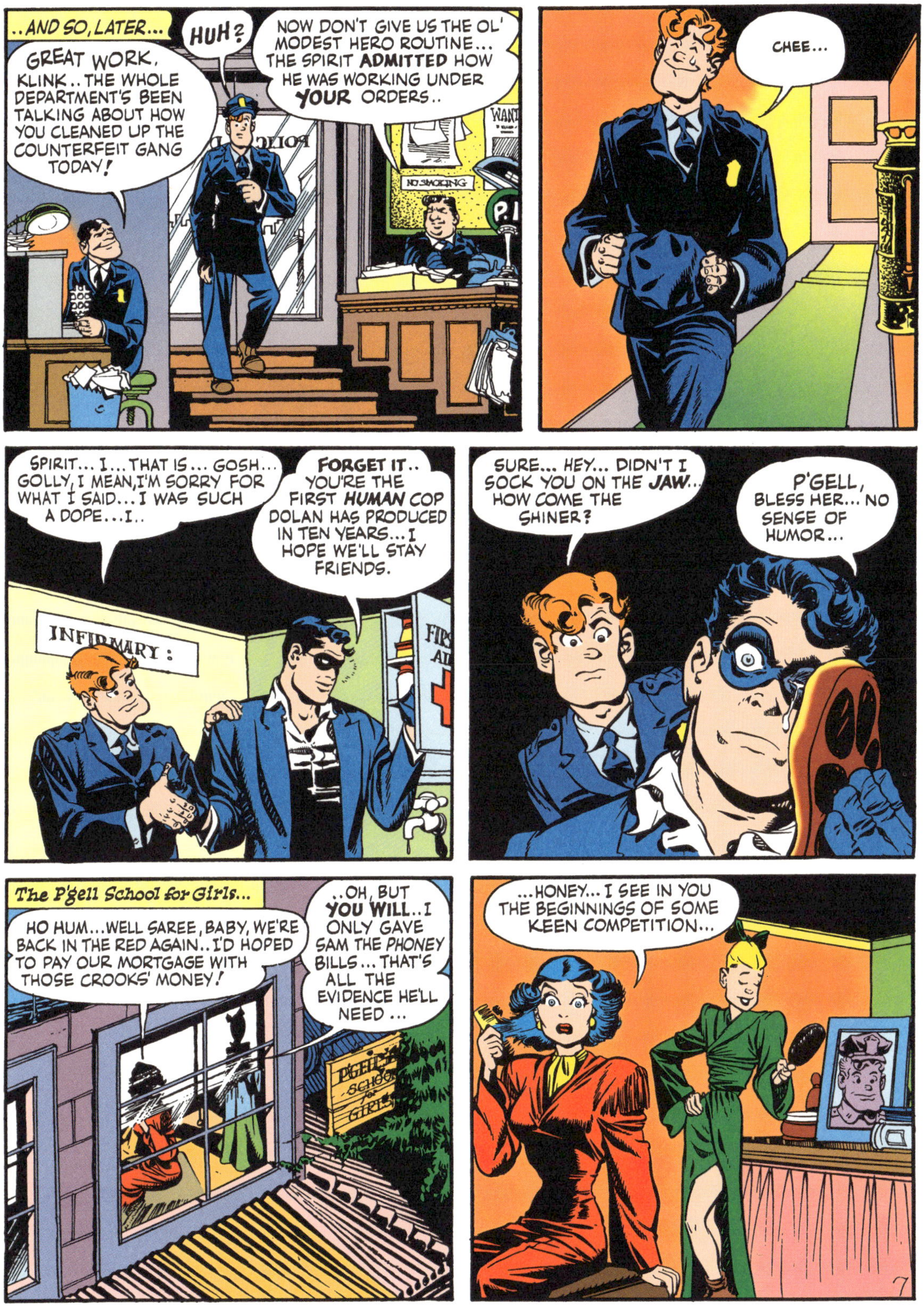
..AND SO, LATER...
GREAT WORK, KLINK.. THE WHOLE DEPARTMENT'S BEEN TALKING ABOUT HOW YOU CLEANED UP THE COUNTERFEIT GANG TODAY!
HUH?
NOW DON'T GIVE US THE OL' MODEST HERO ROUTINE... THE SPIRIT ADMITTED HOW HE WAS WORKING UNDER YOUR ORDERS..
NO SMOKING
CHEE...
SPIRIT... I... THAT IS... GOSH... GOLLY, I MEAN, I'M SORRY FOR WHAT I SAID... I WAS SUCH A DOPE... I..
FORGET IT.. YOU'RE THE FIRST HUMAN COP DOLAN HAS PRODUCED IN TEN YEARS... I HOPE WE'LL STAY FRIENDS.
INFIRMARY :
SURE... HEY... DIDN'T I SOCK YOU ON THE JAW... HOW COME THE SHINER?
P'GELL, BLESS HER... NO SENSE OF HUMOR...
The P'gell School for Girls...
HO HUM... WELL SAREE, BABY, WE'RE BACK IN THE RED AGAIN.. I'D HOPED TO PAY OUR MORTGAGE WITH THOSE CROOKS' MONEY!
..OH, BUT YOU WILL.. I ONLY GAVE SAM THE PHONEY BILLS... THAT'S ALL THE EVIDENCE HE'LL NEED ...
...HONEY... I SEE IN YOU THE BEGINNINGS OF SOME KEEN COMPETITION...
7

COMIC BOOK SECTION

SIGN OF THE OCTOPUS

August 10 1947

ACTION Mystery ADVENTURE

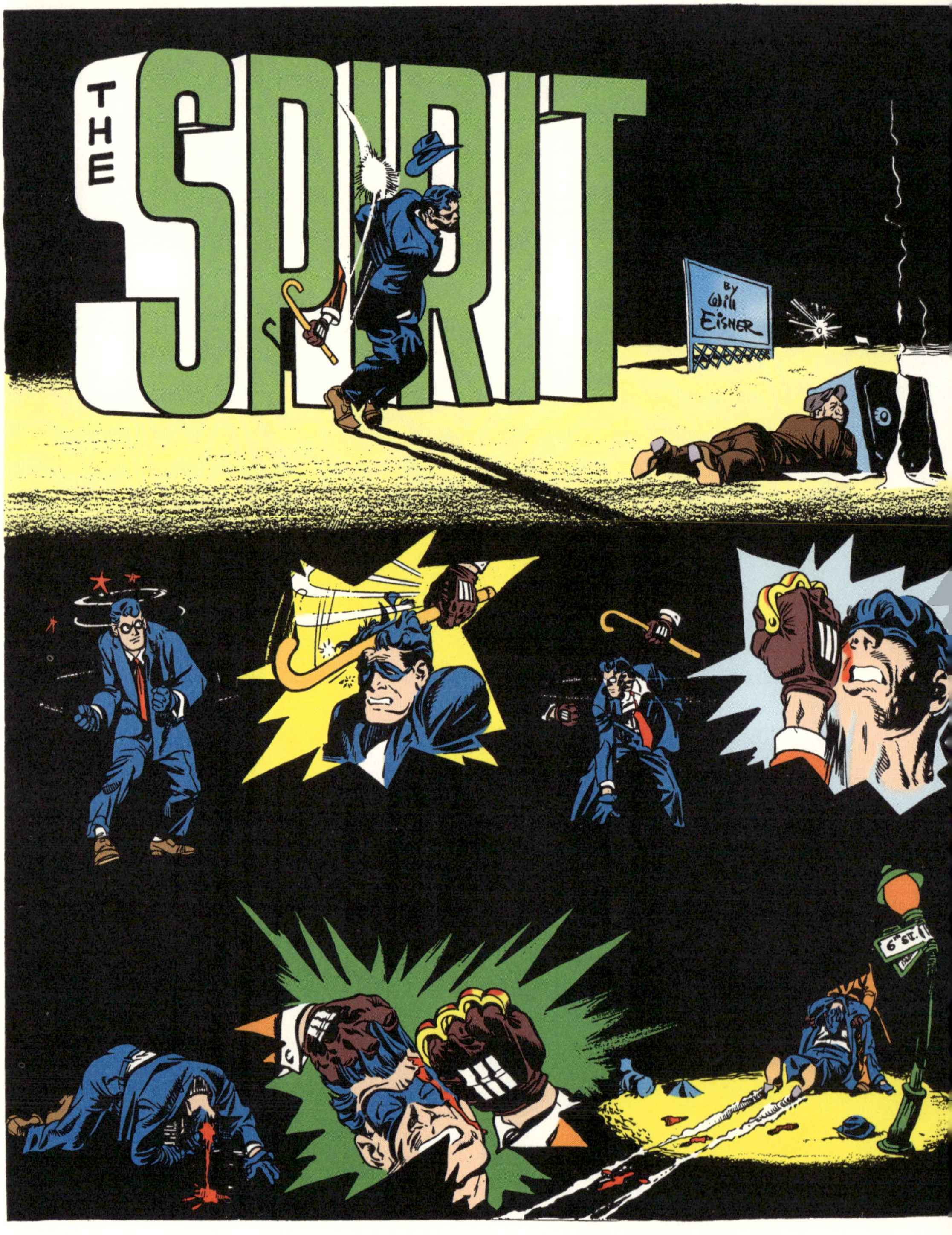

THE SPIRIT
BY Will EISNER
6th ST.

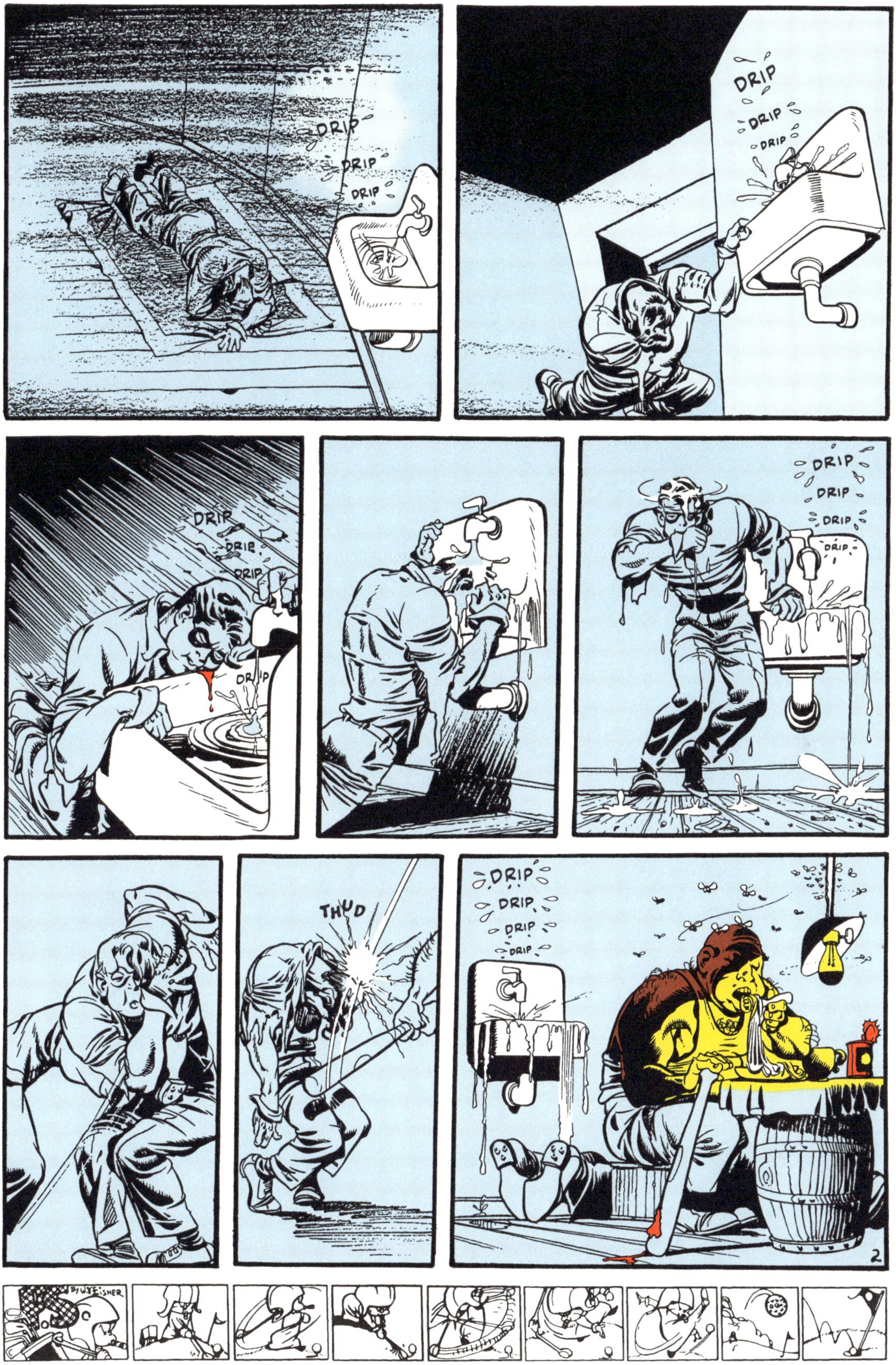
DRIP
DRIP
DRIP
DRIP
DRIP
DRIP
DRIP
DRIP
DRIP
DRIP
DRIP
DRIP
DRIP
DRIP
DRIP
THUD
DRIP
DRIP
DRIP
DRIP
2

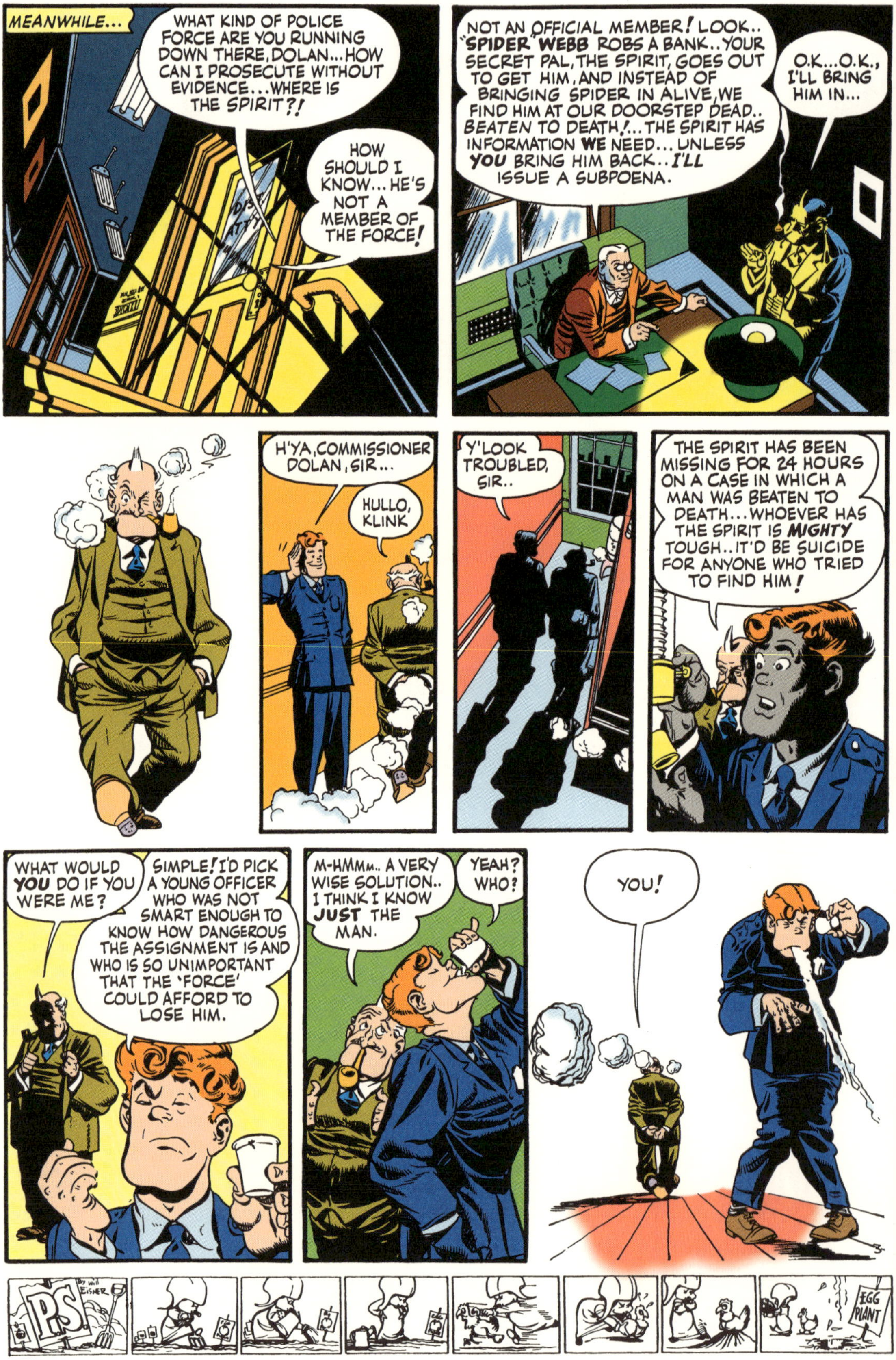

MEANWHILE...
WHAT KIND OF POLICE FORCE ARE YOU RUNNING DOWN THERE, DOLAN...HOW CAN I PROSECUTE WITHOUT EVIDENCE...WHERE IS THE SPIRIT?!
HOW SHOULD I KNOW...HE'S NOT A MEMBER OF THE FORCE!
NOT AN OFFICIAL MEMBER! LOOK.. "SPIDER" WEBB ROBS A BANK..YOUR SECRET PAL, THE SPIRIT, GOES OUT TO GET HIM, AND INSTEAD OF BRINGING SPIDER IN ALIVE, WE FIND HIM AT OUR DOORSTEP DEAD.. BEATEN TO DEATH!...THE SPIRIT HAS INFORMATION WE NEED...UNLESS YOU BRING HIM BACK..I'LL ISSUE A SUBPOENA.
O.K...O.K., I'LL BRING HIM IN...
H'YA, COMMISSIONER DOLAN, SIR...
HULLO, KLINK
Y'LOOK TROUBLED, SIR..
THE SPIRIT HAS BEEN MISSING FOR 24 HOURS ON A CASE IN WHICH A MAN WAS BEATEN TO DEATH...WHOEVER HAS THE SPIRIT IS MIGHTY TOUGH..IT'D BE SUICIDE FOR ANYONE WHO TRIED TO FIND HIM!
WHAT WOULD YOU DO IF YOU WERE ME?
SIMPLE! I'D PICK A YOUNG OFFICER WHO WAS NOT SMART ENOUGH TO KNOW HOW DANGEROUS THE ASSIGNMENT IS AND WHO IS SO UNIMPORTANT THAT THE 'FORCE' COULD AFFORD TO LOSE HIM.
M-HMMm.. A VERY WISE SOLUTION.. I THINK I KNOW JUST THE MAN.
YEAH? WHO?
YOU!
P.S.
By Will Eisner
EGG PLANT

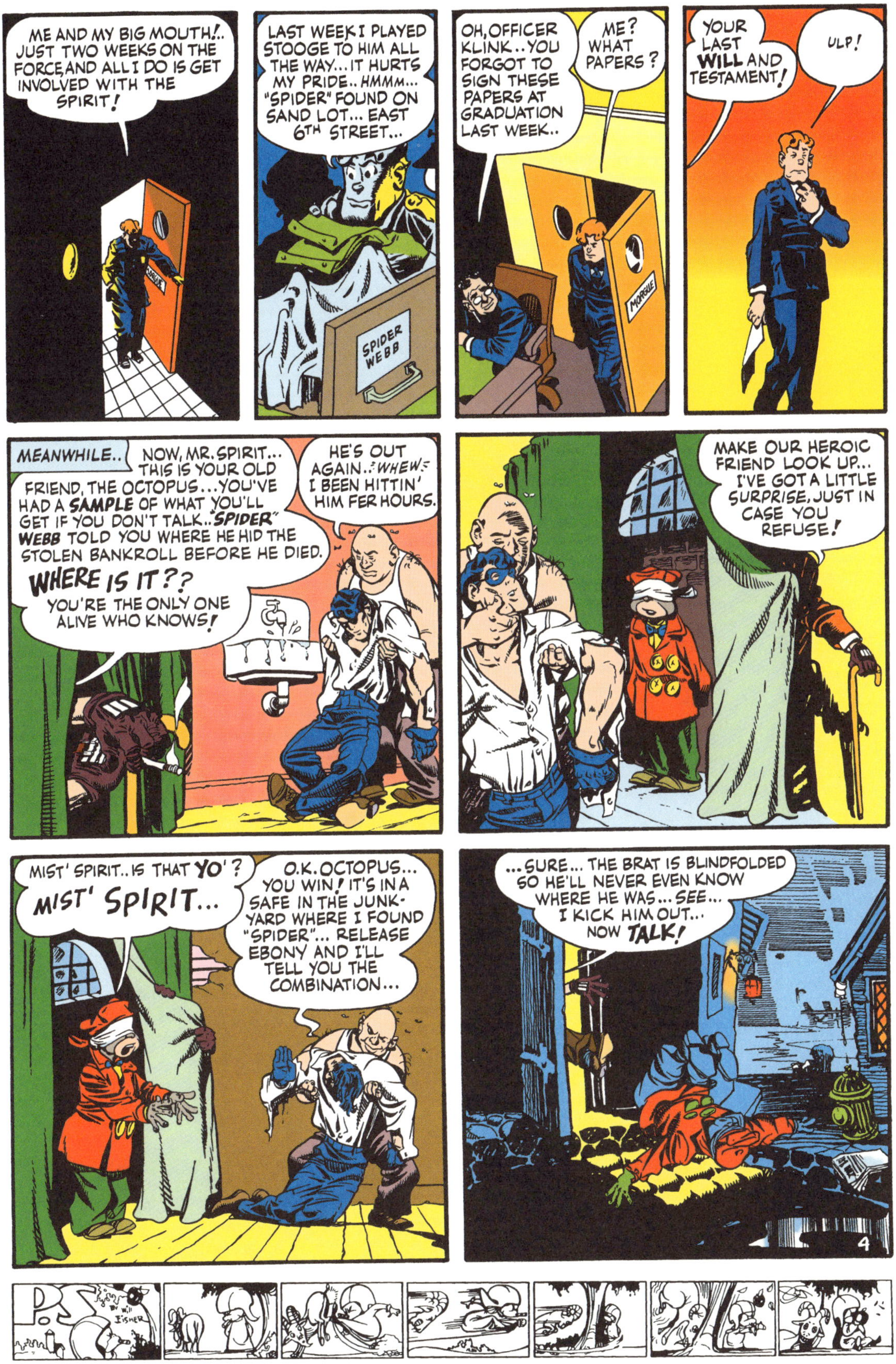
ME AND MY BIG MOUTH!.. JUST TWO WEEKS ON THE FORCE, AND ALL I DO IS GET INVOLVED WITH THE SPIRIT!
LAST WEEK I PLAYED STOOGE TO HIM ALL THE WAY... IT HURTS MY PRIDE.. HMMM... "SPIDER" FOUND ON SAND LOT... EAST 6TH STREET...
SPIDER WEBB
OH, OFFICER KLINK.. YOU FORGOT TO SIGN THESE PAPERS AT GRADUATION LAST WEEK..
ME? WHAT PAPERS?
MORGUE
YOUR LAST WILL AND TESTAMENT!
ULP!
MEANWHILE..
NOW, MR. SPIRIT... THIS IS YOUR OLD FRIEND, THE OCTOPUS... YOU'VE HAD A SAMPLE OF WHAT YOU'LL GET IF YOU DON'T TALK.."SPIDER" WEBB TOLD YOU WHERE HE HID THE STOLEN BANKROLL BEFORE HE DIED. WHERE IS IT?? YOU'RE THE ONLY ONE ALIVE WHO KNOWS!
HE'S OUT AGAIN..WHEW! I BEEN HITTIN' HIM FER HOURS.
MAKE OUR HEROIC FRIEND LOOK UP... I'VE GOT A LITTLE SURPRISE, JUST IN CASE YOU REFUSE!
MIST' SPIRIT.. IS THAT YO'? MIST' SPIRIT...
O.K. OCTOPUS... YOU WIN! IT'S IN A SAFE IN THE JUNK-YARD WHERE I FOUND "SPIDER"... RELEASE EBONY AND I'LL TELL YOU THE COMBINATION...
...SURE... THE BRAT IS BLINDFOLDED SO HE'LL NEVER EVEN KNOW WHERE HE WAS... SEE... I KICK HIM OUT... NOW TALK!
4
P.S. BY Wil EISNER

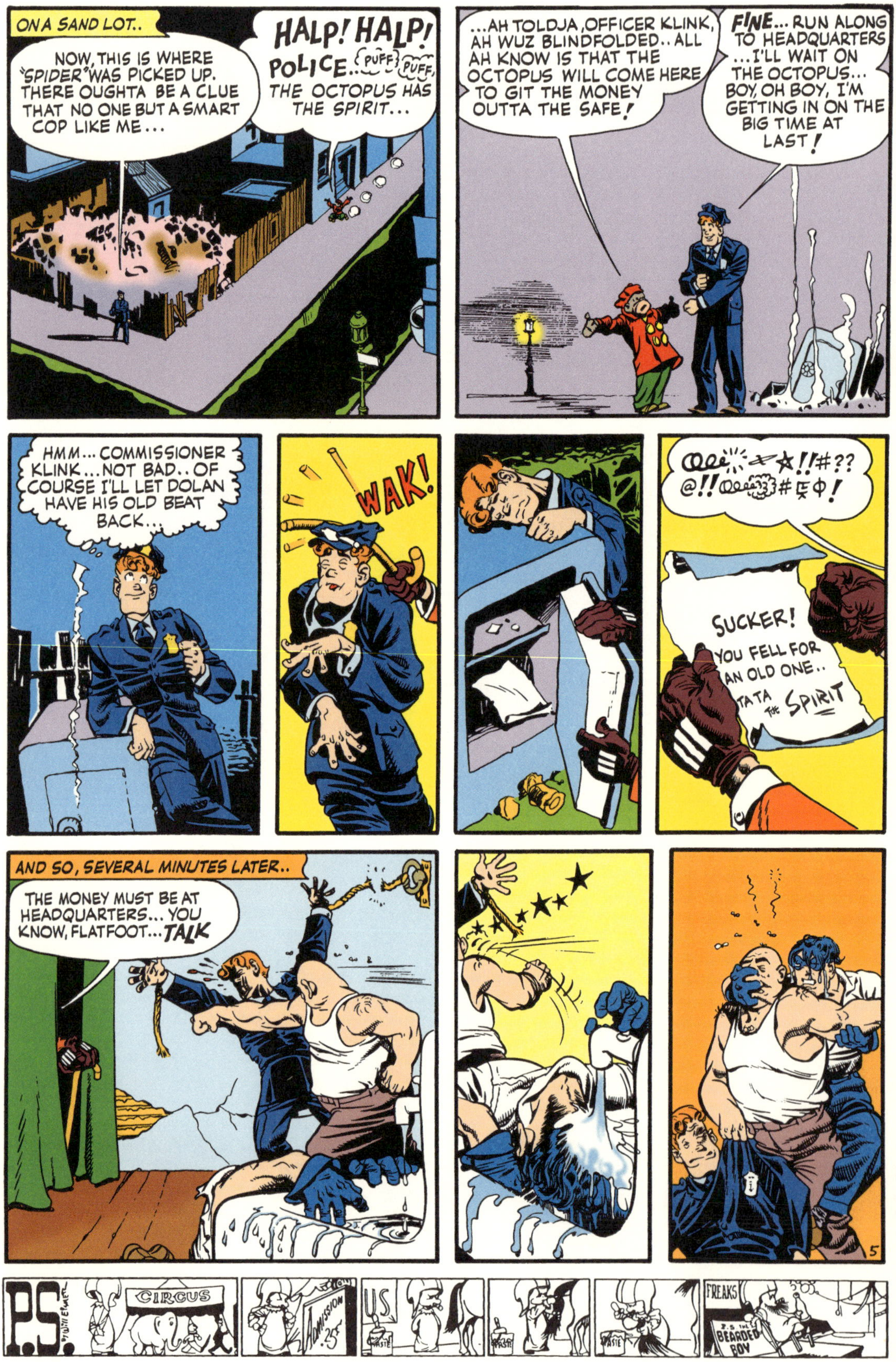
ON A SAND LOT..
NOW, THIS IS WHERE "SPIDER" WAS PICKED UP. THERE OUGHTA BE A CLUE THAT NO ONE BUT A SMART COP LIKE ME...
HALP! HALP! POLICE.. PUFF PUFF, THE OCTOPUS HAS THE SPIRIT...
...AH TOLDJA, OFFICER KLINK, AH WUZ BLINDFOLDED.. ALL AH KNOW IS THAT THE OCTOPUS WILL COME HERE TO GIT THE MONEY OUTTA THE SAFE!
FINE... RUN ALONG TO HEADQUARTERS ...I'LL WAIT ON THE OCTOPUS... BOY, OH BOY, I'M GETTING IN ON THE BIG TIME AT LAST!
HMM... COMMISSIONER KLINK... NOT BAD.. OF COURSE I'LL LET DOLAN HAVE HIS OLD BEAT BACK...
WAK!
SUCKER! YOU FELL FOR AN OLD ONE.. TA TA THE SPIRIT
AND SO, SEVERAL MINUTES LATER..
THE MONEY MUST BE AT HEADQUARTERS... YOU KNOW, FLATFOOT... TALK
5
P.S.
CIRCUS
ADMISSION 35¢
U.S.
PASTE
FREAKS
P.S. THE BEARDED BOY

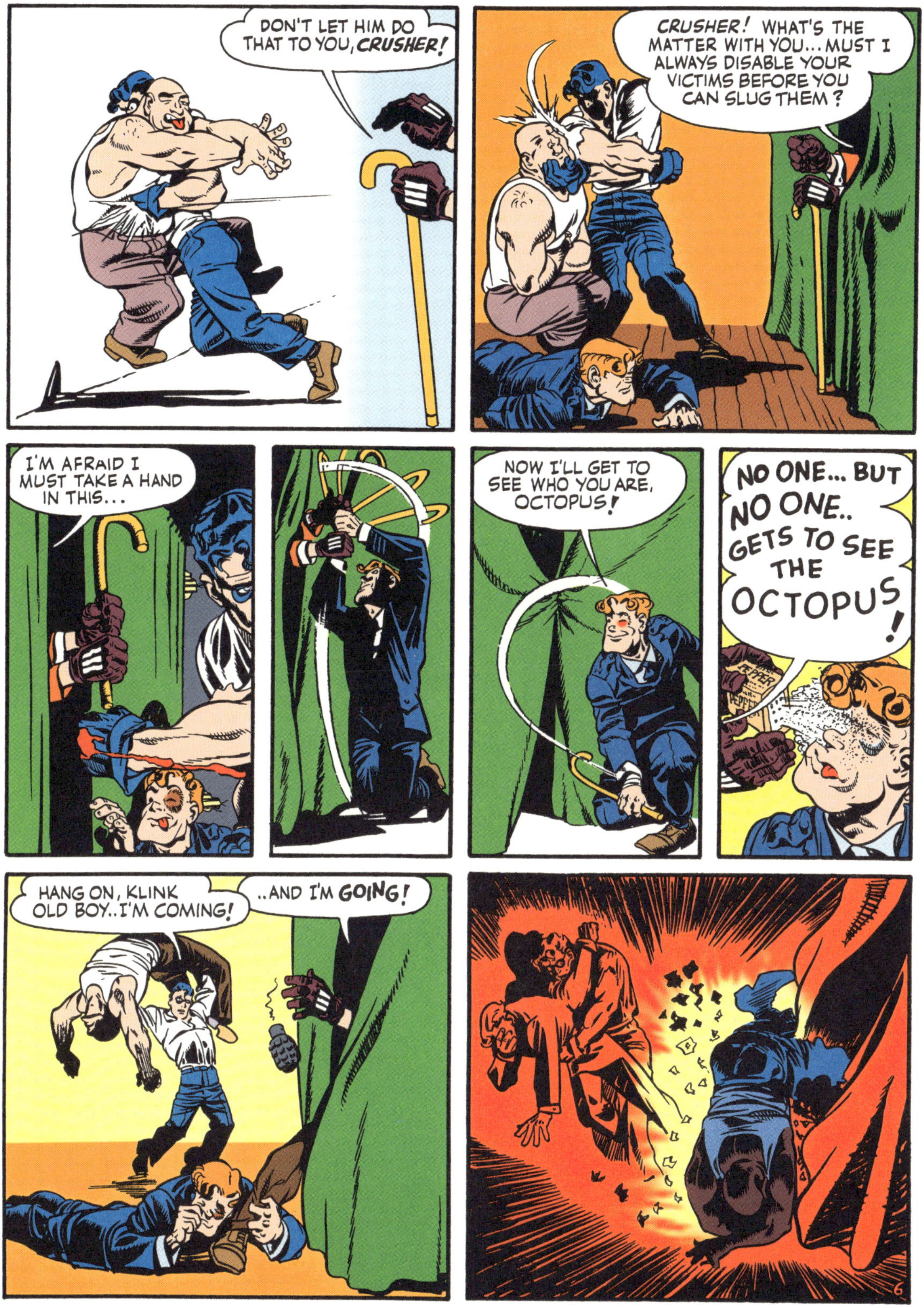
DON'T LET HIM DO THAT TO YOU, CRUSHER!
CRUSHER! WHAT'S THE MATTER WITH YOU... MUST I ALWAYS DISABLE YOUR VICTIMS BEFORE YOU CAN SLUG THEM?
I'M AFRAID I MUST TAKE A HAND IN THIS...
NOW I'LL GET TO SEE WHO YOU ARE, OCTOPUS!
NO ONE... BUT NO ONE.. GETS TO SEE THE OCTOPUS!
PEPPER
HANG ON, KLINK OLD BOY.. I'M COMING!
..AND I'M GOING!
6

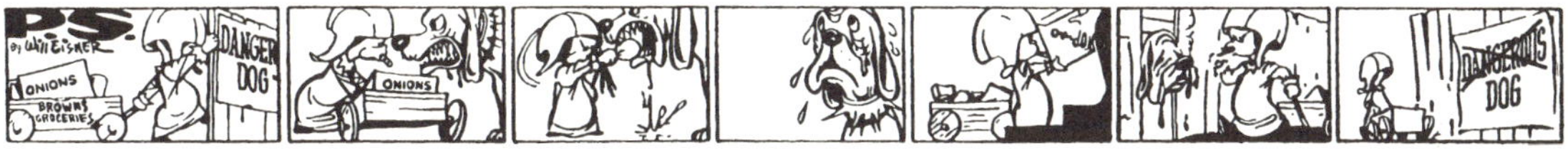
P.S.
by Will Eisner
DANGER DOG
ONIONS
BROWN'S GROCERIES
ONIONS
DANGEROUS DOG

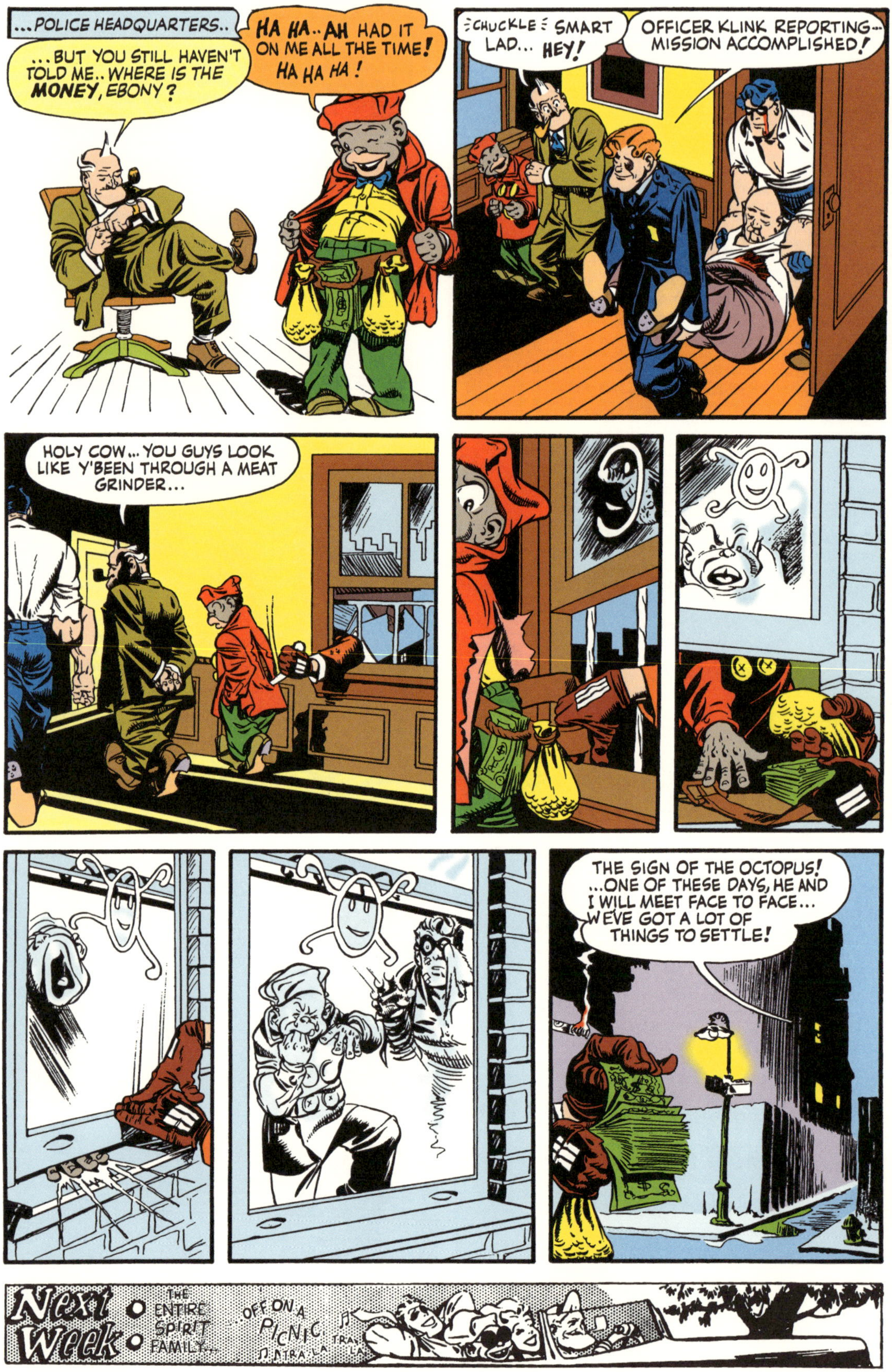
...POLICE HEADQUARTERS..
...BUT YOU STILL HAVEN'T TOLD ME.. WHERE IS THE MONEY, EBONY?
HA HA..AH HAD IT ON ME ALL THE TIME! HA HA HA!
CHUCKLE SMART LAD... HEY!
OFFICER KLINK REPORTING... MISSION ACCOMPLISHED!
HOLY COW... YOU GUYS LOOK LIKE Y'BEEN THROUGH A MEAT GRINDER...
THE SIGN OF THE OCTOPUS! ...ONE OF THESE DAYS, HE AND I WILL MEET FACE TO FACE... WE'VE GOT A LOT OF THINGS TO SETTLE!
Next Week
THE ENTIRE SPIRIT FAMILY...
OFF ON A PICNIC
TRA LA TRA LA

COMIC BOOK SECTION

ACTION Mystery ADVENTURE

THE PICNIC

August 17 1947

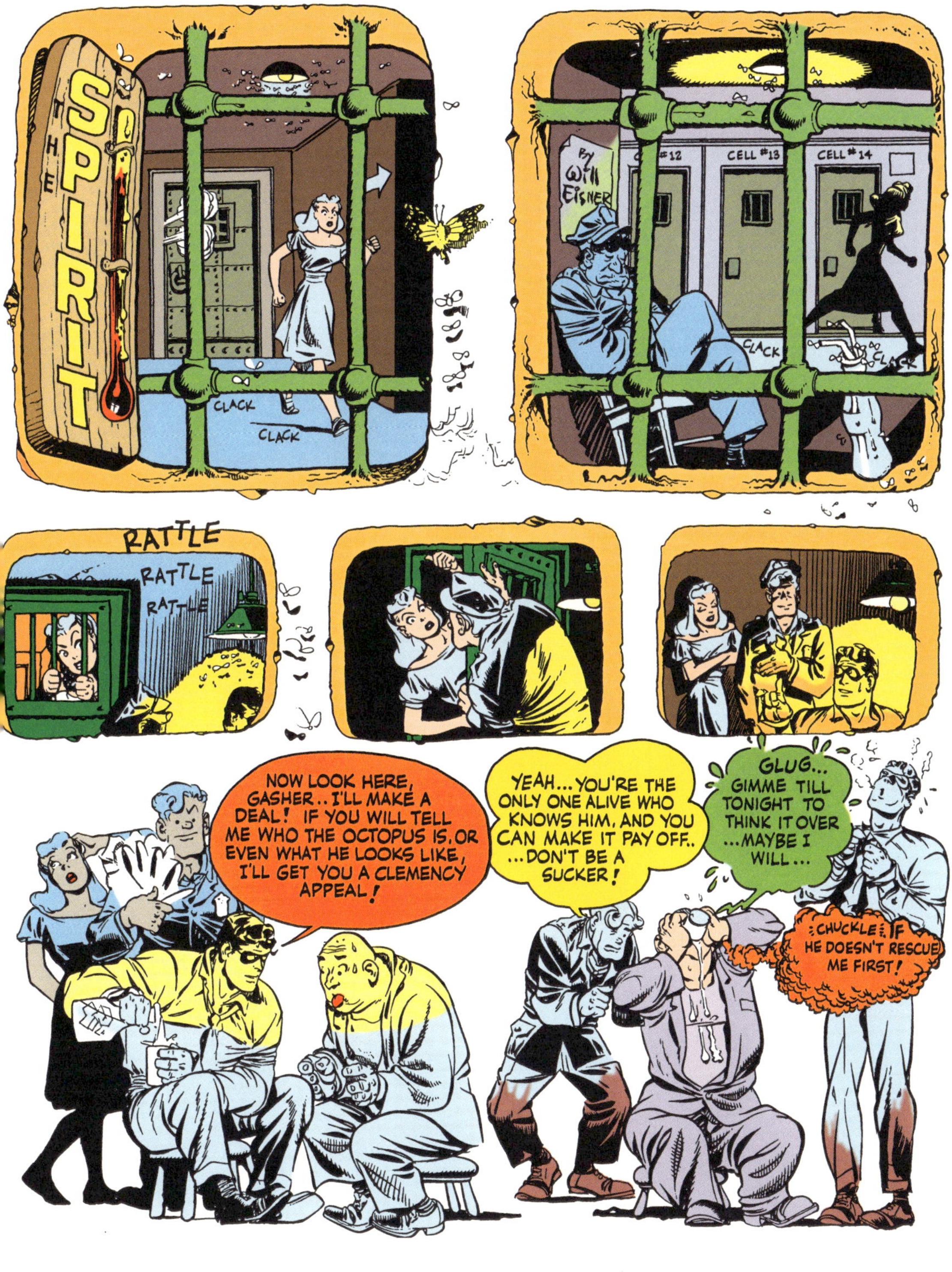

THE SPIRIT
CLACK
CLACK
By Will Eisner
CELL #12
CELL #13
CELL #14
CLACK
CLACK
RATTLE
RATTLE
RATTLE
NOW LOOK HERE, GASHER.. I'LL MAKE A DEAL! IF YOU WILL TELL ME WHO THE OCTOPUS IS, OR EVEN WHAT HE LOOKS LIKE, I'LL GET YOU A CLEMENCY APPEAL!
YEAH... YOU'RE THE ONLY ONE ALIVE WHO KNOWS HIM, AND YOU CAN MAKE IT PAY OFF.. ...DON'T BE A SUCKER!
GLUG... GIMME TILL TONIGHT TO THINK IT OVER ...MAYBE I WILL...
CHUCKLE! IF HE DOESN'T RESCUE ME FIRST!

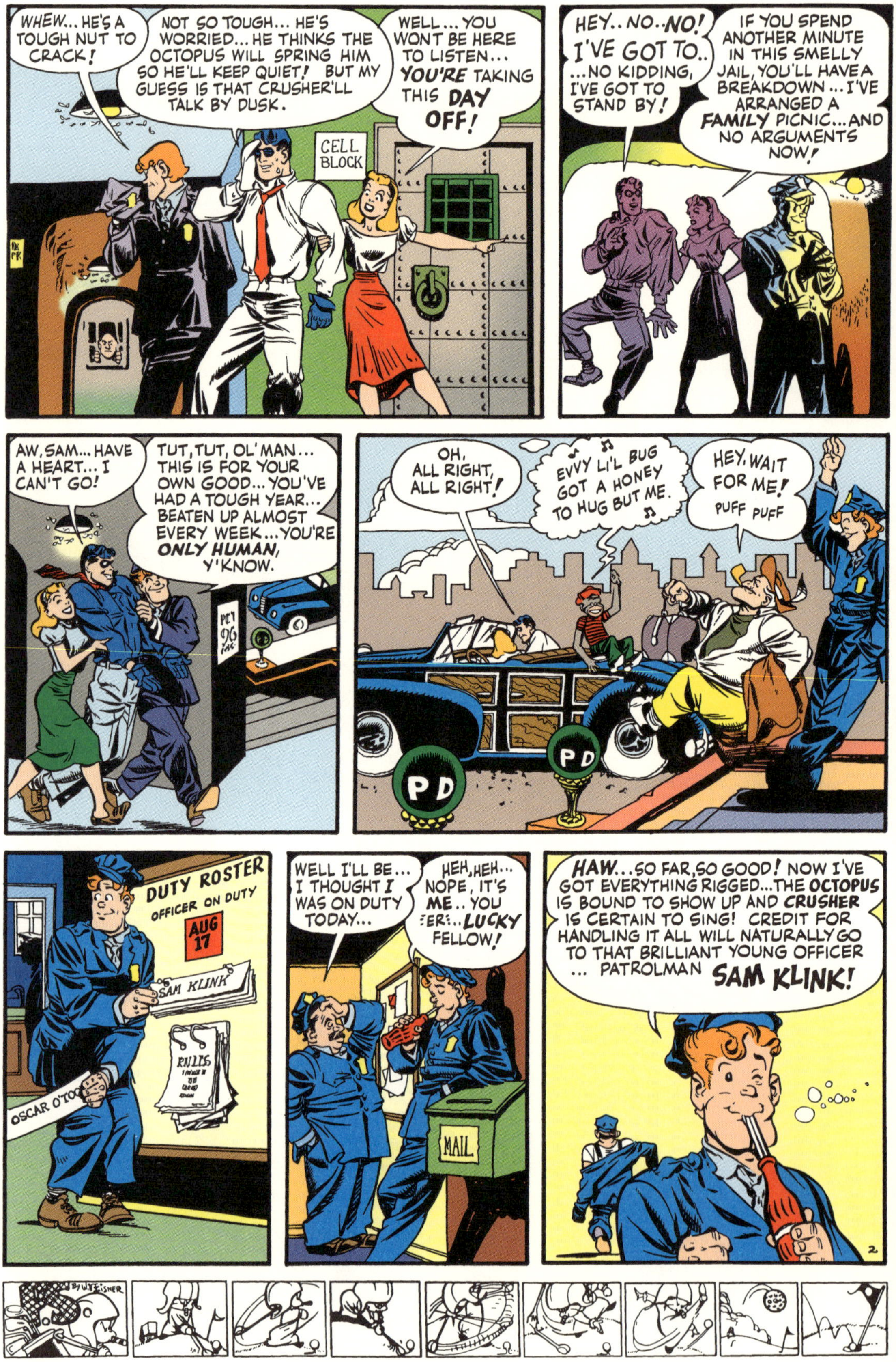
WHEW... HE'S A TOUGH NUT TO CRACK!
NOT SO TOUGH... HE'S WORRIED... HE THINKS THE OCTOPUS WILL SPRING HIM SO HE'LL KEEP QUIET! BUT MY GUESS IS THAT CRUSHER'LL TALK BY DUSK.
CELL BLOCK
WELL... YOU WONT BE HERE TO LISTEN... YOU'RE TAKING THIS DAY OFF!
HEY.. NO.. NO! I'VE GOT TO.. ...NO KIDDING, I'VE GOT TO STAND BY!
IF YOU SPEND ANOTHER MINUTE IN THIS SMELLY JAIL, YOU'LL HAVE A BREAKDOWN... I'VE ARRANGED A FAMILY PICNIC...AND NO ARGUMENTS NOW!
AW, SAM... HAVE A HEART... I CAN'T GO!
TUT, TUT, OL' MAN... THIS IS FOR YOUR OWN GOOD... YOU'VE HAD A TOUGH YEAR... BEATEN UP ALMOST EVERY WEEK... YOU'RE ONLY HUMAN, Y'KNOW.
OH, ALL RIGHT, ALL RIGHT!
EVVY LI'L BUG GOT A HONEY TO HUG BUT ME.
HEY, WAIT FOR ME! PUFF PUFF
PD
PD
DUTY ROSTER
OFFICER ON DUTY
AUG 17
SAM KLINK
OSCAR O'TOO
WELL I'LL BE... I THOUGHT I WAS ON DUTY TODAY...
HEH, HEH... NOPE, IT'S ME.. YOU ER... LUCKY FELLOW!
MAIL
HAW... SO FAR, SO GOOD! NOW I'VE GOT EVERYTHING RIGGED... THE OCTOPUS IS BOUND TO SHOW UP AND CRUSHER IS CERTAIN TO SING! CREDIT FOR HANDLING IT ALL WILL NATURALLY GO TO THAT BRILLIANT YOUNG OFFICER ... PATROLMAN SAM KLINK!
2

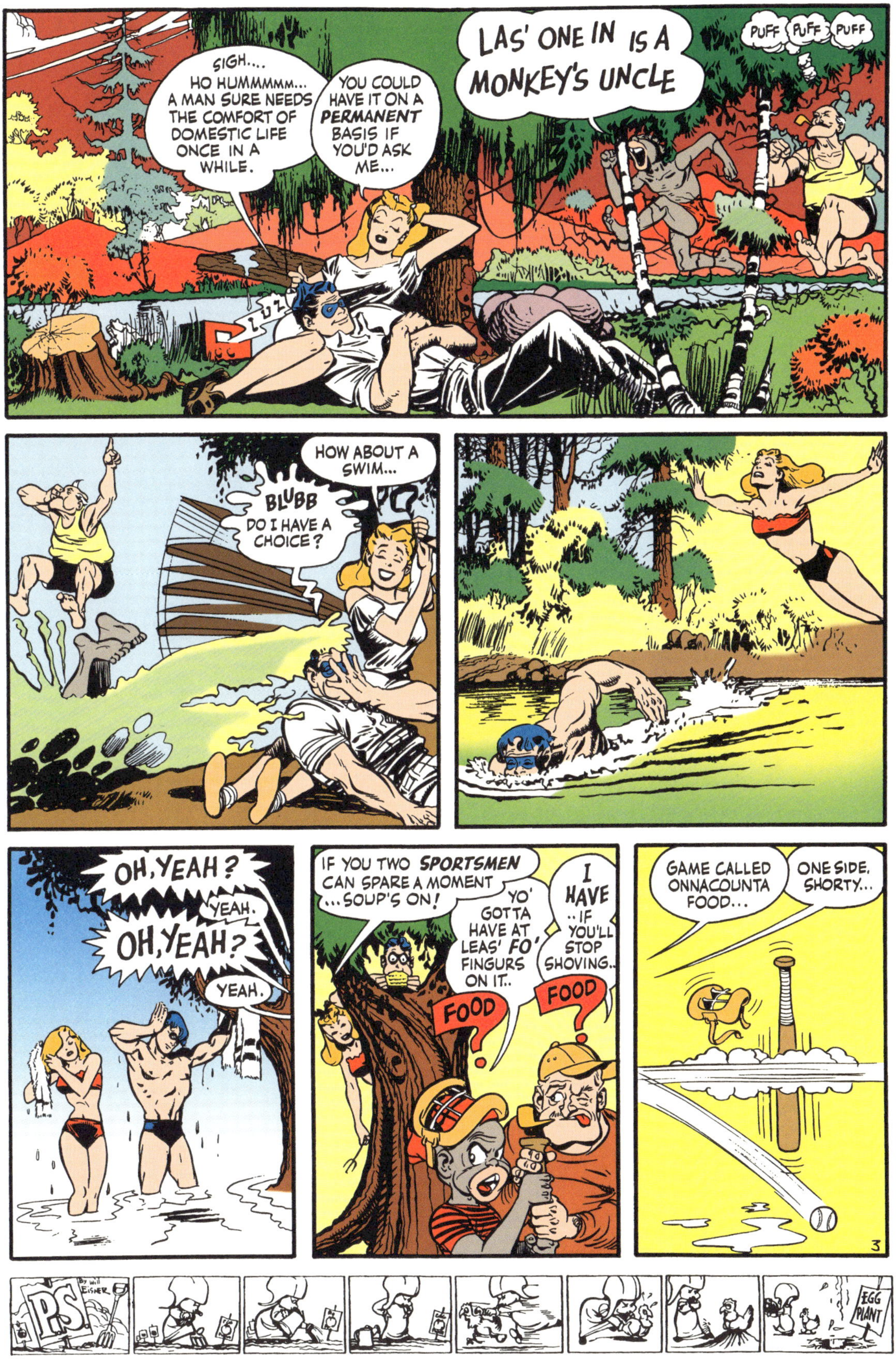
SIGH.... HO HUMMMMM... A MAN SURE NEEDS THE COMFORT OF DOMESTIC LIFE ONCE IN A WHILE.
YOU COULD HAVE IT ON A **PERMANENT** BASIS IF YOU'D ASK ME...
LAS' ONE IN IS A MONKEY'S UNCLE
PUFF PUFF PUFF
HOW ABOUT A SWIM...
BLUBB
DO I HAVE A CHOICE?
OH, YEAH?
YEAH.
OH, YEAH?
YEAH.
IF YOU TWO **SPORTSMEN** CAN SPARE A MOMENT ...SOUP'S ON!
YO' GOTTA HAVE AT LEAS' **FO'** FINGURS ON IT..
I HAVE ..IF YOU'LL STOP SHOVING..
FOOD
FOOD
GAME CALLED ONNACOUNTA FOOD...
ONE SIDE, SHORTY...
3
P.S. By Will Eisner
EGG PLANT

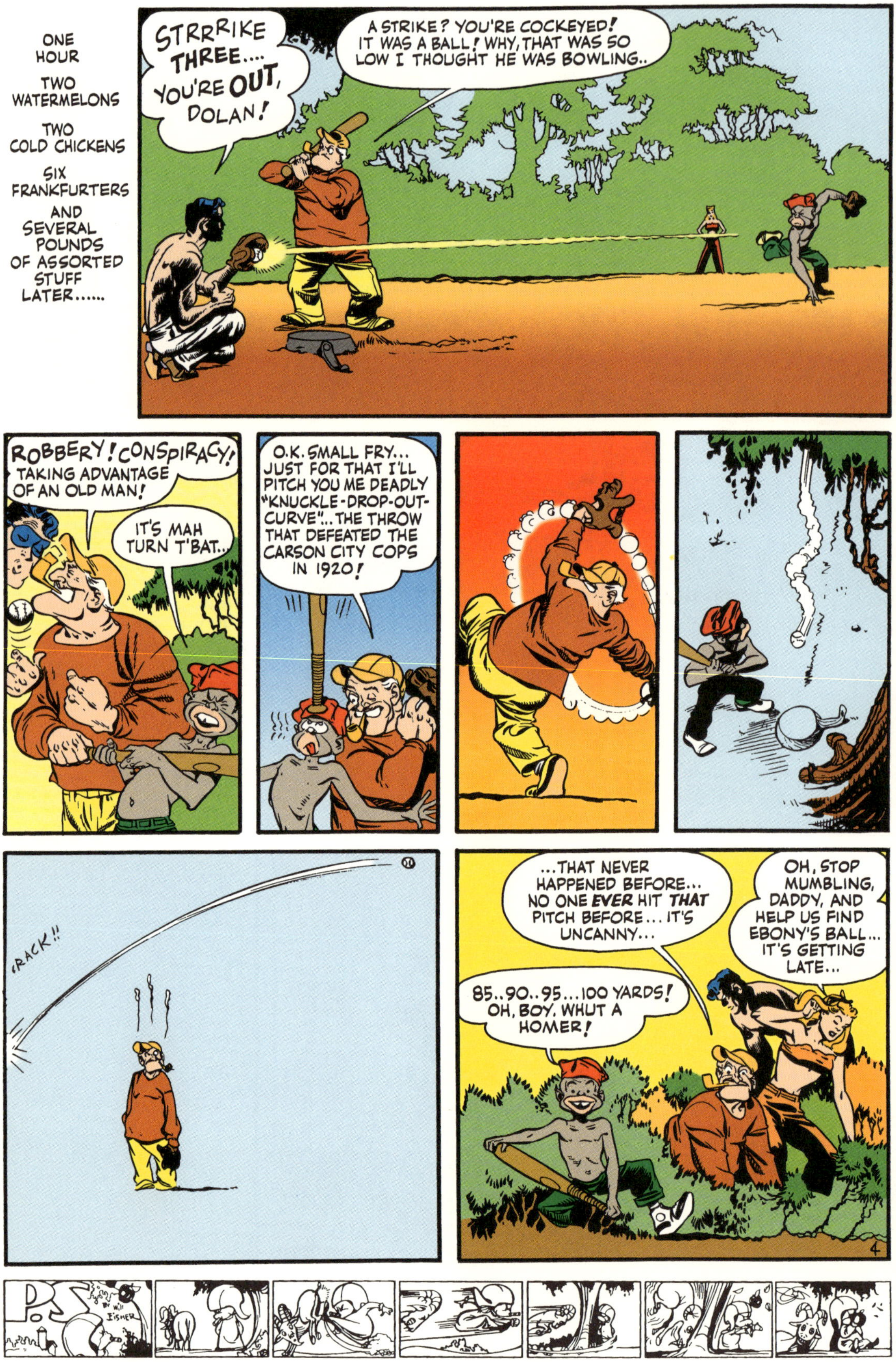
ONE HOUR
TWO WATERMELONS
TWO COLD CHICKENS
SIX FRANKFURTERS
AND SEVERAL POUNDS OF ASSORTED STUFF LATER......
STRRRIKE THREE.... YOU'RE OUT, DOLAN!
A STRIKE? YOU'RE COCKEYED! IT WAS A BALL! WHY, THAT WAS SO LOW I THOUGHT HE WAS BOWLING..
ROBBERY! CONSPIRACY! TAKING ADVANTAGE OF AN OLD MAN!
IT'S MAH TURN T'BAT..
O.K. SMALL FRY... JUST FOR THAT I'LL PITCH YOU ME DEADLY "KNUCKLE-DROP-OUT-CURVE"... THE THROW THAT DEFEATED THE CARSON CITY COPS IN 1920!
CRACK!!
...THAT NEVER HAPPENED BEFORE... NO ONE EVER HIT THAT PITCH BEFORE... IT'S UNCANNY...
OH, STOP MUMBLING, DADDY, AND HELP US FIND EBONY'S BALL... IT'S GETTING LATE...
85..90..95...100 YARDS! OH, BOY, WHUT A HOMER!
4
P.S.
BY Will EISNER

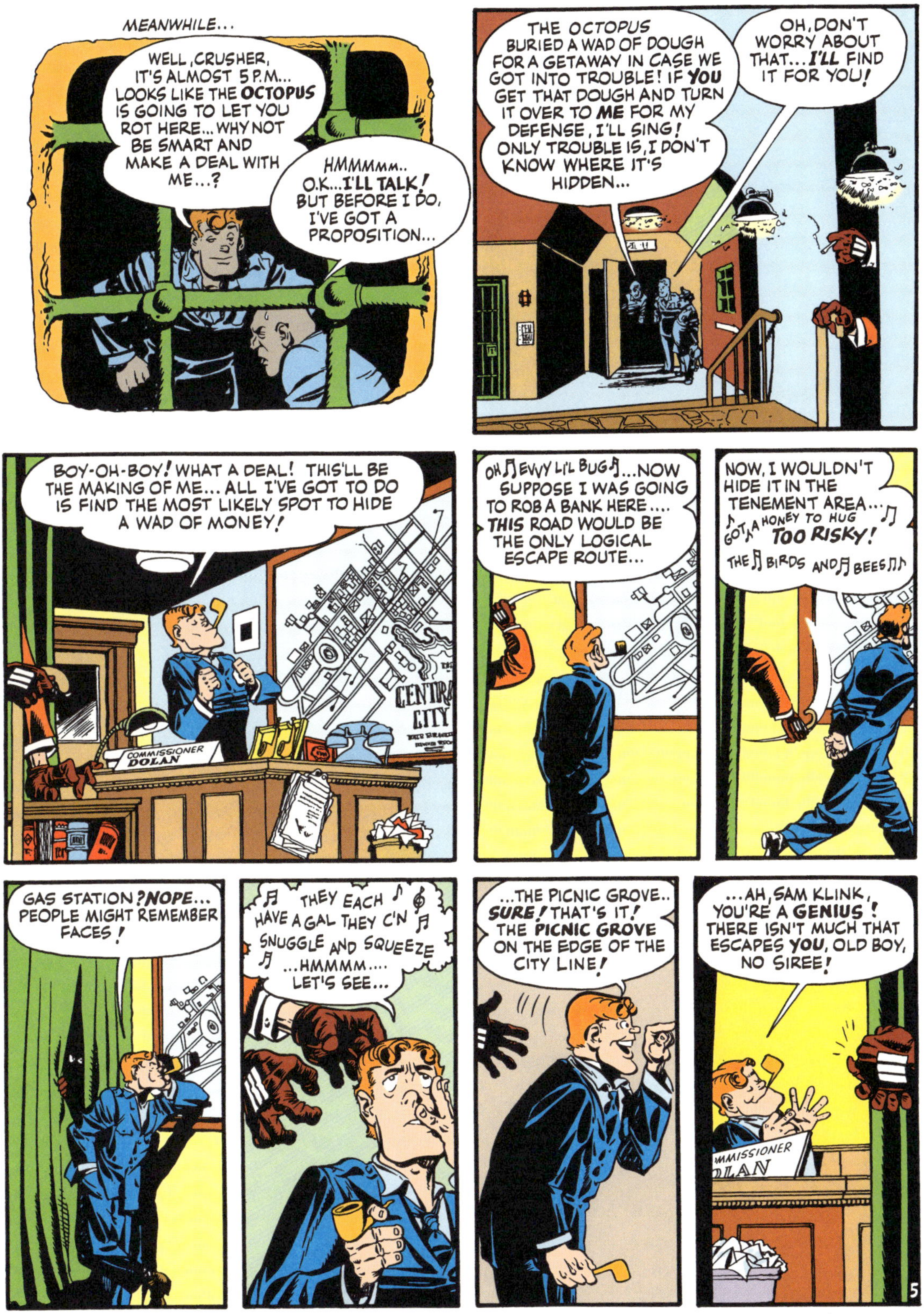
MEANWHILE...
WELL, CRUSHER, IT'S ALMOST 5 P.M... LOOKS LIKE THE OCTOPUS IS GOING TO LET YOU ROT HERE... WHY NOT BE SMART AND MAKE A DEAL WITH ME...?
HMMMMM.. O.K... I'LL TALK! BUT BEFORE I DO, I'VE GOT A PROPOSITION...
THE OCTOPUS BURIED A WAD OF DOUGH FOR A GETAWAY IN CASE WE GOT INTO TROUBLE! IF YOU GET THAT DOUGH AND TURN IT OVER TO ME FOR MY DEFENSE, I'LL SING! ONLY TROUBLE IS, I DON'T KNOW WHERE IT'S HIDDEN...
OH, DON'T WORRY ABOUT THAT... I'LL FIND IT FOR YOU!
BOY-OH-BOY! WHAT A DEAL! THIS'LL BE THE MAKING OF ME... ALL I'VE GOT TO DO IS FIND THE MOST LIKELY SPOT TO HIDE A WAD OF MONEY!
COMMISSIONER DOLAN
CENTRAL CITY
OH ♫ EVVY LI'L BUG ♫ ...NOW SUPPOSE I WAS GOING TO ROB A BANK HERE.... THIS ROAD WOULD BE THE ONLY LOGICAL ESCAPE ROUTE...
NOW, I WOULDN'T HIDE IT IN THE TENEMENT AREA... ♫ GOT A HONEY TO HUG ♫ TOO RISKY! THE ♫ BIRDS AND ♫ BEES ♫♫
GAS STATION? NOPE... PEOPLE MIGHT REMEMBER FACES!
♫ THEY EACH HAVE A GAL THEY C'N ♫ SNUGGLE AND SQUEEZE ♫ ...HMMMM.... LET'S SEE...
...THE PICNIC GROVE.. SURE! THAT'S IT! THE PICNIC GROVE ON THE EDGE OF THE CITY LINE!
...AH, SAM KLINK, YOU'RE A GENIUS! THERE ISN'T MUCH THAT ESCAPES YOU, OLD BOY, NO SIREE!
MMISSIONER DLAN
5

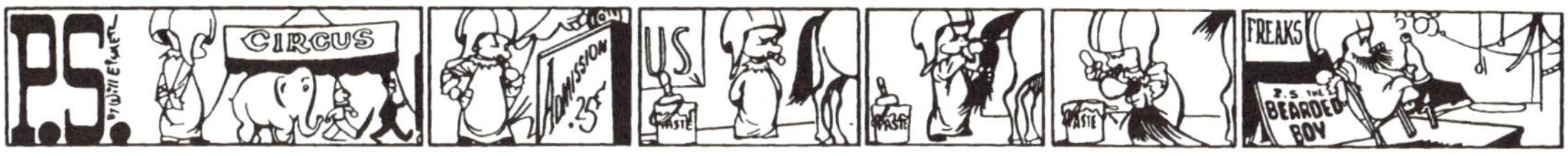
P.S.
CIRCUS
ADMISSION 25¢
U.S.
PASTE
FREAKS
P.S. THE BEARDED BOY

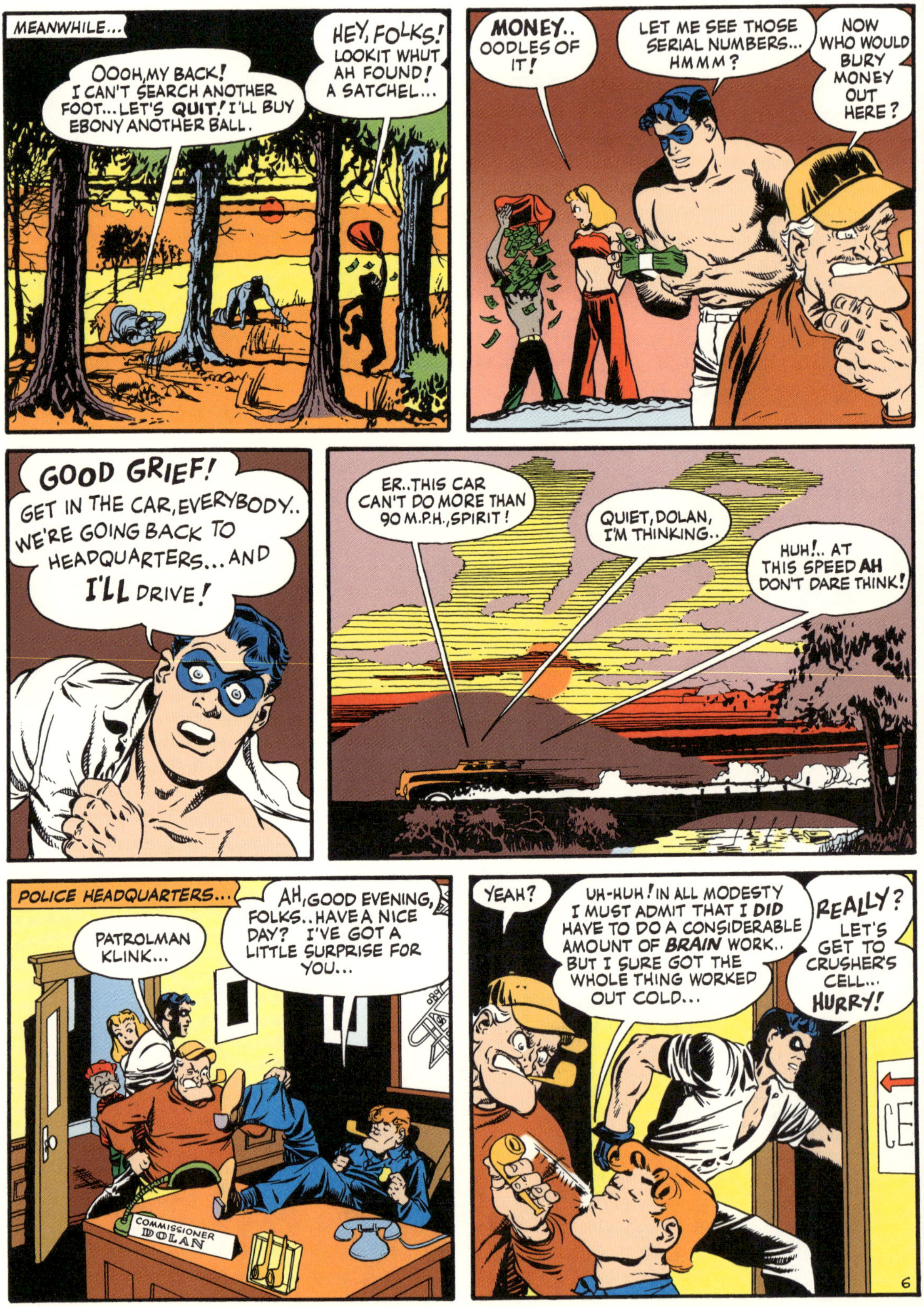
MEANWHILE...
OOOH, MY BACK! I CAN'T SEARCH ANOTHER FOOT... LET'S QUIT! I'LL BUY EBONY ANOTHER BALL.
HEY, FOLKS! LOOKIT WHUT AH FOUND! A SATCHEL...
MONEY.. OODLES OF IT!
LET ME SEE THOSE SERIAL NUMBERS... HMMM?
NOW WHO WOULD BURY MONEY OUT HERE?
GOOD GRIEF! GET IN THE CAR, EVERYBODY.. WE'RE GOING BACK TO HEADQUARTERS... AND I'LL DRIVE!
ER.. THIS CAR CAN'T DO MORE THAN 90 M.P.H., SPIRIT!
QUIET, DOLAN, I'M THINKING..
HUH!.. AT THIS SPEED AH DON'T DARE THINK!
POLICE HEADQUARTERS...
PATROLMAN KLINK...
AH, GOOD EVENING, FOLKS.. HAVE A NICE DAY? I'VE GOT A LITTLE SURPRISE FOR YOU...
COMMISSIONER DOLAN
YEAH?
UH-HUH! IN ALL MODESTY I MUST ADMIT THAT I DID HAVE TO DO A CONSIDERABLE AMOUNT OF BRAIN WORK.. BUT I SURE GOT THE WHOLE THING WORKED OUT COLD...
REALLY? LET'S GET TO CRUSHER'S CELL... HURRY!
CE
6

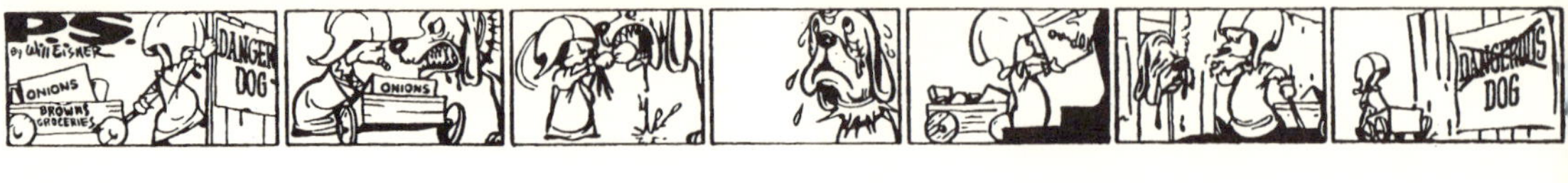
P.S.
DANGER DOG
ONIONS
ONIONS
DANGEROUS DOG

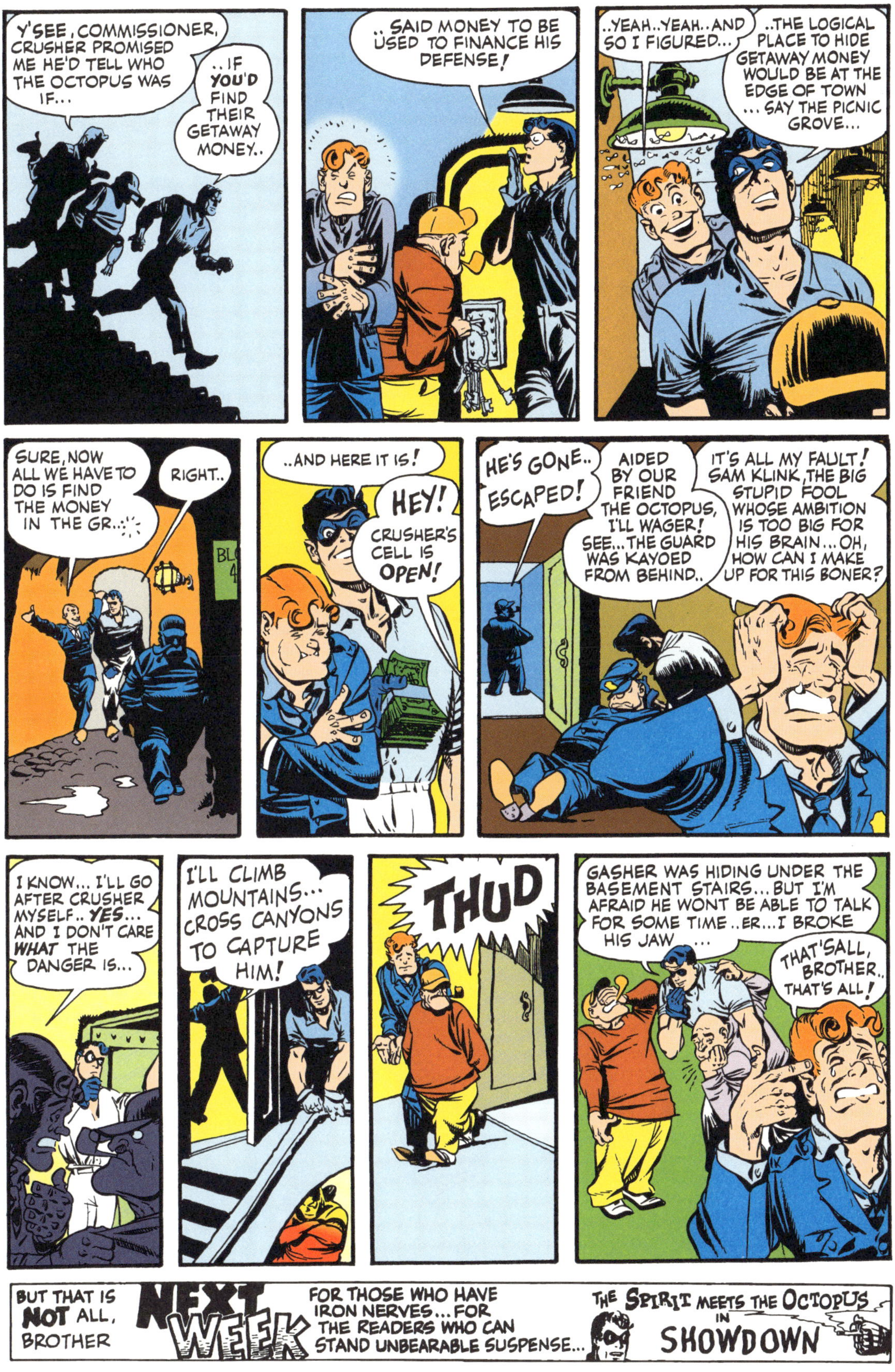
Y'SEE, COMMISSIONER, CRUSHER PROMISED ME HE'D TELL WHO THE OCTOPUS WAS IF...
..IF YOU'D FIND THEIR GETAWAY MONEY..
.. SAID MONEY TO BE USED TO FINANCE HIS DEFENSE!
..YEAH..YEAH..AND SO I FIGURED...
..THE LOGICAL PLACE TO HIDE GETAWAY MONEY WOULD BE AT THE EDGE OF TOWN ... SAY THE PICNIC GROVE...
SURE, NOW ALL WE HAVE TO DO IS FIND THE MONEY IN THE GR..
RIGHT..
..AND HERE IT IS!
HEY! CRUSHER'S CELL IS OPEN!
HE'S GONE.. ESCAPED!
AIDED BY OUR FRIEND THE OCTOPUS, I'LL WAGER! SEE...THE GUARD WAS KAYOED FROM BEHIND..
IT'S ALL MY FAULT! SAM KLINK, THE BIG STUPID FOOL WHOSE AMBITION IS TOO BIG FOR HIS BRAIN...OH, HOW CAN I MAKE UP FOR THIS BONER?
I KNOW... I'LL GO AFTER CRUSHER MYSELF.. YES... AND I DON'T CARE WHAT THE DANGER IS...
I'LL CLIMB MOUNTAINS... CROSS CANYONS TO CAPTURE HIM!
THUD
GASHER WAS HIDING UNDER THE BASEMENT STAIRS... BUT I'M AFRAID HE WONT BE ABLE TO TALK FOR SOME TIME ..ER...I BROKE HIS JAW ...
THAT'SALL, BROTHER.. THAT'S ALL!
BUT THAT IS NOT ALL, BROTHER
NEXT WEEK
FOR THOSE WHO HAVE IRON NERVES...FOR THE READERS WHO CAN STAND UNBEARABLE SUSPENSE...
THE SPIRIT MEETS THE OCTOPUS IN SHOWDOWN

SHOWDOWN WITH THE OCTOPUS

August 24 1947

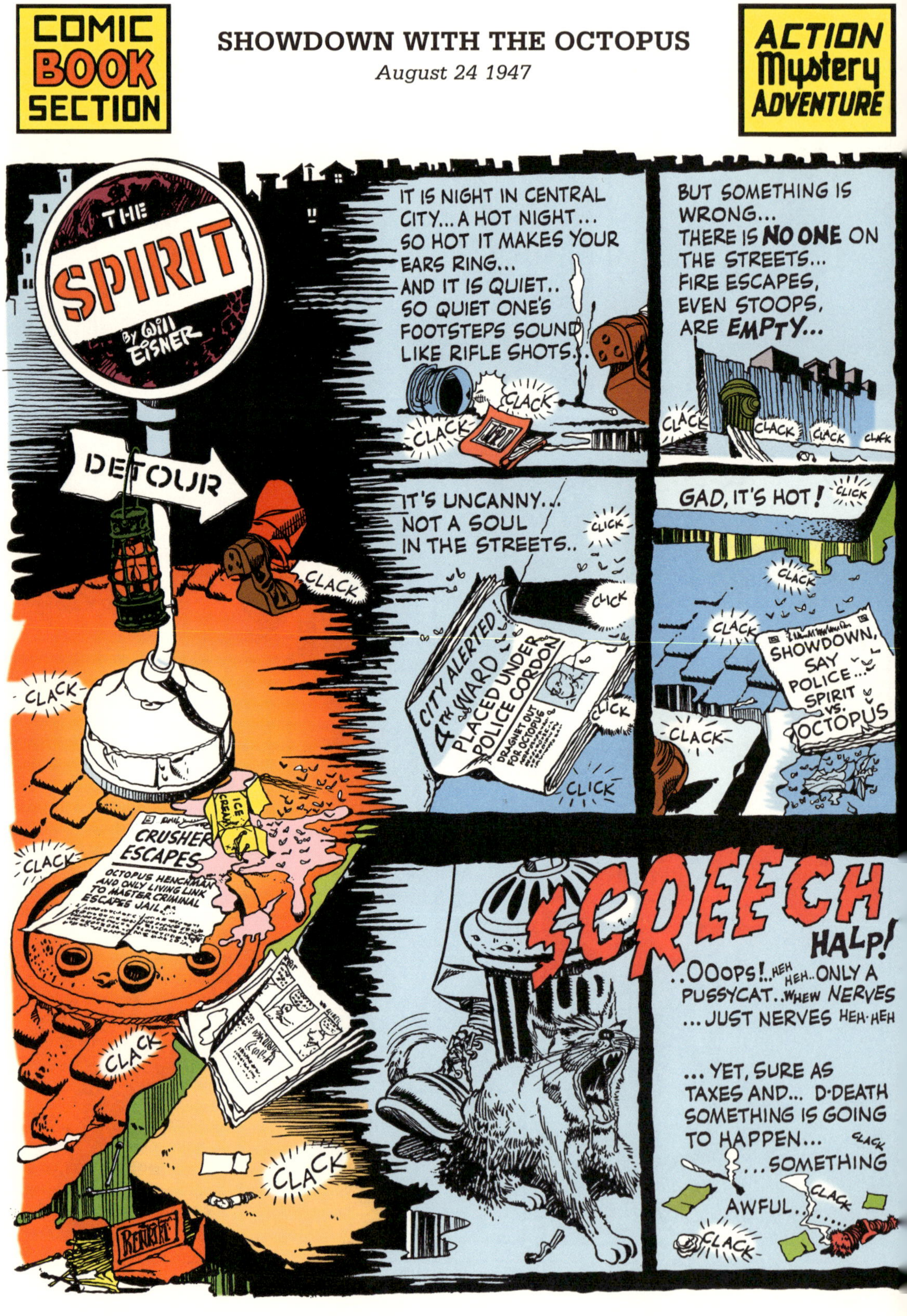

COMIC BOOK SECTION
ACTION Mystery ADVENTURE
THE SPIRIT BY Will EISNER
DETOUR
IT IS NIGHT IN CENTRAL CITY... A HOT NIGHT... SO HOT IT MAKES YOUR EARS RING... AND IT IS QUIET.. SO QUIET ONE'S FOOTSTEPS SOUND LIKE RIFLE SHOTS...
CLACK
CLACK
BUT SOMETHING IS WRONG... THERE IS NO ONE ON THE STREETS... FIRE ESCAPES, EVEN STOOPS, ARE EMPTY...
CLACK
CLACK
CLACK
CLACK
IT'S UNCANNY... NOT A SOUL IN THE STREETS..
CLICK
CLICK
CITY ALERTED! 4TH WARD PLACED UNDER POLICE CORDON
DRAGNET OUT FOR OCTOPUS
CLICK
CLICK
GAD, IT'S HOT!
CLICK
CLACK
CLACK
SHOWDOWN, SAY POLICE... SPIRIT VS. OCTOPUS
CLACK
CLACK
CLACK
CRUSHER ESCAPES
OCTOPUS HENCHMAN AND ONLY LIVING LINK TO MASTER CRIMINAL ESCAPES JAIL
ICE CREAM
CLACK
CLACK
SCREECH
HALP!
..OOops!..HEH HEH..ONLY A PUSSYCAT..WHEW NERVES ...JUST NERVES HEH-HEH
... YET, SURE AS TAXES AND... D-DEATH SOMETHING IS GOING TO HAPPEN...
CLACK
...SOMETHING AWFUL..
CLACK
CLACK

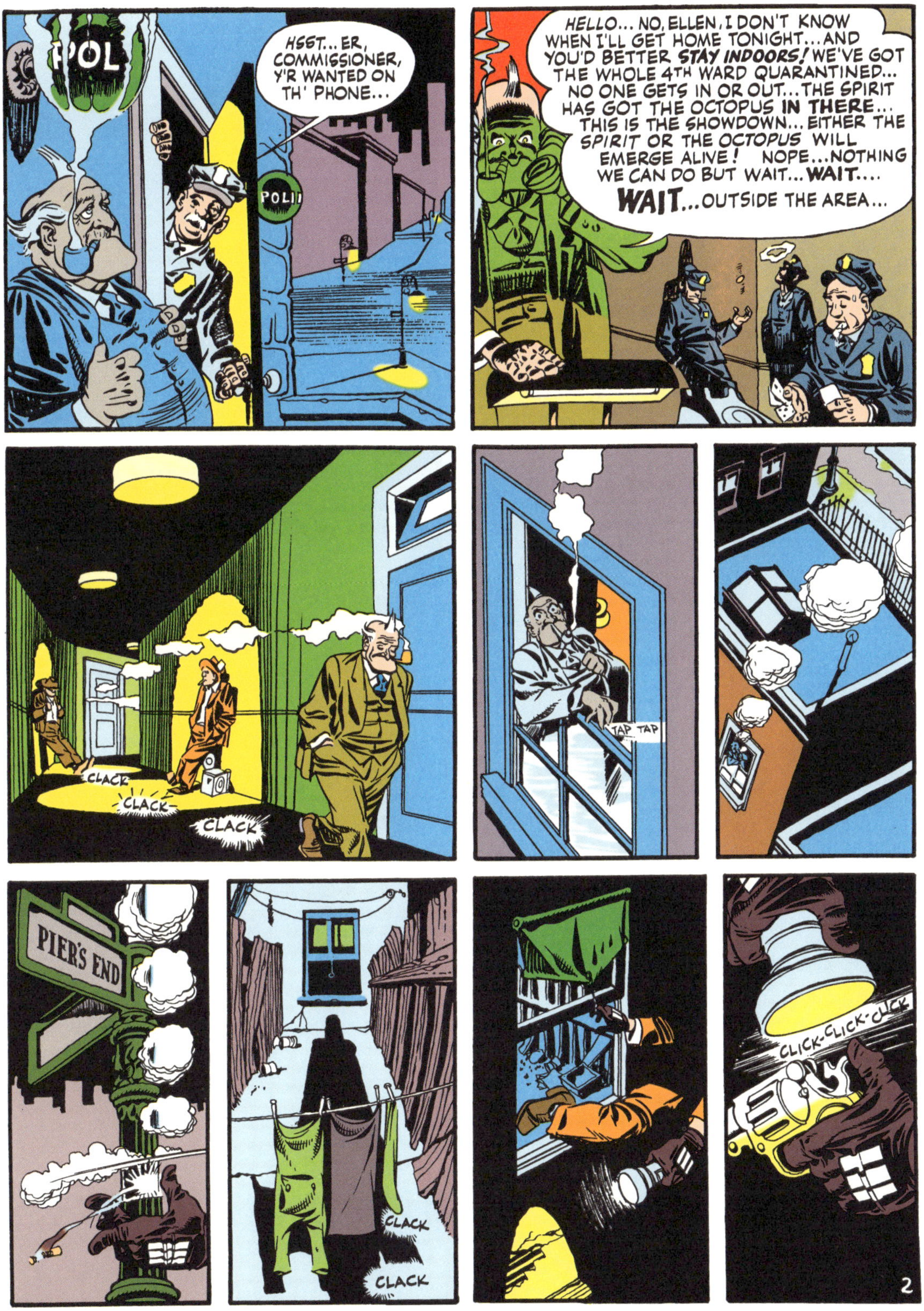
POL
HSST...ER, COMMISSIONER, Y'R WANTED ON TH' PHONE...
POLI
HELLO... NO, ELLEN, I DON'T KNOW WHEN I'LL GET HOME TONIGHT...AND YOU'D BETTER STAY INDOORS! WE'VE GOT THE WHOLE 4TH WARD QUARANTINED... NO ONE GETS IN OR OUT...THE SPIRIT HAS GOT THE OCTOPUS IN THERE... THIS IS THE SHOWDOWN... EITHER THE SPIRIT OR THE OCTOPUS WILL EMERGE ALIVE! NOPE...NOTHING WE CAN DO BUT WAIT...WAIT.... WAIT...OUTSIDE THE AREA...
CLACK
CLACK
CLACK
TAP TAP
PIER'S END
CLACK
CLACK
CLICK-CLICK-CLICK
2

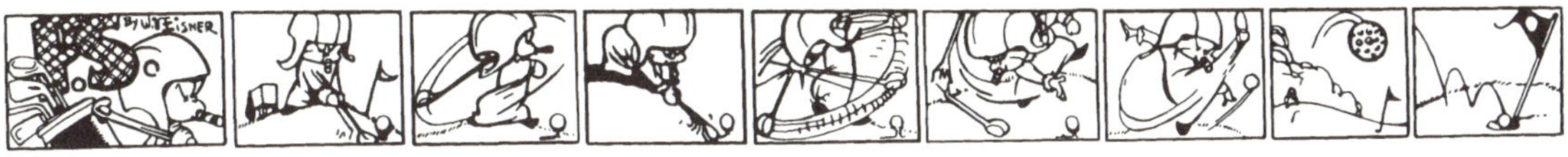
By W. Eisner

CREAK
CREAK
HMM...ODD! ALL EXITS CAREFULLY BARRED... THERE'S BEEN A FIGHT, TOO...
AH...
?!
SLAM
CLICK
SOMEONE'S IN HERE...
CREAK
CRUSHER! YOU MADE IT... YOU ESCAPED...
YES, BUT I CAUGHT HIM AGAIN... THEN IT OCCURRED TO ME WHAT A NEAT TRAP THIS WOULD MAKE... SO I WAITED FOR YOU, MR. OCTOPUS!
!!! CURSE ME FOR A STUPID FOOL!
3

PS
By Will Eisner
EGG PLANT

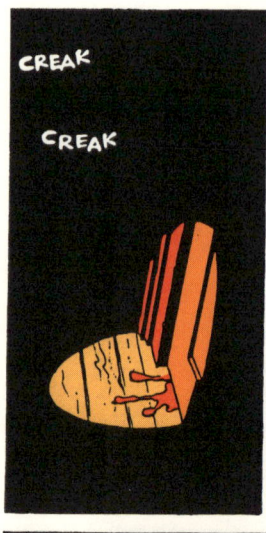

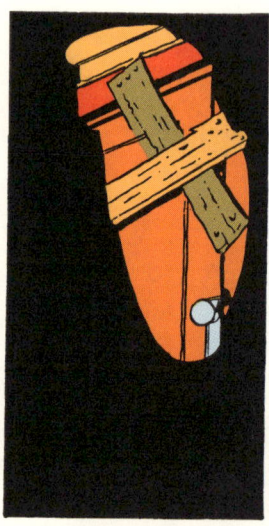

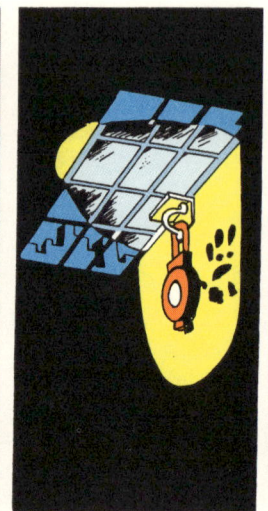

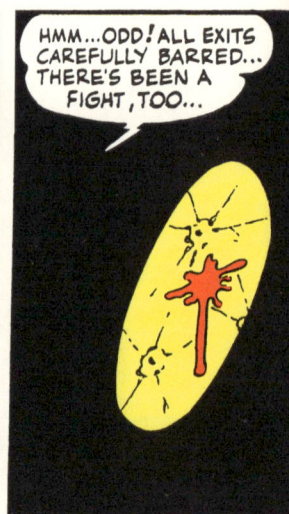

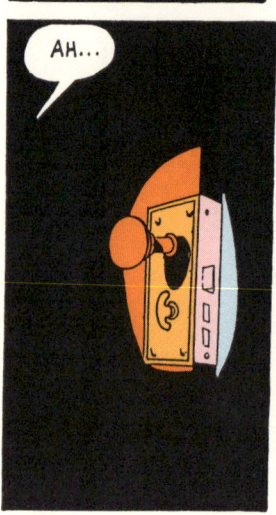

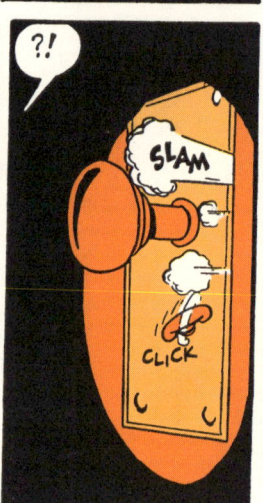

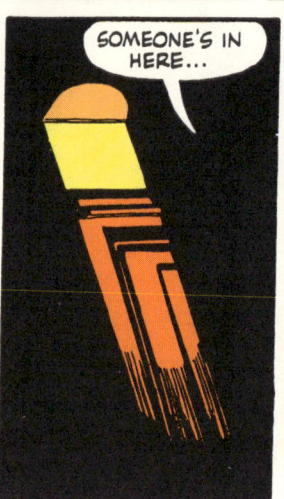

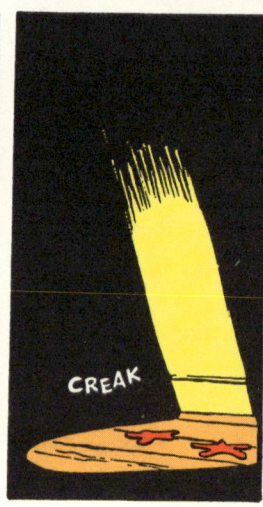

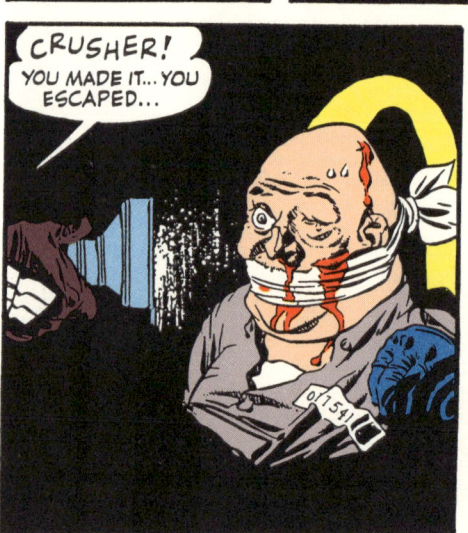

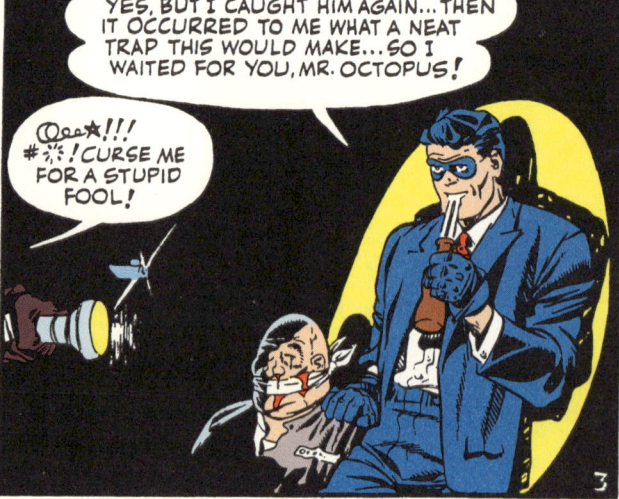

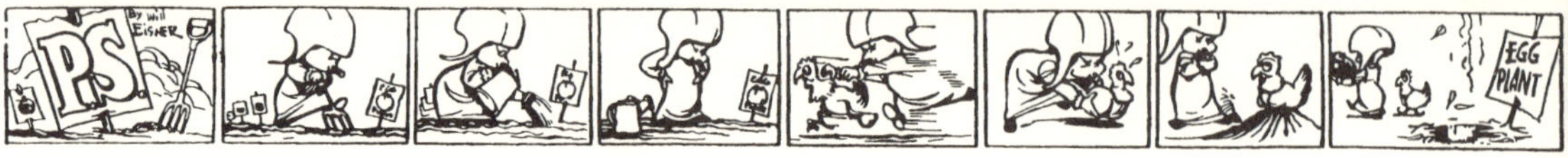

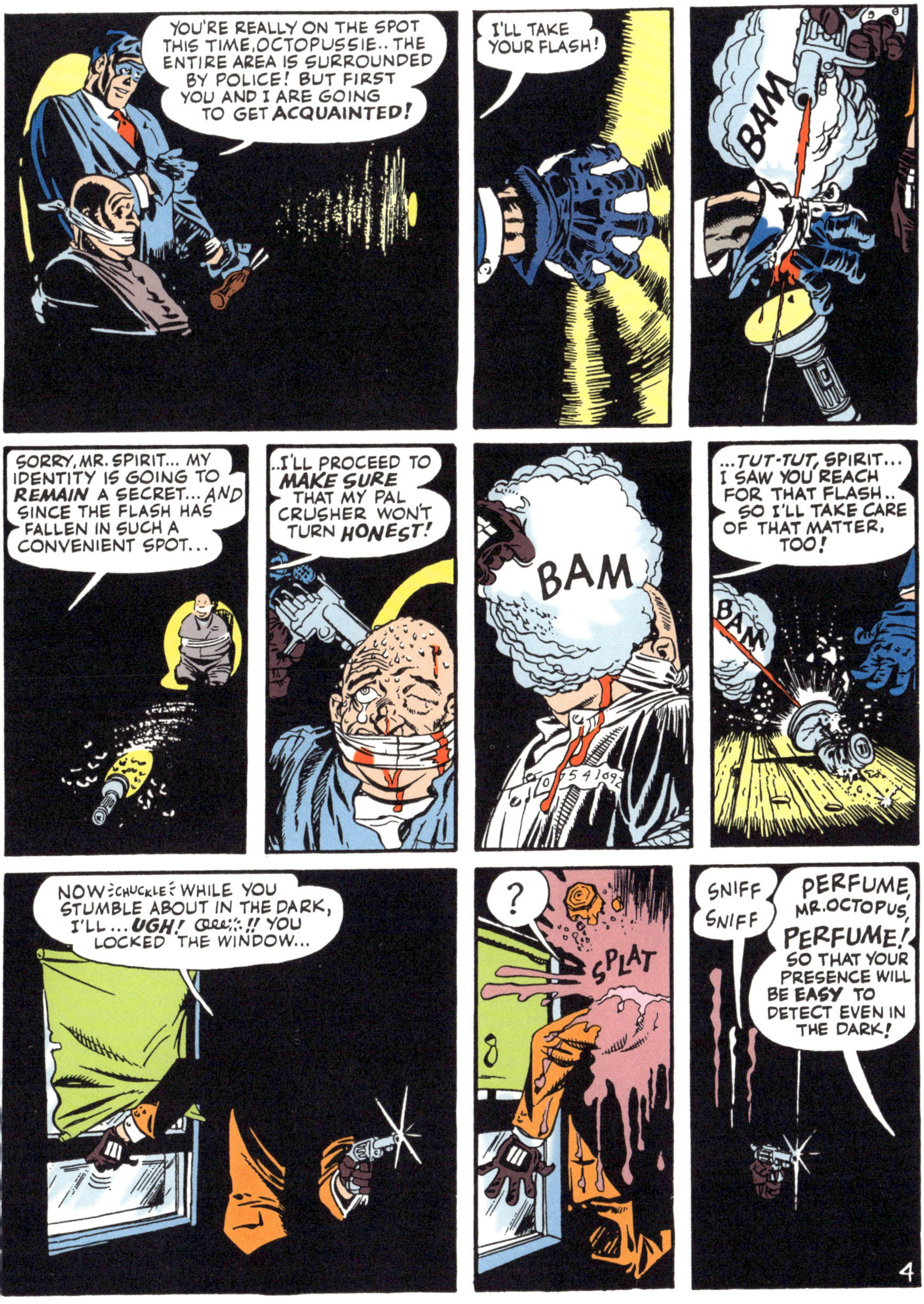
YOU'RE REALLY ON THE SPOT THIS TIME, OCTOPUSSIE.. THE ENTIRE AREA IS SURROUNDED BY POLICE! BUT FIRST YOU AND I ARE GOING TO GET ACQUAINTED!
I'LL TAKE YOUR FLASH!
BAM
SORRY, MR. SPIRIT... MY IDENTITY IS GOING TO REMAIN A SECRET... AND SINCE THE FLASH HAS FALLEN IN SUCH A CONVENIENT SPOT...
..I'LL PROCEED TO MAKE SURE THAT MY PAL CRUSHER WON'T TURN HONEST!
BAM
...TUT-TUT, SPIRIT... I SAW YOU REACH FOR THAT FLASH.. SO I'LL TAKE CARE OF THAT MATTER, TOO!
BAM
NOW :CHUCKLE: WHILE YOU STUMBLE ABOUT IN THE DARK, I'LL ... UGH! !! YOU LOCKED THE WINDOW...
?
SPLAT
SNIFF SNIFF
PERFUME, MR. OCTOPUS, PERFUME! SO THAT YOUR PRESENCE WILL BE EASY TO DETECT EVEN IN THE DARK!
4

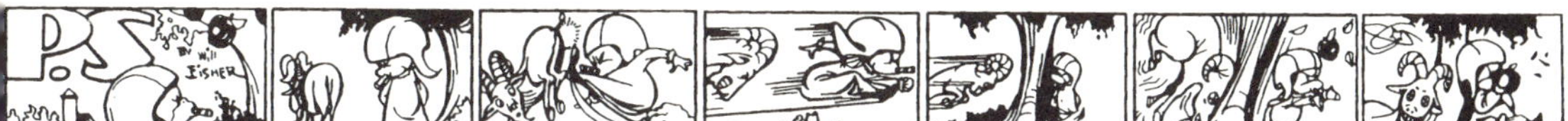
P.S.
BY WILL EISNER

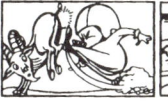

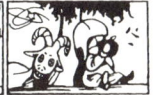

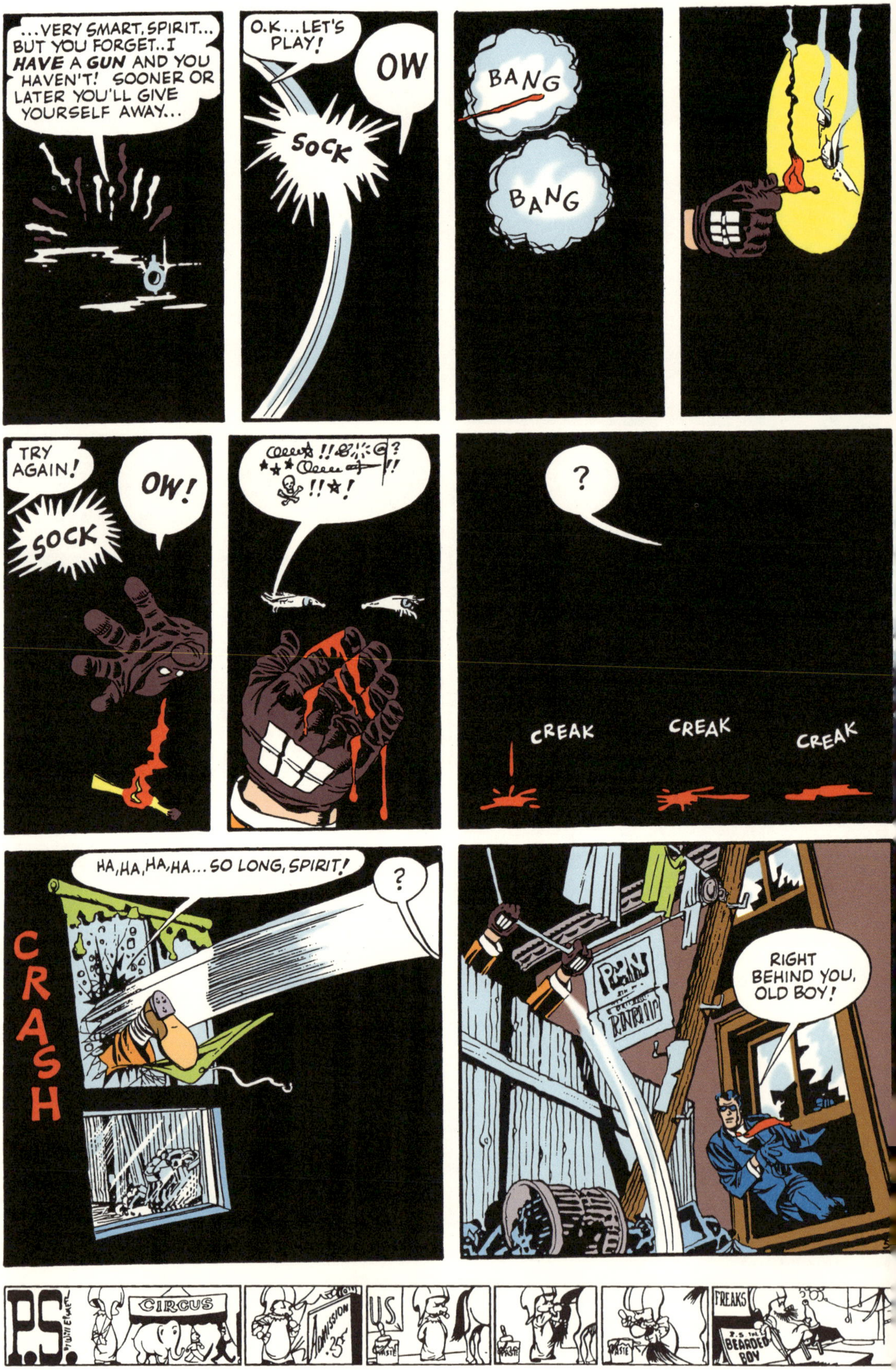
...VERY SMART, SPIRIT... BUT YOU FORGET..I HAVE A GUN AND YOU HAVEN'T! SOONER OR LATER YOU'LL GIVE YOURSELF AWAY...
O.K... LET'S PLAY!
SOCK
OW
BANG
BANG
TRY AGAIN!
SOCK
OW!
?
CREAK
CREAK
CREAK
CRASH
HA, HA, HA, HA... SO LONG, SPIRIT!
?
RIGHT BEHIND YOU, OLD BOY!
P.S.
CIRCUS
ADMISSION 25¢
PASTE
FREAKS
P.S THE BEARDED BOY

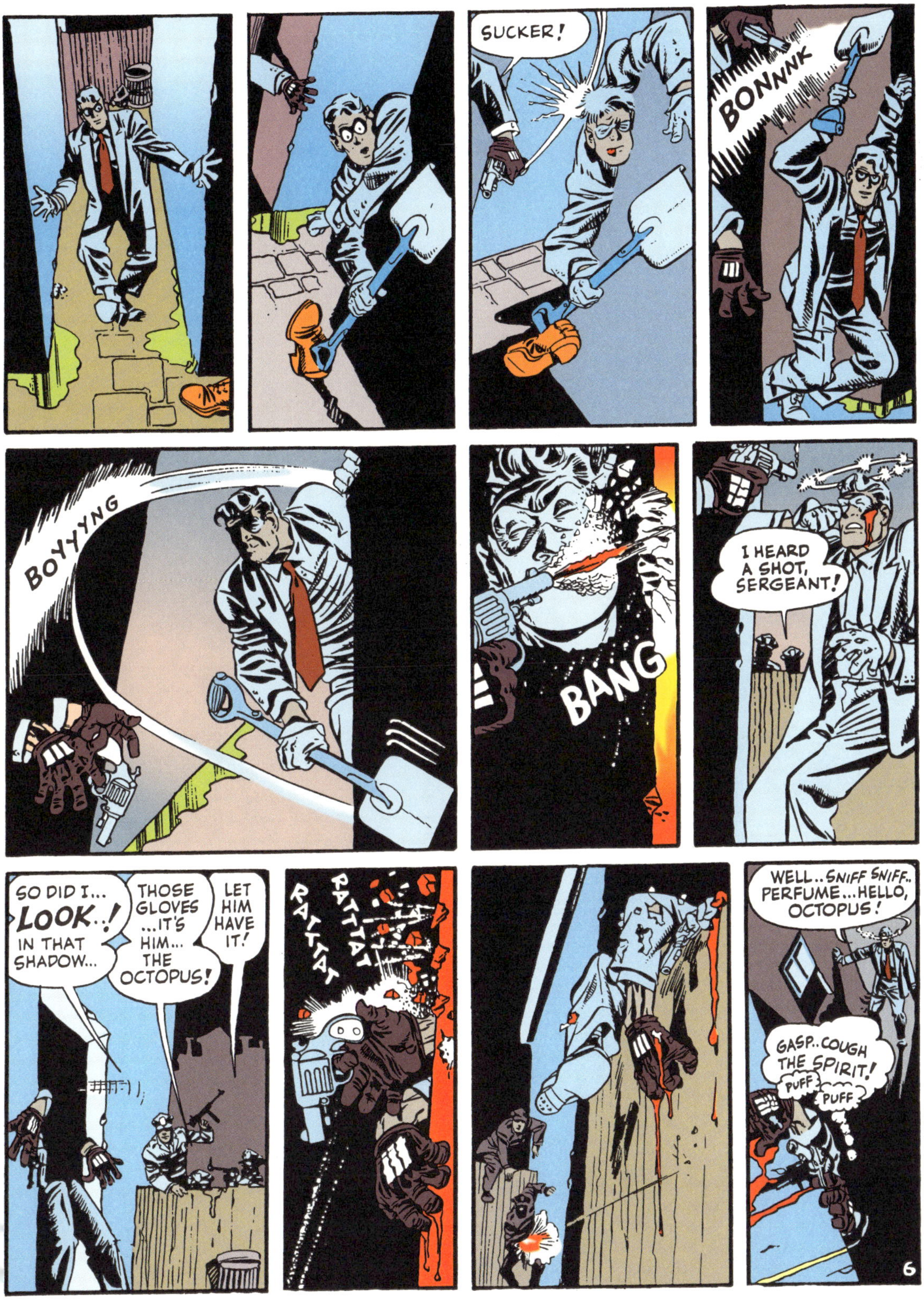
SUCKER!
BONNNK
BOYYYNG
BANG
I HEARD A SHOT, SERGEANT!
SO DID I... LOOK..! IN THAT SHADOW...
THOSE GLOVES ...IT'S HIM... THE OCTOPUS!
LET HIM HAVE IT!
RATTAT RATTAT
WELL..SNIFF SNIFF.. PERFUME...HELLO, OCTOPUS!
GASP..COUGH THE SPIRIT!
PUFF
PUFF
6

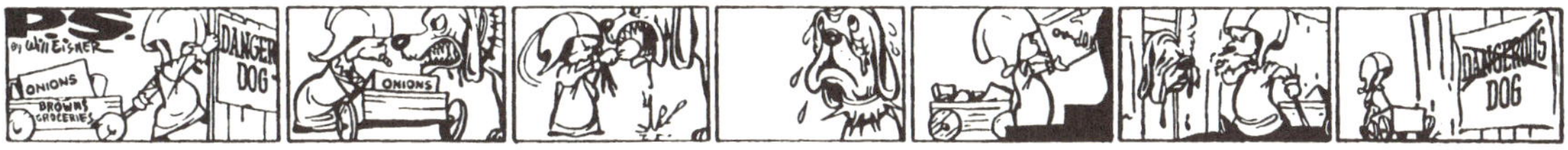
P.S.
BY Will Eisner
ONIONS
BROWNS GROCERIES
DANGER DOG
ONIONS
DANGEROUS DOG

NOW, AT LAST, I'VE GOT YOU!
HE GASP...HE CAN'T SEE... HE'S STILL BLINDED BY MY GUN FLASH!
SNIFF SNIFF
CLICK CLICK
!!*! EMPTY... MY GUN IS EMPTY... OOOH... I'M... COUGH COUGH COUGH COUGH
THUD
SPIRIT!... HANG ON... WE'RE COMING!
POK
CLINK
LOOK OUT IT'S THE FIRING PIN OF A GRENADE
BOOM
...AND SO, THE NEXT DAY...
WELL, THIS TIME THERE CAN BE NO DOUBT ABOUT IT... WE EVEN HAVE THE BODY! YOU'LL SEE FOR YOURSELF IN A DAY OR SO!
FINE... HAVE YOU PHOTOGRAPHED HIS FACE... AND TAKEN HIS FINGERPRINTS?
WELL..ER...NO.. YOU SEE, THE BODY WE FOUND WAS A MESS..HANDS AND FACE BLOWN TO RIBBONS! SHUCKS..WHAT MORE DO YOU WANT?
OCTOPUS FINALLY KILLED BY OWN HAND
AND SO...THAT IS THE END OF THE OCTOPUS...
THERE CAN BE NO DOUBT ABOUT IT. THE EXPLOSION TOOK PLACE BEFORE OUR EYES....DIDN'T IT?...YOU SAW IT FOR YOURSELF...
OF COURSE, SOME SMART ALEC WILL SAY HE COULD HAVE LEFT ANOTHER BODY... SAY, A PASSER-BY! SURE, IT'S POSSIBLE TO SURVIVE A GRENADE BLOW...ER...ER... GOSH...DO YOU SUPPOSE HE COULD HAVE.. AW...THAT'S TOO MUCH TO EXPECT OF A MAN...
sure, that's impossible
WELL, WHAT DID YOU EXPECT? DON'T YA THINK WE'D LIKE TO SEE HIS FACE, TOO?
DO YOU THINK IT'S EASY FOR ME :SOB: SEEING THE CHARACTER I CREATED OUT OF MY OWN INK
BEATEN UP WEEK AFTER WEEK BY A FIEND WHO KEEPS ELUDING MY PEN? DO YOU THINK IT'S FUN? HA HA FUN? :SOB:
WELL.. Next Week: WE BRING YOU THE SPIRIT IN... "THE WELL OF DARKNESS"

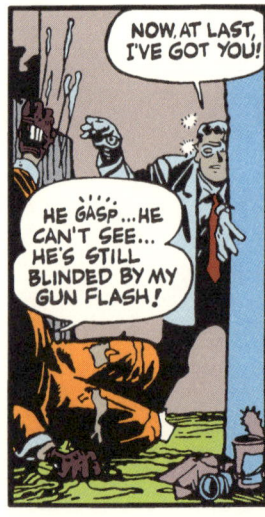

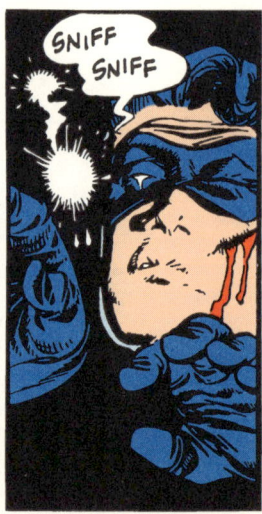

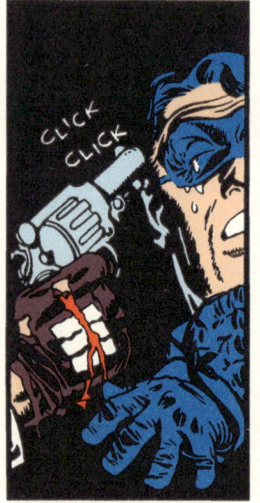

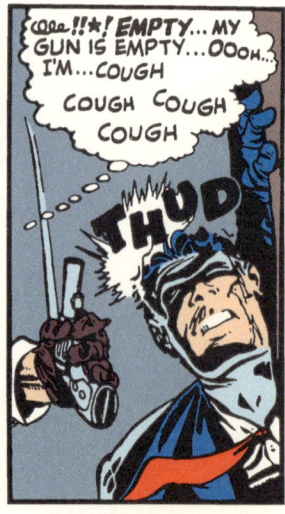

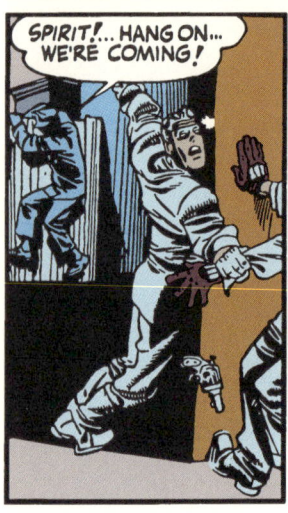

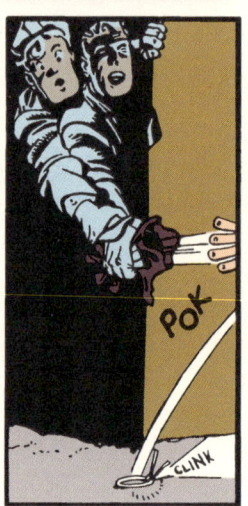

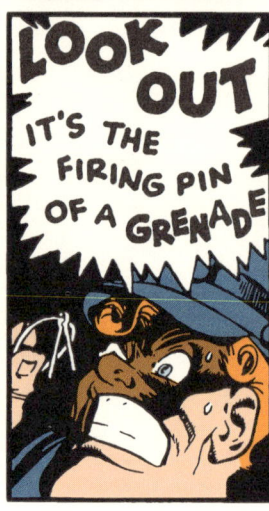

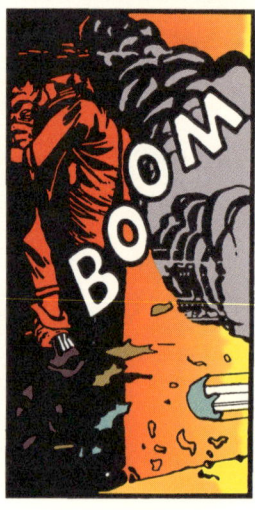

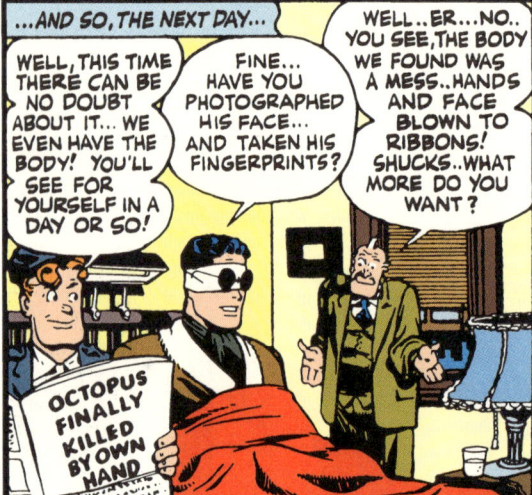

COMIC BOOK SECTION

BLIND

August 31 1947

ACTION Mystery ADVENTURE

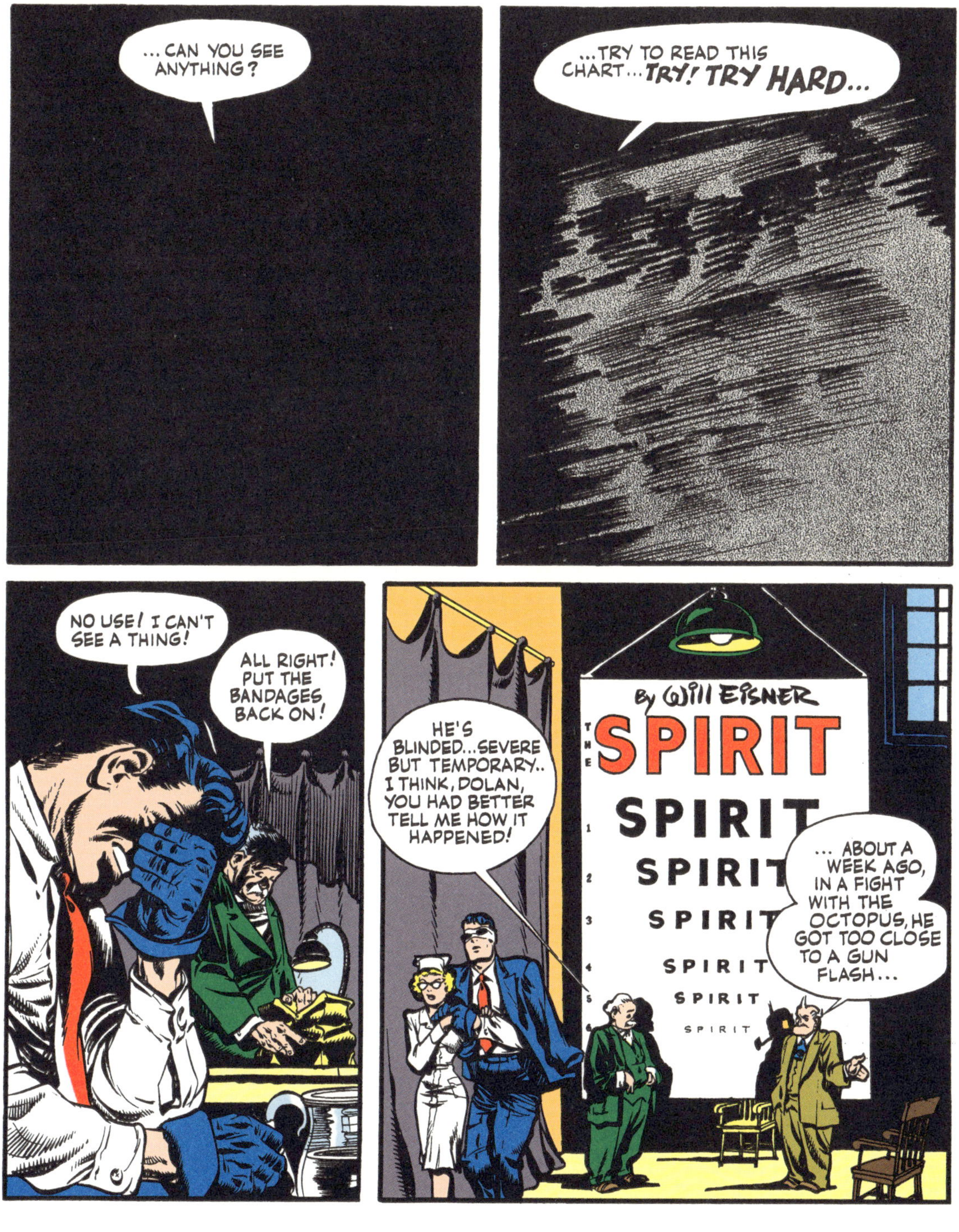
...CAN YOU SEE ANYTHING?
...TRY TO READ THIS CHART...TRY! TRY HARD...
NO USE! I CAN'T SEE A THING!
ALL RIGHT! PUT THE BANDAGES BACK ON!
By Will Eisner
THE SPIRIT
SPIRIT
SPIRIT
SPIRIT
SPIRIT
SPIRIT
SPIRIT
HE'S BLINDED...SEVERE BUT TEMPORARY.. I THINK, DOLAN, YOU HAD BETTER TELL ME HOW IT HAPPENED!
...ABOUT A WEEK AGO, IN A FIGHT WITH THE OCTOPUS, HE GOT TOO CLOSE TO A GUN FLASH...

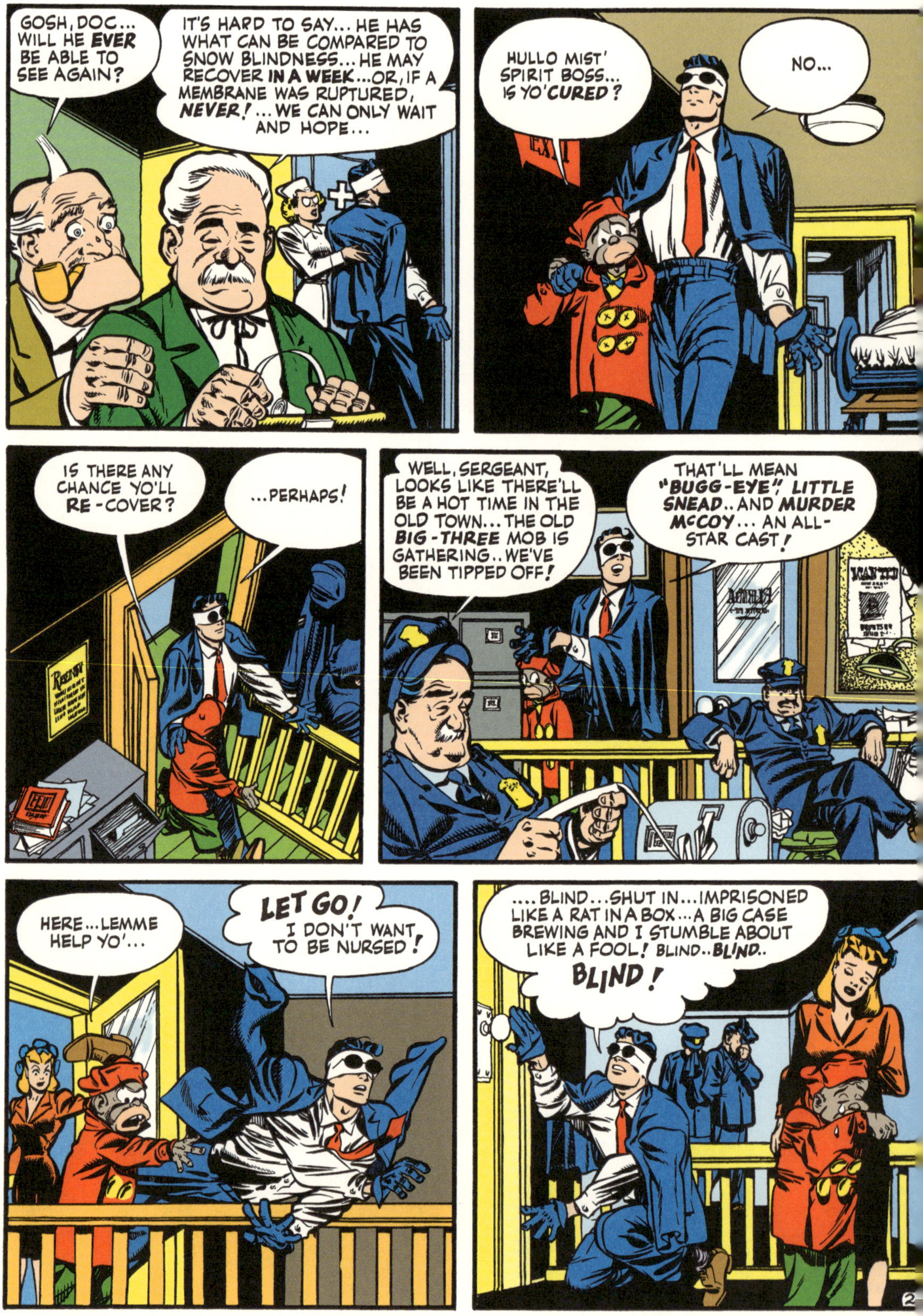
GOSH, DOC... WILL HE EVER BE ABLE TO SEE AGAIN?
IT'S HARD TO SAY... HE HAS WHAT CAN BE COMPARED TO SNOW BLINDNESS... HE MAY RECOVER IN A WEEK...OR, IF A MEMBRANE WAS RUPTURED, NEVER! ... WE CAN ONLY WAIT AND HOPE...
HULLO MIST' SPIRIT BOSS... IS YO' CURED?
NO...
EXIT
IS THERE ANY CHANCE YO'LL RE-COVER?
...PERHAPS!
WELL, SERGEANT, LOOKS LIKE THERE'LL BE A HOT TIME IN THE OLD TOWN... THE OLD BIG-THREE MOB IS GATHERING.. WE'VE BEEN TIPPED OFF!
THAT'LL MEAN "BUGG-EYE", LITTLE SNEAD.. AND MURDER McCOY... AN ALL-STAR CAST!
HERE...LEMME HELP YO'...
LET GO! I DON'T WANT TO BE NURSED!
....BLIND...SHUT IN...IMPRISONED LIKE A RAT IN A BOX...A BIG CASE BREWING AND I STUMBLE ABOUT LIKE A FOOL! BLIND..BLIND..
BLIND!
2

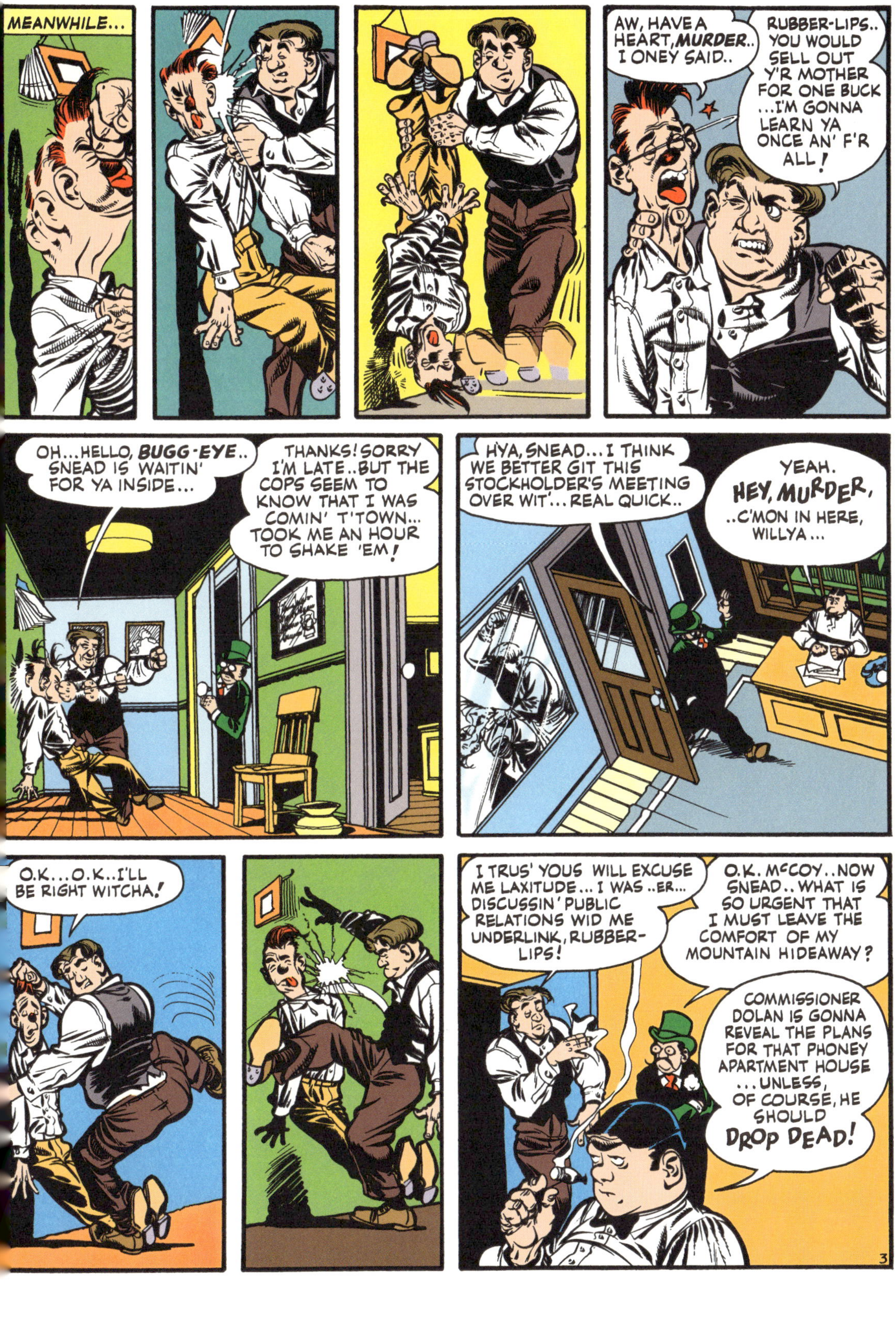
MEANWHILE...
AW, HAVE A HEART, MURDER.. I ONEY SAID..
RUBBER-LIPS.. YOU WOULD SELL OUT Y'R MOTHER FOR ONE BUCK ...I'M GONNA LEARN YA ONCE AN' F'R ALL!
OH...HELLO, BUGG-EYE.. SNEAD IS WAITIN' FOR YA INSIDE...
THANKS! SORRY I'M LATE..BUT THE COPS SEEM TO KNOW THAT I WAS COMIN' T'TOWN... TOOK ME AN HOUR TO SHAKE 'EM!
HYA, SNEAD... I THINK WE BETTER GIT THIS STOCKHOLDER'S MEETING OVER WIT'... REAL QUICK..
YEAH. HEY, MURDER, ..C'MON IN HERE, WILLYA...
O.K...O.K..I'LL BE RIGHT WITCHA!
I TRUS' YOUS WILL EXCUSE ME LAXITUDE... I WAS ..ER... DISCUSSIN' PUBLIC RELATIONS WID ME UNDERLINK, RUBBER-LIPS!
O.K. McCOY..NOW SNEAD..WHAT IS SO URGENT THAT I MUST LEAVE THE COMFORT OF MY MOUNTAIN HIDEAWAY?
COMMISSIONER DOLAN IS GONNA REVEAL THE PLANS FOR THAT PHONEY APARTMENT HOUSE ...UNLESS, OF COURSE, HE SHOULD DROP DEAD!
3

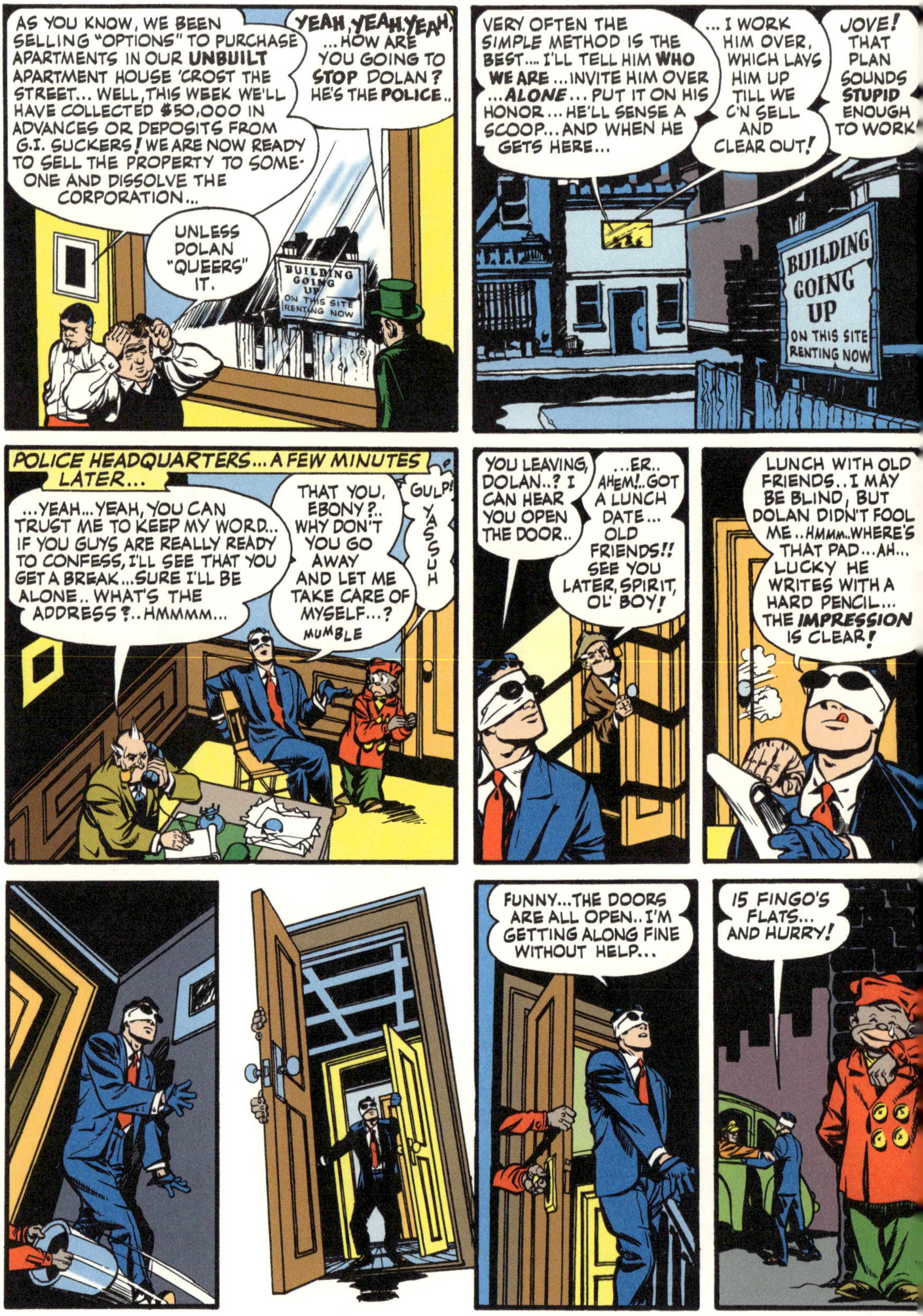
AS YOU KNOW, WE BEEN SELLING "OPTIONS" TO PURCHASE APARTMENTS IN OUR UNBUILT APARTMENT HOUSE 'CROST THE STREET... WELL, THIS WEEK WE'LL HAVE COLLECTED $50,000 IN ADVANCES OR DEPOSITS FROM G.I. SUCKERS! WE ARE NOW READY TO SELL THE PROPERTY TO SOMEONE AND DISSOLVE THE CORPORATION...
YEAH, YEAH, YEAH, ...HOW ARE YOU GOING TO STOP DOLAN? HE'S THE POLICE..
UNLESS DOLAN "QUEERS" IT.
BUILDING GOING UP ON THIS SITE RENTING NOW
VERY OFTEN THE SIMPLE METHOD IS THE BEST.... I'LL TELL HIM WHO WE ARE ...INVITE HIM OVER ...ALONE... PUT IT ON HIS HONOR... HE'LL SENSE A SCOOP... AND WHEN HE GETS HERE...
... I WORK HIM OVER, WHICH LAYS HIM UP TILL WE C'N SELL AND CLEAR OUT!
JOVE! THAT PLAN SOUNDS STUPID ENOUGH TO WORK
BUILDING GOING UP ON THIS SITE RENTING NOW
POLICE HEADQUARTERS... A FEW MINUTES LATER...
...YEAH...YEAH, YOU CAN TRUST ME TO KEEP MY WORD... IF YOU GUYS ARE REALLY READY TO CONFESS, I'LL SEE THAT YOU GET A BREAK...SURE I'LL BE ALONE.. WHAT'S THE ADDRESS?..HMMMM...
THAT YOU, EBONY?.. WHY DON'T YOU GO AWAY AND LET ME TAKE CARE OF MYSELF...? MUMBLE
GULP! YASSUH
YOU LEAVING, DOLAN..? I CAN HEAR YOU OPEN THE DOOR..
...ER.. AHEM!..GOT A LUNCH DATE... OLD FRIENDS!! SEE YOU LATER, SPIRIT, OL' BOY!
LUNCH WITH OLD FRIENDS..I MAY BE BLIND, BUT DOLAN DIDN'T FOOL ME..HMMM..WHERE'S THAT PAD...AH... LUCKY HE WRITES WITH A HARD PENCIL... THE IMPRESSION IS CLEAR!
FUNNY...THE DOORS ARE ALL OPEN..I'M GETTING ALONG FINE WITHOUT HELP...
15 FINGO'S FLATS... AND HURRY!

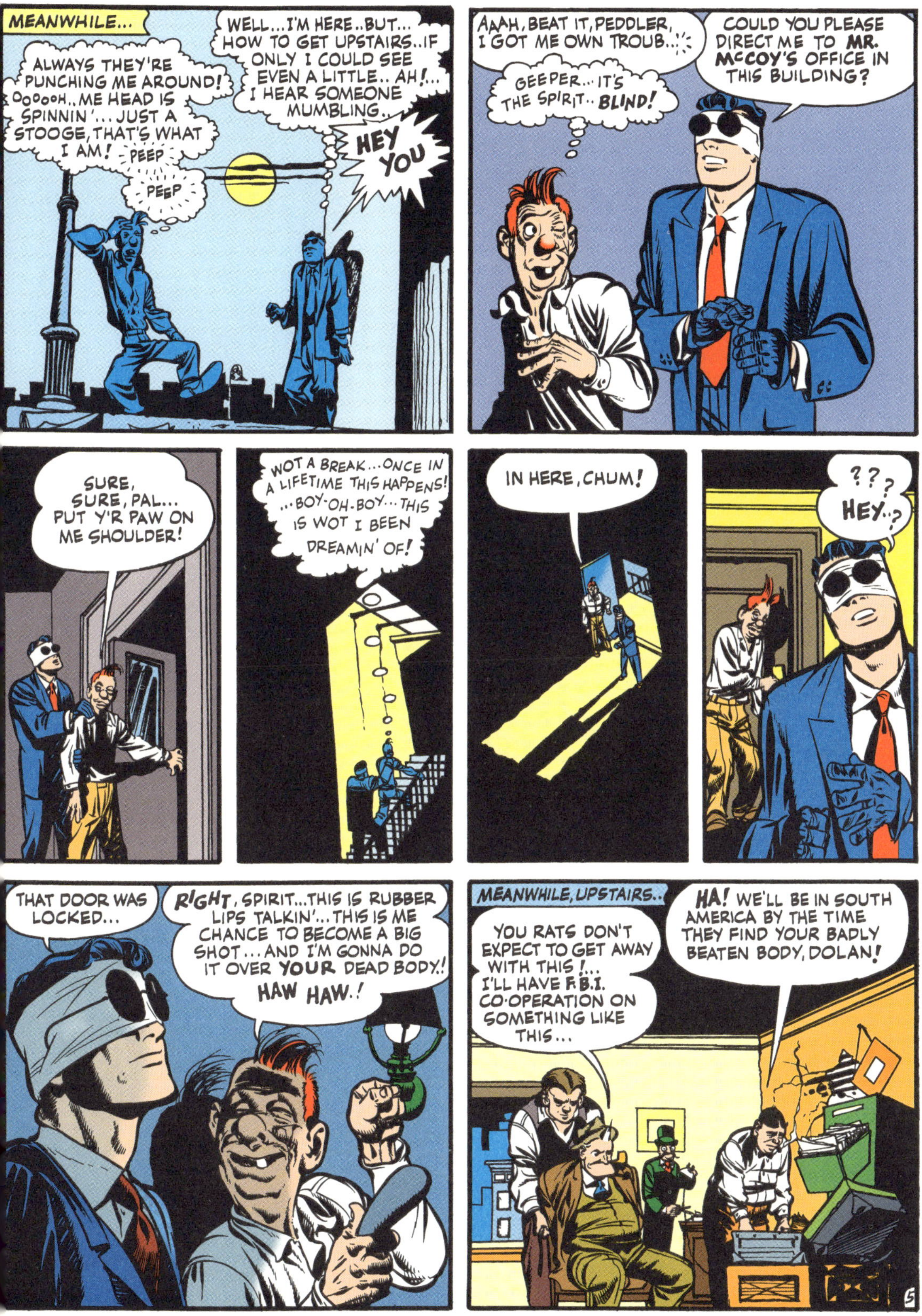

MEANWHILE...
ALWAYS THEY'RE PUNCHING ME AROUND! OOOOOH.. ME HEAD IS SPINNIN'... JUST A STOOGE, THAT'S WHAT I AM!
PEEP
PEEP
WELL... I'M HERE.. BUT... HOW TO GET UPSTAIRS.. IF ONLY I COULD SEE EVEN A LITTLE.. AH!... I HEAR SOMEONE MUMBLING..
HEY YOU
AAAH, BEAT IT, PEDDLER, I GOT ME OWN TROUB..!
GEEPER... IT'S THE SPIRIT.. BLIND!
COULD YOU PLEASE DIRECT ME TO MR. McCOY'S OFFICE IN THIS BUILDING?
SURE, SURE, PAL... PUT Y'R PAW ON ME SHOULDER!
WOT A BREAK... ONCE IN A LIFETIME THIS HAPPENS! ...BOY-OH-BOY... THIS IS WOT I BEEN DREAMIN' OF!
IN HERE, CHUM!
??? HEY..?
THAT DOOR WAS LOCKED...
RIGHT, SPIRIT... THIS IS RUBBER LIPS TALKIN'... THIS IS ME CHANCE TO BECOME A BIG SHOT... AND I'M GONNA DO IT OVER YOUR DEAD BODY! HAW HAW.!
MEANWHILE, UPSTAIRS..
YOU RATS DON'T EXPECT TO GET AWAY WITH THIS!... I'LL HAVE F.B.I. CO-OPERATION ON SOMETHING LIKE THIS...
HA! WE'LL BE IN SOUTH AMERICA BY THE TIME THEY FIND YOUR BADLY BEATEN BODY, DOLAN!
5

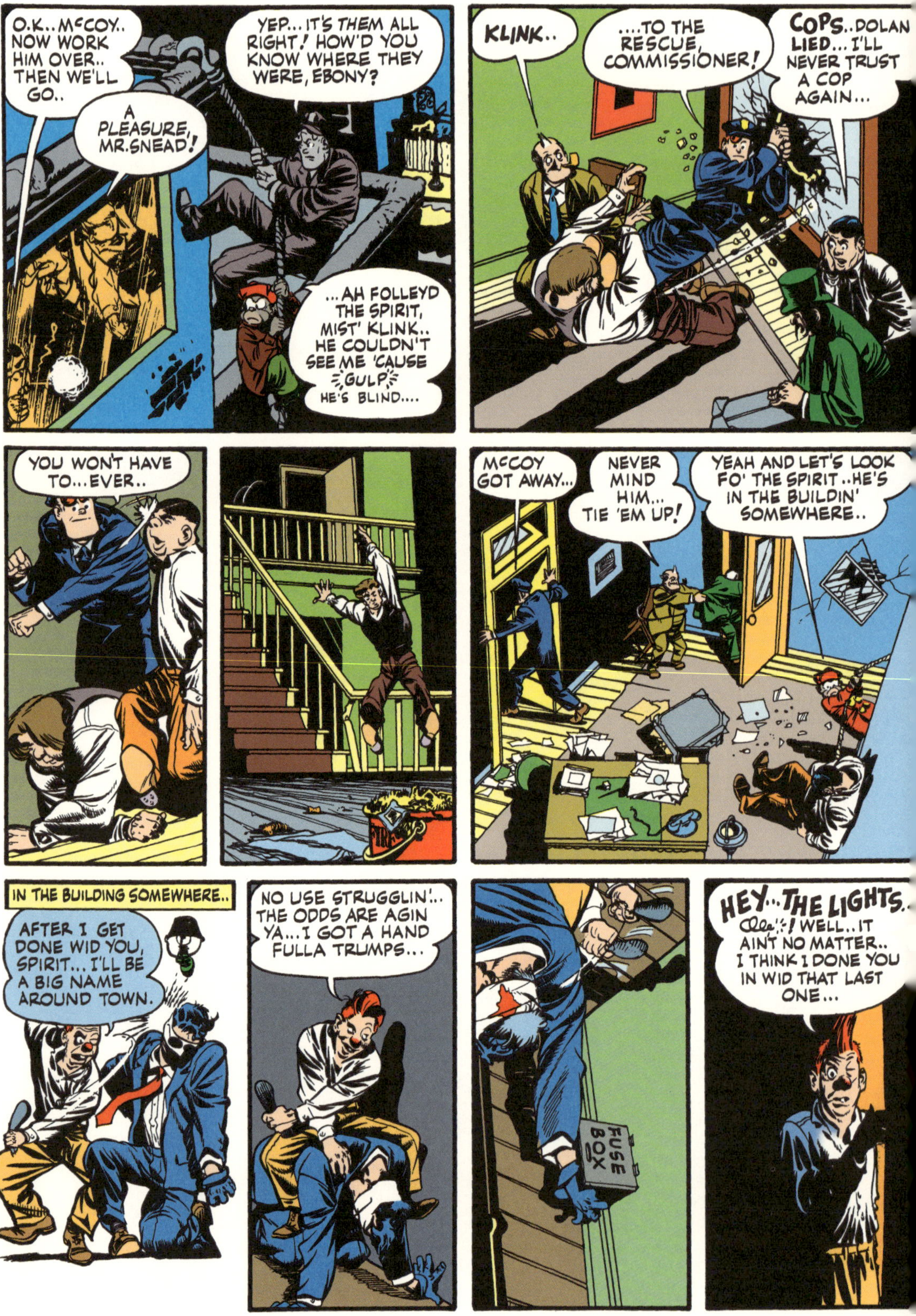
O.K.. McCOY.. NOW WORK HIM OVER.. THEN WE'LL GO..
A PLEASURE, MR. SNEAD!
YEP... IT'S THEM ALL RIGHT! HOW'D YOU KNOW WHERE THEY WERE, EBONY?
...AH FOLLEYD THE SPIRIT, MIST' KLINK.. HE COULDN'T SEE ME 'CAUSE GULP HE'S BLIND....
KLINK..
....TO THE RESCUE, COMMISSIONER!
COPS.. DOLAN LIED... I'LL NEVER TRUST A COP AGAIN...
YOU WON'T HAVE TO... EVER..
McCOY GOT AWAY...
NEVER MIND HIM... TIE 'EM UP!
YEAH AND LET'S LOOK FO' THE SPIRIT.. HE'S IN THE BUILDIN' SOMEWHERE..
IN THE BUILDING SOMEWHERE..
AFTER I GET DONE WID YOU, SPIRIT... I'LL BE A BIG NAME AROUND TOWN.
NO USE STRUGGLIN'.. THE ODDS ARE AGIN YA... I GOT A HAND FULLA TRUMPS...
FUSE BOX
HEY.. THE LIGHTS.. ! WELL.. IT AIN'T NO MATTER.. I THINK I DONE YOU IN WID THAT LAST ONE...

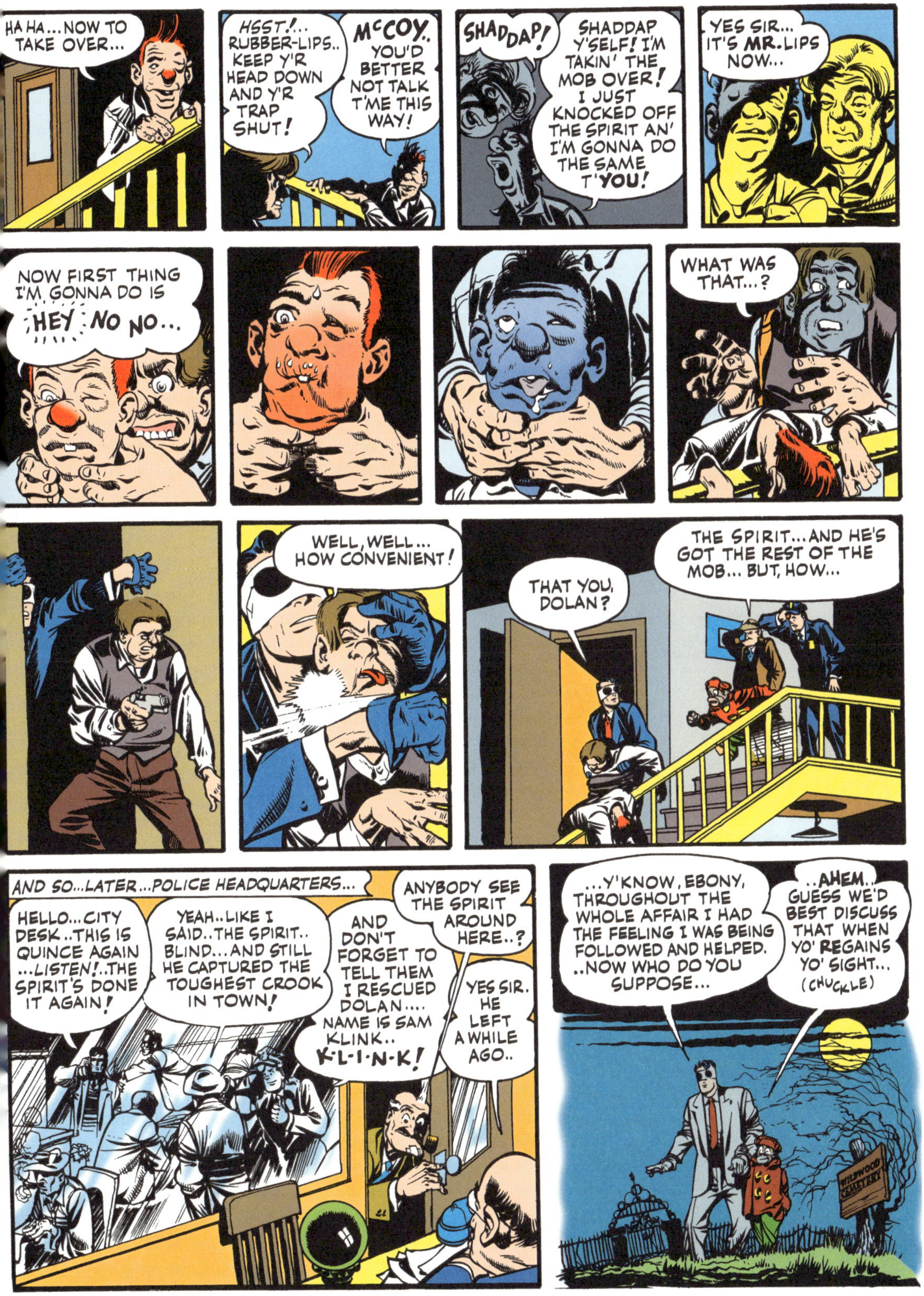
HA HA... NOW TO TAKE OVER...
HSST!.. RUBBER-LIPS.. KEEP Y'R HEAD DOWN AND Y'R TRAP SHUT!
McCOY.. YOU'D BETTER NOT TALK T'ME THIS WAY!
SHADDAP!
SHADDAP Y'SELF! I'M TAKIN' THE MOB OVER! I JUST KNOCKED OFF THE SPIRIT AN' I'M GONNA DO THE SAME T'YOU!
YES SIR... IT'S MR. LIPS NOW...
NOW FIRST THING I'M GONNA DO IS HEY NO NO...
WHAT WAS THAT...?
WELL, WELL... HOW CONVENIENT!
THAT YOU, DOLAN?
THE SPIRIT... AND HE'S GOT THE REST OF THE MOB... BUT, HOW...
AND SO... LATER... POLICE HEADQUARTERS...
HELLO... CITY DESK.. THIS IS QUINCE AGAIN ...LISTEN!.. THE SPIRIT'S DONE IT AGAIN!
YEAH.. LIKE I SAID.. THE SPIRIT.. BLIND... AND STILL HE CAPTURED THE TOUGHEST CROOK IN TOWN!
AND DON'T FORGET TO TELL THEM I RESCUED DOLAN.... NAME IS SAM KLINK.. K-L-I-N-K!
ANYBODY SEE THE SPIRIT AROUND HERE..?
YES SIR. HE LEFT A WHILE AGO..
...Y'KNOW, EBONY, THROUGHOUT THE WHOLE AFFAIR I HAD THE FEELING I WAS BEING FOLLOWED AND HELPED. ..NOW WHO DO YOU SUPPOSE...
..AHEM.. GUESS WE'D BEST DISCUSS THAT WHEN YO' REGAINS YO' SIGHT... (CHUCKLE)

A KILLER AT LARGE

September 7 1947

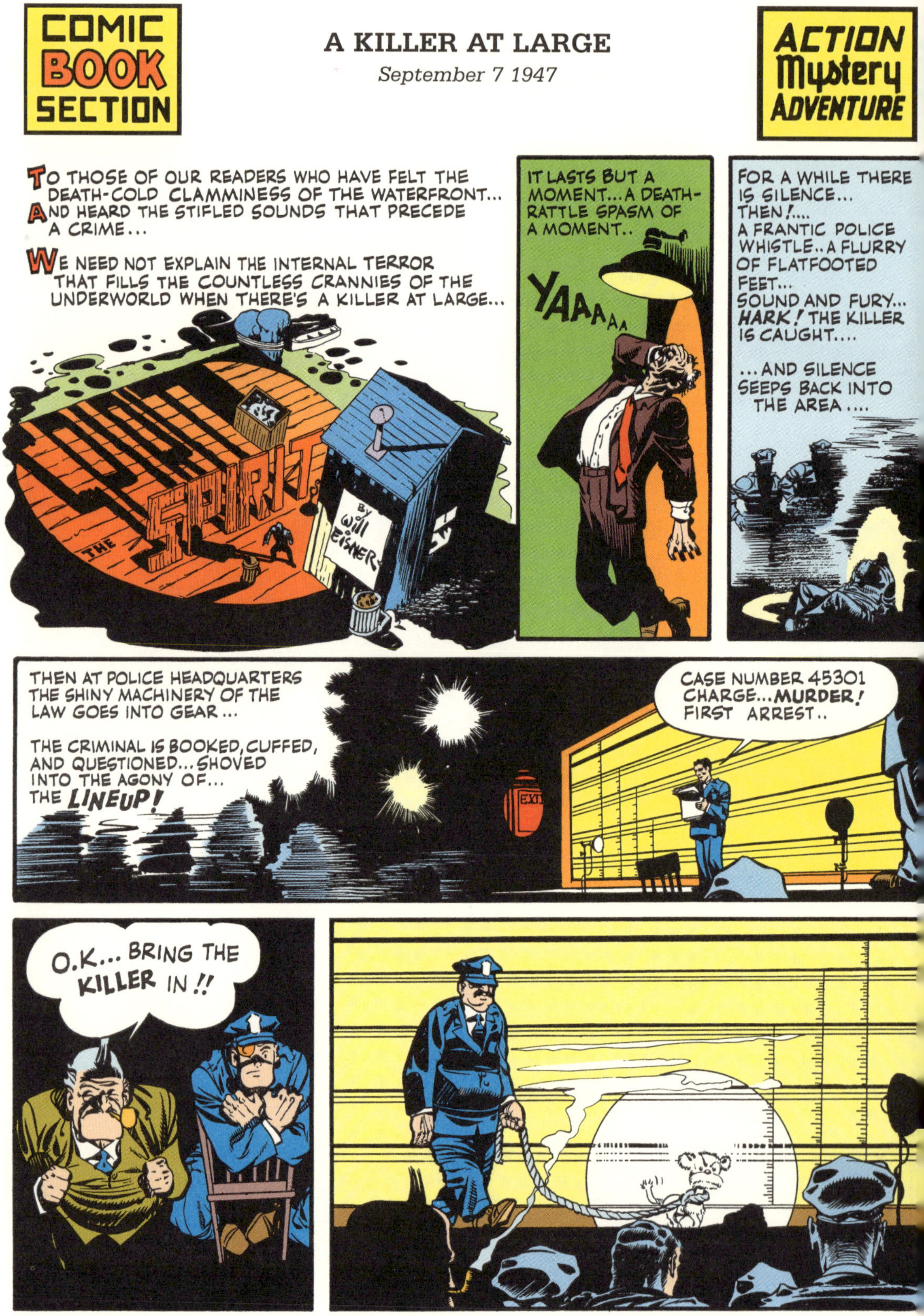
COMIC BOOK SECTION
ACTION Mystery ADVENTURE
TO THOSE OF OUR READERS WHO HAVE FELT THE DEATH-COLD CLAMMINESS OF THE WATERFRONT... AND HEARD THE STIFLED SOUNDS THAT PRECEDE A CRIME...
WE NEED NOT EXPLAIN THE INTERNAL TERROR THAT FILLS THE COUNTLESS CRANNIES OF THE UNDERWORLD WHEN THERE'S A KILLER AT LARGE...
THE SPIRIT
BY WILL EISNER
IT LASTS BUT A MOMENT...A DEATH-RATTLE SPASM OF A MOMENT..
YAAAAAA
FOR A WHILE THERE IS SILENCE... THEN!.... A FRANTIC POLICE WHISTLE..A FLURRY OF FLATFOOTED FEET... SOUND AND FURY... HARK! THE KILLER IS CAUGHT....
...AND SILENCE SEEPS BACK INTO THE AREA....
THEN AT POLICE HEADQUARTERS THE SHINY MACHINERY OF THE LAW GOES INTO GEAR...
THE CRIMINAL IS BOOKED, CUFFED, AND QUESTIONED...SHOVED INTO THE AGONY OF... THE LINEUP!
EXIT
CASE NUMBER 45301 CHARGE...MURDER! FIRST ARREST..
O.K... BRING THE KILLER IN!!

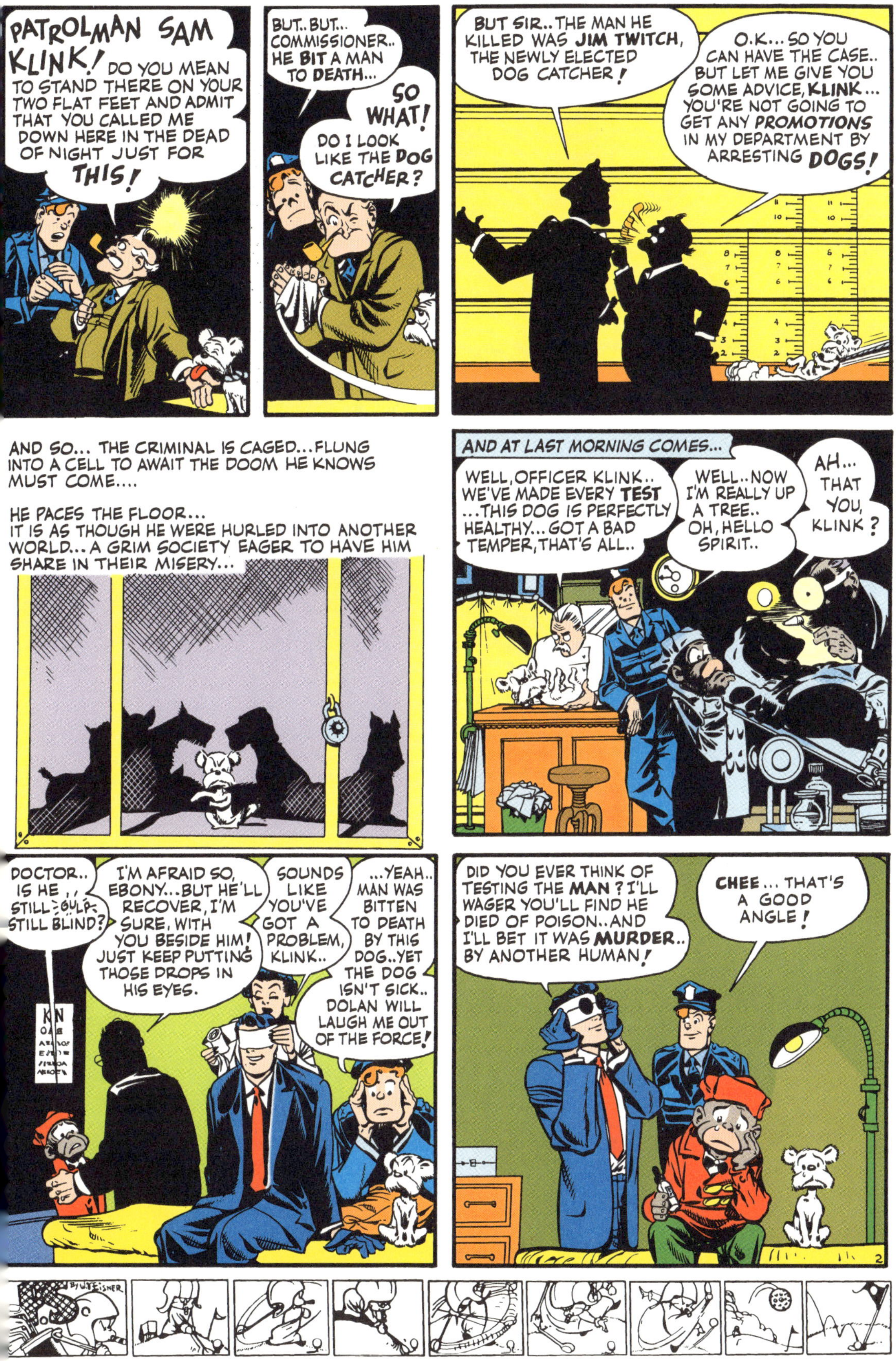
PATROLMAN SAM KLINK! DO YOU MEAN TO STAND THERE ON YOUR TWO FLAT FEET AND ADMIT THAT YOU CALLED ME DOWN HERE IN THE DEAD OF NIGHT JUST FOR THIS!
BUT..BUT.. COMMISSIONER.. HE BIT A MAN TO DEATH...
SO WHAT! DO I LOOK LIKE THE DOG CATCHER?
BUT SIR..THE MAN HE KILLED WAS JIM TWITCH, THE NEWLY ELECTED DOG CATCHER!
O.K...SO YOU CAN HAVE THE CASE.. BUT LET ME GIVE YOU SOME ADVICE, KLINK... YOU'RE NOT GOING TO GET ANY PROMOTIONS IN MY DEPARTMENT BY ARRESTING DOGS!
AND SO... THE CRIMINAL IS CAGED...FLUNG INTO A CELL TO AWAIT THE DOOM HE KNOWS MUST COME....
HE PACES THE FLOOR... IT IS AS THOUGH HE WERE HURLED INTO ANOTHER WORLD...A GRIM SOCIETY EAGER TO HAVE HIM SHARE IN THEIR MISERY...
AND AT LAST MORNING COMES...
WELL, OFFICER KLINK.. WE'VE MADE EVERY TEST ...THIS DOG IS PERFECTLY HEALTHY...GOT A BAD TEMPER, THAT'S ALL..
WELL..NOW I'M REALLY UP A TREE.. OH, HELLO SPIRIT..
AH... THAT YOU, KLINK?
DOCTOR.. IS HE.. STILL -GULP- STILL BLIND?
I'M AFRAID SO, EBONY...BUT HE'LL RECOVER, I'M SURE, WITH YOU BESIDE HIM! JUST KEEP PUTTING THOSE DROPS IN HIS EYES.
SOUNDS LIKE YOU'VE GOT A PROBLEM, KLINK..
...YEAH.. MAN WAS BITTEN TO DEATH BY THIS DOG..YET THE DOG ISN'T SICK.. DOLAN WILL LAUGH ME OUT OF THE FORCE!
DID YOU EVER THINK OF TESTING THE MAN? I'LL WAGER YOU'LL FIND HE DIED OF POISON..AND I'LL BET IT WAS MURDER.. BY ANOTHER HUMAN!
CHEE... THAT'S A GOOD ANGLE!
2
BY W. EISNER

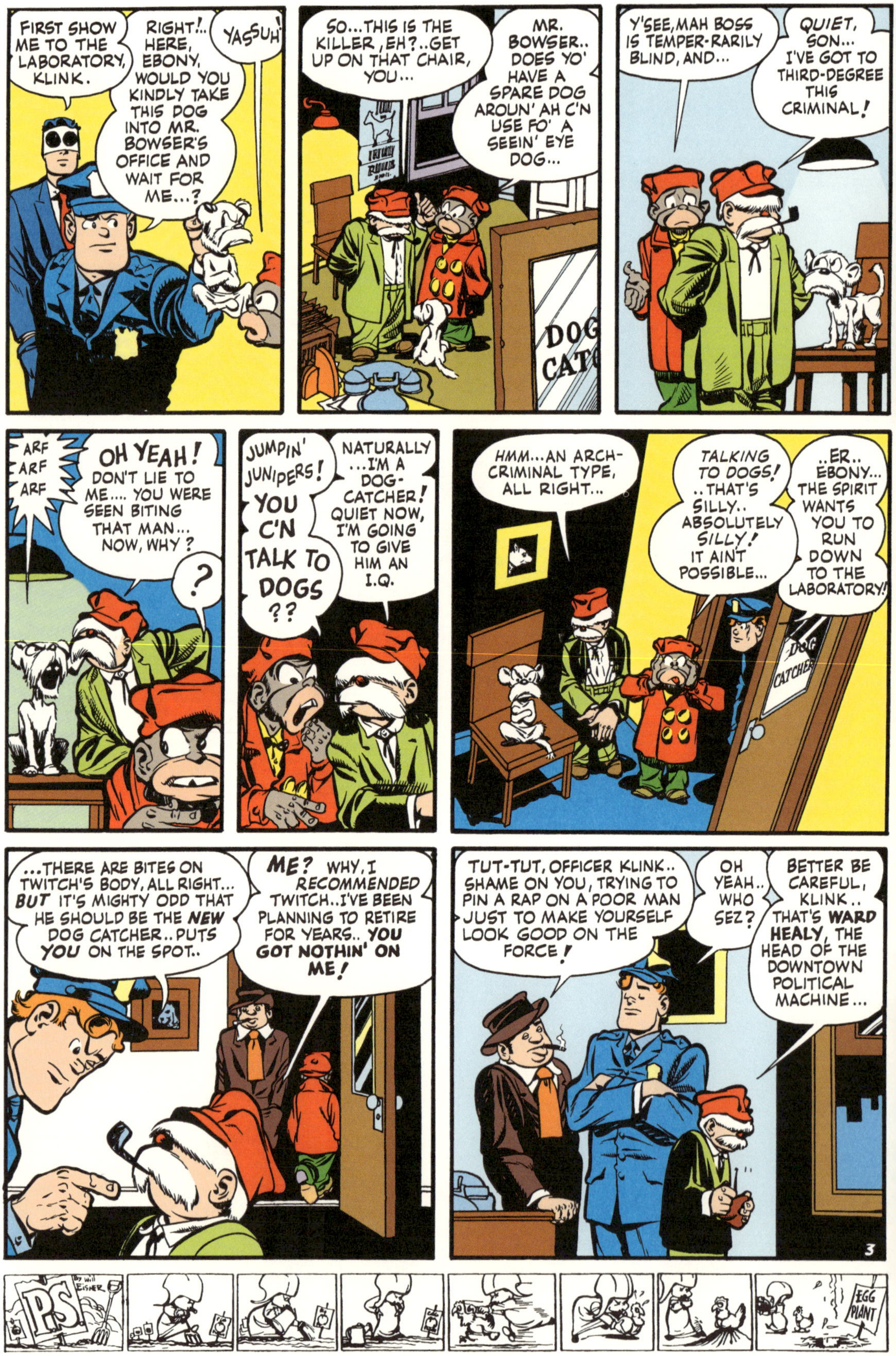

FIRST SHOW ME TO THE LABORATORY, KLINK.
RIGHT!.. HERE, EBONY, WOULD YOU KINDLY TAKE THIS DOG INTO MR. BOWSER'S OFFICE AND WAIT FOR ME...?
YASSUH!
SO...THIS IS THE KILLER, EH?..GET UP ON THAT CHAIR, YOU...
MR. BOWSER.. DOES YO' HAVE A SPARE DOG AROUN' AH C'N USE FO' A SEEIN' EYE DOG...
DOG CATC
Y'SEE, MAH BOSS IS TEMPER-RARILY BLIND, AND...
QUIET, SON... I'VE GOT TO THIRD-DEGREE THIS CRIMINAL!
ARF ARF ARF
OH YEAH! DON'T LIE TO ME.... YOU WERE SEEN BITING THAT MAN... NOW, WHY?
?
JUMPIN' JUNIPERS! YOU C'N TALK TO DOGS ??
NATURALLY ...I'M A DOG-CATCHER! QUIET NOW, I'M GOING TO GIVE HIM AN I.Q.
HMM...AN ARCH-CRIMINAL TYPE, ALL RIGHT...
TALKING TO DOGS! ..THAT'S SILLY.. ABSOLUTELY SILLY! IT AIN'T POSSIBLE...
..ER.. EBONY... THE SPIRIT WANTS YOU TO RUN DOWN TO THE LABORATORY!
DOG CATCHER
...THERE ARE BITES ON TWITCH'S BODY, ALL RIGHT... BUT IT'S MIGHTY ODD THAT HE SHOULD BE THE NEW DOG CATCHER.. PUTS YOU ON THE SPOT..
ME? WHY, I RECOMMENDED TWITCH..I'VE BEEN PLANNING TO RETIRE FOR YEARS.. YOU GOT NOTHIN' ON ME!
TUT-TUT, OFFICER KLINK.. SHAME ON YOU, TRYING TO PIN A RAP ON A POOR MAN JUST TO MAKE YOURSELF LOOK GOOD ON THE FORCE!
OH YEAH.. WHO SEZ?
BETTER BE CAREFUL, KLINK.. THAT'S WARD HEALY, THE HEAD OF THE DOWNTOWN POLITICAL MACHINE...
3
P.S.
By Will Eisner
EGG PLANT

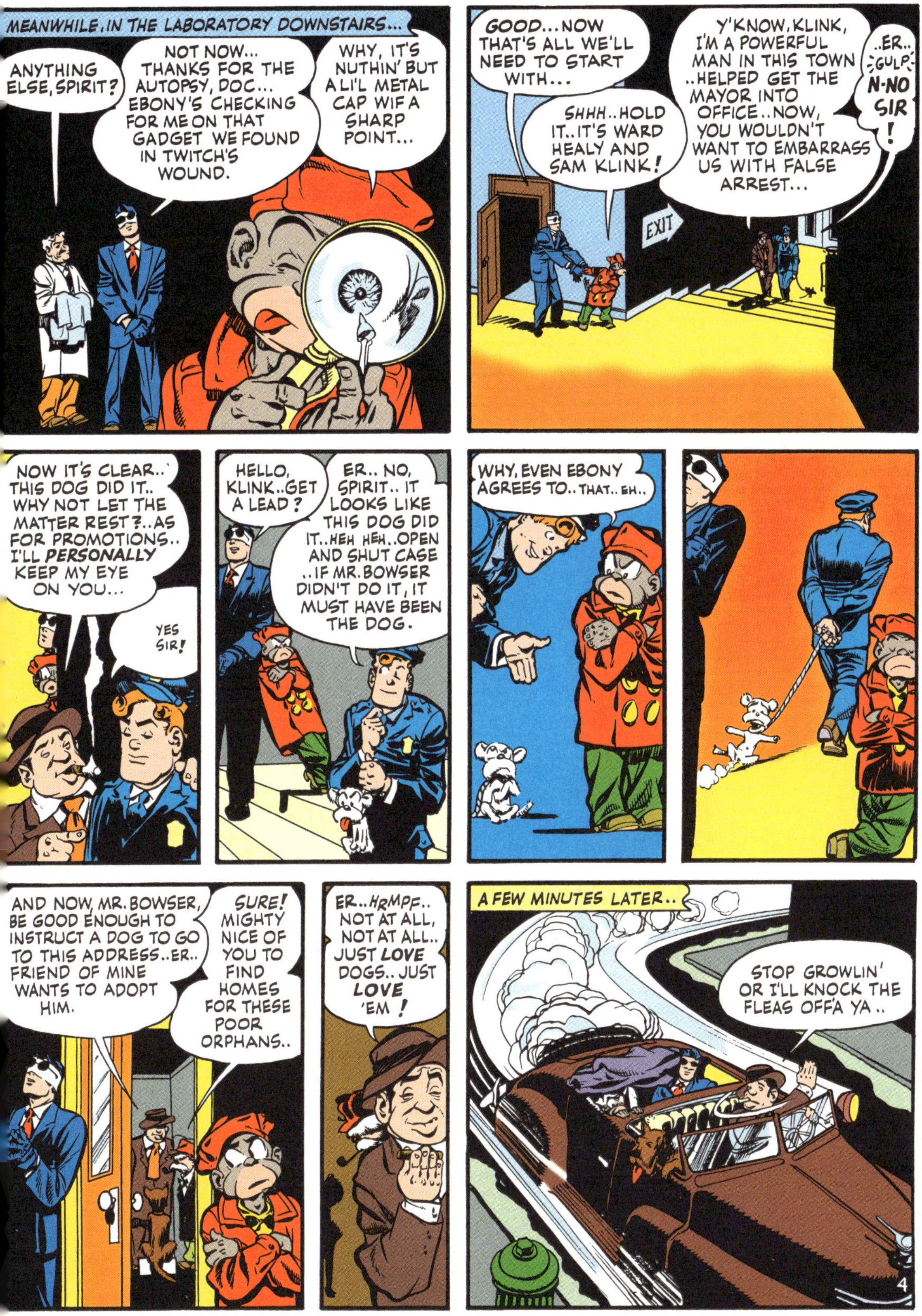
MEANWHILE, IN THE LABORATORY DOWNSTAIRS...
ANYTHING ELSE, SPIRIT?
NOT NOW... THANKS FOR THE AUTOPSY, DOC... EBONY'S CHECKING FOR ME ON THAT GADGET WE FOUND IN TWITCH'S WOUND.
WHY, IT'S NUTHIN' BUT A LI'L METAL CAP WIF A SHARP POINT...
GOOD... NOW THAT'S ALL WE'LL NEED TO START WITH...
SHHH.. HOLD IT.. IT'S WARD HEALY AND SAM KLINK!
EXIT
Y'KNOW, KLINK, I'M A POWERFUL MAN IN THIS TOWN ..HELPED GET THE MAYOR INTO OFFICE.. NOW, YOU WOULDN'T WANT TO EMBARRASS US WITH FALSE ARREST...
..ER.. GULP. N-NO SIR!
NOW IT'S CLEAR.. THIS DOG DID IT.. WHY NOT LET THE MATTER REST?.. AS FOR PROMOTIONS.. I'LL PERSONALLY KEEP MY EYE ON YOU...
YES SIR!
HELLO, KLINK.. GET A LEAD?
ER.. NO, SPIRIT.. IT LOOKS LIKE THIS DOG DID IT.. HEH HEH.. OPEN AND SHUT CASE ..IF MR. BOWSER DIDN'T DO IT, IT MUST HAVE BEEN THE DOG.
WHY, EVEN EBONY AGREES TO.. THAT.. EH..
AND NOW, MR. BOWSER, BE GOOD ENOUGH TO INSTRUCT A DOG TO GO TO THIS ADDRESS.. ER.. FRIEND OF MINE WANTS TO ADOPT HIM.
SURE! MIGHTY NICE OF YOU TO FIND HOMES FOR THESE POOR ORPHANS..
ER.. HRMPF.. NOT AT ALL, NOT AT ALL.. JUST LOVE DOGS.. JUST LOVE 'EM!
A FEW MINUTES LATER..
STOP GROWLIN' OR I'LL KNOCK THE FLEAS OFF'A YA..
4

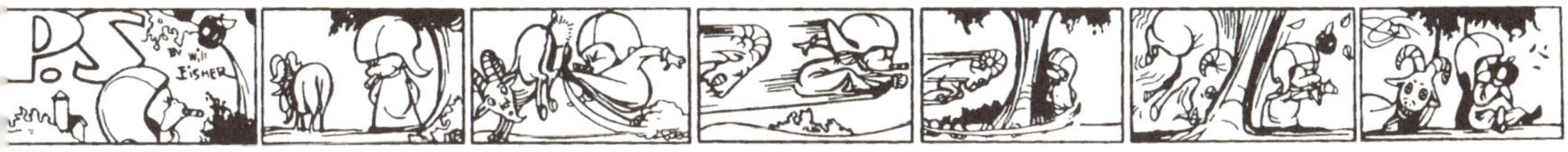
P.S. BY WILL EISNER

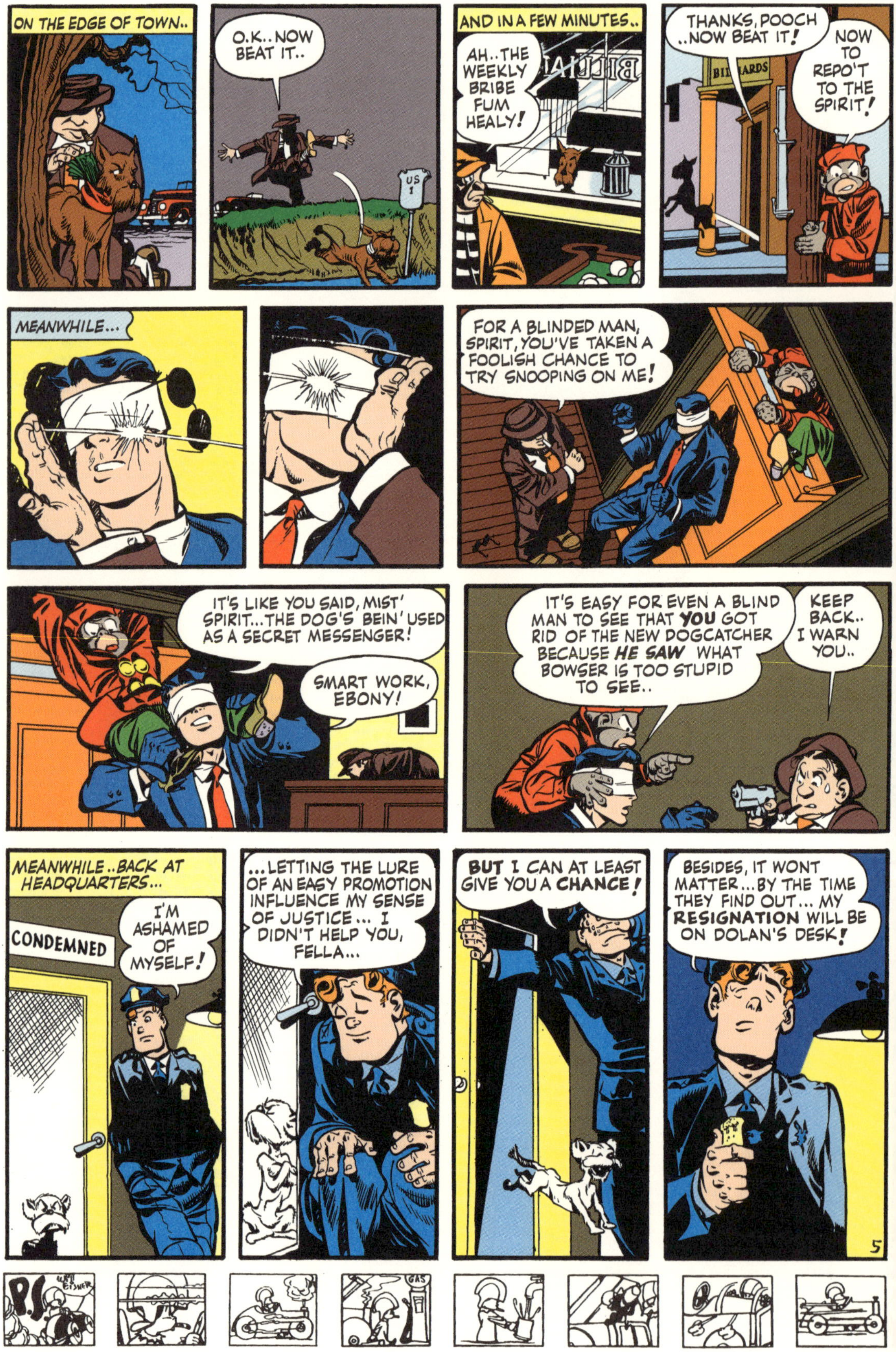
ON THE EDGE OF TOWN..
O.K.. NOW BEAT IT..
US 1
AND IN A FEW MINUTES..
AH.. THE WEEKLY BRIBE FUM HEALY!
THANKS, POOCH ..NOW BEAT IT!
NOW TO REPO'T TO THE SPIRIT!
MEANWHILE...
FOR A BLINDED MAN, SPIRIT, YOU'VE TAKEN A FOOLISH CHANCE TO TRY SNOOPING ON ME!
IT'S LIKE YOU SAID, MIST' SPIRIT...THE DOG'S BEIN' USED AS A SECRET MESSENGER!
SMART WORK, EBONY!
IT'S EASY FOR EVEN A BLIND MAN TO SEE THAT YOU GOT RID OF THE NEW DOGCATCHER BECAUSE HE SAW WHAT BOWSER IS TOO STUPID TO SEE..
KEEP BACK.. I WARN YOU..
MEANWHILE ..BACK AT HEADQUARTERS...
CONDEMNED
I'M ASHAMED OF MYSELF!
...LETTING THE LURE OF AN EASY PROMOTION INFLUENCE MY SENSE OF JUSTICE... I DIDN'T HELP YOU, FELLA...
BUT I CAN AT LEAST GIVE YOU A CHANCE!
BESIDES, IT WONT MATTER... BY THE TIME THEY FIND OUT... MY RESIGNATION WILL BE ON DOLAN'S DESK!
5
P.S.
GAS

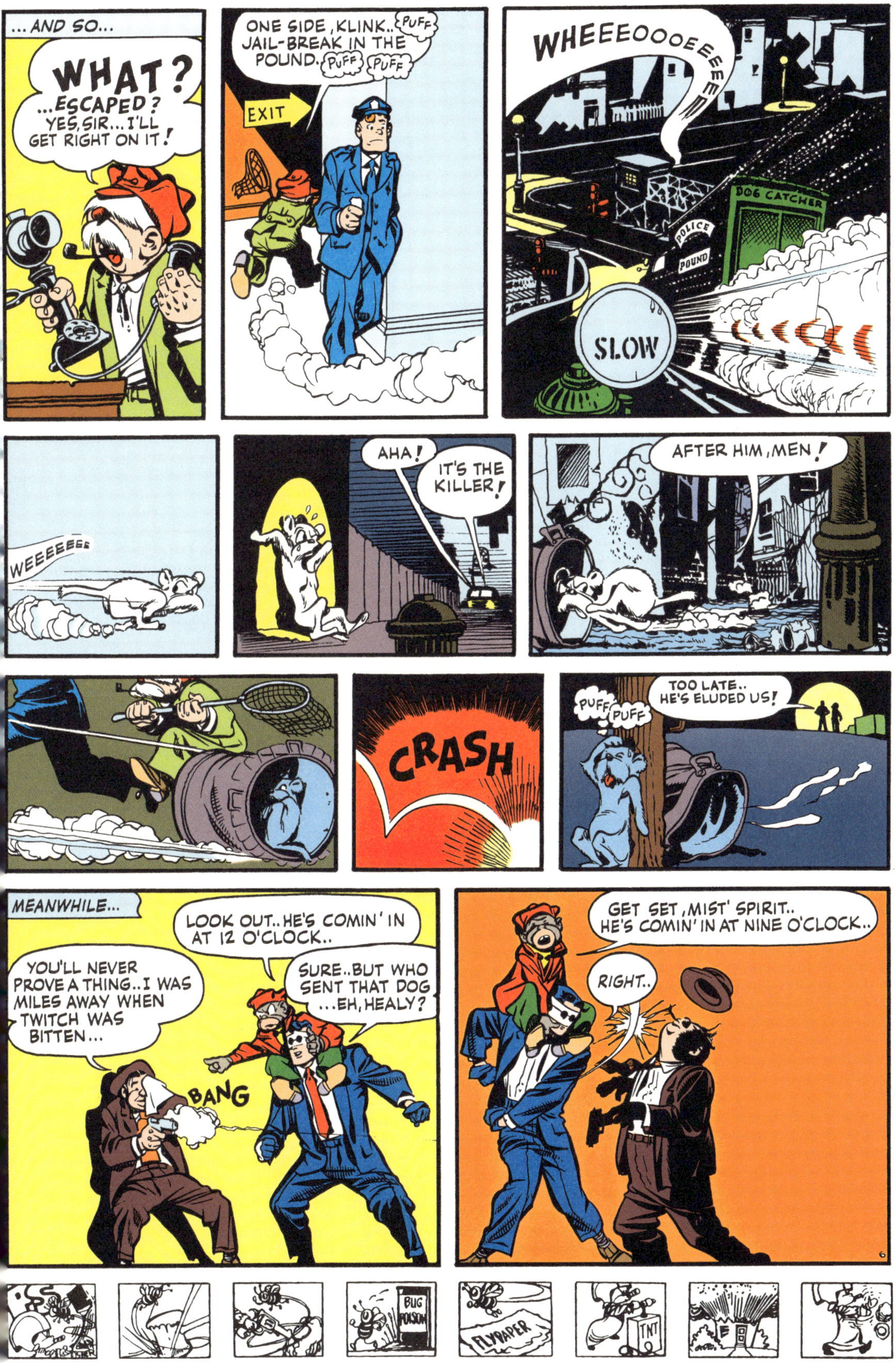

...AND SO...
WHAT? ...ESCAPED? YES, SIR... I'LL GET RIGHT ON IT!
ONE SIDE, KLINK.. PUFF JAIL-BREAK IN THE POUND. PUFF PUFF
EXIT
WHEEEOOOEEEEEE
DOG CATCHER
POLICE
POUND
SLOW
WEEEEEEEE
AHA!
IT'S THE KILLER!
AFTER HIM, MEN!
CRASH
PUFF PUFF
TOO LATE.. HE'S ELUDED US!
MEANWHILE...
LOOK OUT.. HE'S COMIN' IN AT 12 O'CLOCK..
YOU'LL NEVER PROVE A THING.. I WAS MILES AWAY WHEN TWITCH WAS BITTEN...
SURE.. BUT WHO SENT THAT DOG ...EH, HEALY?
BANG
GET SET, MIST' SPIRIT.. HE'S COMIN' IN AT NINE O'CLOCK..
RIGHT..
BUG POISON
FLYPAPER
TNT

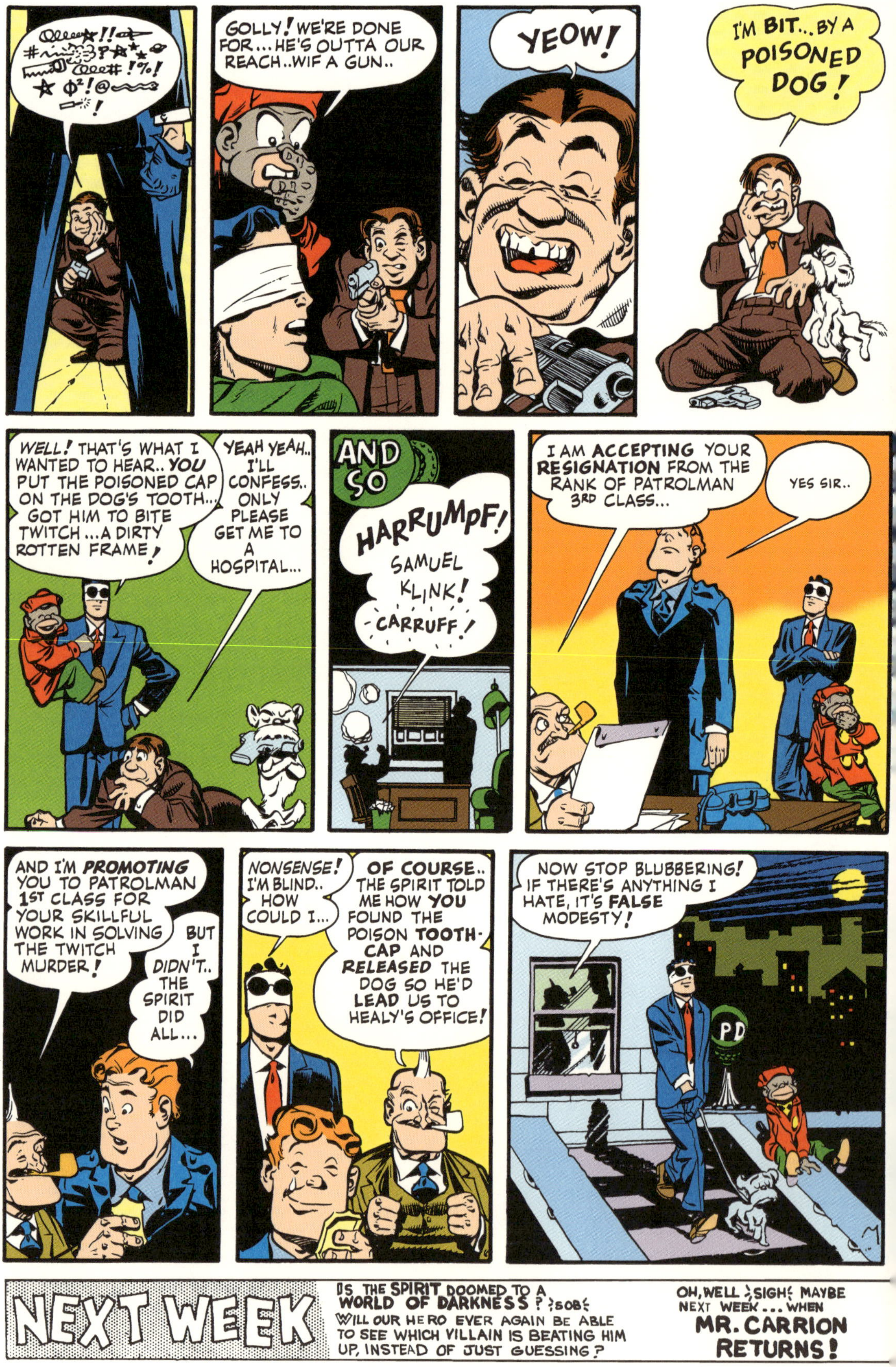
GOLLY! WE'RE DONE FOR... HE'S OUTTA OUR REACH..WIF A GUN..
YEOW!
I'M BIT... BY A POISONED DOG!
WELL! THAT'S WHAT I WANTED TO HEAR.. YOU PUT THE POISONED CAP ON THE DOG'S TOOTH... GOT HIM TO BITE TWITCH ...A DIRTY ROTTEN FRAME!
YEAH YEAH.. I'LL CONFESS.. ONLY PLEASE GET ME TO A HOSPITAL...
AND SO
HARRUMPF! SAMUEL KLINK!
-CARRUFF!
I AM ACCEPTING YOUR RESIGNATION FROM THE RANK OF PATROLMAN 3RD CLASS...
YES SIR..
AND I'M PROMOTING YOU TO PATROLMAN 1ST CLASS FOR YOUR SKILLFUL WORK IN SOLVING THE TWITCH MURDER!
BUT I DIDN'T.. THE SPIRIT DID ALL...
NONSENSE! I'M BLIND.. HOW COULD I...
OF COURSE.. THE SPIRIT TOLD ME HOW YOU FOUND THE POISON TOOTH-CAP AND RELEASED THE DOG SO HE'D LEAD US TO HEALY'S OFFICE!
NOW STOP BLUBBERING! IF THERE'S ANYTHING I HATE, IT'S FALSE MODESTY!
PD
NEXT WEEK
IS THE SPIRIT DOOMED TO A WORLD OF DARKNESS? {SOB} WILL OUR HERO EVER AGAIN BE ABLE TO SEE WHICH VILLAIN IS BEATING HIM UP, INSTEAD OF JUST GUESSING?
OH, WELL {SIGH} MAYBE NEXT WEEK... WHEN MR. CARRION RETURNS!

COMIC BOOK SECTION

INTO THE LIGHT

September 14 1947

ACTION Mystery ADVENTURE

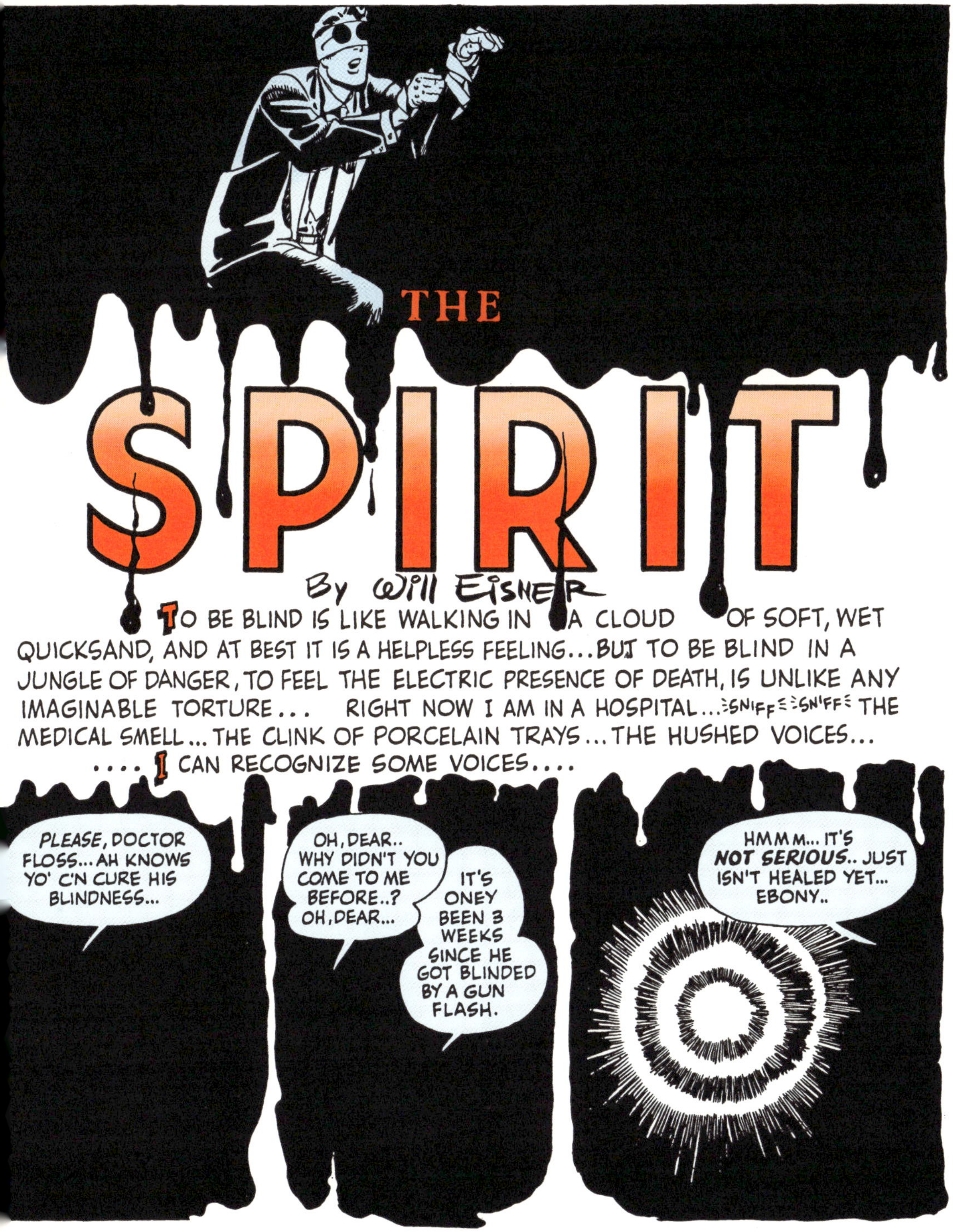
THE SPIRIT
By Will Eisner
TO BE BLIND IS LIKE WALKING IN A CLOUD OF SOFT, WET QUICKSAND, AND AT BEST IT IS A HELPLESS FEELING...BUT TO BE BLIND IN A JUNGLE OF DANGER, TO FEEL THE ELECTRIC PRESENCE OF DEATH, IS UNLIKE ANY IMAGINABLE TORTURE... RIGHT NOW I AM IN A HOSPITAL...SNIFF SNIFF THE MEDICAL SMELL... THE CLINK OF PORCELAIN TRAYS... THE HUSHED VOICES... ....I CAN RECOGNIZE SOME VOICES....
PLEASE, DOCTOR FLOSS...AH KNOWS YO' C'N CURE HIS BLINDNESS...
OH, DEAR.. WHY DIDN'T YOU COME TO ME BEFORE..? OH, DEAR...
IT'S ONEY BEEN 3 WEEKS SINCE HE GOT BLINDED BY A GUN FLASH.
HMMM... IT'S NOT SERIOUS.. JUST ISN'T HEALED YET... EBONY..

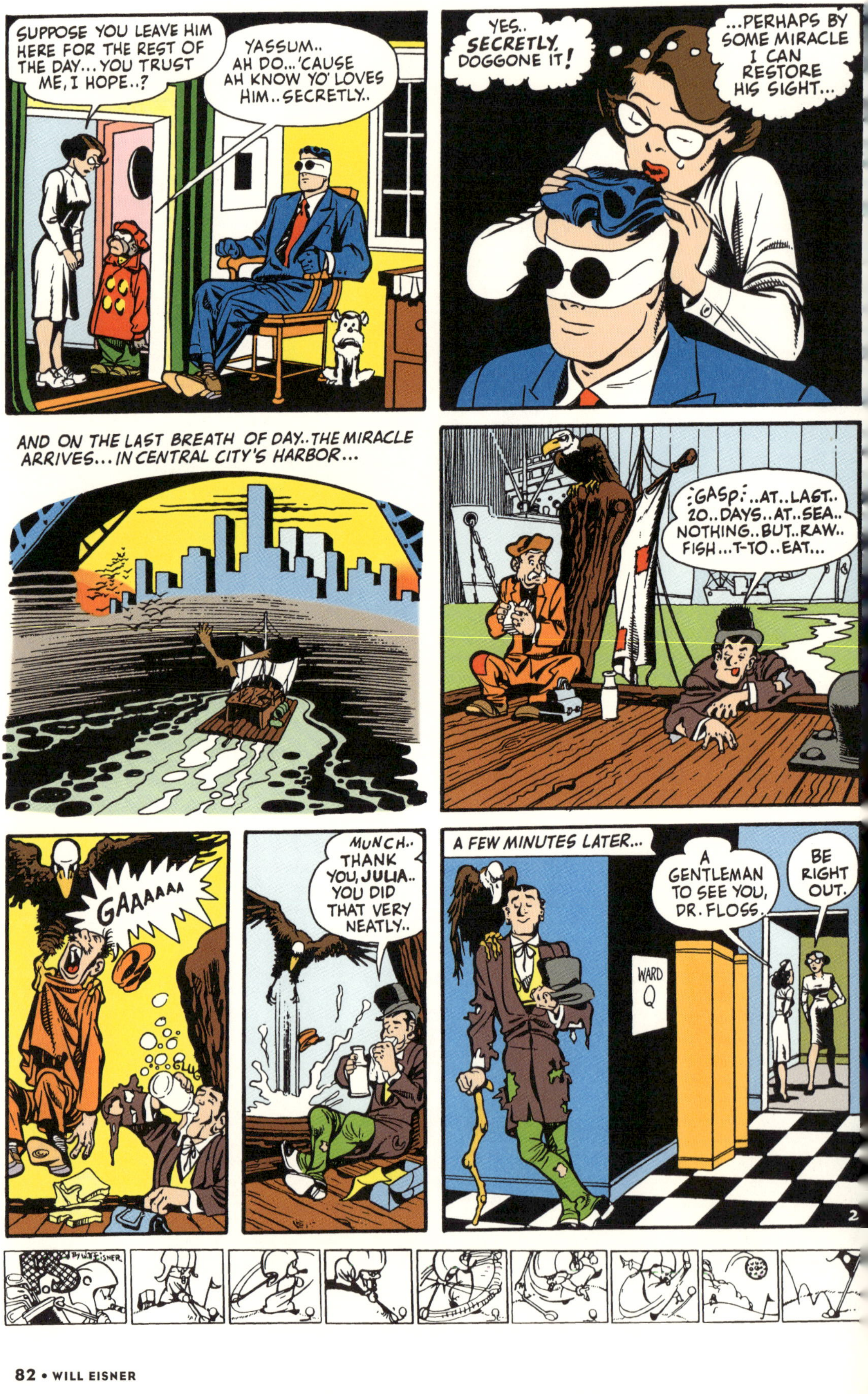
SUPPOSE YOU LEAVE HIM HERE FOR THE REST OF THE DAY... YOU TRUST ME, I HOPE..?
YASSUM.. AH DO...'CAUSE AH KNOW YO' LOVES HIM..SECRETLY..
YES.. SECRETLY, DOGGONE IT!
...PERHAPS BY SOME MIRACLE I CAN RESTORE HIS SIGHT...
AND ON THE LAST BREATH OF DAY..THE MIRACLE ARRIVES... IN CENTRAL CITY'S HARBOR...
:GASP:..AT..LAST.. 20..DAYS..AT..SEA.. NOTHING..BUT..RAW.. FISH...T-TO..EAT...
GAAAAAA
GLUG
MUNCH.. THANK YOU, JULIA.. YOU DID THAT VERY NEATLY..
A FEW MINUTES LATER...
A GENTLEMAN TO SEE YOU, DR. FLOSS.
BE RIGHT OUT.
WARD Q
2
BY W. EISNER

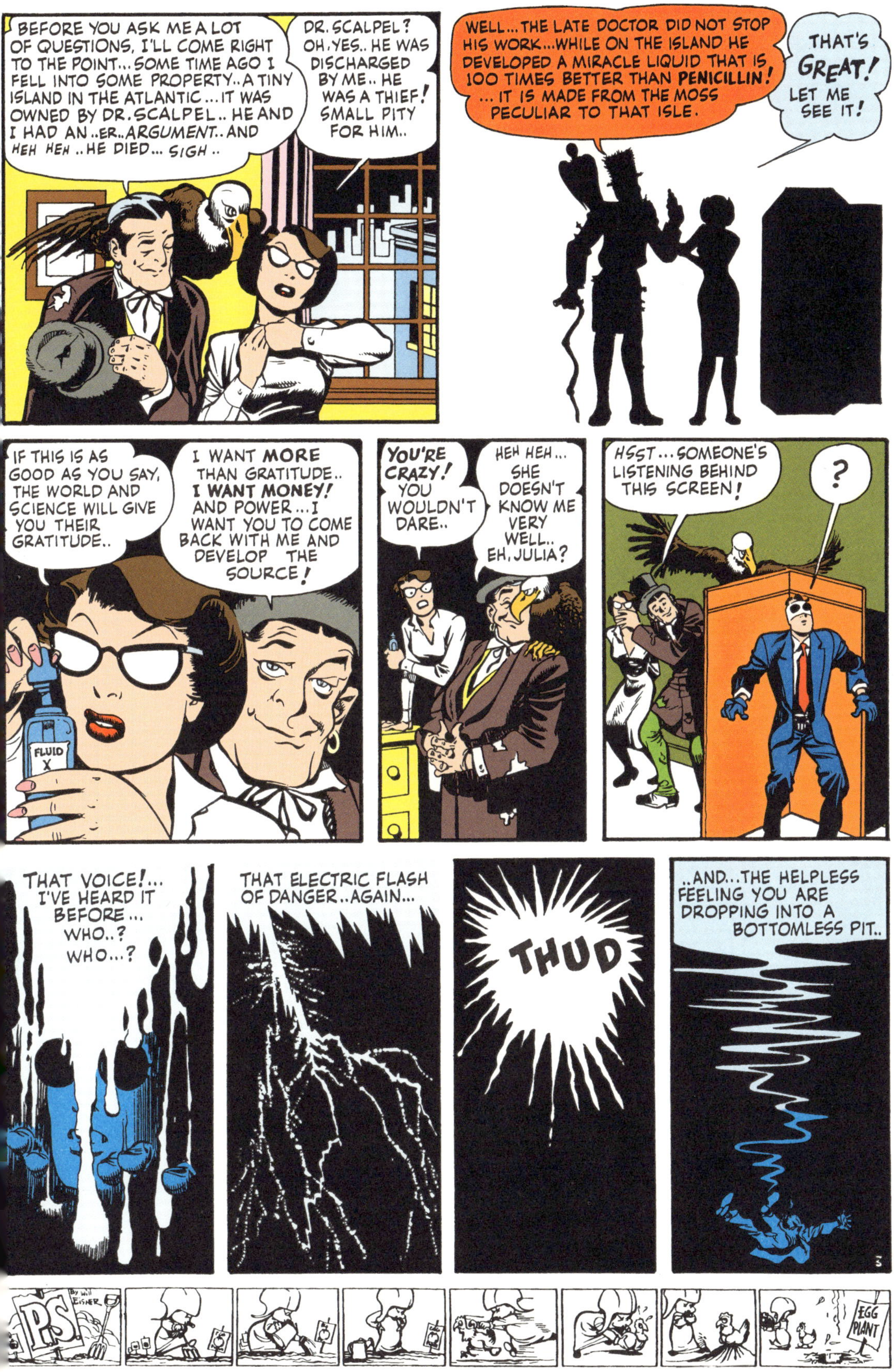

BEFORE YOU ASK ME A LOT OF QUESTIONS, I'LL COME RIGHT TO THE POINT... SOME TIME AGO I FELL INTO SOME PROPERTY.. A TINY ISLAND IN THE ATLANTIC... IT WAS OWNED BY DR. SCALPEL.. HE AND I HAD AN ..ER.. ARGUMENT.. AND HEH HEH ..HE DIED... SIGH ..
DR. SCALPEL? OH, YES.. HE WAS DISCHARGED BY ME.. HE WAS A THIEF! SMALL PITY FOR HIM..
WELL... THE LATE DOCTOR DID NOT STOP HIS WORK... WHILE ON THE ISLAND HE DEVELOPED A MIRACLE LIQUID THAT IS 100 TIMES BETTER THAN PENICILLIN! ... IT IS MADE FROM THE MOSS PECULIAR TO THAT ISLE.
THAT'S GREAT! LET ME SEE IT!
IF THIS IS AS GOOD AS YOU SAY, THE WORLD AND SCIENCE WILL GIVE YOU THEIR GRATITUDE..
I WANT MORE THAN GRATITUDE.. I WANT MONEY! AND POWER... I WANT YOU TO COME BACK WITH ME AND DEVELOP THE SOURCE!
FLUID X
YOU'RE CRAZY! YOU WOULDN'T DARE..
HEH HEH... SHE DOESN'T KNOW ME VERY WELL.. EH, JULIA?
HSST... SOMEONE'S LISTENING BEHIND THIS SCREEN!
?
THAT VOICE!... I'VE HEARD IT BEFORE... WHO..? WHO...?
THAT ELECTRIC FLASH OF DANGER.. AGAIN...
THUD
..AND... THE HELPLESS FEELING YOU ARE DROPPING INTO A BOTTOMLESS PIT..
3
P.S.
By Will Eisner
EGG PLANT

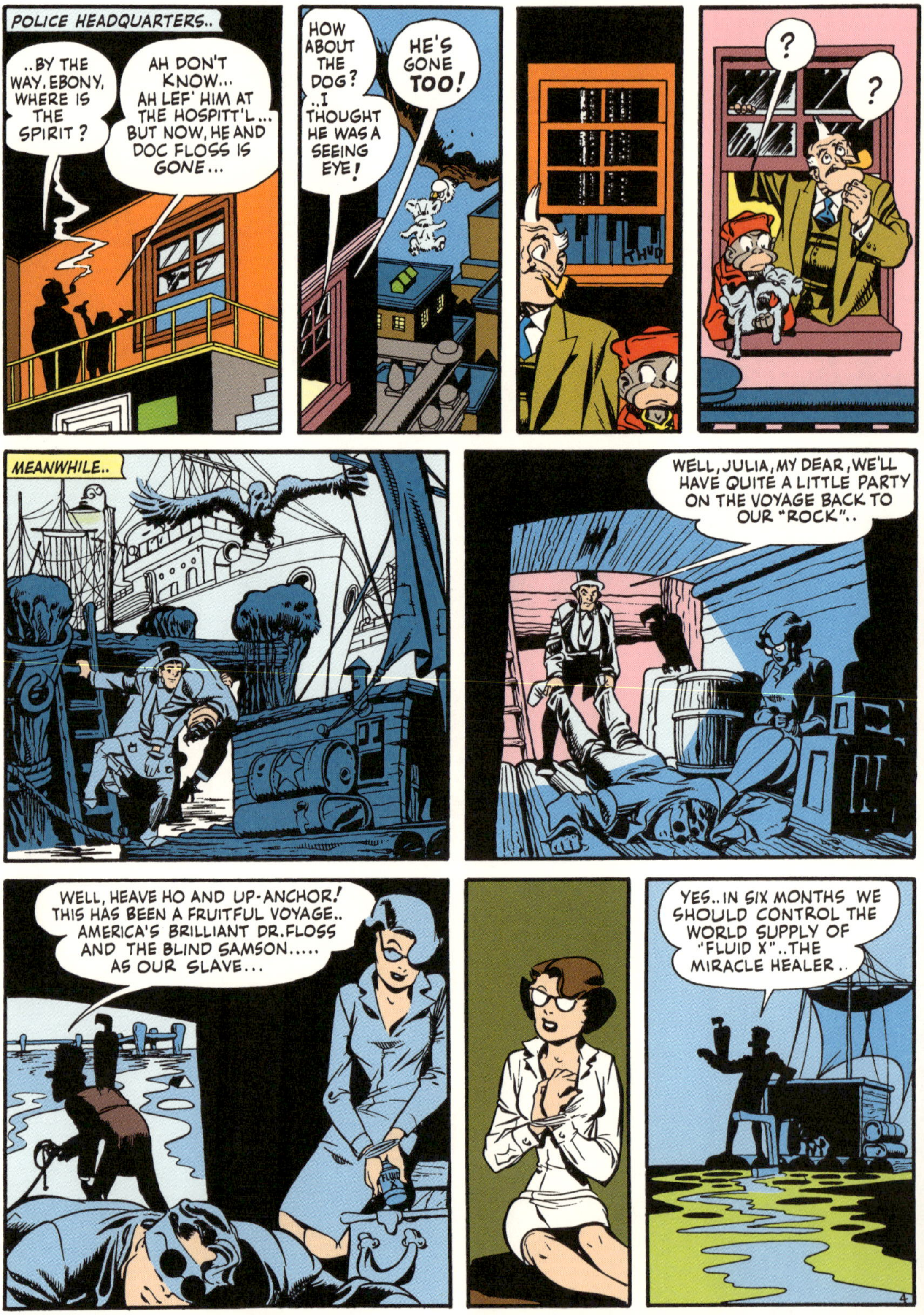
POLICE HEADQUARTERS..
..BY THE WAY, EBONY, WHERE IS THE SPIRIT ?
AH DON'T KNOW... AH LEF' HIM AT THE HOSPITT'L... BUT NOW, HE AND DOC FLOSS IS GONE...
HOW ABOUT THE DOG ? ..I THOUGHT HE WAS A SEEING EYE!
HE'S GONE TOO!
THUD
?
?
MEANWHILE..
WELL, JULIA, MY DEAR, WE'LL HAVE QUITE A LITTLE PARTY ON THE VOYAGE BACK TO OUR "ROCK"..
WELL, HEAVE HO AND UP-ANCHOR! THIS HAS BEEN A FRUITFUL VOYAGE.. AMERICA'S BRILLIANT DR. FLOSS AND THE BLIND SAMSON..... AS OUR SLAVE...
YES.. IN SIX MONTHS WE SHOULD CONTROL THE WORLD SUPPLY OF "FLUID X".. THE MIRACLE HEALER..
4

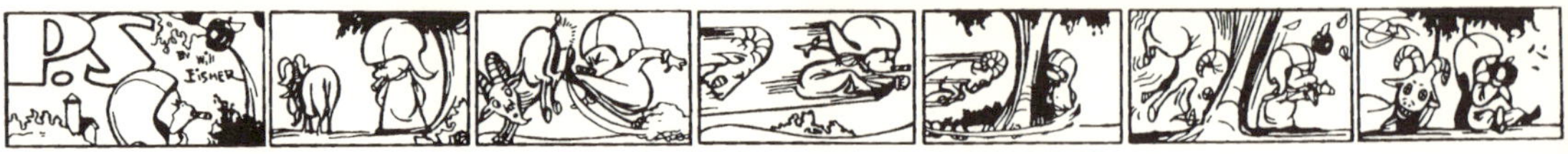
P.S.

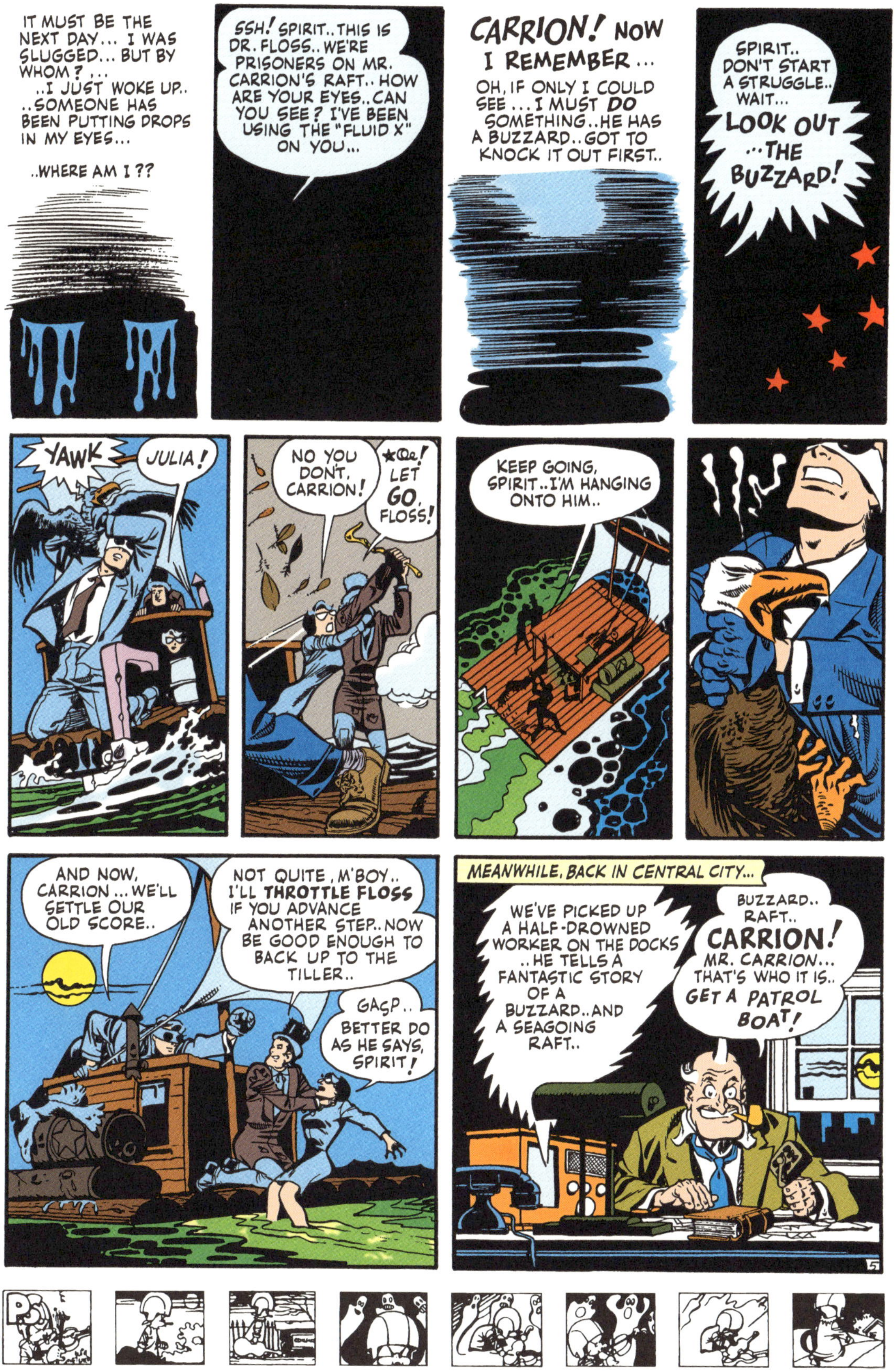
IT MUST BE THE NEXT DAY... I WAS SLUGGED... BUT BY WHOM?... ..I JUST WOKE UP.. ..SOMEONE HAS BEEN PUTTING DROPS IN MY EYES...
..WHERE AM I??
SSH! SPIRIT..THIS IS DR. FLOSS..WE'RE PRISONERS ON MR. CARRION'S RAFT..HOW ARE YOUR EYES..CAN YOU SEE? I'VE BEEN USING THE "FLUID X" ON YOU...
CARRION! NOW I REMEMBER...
OH, IF ONLY I COULD SEE... I MUST DO SOMETHING..HE HAS A BUZZARD..GOT TO KNOCK IT OUT FIRST..
SPIRIT.. DON'T START A STRUGGLE.. WAIT...
LOOK OUT ...THE BUZZARD!
YAWK
JULIA!
NO YOU DON'T, CARRION!
LET GO, FLOSS!
KEEP GOING, SPIRIT..I'M HANGING ONTO HIM..
AND NOW, CARRION... WE'LL SETTLE OUR OLD SCORE..
NOT QUITE, M'BOY.. I'LL THROTTLE FLOSS IF YOU ADVANCE ANOTHER STEP..NOW BE GOOD ENOUGH TO BACK UP TO THE TILLER..
GASP.. BETTER DO AS HE SAYS, SPIRIT!
MEANWHILE, BACK IN CENTRAL CITY...
WE'VE PICKED UP A HALF-DROWNED WORKER ON THE DOCKS ..HE TELLS A FANTASTIC STORY OF A BUZZARD..AND A SEAGOING RAFT..
BUZZARD.. RAFT.. CARRION! MR. CARRION... THAT'S WHO IT IS.. GET A PATROL BOAT!
5

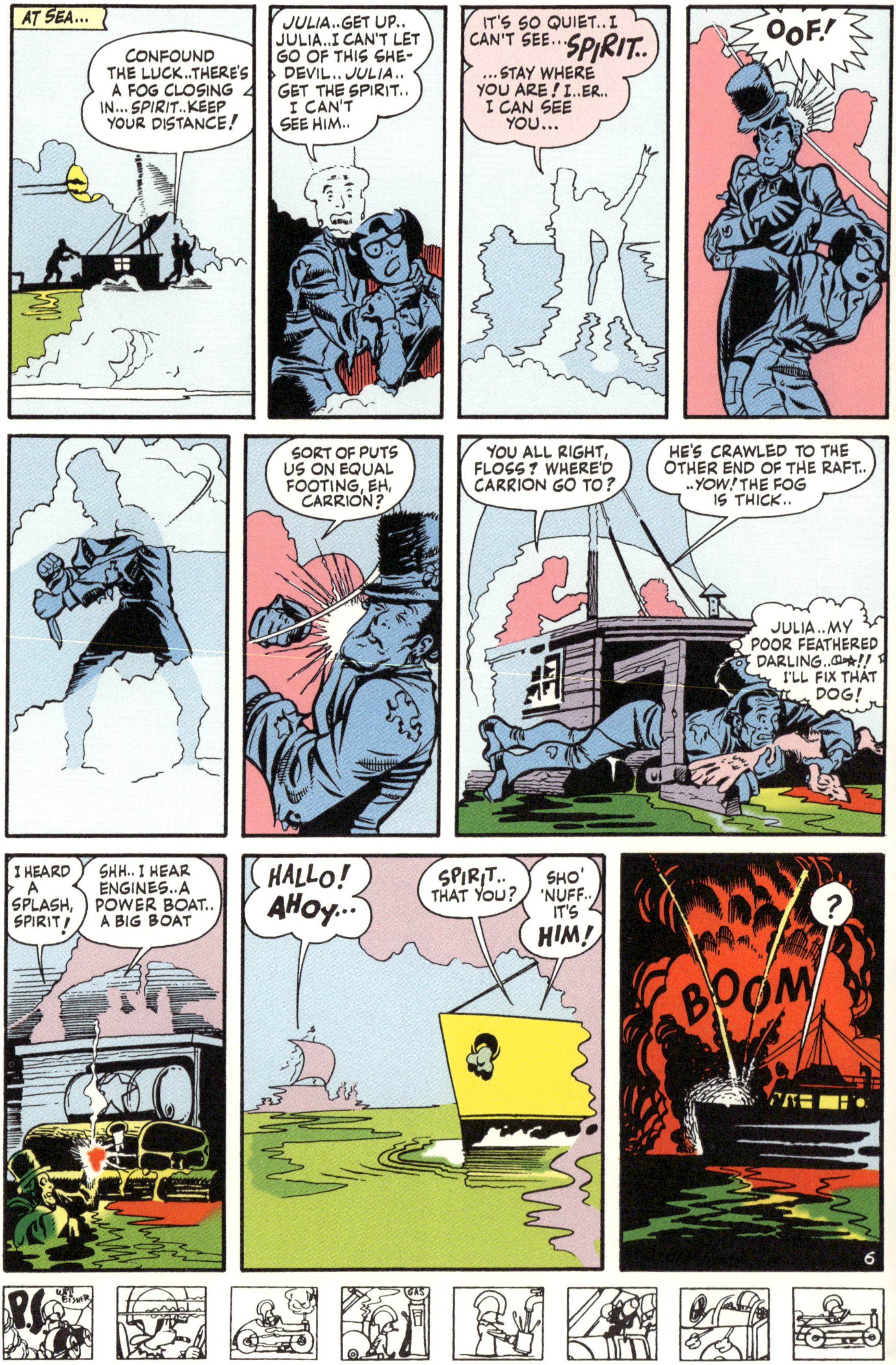
AT SEA...
CONFOUND THE LUCK..THERE'S A FOG CLOSING IN... SPIRIT..KEEP YOUR DISTANCE!
JULIA..GET UP.. JULIA..I CAN'T LET GO OF THIS SHE-DEVIL.. JULIA.. GET THE SPIRIT.. I CAN'T SEE HIM..
IT'S SO QUIET.. I CAN'T SEE... SPIRIT..
...STAY WHERE YOU ARE! I..ER.. I CAN SEE YOU...
OOF!
SORT OF PUTS US ON EQUAL FOOTING, EH, CARRION?
YOU ALL RIGHT, FLOSS? WHERE'D CARRION GO TO?
HE'S CRAWLED TO THE OTHER END OF THE RAFT.. ..YOW! THE FOG IS THICK..
JULIA..MY POOR FEATHERED DARLING..!! I'LL FIX THAT DOG!
I HEARD A SPLASH, SPIRIT!
SHH.. I HEAR ENGINES..A POWER BOAT.. A BIG BOAT
HALLO! AHOY...
SPIRIT.. THAT YOU?
SHO' 'NUFF.. IT'S HIM!
?
BOOM
6
P.S.
GAS

GOOD GRIEF.. NOT AGAIN... I MUST HAVE BEEN BLOWN TO BITS ...DO YOU HAVE ANY IDEA OF WHAT IT'S LIKE TO REGAIN CONSCIOUSNESS? IT'S LIKE CLIMBING UP A STEEP CLIFF!
LOOK HE IS WAKING UP..
SPIRIT.. SPEAK TO US... YOU O.K.?
AH..EBONY.. AND THAT'S DOLAN'S VOICE..UGH! I DON'T FEEL LIKE TALKING...I'M STILL BLIND..
NO...MY EYES ARE CLOSED...BUT WHY KID MYSELF... YET MAYBE.. OH..I..I... I'LL OPEN THEM.. ONE..TWO...
THREE... FOOEY.. STILL BLIND... STILL..
NO..WAIT! WAIT A MINUTE..
I CAN SEE AGAIN...
HE CAN SEE!
IT WORKED! THE FLUID X" WORKED!
AND WE SURVIVED THE BLAST! WHERE'S CARRION, DOLAN?
COUGH..COUGH ..OH HIM.. HE MUST HAVE DROWNED WITH THE FLUID'S SECRET, I'M AFRAID..
WOTCHA CRYIN' ABOUT, EBONY?
WHO'S CRYIN'... AH.. AH JES' GOT A SPECK IN MY EYE, THASSALL...
QUIET
AND FAR OUT AT SEA, ANOTHER JOYOUS REUNION IS CELEBRATED..
JULIA.. JULIA... YOU'RE ALIVE..OH, THANK GOODNESS..YOU'RE ALIVE ..MY LITTLE FEATHERED DARLING..
RAWK
NEXT WEEK:
The RETURN OF THE RAVEN
A STRANGE AND UNEARTHLY TALE OF A KILLER SHIP.. THOSE WHO HAVE FOLLOWED "THE SPIRIT" FOR MANY YEARS WILL REMEMBER THAT ACCURSED VESSEL... THE RAVEN!

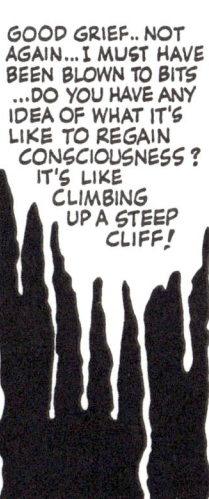

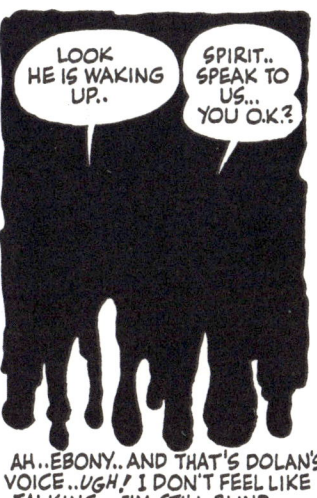

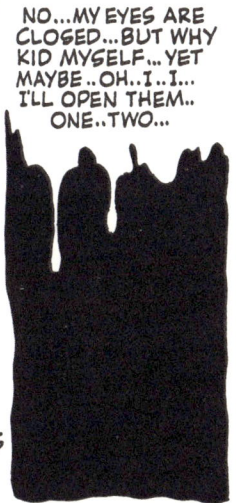

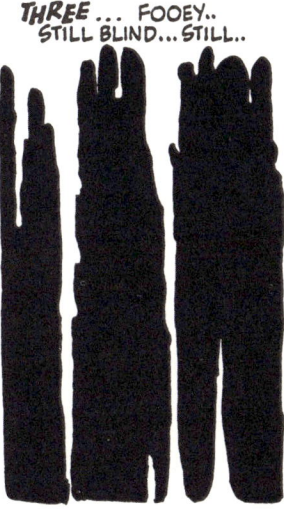

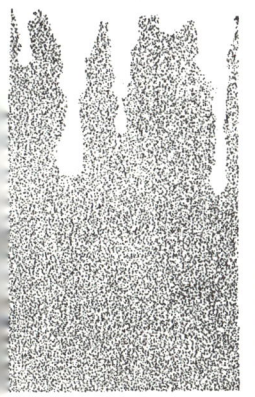

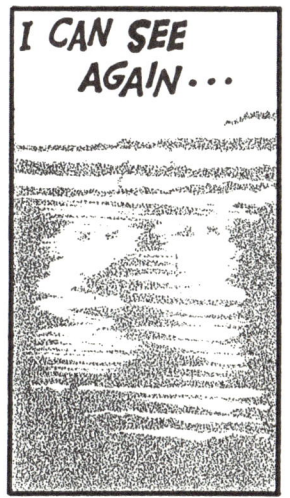

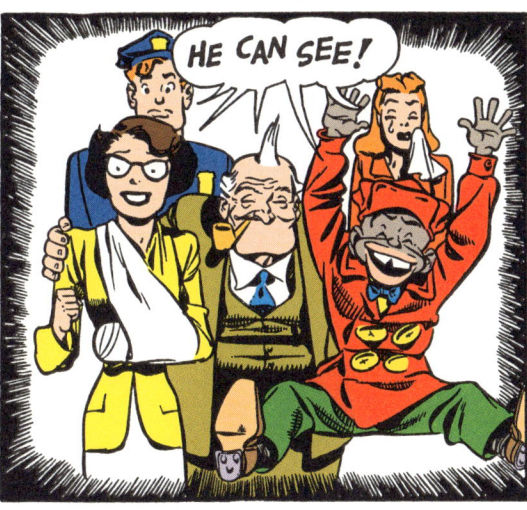

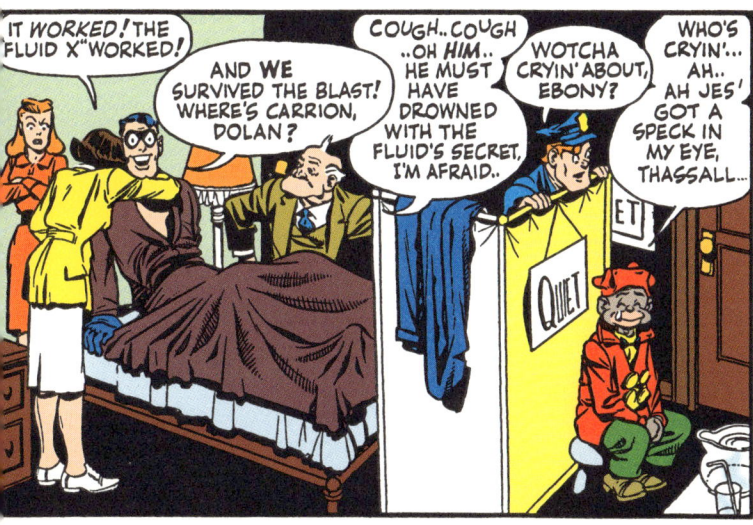

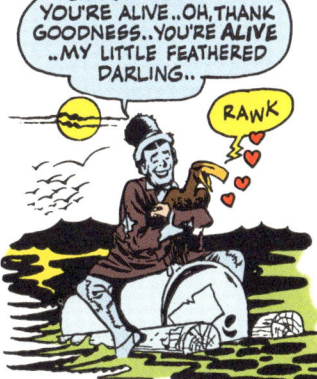

COMIC BOOK SECTION

END OF The S.S. RAVEN

September 21 1947

ACTION Mystery ADVENTURE

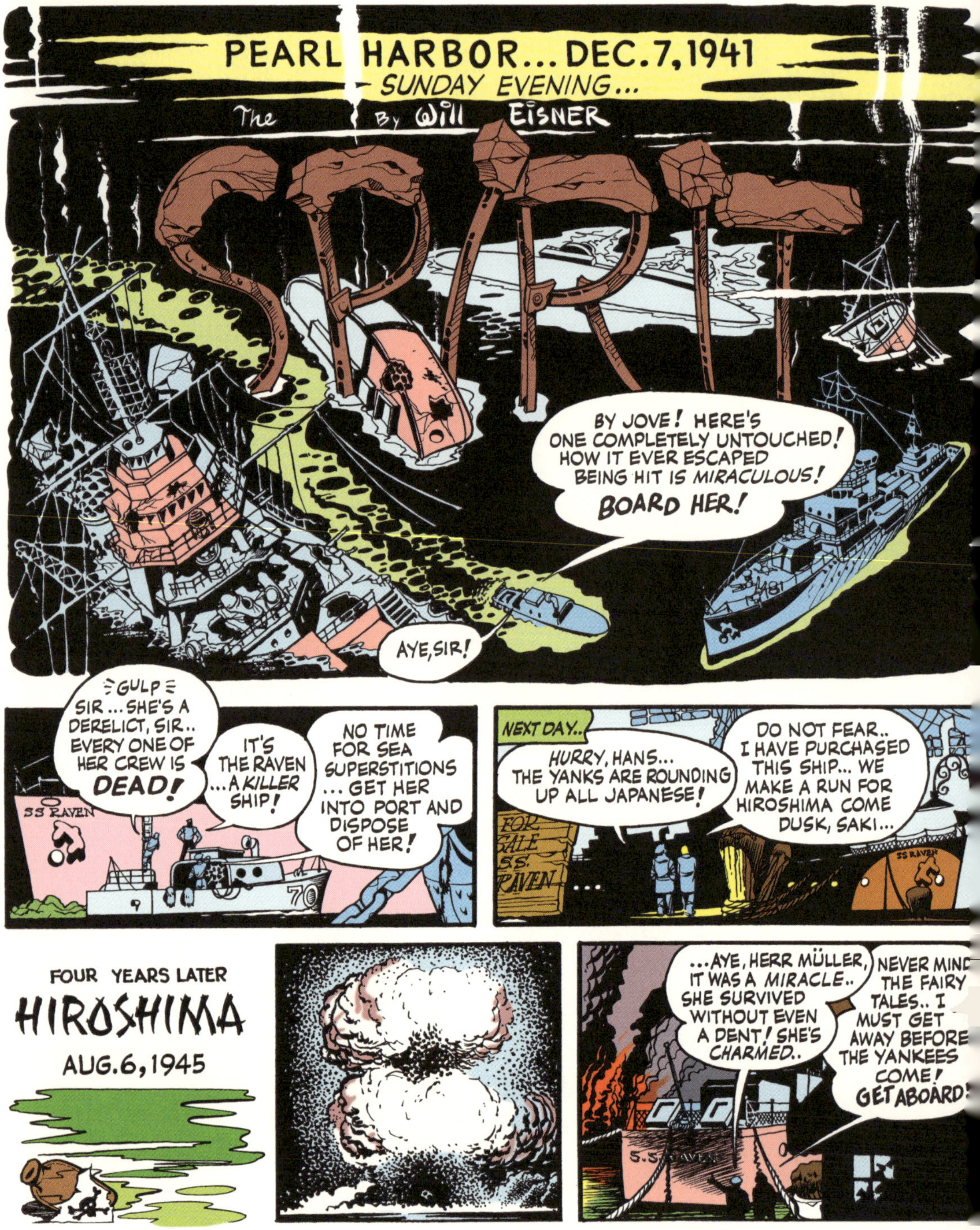
PEARL HARBOR...DEC.7,1941
- SUNDAY EVENING...
The SPIRIT By Will Eisner
BY JOVE! HERE'S ONE COMPLETELY UNTOUCHED! HOW IT EVER ESCAPED BEING HIT IS MIRACULOUS! BOARD HER!
AYE, SIR!
GULP SIR...SHE'S A DERELICT, SIR.. EVERY ONE OF HER CREW IS DEAD!
IT'S THE RAVEN ...A KILLER SHIP!
NO TIME FOR SEA SUPERSTITIONS ... GET HER INTO PORT AND DISPOSE OF HER!
SS RAVEN
NEXT DAY..
HURRY, HANS... THE YANKS ARE ROUNDING UP ALL JAPANESE!
DO NOT FEAR.. I HAVE PURCHASED THIS SHIP... WE MAKE A RUN FOR HIROSHIMA COME DUSK, SAKI...
FOR SALE S.S. RAVEN
FOUR YEARS LATER
HIROSHIMA
AUG.6,1945
...AYE, HERR MÜLLER, IT WAS A MIRACLE.. SHE SURVIVED WITHOUT EVEN A DENT! SHE'S CHARMED..
NEVER MIND THE FAIRY TALES.. I MUST GET AWAY BEFORE THE YANKEES COME! GET ABOARD!

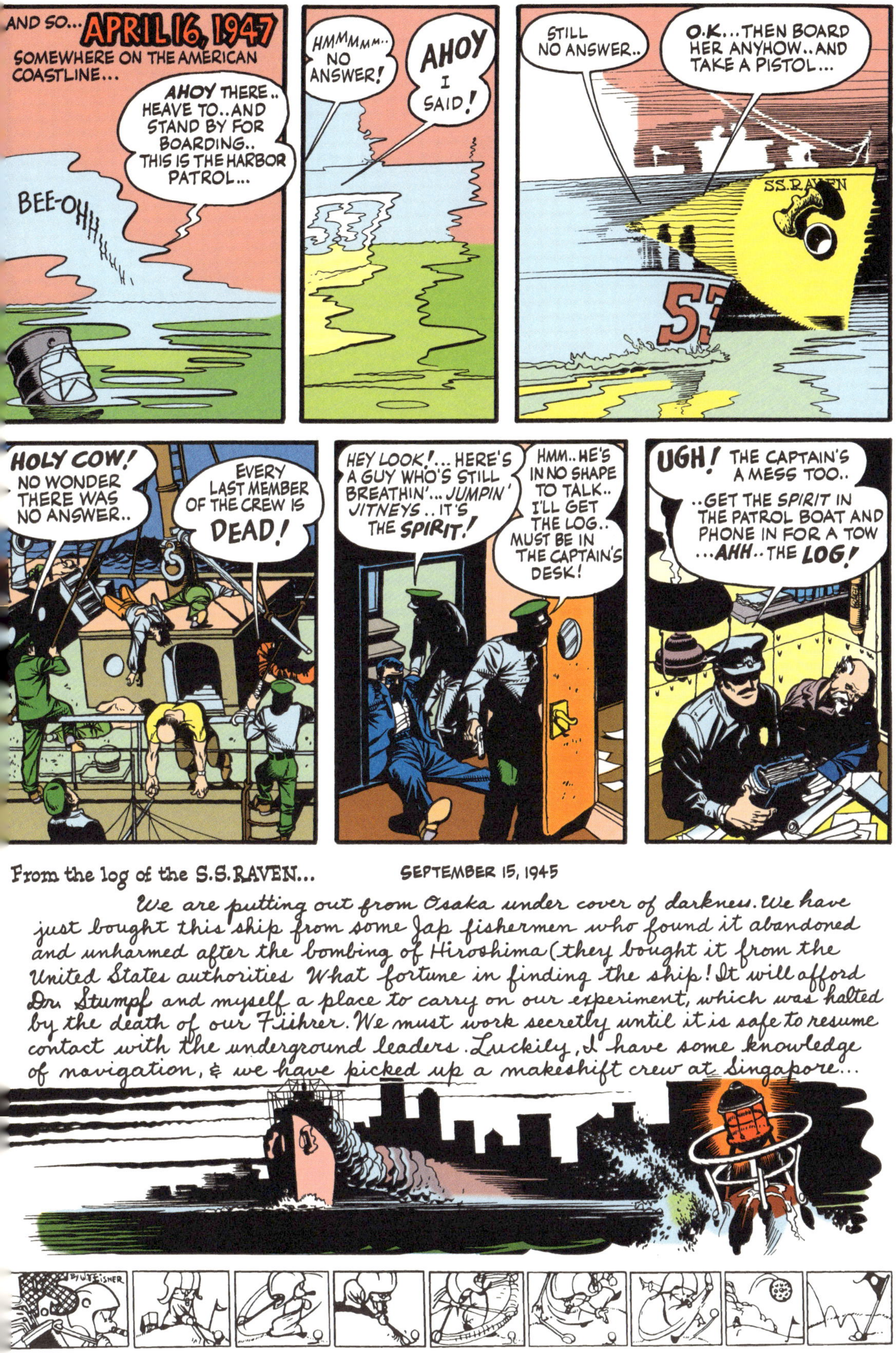
AND SO... APRIL 16, 1947
SOMEWHERE ON THE AMERICAN COASTLINE...
AHOY THERE.. HEAVE TO...AND STAND BY FOR BOARDING.. THIS IS THE HARBOR PATROL...
BEE-OHHHHHHH
HMMMMM.. NO ANSWER!
AHOY I SAID!
STILL NO ANSWER..
O.K...THEN BOARD HER ANYHOW..AND TAKE A PISTOL...
S.S. RAVEN
57
HOLY COW! NO WONDER THERE WAS NO ANSWER..
EVERY LAST MEMBER OF THE CREW IS DEAD!
HEY LOOK!... HERE'S A GUY WHO'S STILL BREATHIN'...JUMPIN' JITNEYS.. IT'S THE SPIRIT!
HMM.. HE'S IN NO SHAPE TO TALK.. I'LL GET THE LOG.. MUST BE IN THE CAPTAIN'S DESK!
UGH! THE CAPTAIN'S A MESS TOO..
..GET THE SPIRIT IN THE PATROL BOAT AND PHONE IN FOR A TOW ...AHH.. THE LOG!
From the log of the S.S. RAVEN... SEPTEMBER 15, 1945
We are putting out from Osaka under cover of darkness. We have
just bought this ship from some Jap fishermen who found it abandoned
and unharmed after the bombing of Hiroshima (they bought it from the
United States authorities What fortune in finding the ship! It will afford
Dr. Stumpf and myself a place to carry on our experiment, which was halted
by the death of our Führer. We must work secretly until it is safe to resume
contact with the underground leaders. Luckily, I have some knowledge
of navigation, & we have picked up a makeshift crew at Singapore...

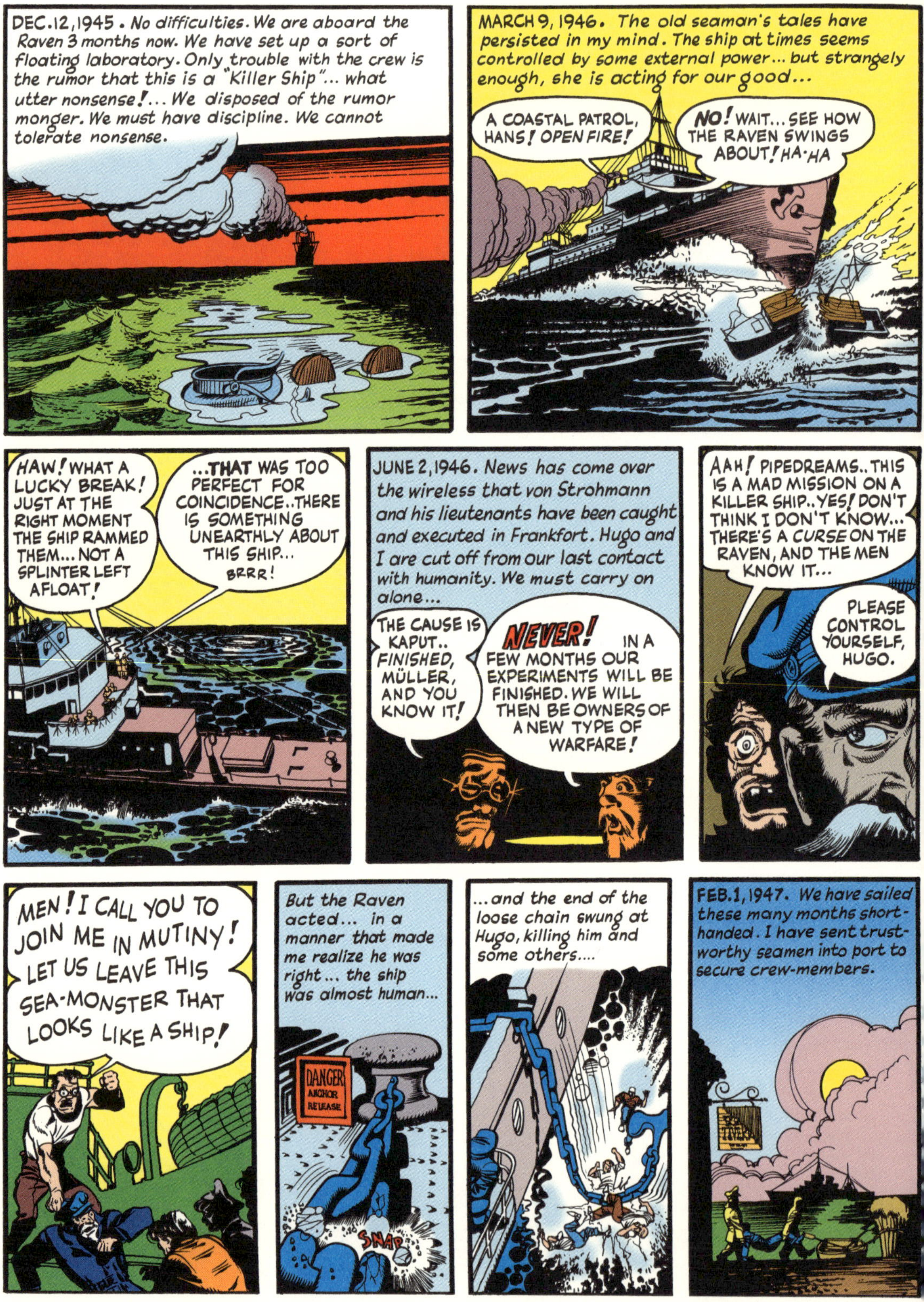
DEC.12,1945 • No difficulties. We are aboard the Raven 3 months now. We have set up a sort of floating laboratory. Only trouble with the crew is the rumor that this is a "Killer Ship"... what utter nonsense!... We disposed of the rumor monger. We must have discipline. We cannot tolerate nonsense.
MARCH 9, 1946 • The old seaman's tales have persisted in my mind. The ship at times seems controlled by some external power... but strangely enough, she is acting for our good...
A COASTAL PATROL, HANS! OPEN FIRE!
NO! WAIT... SEE HOW THE RAVEN SWINGS ABOUT! HA-HA
HAW! WHAT A LUCKY BREAK! JUST AT THE RIGHT MOMENT THE SHIP RAMMED THEM... NOT A SPLINTER LEFT AFLOAT!
...THAT WAS TOO PERFECT FOR COINCIDENCE.. THERE IS SOMETHING UNEARTHLY ABOUT THIS SHIP... BRRR!
JUNE 2, 1946. News has come over the wireless that von Strohmann and his lieutenants have been caught and executed in Frankfort. Hugo and I are cut off from our last contact with humanity. We must carry on alone...
THE CAUSE IS KAPUT.. FINISHED, MÜLLER, AND YOU KNOW IT!
NEVER! IN A FEW MONTHS OUR EXPERIMENTS WILL BE FINISHED. WE WILL THEN BE OWNERS OF A NEW TYPE OF WARFARE!
AAH! PIPEDREAMS.. THIS IS A MAD MISSION ON A KILLER SHIP.. YES! DON'T THINK I DON'T KNOW... THERE'S A CURSE ON THE RAVEN, AND THE MEN KNOW IT...
PLEASE CONTROL YOURSELF, HUGO.
MEN! I CALL YOU TO JOIN ME IN MUTINY! LET US LEAVE THIS SEA-MONSTER THAT LOOKS LIKE A SHIP!
But the Raven acted... in a manner that made me realize he was right... the ship was almost human...
DANGER ANCHOR RELEASE
SNAP
...and the end of the loose chain swung at Hugo, killing him and some others....
FEB.1, 1947. We have sailed these many months short-handed. I have sent trust-worthy seamen into port to secure crew-members.

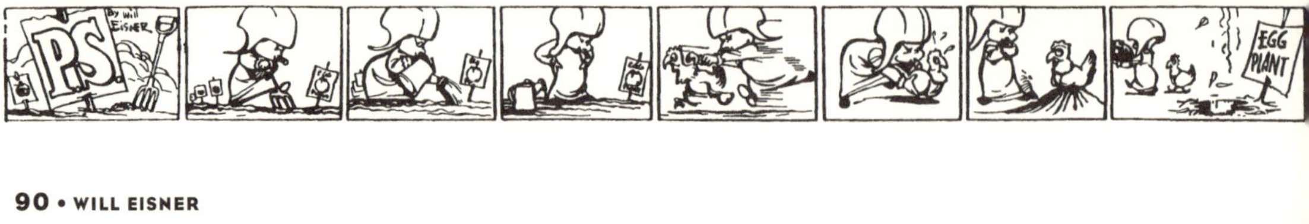
P.S.
By Will Eisner
EGG PLANT

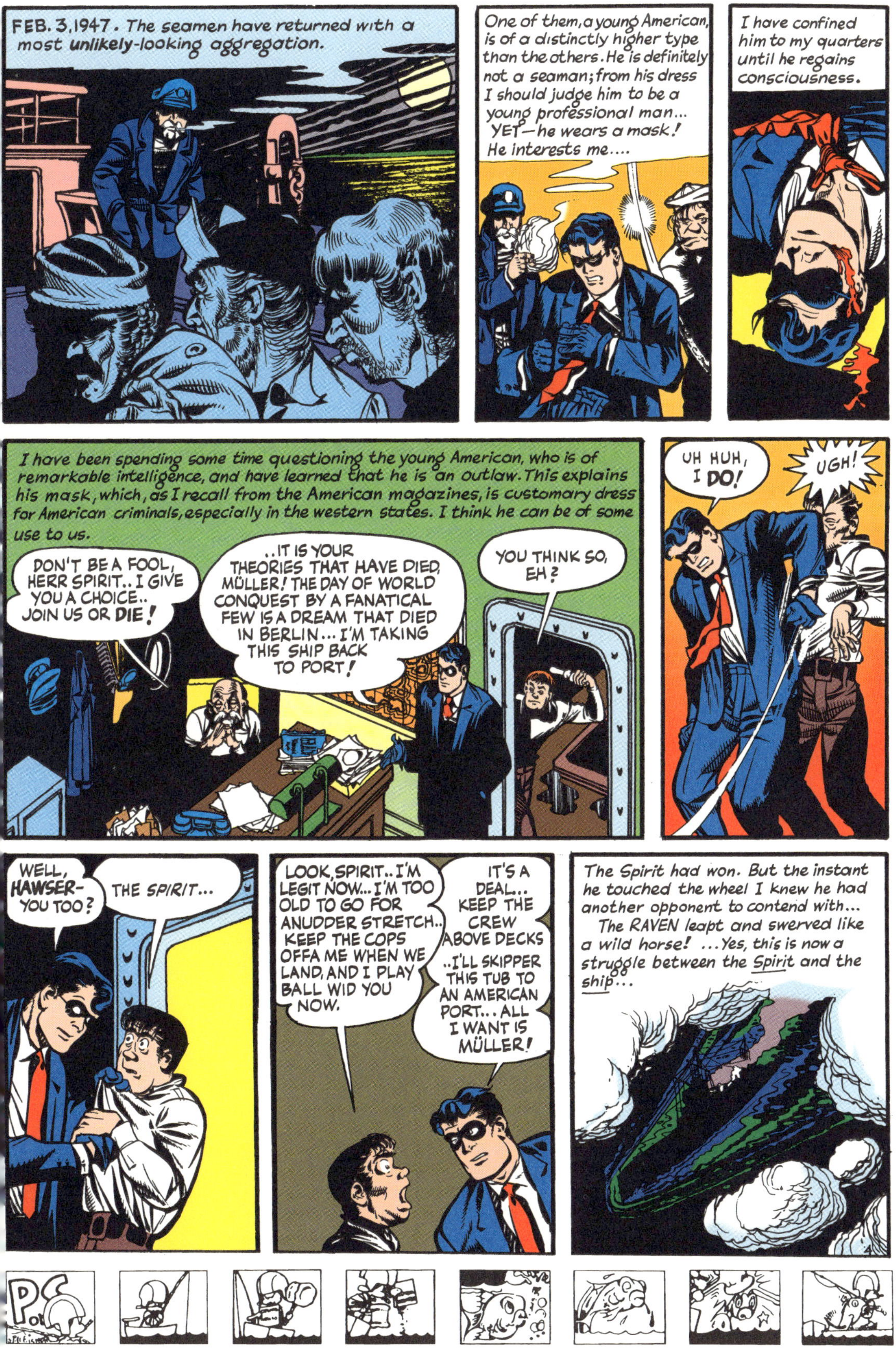
FEB. 3, 1947. The seamen have returned with a most unlikely-looking aggregation.
One of them, a young American, is of a distinctly higher type than the others. He is definitely not a seaman; from his dress I should judge him to be a young professional man... YET—he wears a mask! He interests me....
I have confined him to my quarters until he regains consciousness.
I have been spending some time questioning the young American, who is of remarkable intelligence, and have learned that he is an outlaw. This explains his mask, which, as I recall from the American magazines, is customary dress for American criminals, especially in the western states. I think he can be of some use to us.
DON'T BE A FOOL, HERR SPIRIT.. I GIVE YOU A CHOICE.. JOIN US OR DIE!
..IT IS YOUR THEORIES THAT HAVE DIED, MÜLLER! THE DAY OF WORLD CONQUEST BY A FANATICAL FEW IS A DREAM THAT DIED IN BERLIN... I'M TAKING THIS SHIP BACK TO PORT!
YOU THINK SO, EH?
UH HUH, I DO!
UGH!
WELL, HAWSER- YOU TOO?
THE SPIRIT...
LOOK, SPIRIT.. I'M LEGIT NOW... I'M TOO OLD TO GO FOR ANUDDER STRETCH.. KEEP THE COPS OFFA ME WHEN WE LAND, AND I PLAY BALL WID YOU NOW.
IT'S A DEAL... KEEP THE CREW ABOVE DECKS ..I'LL SKIPPER THIS TUB TO AN AMERICAN PORT... ALL I WANT IS MÜLLER!
The Spirit had won. But the instant he touched the wheel I knew he had another opponent to contend with...
The RAVEN leapt and swerved like a wild horse! ...Yes, this is now a struggle between the Spirit and the ship...
P.S.

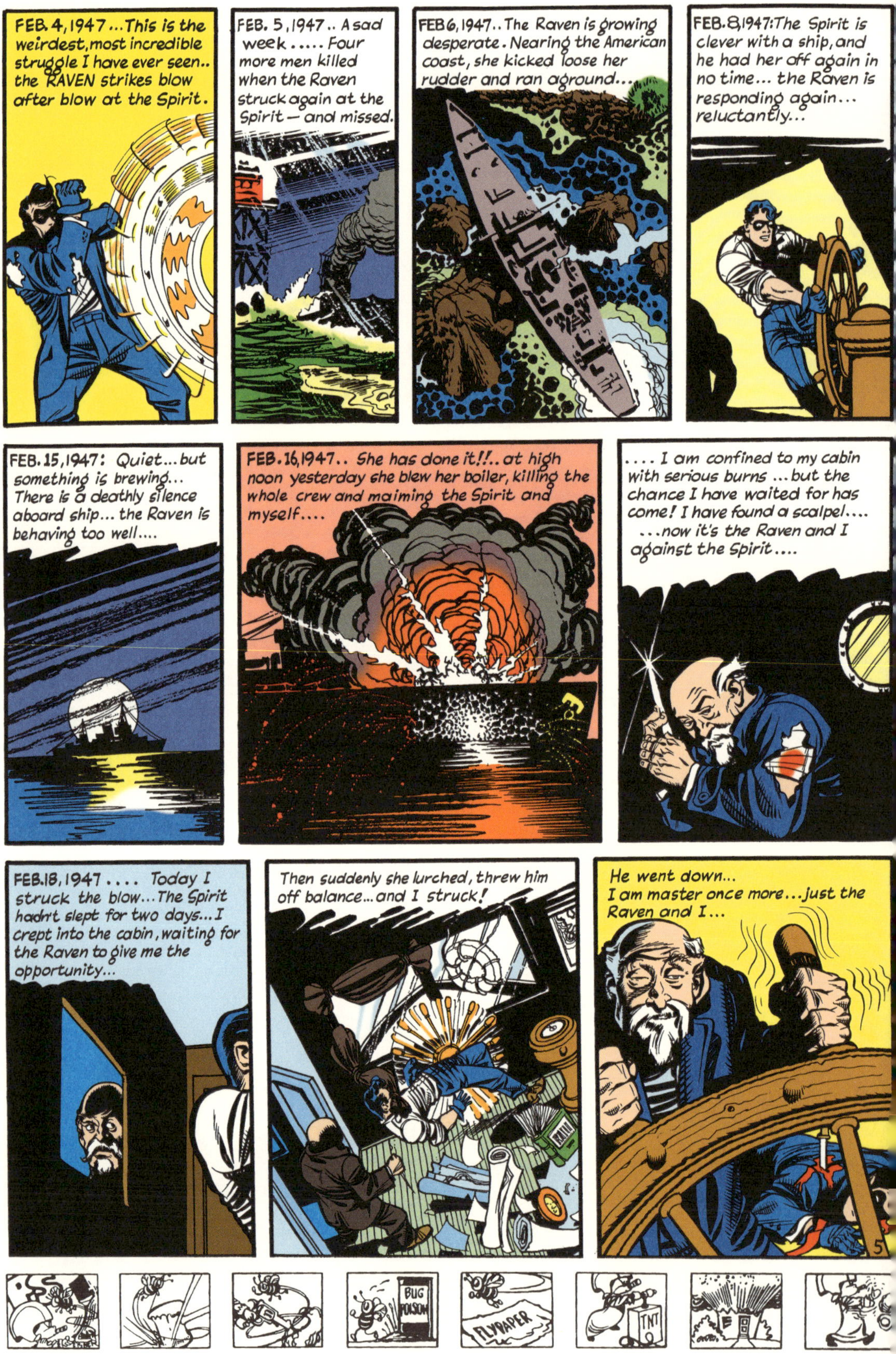
FEB. 4, 1947 ... This is the weirdest, most incredible struggle I have ever seen.. the RAVEN strikes blow after blow at the Spirit.
FEB. 5, 1947 .. A sad week ..... Four more men killed when the Raven struck again at the Spirit — and missed.
FEB 6, 1947.. The Raven is growing desperate. Nearing the American coast, she kicked loose her rudder and ran aground...
FEB. 8, 1947: The Spirit is clever with a ship, and he had her off again in no time... the Raven is responding again... reluctantly...
FEB. 15, 1947: Quiet... but something is brewing... There is a deathly silence aboard ship... the Raven is behaving too well....
FEB. 16, 1947.. She has done it!!.. at high noon yesterday she blew her boiler, killing the whole crew and maiming the Spirit and myself....
.... I am confined to my cabin with serious burns ... but the chance I have waited for has come! I have found a scalpel.... ...now it's the Raven and I against the Spirit....
FEB. 18, 1947 .... Today I struck the blow... The Spirit hadn't slept for two days... I crept into the cabin, waiting for the Raven to give me the opportunity...
Then suddenly she lurched, threw him off balance... and I struck!
He went down... I am master once more... just the Raven and I...
5
BUG POISON
FLYPAPER
TNT

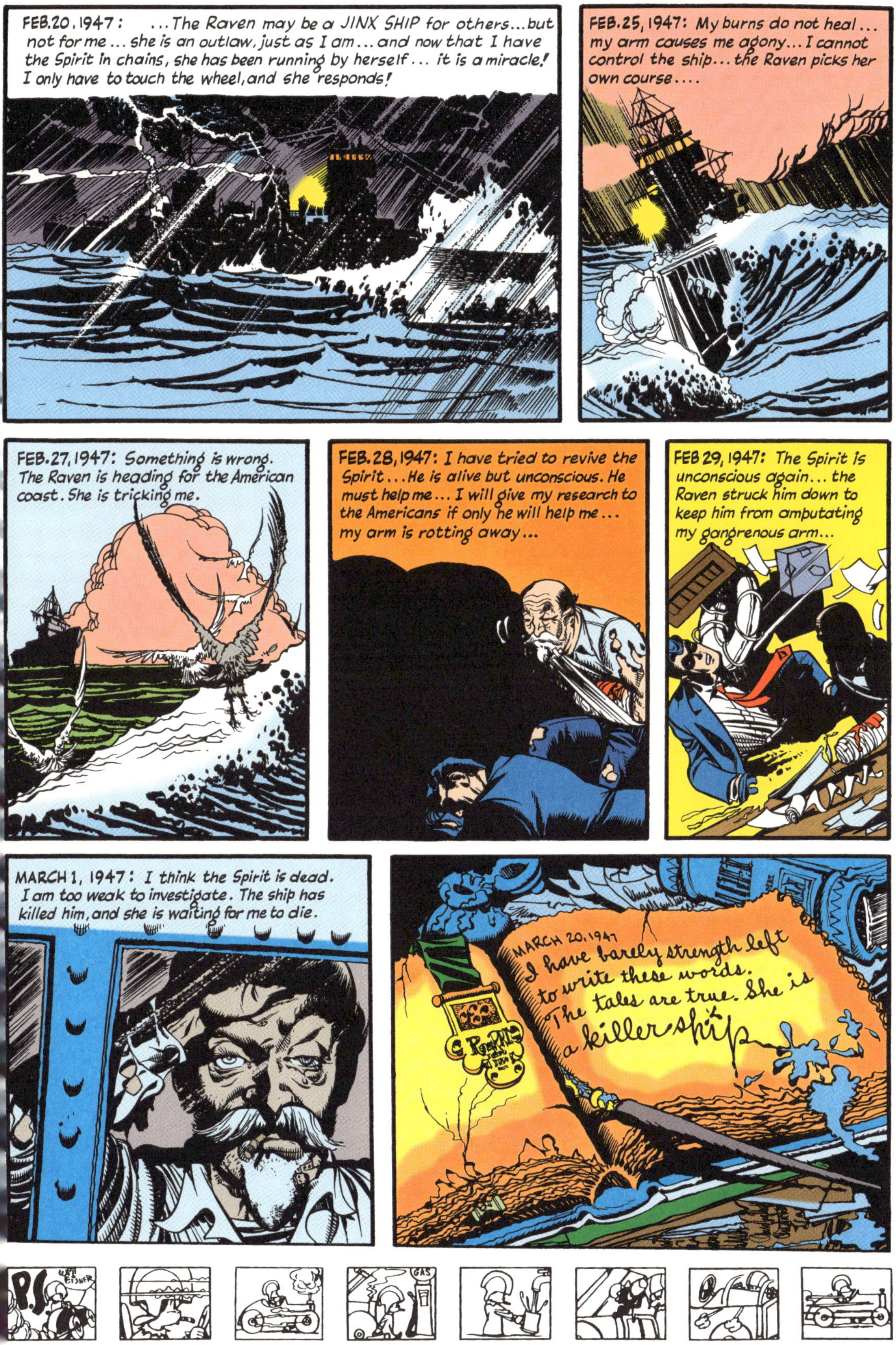
FEB.20, 1947: ...The Raven may be a JINX SHIP for others...but not for me... she is an outlaw, just as I am... and now that I have the Spirit in chains, she has been running by herself... it is a miracle! I only have to touch the wheel, and she responds!
FEB.25, 1947: My burns do not heal... my arm causes me agony... I cannot control the ship... the Raven picks her own course....
FEB.27, 1947: Something is wrong. The Raven is heading for the American coast. She is tricking me.
FEB.28, 1947: I have tried to revive the Spirit... He is alive but unconscious. He must help me... I will give my research to the Americans if only he will help me... my arm is rotting away...
FEB 29, 1947: The Spirit is unconscious again... the Raven struck him down to keep him from amputating my gangrenous arm...
MARCH 1, 1947: I think the Spirit is dead. I am too weak to investigate. The ship has killed him, and she is waiting for me to die.
MARCH 20, 1947
I have barely strength left to write these words. The tales are true. She is a killer ship
P.S.
GAS

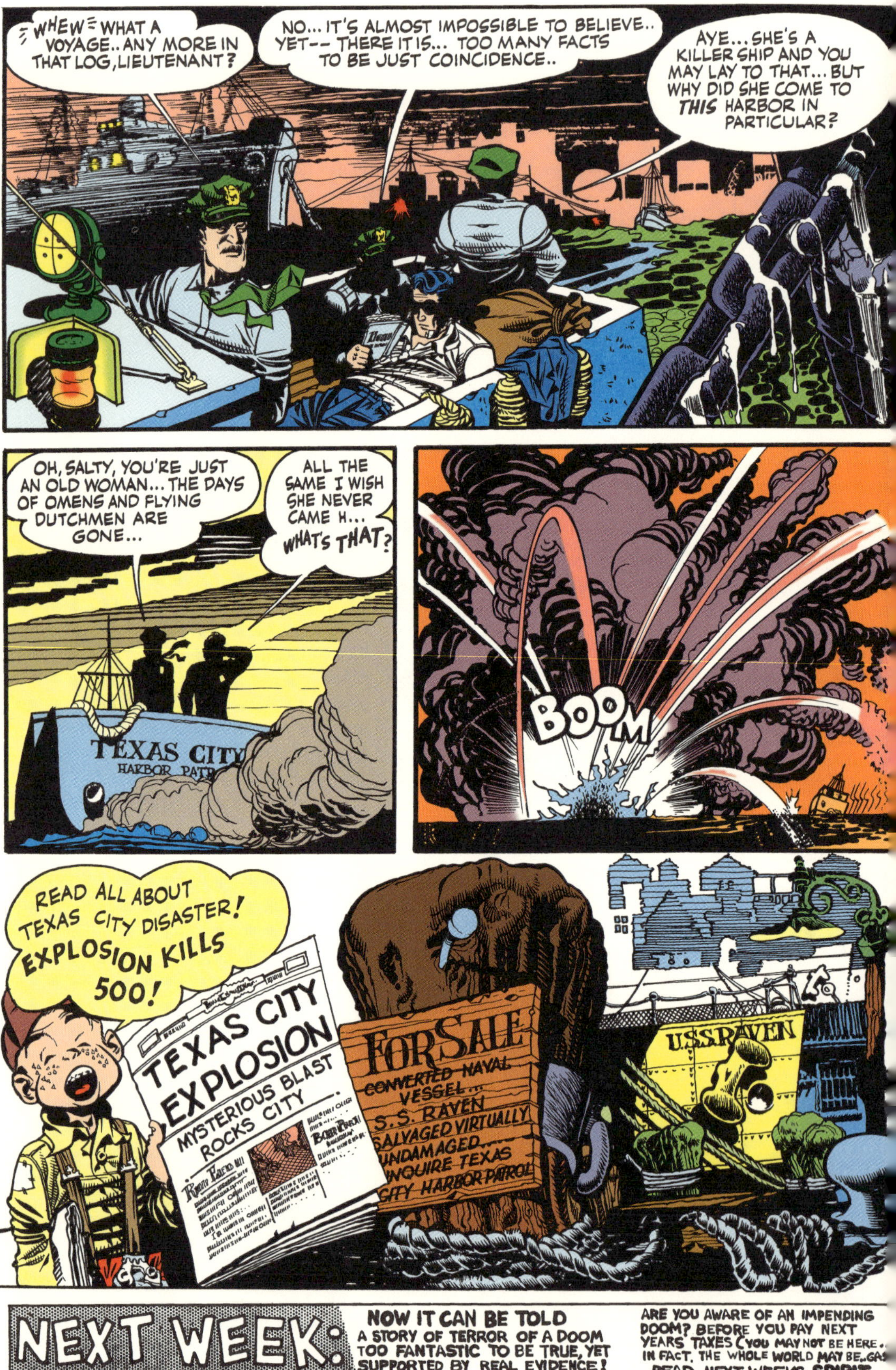
WHEW WHAT A VOYAGE.. ANY MORE IN THAT LOG, LIEUTENANT?
NO... IT'S ALMOST IMPOSSIBLE TO BELIEVE.. YET-- THERE IT IS... TOO MANY FACTS TO BE JUST COINCIDENCE..
AYE... SHE'S A KILLER SHIP AND YOU MAY LAY TO THAT... BUT WHY DID SHE COME TO THIS HARBOR IN PARTICULAR?
OH, SALTY, YOU'RE JUST AN OLD WOMAN... THE DAYS OF OMENS AND FLYING DUTCHMEN ARE GONE...
ALL THE SAME I WISH SHE NEVER CAME H... WHAT'S THAT?
TEXAS CITY
HARBOR PATR
BOOM
READ ALL ABOUT TEXAS CITY DISASTER! EXPLOSION KILLS 500!
TEXAS CITY EXPLOSION
MYSTERIOUS BLAST ROCKS CITY
FOR SALE
CONVERTED NAVAL VESSEL... S.S. RAVEN SALVAGED VIRTUALLY UNDAMAGED... INQUIRE TEXAS CITY HARBOR PATROL
U.S.S. RAVEN
NEXT WEEK:
NOW IT CAN BE TOLD
A STORY OF TERROR OF A DOOM TOO FANTASTIC TO BE TRUE, YET SUPPORTED BY REAL EVIDENCE!
ARE YOU AWARE OF AN IMPENDING DOOM? BEFORE YOU PAY NEXT YEARS TAXES (YOU MAY NOT BE HERE... IN FACT, THE WHOLE WORLD MAY BE..GAS
READ NEXT WEEKS SPIRIT

U.F.O.

September 28 1947

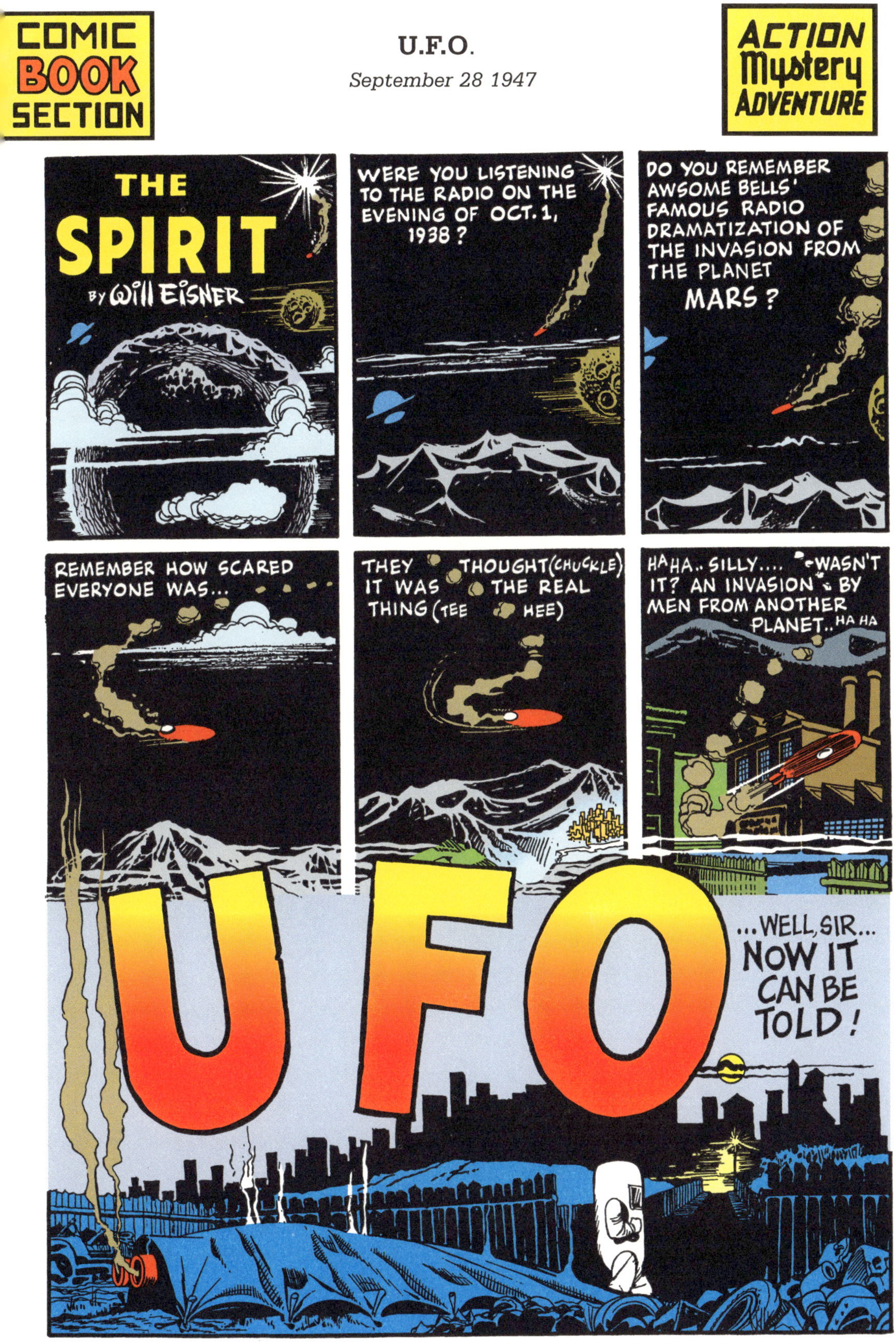
COMIC BOOK SECTION
ACTION Mystery ADVENTURE
THE SPIRIT
BY Will Eisner
WERE YOU LISTENING TO THE RADIO ON THE EVENING OF OCT. 1, 1938?
DO YOU REMEMBER AWSOME BELLS' FAMOUS RADIO DRAMATIZATION OF THE INVASION FROM THE PLANET MARS?
REMEMBER HOW SCARED EVERYONE WAS...
THEY THOUGHT (CHUCKLE) IT WAS THE REAL THING (TEE HEE)
HAHA.. SILLY.... WASN'T IT? AN INVASION BY MEN FROM ANOTHER PLANET.. HA HA
UFO
...WELL, SIR... NOW IT CAN BE TOLD!

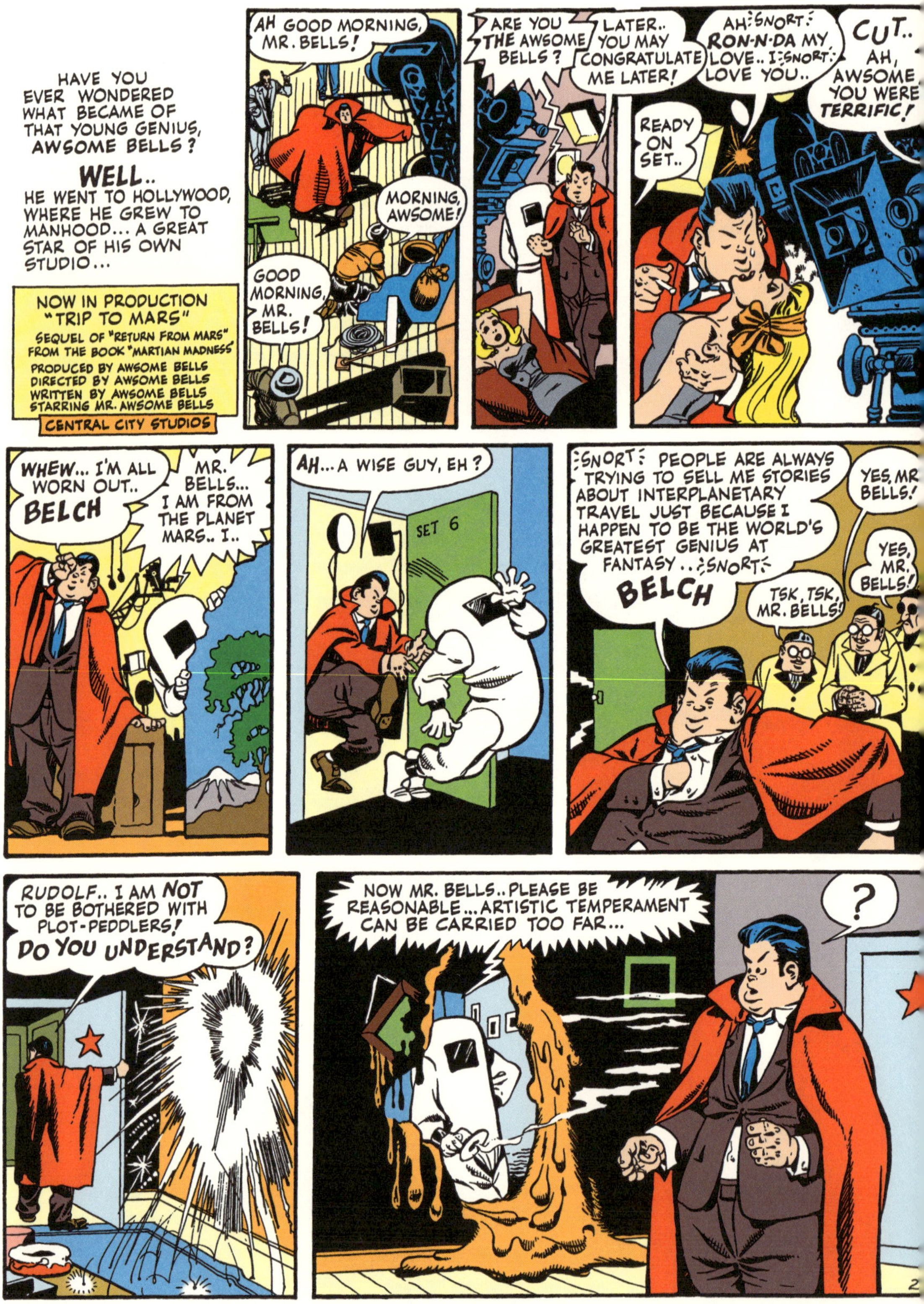
HAVE YOU EVER WONDERED WHAT BECAME OF THAT YOUNG GENIUS, AWSOME BELLS?
WELL.. HE WENT TO HOLLYWOOD, WHERE HE GREW TO MANHOOD... A GREAT STAR OF HIS OWN STUDIO...
NOW IN PRODUCTION "TRIP TO MARS" SEQUEL OF "RETURN FROM MARS" FROM THE BOOK "MARTIAN MADNESS" PRODUCED BY AWSOME BELLS DIRECTED BY AWSOME BELLS WRITTEN BY AWSOME BELLS STARRING MR. AWSOME BELLS
CENTRAL CITY STUDIOS
AH GOOD MORNING, MR. BELLS!
MORNING, AWSOME!
GOOD MORNING, MR. BELLS!
ARE YOU THE AWSOME BELLS?
LATER.. YOU MAY CONGRATULATE ME LATER!
AH:SNORT: RON-N-DA MY LOVE.. I:SNORT: LOVE YOU..
READY ON SET..
CUT.. AH, AWSOME YOU WERE TERRIFIC!
WHEW... I'M ALL WORN OUT.. BELCH
MR. BELLS... I AM FROM THE PLANET MARS.. I..
AH... A WISE GUY, EH?
SET 6
:SNORT: PEOPLE ARE ALWAYS TRYING TO SELL ME STORIES ABOUT INTERPLANETARY TRAVEL JUST BECAUSE I HAPPEN TO BE THE WORLD'S GREATEST GENIUS AT FANTASY..:SNORT: BELCH
YES, MR BELLS!
YES, MR. BELLS!
TSK, TSK, MR. BELLS!
RUDOLF.. I AM NOT TO BE BOTHERED WITH PLOT-PEDDLERS! DO YOU UNDERSTAND?
NOW MR. BELLS.. PLEASE BE REASONABLE... ARTISTIC TEMPERAMENT CAN BE CARRIED TOO FAR...
?
2

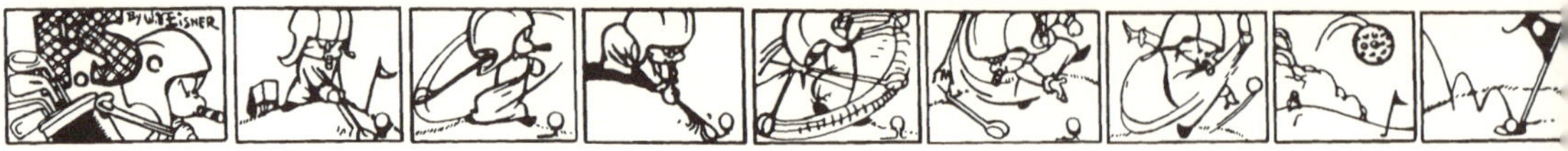

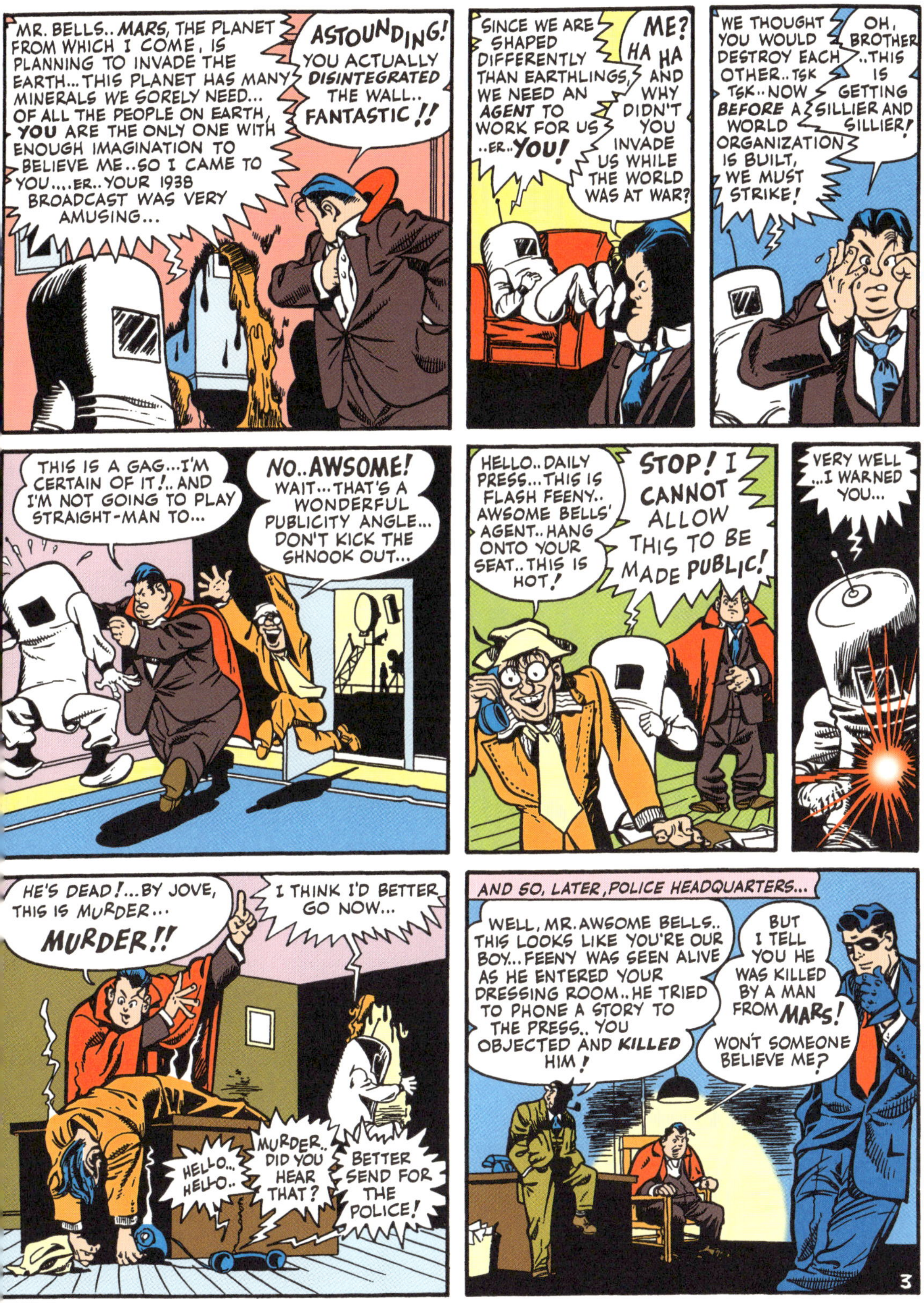
MR. BELLS.. MARS, THE PLANET FROM WHICH I COME, IS PLANNING TO INVADE THE EARTH... THIS PLANET HAS MANY MINERALS WE SORELY NEED... OF ALL THE PEOPLE ON EARTH, YOU ARE THE ONLY ONE WITH ENOUGH IMAGINATION TO BELIEVE ME.. SO I CAME TO YOU.... ER.. YOUR 1938 BROADCAST WAS VERY AMUSING...
ASTOUNDING! YOU ACTUALLY DISINTEGRATED THE WALL.. FANTASTIC!!
SINCE WE ARE SHAPED DIFFERENTLY THAN EARTHLINGS, WE NEED AN AGENT TO WORK FOR US ..ER.. YOU!
ME? HA HA AND WHY DIDN'T YOU INVADE US WHILE THE WORLD WAS AT WAR?
WE THOUGHT YOU WOULD DESTROY EACH OTHER.. TSK TSK.. NOW BEFORE A WORLD ORGANIZATION IS BUILT, WE MUST STRIKE!
OH, BROTHER ..THIS IS GETTING SILLIER AND SILLIER!
THIS IS A GAG...I'M CERTAIN OF IT!.. AND I'M NOT GOING TO PLAY STRAIGHT-MAN TO...
NO.. AWSOME! WAIT... THAT'S A WONDERFUL PUBLICITY ANGLE... DON'T KICK THE SHNOOK OUT...
HELLO.. DAILY PRESS... THIS IS FLASH FEENY.. AWSOME BELLS' AGENT.. HANG ONTO YOUR SEAT.. THIS IS HOT!
STOP! I CANNOT ALLOW THIS TO BE MADE PUBLIC!
VERY WELL ...I WARNED YOU...
HE'S DEAD!... BY JOVE, THIS IS MURDER... MURDER!!
I THINK I'D BETTER GO NOW...
HELLO... HELLO..
MURDER.. DID YOU HEAR THAT?
BETTER SEND FOR THE POLICE!
AND SO, LATER, POLICE HEADQUARTERS...
WELL, MR. AWSOME BELLS.. THIS LOOKS LIKE YOU'RE OUR BOY... FEENY WAS SEEN ALIVE AS HE ENTERED YOUR DRESSING ROOM.. HE TRIED TO PHONE A STORY TO THE PRESS.. YOU OBJECTED AND KILLED HIM!
BUT I TELL YOU HE WAS KILLED BY A MAN FROM MARS!
WON'T SOMEONE BELIEVE ME?
3

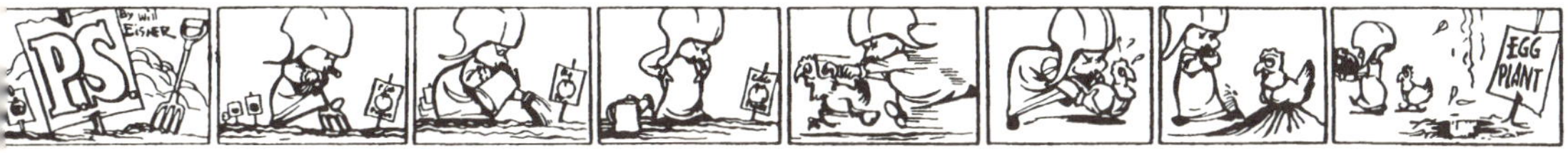
P.S.
By Will Eisner
EGG PLANT

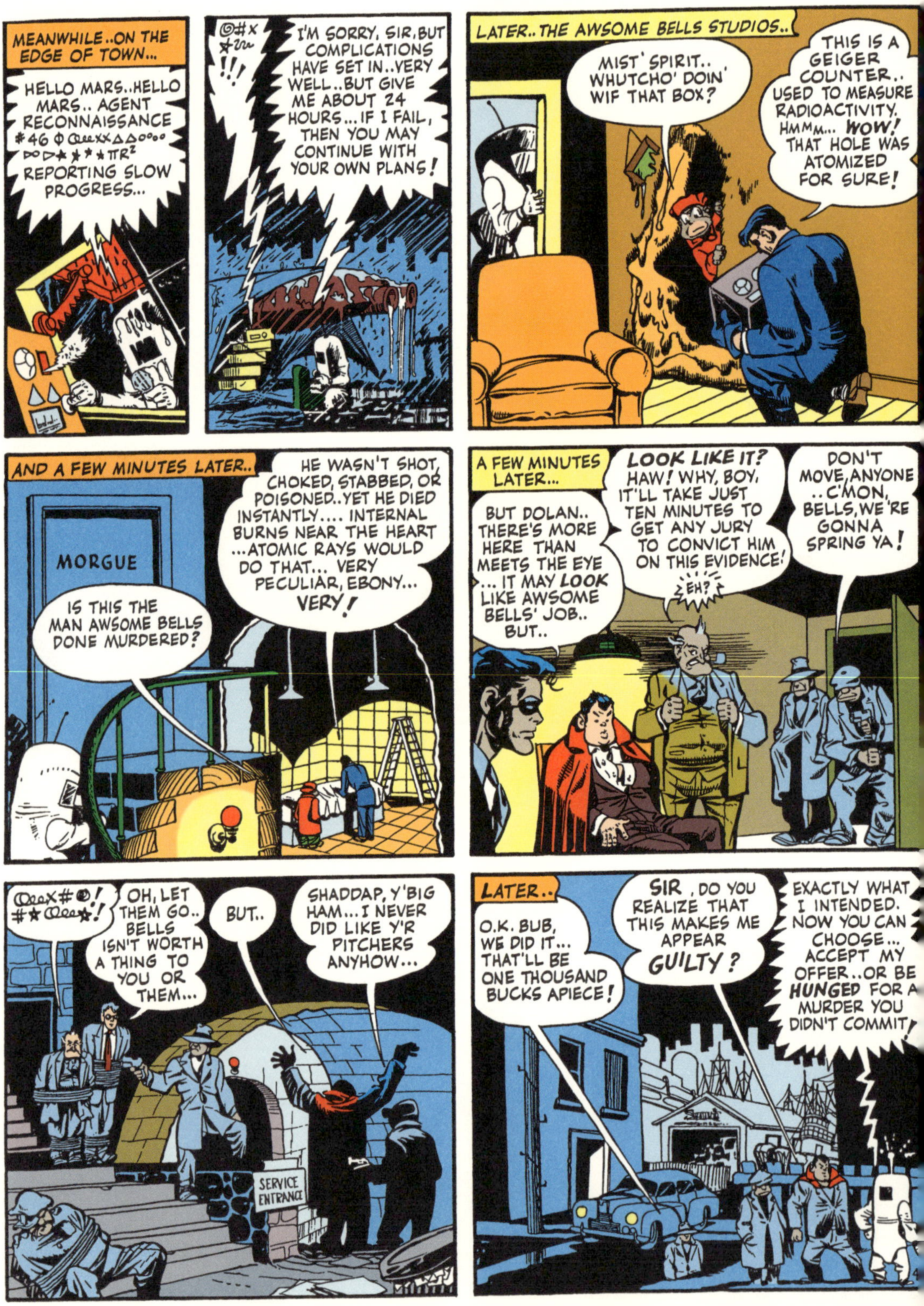
MEANWHILE..ON THE EDGE OF TOWN...
HELLO MARS..HELLO MARS.. AGENT RECONNAISSANCE #46 ... REPORTING SLOW PROGRESS...
!!!
I'M SORRY, SIR, BUT COMPLICATIONS HAVE SET IN..VERY WELL..BUT GIVE ME ABOUT 24 HOURS...IF I FAIL, THEN YOU MAY CONTINUE WITH YOUR OWN PLANS!
LATER.. THE AWSOME BELLS STUDIOS..
MIST' SPIRIT.. WHUTCHO' DOIN' WIF THAT BOX?
THIS IS A GEIGER COUNTER.. USED TO MEASURE RADIOACTIVITY. HMMM... WOW! THAT HOLE WAS ATOMIZED FOR SURE!
AND A FEW MINUTES LATER..
MORGUE
IS THIS THE MAN AWSOME BELLS DONE MURDERED?
HE WASN'T SHOT, CHOKED, STABBED, OR POISONED..YET HE DIED INSTANTLY.... INTERNAL BURNS NEAR THE HEART ...ATOMIC RAYS WOULD DO THAT... VERY PECULIAR, EBONY... VERY!
A FEW MINUTES LATER...
BUT DOLAN.. THERE'S MORE HERE THAN MEETS THE EYE ... IT MAY LOOK LIKE AWSOME BELLS' JOB.. BUT..
LOOK LIKE IT? HAW! WHY, BOY, IT'LL TAKE JUST TEN MINUTES TO GET ANY JURY TO CONVICT HIM ON THIS EVIDENCE!
EH?
DON'T MOVE, ANYONE ..C'MON, BELLS, WE'RE GONNA SPRING YA!
OH, LET THEM GO.. BELLS ISN'T WORTH A THING TO YOU OR THEM...
BUT..
SHADDAP, Y'BIG HAM...I NEVER DID LIKE Y'R PITCHERS ANYHOW...
SERVICE ENTRANCE
LATER..
O.K. BUB, WE DID IT... THAT'LL BE ONE THOUSAND BUCKS APIECE!
SIR, DO YOU REALIZE THAT THIS MAKES ME APPEAR GUILTY?
EXACTLY WHAT I INTENDED. NOW YOU CAN CHOOSE... ACCEPT MY OFFER..OR BE HUNGED FOR A MURDER YOU DIDN'T COMMIT!

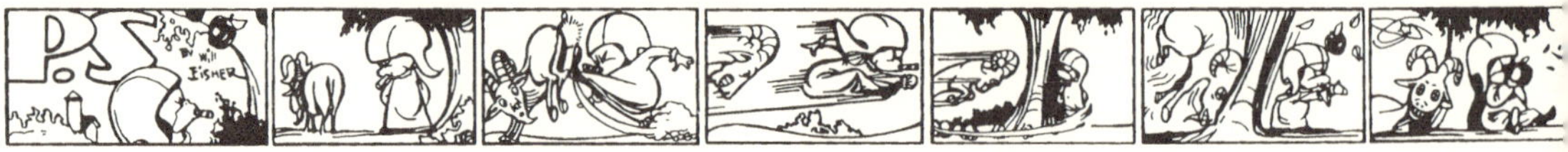
P.S.
BY WILL EISNER

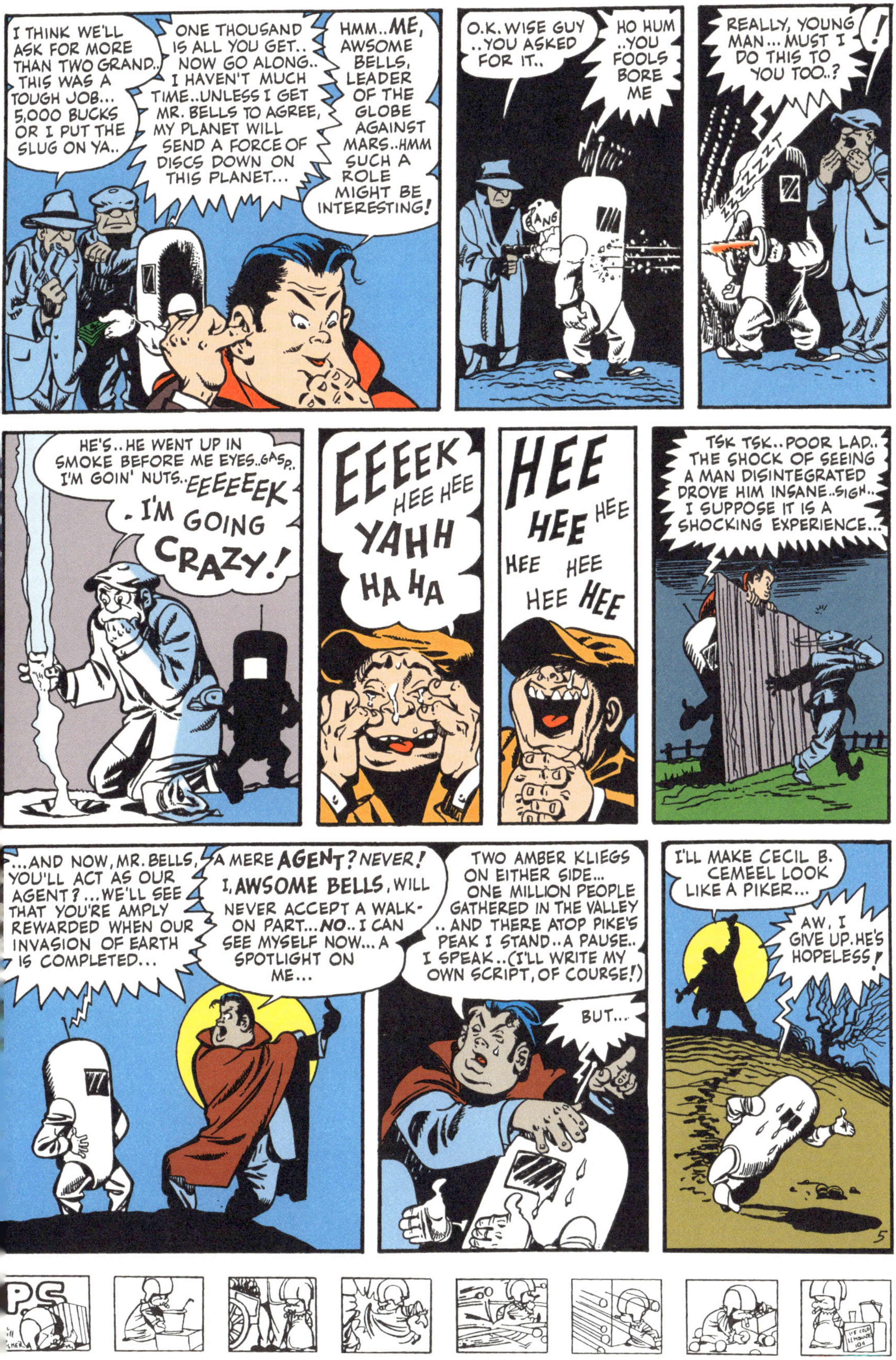
I THINK WE'LL ASK FOR MORE THAN TWO GRAND.. THIS WAS A TOUGH JOB... 5,000 BUCKS OR I PUT THE SLUG ON YA..
ONE THOUSAND IS ALL YOU GET.. NOW GO ALONG.. I HAVEN'T MUCH TIME..UNLESS I GET MR. BELLS TO AGREE, MY PLANET WILL SEND A FORCE OF DISCS DOWN ON THIS PLANET...
HMM..ME, AWSOME BELLS, LEADER OF THE GLOBE AGAINST MARS..HMM SUCH A ROLE MIGHT BE INTERESTING!
O.K. WISE GUY ..YOU ASKED FOR IT..
HO HUM ..YOU FOOLS BORE ME
BANG
REALLY, YOUNG MAN... MUST I DO THIS TO YOU TOO..?
!
ZZZZZZT
HE'S..HE WENT UP IN SMOKE BEFORE ME EYES..GASP.. I'M GOIN' NUTS..EEEEEEK
- I'M GOING CRAZY!
EEEEK HEE HEE YAHH HA HA
HEE HEE HEE HEE HEE HEE HEE
TSK TSK..POOR LAD.. THE SHOCK OF SEEING A MAN DISINTEGRATED DROVE HIM INSANE..SIGH.. I SUPPOSE IT IS A SHOCKING EXPERIENCE...
...AND NOW, MR. BELLS, YOU'LL ACT AS OUR AGENT?...WE'LL SEE THAT YOU'RE AMPLY REWARDED WHEN OUR INVASION OF EARTH IS COMPLETED...
A MERE AGENT? NEVER! I, AWSOME BELLS, WILL NEVER ACCEPT A WALK-ON PART...NO..I CAN SEE MYSELF NOW... A SPOTLIGHT ON ME...
TWO AMBER KLIEGS ON EITHER SIDE... ONE MILLION PEOPLE GATHERED IN THE VALLEY ..AND THERE ATOP PIKE'S PEAK I STAND..A PAUSE.. I SPEAK..(I'LL WRITE MY OWN SCRIPT, OF COURSE!)
BUT...
I'LL MAKE CECIL B. CEMEEL LOOK LIKE A PIKER...
AW, I GIVE UP. HE'S HOPELESS!
5
PS

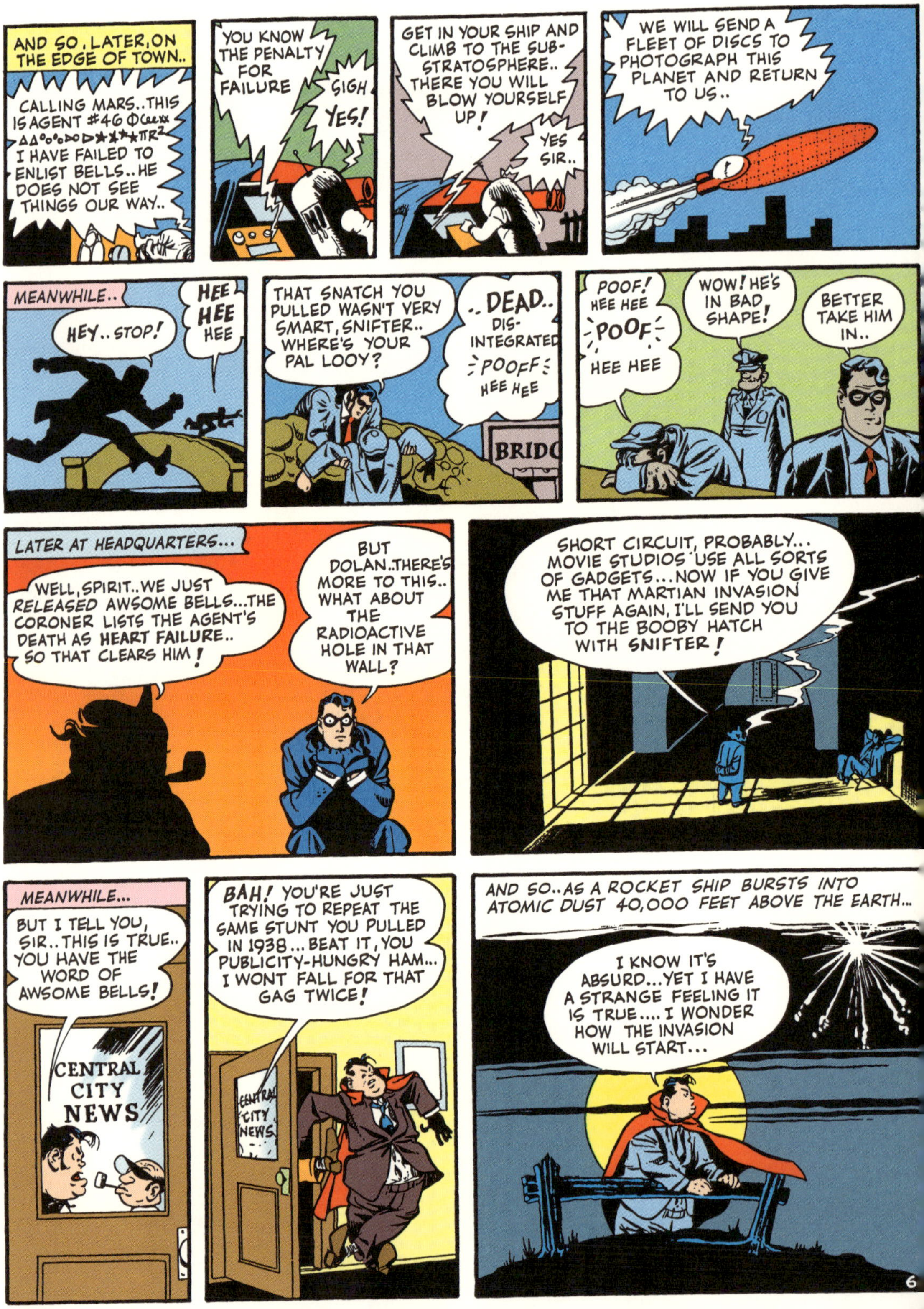
AND SO, LATER, ON THE EDGE OF TOWN..
CALLING MARS..THIS IS AGENT #46
I HAVE FAILED TO ENLIST BELLS..HE DOES NOT SEE THINGS OUR WAY..
YOU KNOW THE PENALTY FOR FAILURE
SIGH YES!
GET IN YOUR SHIP AND CLIMB TO THE SUB-STRATOSPHERE.. THERE YOU WILL BLOW YOURSELF UP!
YES SIR..
WE WILL SEND A FLEET OF DISCS TO PHOTOGRAPH THIS PLANET AND RETURN TO US..
MEANWHILE..
HEY.. STOP!
HEE HEE HEE
THAT SNATCH YOU PULLED WASN'T VERY SMART, SNIFTER.. WHERE'S YOUR PAL LOOY?
.. DEAD.. DIS-INTEGRATED POOFF HEE HEE
BRIDG
POOF! HEE HEE POOF HEE HEE
WOW! HE'S IN BAD SHAPE!
BETTER TAKE HIM IN..
LATER AT HEADQUARTERS...
WELL, SPIRIT..WE JUST RELEASED AWSOME BELLS...THE CORONER LISTS THE AGENT'S DEATH AS HEART FAILURE.. SO THAT CLEARS HIM!
BUT DOLAN..THERE'S MORE TO THIS.. WHAT ABOUT THE RADIOACTIVE HOLE IN THAT WALL?
SHORT CIRCUIT, PROBABLY... MOVIE STUDIOS USE ALL SORTS OF GADGETS...NOW IF YOU GIVE ME THAT MARTIAN INVASION STUFF AGAIN, I'LL SEND YOU TO THE BOOBY HATCH WITH SNIFTER!
MEANWHILE...
BUT I TELL YOU, SIR..THIS IS TRUE.. YOU HAVE THE WORD OF AWSOME BELLS!
CENTRAL CITY NEWS
BAH! YOU'RE JUST TRYING TO REPEAT THE SAME STUNT YOU PULLED IN 1938... BEAT IT, YOU PUBLICITY-HUNGRY HAM... I WONT FALL FOR THAT GAG TWICE!
CENTRAL CITY NEWS
AND SO..AS A ROCKET SHIP BURSTS INTO ATOMIC DUST 40,000 FEET ABOVE THE EARTH...
I KNOW IT'S ABSURD...YET I HAVE A STRANGE FEELING IT IS TRUE.... I WONDER HOW THE INVASION WILL START...
6

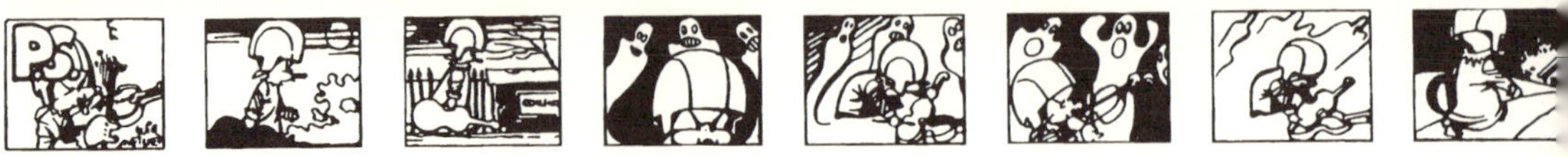

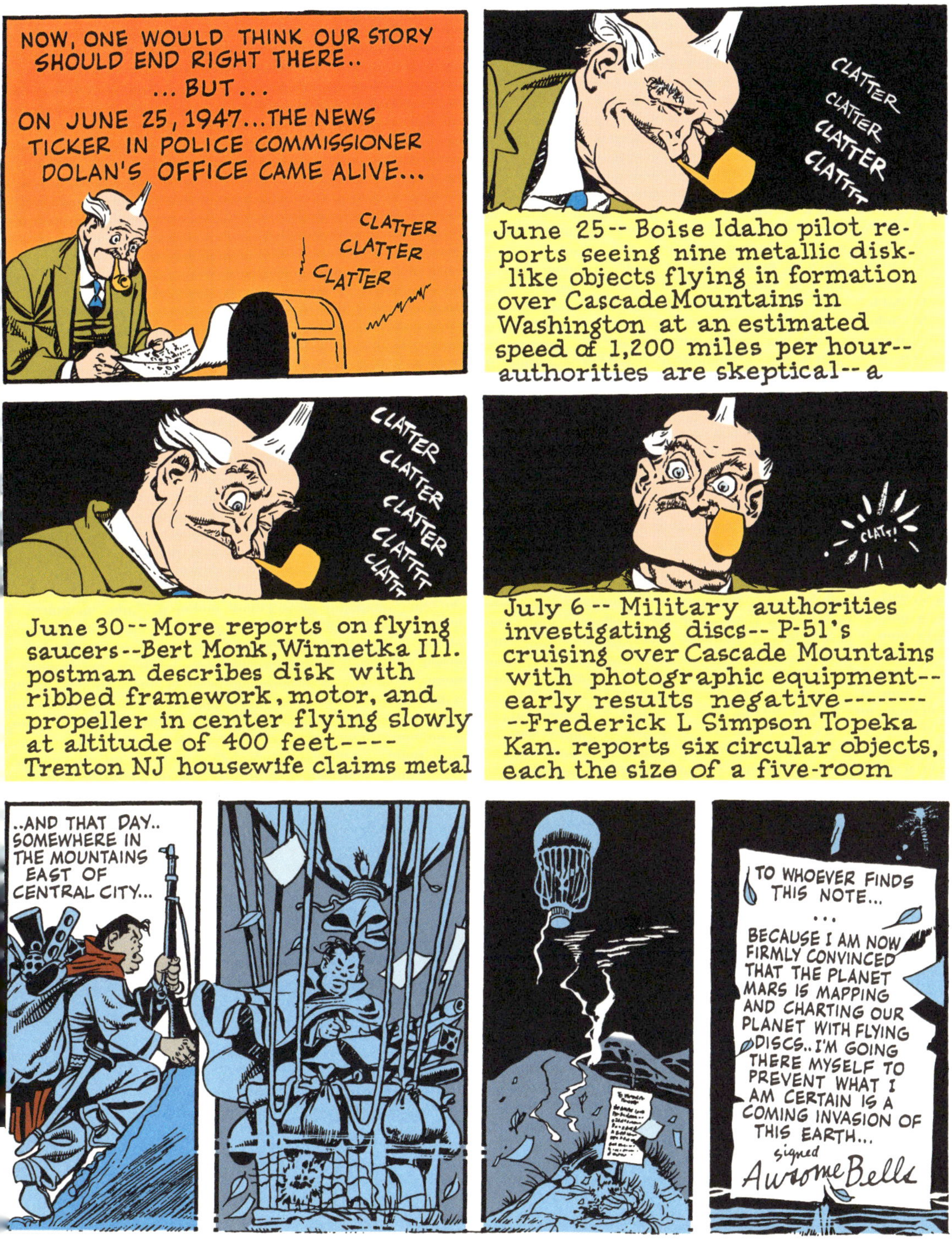

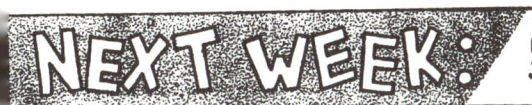

NOW, ONE WOULD THINK OUR STORY SHOULD END RIGHT THERE.. ... BUT ... ON JUNE 25, 1947...THE NEWS TICKER IN POLICE COMMISSIONER DOLAN'S OFFICE CAME ALIVE...
CLATTER CLATTER CLATTER
CLATTER CLATTER CLATTER CLATTTT
June 25-- Boise Idaho pilot reports seeing nine metallic disk-like objects flying in formation over Cascade Mountains in Washington at an estimated speed of 1,200 miles per hour-- authorities are skeptical-- a
CLATTER CLATTER CLATTER CLATTTT CLATTT
June 30--More reports on flying saucers--Bert Monk, Winnetka Ill. postman describes disk with ribbed framework, motor, and propeller in center flying slowly at altitude of 400 feet---- Trenton NJ housewife claims metal
CLAT!!
July 6 -- Military authorities investigating discs-- P-51's cruising over Cascade Mountains with photographic equipment-- early results negative------- --Frederick L Simpson Topeka Kan. reports six circular objects, each the size of a five-room
..AND THAT DAY.. SOMEWHERE IN THE MOUNTAINS EAST OF CENTRAL CITY...
TO WHOEVER FINDS THIS NOTE... ... BECAUSE I AM NOW FIRMLY CONVINCED THAT THE PLANET MARS IS MAPPING AND CHARTING OUR PLANET WITH FLYING DISCS..I'M GOING THERE MYSELF TO PREVENT WHAT I AM CERTAIN IS A COMING INVASION OF THIS EARTH... signed Awsome Bells

ABOUT WHAT HAPPENED SINCE THEN.. BY 1973 THE NUMBER OF AMERICANS WHO REPORTED "SIGHTINGS" OF UFOs REACHED AN ALL-TIME HIGH . . . TWICE AS MANY AS IN 1966. A NATIONALLY RESPECTED POLLING GROUP REPORTED THAT 51% OF AMERICANS SURVEYED IN 1973 BELIEVED THAT EXTRATERRESTRIAL VEHICLES HAVE VISITED EARTH.

NEXT WEEK: THE SPIRIT'S FAVORITE FAIRY TALES FOR JUVENILE DELINQUENTS VOLUME # 2

THE STORY OF CINDERELLA EXCLUSIVE!! ONLY IN "THE SPIRIT" NO OTHER COMIC CAN MAKE THAT STATEMENT!!

THE SPIRIT'S FAVORITE FAIRY TALES FOR JUVENILE DELINQUENTS: CINDERELLA

October 5 1947

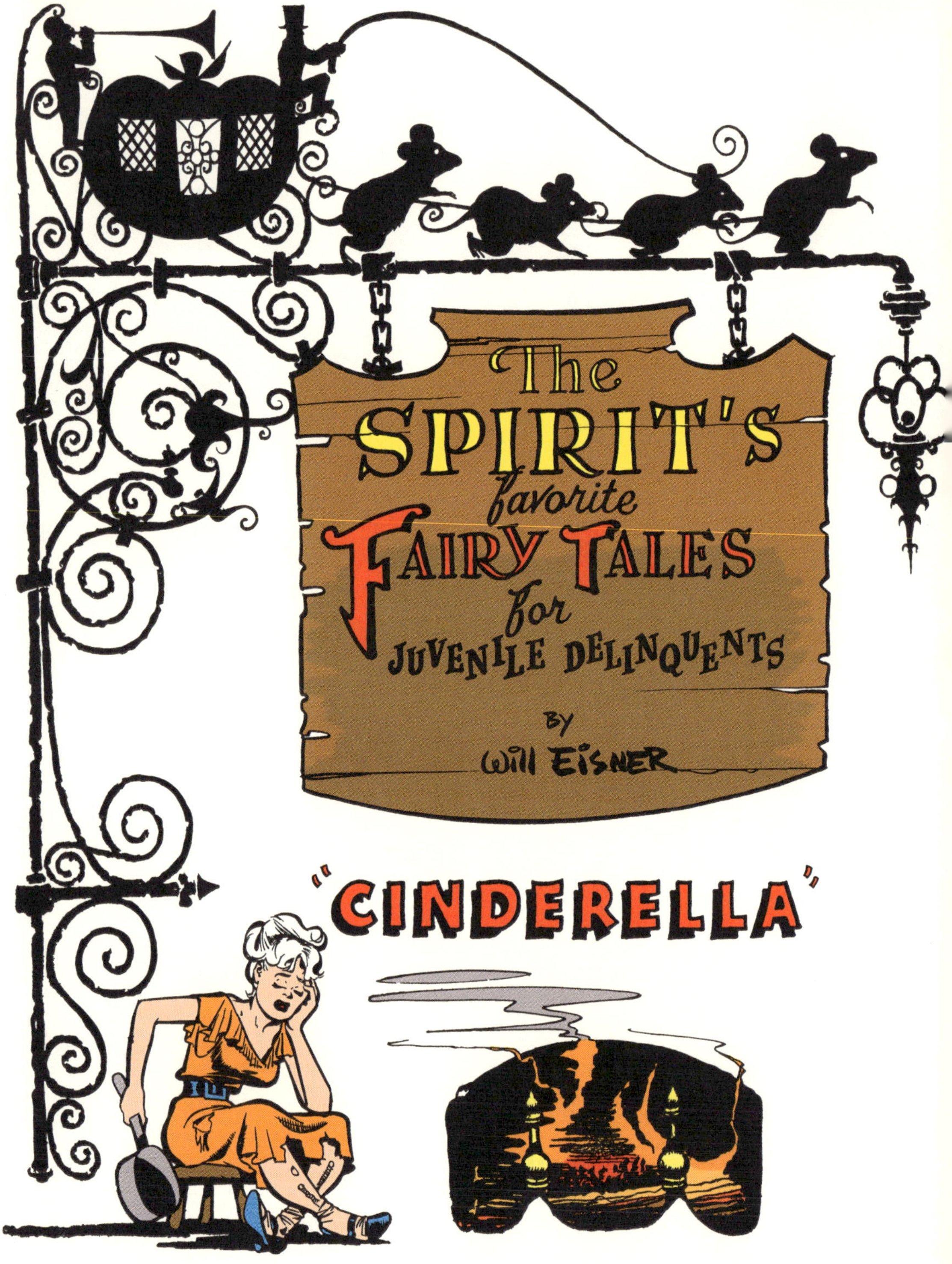
The SPIRIT'S favorite FAIRY TALES for JUVENILE DELINQUENTS
BY Will EISNER
"CINDERELLA"

Once upon a time in Central City there lived an ex-shoplifter named Ma Harridan and her three daughters.

Now **MA** (who was out on parole) had just finished a two-year rap..she was really innocent of everything...she was just trying to change them nylons for a larger size...

Anyhow, Ma decided that crime does not pay, and in an effort to bring her girls up straight, she opened a respectable eatery....

Now her two eldest daughters, **Prudence** and **Desire**, were **perfect ladies**, so Ma kept them at the tables, serving the sitting guests (hoping, of course, they would marry rich husbands.)

But the third, Cinderella, was a stepdaughter, and Ma, knowing her sweet ways and gentle disposition would make the older sisters look like pikers, kept the poor little thing in the kitchen...

There, she had to get along on "leavings"...

...For the cruel stepmother allowed no one near her, and the sweet little thing spent a lonely life amid the pots and pans...

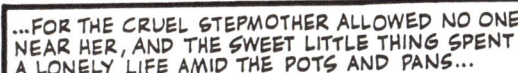
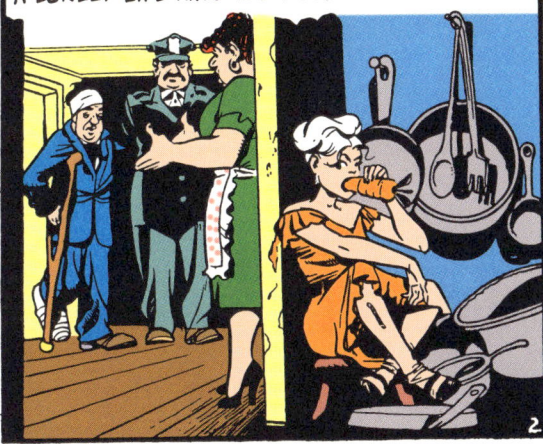

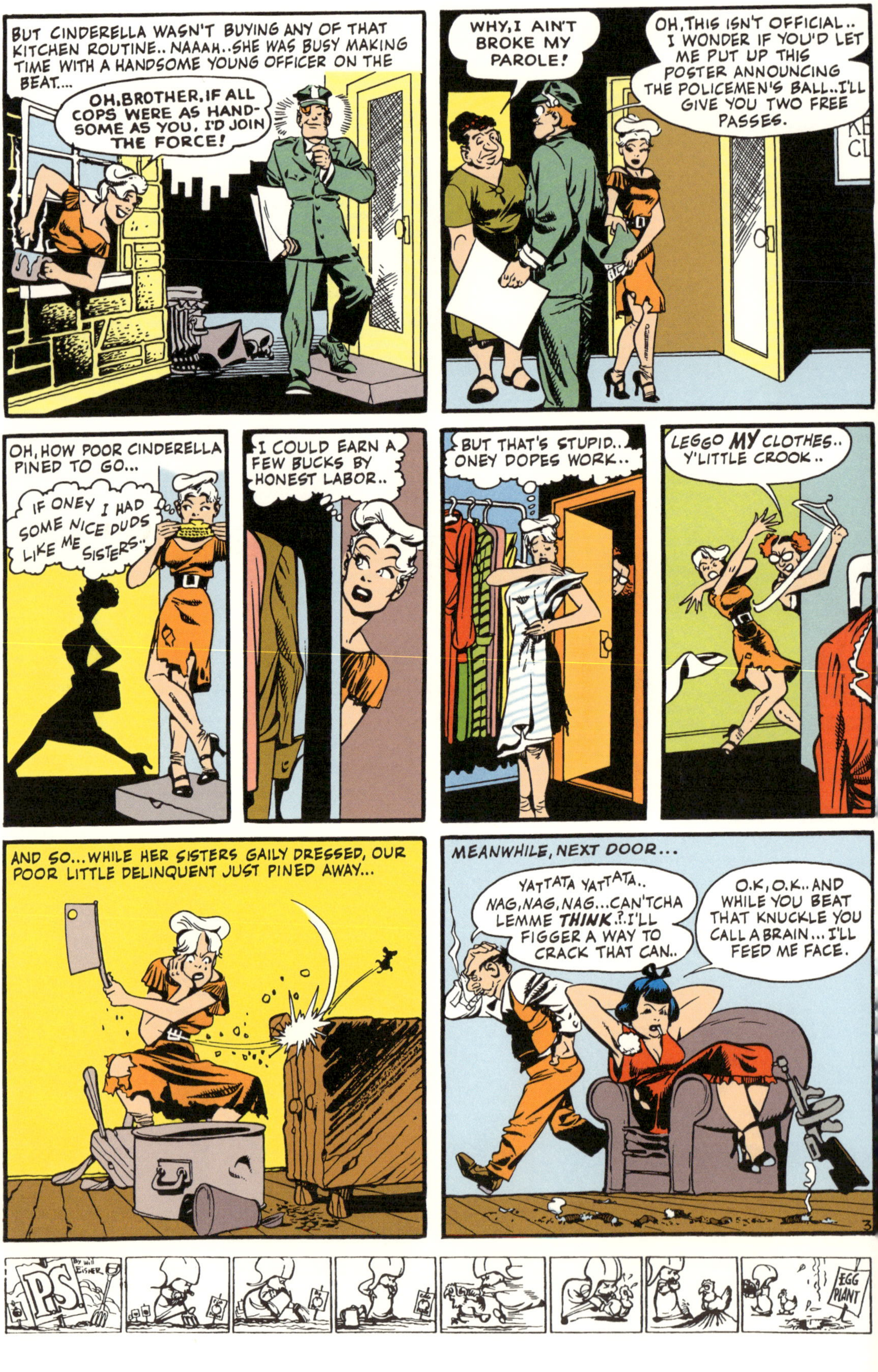
BUT CINDERELLA WASN'T BUYING ANY OF THAT KITCHEN ROUTINE.. NAAAH..SHE WAS BUSY MAKING TIME WITH A HANDSOME YOUNG OFFICER ON THE BEAT....
OH, BROTHER, IF ALL COPS WERE AS HAND-SOME AS YOU, I'D JOIN THE FORCE!
WHY, I AIN'T BROKE MY PAROLE!
OH, THIS ISN'T OFFICIAL.. I WONDER IF YOU'D LET ME PUT UP THIS POSTER ANNOUNCING THE POLICEMEN'S BALL..I'LL GIVE YOU TWO FREE PASSES.
OH, HOW POOR CINDERELLA PINED TO GO...
IF ONEY I HAD SOME NICE DUDS LIKE ME SISTERS..
I COULD EARN A FEW BUCKS BY HONEST LABOR..
BUT THAT'S STUPID.. ONEY DOPES WORK..
LEGGO MY CLOTHES.. Y'LITTLE CROOK..
AND SO...WHILE HER SISTERS GAILY DRESSED, OUR POOR LITTLE DELINQUENT JUST PINED AWAY...
MEANWHILE, NEXT DOOR...
YATTATA YATTATA.. NAG, NAG, NAG...CAN'TCHA LEMME THINK.?.I'LL FIGGER A WAY TO CRACK THAT CAN..
O.K, O.K.. AND WHILE YOU BEAT THAT KNUCKLE YOU CALL A BRAIN... I'LL FEED ME FACE.
P.S.
EGG PLANT

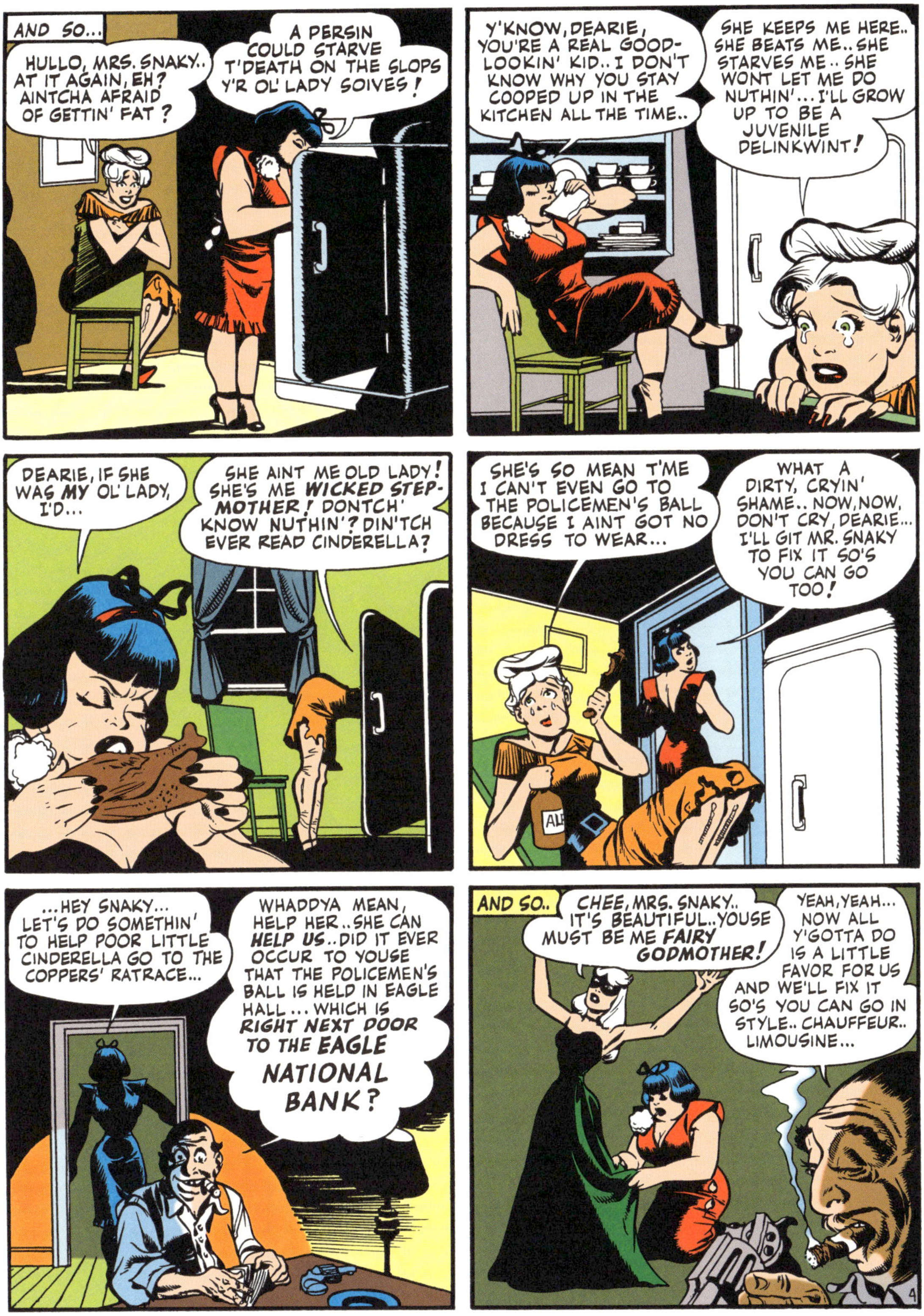
AND SO...
HULLO, MRS. SNAKY.. AT IT AGAIN, EH? AINTCHA AFRAID OF GETTIN' FAT?
A PERSIN COULD STARVE T'DEATH ON THE SLOPS Y'R OL' LADY SOIVES!
Y'KNOW, DEARIE, YOU'RE A REAL GOOD-LOOKIN' KID.. I DON'T KNOW WHY YOU STAY COOPED UP IN THE KITCHEN ALL THE TIME..
SHE KEEPS ME HERE.. SHE BEATS ME.. SHE STARVES ME.. SHE WONT LET ME DO NUTHIN'... I'LL GROW UP TO BE A JUVENILE DELINKWINT!
DEARIE, IF SHE WAS MY OL' LADY, I'D...
SHE AINT ME OLD LADY! SHE'S ME WICKED STEP-MOTHER! DONTCH' KNOW NUTHIN'? DIN'TCH EVER READ CINDERELLA?
SHE'S SO MEAN T'ME I CAN'T EVEN GO TO THE POLICEMEN'S BALL BECAUSE I AINT GOT NO DRESS TO WEAR...
WHAT A DIRTY, CRYIN' SHAME.. NOW, NOW, DON'T CRY, DEARIE... I'LL GIT MR. SNAKY TO FIX IT SO'S YOU CAN GO TOO!
ALE
...HEY SNAKY... LET'S DO SOMETHIN' TO HELP POOR LITTLE CINDERELLA GO TO THE COPPERS' RATRACE...
WHADDYA MEAN, HELP HER.. SHE CAN HELP US.. DID IT EVER OCCUR TO YOUSE THAT THE POLICEMEN'S BALL IS HELD IN EAGLE HALL... WHICH IS RIGHT NEXT DOOR TO THE EAGLE NATIONAL BANK?
AND SO..
CHEE, MRS. SNAKY.. IT'S BEAUTIFUL.. YOUSE MUST BE ME FAIRY GODMOTHER!
YEAH, YEAH... NOW ALL Y'GOTTA DO IS A LITTLE FAVOR FOR US AND WE'LL FIX IT SO'S YOU CAN GO IN STYLE.. CHAUFFEUR.. LIMOUSINE...
4

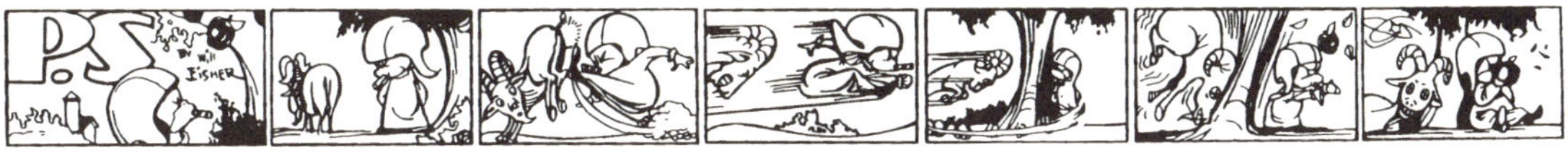
P.S.

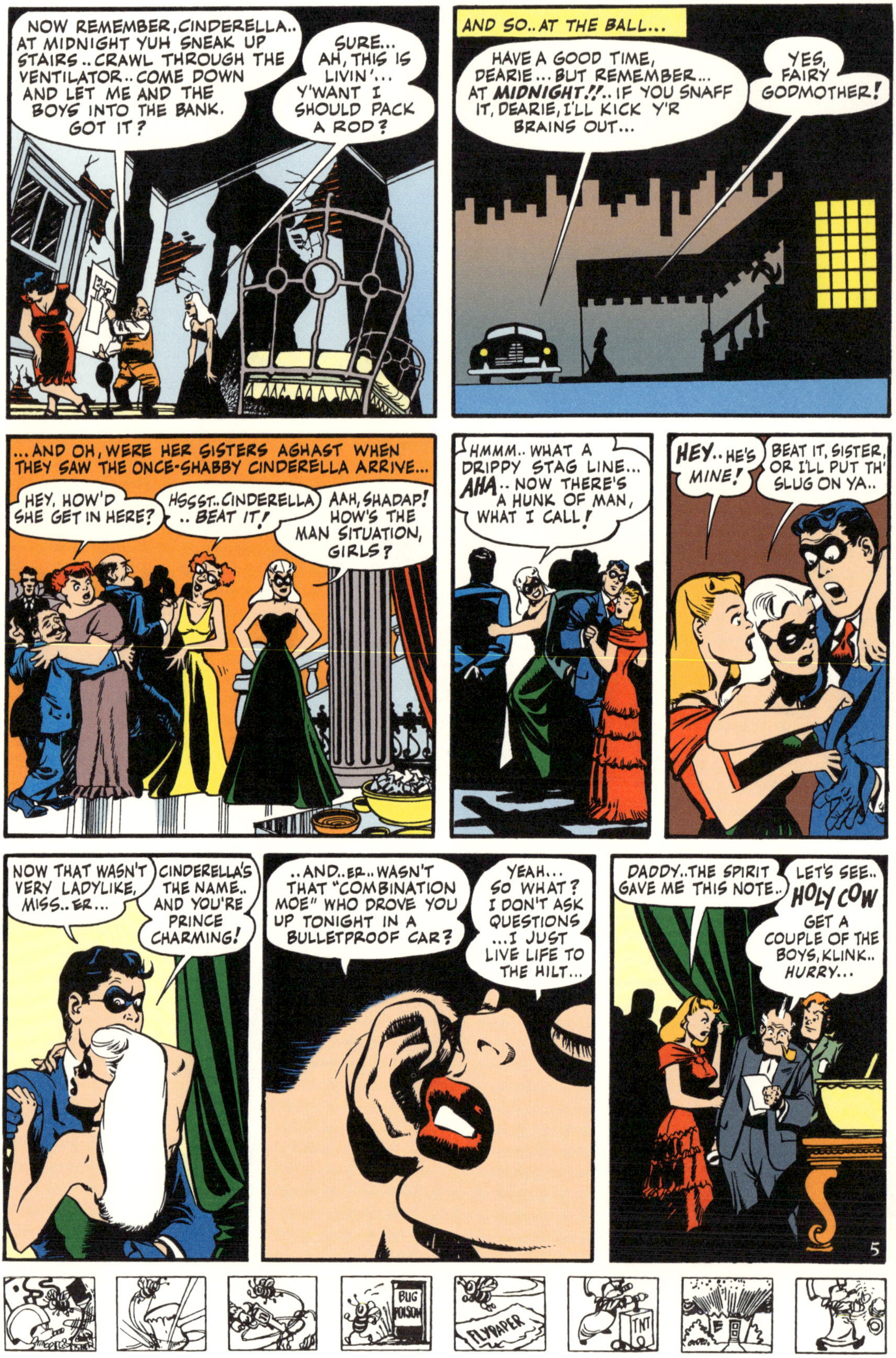
NOW REMEMBER, CINDERELLA.. AT MIDNIGHT YUH SNEAK UP STAIRS.. CRAWL THROUGH THE VENTILATOR.. COME DOWN AND LET ME AND THE BOYS INTO THE BANK. GOT IT?
SURE... AH, THIS IS LIVIN'... Y'WANT I SHOULD PACK A ROD?
AND SO.. AT THE BALL...
HAVE A GOOD TIME, DEARIE... BUT REMEMBER... AT MIDNIGHT!!.. IF YOU SNAFF IT, DEARIE, I'LL KICK Y'R BRAINS OUT...
YES, FAIRY GODMOTHER!
...AND OH, WERE HER SISTERS AGHAST WHEN THEY SAW THE ONCE-SHABBY CINDERELLA ARRIVE...
HEY, HOW'D SHE GET IN HERE?
HSSST.. CINDERELLA .. BEAT IT!
AAH, SHADAP! HOW'S THE MAN SITUATION, GIRLS?
HMMM.. WHAT A DRIPPY STAG LINE... AHA.. NOW THERE'S A HUNK OF MAN, WHAT I CALL!
HEY.. HE'S MINE!
BEAT IT, SISTER, OR I'LL PUT TH' SLUG ON YA..
NOW THAT WASN'T VERY LADYLIKE, MISS.. ER...
CINDERELLA'S THE NAME.. AND YOU'RE PRINCE CHARMING!
..AND.. ER.. WASN'T THAT "COMBINATION MOE" WHO DROVE YOU UP TONIGHT IN A BULLETPROOF CAR?
YEAH... SO WHAT? I DON'T ASK QUESTIONS ...I JUST LIVE LIFE TO THE HILT...
DADDY.. THE SPIRIT GAVE ME THIS NOTE..
LET'S SEE.. HOLY COW GET A COUPLE OF THE BOYS, KLINK.. HURRY...
5
BUG POISON
FLYPAPER
TNT

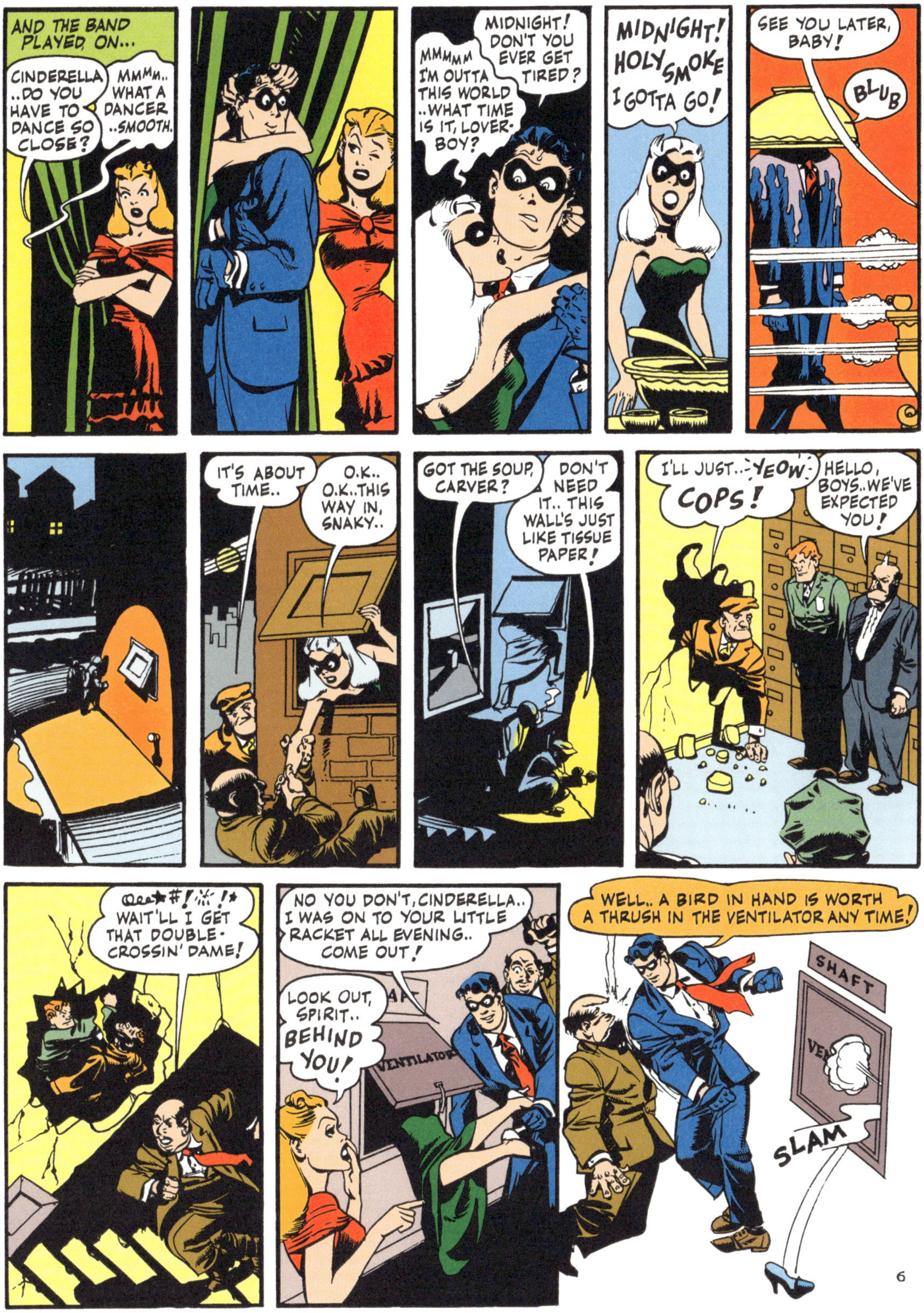
AND THE BAND PLAYED ON...
CINDERELLA ..DO YOU HAVE TO DANCE SO CLOSE?
MMMM.. WHAT A DANCER ..SMOOTH.
MIDNIGHT! DON'T YOU EVER GET TIRED?
MMMMM I'M OUTTA THIS WORLD ..WHAT TIME IS IT, LOVER-BOY?
MIDNIGHT! HOLY SMOKE I GOTTA GO!
SEE YOU LATER, BABY!
BLUB
IT'S ABOUT TIME..
O.K.. O.K..THIS WAY IN, SNAKY..
GOT THE SOUP, CARVER?
DON'T NEED IT.. THIS WALL'S JUST LIKE TISSUE PAPER!
I'LL JUST.. YEOW COPS!
HELLO, BOYS..WE'VE EXPECTED YOU!
WAIT'LL I GET THAT DOUBLE-CROSSIN' DAME!
NO YOU DON'T, CINDERELLA.. I WAS ON TO YOUR LITTLE RACKET ALL EVENING.. COME OUT!
LOOK OUT, SPIRIT.. BEHIND YOU!
VENTILATOR
WELL.. A BIRD IN HAND IS WORTH A THRUSH IN THE VENTILATOR ANY TIME!
SHAFT
SLAM
6

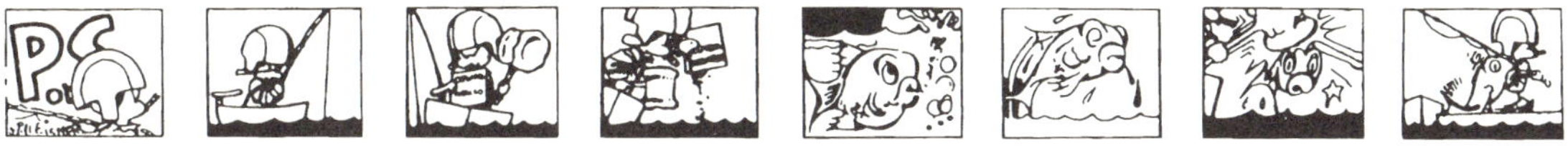

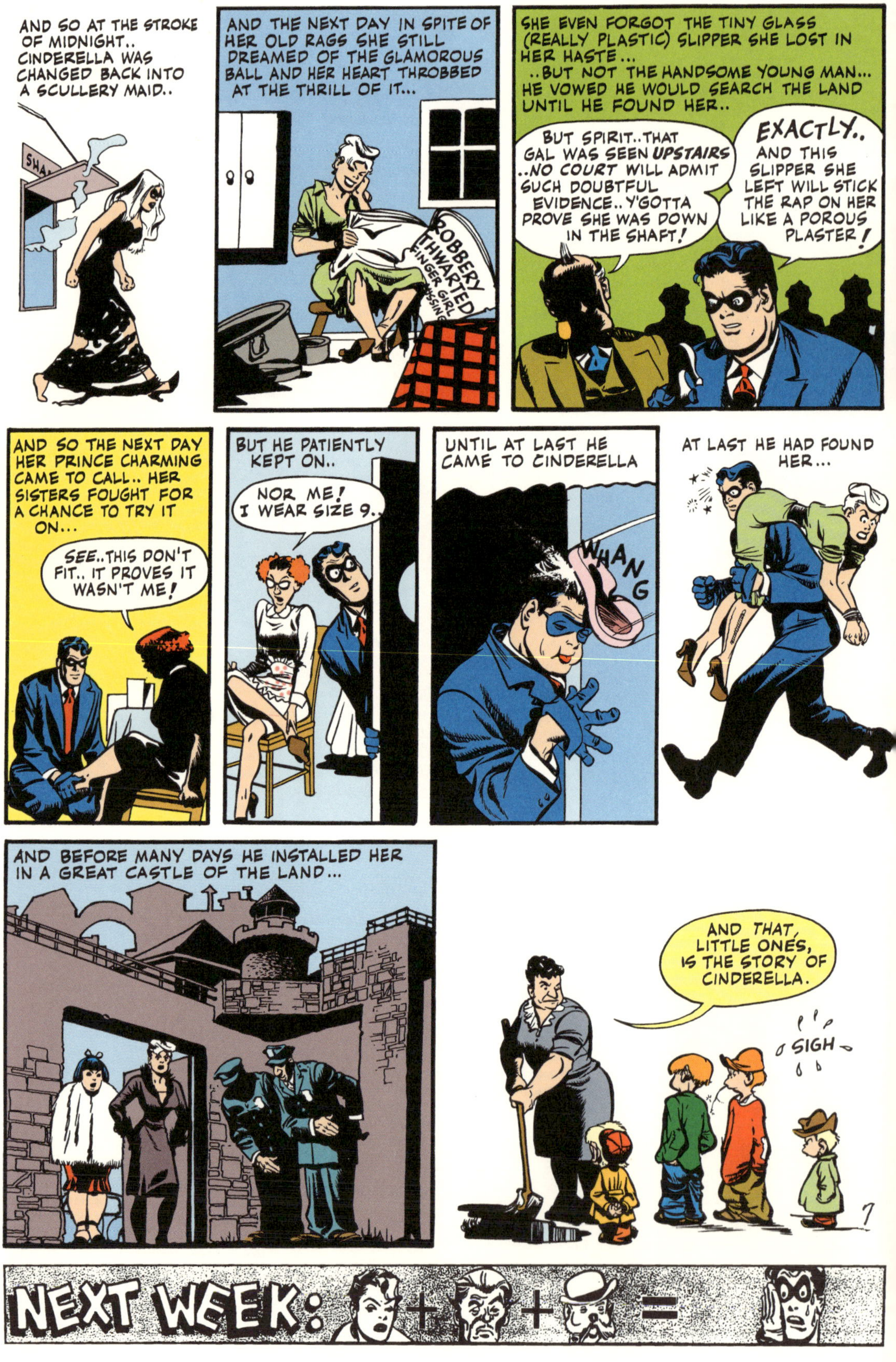
AND SO AT THE STROKE OF MIDNIGHT.. CINDERELLA WAS CHANGED BACK INTO A SCULLERY MAID..
AND THE NEXT DAY IN SPITE OF HER OLD RAGS SHE STILL DREAMED OF THE GLAMOROUS BALL AND HER HEART THROBBED AT THE THRILL OF IT...
ROBBERY THWARTED
SHE EVEN FORGOT THE TINY GLASS (REALLY PLASTIC) SLIPPER SHE LOST IN HER HASTE... ..BUT NOT THE HANDSOME YOUNG MAN... HE VOWED HE WOULD SEARCH THE LAND UNTIL HE FOUND HER..
BUT SPIRIT..THAT GAL WAS SEEN UPSTAIRS ..NO COURT WILL ADMIT SUCH DOUBTFUL EVIDENCE.. Y'GOTTA PROVE SHE WAS DOWN IN THE SHAFT!
EXACTLY.. AND THIS SLIPPER SHE LEFT WILL STICK THE RAP ON HER LIKE A POROUS PLASTER!
AND SO THE NEXT DAY HER PRINCE CHARMING CAME TO CALL.. HER SISTERS FOUGHT FOR A CHANCE TO TRY IT ON...
SEE..THIS DON'T FIT.. IT PROVES IT WASN'T ME!
BUT HE PATIENTLY KEPT ON..
NOR ME! I WEAR SIZE 9..
UNTIL AT LAST HE CAME TO CINDERELLA
WHANG
AT LAST HE HAD FOUND HER...
AND BEFORE MANY DAYS HE INSTALLED HER IN A GREAT CASTLE OF THE LAND...
AND THAT, LITTLE ONES, IS THE STORY OF CINDERELLA.
SIGH
NEXT WEEK: + + =

COMIC BOOK SECTION

ACTION Mystery ADVENTURE

MR. McDOOL

October 12 1947

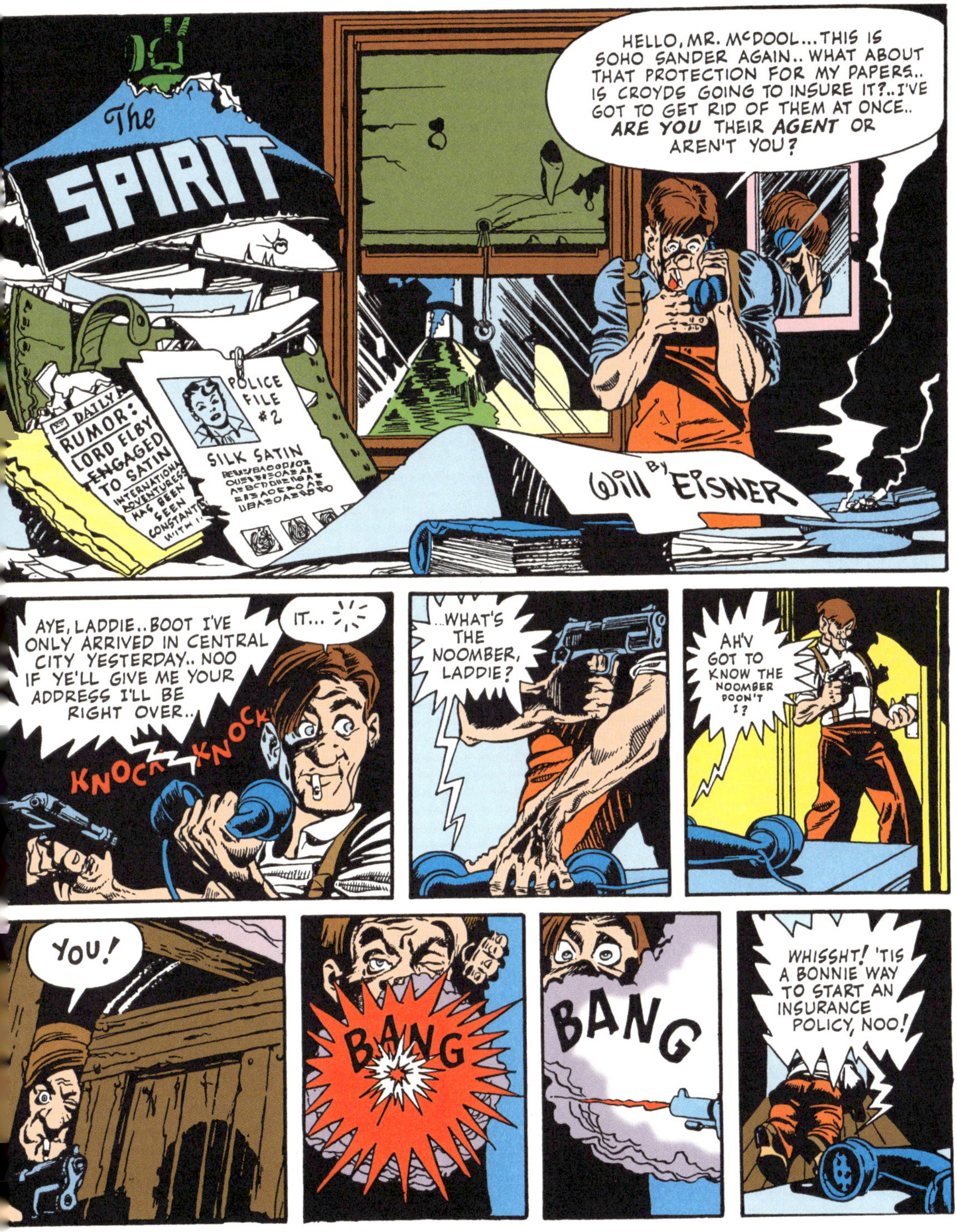

The SPIRIT
HELLO, MR. McDOOL... THIS IS SOHO SANDER AGAIN.. WHAT ABOUT THAT PROTECTION FOR MY PAPERS.. IS CROYDS GOING TO INSURE IT?.. I'VE GOT TO GET RID OF THEM AT ONCE.. ARE YOU THEIR AGENT OR AREN'T YOU?
DAILY
RUMOR: LORD ELBY ENGAGED TO SATIN
INTERNATIONAL ADVENTURESS HAS BEEN SEEN CONSTANTLY WITH
POLICE FILE #2
SILK SATIN
By Will EISNER
AYE, LADDIE.. BOOT I'VE ONLY ARRIVED IN CENTRAL CITY YESTERDAY.. NOO IF YE'LL GIVE ME YOUR ADDRESS I'LL BE RIGHT OVER..
IT...
KNOCK KNOCK
..WHAT'S THE NOOMBER, LADDIE?
AH'V GOT TO KNOW THE NOOMBER DOON'T I?
YOU!
BANG
BANG
WHISSHT! 'TIS A BONNIE WAY TO START AN INSURANCE POLICY, NOO!

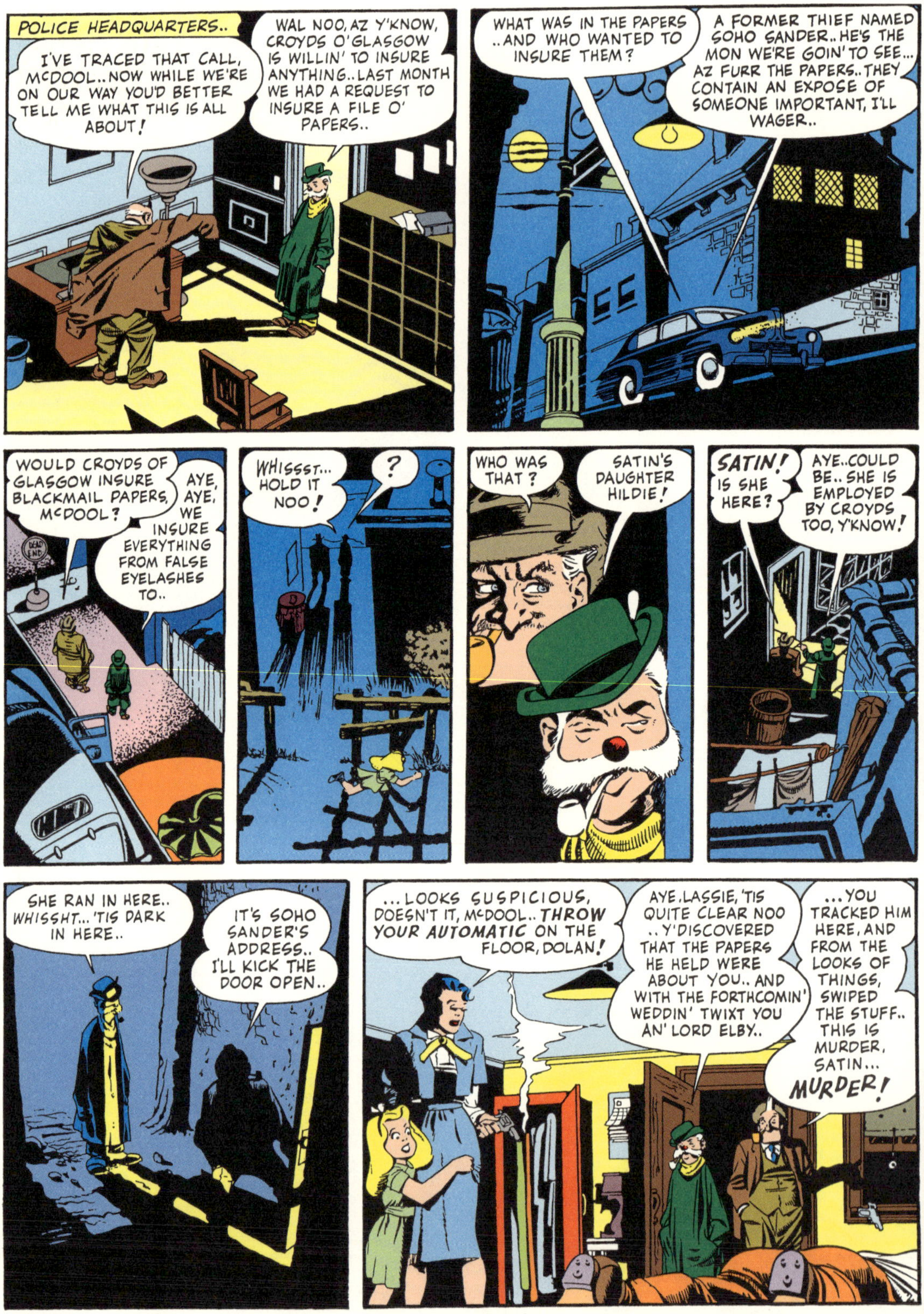
POLICE HEADQUARTERS..
I'VE TRACED THAT CALL, McDOOL..NOW WHILE WE'RE ON OUR WAY YOU'D BETTER TELL ME WHAT THIS IS ALL ABOUT!
WAL NOO, AZ Y'KNOW, CROYDS O'GLASGOW IS WILLIN' TO INSURE ANYTHING..LAST MONTH WE HAD A REQUEST TO INSURE A FILE O' PAPERS..
WHAT WAS IN THE PAPERS ..AND WHO WANTED TO INSURE THEM?
A FORMER THIEF NAMED SOHO SANDER..HE'S THE MON WE'RE GOIN' TO SEE... AZ FURR THE PAPERS..THEY CONTAIN AN EXPOSE OF SOMEONE IMPORTANT, I'LL WAGER..
WOULD CROYDS OF GLASGOW INSURE BLACKMAIL PAPERS, McDOOL?
AYE, AYE, WE INSURE EVERYTHING FROM FALSE EYELASHES TO..
DEAD END
WHISSST... HOLD IT NOO!
?
WHO WAS THAT?
SATIN'S DAUGHTER HILDIE!
SATIN! IS SHE HERE?
AYE..COULD BE..SHE IS EMPLOYED BY CROYDS TOO, Y'KNOW!
SHE RAN IN HERE.. WHISSHT...'TIS DARK IN HERE..
IT'S SOHO SANDER'S ADDRESS.. I'LL KICK THE DOOR OPEN..
...LOOKS SUSPICIOUS, DOESN'T IT, McDOOL..THROW YOUR AUTOMATIC ON THE FLOOR, DOLAN!
AYE.LASSIE, 'TIS QUITE CLEAR NOO ..Y'DISCOVERED THAT THE PAPERS HE HELD WERE ABOUT YOU..AND WITH THE FORTHCOMIN' WEDDIN' TWIXT YOU AN' LORD ELBY..
...YOU TRACKED HIM HERE, AND FROM THE LOOKS OF THINGS, SWIPED THE STUFF.. THIS IS MURDER, SATIN... MURDER!

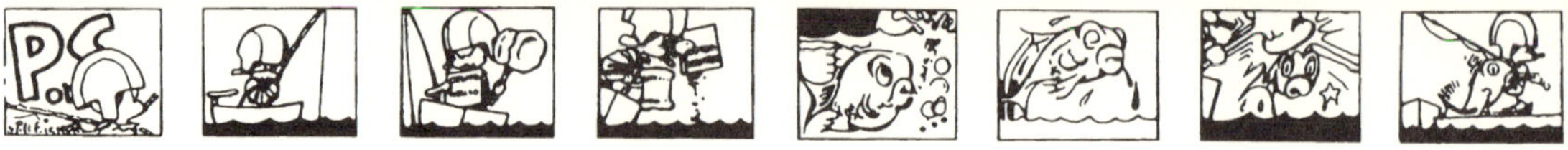

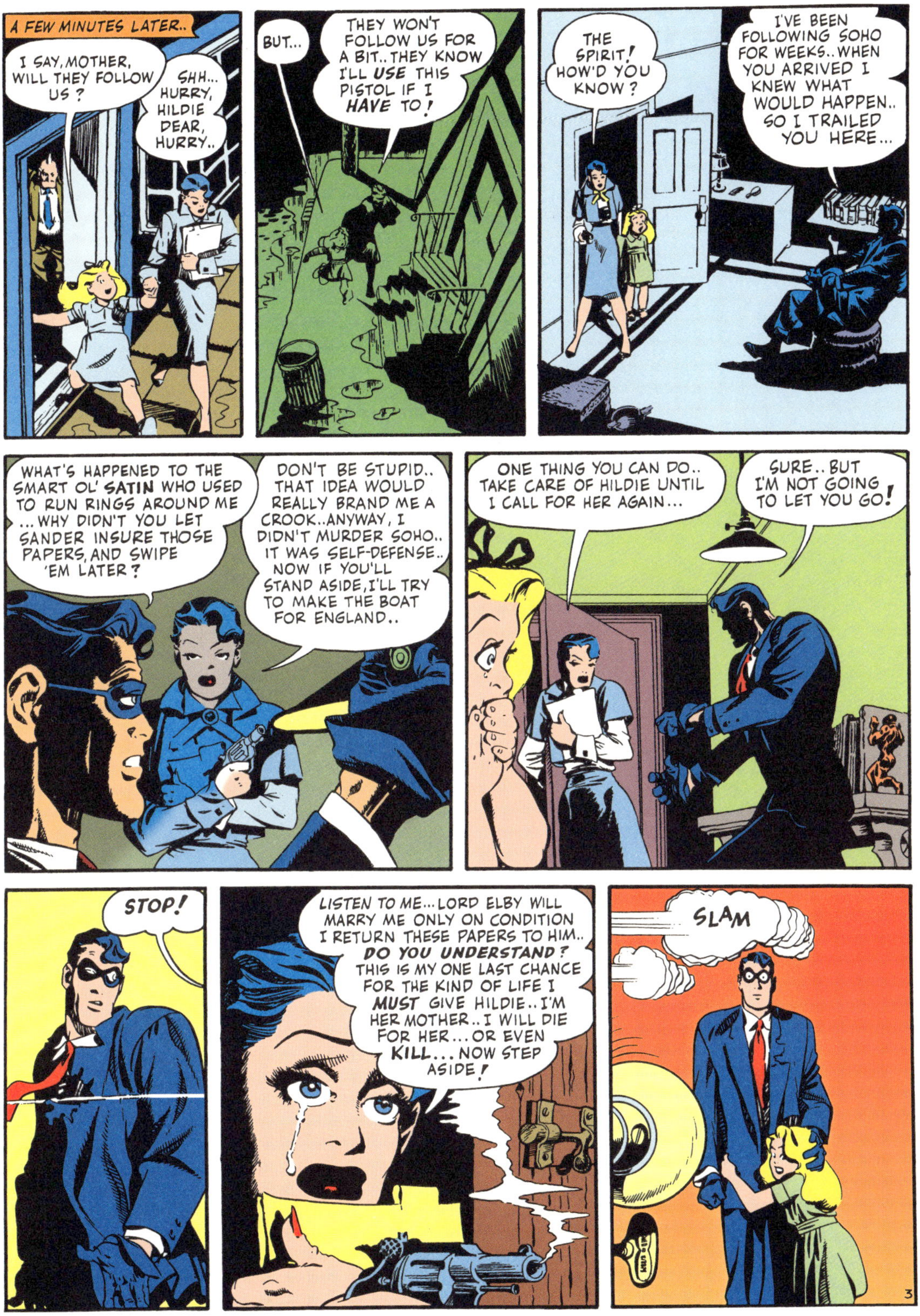
A FEW MINUTES LATER..
I SAY, MOTHER, WILL THEY FOLLOW US ?
SHH... HURRY, HILDIE DEAR, HURRY..
BUT...
THEY WON'T FOLLOW US FOR A BIT.. THEY KNOW I'LL USE THIS PISTOL IF I HAVE TO!
THE SPIRIT! HOW'D YOU KNOW ?
I'VE BEEN FOLLOWING SOHO FOR WEEKS.. WHEN YOU ARRIVED I KNEW WHAT WOULD HAPPEN.. SO I TRAILED YOU HERE...
WHAT'S HAPPENED TO THE SMART OL' SATIN WHO USED TO RUN RINGS AROUND ME ... WHY DIDN'T YOU LET SANDER INSURE THOSE PAPERS, AND SWIPE 'EM LATER ?
DON'T BE STUPID.. THAT IDEA WOULD REALLY BRAND ME A CROOK.. ANYWAY, I DIDN'T MURDER SOHO.. IT WAS SELF-DEFENSE.. NOW IF YOU'LL STAND ASIDE, I'LL TRY TO MAKE THE BOAT FOR ENGLAND..
ONE THING YOU CAN DO.. TAKE CARE OF HILDIE UNTIL I CALL FOR HER AGAIN...
SURE.. BUT I'M NOT GOING TO LET YOU GO!
STOP!
LISTEN TO ME... LORD ELBY WILL MARRY ME ONLY ON CONDITION I RETURN THESE PAPERS TO HIM.. DO YOU UNDERSTAND ? THIS IS MY ONE LAST CHANCE FOR THE KIND OF LIFE I MUST GIVE HILDIE.. I'M HER MOTHER.. I WILL DIE FOR HER... OR EVEN KILL... NOW STEP ASIDE!
SLAM
3

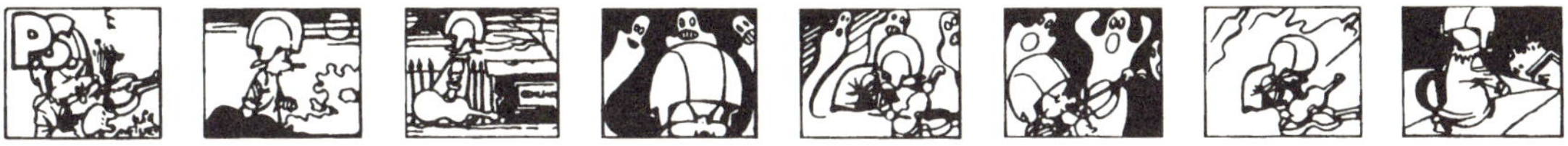

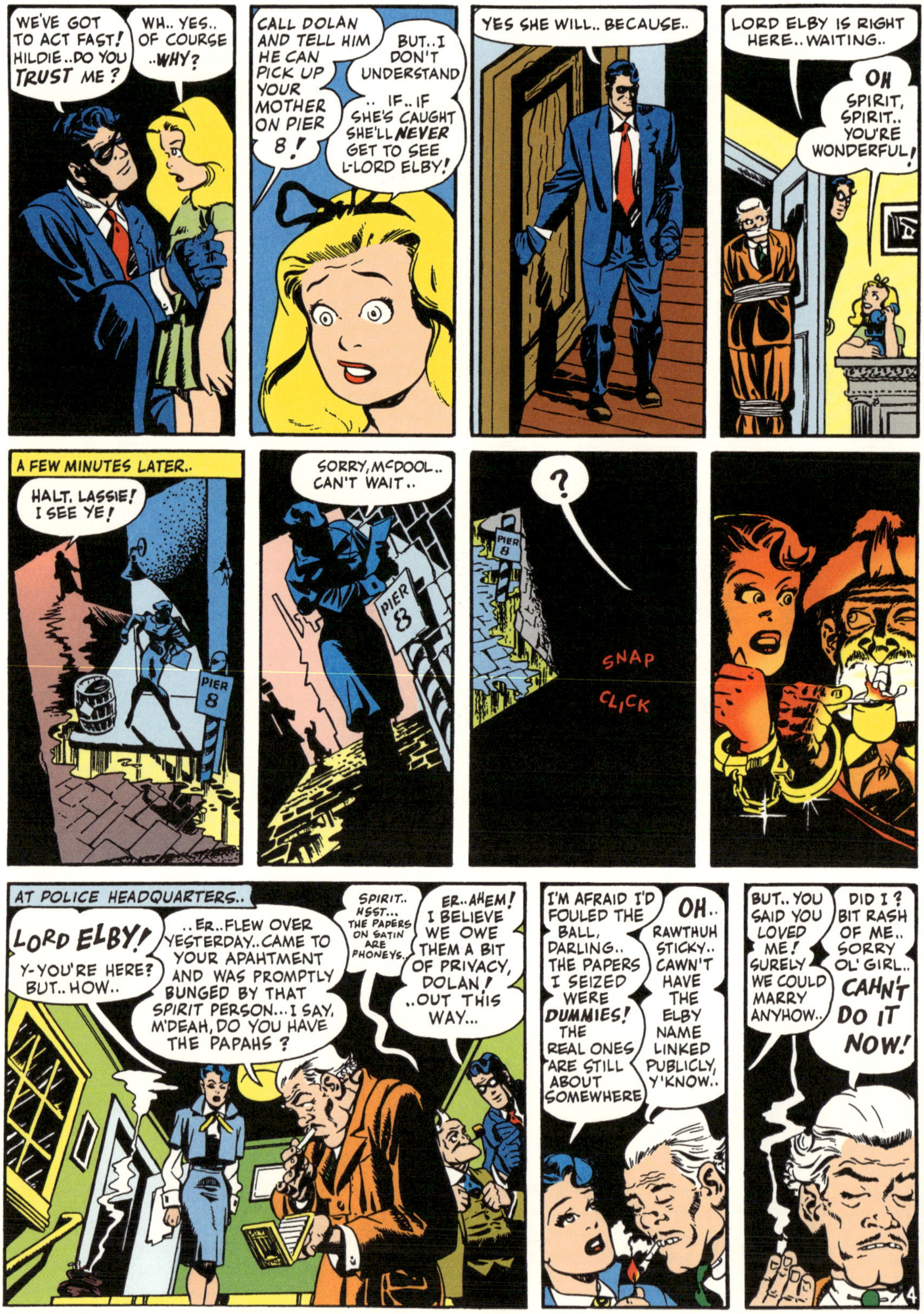
WE'VE GOT TO ACT FAST! HILDIE..DO YOU TRUST ME?
WH.. YES.. OF COURSE ..WHY?
CALL DOLAN AND TELL HIM HE CAN PICK UP YOUR MOTHER ON PIER 8!
BUT..I DON'T UNDERSTAND
.. IF.. IF SHE'S CAUGHT SHE'LL NEVER GET TO SEE L-LORD ELBY!
YES SHE WILL.. BECAUSE..
LORD ELBY IS RIGHT HERE.. WAITING..
OH SPIRIT, SPIRIT.. YOU'RE WONDERFUL!
A FEW MINUTES LATER..
HALT, LASSIE! I SEE YE!
PIER 8
SORRY, McDOOL.. CAN'T WAIT..
PIER 8
?
PIER 8
SNAP
CLICK
AT POLICE HEADQUARTERS..
LORD ELBY! Y-YOU'RE HERE? BUT.. HOW..
..ER..FLEW OVER YESTERDAY..CAME TO YOUR APAHTMENT AND WAS PROMPTLY BUNGED BY THAT SPIRIT PERSON...I SAY, M'DEAH, DO YOU HAVE THE PAPAHS?
SPIRIT.. HSST... THE PAPERS ON SATIN ARE PHONEYS..
ER..AHEM! I BELIEVE WE OWE THEM A BIT OF PRIVACY, DOLAN! ..OUT THIS WAY...
I'M AFRAID I'D FOULED THE BALL, DARLING.. THE PAPERS I SEIZED WERE DUMMIES! THE REAL ONES ARE STILL ABOUT SOMEWHERE
OH.. RAWTHUH STICKY.. CAWN'T HAVE THE ELBY NAME LINKED PUBLICLY, Y'KNOW..
BUT.. YOU SAID YOU LOVED ME! SURELY WE COULD MARRY ANYHOW..
DID I? BIT RASH OF ME.. SORRY OL' GIRL.. CAHN'T DO IT NOW!
4

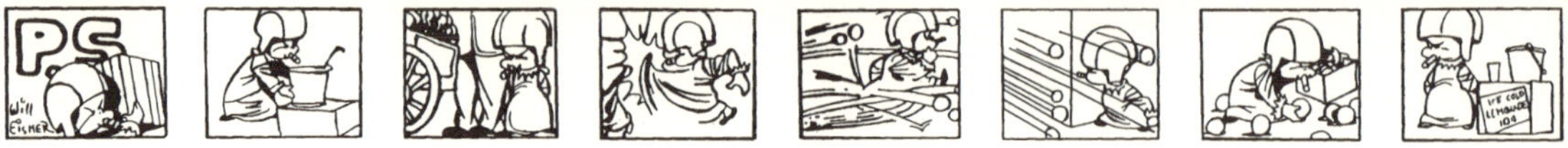
PS
WILL EISNER

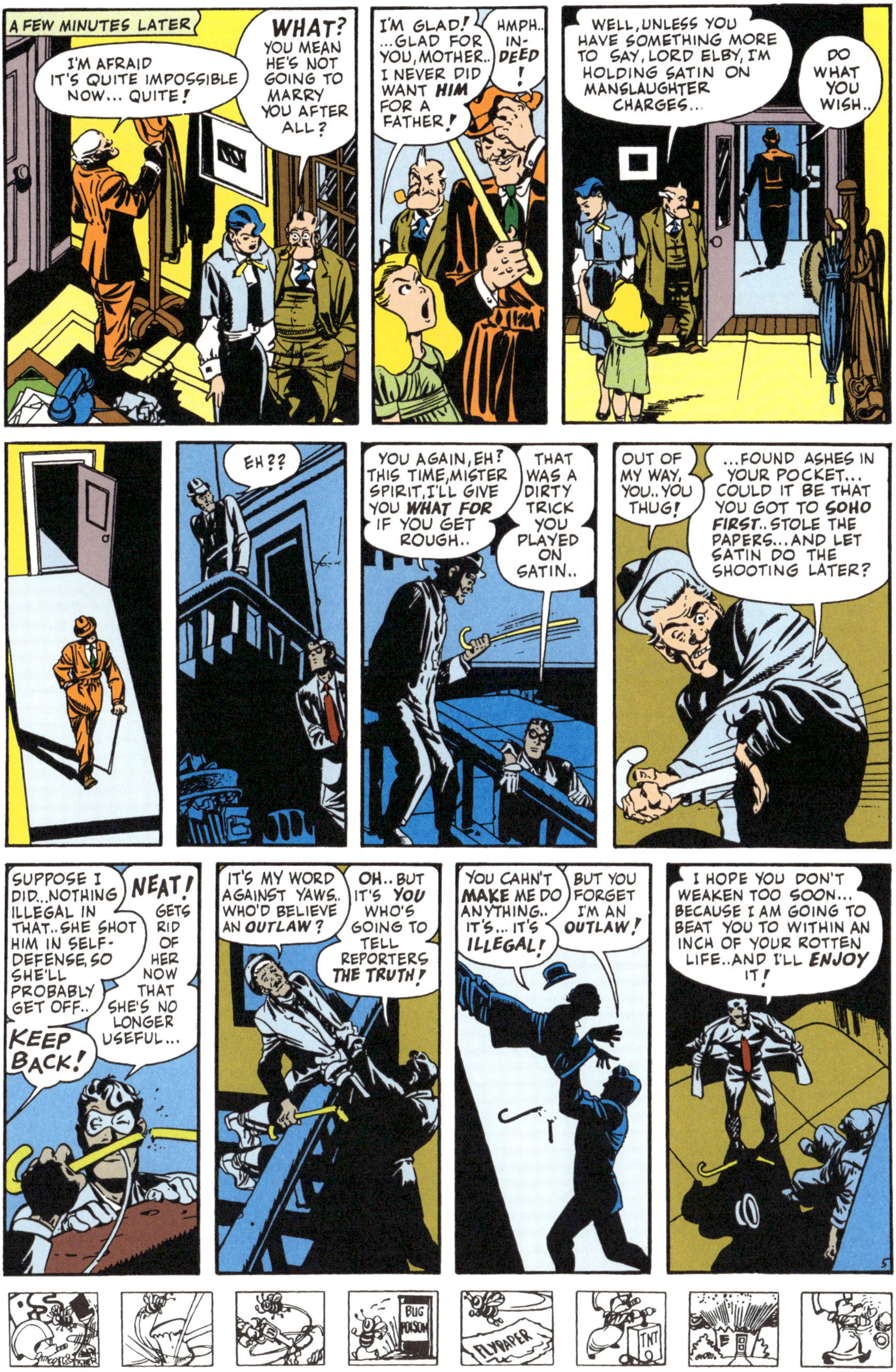

A FEW MINUTES LATER
I'M AFRAID IT'S QUITE IMPOSSIBLE NOW... QUITE!
WHAT? YOU MEAN HE'S NOT GOING TO MARRY YOU AFTER ALL?
I'M GLAD! ...GLAD FOR YOU, MOTHER.. I NEVER DID WANT HIM FOR A FATHER!
HMPH.. IN-DEED!
WELL, UNLESS YOU HAVE SOMETHING MORE TO SAY, LORD ELBY, I'M HOLDING SATIN ON MANSLAUGHTER CHARGES...
DO WHAT YOU WISH..
EH??
YOU AGAIN, EH? THIS TIME, MISTER SPIRIT, I'LL GIVE YOU WHAT FOR IF YOU GET ROUGH..
THAT WAS A DIRTY TRICK YOU PLAYED ON SATIN..
OUT OF MY WAY, YOU.. YOU THUG!
...FOUND ASHES IN YOUR POCKET... COULD IT BE THAT YOU GOT TO SOHO FIRST.. STOLE THE PAPERS... AND LET SATIN DO THE SHOOTING LATER?
SUPPOSE I DID... NOTHING ILLEGAL IN THAT.. SHE SHOT HIM IN SELF-DEFENSE, SO SHE'LL PROBABLY GET OFF..
NEAT! GETS RID OF HER NOW THAT SHE'S NO LONGER USEFUL...
KEEP BACK!
IT'S MY WORD AGAINST YAWS.. WHO'D BELIEVE AN OUTLAW?
OH.. BUT IT'S YOU WHO'S GOING TO TELL REPORTERS THE TRUTH!
YOU CAHN'T MAKE ME DO ANYTHING.. IT'S... IT'S ILLEGAL!
BUT YOU FORGET I'M AN OUTLAW!
I HOPE YOU DON'T WEAKEN TOO SOON... BECAUSE I AM GOING TO BEAT YOU TO WITHIN AN INCH OF YOUR ROTTEN LIFE.. AND I'LL ENJOY IT!
5
BUG POISON
FLYPAPER
TNT

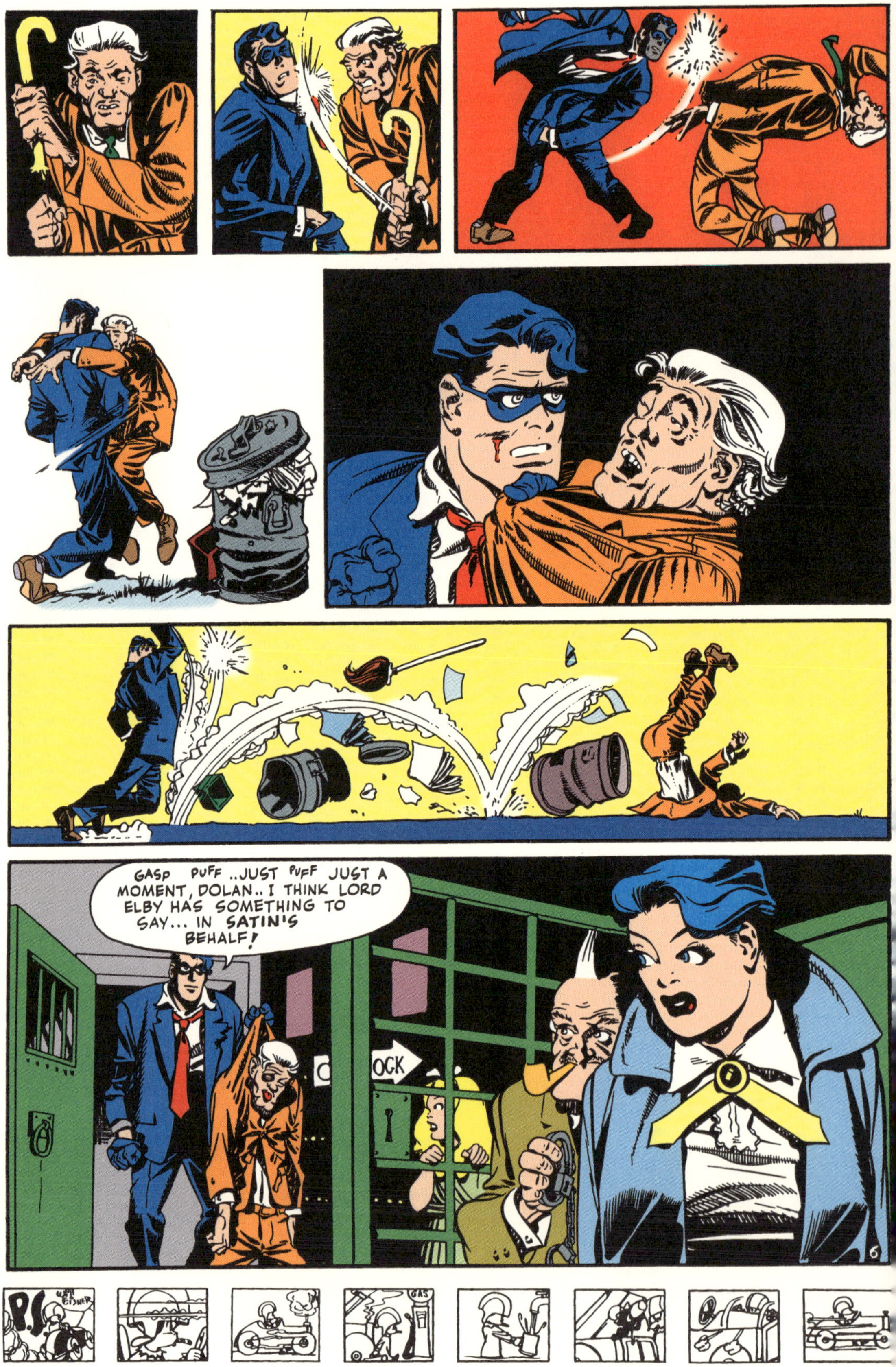
GASP PUFF ..JUST PUFF JUST A MOMENT, DOLAN.. I THINK LORD ELBY HAS SOMETHING TO SAY... IN SATIN'S BEHALF!
OCK
6
P.S.
WILL EISNER
GAS

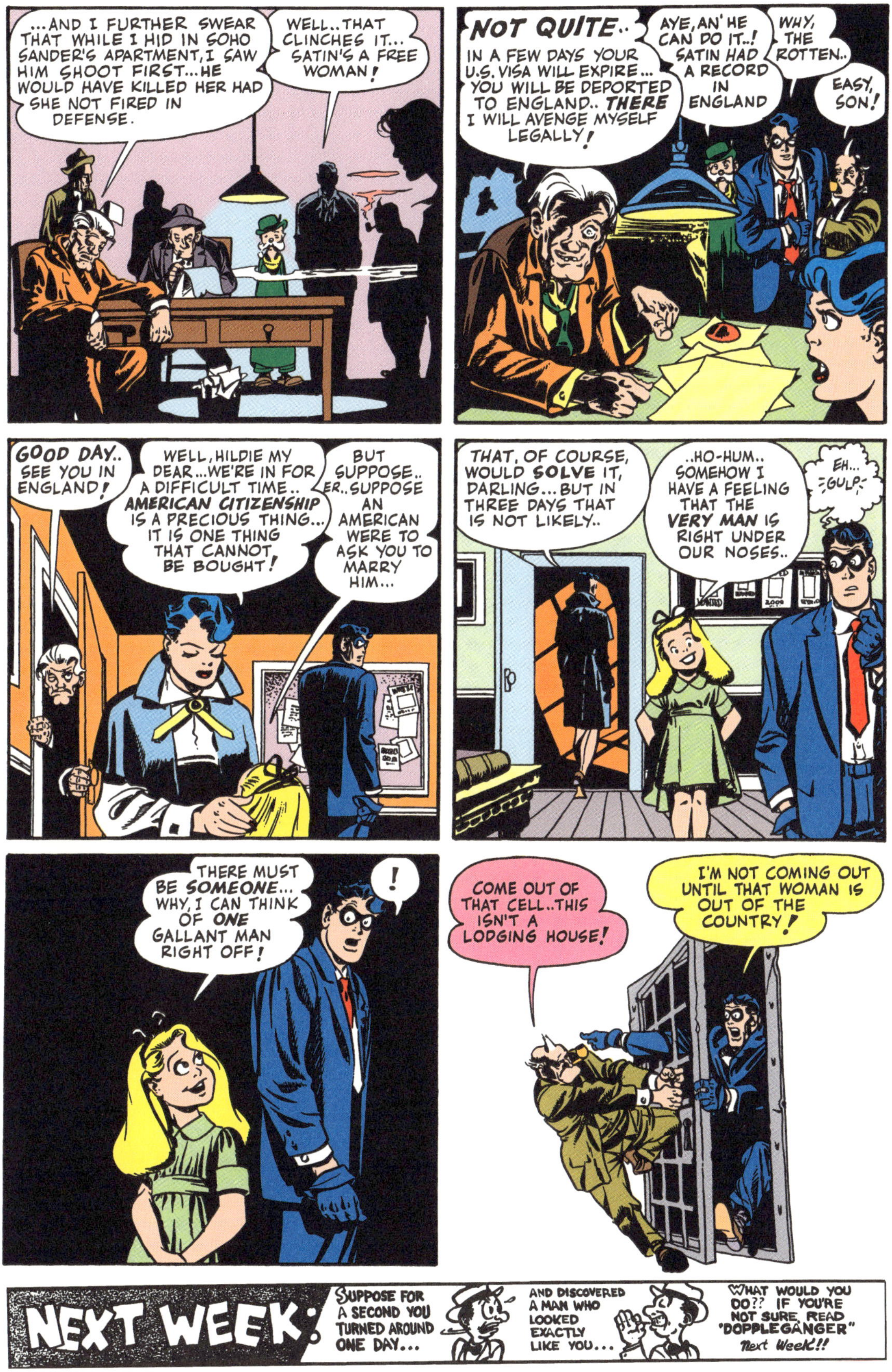
...AND I FURTHER SWEAR THAT WHILE I HID IN SOHO SANDER'S APARTMENT, I SAW HIM SHOOT FIRST...HE WOULD HAVE KILLED HER HAD SHE NOT FIRED IN DEFENSE.
WELL..THAT CLINCHES IT... SATIN'S A FREE WOMAN!
NOT QUITE.. IN A FEW DAYS YOUR U.S. VISA WILL EXPIRE... YOU WILL BE DEPORTED TO ENGLAND.. THERE I WILL AVENGE MYSELF LEGALLY!
AYE, AN' HE CAN DO IT..! SATIN HAD A RECORD IN ENGLAND
WHY, THE ROTTEN..
EASY, SON!
GOOD DAY.. SEE YOU IN ENGLAND!
WELL, HILDIE MY DEAR...WE'RE IN FOR A DIFFICULT TIME.. AMERICAN CITIZENSHIP IS A PRECIOUS THING... IT IS ONE THING THAT CANNOT BE BOUGHT!
BUT SUPPOSE.. ER..SUPPOSE AN AMERICAN WERE TO ASK YOU TO MARRY HIM...
THAT, OF COURSE, WOULD SOLVE IT, DARLING...BUT IN THREE DAYS THAT IS NOT LIKELY..
..HO-HUM.. SOMEHOW I HAVE A FEELING THAT THE VERY MAN IS RIGHT UNDER OUR NOSES..
EH... GULP
THERE MUST BE SOMEONE... WHY, I CAN THINK OF ONE GALLANT MAN RIGHT OFF!
!
COME OUT OF THAT CELL..THIS ISN'T A LODGING HOUSE!
I'M NOT COMING OUT UNTIL THAT WOMAN IS OUT OF THE COUNTRY!
NEXT WEEK:
SUPPOSE FOR A SECOND YOU TURNED AROUND ONE DAY...
AND DISCOVERED A MAN WHO LOOKED EXACTLY LIKE YOU...
WHAT WOULD YOU DO?? IF YOU'RE NOT SURE, READ "DOPPLEGANGER" Next Week!!

COMIC BOOK SECTION

DOPPELGANGER

October 19 1947

ACTION Mystery ADVENTURE

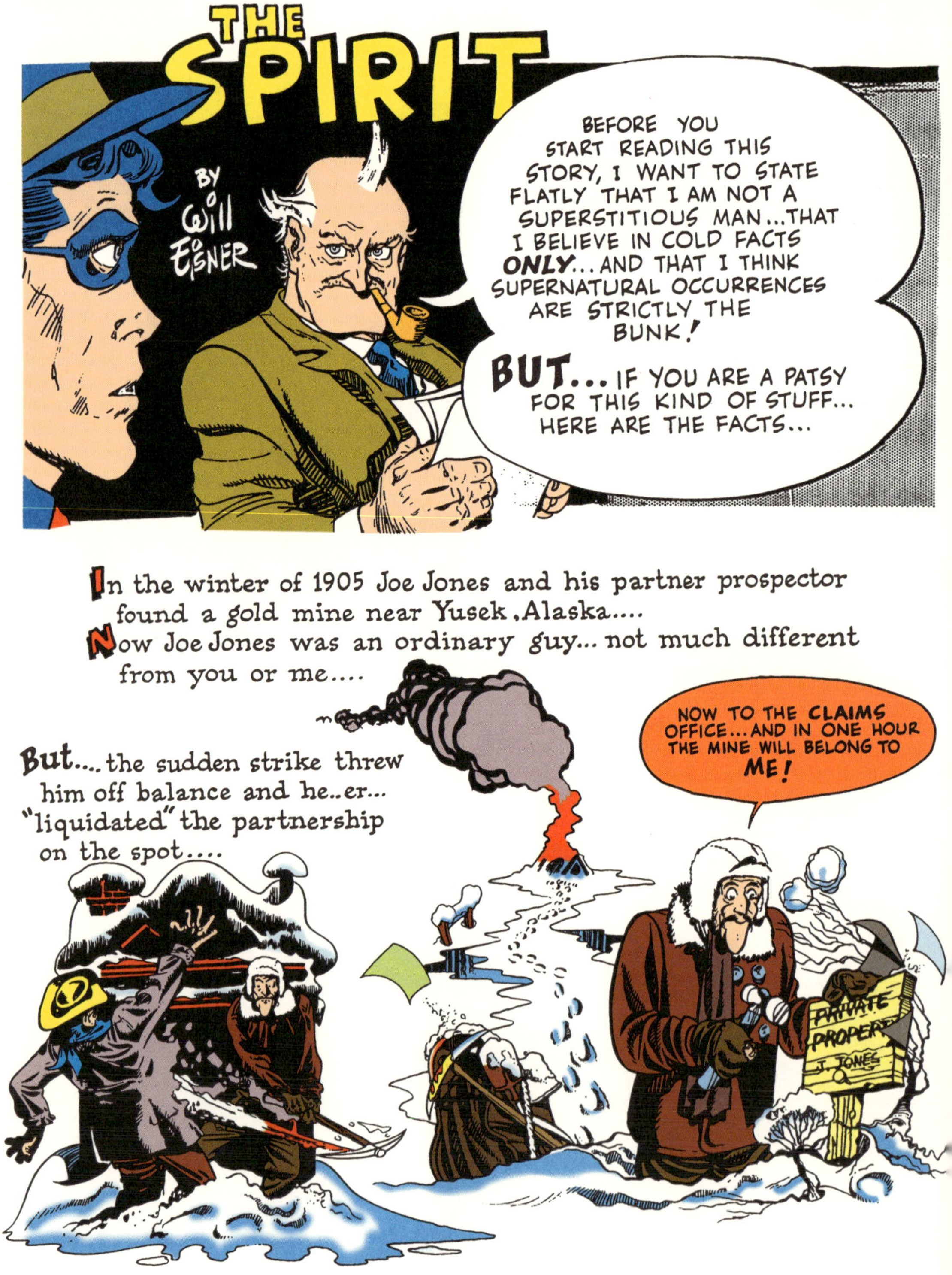
THE SPIRIT
BY Will Eisner
BEFORE YOU START READING THIS STORY, I WANT TO STATE FLATLY THAT I AM NOT A SUPERSTITIOUS MAN...THAT I BELIEVE IN COLD FACTS ONLY...AND THAT I THINK SUPERNATURAL OCCURRENCES ARE STRICTLY THE BUNK!
BUT...IF YOU ARE A PATSY FOR THIS KIND OF STUFF... HERE ARE THE FACTS...
In the winter of 1905 Joe Jones and his partner prospector found a gold mine near Yusek, Alaska....
Now Joe Jones was an ordinary guy... not much different from you or me....
But.... the sudden strike threw him off balance and he..er... "liquidated" the partnership on the spot....
NOW TO THE CLAIMS OFFICE...AND IN ONE HOUR THE MINE WILL BELONG TO ME!
PRIVATE PROPERTY
J. JONES

UNITED STATES CLAIMS OFFICE
Yes, Joe Jones got there, all right...
But watch what happens ..carefully....
HURRY UP WITH THOSE PAPERS... I'M GOING OUT ON A SPREE!
O.K. O.K...
SIGN HERE... IT'S AN AFFIDAVIT OF SOLE DISCOVERY..
SURE.. YIKE
YOU ARE THE VERY DUPLICATE OF ME! LOOK...
SO WHAT.. ER.. HAPPENS EVERY DAY IN THE WEEK.. HERE'S YOUR RECEIPT FOR THE CLAIM!
YOUR NAME...EXACTLY LIKE MINE!!
WHAT'S SO EXCLUSIVE ABOUT "JOE JONES".. ? YAWWWN... SEE YA'AROUN' SOMETIME..
RECEIPT
LAND CLAIM NO. 1235
DEEDED TO Joe Jones
RECORDED BY Joe Jones
Remember that, please!
Read it again... burn it into your memory...
it is important!! because from here on in things move awfully fast...
AWFULLY FAST!
By 1920 Joe Jones the miner had used the revenue to purchase a joint...but things went bad and he began to fix the wheels...
AND NOW, YOU RAT, WHILE MY BOYS BREAK UP Y'R JOINT I'M GONNA TEACH YOU A PERMANENT LESSON...
NO, NO.. HELP.. HELP!
HOLD IT, AJAX!
WHAT.. AHK
?
YOU!? TH..THE CLAIMS AGENT...
JOE JONES IS THE NAME.. SAME'S YOURS.. ANY TIME YOU'RE IN TROUBLE AGAIN I'LL BE GLAD TO HELP!
WAIT! WHY DID YOU HELP ME..?? HEY... OH.. HE'S GONE..

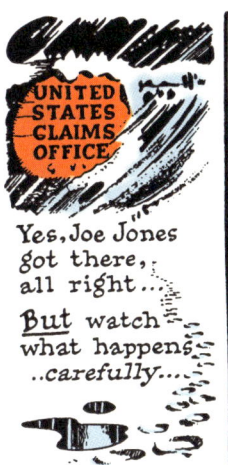

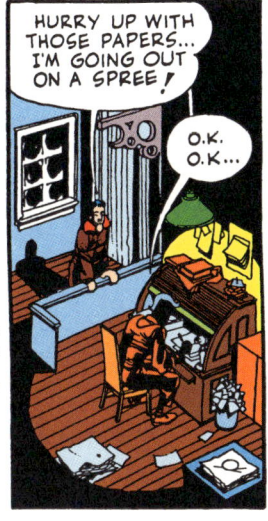

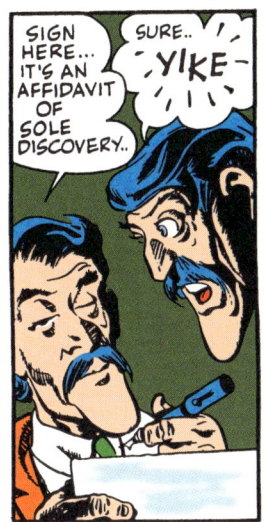

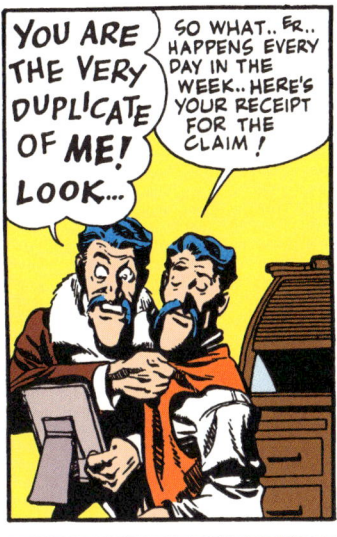

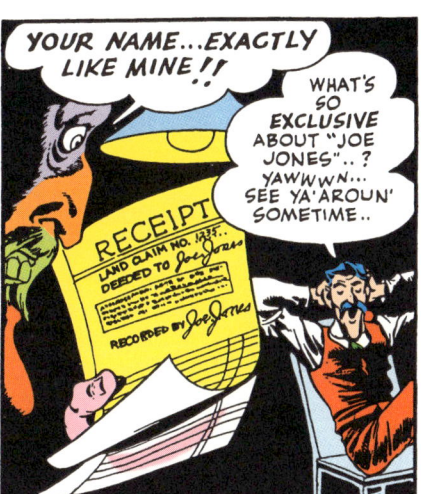

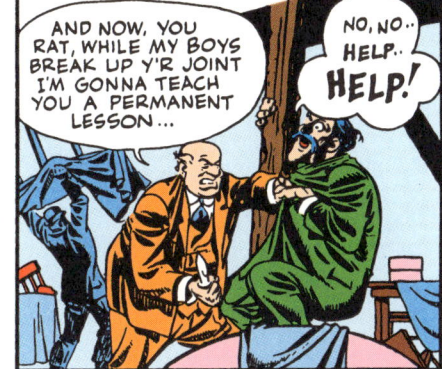

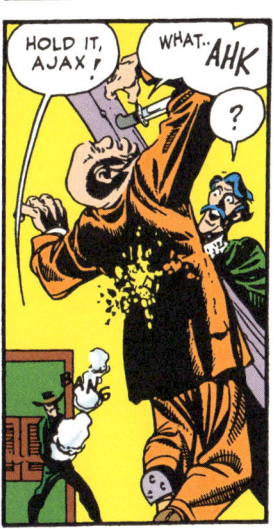

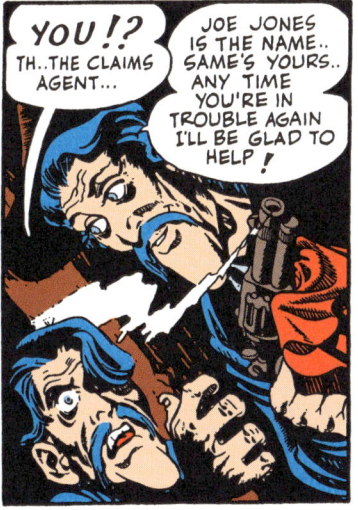

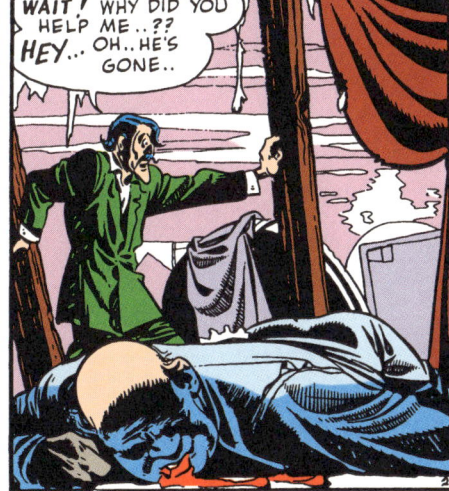

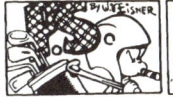

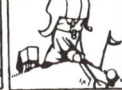

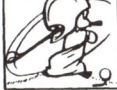

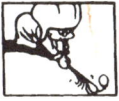

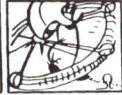

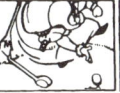

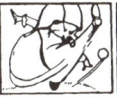

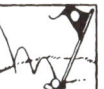

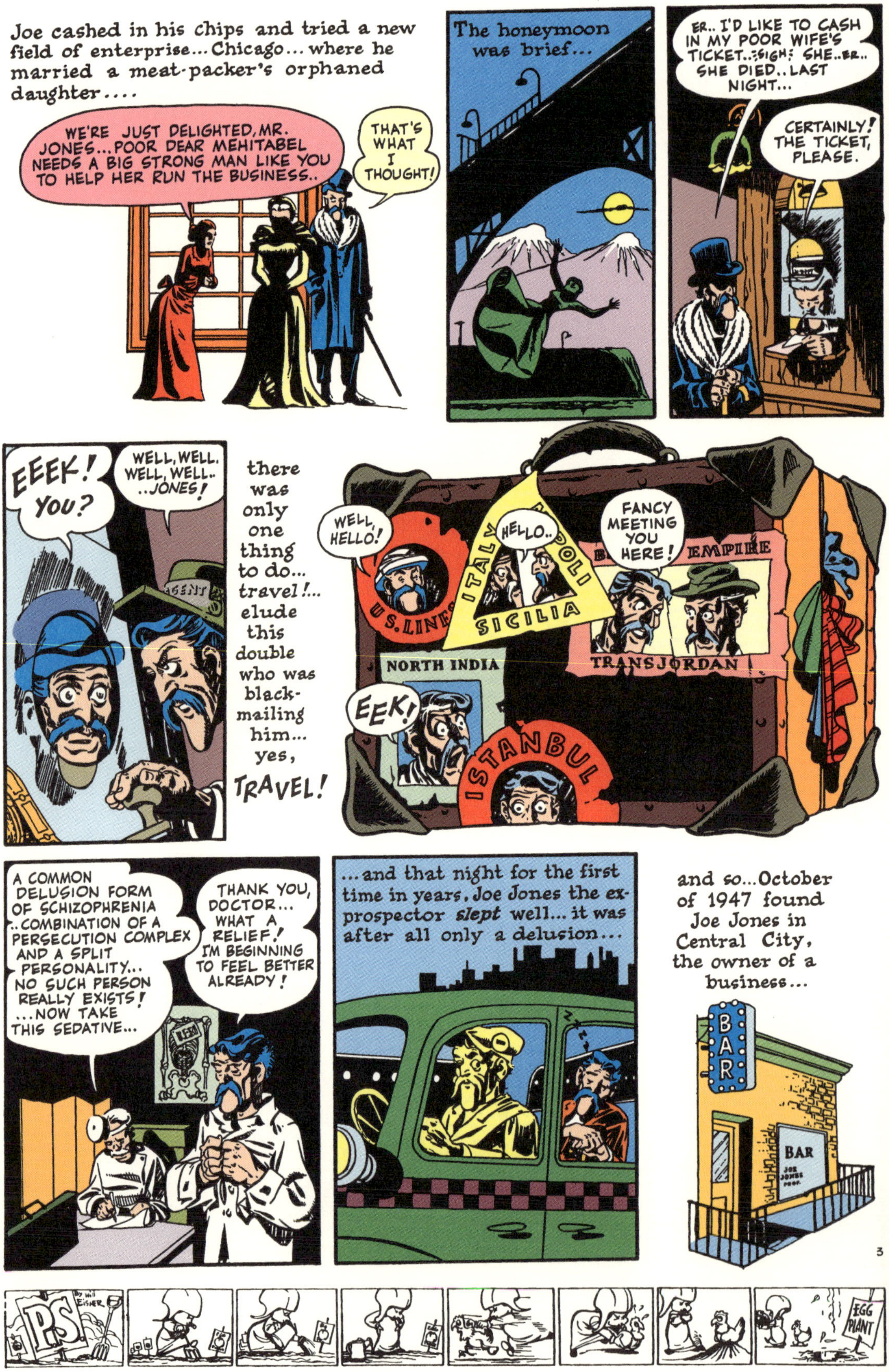
Joe cashed in his chips and tried a new field of enterprise... Chicago... where he married a meat-packer's orphaned daughter....
WE'RE JUST DELIGHTED, MR. JONES... POOR DEAR MEHITABEL NEEDS A BIG STRONG MAN LIKE YOU TO HELP HER RUN THE BUSINESS..
THAT'S WHAT I THOUGHT!
The honeymoon was brief...
ER.. I'D LIKE TO CASH IN MY POOR WIFE'S TICKET..SIGH. SHE..ER.. SHE DIED..LAST NIGHT...
CERTAINLY! THE TICKET, PLEASE.
EEEK! YOU?
WELL, WELL. WELL, WELL.. ..JONES!
AGENT
there was only one thing to do... travel!... elude this double who was black-mailing him... yes, TRAVEL!
WELL, HELLO!
U.S. LINES
ITALY
SICILIA
HELLO..
FANCY MEETING YOU HERE!
EMPIRE
TRANSJORDAN
NORTH INDIA
EEK!
ISTANBUL
A COMMON DELUSION FORM OF SCHIZOPHRENIA ..COMBINATION OF A PERSECUTION COMPLEX AND A SPLIT PERSONALITY... NO SUCH PERSON REALLY EXISTS! ...NOW TAKE THIS SEDATIVE...
THANK YOU, DOCTOR... WHAT A RELIEF! I'M BEGINNING TO FEEL BETTER ALREADY!
...and that night for the first time in years, Joe Jones the ex-prospector slept well... it was after all only a delusion...
and so... October of 1947 found Joe Jones in Central City, the owner of a business...
BAR
BAR
JOE JONES PROP.
3
P.S.
EGG PLANT

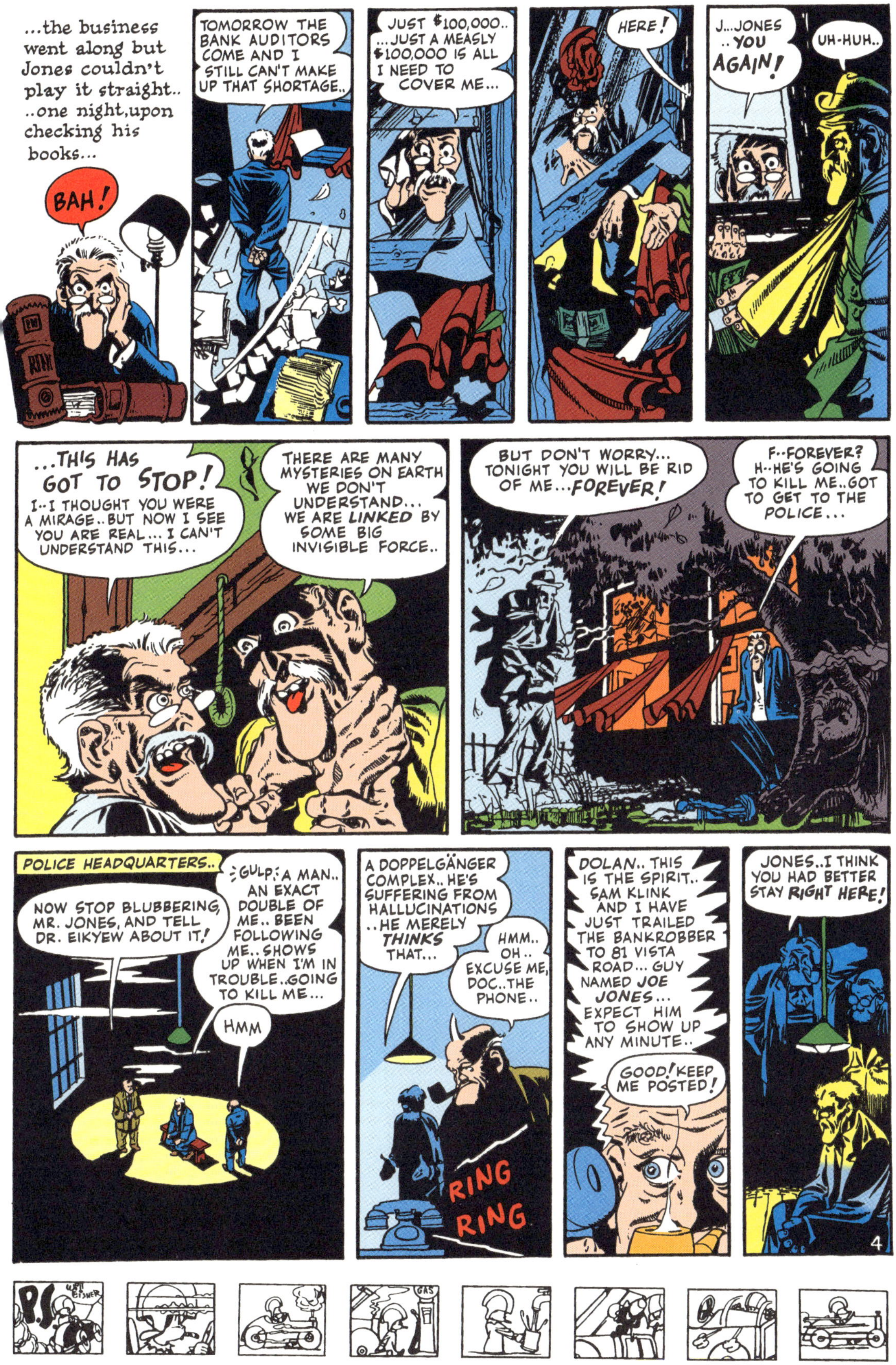

...the business went along but Jones couldn't play it straight.. ..one night, upon checking his books...
BAH!
TOMORROW THE BANK AUDITORS COME AND I STILL CAN'T MAKE UP THAT SHORTAGE..
JUST $100,000.. ...JUST A MEASLY $100,000 IS ALL I NEED TO COVER ME...
HERE!
J...JONES ..YOU AGAIN!
UH-HUH..
...THIS HAS GOT TO STOP! I--I THOUGHT YOU WERE A MIRAGE..BUT NOW I SEE YOU ARE REAL... I CAN'T UNDERSTAND THIS...
THERE ARE MANY MYSTERIES ON EARTH WE DON'T UNDERSTAND... WE ARE LINKED BY SOME BIG INVISIBLE FORCE..
BUT DON'T WORRY... TONIGHT YOU WILL BE RID OF ME...FOREVER!
F--FOREVER? H--HE'S GOING TO KILL ME..GOT TO GET TO THE POLICE...
POLICE HEADQUARTERS..
NOW STOP BLUBBERING, MR. JONES, AND TELL DR. EIKYEW ABOUT IT!
:GULP: A MAN.. AN EXACT DOUBLE OF ME.. BEEN FOLLOWING ME..SHOWS UP WHEN I'M IN TROUBLE..GOING TO KILL ME...
HMM
A DOPPELGÄNGER COMPLEX.. HE'S SUFFERING FROM HALLUCINATIONS ..HE MERELY THINKS THAT...
HMM.. OH.. EXCUSE ME, DOC..THE PHONE..
RING RING
DOLAN.. THIS IS THE SPIRIT.. SAM KLINK AND I HAVE JUST TRAILED THE BANKROBBER TO 81 VISTA ROAD... GUY NAMED JOE JONES... EXPECT HIM TO SHOW UP ANY MINUTE..
GOOD! KEEP ME POSTED!
JONES..I THINK YOU HAD BETTER STAY RIGHT HERE!
4
P.S.
GAS

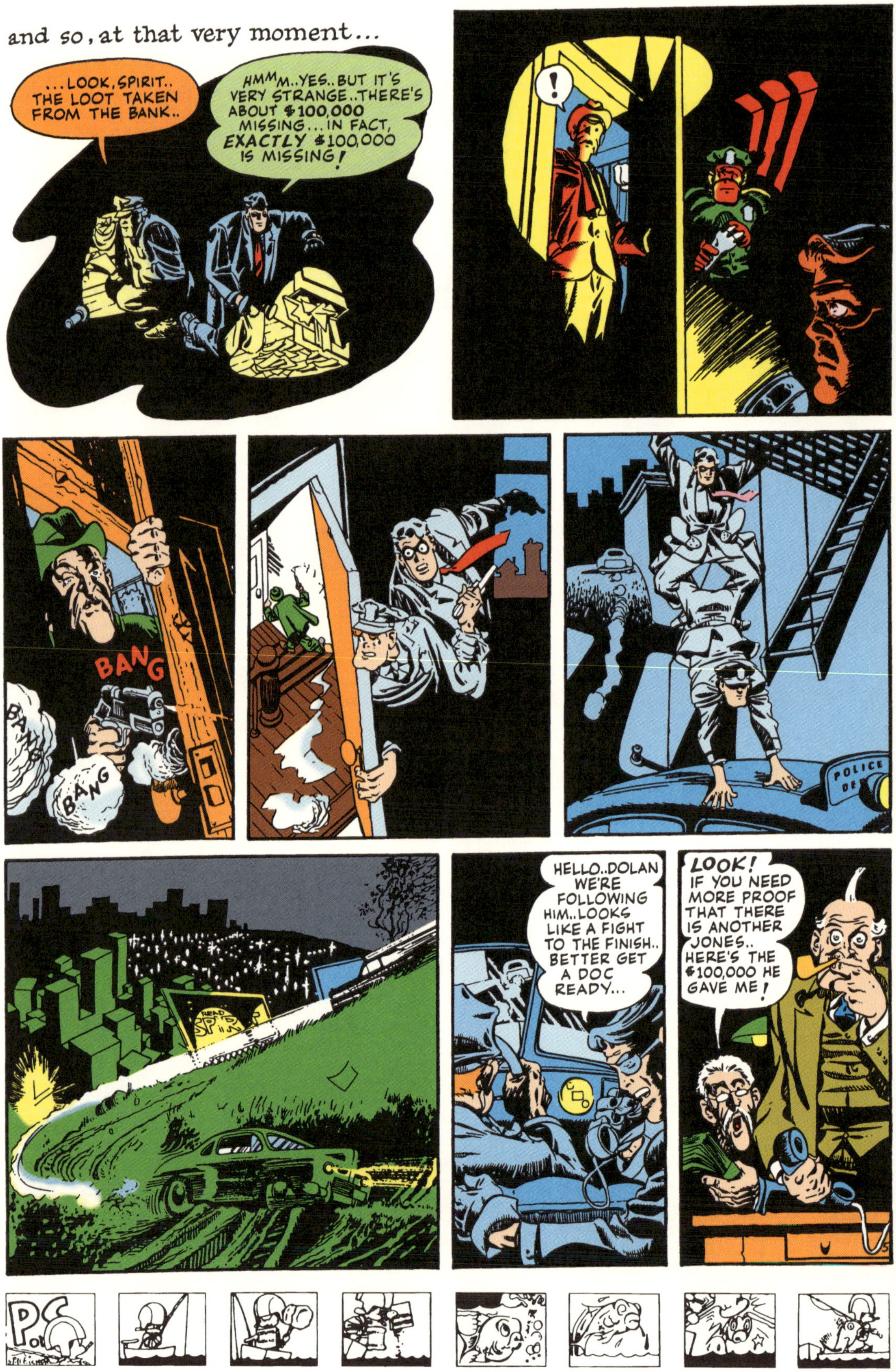
and so, at that very moment...
...LOOK, SPIRIT.. THE LOOT TAKEN FROM THE BANK..
HMMM..YES..BUT IT'S VERY STRANGE..THERE'S ABOUT $100,000 MISSING...IN FACT, EXACTLY $100,000 IS MISSING!
!
BANG
BANG
BANG
HELLO..DOLAN WE'RE FOLLOWING HIM..LOOKS LIKE A FIGHT TO THE FINISH.. BETTER GET A DOC READY...
LOOK! IF YOU NEED MORE PROOF THAT THERE IS ANOTHER JONES.. HERE'S THE $100,000 HE GAVE ME!

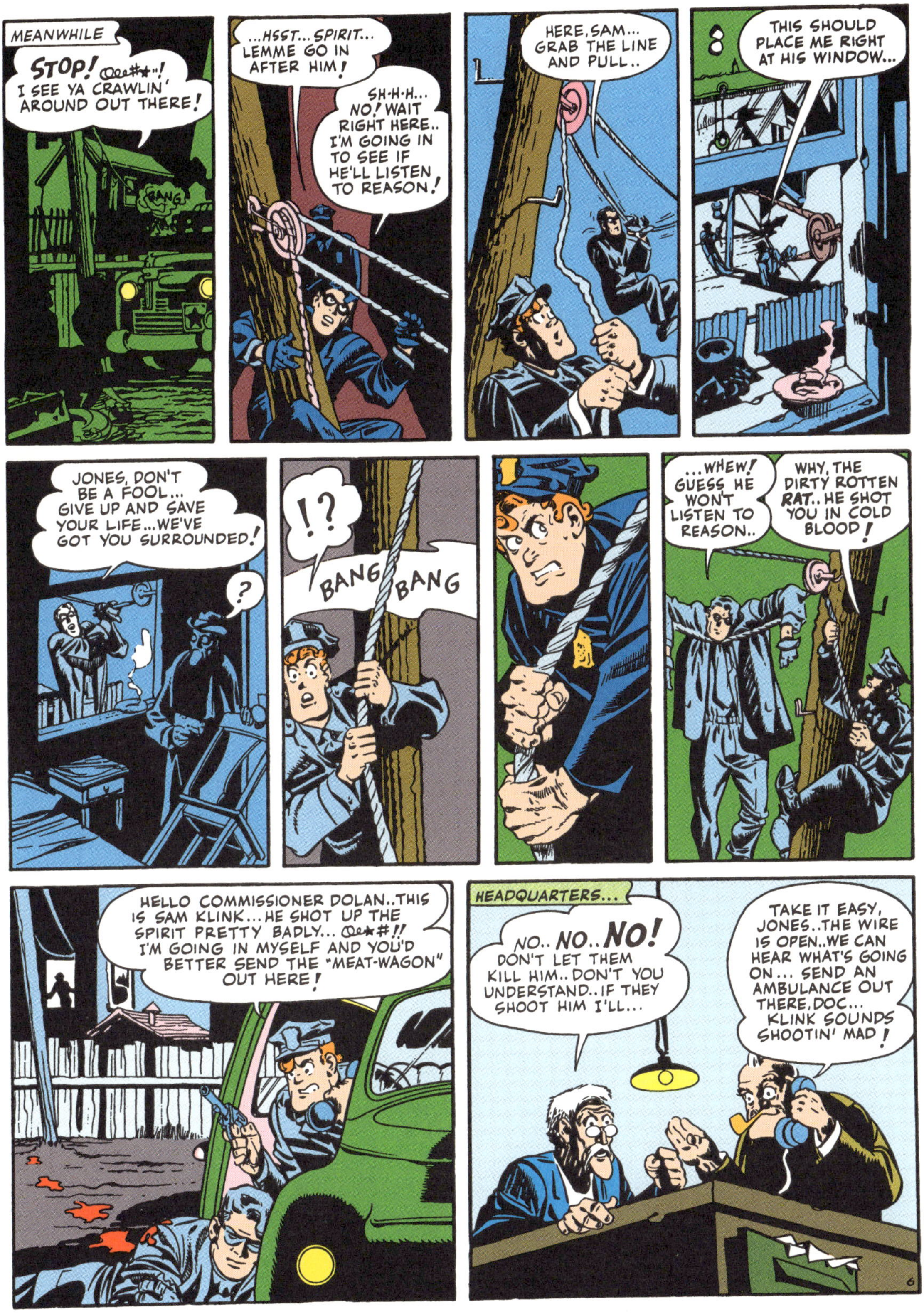
MEANWHILE
STOP! @@#*! I SEE YA CRAWLIN' AROUND OUT THERE!
BANG
...HSST...SPIRIT... LEMME GO IN AFTER HIM!
SH-H-H... NO! WAIT RIGHT HERE.. I'M GOING IN TO SEE IF HE'LL LISTEN TO REASON!
HERE, SAM... GRAB THE LINE AND PULL..
THIS SHOULD PLACE ME RIGHT AT HIS WINDOW...
JONES, DON'T BE A FOOL... GIVE UP AND SAVE YOUR LIFE...WE'VE GOT YOU SURROUNDED!
?
!?
BANG
BANG
...WHEW! GUESS HE WON'T LISTEN TO REASON..
WHY, THE DIRTY ROTTEN RAT.. HE SHOT YOU IN COLD BLOOD!
HELLO COMMISSIONER DOLAN..THIS IS SAM KLINK...HE SHOT UP THE SPIRIT PRETTY BADLY... @@#!! I'M GOING IN MYSELF AND YOU'D BETTER SEND THE "MEAT-WAGON" OUT HERE!
HEADQUARTERS...
NO.. NO.. NO! DON'T LET THEM KILL HIM.. DON'T YOU UNDERSTAND..IF THEY SHOOT HIM I'LL...
TAKE IT EASY, JONES..THE WIRE IS OPEN..WE CAN HEAR WHAT'S GOING ON... SEND AN AMBULANCE OUT THERE, DOC... KLINK SOUNDS SHOOTIN' MAD!
6

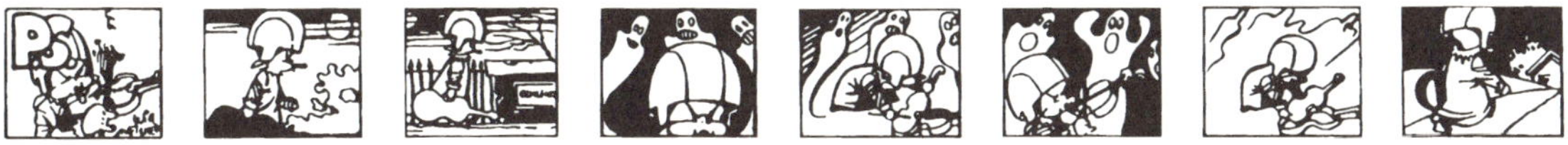

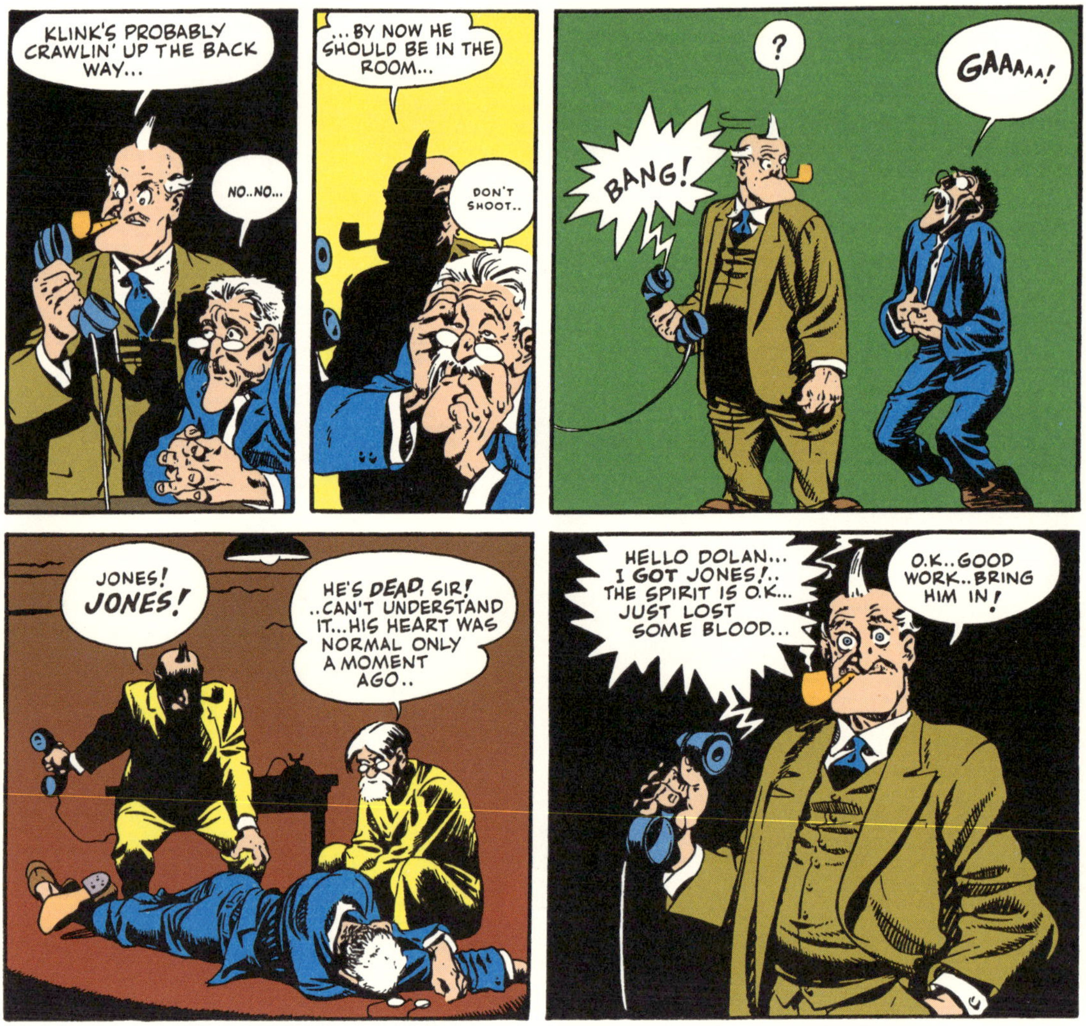
KLINK'S PROBABLY CRAWLIN' UP THE BACK WAY...
NO..NO...
...BY NOW HE SHOULD BE IN THE ROOM...
DON'T SHOOT..
?
BANG!
GAAAAA!
JONES! JONES!
HE'S DEAD, SIR! ..CAN'T UNDERSTAND IT...HIS HEART WAS NORMAL ONLY A MOMENT AGO..
HELLO DOLAN... I GOT JONES!.. THE SPIRIT IS O.K... JUST LOST SOME BLOOD...
O.K..GOOD WORK..BRING HIM IN!

If you care to check...

There's an old legend in German folklore which tells of the "Doppelgänger," who was supposed to be a man's second-self, or an exact physical duplicate who pursues him relentlessly... some laugh and say this shadowy counterpart is a man's evil nature.... some figure it's his conscience... and some say it's just a lot of eyewash....

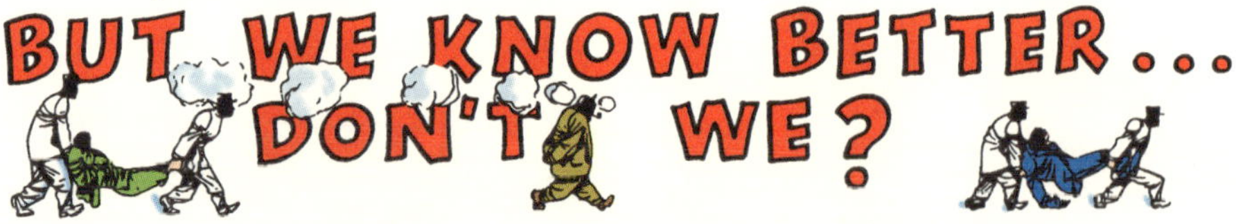
BUT WE KNOW BETTER...
DON'T WE?

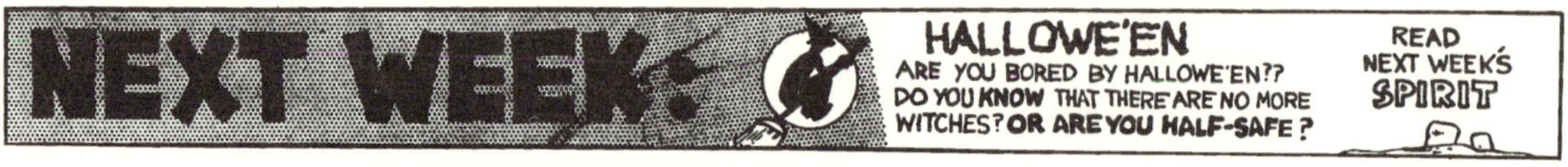
NEXT WEEK:
HALLOWE'EN
ARE YOU BORED BY HALLOWE'EN??
DO YOU KNOW THAT THERE ARE NO MORE WITCHES? OR ARE YOU HALF-SAFE?
READ NEXT WEEK'S SPIRIT

THE HALLOWE'EN SPIRIT OF 1947: THE BURNING OF P.S. 43

October 26 1947

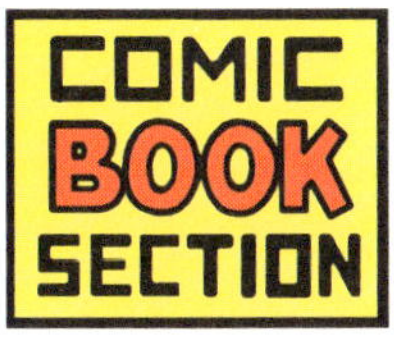

COMIC BOOK SECTION

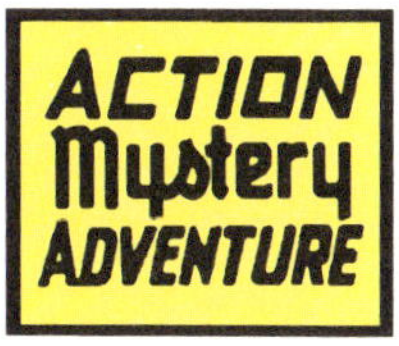

ACTION Mystery ADVENTURE

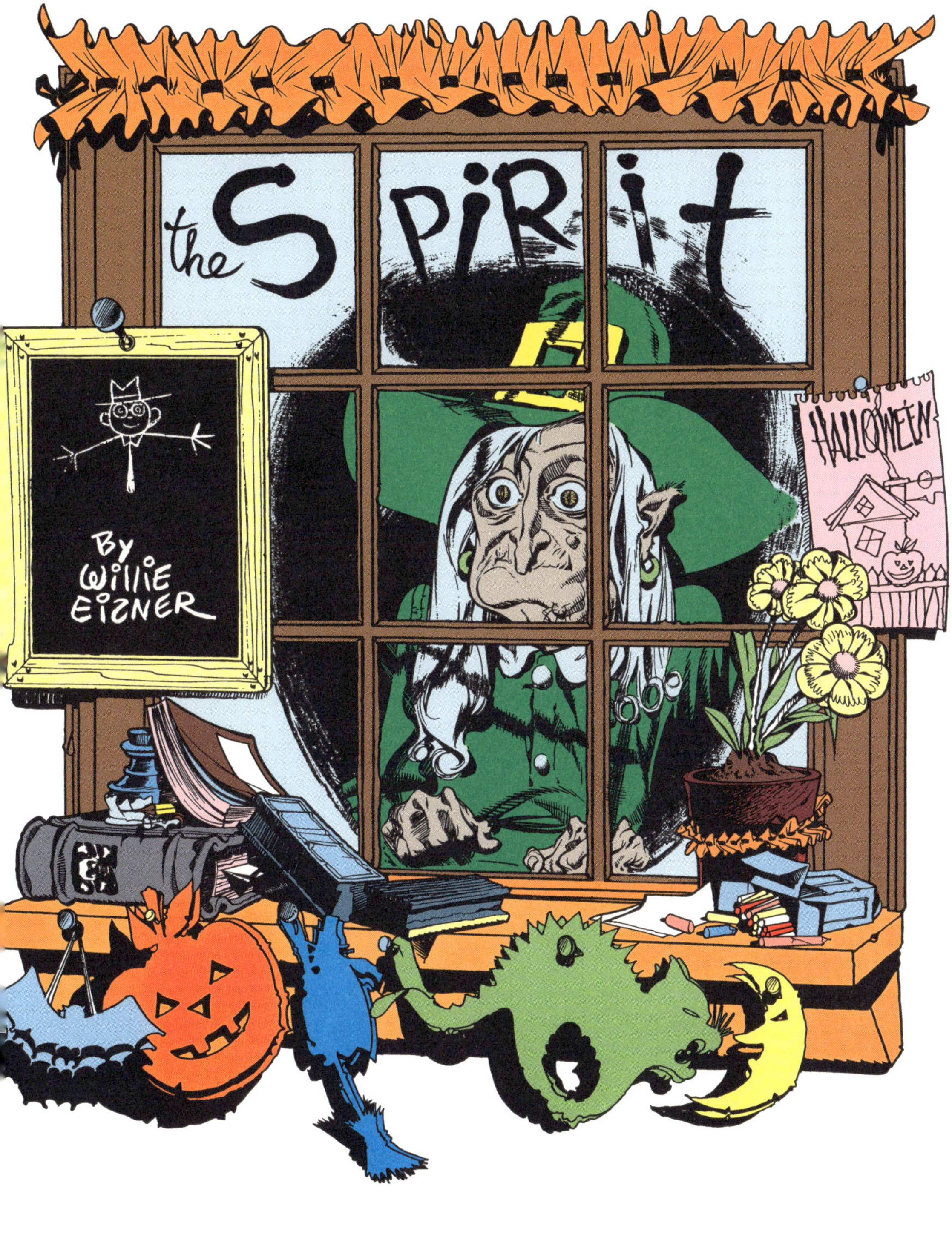

the Spirit
By Willie Eisner
HALLOWEEN

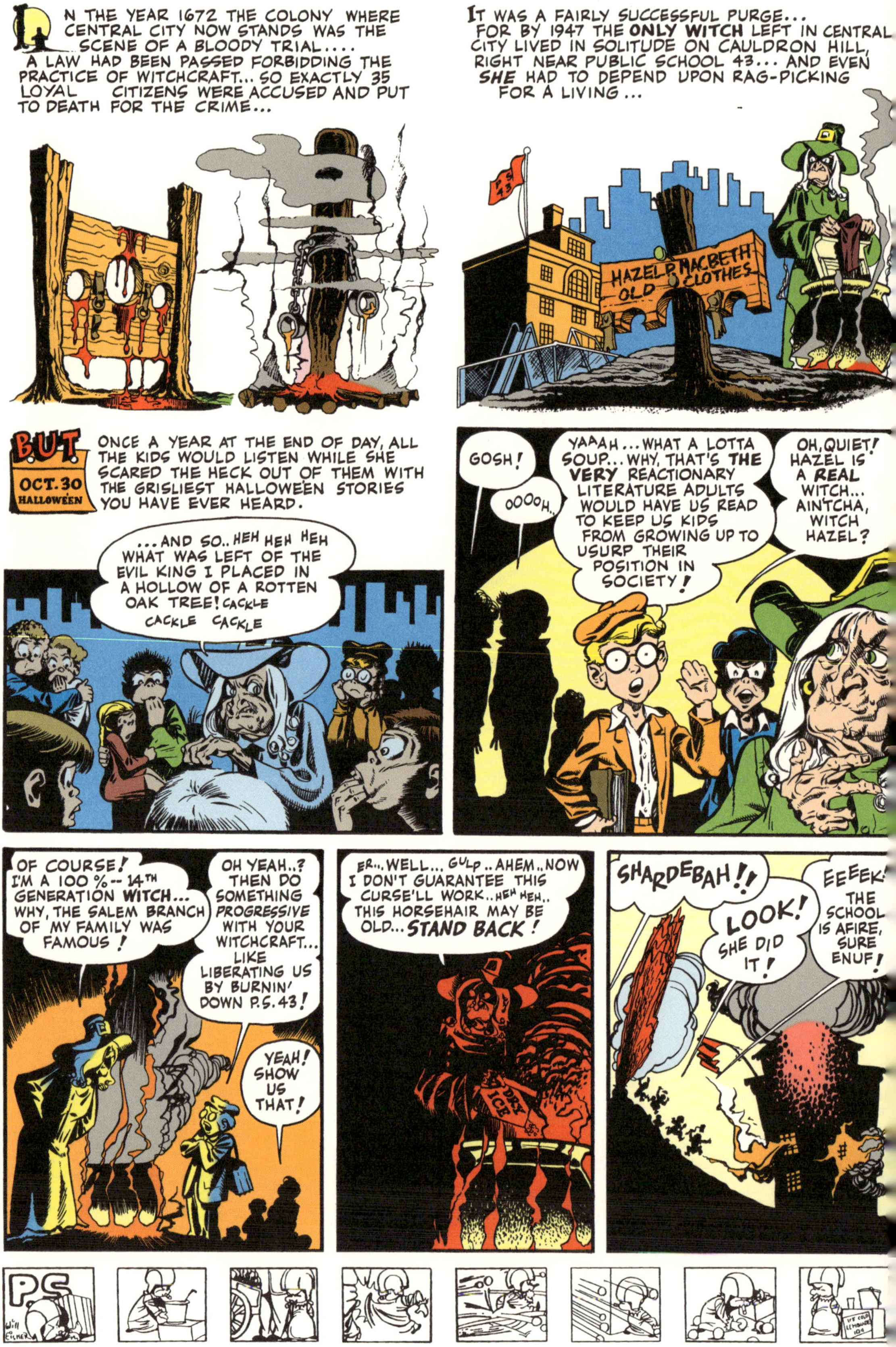
IN THE YEAR 1672 THE COLONY WHERE CENTRAL CITY NOW STANDS WAS THE SCENE OF A BLOODY TRIAL.... A LAW HAD BEEN PASSED FORBIDDING THE PRACTICE OF WITCHCRAFT... SO EXACTLY 35 LOYAL CITIZENS WERE ACCUSED AND PUT TO DEATH FOR THE CRIME...
IT WAS A FAIRLY SUCCESSFUL PURGE... FOR BY 1947 THE ONLY WITCH LEFT IN CENTRAL CITY LIVED IN SOLITUDE ON CAULDRON HILL, RIGHT NEAR PUBLIC SCHOOL 43... AND EVEN SHE HAD TO DEPEND UPON RAG-PICKING FOR A LIVING...
P.S. 43
HAZEL P. MACBETH OLD CLOTHES
B.U.T.
OCT. 30 HALLOWEEN
ONCE A YEAR AT THE END OF DAY, ALL THE KIDS WOULD LISTEN WHILE SHE SCARED THE HECK OUT OF THEM WITH THE GRISLIEST HALLOWEEN STORIES YOU HAVE EVER HEARD.
...AND SO.. HEH HEH HEH WHAT WAS LEFT OF THE EVIL KING I PLACED IN A HOLLOW OF A ROTTEN OAK TREE! CACKLE CACKLE CACKLE
GOSH!
OOOOH..
YAAAH...WHAT A LOTTA SOUP...WHY, THAT'S THE VERY REACTIONARY LITERATURE ADULTS WOULD HAVE US READ TO KEEP US KIDS FROM GROWING UP TO USURP THEIR POSITION IN SOCIETY!
OH, QUIET! HAZEL IS A REAL WITCH... AIN'TCHA, WITCH HAZEL?
OF COURSE! I'M A 100% -- 14TH GENERATION WITCH... WHY, THE SALEM BRANCH OF MY FAMILY WAS FAMOUS!
OH YEAH..? THEN DO SOMETHING PROGRESSIVE WITH YOUR WITCHCRAFT... LIKE LIBERATING US BY BURNIN' DOWN P.S. 43!
YEAH! SHOW US THAT!
ER... WELL... GULP.. AHEM.. NOW I DON'T GUARANTEE THIS CURSE'LL WORK.. HEH HEH.. THIS HORSEHAIR MAY BE OLD... STAND BACK!
DRY ICE
SHARDEBAH!!
LOOK! SHE DID IT!
EEEEK! THE SCHOOL IS AFIRE, SURE ENUF!
P.S.
WILL EISNER

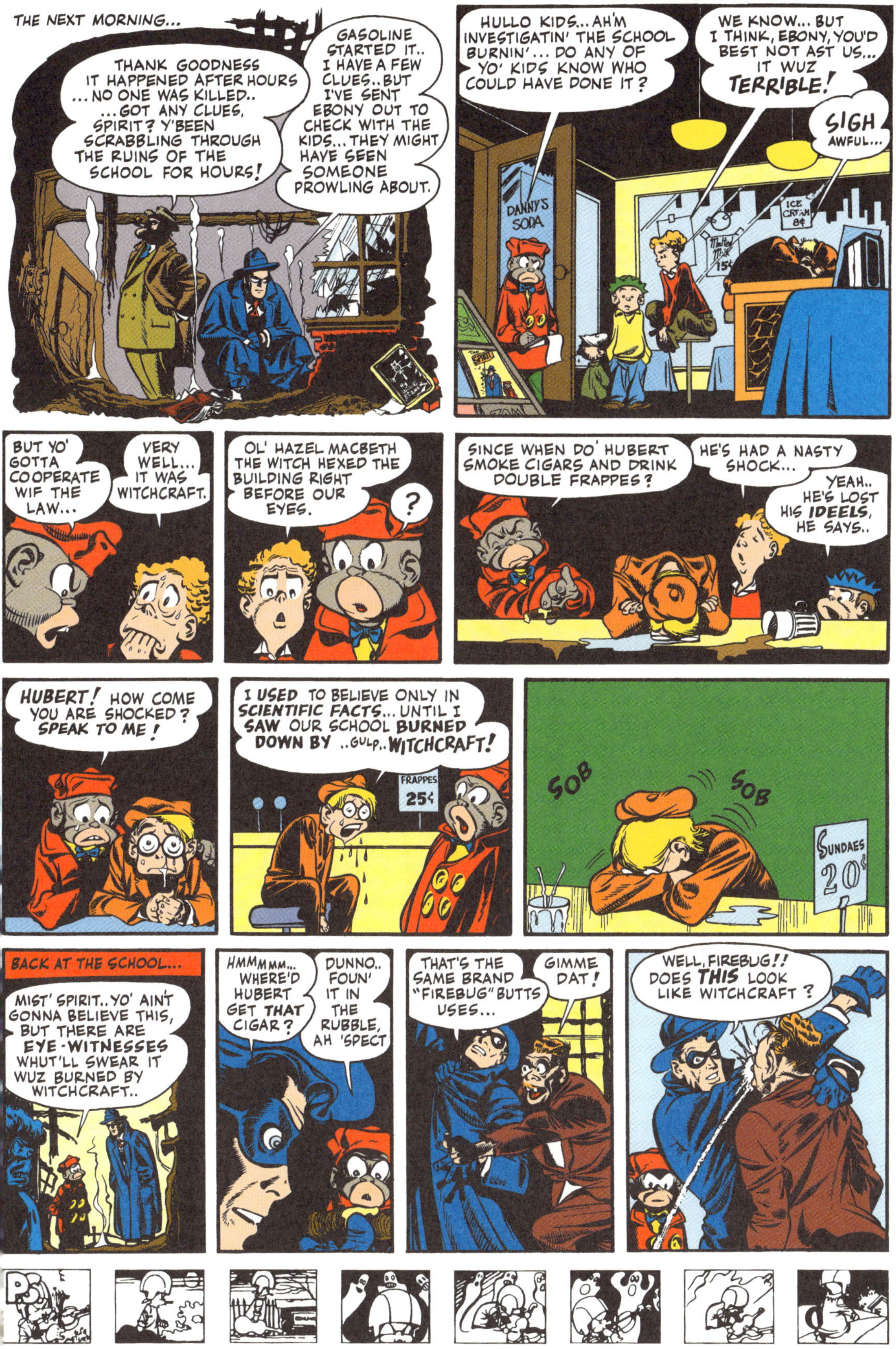
THE NEXT MORNING...
THANK GOODNESS IT HAPPENED AFTER HOURS ... NO ONE WAS KILLED.. ...GOT ANY CLUES, SPIRIT? Y'BEEN SCRABBLING THROUGH THE RUINS OF THE SCHOOL FOR HOURS!
GASOLINE STARTED IT.. I HAVE A FEW CLUES..BUT I'VE SENT EBONY OUT TO CHECK WITH THE KIDS... THEY MIGHT HAVE SEEN SOMEONE PROWLING ABOUT.
HULLO KIDS... AH'M INVESTIGATIN' THE SCHOOL BURNIN'... DO ANY OF YO' KIDS KNOW WHO COULD HAVE DONE IT?
WE KNOW... BUT I THINK, EBONY, YOU'D BEST NOT AST US... IT WUZ TERRIBLE!
SIGH AWFUL...
DANNY'S SODA
BUT YO' GOTTA COOPERATE WIF THE LAW...
VERY WELL... IT WAS WITCHCRAFT.
OL' HAZEL MACBETH THE WITCH HEXED THE BUILDING RIGHT BEFORE OUR EYES.
?
SINCE WHEN DO' HUBERT SMOKE CIGARS AND DRINK DOUBLE FRAPPES?
HE'S HAD A NASTY SHOCK...
YEAH.. HE'S LOST HIS IDEELS, HE SAYS..
HUBERT! HOW COME YOU ARE SHOCKED? SPEAK TO ME!
I USED TO BELIEVE ONLY IN SCIENTIFIC FACTS... UNTIL I SAW OUR SCHOOL BURNED DOWN BY ..GULP.. WITCHCRAFT!
FRAPPES 25¢
SOB SOB
SUNDAES 20¢
BACK AT THE SCHOOL...
MIST' SPIRIT..YO' AIN'T GONNA BELIEVE THIS, BUT THERE ARE EYE-WITNESSES WHUT'LL SWEAR IT WUZ BURNED BY WITCHCRAFT..
HMMMMM... WHERE'D HUBERT GET THAT CIGAR?
DUNNO.. FOUN' IT IN THE RUBBLE, AH 'SPECT
THAT'S THE SAME BRAND "FIREBUG" BUTTS USES...
GIMME DAT!
WELL, FIREBUG!! DOES THIS LOOK LIKE WITCHCRAFT?

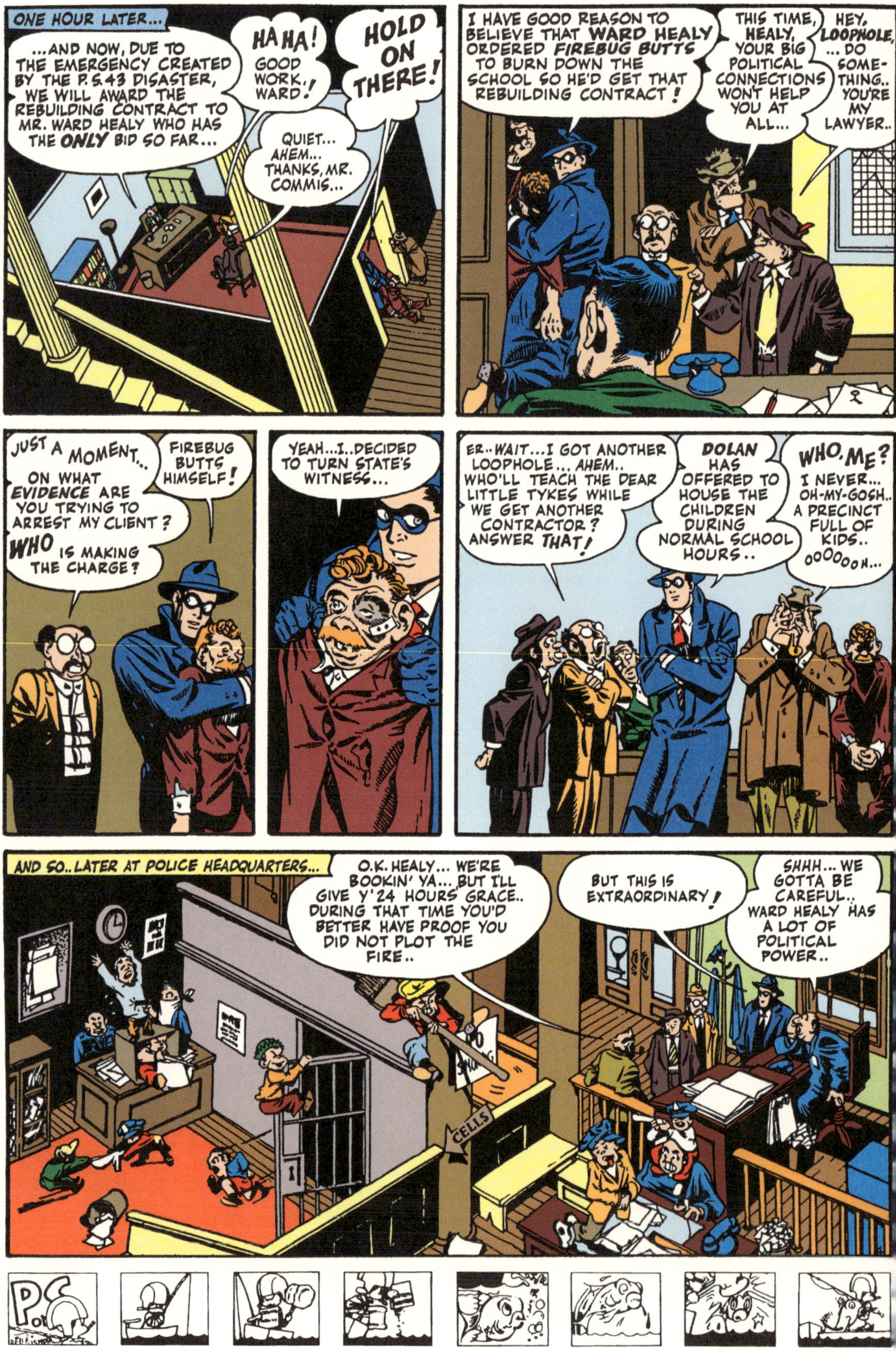
ONE HOUR LATER...
...AND NOW, DUE TO THE EMERGENCY CREATED BY THE P.S.43 DISASTER, WE WILL AWARD THE REBUILDING CONTRACT TO MR. WARD HEALY WHO HAS THE ONLY BID SO FAR...
HA HA! GOOD WORK, WARD!
QUIET... AHEM... THANKS, MR. COMMIS...
HOLD ON THERE!
I HAVE GOOD REASON TO BELIEVE THAT WARD HEALY ORDERED FIREBUG BUTTS TO BURN DOWN THE SCHOOL SO HE'D GET THAT REBUILDING CONTRACT!
THIS TIME, HEALY, YOUR BIG POLITICAL CONNECTIONS WON'T HELP YOU AT ALL...
HEY, LOOPHOLE, ...DO SOME-THING.. YOU'RE MY LAWYER..
JUST A MOMENT... ON WHAT EVIDENCE ARE YOU TRYING TO ARREST MY CLIENT? WHO IS MAKING THE CHARGE?
FIREBUG BUTTS HIMSELF!
YEAH...I..DECIDED TO TURN STATE'S WITNESS...
ER..WAIT...I GOT ANOTHER LOOPHOLE... AHEM.. WHO'LL TEACH THE DEAR LITTLE TYKES WHILE WE GET ANOTHER CONTRACTOR? ANSWER THAT!
DOLAN HAS OFFERED TO HOUSE THE CHILDREN DURING NORMAL SCHOOL HOURS..
WHO, ME? I NEVER... OH-MY-GOSH.. A PRECINCT FULL OF KIDS.. OOOOOOH...
AND SO..LATER AT POLICE HEADQUARTERS...
O.K. HEALY... WE'RE BOOKIN' YA... BUT I'LL GIVE Y'24 HOURS GRACE.. DURING THAT TIME YOU'D BETTER HAVE PROOF YOU DID NOT PLOT THE FIRE..
BUT THIS IS EXTRAORDINARY!
SHHH... WE GOTTA BE CAREFUL.. WARD HEALY HAS A LOT OF POLITICAL POWER..
CELLS
P.S.

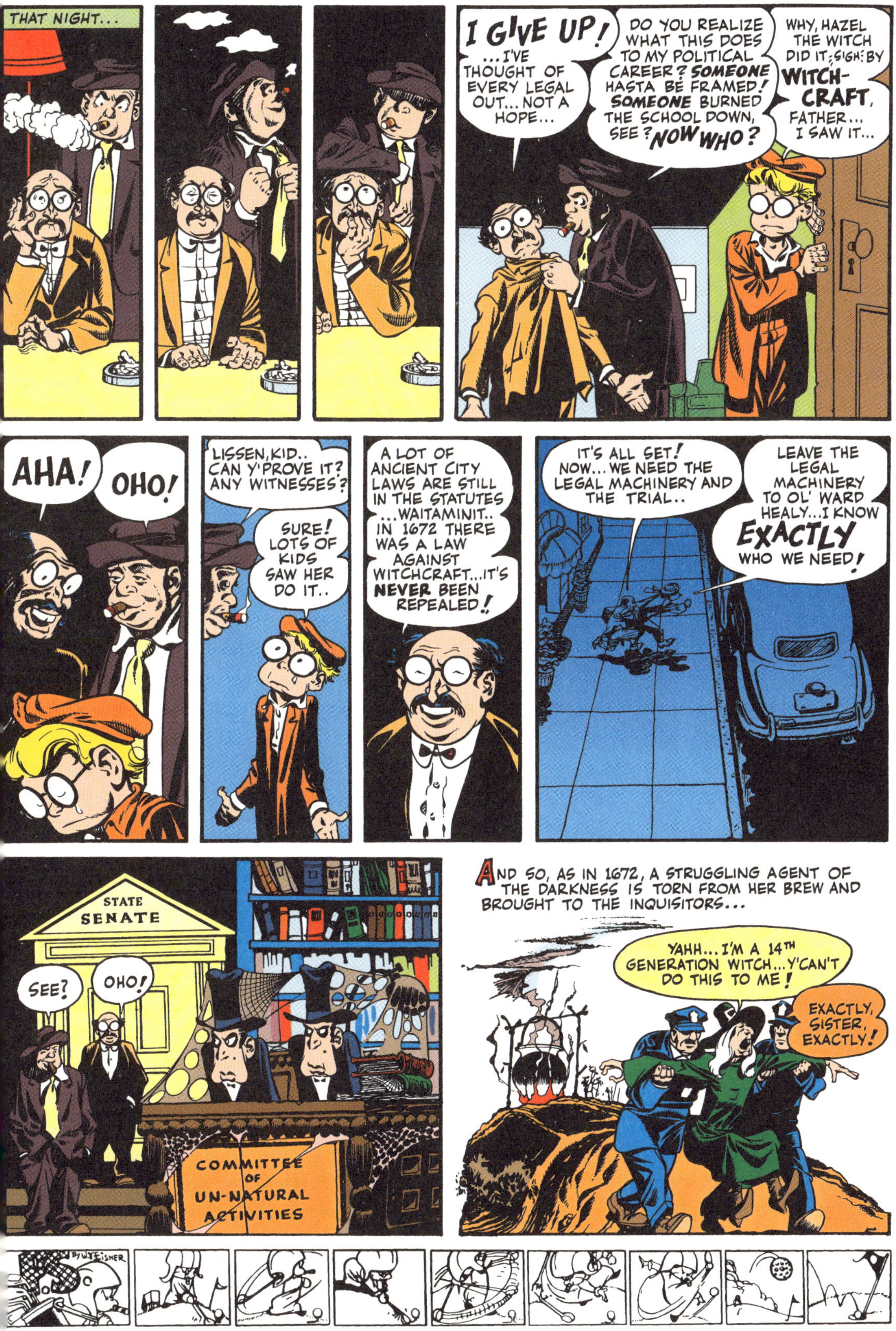
THAT NIGHT...
I GIVE UP! ...I'VE THOUGHT OF EVERY LEGAL OUT...NOT A HOPE...
DO YOU REALIZE WHAT THIS DOES TO MY POLITICAL CAREER? SOMEONE HASTA BE FRAMED! SOMEONE BURNED THE SCHOOL DOWN, SEE? NOW WHO?
WHY, HAZEL THE WITCH DID IT :SIGH: BY WITCH-CRAFT, FATHER... I SAW IT...
AHA!
OHO!
LISSEN, KID.. CAN Y'PROVE IT? ANY WITNESSES?
SURE! LOTS OF KIDS SAW HER DO IT..
A LOT OF ANCIENT CITY LAWS ARE STILL IN THE STATUTES ...WAITAMINIT.. IN 1672 THERE WAS A LAW AGAINST WITCHCRAFT...IT'S NEVER BEEN REPEALED!
IT'S ALL SET! NOW... WE NEED THE LEGAL MACHINERY AND THE TRIAL..
LEAVE THE LEGAL MACHINERY TO OL' WARD HEALY...I KNOW EXACTLY WHO WE NEED!
STATE SENATE
SEE?
OHO!
COMMITTEE OF UN-NATURAL ACTIVITIES
AND SO, AS IN 1672, A STRUGGLING AGENT OF THE DARKNESS IS TORN FROM HER BREW AND BROUGHT TO THE INQUISITORS...
YAHH... I'M A 14TH GENERATION WITCH... Y'CAN'T DO THIS TO ME!
EXACTLY, SISTER, EXACTLY!

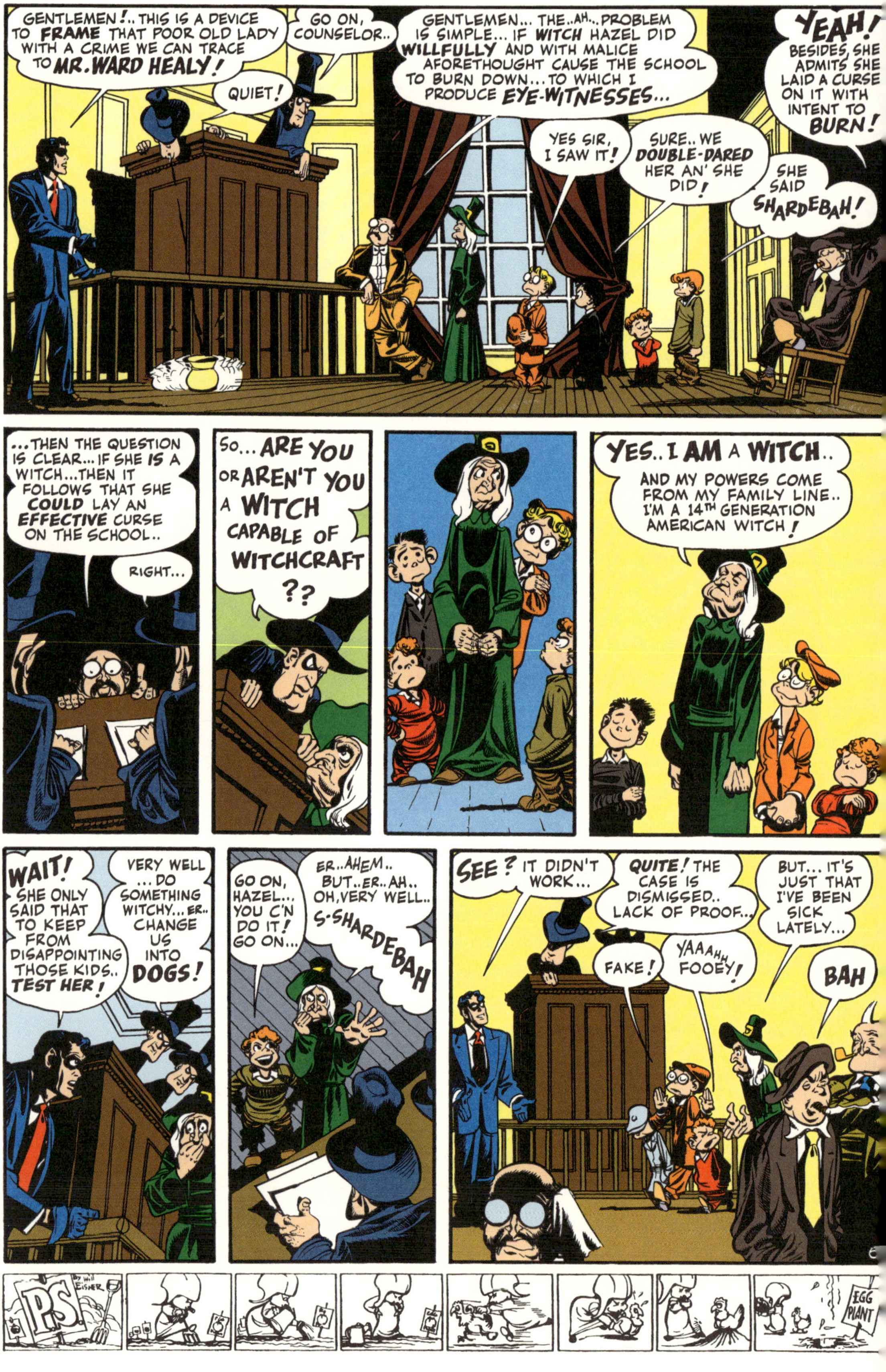
GENTLEMEN!.. THIS IS A DEVICE TO FRAME THAT POOR OLD LADY WITH A CRIME WE CAN TRACE TO MR. WARD HEALY!
QUIET!
GO ON, COUNSELOR..
GENTLEMEN... THE..AH...PROBLEM IS SIMPLE... IF WITCH HAZEL DID WILLFULLY AND WITH MALICE AFORETHOUGHT CAUSE THE SCHOOL TO BURN DOWN... TO WHICH I PRODUCE EYE-WITNESSES...
YES SIR, I SAW IT!
SURE.. WE DOUBLE-DARED HER AN' SHE DID!
YEAH! BESIDES, SHE ADMITS SHE LAID A CURSE ON IT WITH INTENT TO BURN!
SHE SAID SHARDEBAH!
...THEN THE QUESTION IS CLEAR... IF SHE IS A WITCH...THEN IT FOLLOWS THAT SHE COULD LAY AN EFFECTIVE CURSE ON THE SCHOOL..
RIGHT...
SO... ARE YOU OR AREN'T YOU A WITCH CAPABLE OF WITCHCRAFT ??
YES.. I AM A WITCH..
AND MY POWERS COME FROM MY FAMILY LINE.. I'M A 14TH GENERATION AMERICAN WITCH!
WAIT! SHE ONLY SAID THAT TO KEEP FROM DISAPPOINTING THOSE KIDS.. TEST HER!
VERY WELL ... DO SOMETHING WITCHY... ER.. CHANGE US INTO DOGS!
GO ON, HAZEL... YOU C'N DO IT! GO ON...
ER..AHEM.. BUT..ER..AH.. OH, VERY WELL..
S-SHARDEBAH
SEE? IT DIDN'T WORK...
QUITE! THE CASE IS DISMISSED.. LACK OF PROOF...
BUT... IT'S JUST THAT I'VE BEEN SICK LATELY...
FAKE!
YAAAHH FOOEY!
BAH
P.S.
By Will Eisner
EGG PLANT

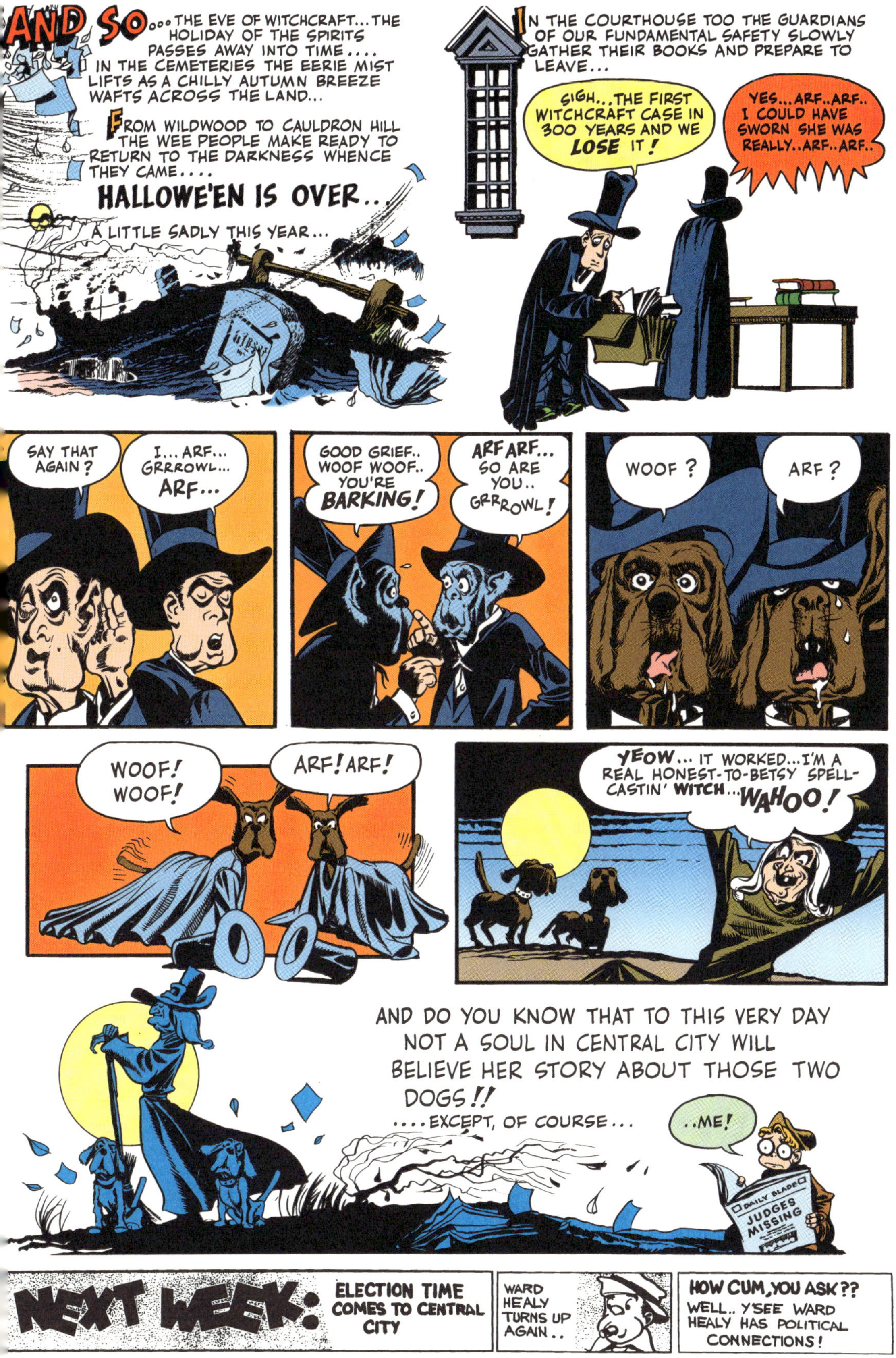
AND SO... THE EVE OF WITCHCRAFT... THE HOLIDAY OF THE SPIRITS PASSES AWAY INTO TIME.... IN THE CEMETERIES THE EERIE MIST LIFTS AS A CHILLY AUTUMN BREEZE WAFTS ACROSS THE LAND...
FROM WILDWOOD TO CAULDRON HILL THE WEE PEOPLE MAKE READY TO RETURN TO THE DARKNESS WHENCE THEY CAME....
HALLOWE'EN IS OVER...
A LITTLE SADLY THIS YEAR...
IN THE COURTHOUSE TOO THE GUARDIANS OF OUR FUNDAMENTAL SAFETY SLOWLY GATHER THEIR BOOKS AND PREPARE TO LEAVE...
SIGH... THE FIRST WITCHCRAFT CASE IN 300 YEARS AND WE LOSE IT!
YES... ARF.. ARF.. I COULD HAVE SWORN SHE WAS REALLY.. ARF.. ARF..
SAY THAT AGAIN?
I... ARF... GRRROWL... ARF...
GOOD GRIEF.. WOOF WOOF.. YOU'RE BARKING!
ARF ARF... SO ARE YOU.. GRRROWL!
WOOF?
ARF?
WOOF! WOOF!
ARF! ARF!
YEOW... IT WORKED... I'M A REAL HONEST-TO-BETSY SPELL-CASTIN' WITCH... WAHOO!
AND DO YOU KNOW THAT TO THIS VERY DAY NOT A SOUL IN CENTRAL CITY WILL BELIEVE HER STORY ABOUT THOSE TWO DOGS!!
....EXCEPT, OF COURSE...
..ME!
DAILY BLADE
JUDGES MISSING
NEXT WEEK:
ELECTION TIME COMES TO CENTRAL CITY
WARD HEALY TURNS UP AGAIN..
HOW CUM, YOU ASK??
WELL.. Y'SEE WARD HEALY HAS POLITICAL CONNECTIONS!

COMIC BOOK SECTION

THE CRIMINAL

November 2 1947

ACTION Mystery ADVENTURE

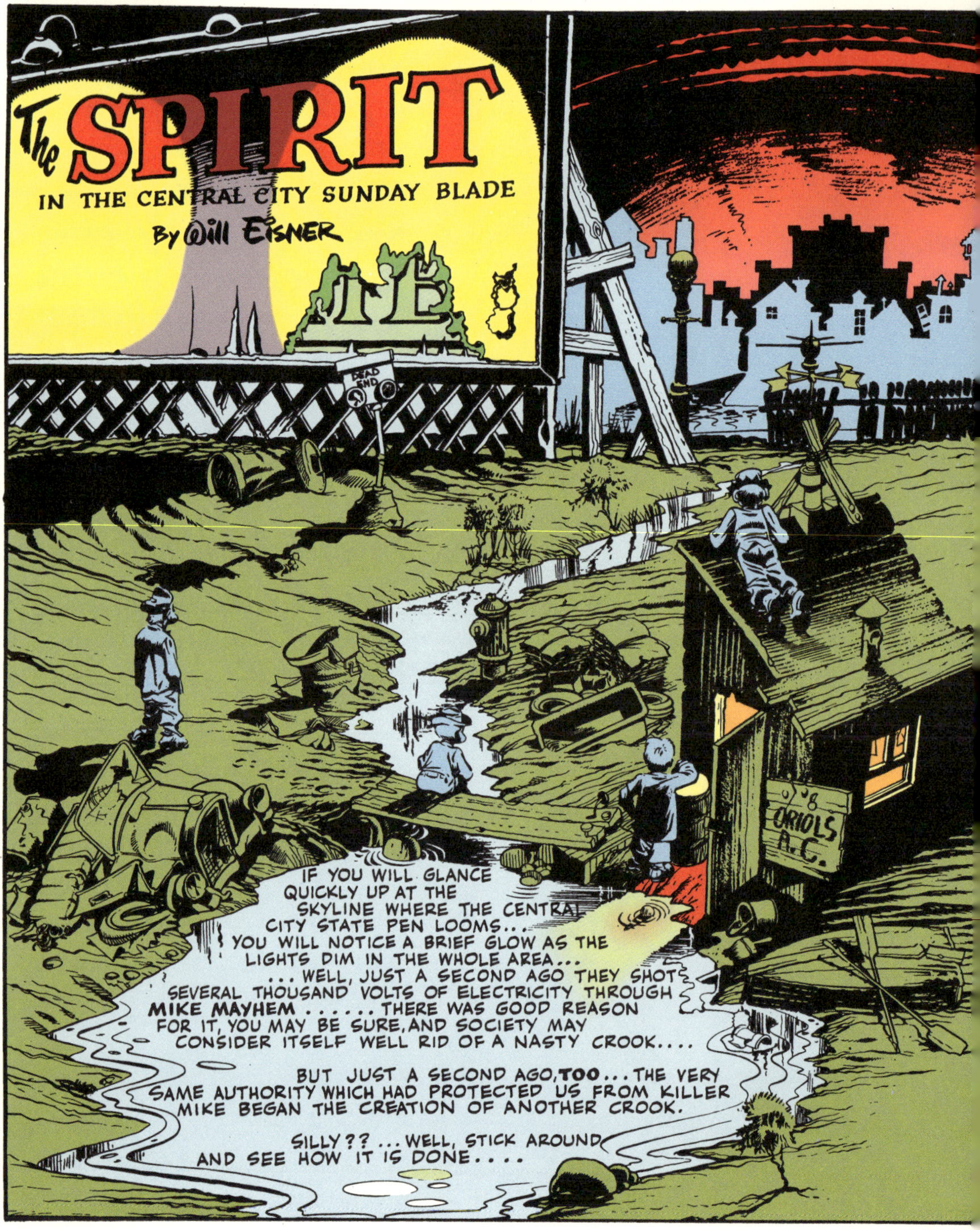
The SPIRIT
IN THE CENTRAL CITY SUNDAY BLADE
By Will Eisner
DEAD END
ORIOLS A.C.
IF YOU WILL GLANCE QUICKLY UP AT THE SKYLINE WHERE THE CENTRAL CITY STATE PEN LOOMS... YOU WILL NOTICE A BRIEF GLOW AS THE LIGHTS DIM IN THE WHOLE AREA... ... WELL, JUST A SECOND AGO THEY SHOT SEVERAL THOUSAND VOLTS OF ELECTRICITY THROUGH **MIKE MAYHEM** ...... THERE WAS GOOD REASON FOR IT, YOU MAY BE SURE, AND SOCIETY MAY CONSIDER ITSELF WELL RID OF A NASTY CROOK....
BUT JUST A SECOND AGO, **TOO**... THE VERY SAME AUTHORITY WHICH HAD PROTECTED US FROM KILLER MIKE BEGAN THE CREATION OF ANOTHER CROOK.
SILLY?? ... WELL, STICK AROUND AND SEE HOW IT IS DONE....

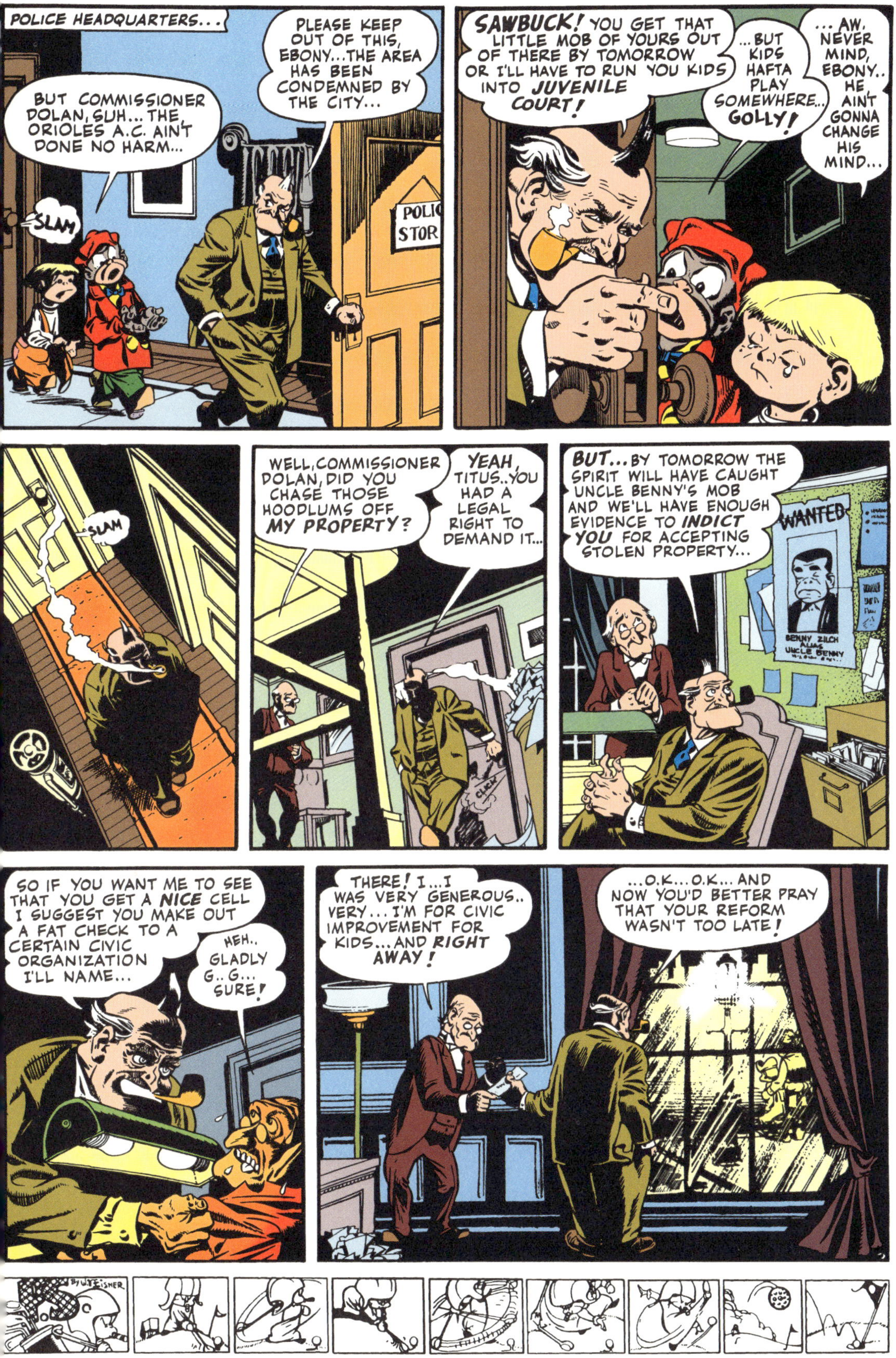
POLICE HEADQUARTERS...
BUT COMMISSIONER DOLAN, SUH... THE ORIOLES A.C. AIN'T DONE NO HARM...
PLEASE KEEP OUT OF THIS, EBONY...THE AREA HAS BEEN CONDEMNED BY THE CITY...
SLAM
POLIC STOR
SAWBUCK! YOU GET THAT LITTLE MOB OF YOURS OUT OF THERE BY TOMORROW OR I'LL HAVE TO RUN YOU KIDS INTO JUVENILE COURT!
...BUT KIDS HAFTA PLAY SOMEWHERE... GOLLY!
...AW, NEVER MIND, EBONY.. HE AIN'T GONNA CHANGE HIS MIND...
SLAM
WELL,COMMISSIONER DOLAN, DID YOU CHASE THOSE HOODLUMS OFF MY PROPERTY?
YEAH, TITUS..YOU HAD A LEGAL RIGHT TO DEMAND IT...
CLICK
BUT... BY TOMORROW THE SPIRIT WILL HAVE CAUGHT UNCLE BENNY'S MOB AND WE'LL HAVE ENOUGH EVIDENCE TO INDICT YOU FOR ACCEPTING STOLEN PROPERTY...
WANTED
BENNY ZILCH ALIAS UNCLE BENNY
SO IF YOU WANT ME TO SEE THAT YOU GET A NICE CELL I SUGGEST YOU MAKE OUT A FAT CHECK TO A CERTAIN CIVIC ORGANIZATION I'LL NAME...
HEH.. GLADLY G.. G... SURE!
THERE! I...I WAS VERY GENEROUS.. VERY... I'M FOR CIVIC IMPROVEMENT FOR KIDS...AND RIGHT AWAY!
...O.K...O.K... AND NOW YOU'D BETTER PRAY THAT YOUR REFORM WASN'T TOO LATE!
BY WILL EISNER

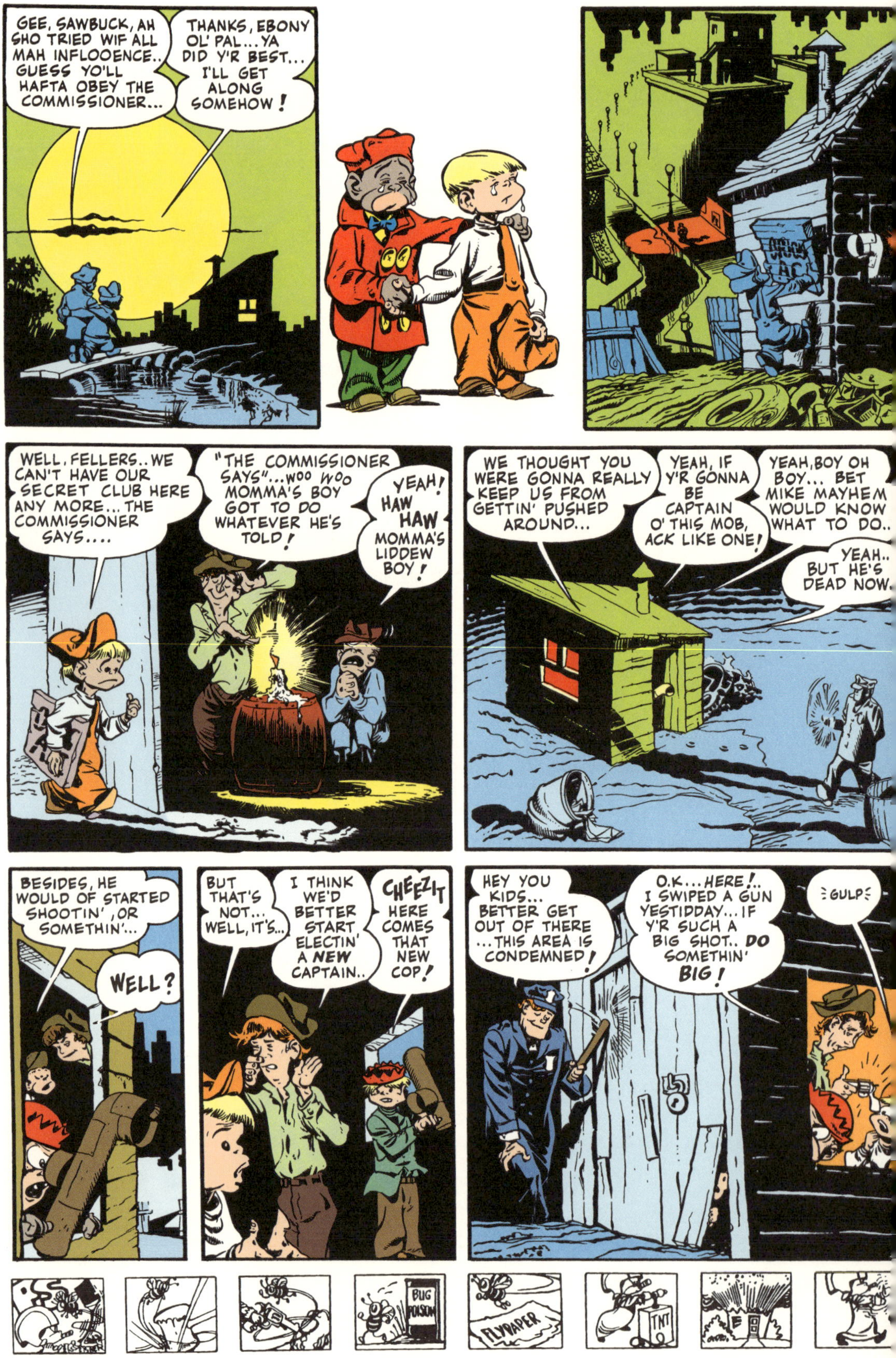
GEE, SAWBUCK, AH SHO TRIED WIF ALL MAH INFLOOENCE.. GUESS YO'LL HAFTA OBEY THE COMMISSIONER...
THANKS, EBONY OL' PAL... YA DID Y'R BEST... I'LL GET ALONG SOMEHOW!
WELL, FELLERS.. WE CAN'T HAVE OUR SECRET CLUB HERE ANY MORE... THE COMMISSIONER SAYS....
"THE COMMISSIONER SAYS"... WOO WOO MOMMA'S BOY GOT TO DO WHATEVER HE'S TOLD!
YEAH! HAW HAW MOMMA'S LIDDEW BOY!
WE THOUGHT YOU WERE GONNA REALLY KEEP US FROM GETTIN' PUSHED AROUND...
YEAH, IF Y'R GONNA BE CAPTAIN O' THIS MOB, ACK LIKE ONE!
YEAH, BOY OH BOY... BET MIKE MAYHEM WOULD KNOW WHAT TO DO..
YEAH.. BUT HE'S DEAD NOW.
BESIDES, HE WOULD OF STARTED SHOOTIN', OR SOMETHIN'...
WELL?
BUT THAT'S NOT... WELL, IT'S...
I THINK WE'D BETTER START ELECTIN' A NEW CAPTAIN..
CHEEZIT HERE COMES THAT NEW COP!
HEY YOU KIDS... BETTER GET OUT OF THERE ...THIS AREA IS CONDEMNED!
O.K... HERE!.. I SWIPED A GUN YESTIDDAY... IF Y'R SUCH A BIG SHOT.. DO SOMETHIN' BIG!
GULP
BUG POISON
FLYPAPER
TNT

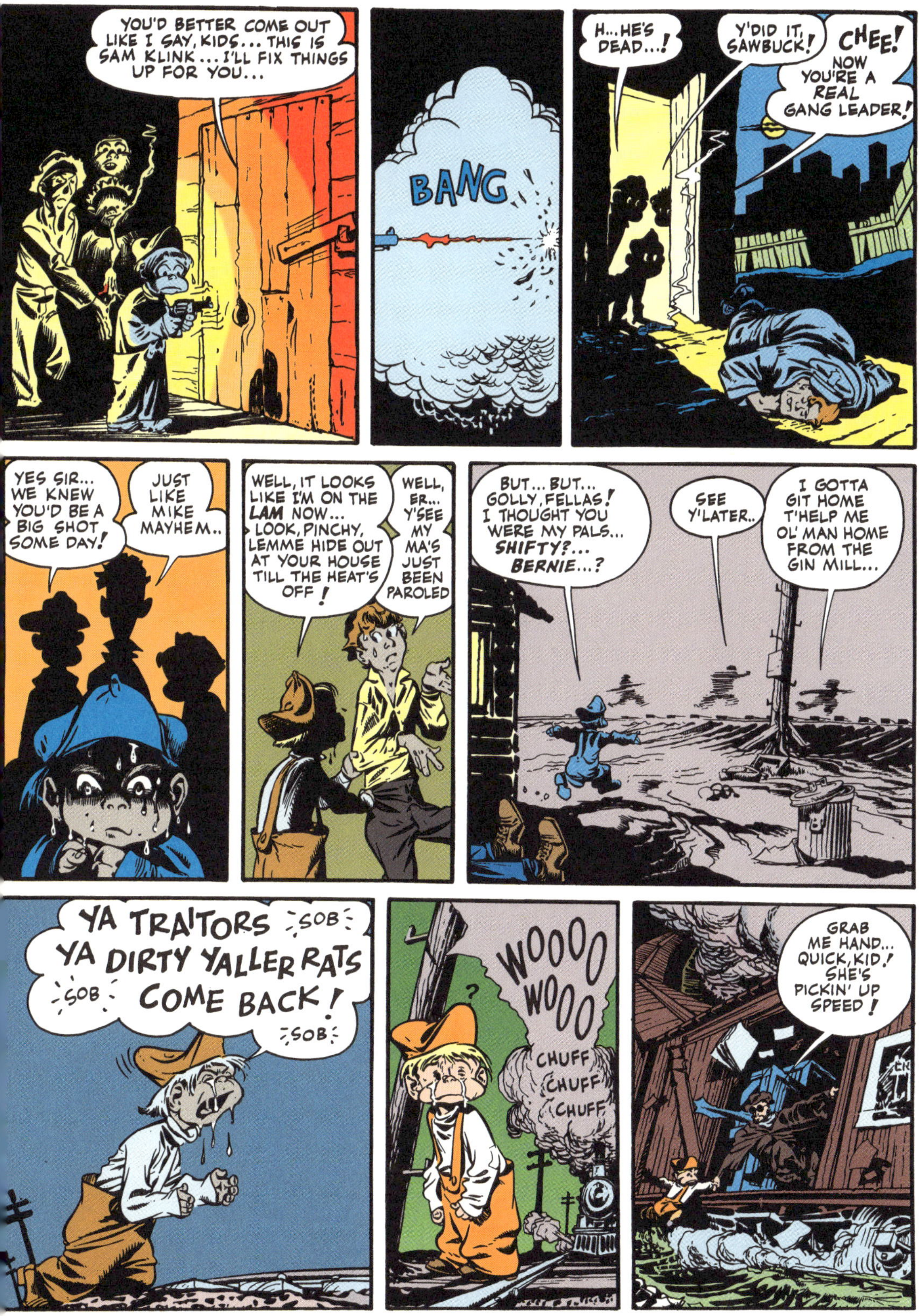
YOU'D BETTER COME OUT LIKE I SAY, KIDS... THIS IS SAM KLINK... I'LL FIX THINGS UP FOR YOU...
BANG
H...HE'S DEAD...!
Y'DID IT, SAWBUCK!
CHEE! NOW YOU'RE A REAL GANG LEADER!
YES SIR... WE KNEW YOU'D BE A BIG SHOT SOME DAY!
JUST LIKE MIKE MAYHEM..
WELL, IT LOOKS LIKE I'M ON THE LAM NOW... LOOK, PINCHY, LEMME HIDE OUT AT YOUR HOUSE TILL THE HEAT'S OFF!
WELL, ER... Y'SEE MY MA'S JUST BEEN PAROLED
BUT... BUT... GOLLY, FELLAS! I THOUGHT YOU WERE MY PALS... SHIFTY?... BERNIE...?
SEE Y'LATER..
I GOTTA GIT HOME T'HELP ME OL' MAN HOME FROM THE GIN MILL...
YA TRAITORS SOB YA DIRTY YALLER RATS SOB COME BACK! SOB
?
WOOOO WOOO
CHUFF CHUFF CHUFF
GRAB ME HAND... QUICK, KID! SHE'S PICKIN' UP SPEED!

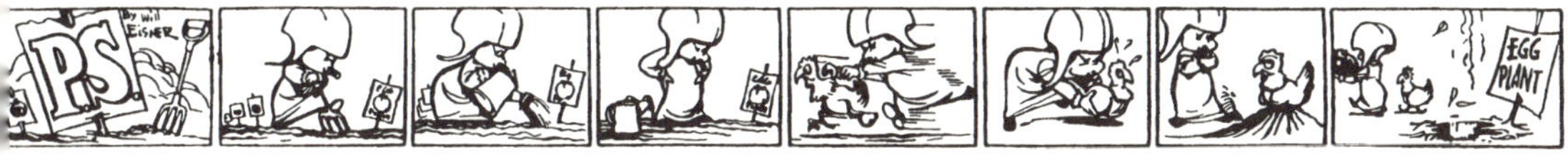
PS
By Wil Eisner
EGG PLANT

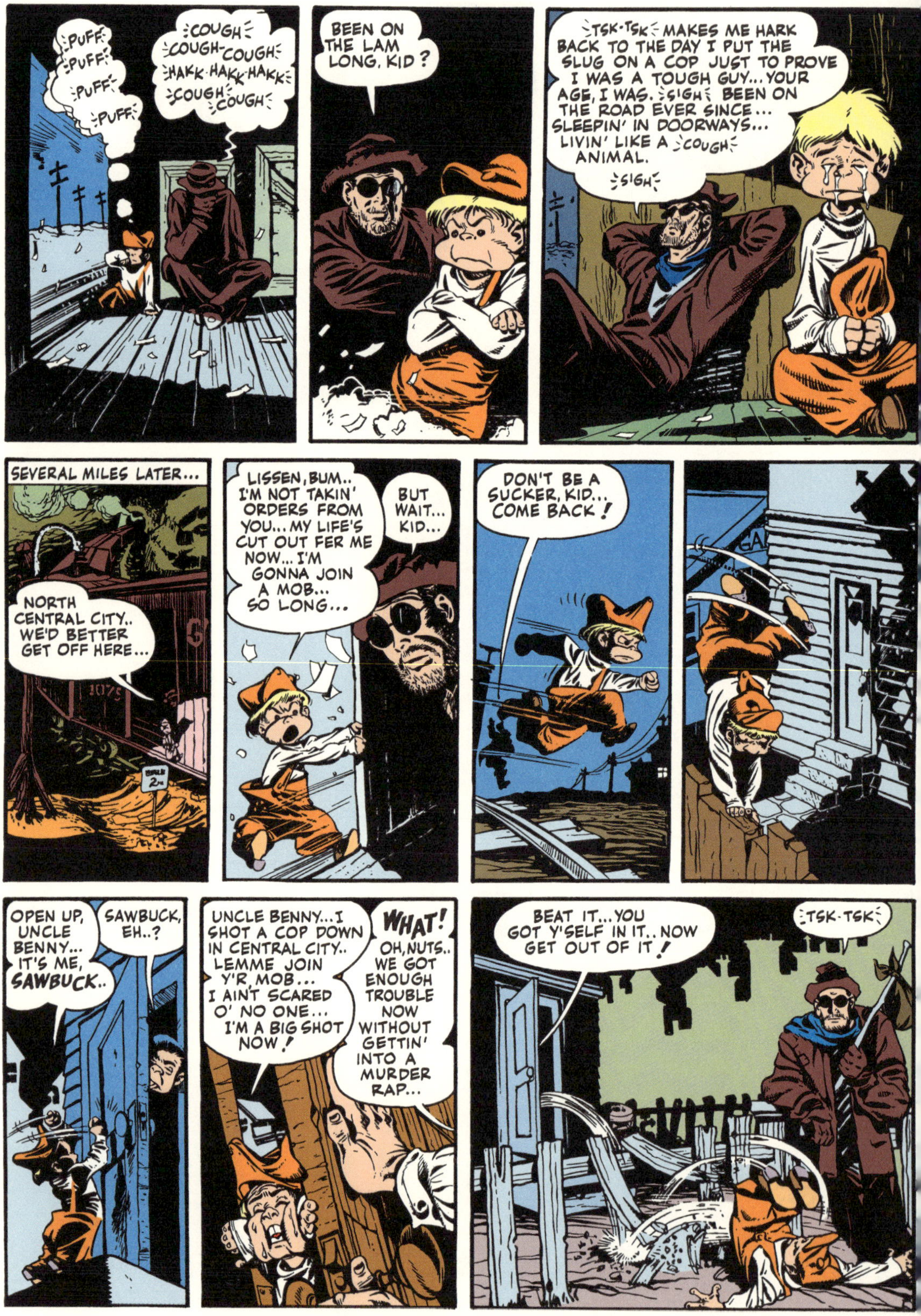
PUFF PUFF PUFF PUFF
COUGH COUGH-COUGH HAKK-HAKK-HAKK COUGH COUGH
BEEN ON THE LAM LONG, KID ?
TSK-TSK MAKES ME HARK BACK TO THE DAY I PUT THE SLUG ON A COP JUST TO PROVE I WAS A TOUGH GUY... YOUR AGE, I WAS. SIGH BEEN ON THE ROAD EVER SINCE... SLEEPIN' IN DOORWAYS... LIVIN' LIKE A COUGH ANIMAL.
SIGH
SEVERAL MILES LATER...
NORTH CENTRAL CITY.. WE'D BETTER GET OFF HERE...
LISSEN, BUM.. I'M NOT TAKIN' ORDERS FROM YOU... MY LIFE'S CUT OUT FER ME NOW... I'M GONNA JOIN A MOB... SO LONG...
BUT WAIT... KID...
DON'T BE A SUCKER, KID... COME BACK !
OPEN UP, UNCLE BENNY... IT'S ME, SAWBUCK..
SAWBUCK, EH..?
UNCLE BENNY...I SHOT A COP DOWN IN CENTRAL CITY.. LEMME JOIN Y'R MOB... I AIN'T SCARED O' NO ONE... I'M A BIG SHOT NOW !
WHAT!
OH, NUTS.. WE GOT ENOUGH TROUBLE NOW WITHOUT GETTIN' INTO A MURDER RAP...
BEAT IT...YOU GOT Y'SELF IN IT.. NOW GET OUT OF IT !
TSK-TSK

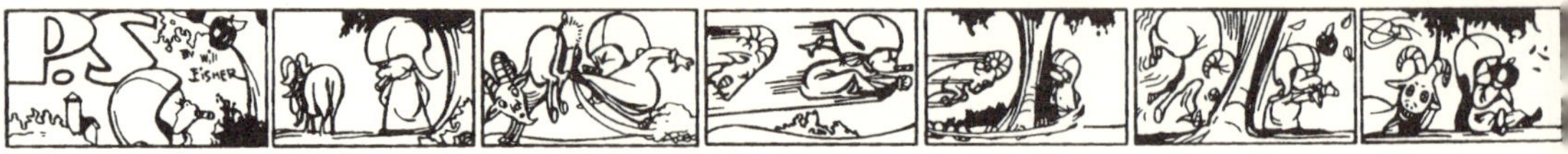

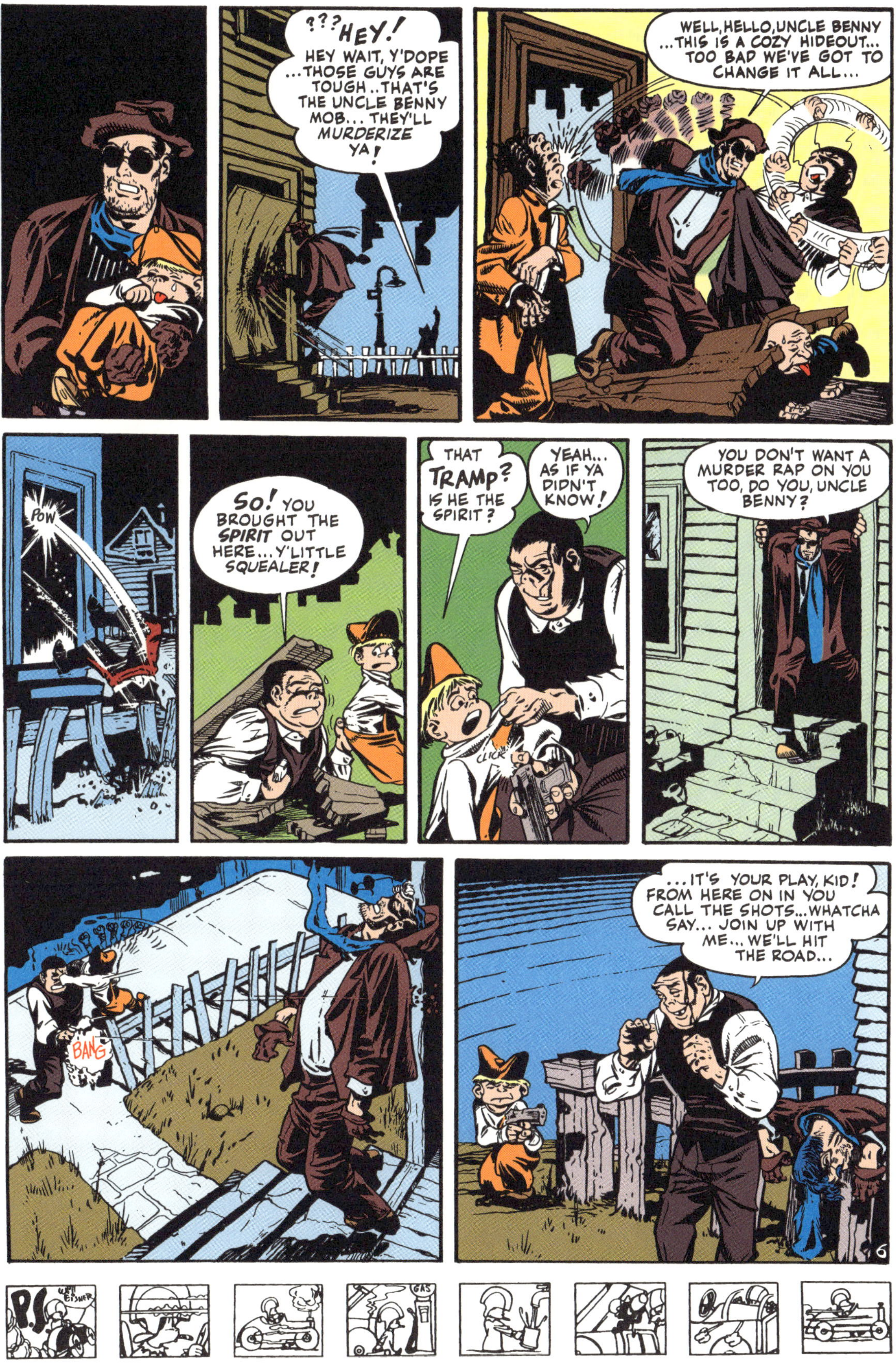
???HEY! HEY WAIT, Y'DOPE ...THOSE GUYS ARE TOUGH..THAT'S THE UNCLE BENNY MOB... THEY'LL MURDERIZE YA!
WELL, HELLO, UNCLE BENNY ...THIS IS A COZY HIDEOUT... TOO BAD WE'VE GOT TO CHANGE IT ALL...
POW
SO! YOU BROUGHT THE SPIRIT OUT HERE...Y'LITTLE SQUEALER!
THAT TRAMP? IS HE THE SPIRIT?
YEAH... AS IF YA DIDN'T KNOW!
CLICK
YOU DON'T WANT A MURDER RAP ON YOU TOO, DO YOU, UNCLE BENNY?
BANG
...IT'S YOUR PLAY, KID! FROM HERE ON IN YOU CALL THE SHOTS...WHATCHA SAY... JOIN UP WITH ME... WE'LL HIT THE ROAD...
6
P.S.
GAS

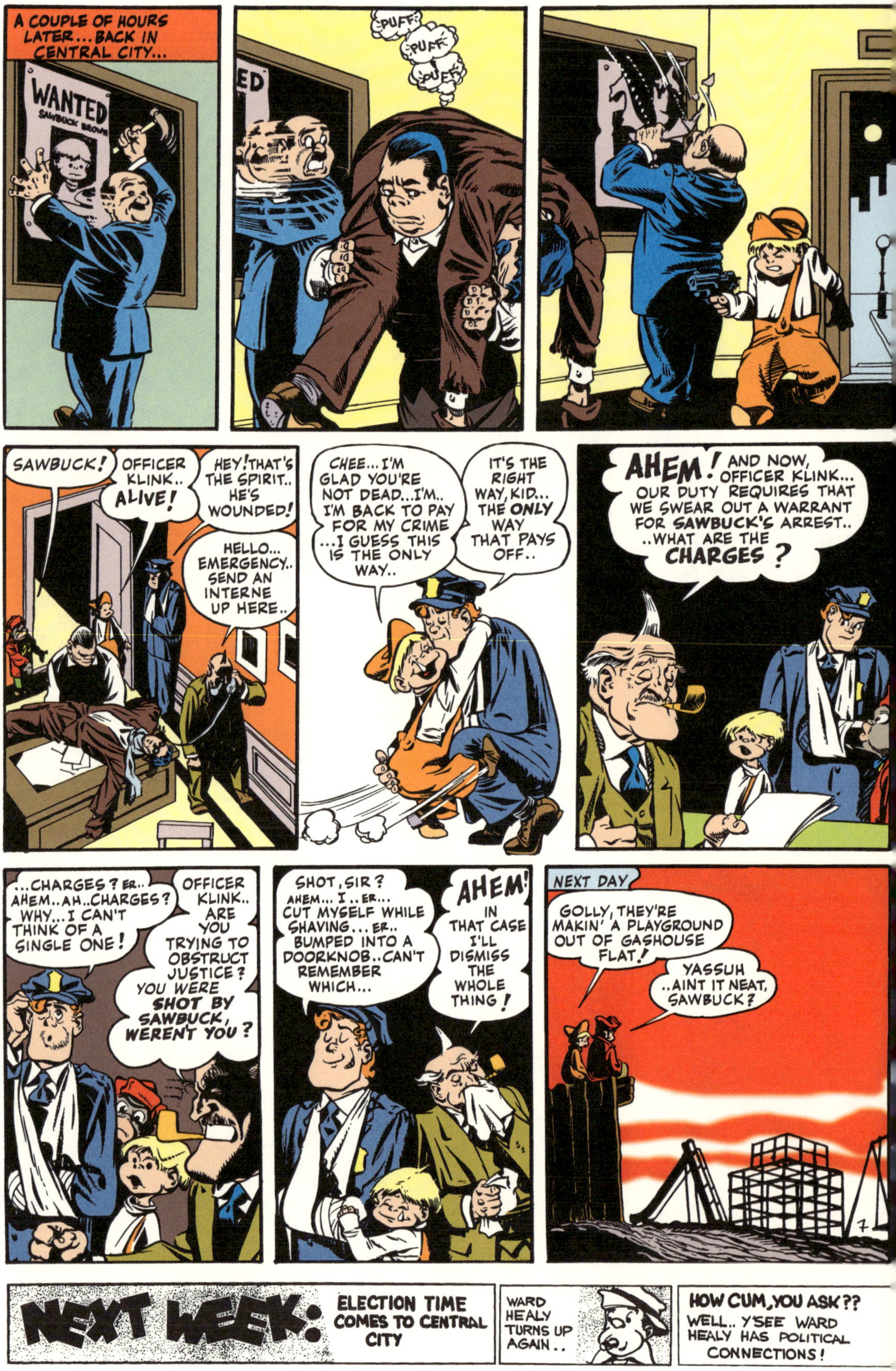
A COUPLE OF HOURS LATER... BACK IN CENTRAL CITY...
WANTED
PUFF
PUFF
PUFF
SAWBUCK!
OFFICER KLINK.. ALIVE!
HEY! THAT'S THE SPIRIT.. HE'S WOUNDED!
HELLO... EMERGENCY.. SEND AN INTERNE UP HERE..
CHEE... I'M GLAD YOU'RE NOT DEAD... I'M.. I'M BACK TO PAY FOR MY CRIME ...I GUESS THIS IS THE ONLY WAY..
IT'S THE RIGHT WAY, KID... THE ONLY WAY THAT PAYS OFF..
AHEM! AND NOW, OFFICER KLINK... OUR DUTY REQUIRES THAT WE SWEAR OUT A WARRANT FOR SAWBUCK'S ARREST.. ..WHAT ARE THE CHARGES?
...CHARGES? ER.. AHEM..AH..CHARGES? WHY...I CAN'T THINK OF A SINGLE ONE!
OFFICER KLINK.. ARE YOU TRYING TO OBSTRUCT JUSTICE? YOU WERE SHOT BY SAWBUCK, WEREN'T YOU?
SHOT, SIR? AHEM... I.. ER... CUT MYSELF WHILE SHAVING... ER.. BUMPED INTO A DOORKNOB..CAN'T REMEMBER WHICH...
AHEM! IN THAT CASE I'LL DISMISS THE WHOLE THING!
NEXT DAY
GOLLY, THEY'RE MAKIN' A PLAYGROUND OUT OF GASHOUSE FLAT!
YASSUH ..AINT IT NEAT, SAWBUCK?
7
NEXT WEEK:
ELECTION TIME COMES TO CENTRAL CITY
WARD HEALY TURNS UP AGAIN..
HOW CUM, YOU ASK?? WELL.. Y'SEE WARD HEALY HAS POLITICAL CONNECTIONS!

COMIC BOOK SECTION

MR. BOWSER'S ELECTION

November 9 1947

ACTION Mystery ADVENTURE

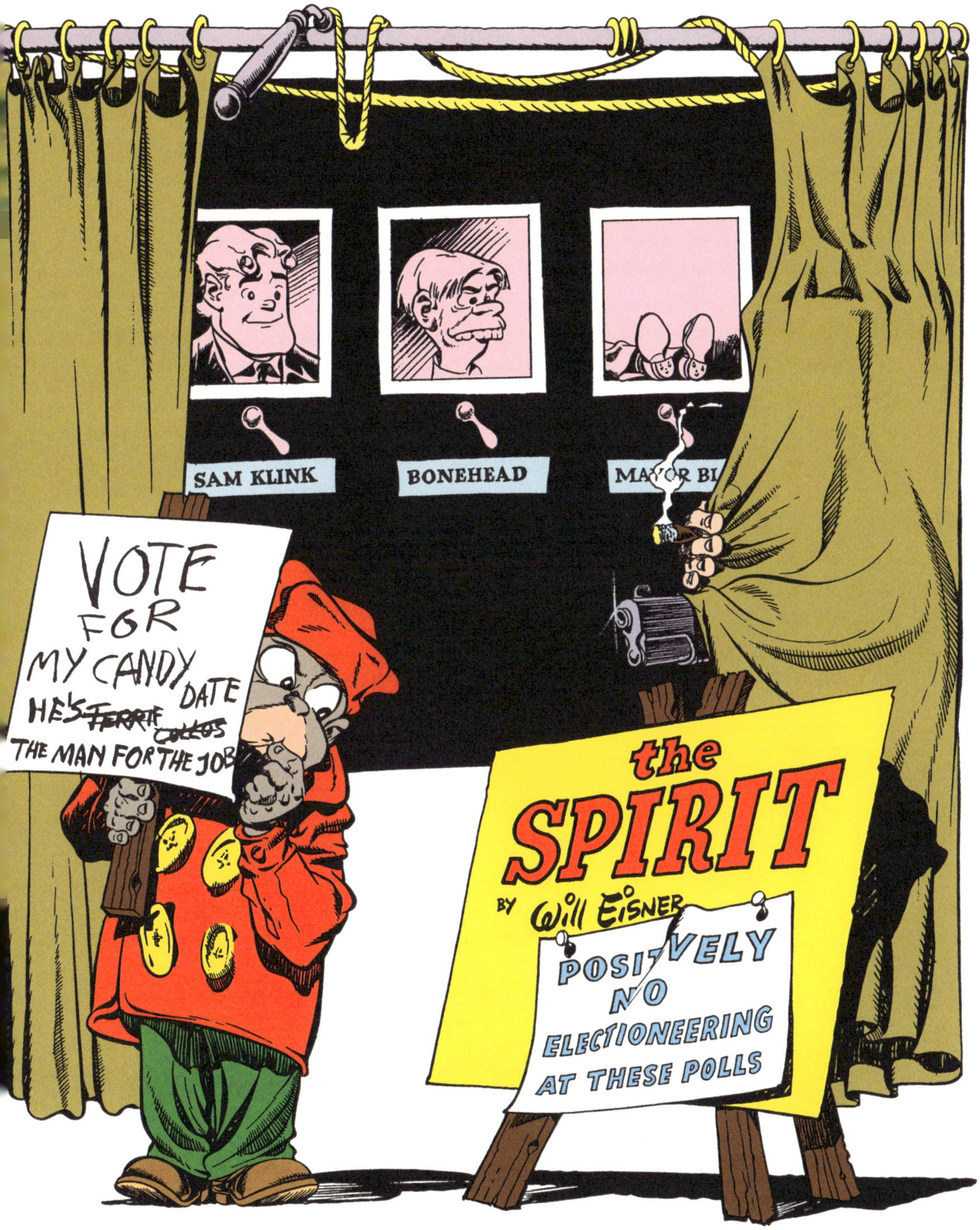

SAM KLINK
BONEHEAD
VOTE FOR MY CANDY DATE HE'S ~~TERRIF~~ ~~COLLOS~~ THE MAN FOR THE JOB
the SPIRIT
BY Will Eisner
POSITIVELY NO ELECTIONEERING AT THESE POLLS

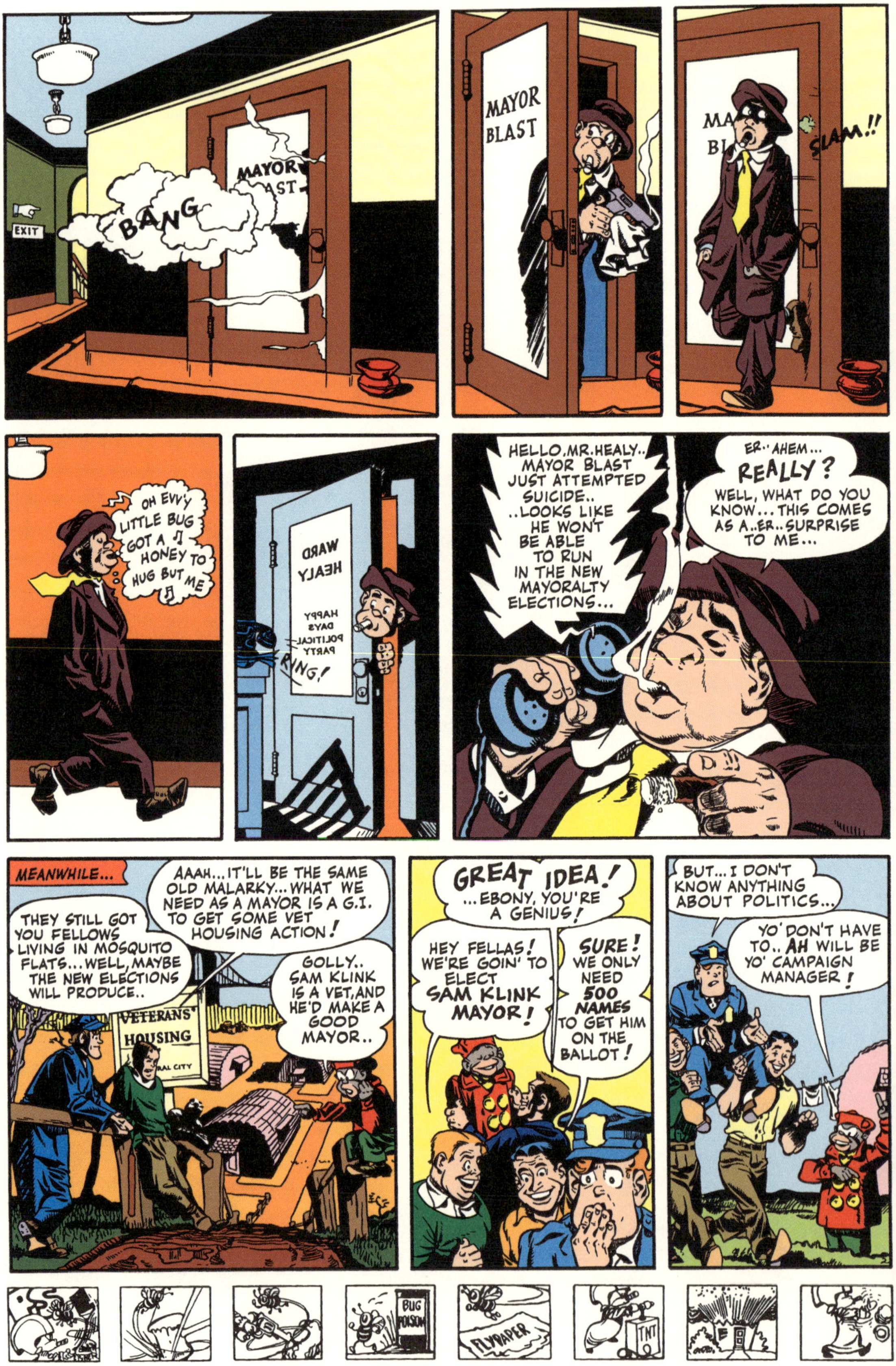
MAYOR BLAST
BANG
MAYOR BLAST
SLAM!!
OH EV'Y LITTLE BUG GOT A HONEY TO HUG BUT ME
WARD HEALY
HAPPY DAYS POLITICAL PARTY
RING!
HELLO, MR. HEALY.. MAYOR BLAST JUST ATTEMPTED SUICIDE.. ..LOOKS LIKE HE WON'T BE ABLE TO RUN IN THE NEW MAYORALTY ELECTIONS...
ER.. AHEM... REALLY? WELL, WHAT DO YOU KNOW... THIS COMES AS A..ER..SURPRISE TO ME...
MEANWHILE...
THEY STILL GOT YOU FELLOWS LIVING IN MOSQUITO FLATS...WELL, MAYBE THE NEW ELECTIONS WILL PRODUCE..
AAAH...IT'LL BE THE SAME OLD MALARKY...WHAT WE NEED AS A MAYOR IS A G.I. TO GET SOME VET HOUSING ACTION!
VETERANS' HOUSING
GOLLY.. SAM KLINK IS A VET, AND HE'D MAKE A GOOD MAYOR..
GREAT IDEA! ...EBONY, YOU'RE A GENIUS!
HEY FELLAS! WE'RE GOIN' TO ELECT SAM KLINK MAYOR!
SURE! WE ONLY NEED 500 NAMES TO GET HIM ON THE BALLOT!
BUT... I DON'T KNOW ANYTHING ABOUT POLITICS...
YO' DON'T HAVE TO.. AH WILL BE YO' CAMPAIGN MANAGER!
BUG POISON
FLYPAPER
TNT

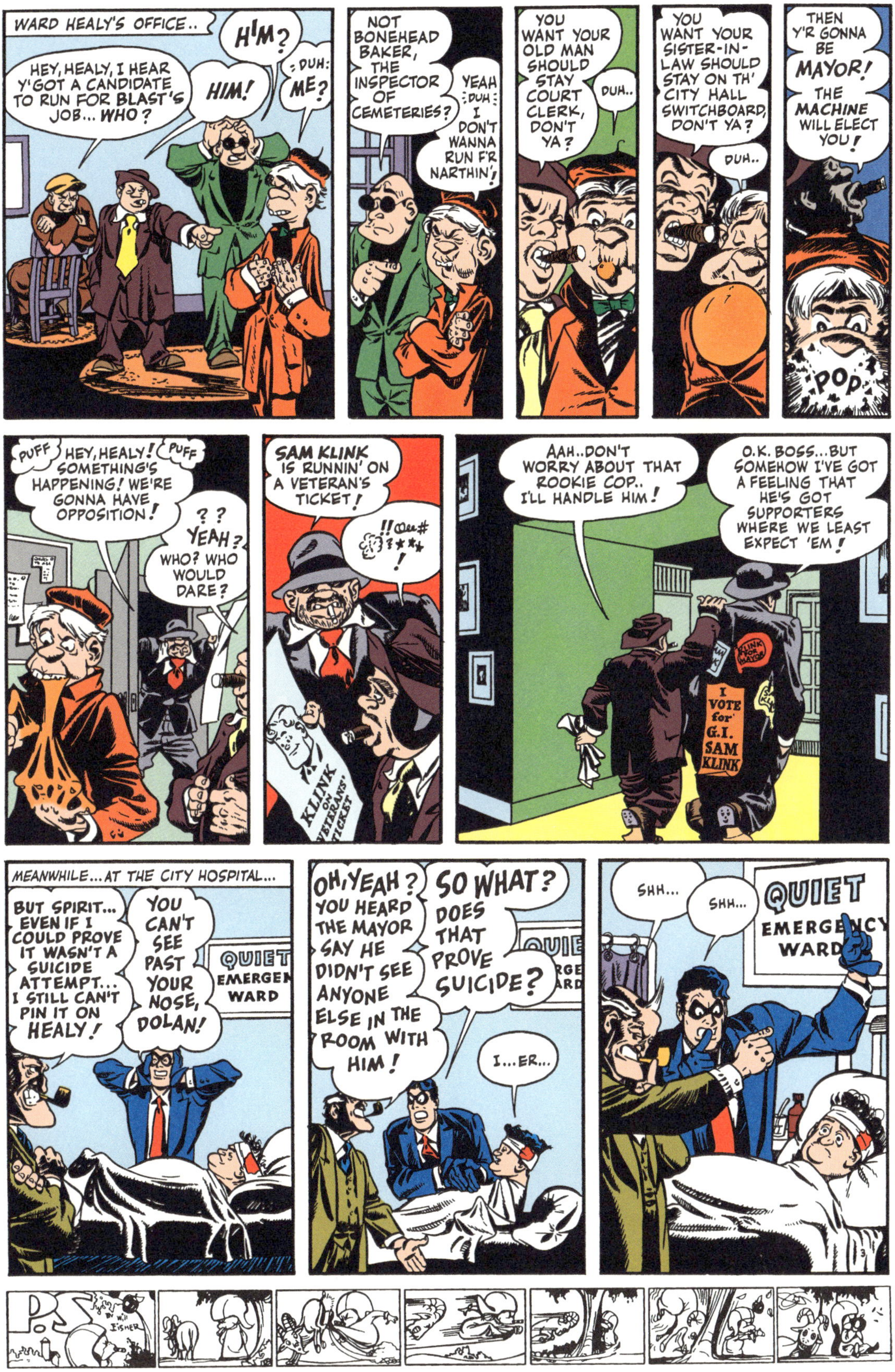
WARD HEALY'S OFFICE..
HEY, HEALY, I HEAR Y'GOT A CANDIDATE TO RUN FOR BLAST'S JOB... WHO?
HIM!
HIM?
DUH: ME?
NOT BONEHEAD BAKER, THE INSPECTOR OF CEMETERIES?
YEAH DUH: I DON'T WANNA RUN F'R NARTHIN'!
YOU WANT YOUR OLD MAN SHOULD STAY COURT CLERK, DON'T YA?
DUH..
YOU WANT YOUR SISTER-IN-LAW SHOULD STAY ON TH' CITY HALL SWITCHBOARD, DON'T YA?
DUH..
THEN Y'R GONNA BE MAYOR! THE MACHINE WILL ELECT YOU!
POP
PUFF HEY, HEALY! PUFF SOMETHING'S HAPPENING! WE'RE GONNA HAVE OPPOSITION!
? ? YEAH? WHO? WHO WOULD DARE?
SAM KLINK IS RUNNIN' ON A VETERAN'S TICKET!
!!@#?**!
KLINK ON VETERANS' TICKET
AAH..DON'T WORRY ABOUT THAT ROOKIE COP.. I'LL HANDLE HIM!
O.K. BOSS...BUT SOMEHOW I'VE GOT A FEELING THAT HE'S GOT SUPPORTERS WHERE WE LEAST EXPECT 'EM!
I VOTE for G.I. SAM KLINK
KLINK FOR MAYOR
MEANWHILE... AT THE CITY HOSPITAL...
BUT SPIRIT... EVEN IF I COULD PROVE IT WASN'T A SUICIDE ATTEMPT... I STILL CAN'T PIN IT ON HEALY!
YOU CAN'T SEE PAST YOUR NOSE, DOLAN!
QUIET EMERGEN WARD
OH, YEAH? YOU HEARD THE MAYOR SAY HE DIDN'T SEE ANYONE ELSE IN THE ROOM WITH HIM!
SO WHAT? DOES THAT PROVE SUICIDE?
I...ER...
SHH...
SHH...
QUIET EMERGENCY WARD
P.S. BY Will Eisner

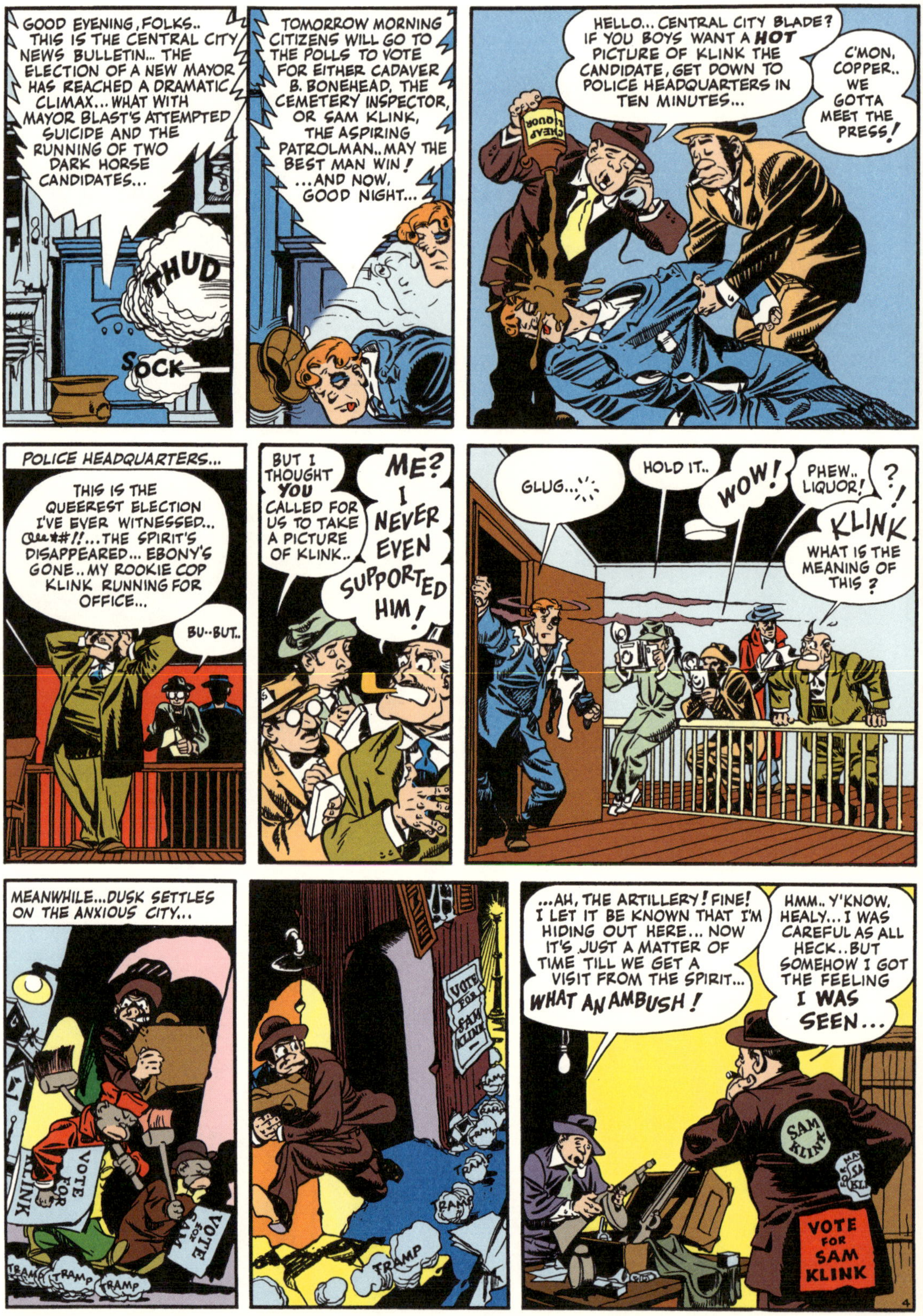
GOOD EVENING, FOLKS.. THIS IS THE CENTRAL CITY NEWS BULLETIN... THE ELECTION OF A NEW MAYOR HAS REACHED A DRAMATIC CLIMAX... WHAT WITH MAYOR BLAST'S ATTEMPTED SUICIDE AND THE RUNNING OF TWO DARK HORSE CANDIDATES...
THUD
SOCK
TOMORROW MORNING CITIZENS WILL GO TO THE POLLS TO VOTE FOR EITHER CADAVER B. BONEHEAD, THE CEMETERY INSPECTOR, OR SAM KLINK, THE ASPIRING PATROLMAN.. MAY THE BEST MAN WIN! ...AND NOW, GOOD NIGHT...
HELLO... CENTRAL CITY BLADE? IF YOU BOYS WANT A HOT PICTURE OF KLINK THE CANDIDATE, GET DOWN TO POLICE HEADQUARTERS IN TEN MINUTES...
C'MON, COPPER.. WE GOTTA MEET THE PRESS!
CHEAP LIQUOR
POLICE HEADQUARTERS...
THIS IS THE QUEEREST ELECTION I'VE EVER WITNESSED... ...THE SPIRIT'S DISAPPEARED... EBONY'S GONE.. MY ROOKIE COP KLINK RUNNING FOR OFFICE...
BU--BUT..
BUT I THOUGHT YOU CALLED FOR US TO TAKE A PICTURE OF KLINK..
ME? I NEVER EVEN SUPPORTED HIM!
GLUG...
HOLD IT..
WOW!
PHEW.. LIQUOR!
?!
KLINK WHAT IS THE MEANING OF THIS?
MEANWHILE...DUSK SETTLES ON THE ANXIOUS CITY...
VOTE FOR KLINK
VOTE FOR
TRAMP TRAMP TRAMP
VOTE FOR SAM KLINK
TRAMP
...AH, THE ARTILLERY! FINE! I LET IT BE KNOWN THAT I'M HIDING OUT HERE... NOW IT'S JUST A MATTER OF TIME TILL WE GET A VISIT FROM THE SPIRIT... WHAT AN AMBUSH!
HMM.. Y'KNOW, HEALY... I WAS CAREFUL AS ALL HECK..BUT SOMEHOW I GOT THE FEELING I WAS SEEN...
SAM KLINK
VOTE FOR SAM KLINK
4

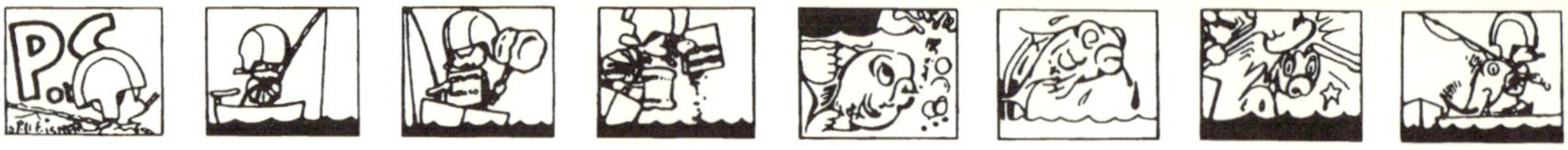

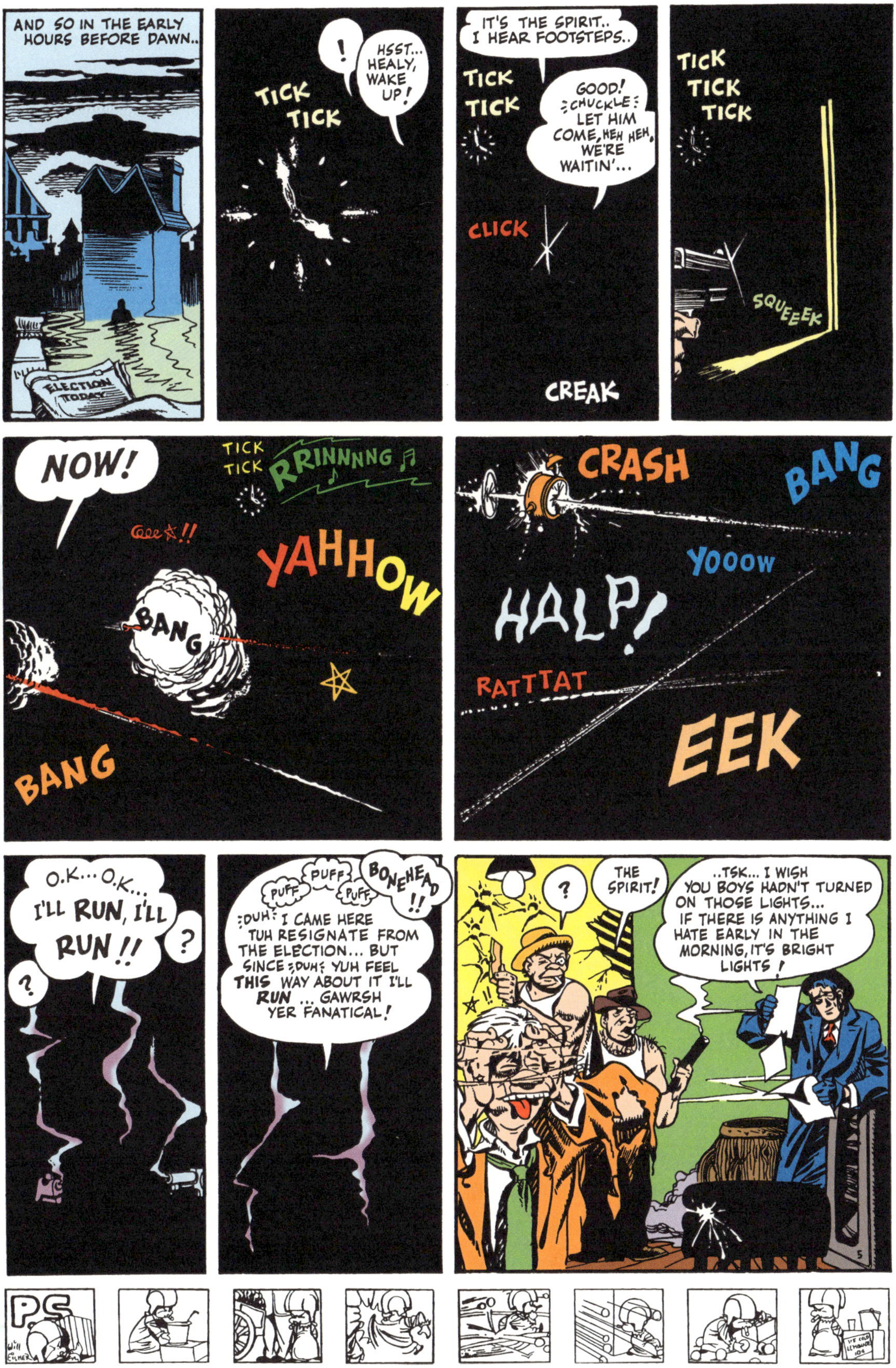
AND SO IN THE EARLY HOURS BEFORE DAWN..
ELECTION TODAY
TICK TICK
!
HSST... HEALY, WAKE UP!
IT'S THE SPIRIT.. I HEAR FOOTSTEPS..
TICK TICK
GOOD! :CHUCKLE: LET HIM COME, HEH HEH, WE'RE WAITIN'...
CLICK
CREAK
TICK TICK TICK
SQUEEEK
NOW!
TICK TICK
RRINNNNG
YAHHOW
BANG
BANG
CRASH
BANG
YOOOW
HALP!
RATTTAT
EEK
O.K... O.K... I'LL RUN, I'LL RUN!!
?
?
PUFF PUFF PUFF
BONEHEAD!!
:DUH: I CAME HERE TUH RESIGNATE FROM THE ELECTION... BUT SINCE :DUH: YUH FEEL THIS WAY ABOUT IT I'LL RUN ... GAWRSH YER FANATICAL!
?
THE SPIRIT!
..TSK... I WISH YOU BOYS HADN'T TURNED ON THOSE LIGHTS... IF THERE IS ANYTHING I HATE EARLY IN THE MORNING, IT'S BRIGHT LIGHTS!
5
PS
Will Eisner

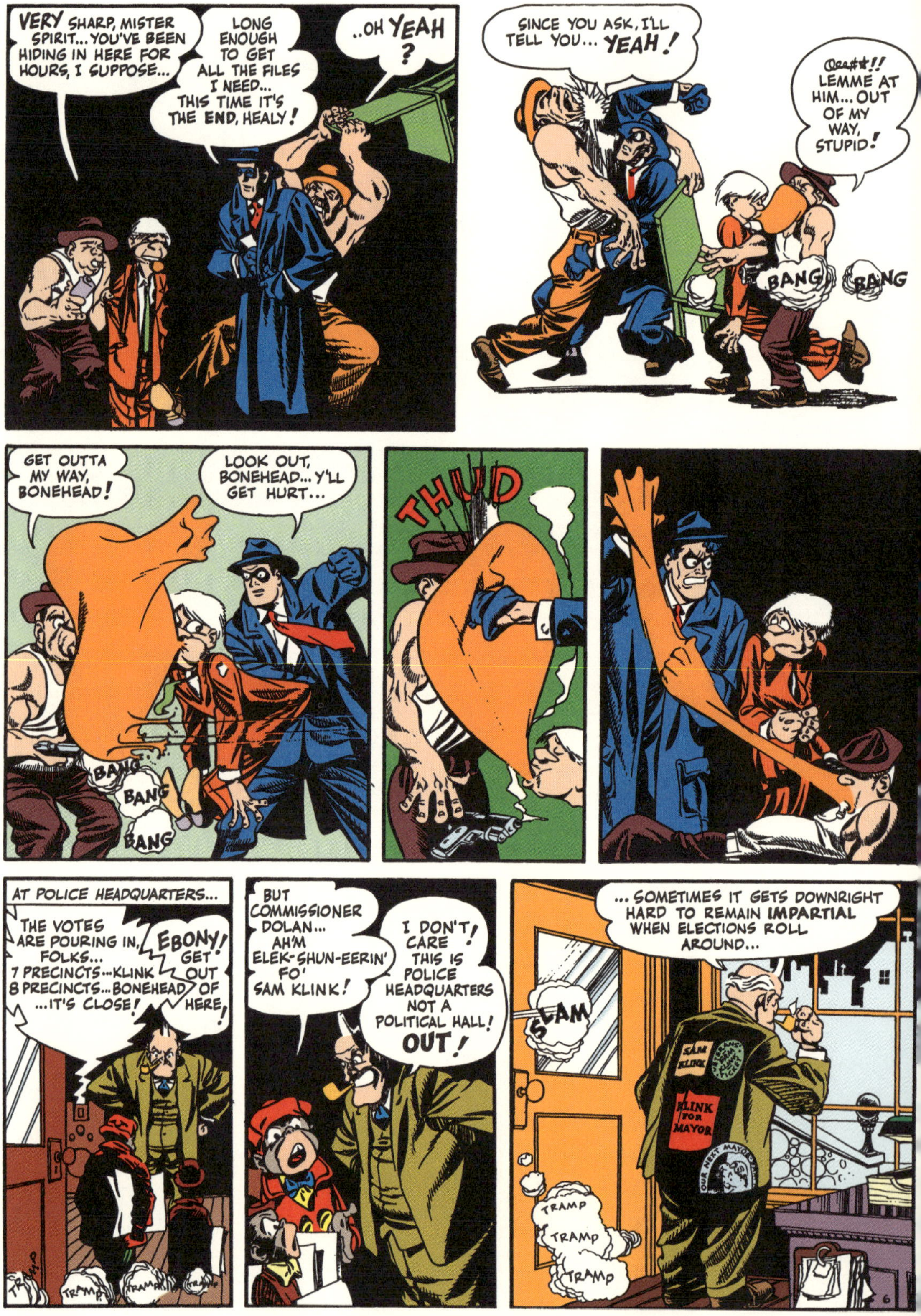
VERY SHARP, MISTER SPIRIT... YOU'VE BEEN HIDING IN HERE FOR HOURS, I SUPPOSE...
LONG ENOUGH TO GET ALL THE FILES I NEED... THIS TIME IT'S THE END, HEALY!
..OH YEAH ?
SINCE YOU ASK, I'LL TELL YOU... YEAH!
LEMME AT HIM... OUT OF MY WAY, STUPID!
BANG
BANG
GET OUTTA MY WAY, BONEHEAD!
LOOK OUT, BONEHEAD... Y'LL GET HURT...
BANG
BANG
BANG
THUD
AT POLICE HEADQUARTERS...
THE VOTES ARE POURING IN, FOLKS... 7 PRECINCTS...KLINK 8 PRECINCTS...BONEHEAD ...IT'S CLOSE!
EBONY! GET OUT OF HERE!
TRAMP
TRAMP
TRAMP
TRAMP
BUT COMMISSIONER DOLAN... AH'M ELEK-SHUN-EERIN' FO' SAM KLINK!
I DON'T CARE! THIS IS POLICE HEADQUARTERS NOT A POLITICAL HALL! OUT!
... SOMETIMES IT GETS DOWNRIGHT HARD TO REMAIN IMPARTIAL WHEN ELECTIONS ROLL AROUND...
SLAM
SAM KLINK
KLINK FOR MAYOR
OUR NEXT MAYOR
TRAMP
TRAMP
TRAMP
6

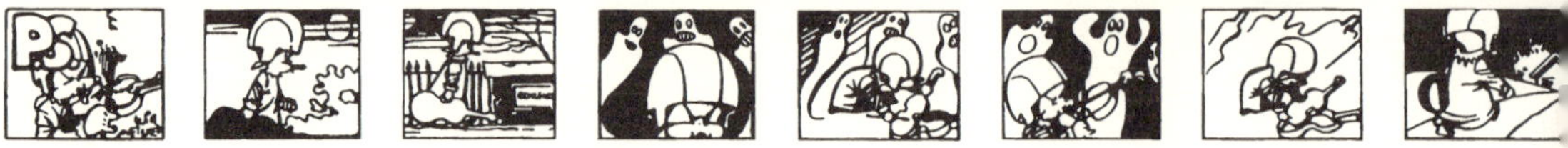

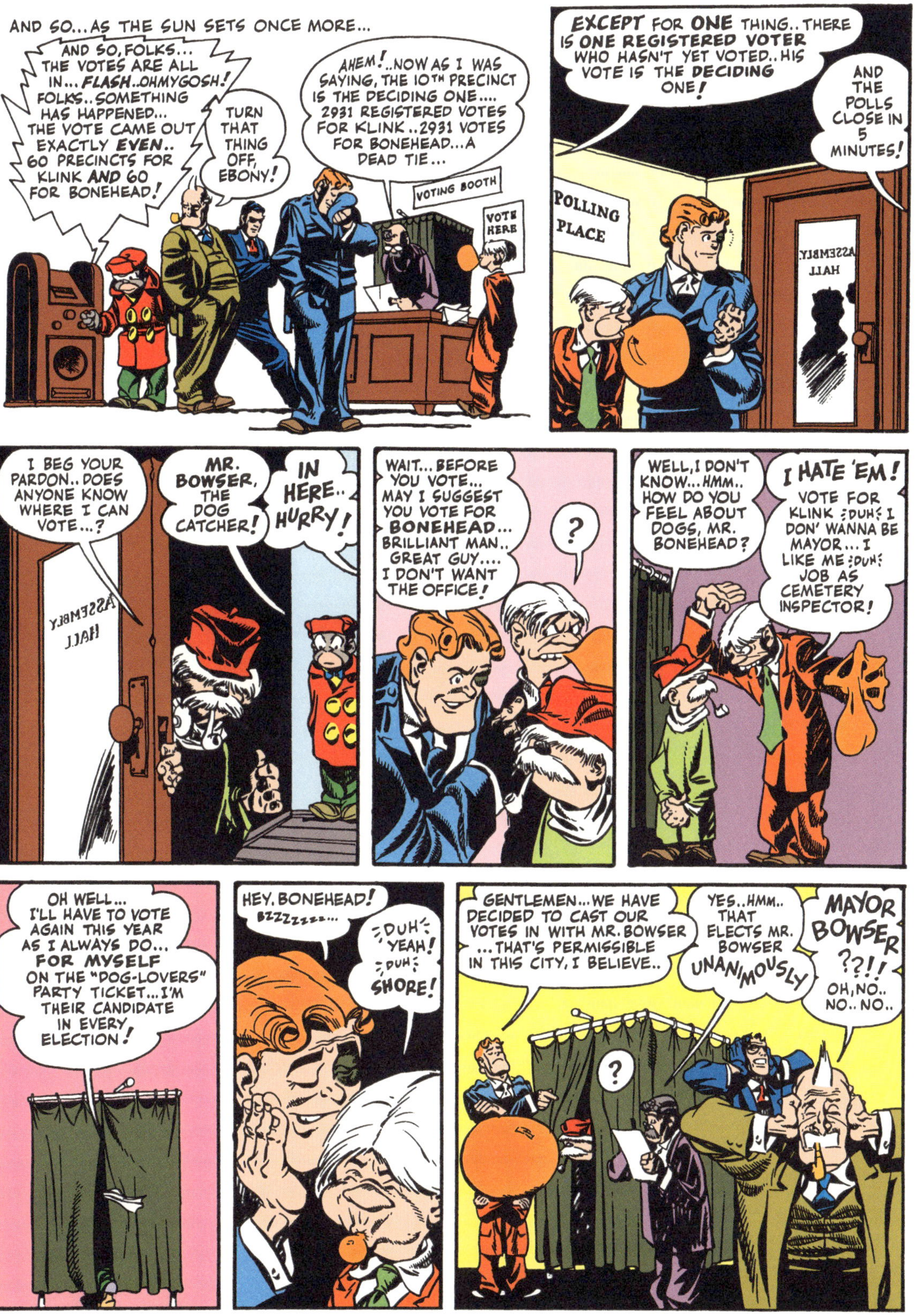
AND SO... AS THE SUN SETS ONCE MORE...
AND SO, FOLKS... THE VOTES ARE ALL IN... FLASH..OHMYGOSH! FOLKS..SOMETHING HAS HAPPENED... THE VOTE CAME OUT EXACTLY EVEN.. 60 PRECINCTS FOR KLINK AND 60 FOR BONEHEAD!
TURN THAT THING OFF, EBONY!
AHEM!..NOW AS I WAS SAYING, THE 10TH PRECINCT IS THE DECIDING ONE.... 2931 REGISTERED VOTES FOR KLINK..2931 VOTES FOR BONEHEAD...A DEAD TIE...
VOTING BOOTH
VOTE HERE
EXCEPT FOR ONE THING.. THERE IS ONE REGISTERED VOTER WHO HASN'T YET VOTED.. HIS VOTE IS THE DECIDING ONE!
AND THE POLLS CLOSE IN 5 MINUTES!
POLLING PLACE
ASSEMBLY HALL
I BEG YOUR PARDON.. DOES ANYONE KNOW WHERE I CAN VOTE...?
MR. BOWSER, THE DOG CATCHER!
IN HERE.. HURRY!
ASSEMBLY HALL
WAIT... BEFORE YOU VOTE... MAY I SUGGEST YOU VOTE FOR BONEHEAD... BRILLIANT MAN.. GREAT GUY.... I DON'T WANT THE OFFICE!
?
WELL, I DON'T KNOW... HMM.. HOW DO YOU FEEL ABOUT DOGS, MR. BONEHEAD?
I HATE 'EM!
VOTE FOR KLINK :DUH: I DON' WANNA BE MAYOR... I LIKE ME :DUH: JOB AS CEMETERY INSPECTOR!
OH WELL... I'LL HAVE TO VOTE AGAIN THIS YEAR AS I ALWAYS DO... FOR MYSELF ON THE "DOG-LOVERS" PARTY TICKET... I'M THEIR CANDIDATE IN EVERY ELECTION!
HEY, BONEHEAD! BZZZZZZZ...
:DUH: YEAH! :DUH: SHORE!
GENTLEMEN... WE HAVE DECIDED TO CAST OUR VOTES IN WITH MR. BOWSER ...THAT'S PERMISSIBLE IN THIS CITY, I BELIEVE..
YES..HMM.. THAT ELECTS MR. BOWSER UNANIMOUSLY
MAYOR BOWSER ??!! OH, NO.. NO.. NO..
?

Next Week

A BONE-CRUSHING, BLOOD-LETTING, NOSE-SMASHING STORY OF 10 ROUNDS IN WHICH THE SPIRIT PROVES... GAD!... HE CAN TAKE IT.
Don't miss "THE FIGHTING MACHINE"

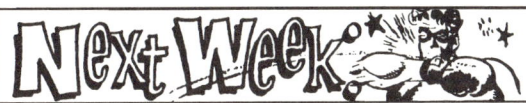

THE FIGHTING MACHINE

November 16 1947

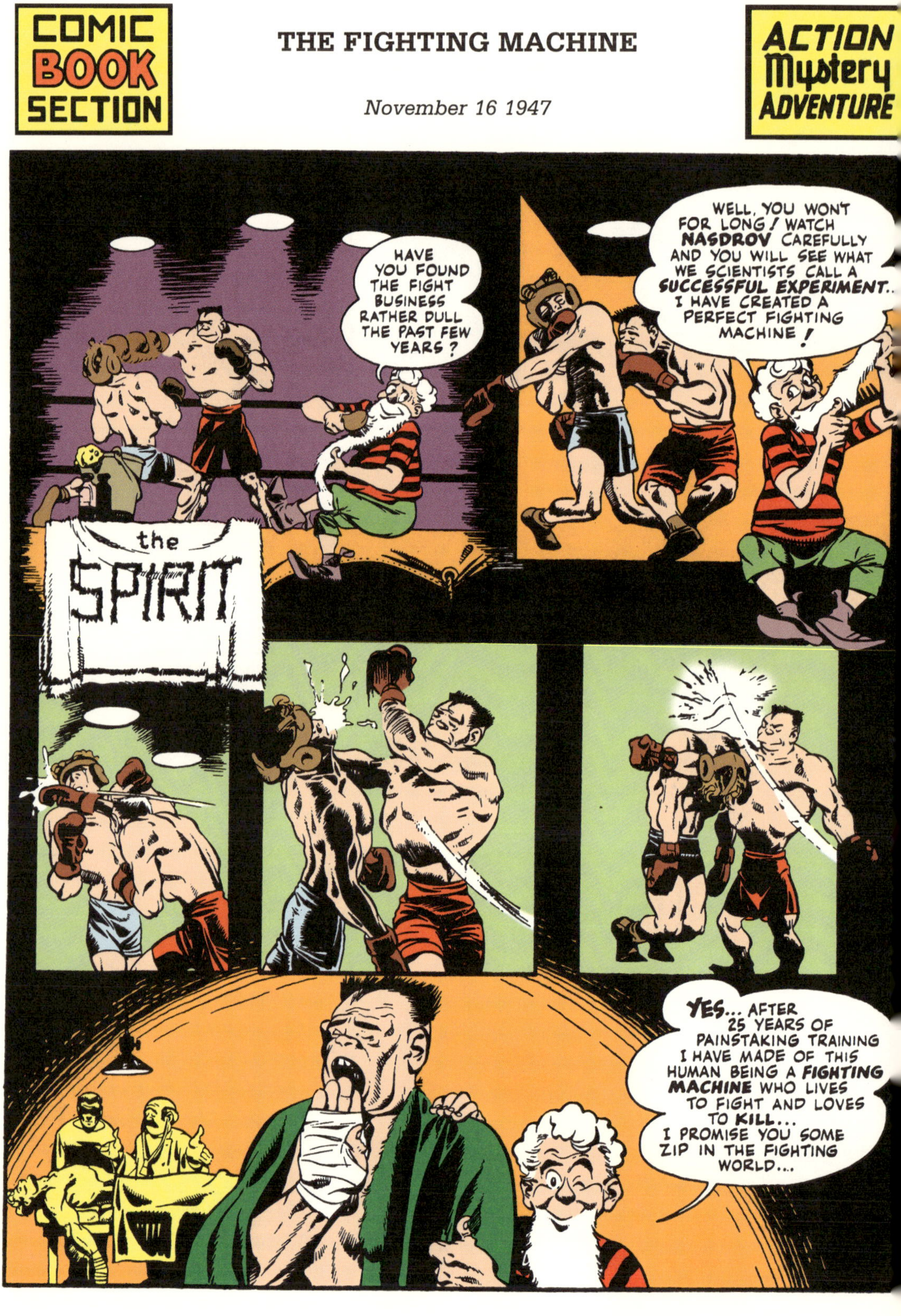

COMIC BOOK SECTION
ACTION Mystery ADVENTURE
the SPIRIT
HAVE YOU FOUND THE FIGHT BUSINESS RATHER DULL THE PAST FEW YEARS?
WELL, YOU WON'T FOR LONG! WATCH NASDROV CAREFULLY AND YOU WILL SEE WHAT WE SCIENTISTS CALL A SUCCESSFUL EXPERIMENT.. I HAVE CREATED A PERFECT FIGHTING MACHINE!
YES... AFTER 25 YEARS OF PAINSTAKING TRAINING I HAVE MADE OF THIS HUMAN BEING A FIGHTING MACHINE WHO LIVES TO FIGHT AND LOVES TO KILL... I PROMISE YOU SOME ZIP IN THE FIGHTING WORLD...

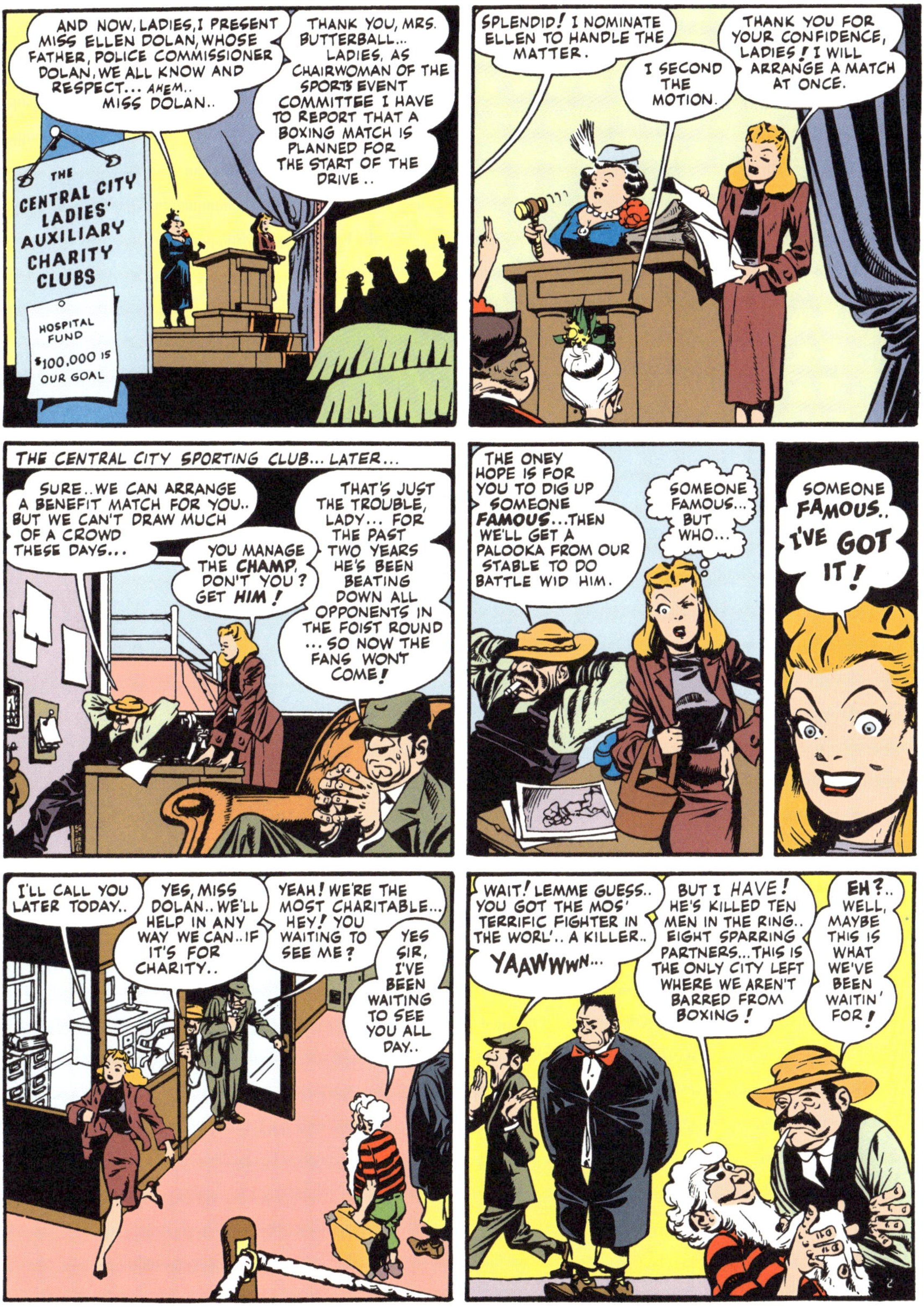
AND NOW, LADIES, I PRESENT MISS ELLEN DOLAN, WHOSE FATHER, POLICE COMMISSIONER DOLAN, WE ALL KNOW AND RESPECT... AHEM.. MISS DOLAN..
THANK YOU, MRS. BUTTERBALL... LADIES, AS CHAIRWOMAN OF THE SPORTS EVENT COMMITTEE I HAVE TO REPORT THAT A BOXING MATCH IS PLANNED FOR THE START OF THE DRIVE..
THE CENTRAL CITY LADIES' AUXILIARY CHARITY CLUBS
HOSPITAL FUND $100,000 IS OUR GOAL
SPLENDID! I NOMINATE ELLEN TO HANDLE THE MATTER.
I SECOND THE MOTION.
THANK YOU FOR YOUR CONFIDENCE, LADIES! I WILL ARRANGE A MATCH AT ONCE.
THE CENTRAL CITY SPORTING CLUB... LATER...
SURE.. WE CAN ARRANGE A BENEFIT MATCH FOR YOU.. BUT WE CAN'T DRAW MUCH OF A CROWD THESE DAYS...
YOU MANAGE THE CHAMP, DON'T YOU? GET HIM!
THAT'S JUST THE TROUBLE, LADY... FOR THE PAST TWO YEARS HE'S BEEN BEATING DOWN ALL OPPONENTS IN THE FOIST ROUND ... SO NOW THE FANS WON'T COME!
THE ONEY HOPE IS FOR YOU TO DIG UP SOMEONE FAMOUS... THEN WE'LL GET A PALOOKA FROM OUR STABLE TO DO BATTLE WID HIM.
SOMEONE FAMOUS... BUT WHO...
SOMEONE FAMOUS.. I'VE GOT IT!
I'LL CALL YOU LATER TODAY..
YES, MISS DOLAN.. WE'LL HELP IN ANY WAY WE CAN.. IF IT'S FOR CHARITY..
YEAH! WE'RE THE MOST CHARITABLE... HEY! YOU WAITING TO SEE ME?
YES SIR, I'VE BEEN WAITING TO SEE YOU ALL DAY..
WAIT! LEMME GUESS.. YOU GOT THE MOS' TERRIFIC FIGHTER IN THE WORL'.. A KILLER..
YAAWWWN...
BUT I HAVE! HE'S KILLED TEN MEN IN THE RING.. EIGHT SPARRING PARTNERS... THIS IS THE ONLY CITY LEFT WHERE WE AREN'T BARRED FROM BOXING!
EH?.. WELL, MAYBE THIS IS WHAT WE'VE BEEN WAITIN' FOR!

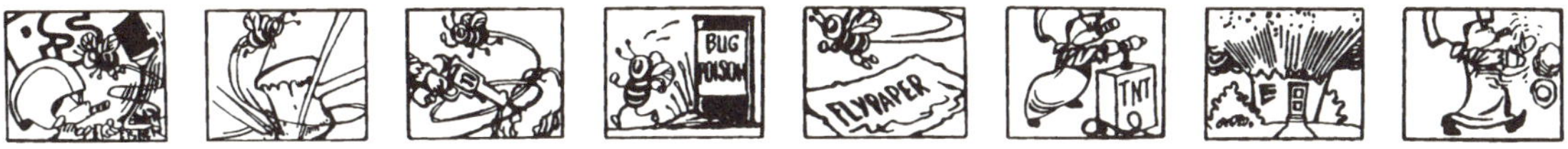
BUG POISON
FLYPAPER
TNT

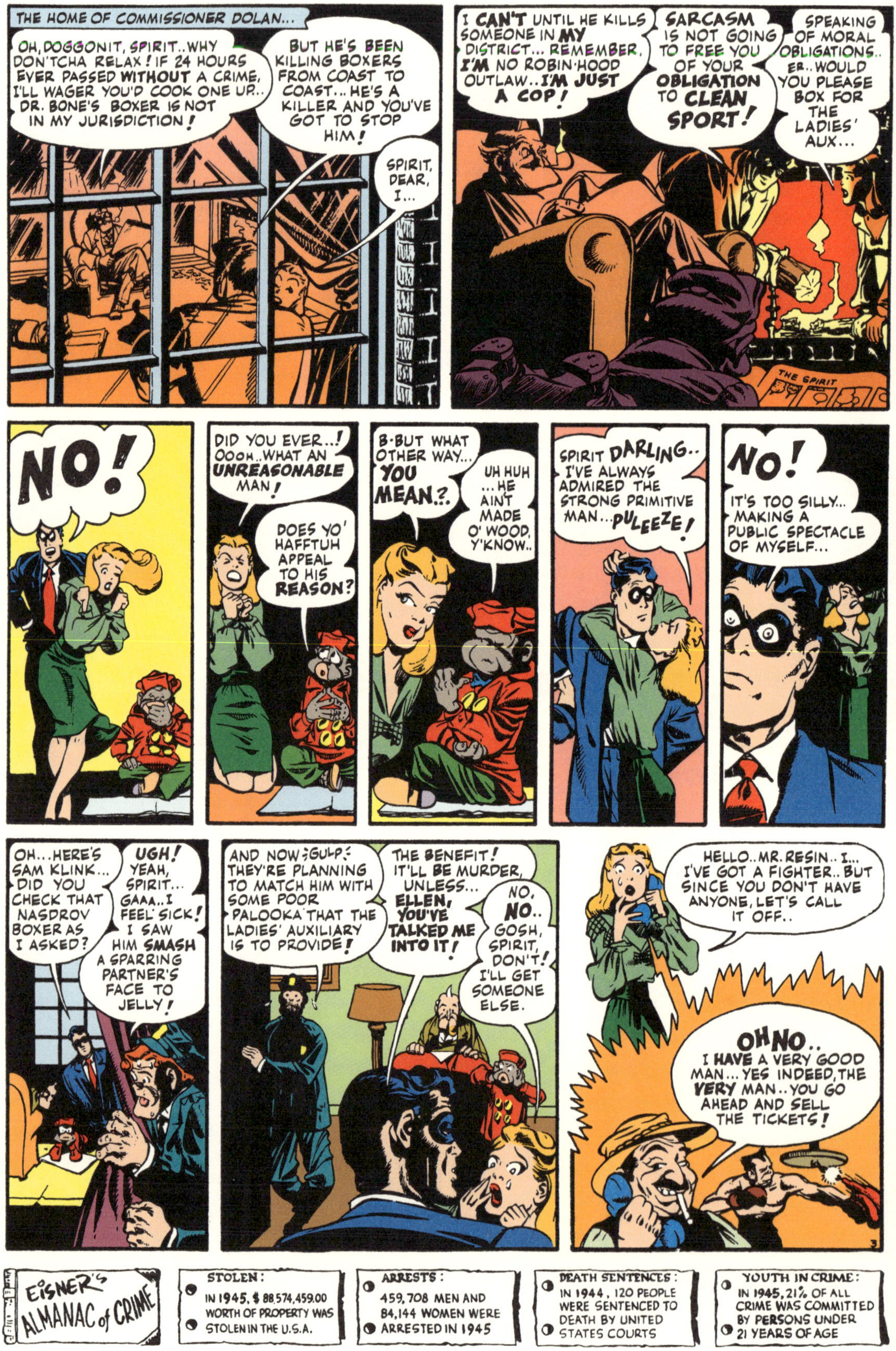

THE HOME OF COMMISSIONER DOLAN...
OH, DOGGONIT, SPIRIT..WHY DON'TCHA RELAX! IF 24 HOURS EVER PASSED WITHOUT A CRIME, I'LL WAGER YOU'D COOK ONE UP.. DR. BONE'S BOXER IS NOT IN MY JURISDICTION!
BUT HE'S BEEN KILLING BOXERS FROM COAST TO COAST... HE'S A KILLER AND YOU'VE GOT TO STOP HIM!
SPIRIT, DEAR, I...
I CAN'T UNTIL HE KILLS SOMEONE IN MY DISTRICT... REMEMBER, I'M NO ROBIN·HOOD OUTLAW..I'M JUST A COP!
SARCASM IS NOT GOING TO FREE YOU OF YOUR OBLIGATION TO CLEAN SPORT!
SPEAKING OF MORAL OBLIGATIONS.. ER..WOULD YOU PLEASE BOX FOR THE LADIES' AUX...
THE SPIRIT
NO!
DID YOU EVER..! OOOH..WHAT AN UNREASONABLE MAN!
DOES YO' HAFFTUH APPEAL TO HIS REASON?
B-BUT WHAT OTHER WAY... YOU MEAN..?
UH HUH ...HE AIN'T MADE O' WOOD, Y'KNOW..
SPIRIT DARLING.. I'VE ALWAYS ADMIRED THE STRONG PRIMITIVE MAN...PULEEZE!
NO! IT'S TOO SILLY... MAKING A PUBLIC SPECTACLE OF MYSELF...
OH...HERE'S SAM KLINK... DID YOU CHECK THAT NASDROV BOXER AS I ASKED?
UGH! YEAH, SPIRIT... GAAA..I FEEL SICK! I SAW HIM SMASH A SPARRING PARTNER'S FACE TO JELLY!
AND NOW -GULP- THEY'RE PLANNING TO MATCH HIM WITH SOME POOR PALOOKA THAT THE LADIES' AUXILIARY IS TO PROVIDE!
THE BENEFIT! IT'LL BE MURDER, UNLESS... ELLEN, YOU'VE TALKED ME INTO IT!
NO, NO.. GOSH, SPIRIT, DON'T! I'LL GET SOMEONE ELSE.
HELLO..MR. RESIN.. I... I'VE GOT A FIGHTER.. BUT SINCE YOU DON'T HAVE ANYONE, LET'S CALL IT OFF..
OH NO.. I HAVE A VERY GOOD MAN... YES INDEED, THE VERY MAN.. YOU GO AHEAD AND SELL THE TICKETS!
3
EISNER'S ALMANAC of CRIME
STOLEN: IN 1945, $ 88,574,459.00 WORTH OF PROPERTY WAS STOLEN IN THE U.S.A.
ARRESTS: 459,708 MEN AND 84,144 WOMEN WERE ARRESTED IN 1945
DEATH SENTENCES: IN 1944, 120 PEOPLE WERE SENTENCED TO DEATH BY UNITED STATES COURTS
YOUTH IN CRIME: IN 1945, 21% OF ALL CRIME WAS COMMITTED BY PERSONS UNDER 21 YEARS OF AGE

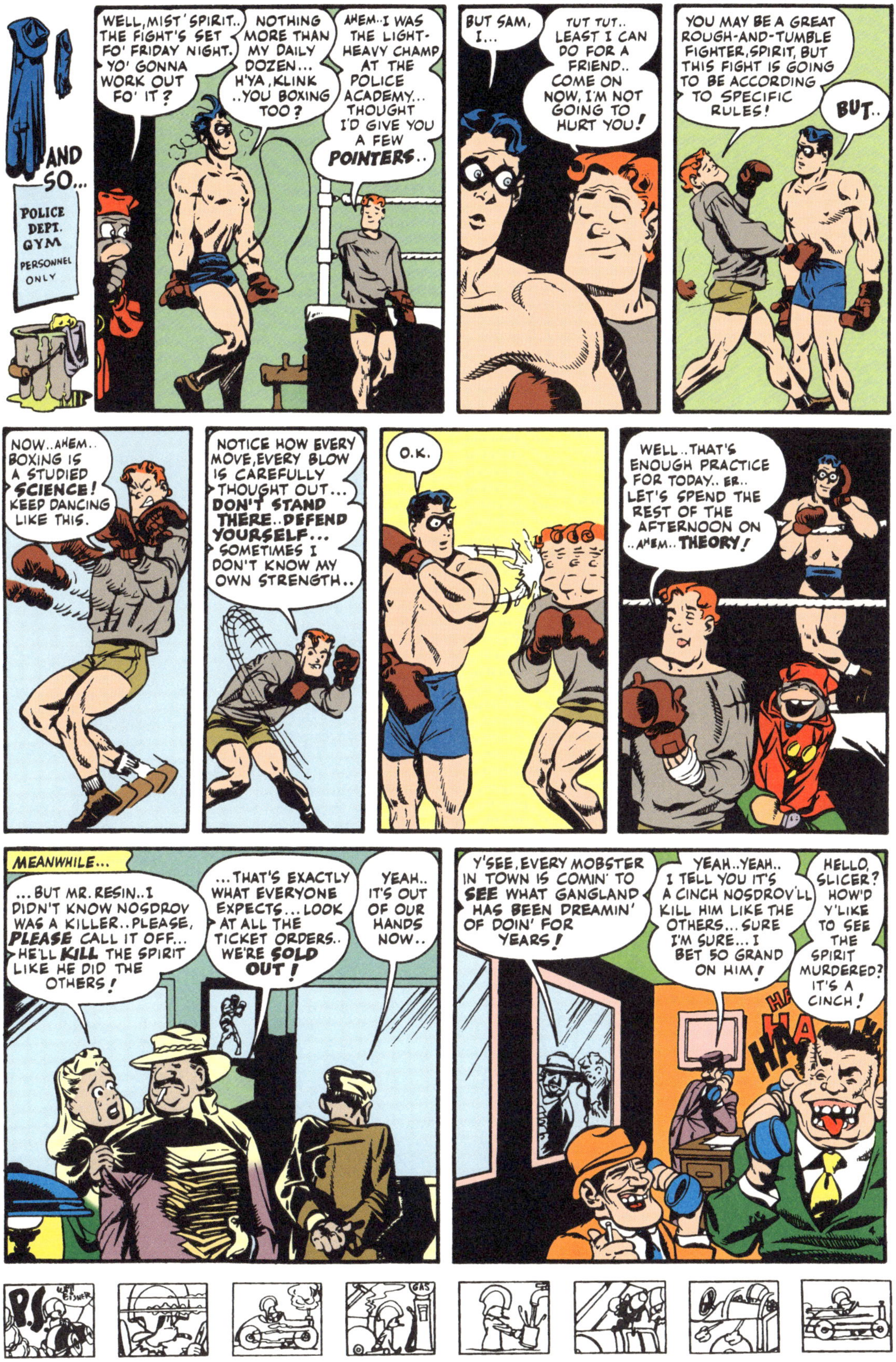
AND SO...
POLICE DEPT. GYM PERSONNEL ONLY
WELL, MIST' SPIRIT.. THE FIGHT'S SET FO' FRIDAY NIGHT. YO' GONNA WORK OUT FO' IT?
NOTHING MORE THAN MY DAILY DOZEN... H'YA, KLINK ..YOU BOXING TOO?
AHEM..I WAS THE LIGHT-HEAVY CHAMP AT THE POLICE ACADEMY... THOUGHT I'D GIVE YOU A FEW POINTERS..
BUT SAM, I...
TUT TUT.. LEAST I CAN DO FOR A FRIEND.. COME ON NOW, I'M NOT GOING TO HURT YOU!
YOU MAY BE A GREAT ROUGH-AND-TUMBLE FIGHTER, SPIRIT, BUT THIS FIGHT IS GOING TO BE ACCORDING TO SPECIFIC RULES!
BUT..
NOW..AHEM.. BOXING IS A STUDIED SCIENCE! KEEP DANCING LIKE THIS.
NOTICE HOW EVERY MOVE, EVERY BLOW IS CAREFULLY THOUGHT OUT... DON'T STAND THERE..DEFEND YOURSELF... SOMETIMES I DON'T KNOW MY OWN STRENGTH..
O.K.
WELL..THAT'S ENOUGH PRACTICE FOR TODAY.. ER.. LET'S SPEND THE REST OF THE AFTERNOON ON ..AHEM.. THEORY!
MEANWHILE...
...BUT MR. RESIN..I DIDN'T KNOW NOSDROV WAS A KILLER..PLEASE, PLEASE CALL IT OFF... HE'LL KILL THE SPIRIT LIKE HE DID THE OTHERS!
...THAT'S EXACTLY WHAT EVERYONE EXPECTS...LOOK AT ALL THE TICKET ORDERS.. WE'RE SOLD OUT!
YEAH.. IT'S OUT OF OUR HANDS NOW..
Y'SEE, EVERY MOBSTER IN TOWN IS COMIN' TO SEE WHAT GANGLAND HAS BEEN DREAMIN' OF DOIN' FOR YEARS!
YEAH..YEAH.. I TELL YOU IT'S A CINCH NOSDROV'LL KILL HIM LIKE THE OTHERS... SURE I'M SURE... I BET 50 GRAND ON HIM!
HELLO, SLICER? HOW'D Y'LIKE TO SEE THE SPIRIT MURDERED? IT'S A CINCH!
HA HA HA
P.S.
GAS

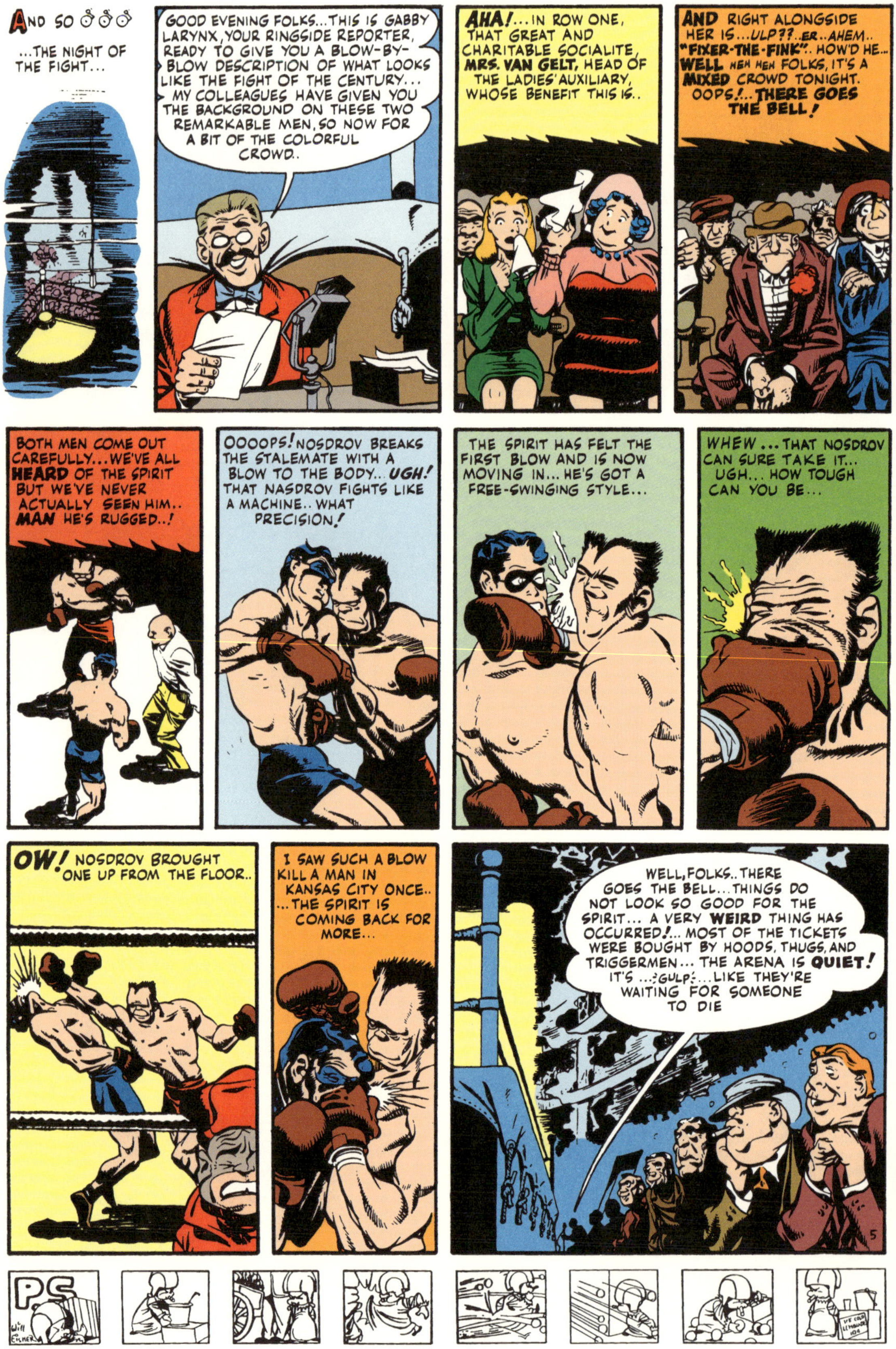
AND SO ...
...THE NIGHT OF THE FIGHT...
GOOD EVENING FOLKS...THIS IS GABBY LARYNX, YOUR RINGSIDE REPORTER, READY TO GIVE YOU A BLOW-BY-BLOW DESCRIPTION OF WHAT LOOKS LIKE THE FIGHT OF THE CENTURY... MY COLLEAGUES HAVE GIVEN YOU THE BACKGROUND ON THESE TWO REMARKABLE MEN, SO NOW FOR A BIT OF THE COLORFUL CROWD..
AHA!... IN ROW ONE, THAT GREAT AND CHARITABLE SOCIALITE, MRS. VAN GELT, HEAD OF THE LADIES' AUXILIARY, WHOSE BENEFIT THIS IS..
AND RIGHT ALONGSIDE HER IS...ULP??..ER..AHEM.. "FIXER-THE-FINK".. HOW'D HE... WELL HEH HEH FOLKS, IT'S A MIXED CROWD TONIGHT. OOPS!...THERE GOES THE BELL!
BOTH MEN COME OUT CAREFULLY...WE'VE ALL HEARD OF THE SPIRIT BUT WE'VE NEVER ACTUALLY SEEN HIM.. MAN HE'S RUGGED..!
OOOOPS! NOSDROV BREAKS THE STALEMATE WITH A BLOW TO THE BODY.. UGH! THAT NASDROV FIGHTS LIKE A MACHINE.. WHAT PRECISION!
THE SPIRIT HAS FELT THE FIRST BLOW AND IS NOW MOVING IN... HE'S GOT A FREE-SWINGING STYLE...
WHEW ... THAT NOSDROV CAN SURE TAKE IT... UGH... HOW TOUGH CAN YOU BE...
OW! NOSDROV BROUGHT ONE UP FROM THE FLOOR..
I SAW SUCH A BLOW KILL A MAN IN KANSAS CITY ONCE.. ...THE SPIRIT IS COMING BACK FOR MORE...
WELL, FOLKS.. THERE GOES THE BELL... THINGS DO NOT LOOK SO GOOD FOR THE SPIRIT... A VERY WEIRD THING HAS OCCURRED!... MOST OF THE TICKETS WERE BOUGHT BY HOODS, THUGS, AND TRIGGERMEN... THE ARENA IS QUIET! IT'S ...GULP... LIKE THEY'RE WAITING FOR SOMEONE TO DIE
5
PS
WILL EISNER

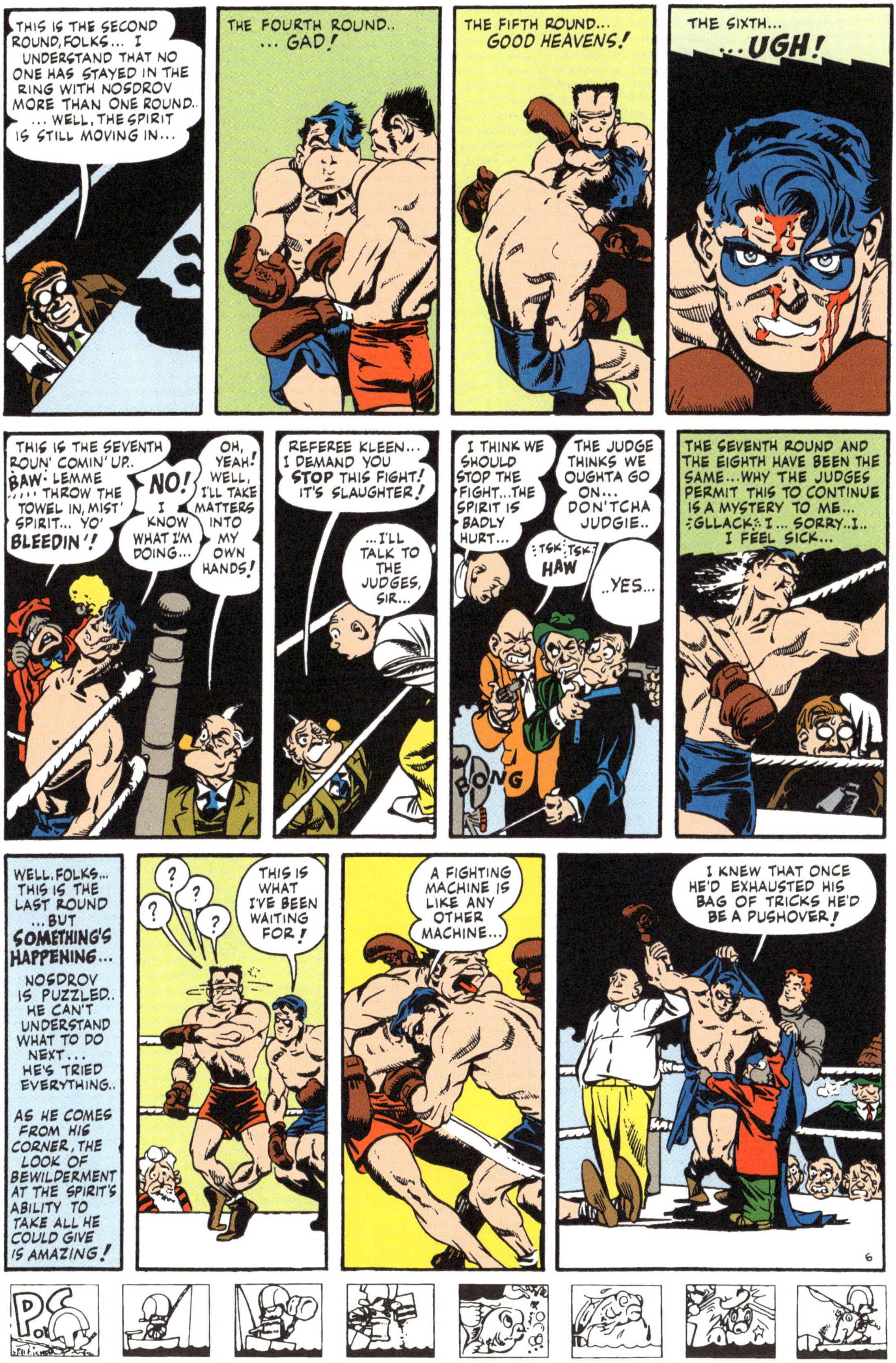
THIS IS THE SECOND ROUND, FOLKS... I UNDERSTAND THAT NO ONE HAS STAYED IN THE RING WITH NOSDROV MORE THAN ONE ROUND.. ...WELL, THE SPIRIT IS STILL MOVING IN...
THE FOURTH ROUND.. ...GAD!
THE FIFTH ROUND... GOOD HEAVENS!
THE SIXTH... ...UGH!
THIS IS THE SEVENTH ROUN' COMIN' UP.. BAW! LEMME THROW THE TOWEL IN, MIST' SPIRIT... YO' BLEEDIN'!
NO! I KNOW WHAT I'M DOING...
OH, YEAH! WELL, I'LL TAKE MATTERS INTO MY OWN HANDS!
REFEREE KLEEN... I DEMAND YOU STOP THIS FIGHT! IT'S SLAUGHTER!
...I'LL TALK TO THE JUDGES, SIR...
I THINK WE SHOULD STOP THE FIGHT...THE SPIRIT IS BADLY HURT...
THE JUDGE THINKS WE OUGHTA GO ON... DON'TCHA JUDGIE..
TSK TSK HAW
..YES...
BONG
THE SEVENTH ROUND AND THE EIGHTH HAVE BEEN THE SAME...WHY THE JUDGES PERMIT THIS TO CONTINUE IS A MYSTERY TO ME... GLLACK! I... SORRY..I.. I FEEL SICK...
WELL, FOLKS... THIS IS THE LAST ROUND ...BUT SOMETHING'S HAPPENING... NOSDROV IS PUZZLED.. HE CAN'T UNDERSTAND WHAT TO DO NEXT... HE'S TRIED EVERYTHING.. AS HE COMES FROM HIS CORNER, THE LOOK OF BEWILDERMENT AT THE SPIRIT'S ABILITY TO TAKE ALL HE COULD GIVE IS AMAZING!
? ? ? ?
THIS IS WHAT I'VE BEEN WAITING FOR!
A FIGHTING MACHINE IS LIKE ANY OTHER MACHINE...
I KNEW THAT ONCE HE'D EXHAUSTED HIS BAG OF TRICKS HE'D BE A PUSHOVER!
6
P.S.

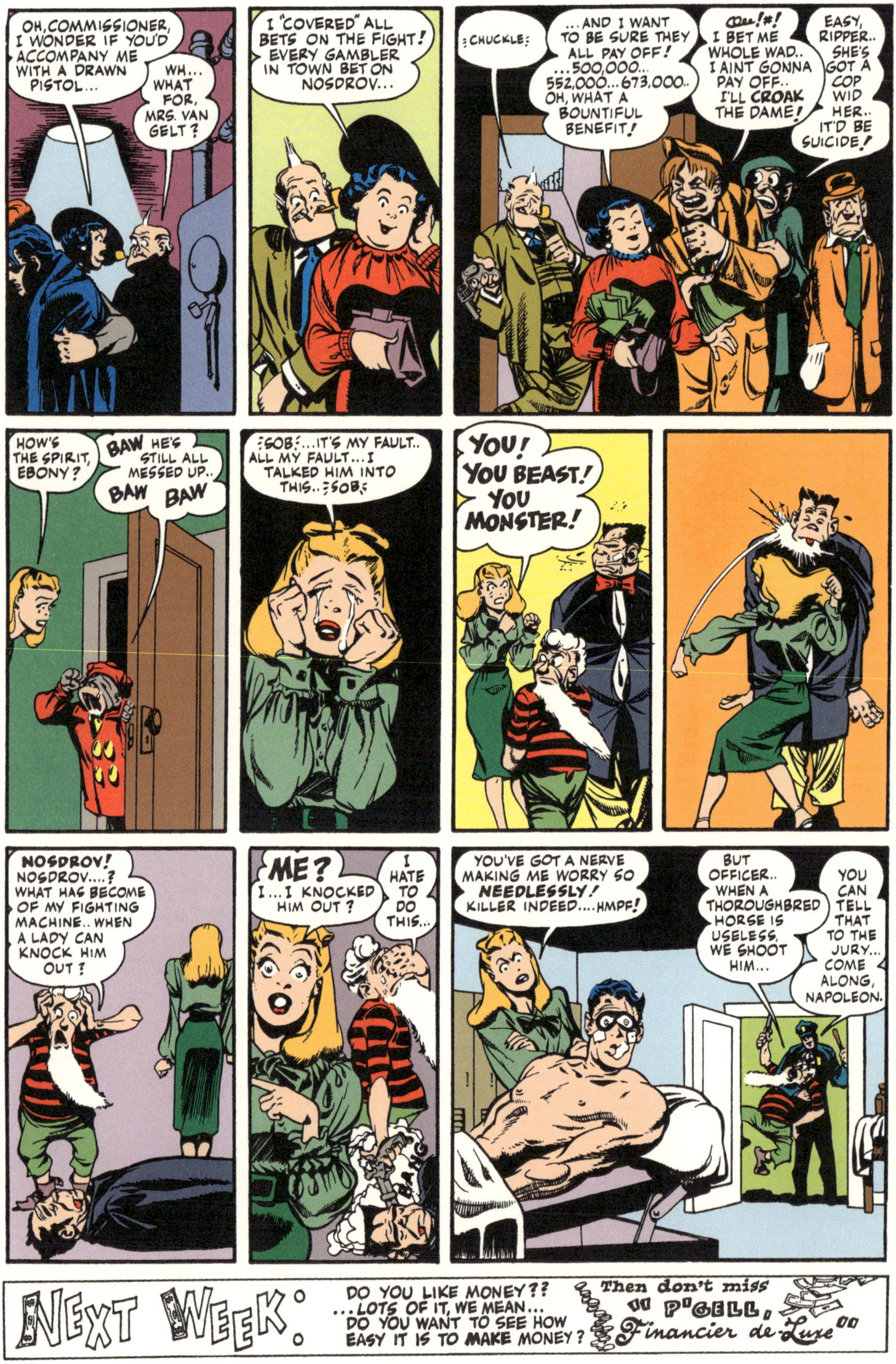

OH, COMMISSIONER, I WONDER IF YOU'D ACCOMPANY ME WITH A DRAWN PISTOL...
WH... WHAT FOR, MRS. VAN GELT?
I "COVERED" ALL BETS ON THE FIGHT! EVERY GAMBLER IN TOWN BET ON NOSDROV...
CHUCKLE
...AND I WANT TO BE SURE THEY ALL PAY OFF! ...500,000.. 552,000...673,000.. OH, WHAT A BOUNTIFUL BENEFIT!
I BET ME WHOLE WAD.. I AINT GONNA PAY OFF.. I'LL CROAK THE DAME!
EASY, RIPPER.. SHE'S GOT A COP WID HER.. IT'D BE SUICIDE!
HOW'S THE SPIRIT, EBONY?
BAW HE'S STILL ALL MESSED UP.. BAW BAW
SOB ...IT'S MY FAULT.. ALL MY FAULT... I TALKED HIM INTO THIS.. SOB
YOU! YOU BEAST! YOU MONSTER!
NOSDROV! NOSDROV....? WHAT HAS BECOME OF MY FIGHTING MACHINE.. WHEN A LADY CAN KNOCK HIM OUT?
ME? I...I KNOCKED HIM OUT?
I HATE TO DO THIS...
BANG
YOU'VE GOT A NERVE MAKING ME WORRY SO NEEDLESSLY! KILLER INDEED....HMPF!
BUT OFFICER.. WHEN A THOROUGHBRED HORSE IS USELESS, WE SHOOT HIM...
YOU CAN TELL THAT TO THE JURY... COME ALONG, NAPOLEON.
NEXT WEEK:
DO YOU LIKE MONEY?? ...LOTS OF IT, WE MEAN... DO YOU WANT TO SEE HOW EASY IT IS TO MAKE MONEY?
Then don't miss "P'GELL, Financier de Luxe"

COMIC BOOK SECTION

MONEY, MONEY

November 23 1947

ACTION Mystery ADVENTURE

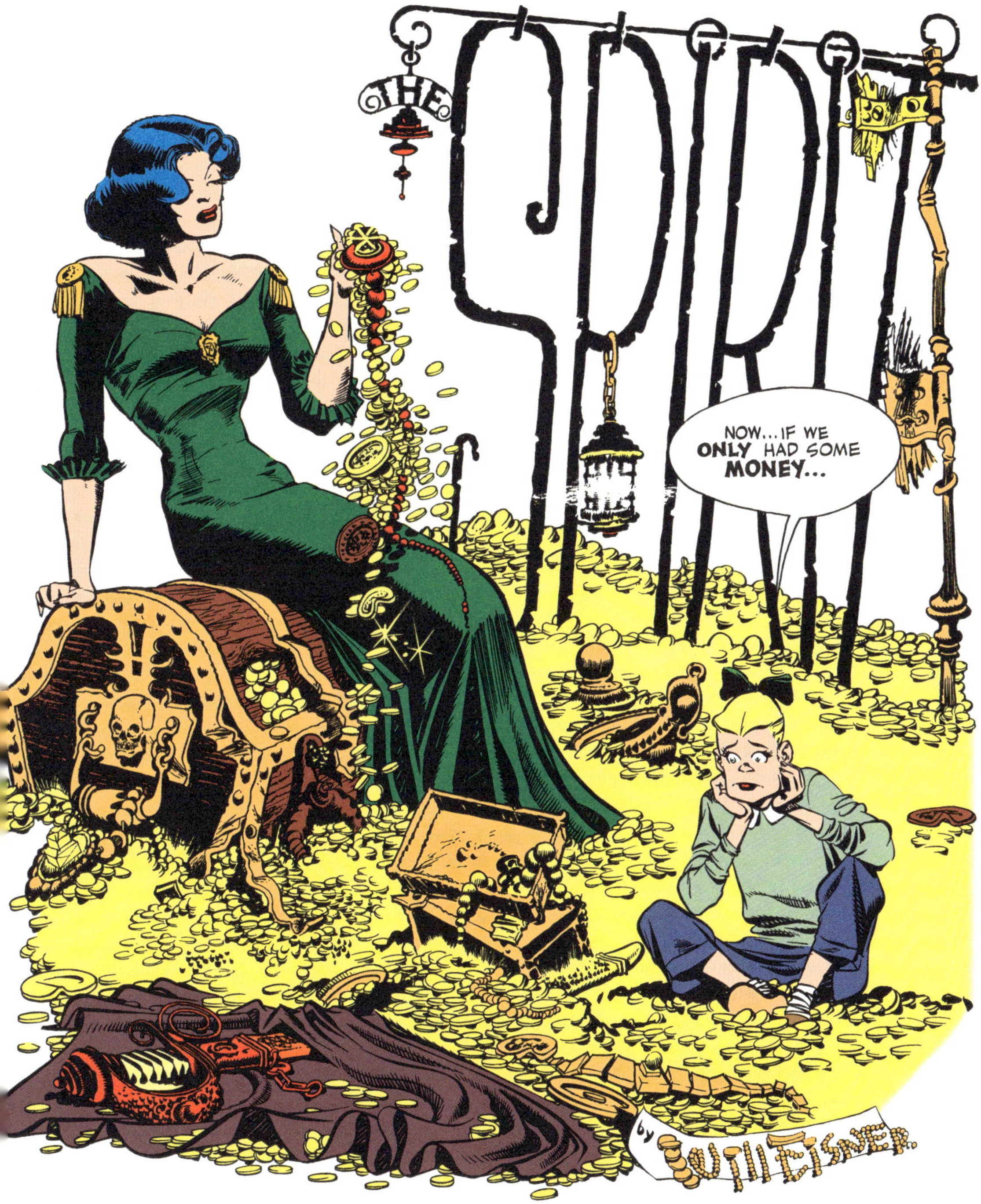

THE SPIRIT
NOW... IF WE ONLY HAD SOME MONEY...
by Will Eisner

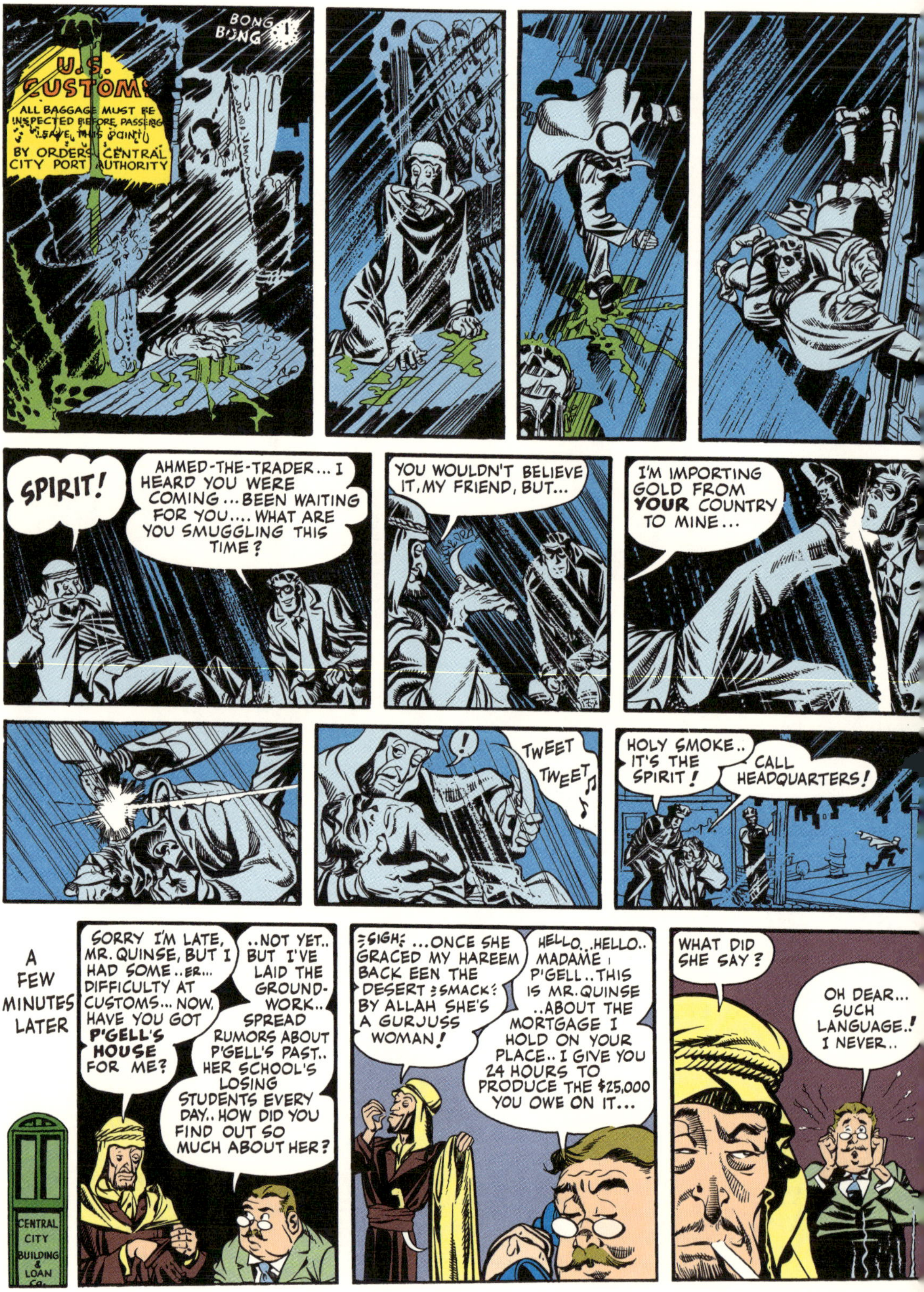
BONG BONG
U.S. CUSTOMS
ALL BAGGAGE MUST BE INSPECTED BEFORE PASSENGERS LEAVE THIS POINT
BY ORDER CENTRAL CITY PORT AUTHORITY
SPIRIT!
AHMED-THE-TRADER... I HEARD YOU WERE COMING... BEEN WAITING FOR YOU.... WHAT ARE YOU SMUGGLING THIS TIME?
YOU WOULDN'T BELIEVE IT, MY FRIEND, BUT...
I'M IMPORTING GOLD FROM YOUR COUNTRY TO MINE...
!
TWEET TWEET
HOLY SMOKE.. IT'S THE SPIRIT!
CALL HEADQUARTERS!
A FEW MINUTES LATER
SORRY I'M LATE, MR. QUINSE, BUT I HAD SOME.. ER... DIFFICULTY AT CUSTOMS... NOW, HAVE YOU GOT P'GELL'S HOUSE FOR ME?
..NOT YET.. BUT I'VE LAID THE GROUND-WORK.. SPREAD RUMORS ABOUT P'GELL'S PAST.. HER SCHOOL'S LOSING STUDENTS EVERY DAY.. HOW DID YOU FIND OUT SO MUCH ABOUT HER?
CENTRAL CITY BUILDING & LOAN Co.
≑SIGH≑ ...ONCE SHE GRACED MY HAREEM BACK EEN THE DESERT ≑SMACK≑ BY ALLAH SHE'S A GURJUSS WOMAN!
HELLO..HELLO.. MADAME P'GELL..THIS IS MR. QUINSE ..ABOUT THE MORTGAGE I HOLD ON YOUR PLACE.. I GIVE YOU 24 HOURS TO PRODUCE THE $25,000 YOU OWE ON IT...
WHAT DID SHE SAY?
OH DEAR... SUCH LANGUAGE..! I NEVER..

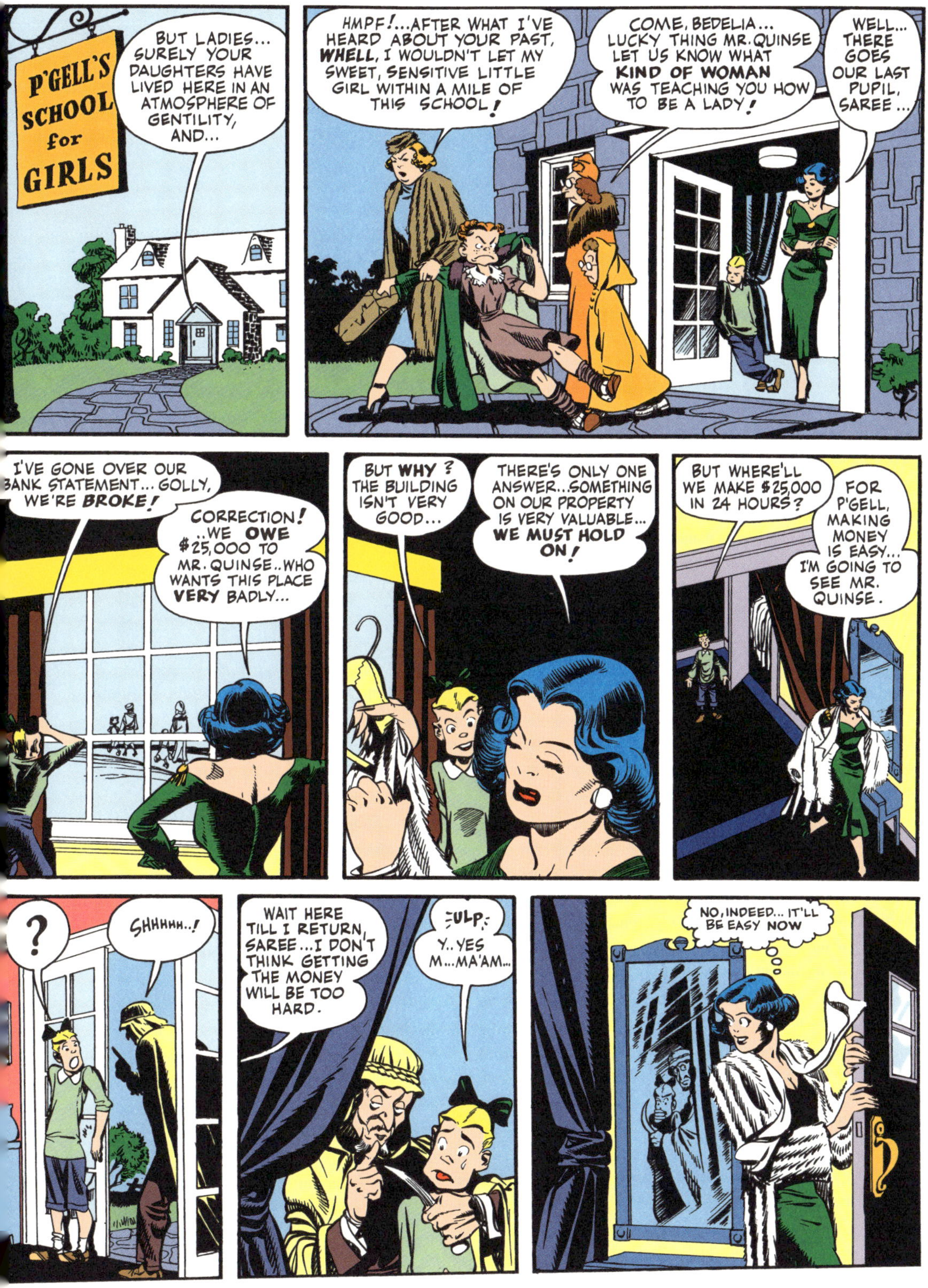
P'GELL'S SCHOOL for GIRLS
BUT LADIES... SURELY YOUR DAUGHTERS HAVE LIVED HERE IN AN ATMOSPHERE OF GENTILITY, AND...
HMPF!...AFTER WHAT I'VE HEARD ABOUT YOUR PAST, WHELL, I WOULDN'T LET MY SWEET, SENSITIVE LITTLE GIRL WITHIN A MILE OF THIS SCHOOL!
COME, BEDELIA... LUCKY THING MR. QUINSE LET US KNOW WHAT KIND OF WOMAN WAS TEACHING YOU HOW TO BE A LADY!
WELL... THERE GOES OUR LAST PUPIL, SAREE...
I'VE GONE OVER OUR BANK STATEMENT... GOLLY, WE'RE BROKE!
CORRECTION! ..WE OWE $25,000 TO MR. QUINSE..WHO WANTS THIS PLACE VERY BADLY...
BUT WHY? THE BUILDING ISN'T VERY GOOD...
THERE'S ONLY ONE ANSWER...SOMETHING ON OUR PROPERTY IS VERY VALUABLE... WE MUST HOLD ON!
BUT WHERE'LL WE MAKE $25,000 IN 24 HOURS?
FOR P'GELL, MAKING MONEY IS EASY... I'M GOING TO SEE MR. QUINSE.
?
SHHHHH..!
WAIT HERE TILL I RETURN, SAREE...I DON'T THINK GETTING THE MONEY WILL BE TOO HARD.
ULP
Y.. YES M...MA'AM...
NO, INDEED... IT'LL BE EASY NOW

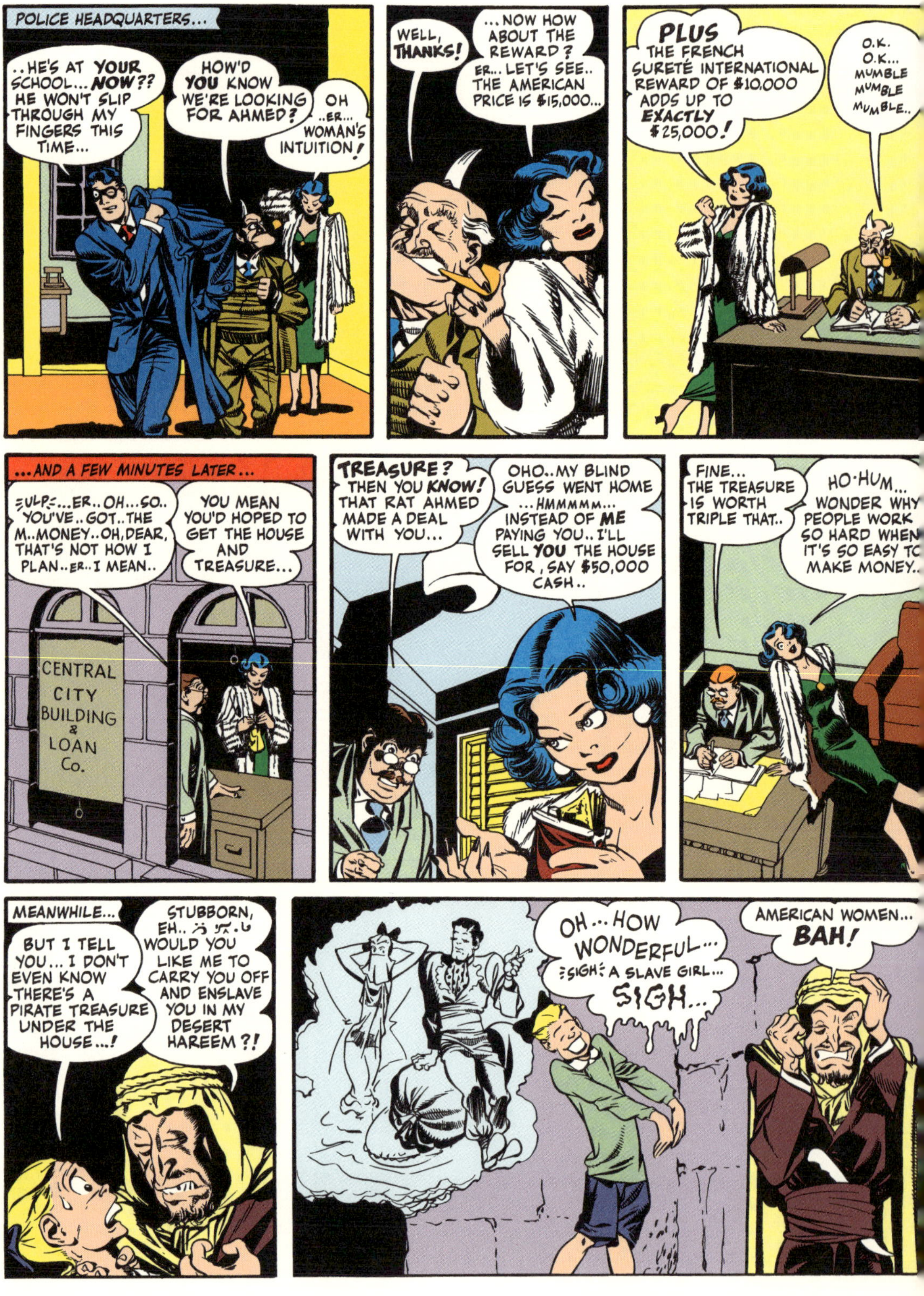
POLICE HEADQUARTERS...
..HE'S AT YOUR SCHOOL... NOW?? HE WON'T SLIP THROUGH MY FINGERS THIS TIME...
HOW'D YOU KNOW WE'RE LOOKING FOR AHMED?
OH ..ER... WOMAN'S INTUITION!
WELL, THANKS!
...NOW HOW ABOUT THE REWARD? ER... LET'S SEE.. THE AMERICAN PRICE IS $15,000...
PLUS THE FRENCH SURETÉ INTERNATIONAL REWARD OF $10,000 ADDS UP TO EXACTLY $25,000!
O.K. O.K... MUMBLE MUMBLE MUMBLE..
...AND A FEW MINUTES LATER...
ULP... ER.. OH... SO.. YOU'VE.. GOT.. THE M..MONEY..OH, DEAR, THAT'S NOT HOW I PLAN..ER..I MEAN..
YOU MEAN YOU'D HOPED TO GET THE HOUSE AND TREASURE...
CENTRAL CITY BUILDING & LOAN Co.
TREASURE? THEN YOU KNOW! THAT RAT AHMED MADE A DEAL WITH YOU...
OHO..MY BLIND GUESS WENT HOME ...HMMMMM... INSTEAD OF ME PAYING YOU.. I'LL SELL YOU THE HOUSE FOR, SAY $50,000 CASH..
FINE... THE TREASURE IS WORTH TRIPLE THAT..
HO-HUM... WONDER WHY PEOPLE WORK SO HARD WHEN IT'S SO EASY TO MAKE MONEY...
MEANWHILE...
BUT I TELL YOU... I DON'T EVEN KNOW THERE'S A PIRATE TREASURE UNDER THE HOUSE...!
STUBBORN, EH.. WOULD YOU LIKE ME TO CARRY YOU OFF AND ENSLAVE YOU IN MY DESERT HAREEM?!
OH... HOW WONDERFUL... SIGH A SLAVE GIRL... SIGH...
AMERICAN WOMEN... BAH!

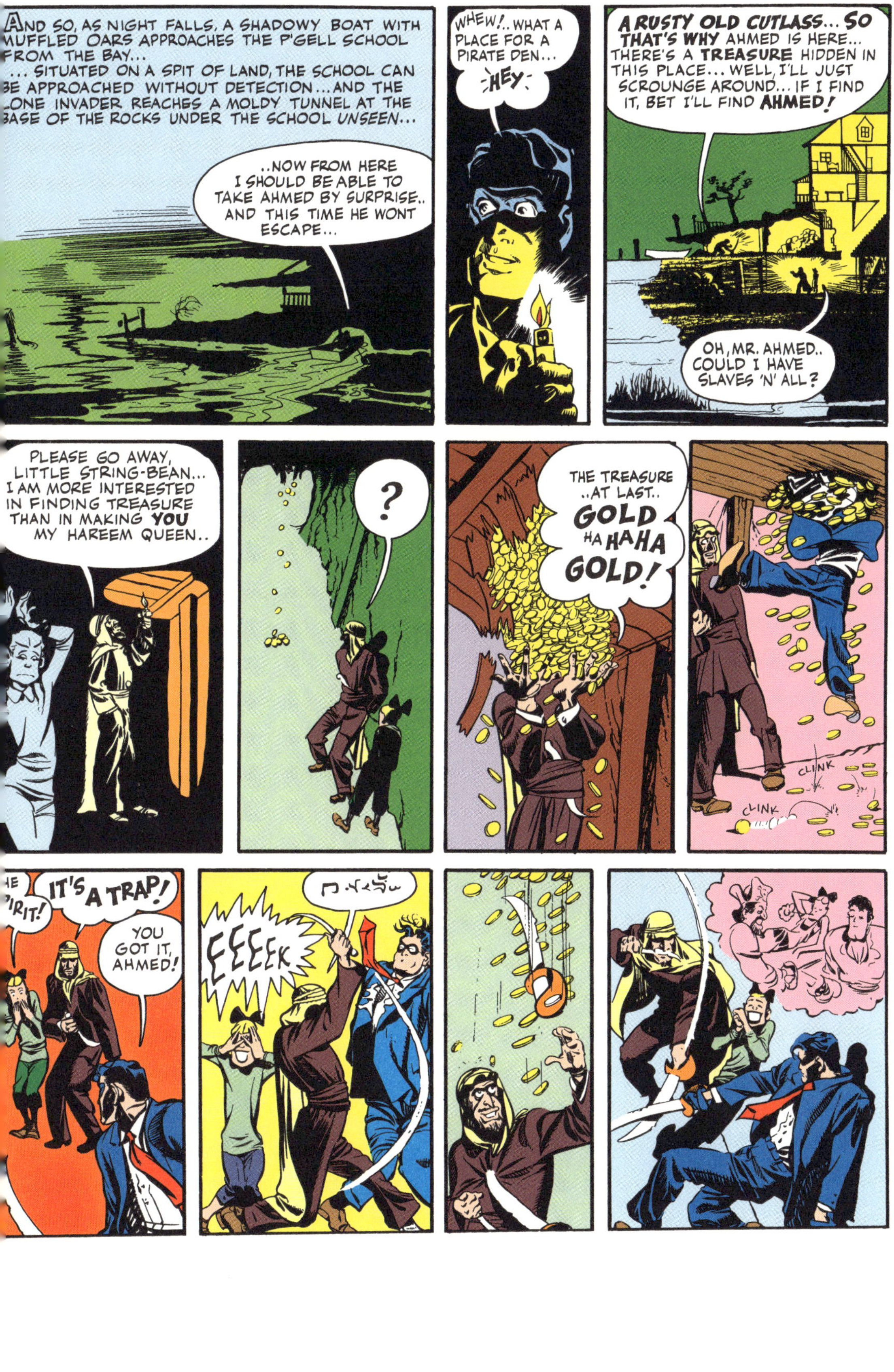

AND SO, AS NIGHT FALLS, A SHADOWY BOAT WITH MUFFLED OARS APPROACHES THE P'GELL SCHOOL FROM THE BAY... ... SITUATED ON A SPIT OF LAND, THE SCHOOL CAN BE APPROACHED WITHOUT DETECTION... AND THE LONE INVADER REACHES A MOLDY TUNNEL AT THE BASE OF THE ROCKS UNDER THE SCHOOL UNSEEN...
..NOW FROM HERE I SHOULD BE ABLE TO TAKE AHMED BY SURPRISE.. AND THIS TIME HE WONT ESCAPE...
WHEW!.. WHAT A PLACE FOR A PIRATE DEN... HEY
A RUSTY OLD CUTLASS... SO THAT'S WHY AHMED IS HERE... THERE'S A TREASURE HIDDEN IN THIS PLACE... WELL, I'LL JUST SCROUNGE AROUND... IF I FIND IT, BET I'LL FIND AHMED!
OH, MR. AHMED.. COULD I HAVE SLAVES 'N' ALL?
PLEASE GO AWAY, LITTLE STRING-BEAN... I AM MORE INTERESTED IN FINDING TREASURE THAN IN MAKING YOU MY HAREEM QUEEN..
?
THE TREASURE ..AT LAST.. GOLD HA HAHA GOLD!
CLINK
CLINK
IT'S A TRAP!
YOU GOT IT, AHMED!
EEEEK

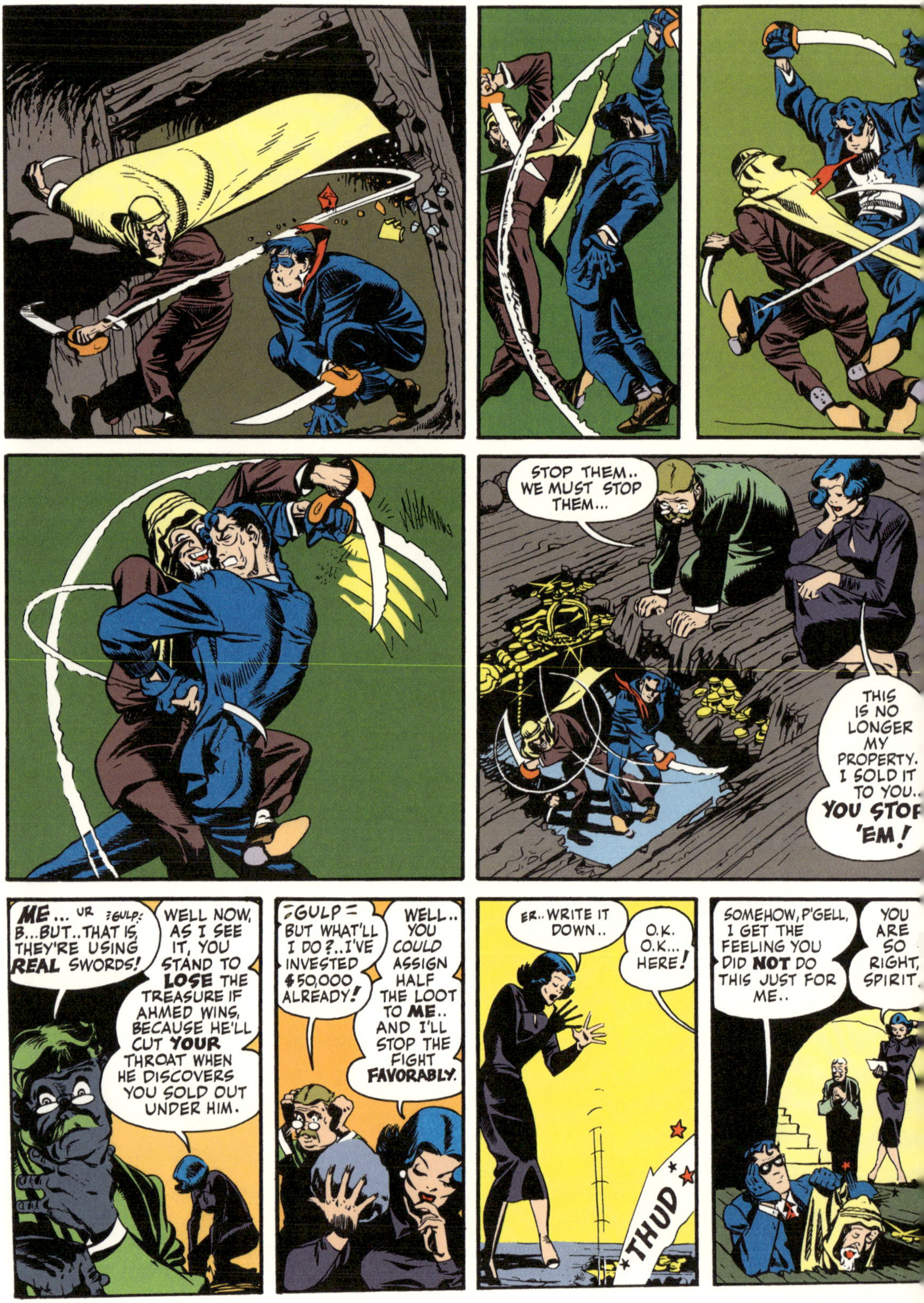
STOP THEM.. WE MUST STOP THEM...
THIS IS NO LONGER MY PROPERTY. I SOLD IT TO YOU.. YOU STOP 'EM!
ME... UR =GULP= B...BUT..THAT IS, THEY'RE USING REAL SWORDS!
WELL NOW, AS I SEE IT, YOU STAND TO LOSE THE TREASURE IF AHMED WINS, BECAUSE HE'LL CUT YOUR THROAT WHEN HE DISCOVERS YOU SOLD OUT UNDER HIM.
=GULP= BUT WHAT'LL I DO?..I'VE INVESTED $50,000 ALREADY!
WELL.. YOU COULD ASSIGN HALF THE LOOT TO ME.. AND I'LL STOP THE FIGHT FAVORABLY.
ER.. WRITE IT DOWN..
O.K. O.K... HERE!
THUD
SOMEHOW, P'GELL, I GET THE FEELING YOU DID NOT DO THIS JUST FOR ME..
YOU ARE SO RIGHT, SPIRIT

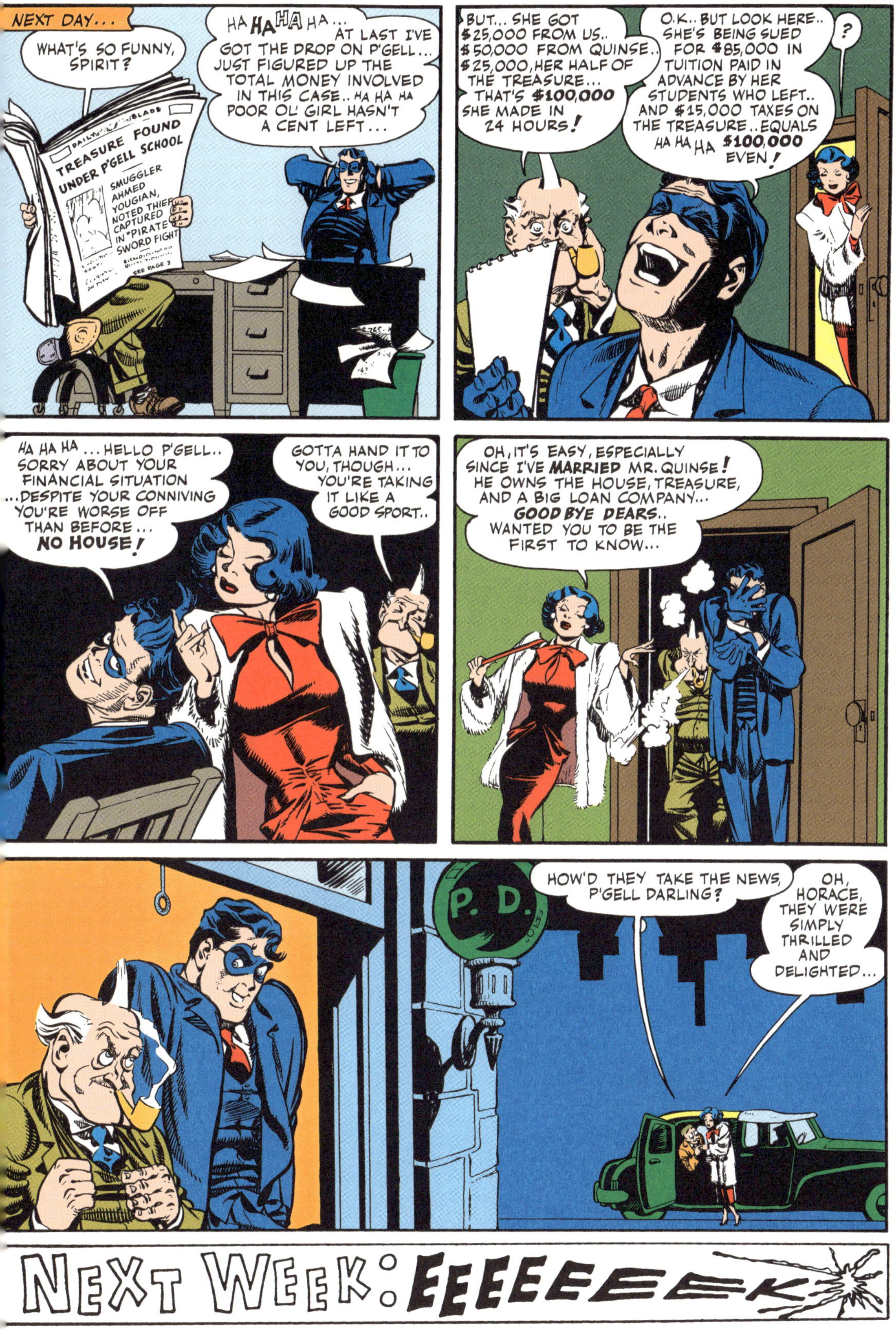

NEXT DAY...
WHAT'S SO FUNNY, SPIRIT?
TREASURE FOUND UNDER P'GELL SCHOOL
SMUGGLER AHMED YOUGIAN, NOTED THIEF CAPTURED IN "PIRATE" SWORD FIGHT
SEE PAGE 3
HA HA HA HA HA... AT LAST I'VE GOT THE DROP ON P'GELL... JUST FIGURED UP THE TOTAL MONEY INVOLVED IN THIS CASE.. HA HA HA POOR OL' GIRL HASN'T A CENT LEFT...
BUT... SHE GOT $25,000 FROM US.. $50,000 FROM QUINSE.. $25,000, HER HALF OF THE TREASURE... THAT'S $100,000 SHE MADE IN 24 HOURS!
O.K.. BUT LOOK HERE.. SHE'S BEING SUED FOR $85,000 IN TUITION PAID IN ADVANCE BY HER STUDENTS WHO LEFT.. AND $15,000 TAXES ON THE TREASURE.. EQUALS HA HA HA $100,000 EVEN!
?
HA HA HA ... HELLO P'GELL.. SORRY ABOUT YOUR FINANCIAL SITUATION ...DESPITE YOUR CONNIVING YOU'RE WORSE OFF THAN BEFORE... NO HOUSE!
GOTTA HAND IT TO YOU, THOUGH... YOU'RE TAKING IT LIKE A GOOD SPORT..
OH, IT'S EASY, ESPECIALLY SINCE I'VE MARRIED MR. QUINSE! HE OWNS THE HOUSE, TREASURE, AND A BIG LOAN COMPANY... GOOD BYE DEARS.. WANTED YOU TO BE THE FIRST TO KNOW...
P. D.
HOW'D THEY TAKE THE NEWS, P'GELL DARLING?
OH, HORACE, THEY WERE SIMPLY THRILLED AND DELIGHTED...
NEXT WEEK: EEEEEEEEK

COMIC BOOK SECTION

SLIPPERY EALL

November 30 1947

ACTION Mystery ADVENTURE

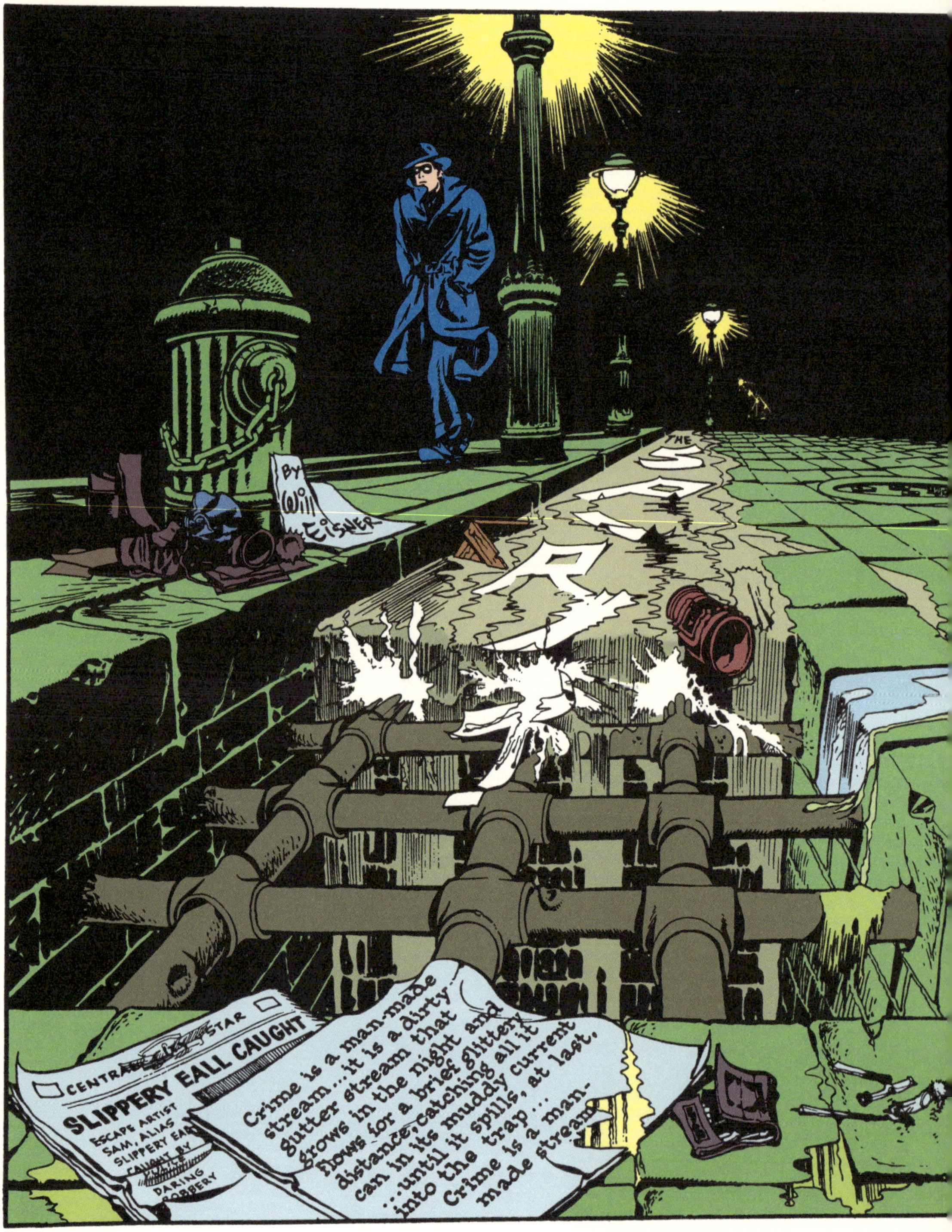
THE
By Will Eisner
SLIPPERY EALL CAUGHT
ESCAPE ARTIST SAM, ALIAS SLIPPERY EA
DARING ROBBERY
Crime is a man-made stream... it is a dirty gutter stream that grows in the night and flows for a brief glittery distance, catching all it can in its muddy current ...until it spills, at last, into the trap... Crime is a man-made stream.

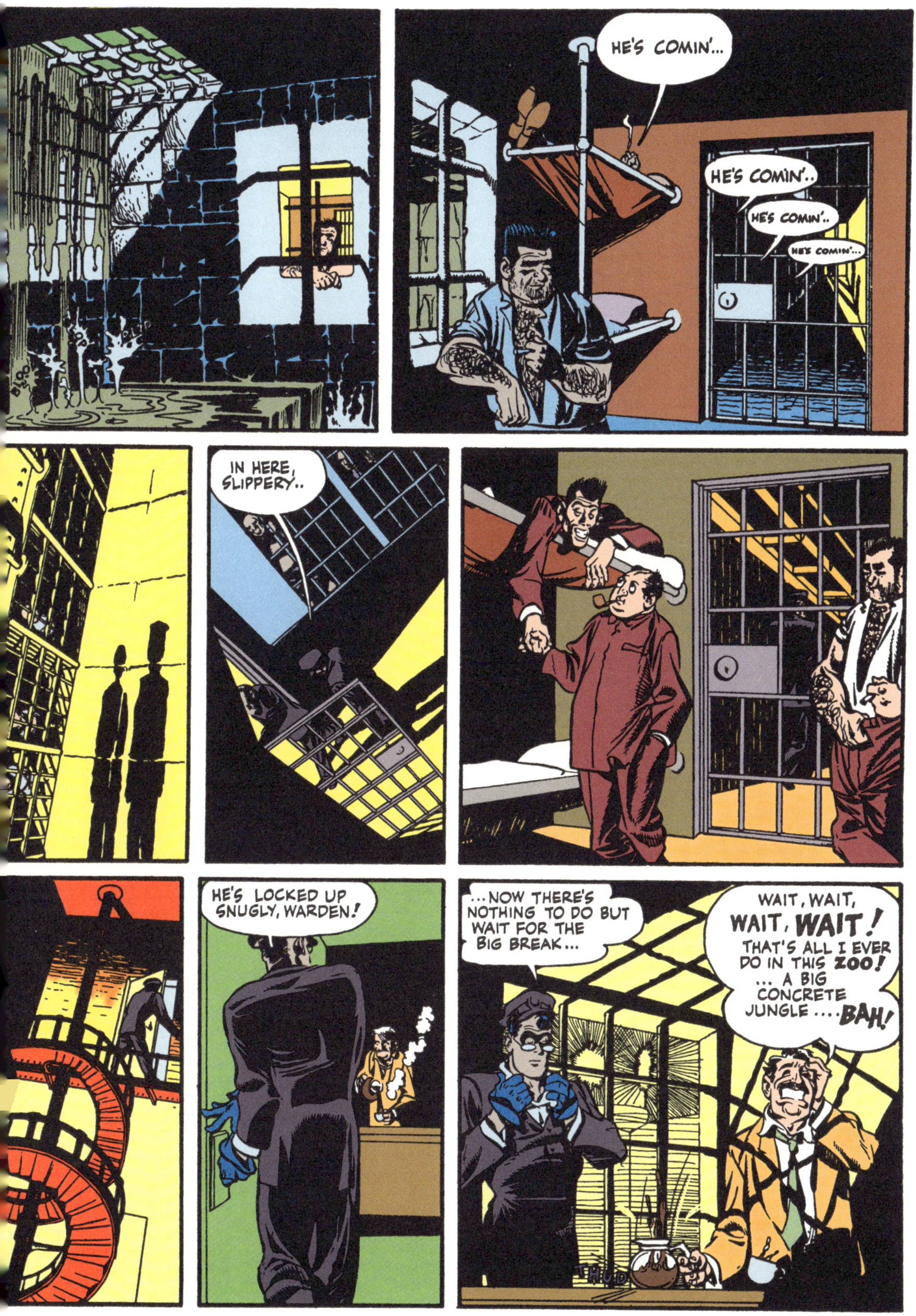
BLOOP
PLOP
HE'S COMIN'...
HE'S COMIN'..
HE'S COMIN'..
HE'S COMIN'...
IN HERE, SLIPPERY..
HE'S LOCKED UP SNUGLY, WARDEN!
...NOW THERE'S NOTHING TO DO BUT WAIT FOR THE BIG BREAK...
WAIT, WAIT, WAIT, WAIT! THAT'S ALL I EVER DO IN THIS ZOO! ... A BIG CONCRETE JUNGLE .... BAH!
THUD

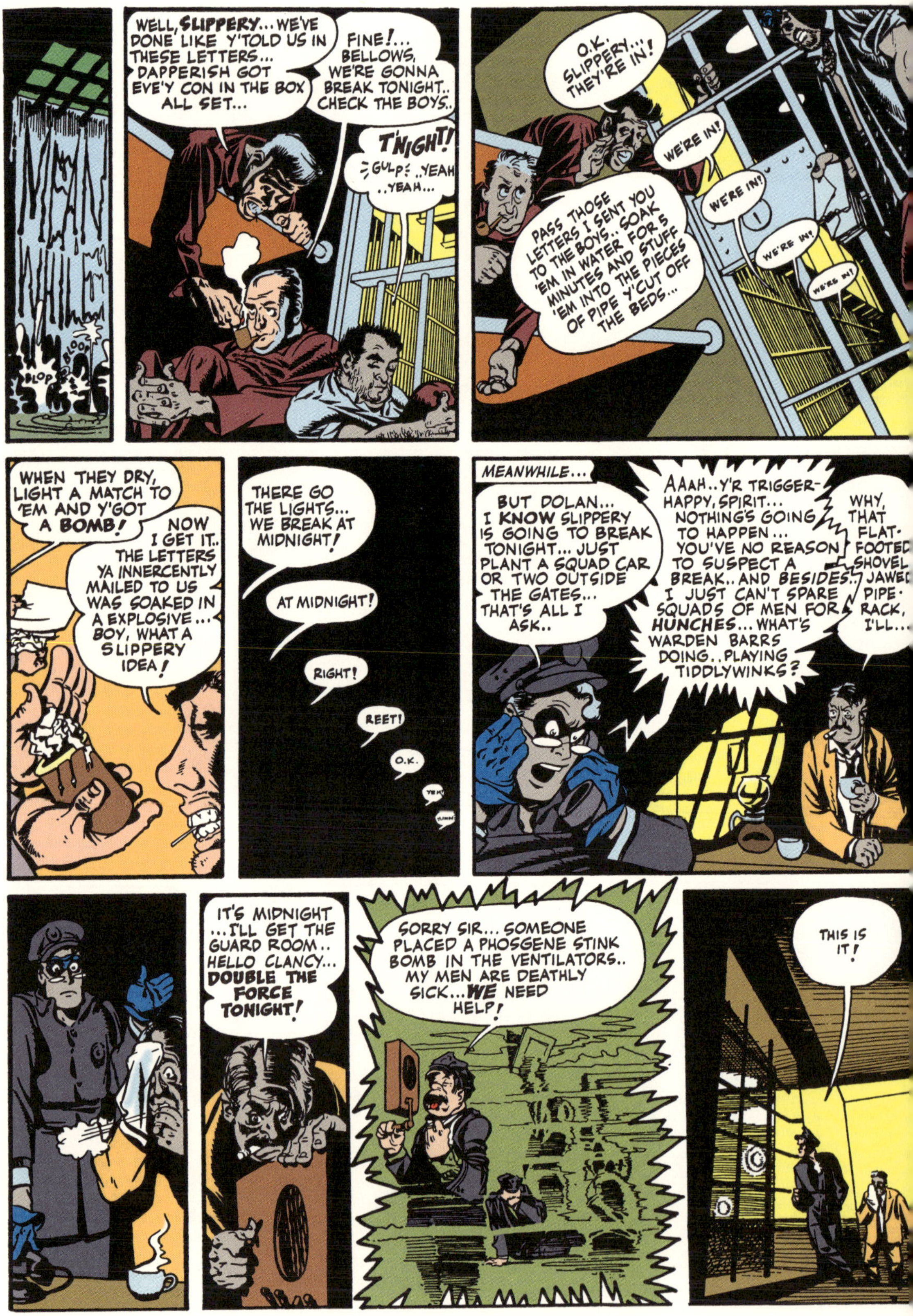

WELL, SLIPPERY... WE'VE DONE LIKE Y'TOLD US IN THESE LETTERS... DAPPERISH GOT EVE'Y CON IN THE BOX ALL SET...
FINE!... BELLOWS, WE'RE GONNA BREAK TONIGHT.. CHECK THE BOYS..
T'NIGHT!
GULP! ..YEAH ..YEAH...
O.K. SLIPPERY... THEY'RE IN!
WE'RE IN!
WE'RE IN!
WE'RE IN!
WE'RE IN!
PASS THOSE LETTERS I SENT YOU TO THE BOYS.. SOAK 'EM IN WATER FOR 5 MINUTES AND STUFF 'EM INTO THE PIECES OF PIPE Y'CUT OFF THE BEDS...
WHEN THEY DRY, LIGHT A MATCH TO 'EM AND Y'GOT A BOMB!
NOW I GET IT.. THE LETTERS YA INNERCENTLY MAILED TO US WAS SOAKED IN A EXPLOSIVE... BOY, WHAT A SLIPPERY IDEA!
THERE GO THE LIGHTS... WE BREAK AT MIDNIGHT!
AT MIDNIGHT!
RIGHT!
REET!
O.K.
MEANWHILE...
BUT DOLAN... I KNOW SLIPPERY IS GOING TO BREAK TONIGHT... JUST PLANT A SQUAD CAR OR TWO OUTSIDE THE GATES... THAT'S ALL I ASK..
AAAH..Y'R TRIGGER-HAPPY, SPIRIT... NOTHING'S GOING TO HAPPEN... YOU'VE NO REASON TO SUSPECT A BREAK.. AND BESIDES.. I JUST CAN'T SPARE SQUADS OF MEN FOR HUNCHES... WHAT'S WARDEN BARRS DOING.. PLAYING TIDDLYWINKS?
WHY, THAT FLAT-FOOTED SHOVEL JAWED PIPE-RACK, I'LL...
IT'S MIDNIGHT ...I'LL GET THE GUARD ROOM.. HELLO CLANCY... DOUBLE THE FORCE TONIGHT!
SORRY SIR... SOMEONE PLACED A PHOSGENE STINK BOMB IN THE VENTILATORS.. MY MEN ARE DEATHLY SICK... WE NEED HELP!
THIS IS IT!

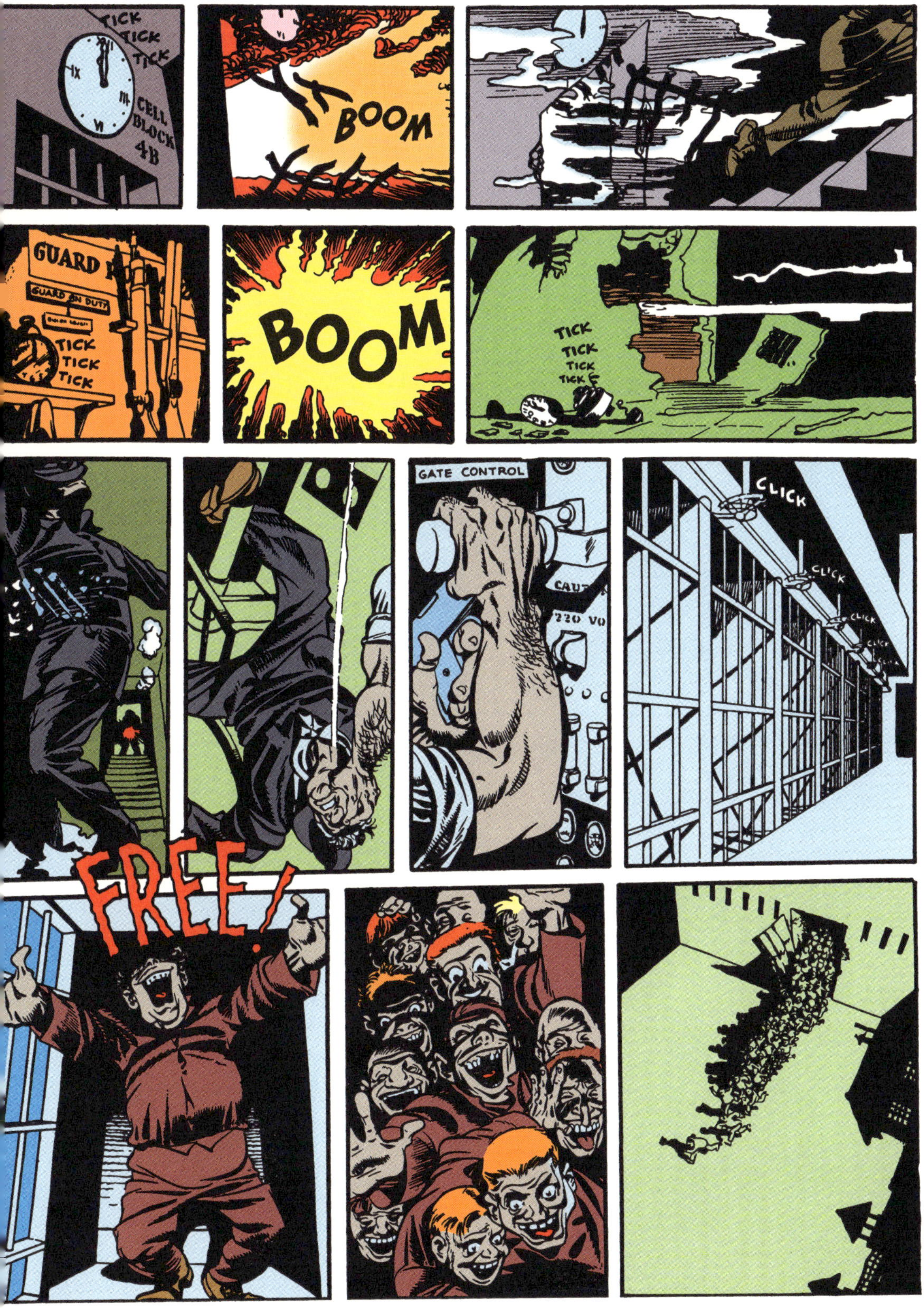
TICK
TICK
TICK
CELL BLOCK 4B
BOOM
GUARD
GUARD ON DUTY
TICK
TICK
TICK
BOOM
TICK
TICK
TICK
TICK
GATE CONTROL
CLICK
CLICK
CLICK
FREE!

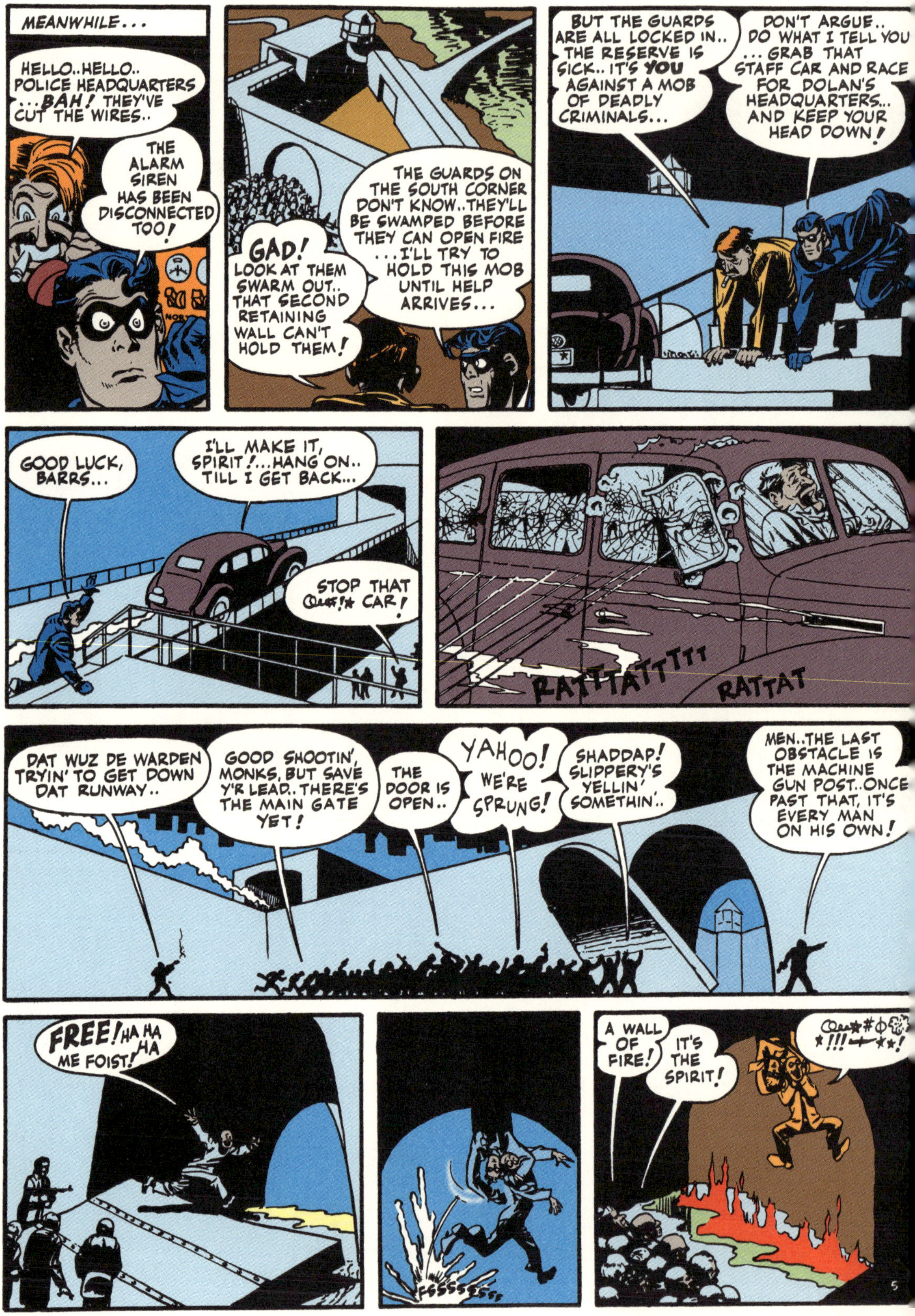

MEANWHILE...
HELLO..HELLO.. POLICE HEADQUARTERS ...BAH! THEY'VE CUT THE WIRES..
THE ALARM SIREN HAS BEEN DISCONNECTED TOO!
GAD! LOOK AT THEM SWARM OUT.. THAT SECOND RETAINING WALL CAN'T HOLD THEM!
THE GUARDS ON THE SOUTH CORNER DON'T KNOW..THEY'LL BE SWAMPED BEFORE THEY CAN OPEN FIRE ...I'LL TRY TO HOLD THIS MOB UNTIL HELP ARRIVES...
BUT THE GUARDS ARE ALL LOCKED IN.. THE RESERVE IS SICK.. IT'S YOU AGAINST A MOB OF DEADLY CRIMINALS...
DON'T ARGUE.. DO WHAT I TELL YOU ...GRAB THAT STAFF CAR AND RACE FOR DOLAN'S HEADQUARTERS... AND KEEP YOUR HEAD DOWN!
GOOD LUCK, BARRS...
I'LL MAKE IT, SPIRIT!...HANG ON.. TILL I GET BACK...
STOP THAT CAR!
RATTATTTTT
RATTAT
DAT WUZ DE WARDEN TRYIN' TO GET DOWN DAT RUNWAY..
GOOD SHOOTIN', MONKS, BUT SAVE Y'R LEAD..THERE'S THE MAIN GATE YET!
THE DOOR IS OPEN..
YAHOO! WE'RE SPRUNG!
SHADDAP! SLIPPERY'S YELLIN' SOMETHIN'..
MEN..THE LAST OBSTACLE IS THE MACHINE GUN POST..ONCE PAST THAT, IT'S EVERY MAN ON HIS OWN!
FREE! HA HA HA ME FOIST!
FSSSSSsss
A WALL OF FIRE!
IT'S THE SPIRIT!

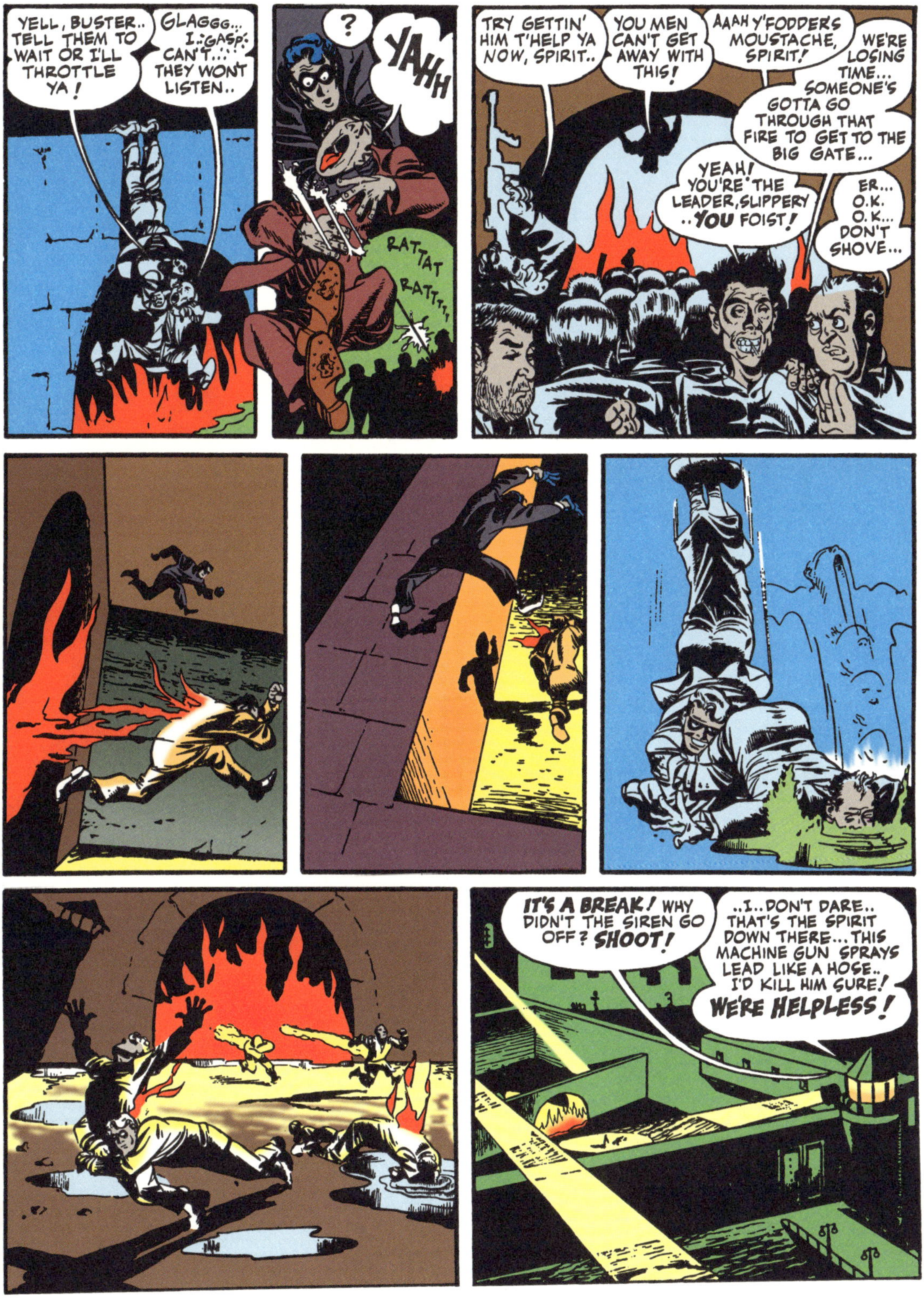
YELL, BUSTER.. TELL THEM TO WAIT OR I'LL THROTTLE YA!
GLAGGG... I..GASP.. CAN'T..! THEY WON'T LISTEN..
?
YAHH
RAT TAT RATT
TRY GETTIN' HIM T'HELP YA NOW, SPIRIT..
YOU MEN CAN'T GET AWAY WITH THIS!
AAAH Y'FODDER'S MOUSTACHE, SPIRIT!
WE'RE LOSING TIME... SOMEONE'S GOTTA GO THROUGH THAT FIRE TO GET TO THE BIG GATE...
YEAH! YOU'RE THE LEADER, SLIPPERY ..YOU FOIST!
ER... O.K. O.K... DON'T SHOVE...
IT'S A BREAK! WHY DIDN'T THE SIREN GO OFF? SHOOT!
..I..DON'T DARE.. THAT'S THE SPIRIT DOWN THERE... THIS MACHINE GUN SPRAYS LEAD LIKE A HOSE.. I'D KILL HIM SURE! WE'RE HELPLESS!

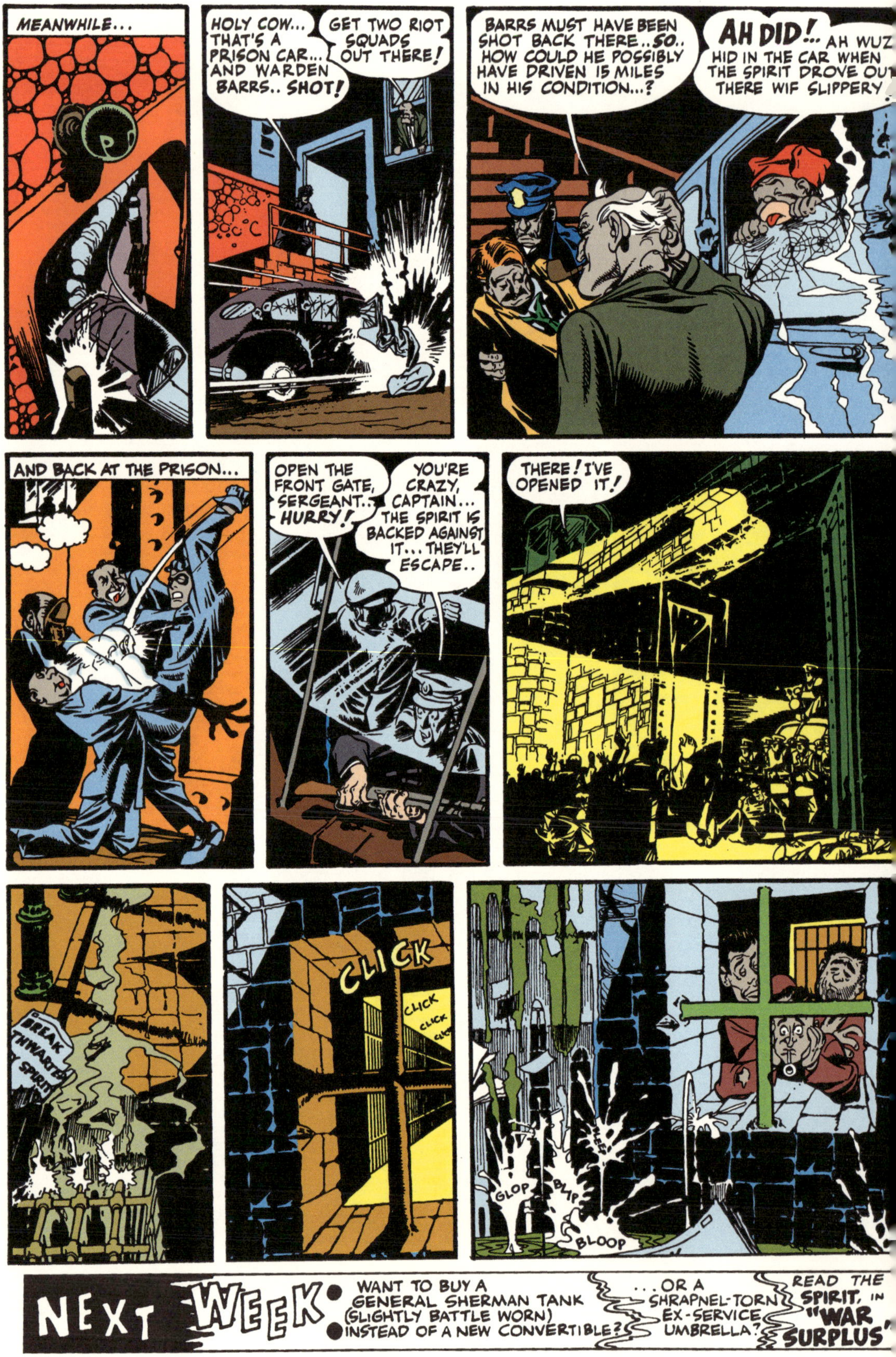
MEANWHILE...
HOLY COW... THAT'S A PRISON CAR... AND WARDEN BARRS.. SHOT!
GET TWO RIOT SQUADS OUT THERE!
BARRS MUST HAVE BEEN SHOT BACK THERE.. SO.. HOW COULD HE POSSIBLY HAVE DRIVEN 15 MILES IN HIS CONDITION...?
AH DID!.. AH WUZ HID IN THE CAR WHEN THE SPIRIT DROVE OU THERE WIF SLIPPERY
AND BACK AT THE PRISON...
OPEN THE FRONT GATE, SERGEANT.. HURRY!
YOU'RE CRAZY, CAPTAIN... THE SPIRIT IS BACKED AGAINST IT... THEY'LL ESCAPE..
THERE! I'VE OPENED IT!
BREAK
THWARTED
SPIRIT
CLICK
CLICK
CLICK
GLOP
BLIP
BLOOP
NEXT WEEK:
WANT TO BUY A GENERAL SHERMAN TANK (SLIGHTLY BATTLE WORN) INSTEAD OF A NEW CONVERTIBLE?
...OR A SHRAPNEL-TORN EX-SERVICE UMBRELLA?
READ THE SPIRIT, IN "WAR SURPLUS"

COMIC BOOK SECTION

DEATH OF HUGO

December 7 1947

ACTION Mystery ADVENTURE

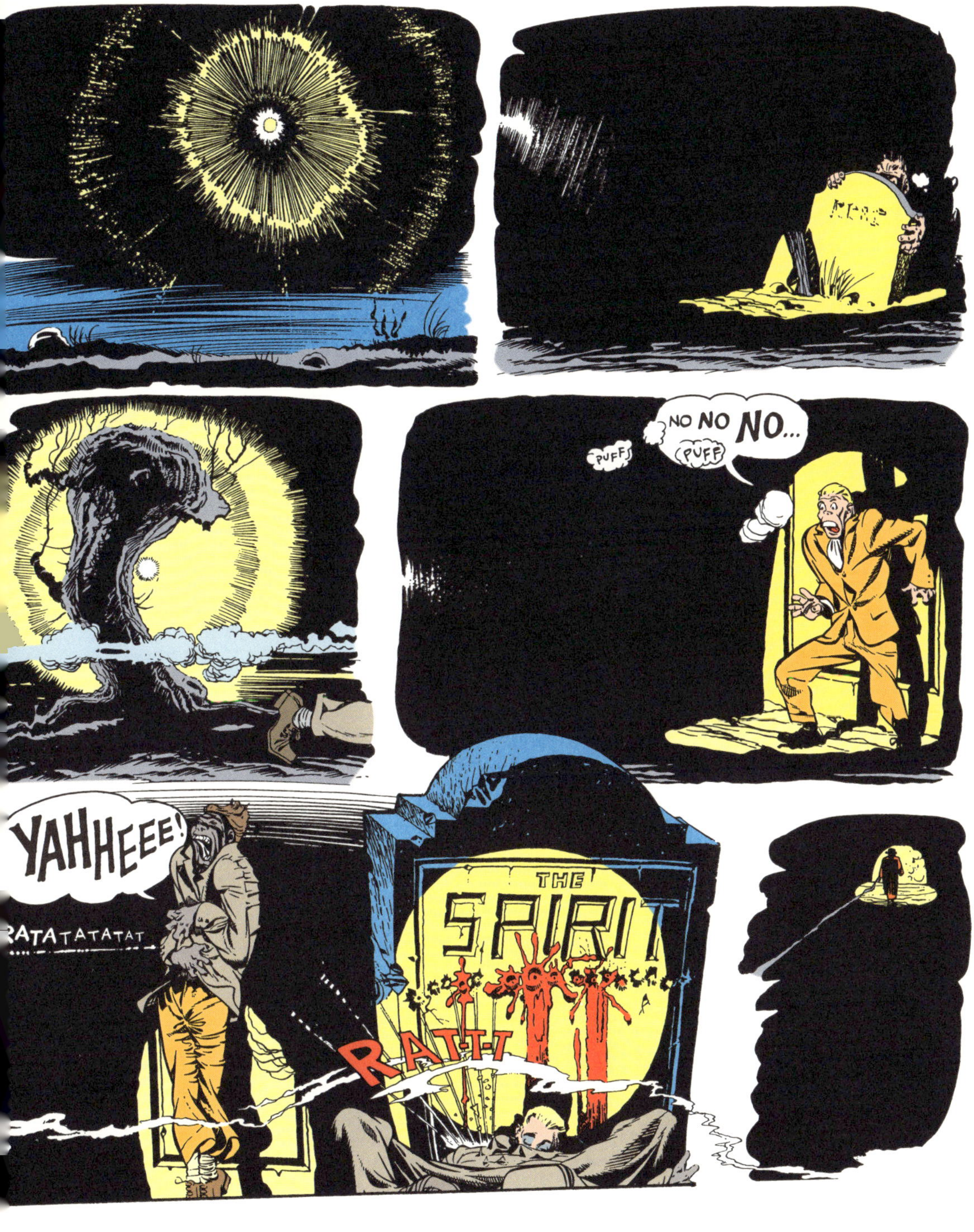

PUFF
NO NO NO...
PUFF
YAHHEEE!
RATATATATATAT
THE SPIRIT
RAT-T-T

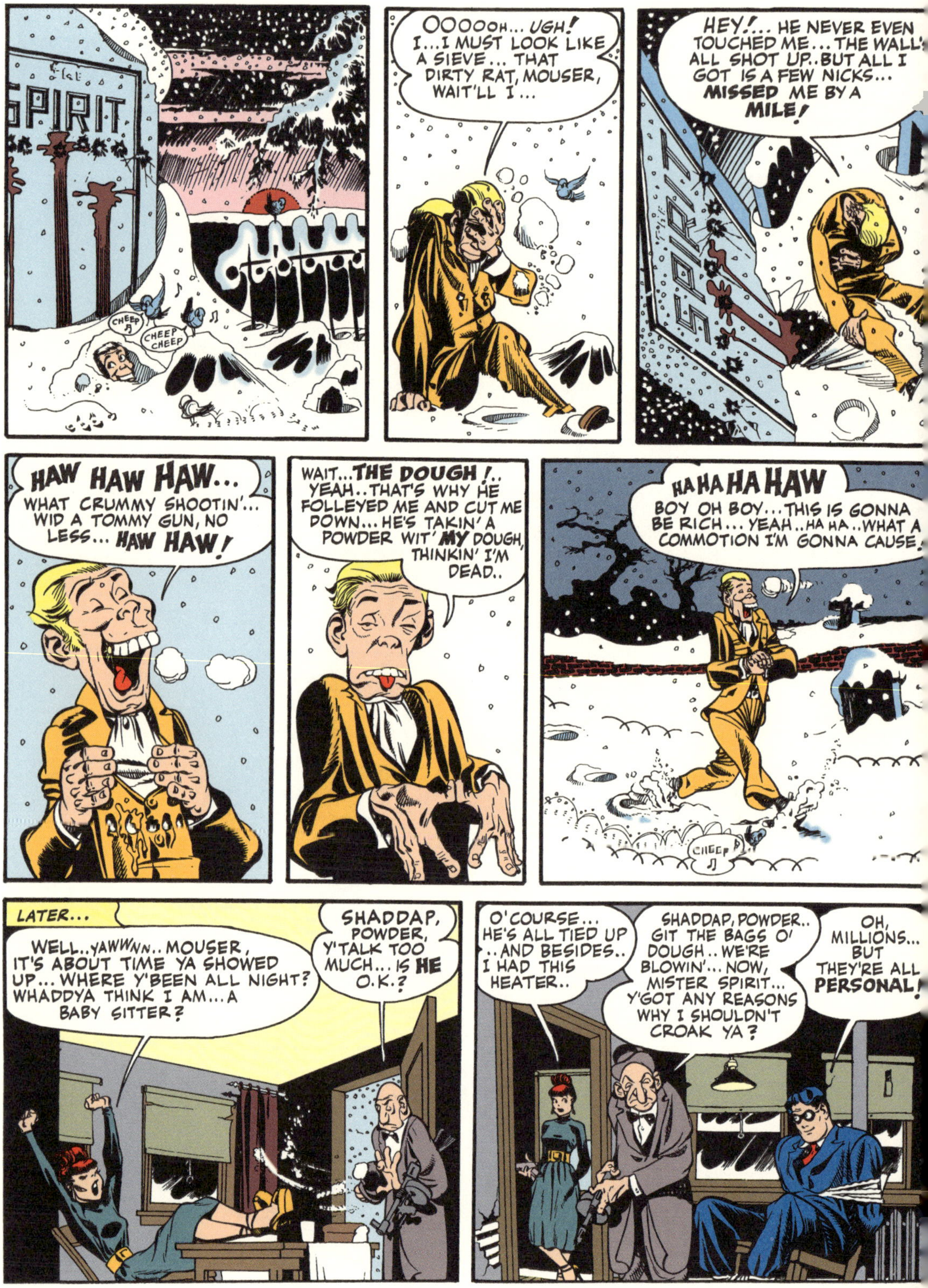
SPIRIT
CHEEP
CHEEP CHEEP
OOOOOH... UGH! I...I MUST LOOK LIKE A SIEVE... THAT DIRTY RAT, MOUSER, WAIT'LL I...
HEY!... HE NEVER EVEN TOUCHED ME... THE WALL'S ALL SHOT UP..BUT ALL I GOT IS A FEW NICKS... MISSED ME BY A MILE!
HAW HAW HAW... WHAT CRUMMY SHOOTIN'... WID A TOMMY GUN, NO LESS... HAW HAW!
WAIT... THE DOUGH!.. YEAH..THAT'S WHY HE FOLLEYED ME AND CUT ME DOWN... HE'S TAKIN' A POWDER WIT' MY DOUGH, THINKIN' I'M DEAD..
HA HA HA HAW
BOY OH BOY... THIS IS GONNA BE RICH... YEAH..HA HA..WHAT A COMMOTION I'M GONNA CAUSE.
CHEEP
LATER...
WELL..YAWWNN..MOUSER, IT'S ABOUT TIME YA SHOWED UP... WHERE Y'BEEN ALL NIGHT? WHADDYA THINK I AM... A BABY SITTER?
SHADDAP, POWDER, Y'TALK TOO MUCH... IS HE O.K.?
O'COURSE... HE'S ALL TIED UP ..AND BESIDES.. I HAD THIS HEATER..
SHADDAP, POWDER.. GIT THE BAGS O' DOUGH.. WE'RE BLOWIN'... NOW, MISTER SPIRIT... Y'GOT ANY REASONS WHY I SHOULDN'T CROAK YA?
OH, MILLIONS... BUT THEY'RE ALL PERSONAL!

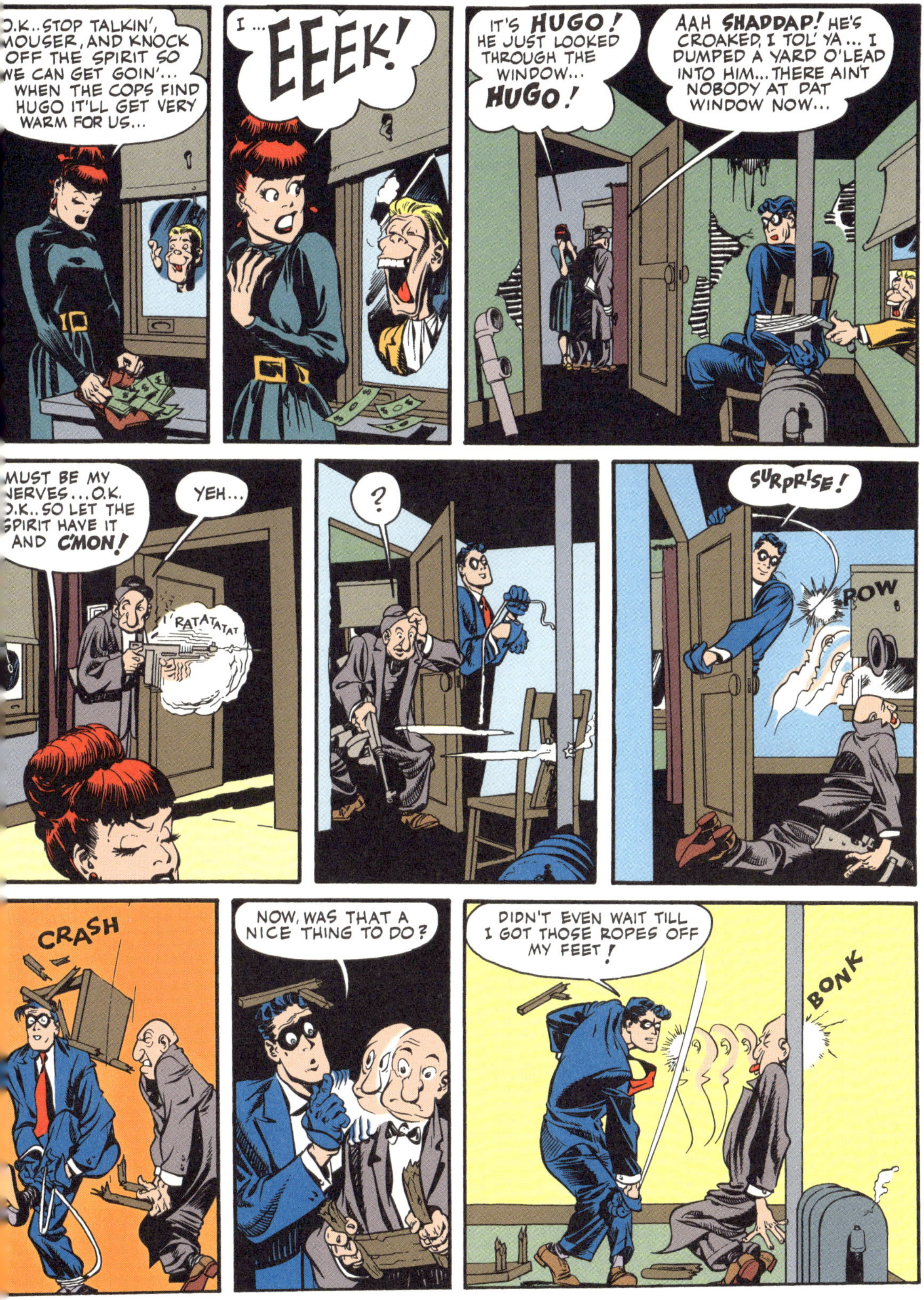
O.K.. STOP TALKIN', MOUSER, AND KNOCK OFF THE SPIRIT SO WE CAN GET GOIN'... WHEN THE COPS FIND HUGO IT'LL GET VERY WARM FOR US...
I ... EEEK!
IT'S HUGO! HE JUST LOOKED THROUGH THE WINDOW... HUGO!
AAH SHADDAP! HE'S CROAKED, I TOL' YA ... I DUMPED A YARD O'LEAD INTO HIM... THERE AIN'T NOBODY AT DAT WINDOW NOW...
MUST BE MY NERVES...O.K. O.K.. SO LET THE SPIRIT HAVE IT AND C'MON!
YEH...
RATATATATAT
?
SURPRISE!
POW
CRASH
NOW, WAS THAT A NICE THING TO DO?
DIDN'T EVEN WAIT TILL I GOT THOSE ROPES OFF MY FEET!
BONK

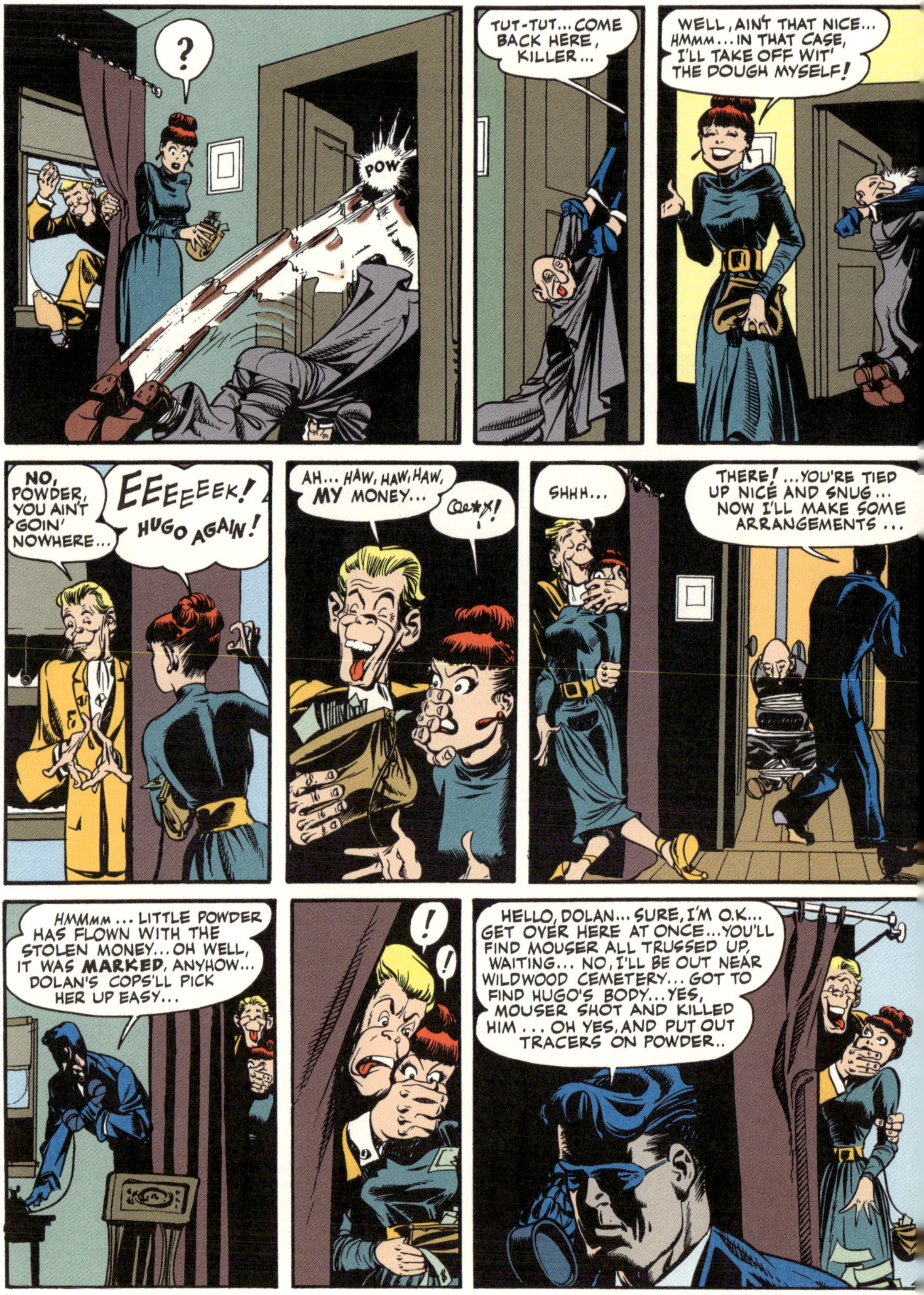
?
POW
TUT-TUT... COME BACK HERE, KILLER...
WELL, AIN'T THAT NICE... HMMM... IN THAT CASE, I'LL TAKE OFF WIT' THE DOUGH MYSELF!
NO, POWDER, YOU AIN'T GOIN' NOWHERE...
EEEEEEEK! HUGO AGAIN!
AH... HAW, HAW, HAW, MY MONEY...
SHHH...
THERE! ...YOU'RE TIED UP NICE AND SNUG... NOW I'LL MAKE SOME ARRANGEMENTS...
HMMMM... LITTLE POWDER HAS FLOWN WITH THE STOLEN MONEY... OH WELL, IT WAS MARKED, ANYHOW... DOLAN'S COPS'LL PICK HER UP EASY...
!
!
HELLO, DOLAN... SURE, I'M O.K... GET OVER HERE AT ONCE... YOU'LL FIND MOUSER ALL TRUSSED UP, WAITING... NO, I'LL BE OUT NEAR WILDWOOD CEMETERY... GOT TO FIND HUGO'S BODY... YES, MOUSER SHOT AND KILLED HIM... OH YES, AND PUT OUT TRACERS ON POWDER..

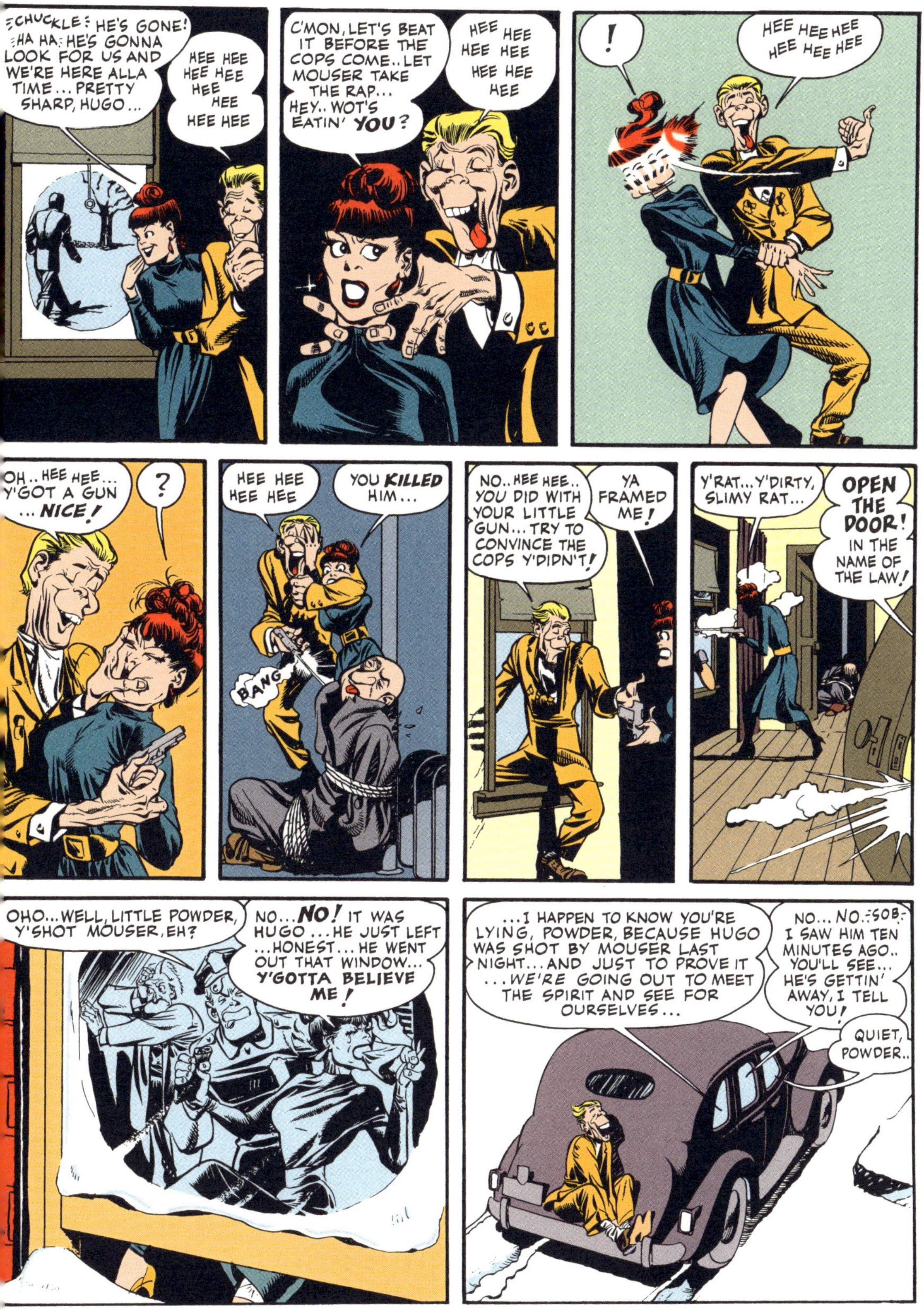

=CHUCKLE= HE'S GONE! =HA HA= HE'S GONNA LOOK FOR US AND WE'RE HERE ALLA TIME... PRETTY SHARP, HUGO...
HEE HEE HEE HEE HEE HEE HEE HEE
C'MON, LET'S BEAT IT BEFORE THE COPS COME.. LET MOUSER TAKE THE RAP... HEY.. WOT'S EATIN' YOU?
HEE HEE HEE HEE HEE HEE HEE
!
HEE HEE HEE HEE HEE HEE
OH.. HEE HEE... Y'GOT A GUN ... NICE!
?
HEE HEE HEE HEE
YOU KILLED HIM...
BANG
NO.. HEE HEE.. YOU DID WITH YOUR LITTLE GUN... TRY TO CONVINCE THE COPS Y'DIDN'T!
YA FRAMED ME!
Y'RAT... Y'DIRTY, SLIMY RAT...
OPEN THE DOOR! IN THE NAME OF THE LAW!
OHO... WELL, LITTLE POWDER, Y'SHOT MOUSER, EH?
NO... NO! IT WAS HUGO... HE JUST LEFT ...HONEST... HE WENT OUT THAT WINDOW... Y'GOTTA BELIEVE ME!
...I HAPPEN TO KNOW YOU'RE LYING, POWDER, BECAUSE HUGO WAS SHOT BY MOUSER LAST NIGHT... AND JUST TO PROVE IT ...WE'RE GOING OUT TO MEET THE SPIRIT AND SEE FOR OURSELVES...
NO... NO... =SOB= I SAW HIM TEN MINUTES AGO.. YOU'LL SEE... HE'S GETTIN' AWAY, I TELL YOU!
QUIET, POWDER..

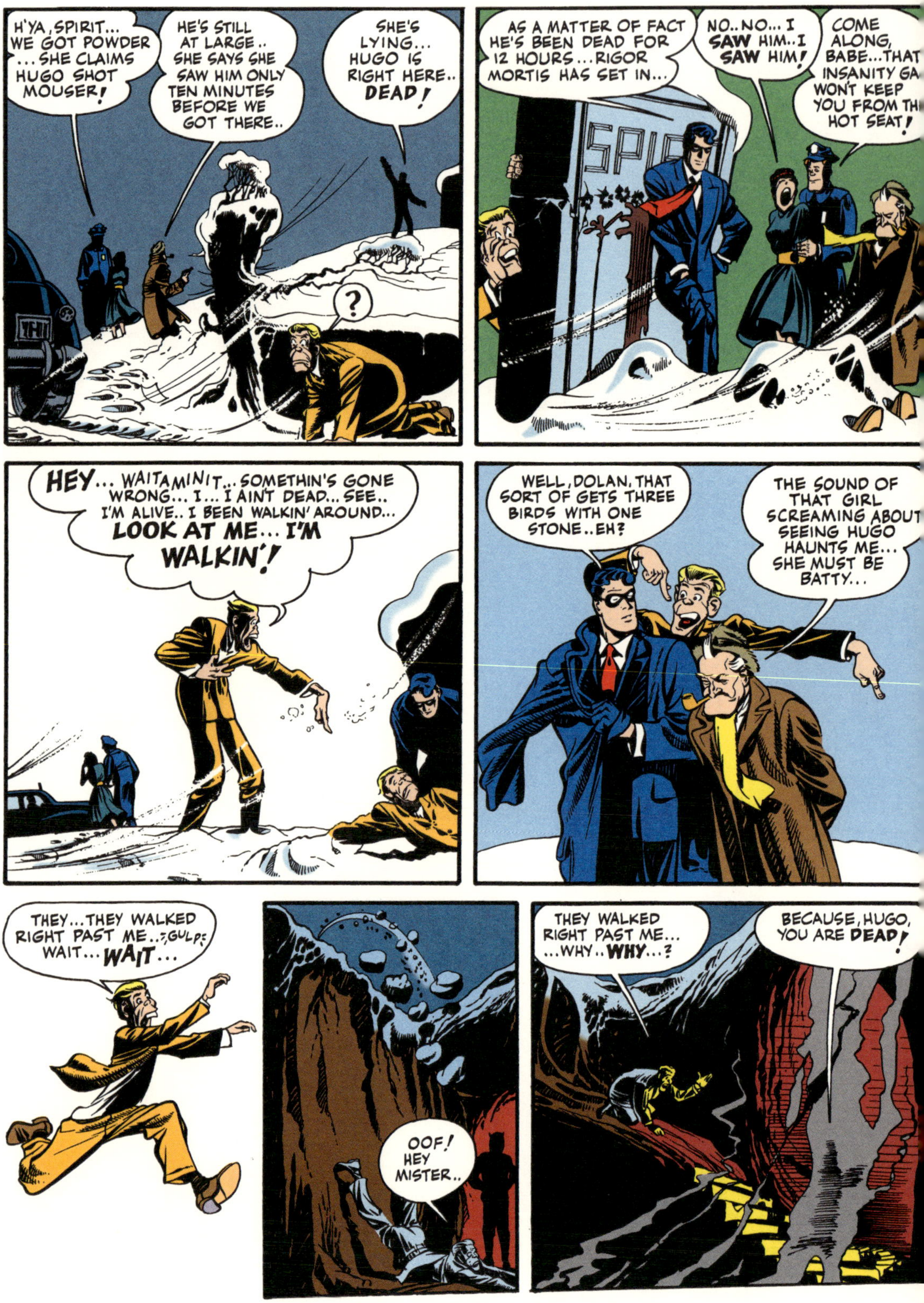

H'YA, SPIRIT... WE GOT POWDER ...SHE CLAIMS HUGO SHOT MOUSER!
HE'S STILL AT LARGE.. SHE SAYS SHE SAW HIM ONLY TEN MINUTES BEFORE WE GOT THERE..
SHE'S LYING... HUGO IS RIGHT HERE.. DEAD!
?
AS A MATTER OF FACT HE'S BEEN DEAD FOR 12 HOURS... RIGOR MORTIS HAS SET IN...
NO..NO... I SAW HIM..I SAW HIM!
COME ALONG, BABE...THAT INSANITY GA WON'T KEEP YOU FROM TH HOT SEAT!
HEY... WAITAMINIT... SOMETHIN'S GONE WRONG... I... I AIN'T DEAD... SEE.. I'M ALIVE.. I BEEN WALKIN' AROUND... LOOK AT ME... I'M WALKIN'!
WELL, DOLAN, THAT SORT OF GETS THREE BIRDS WITH ONE STONE..EH?
THE SOUND OF THAT GIRL SCREAMING ABOUT SEEING HUGO HAUNTS ME... SHE MUST BE BATTY...
THEY...THEY WALKED RIGHT PAST ME..GULP WAIT... WAIT...
OOF! HEY MISTER..
THEY WALKED RIGHT PAST ME... ...WHY..WHY...?
BECAUSE, HUGO, YOU ARE DEAD!

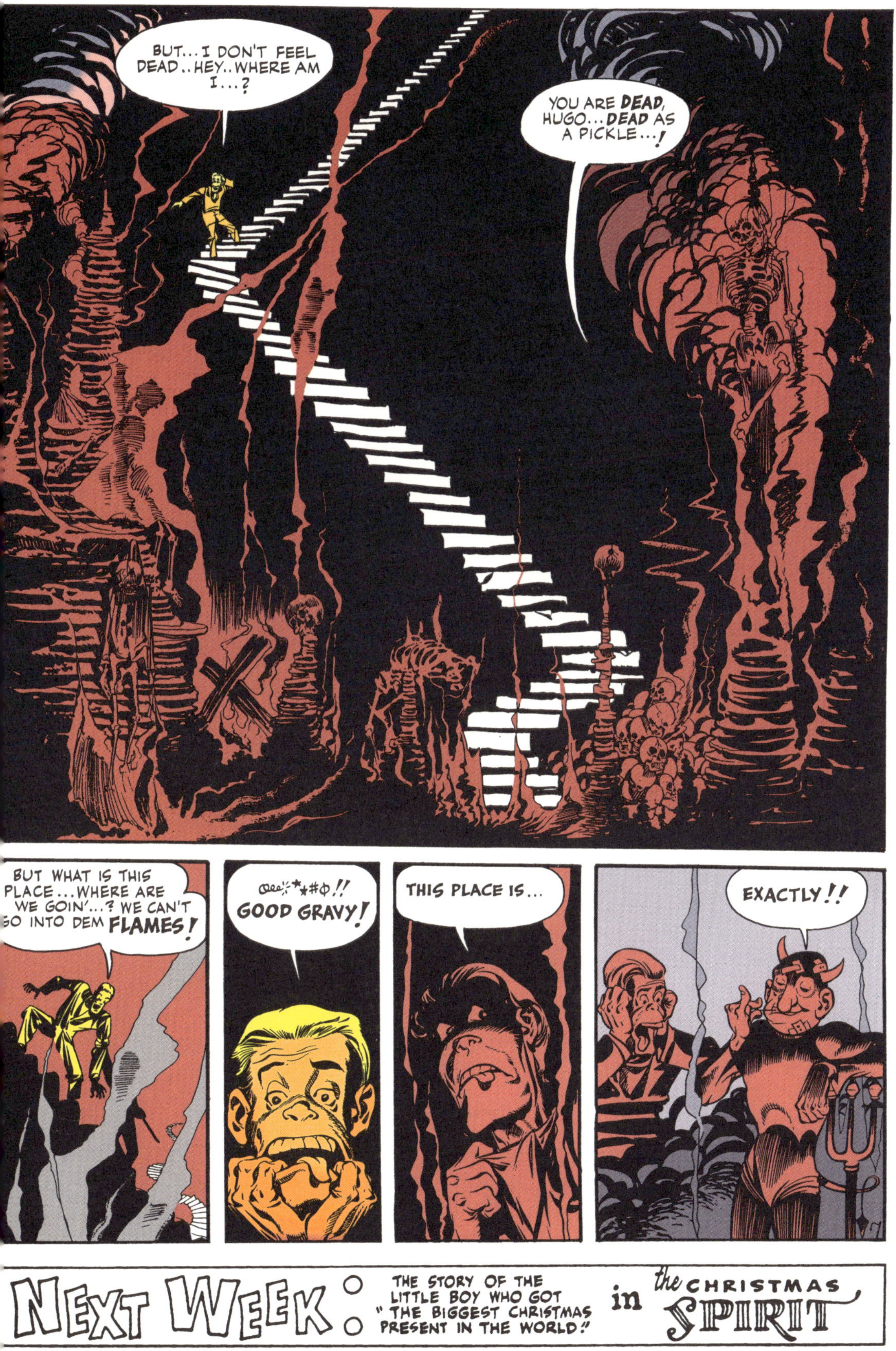
BUT... I DON'T FEEL DEAD.. HEY.. WHERE AM I...?
YOU ARE DEAD, HUGO... DEAD AS A PICKLE...!
BUT WHAT IS THIS PLACE... WHERE ARE WE GOIN'...? WE CAN'T GO INTO DEM FLAMES!
GOOD GRAVY!
THIS PLACE IS...
EXACTLY!!
NEXT WEEK:
THE STORY OF THE LITTLE BOY WHO GOT "THE BIGGEST CHRISTMAS PRESENT IN THE WORLD."
in the CHRISTMAS SPIRIT

COMIC BOOK SECTION

SNOW

December 14 1947

ACTION Mystery ADVENTURE

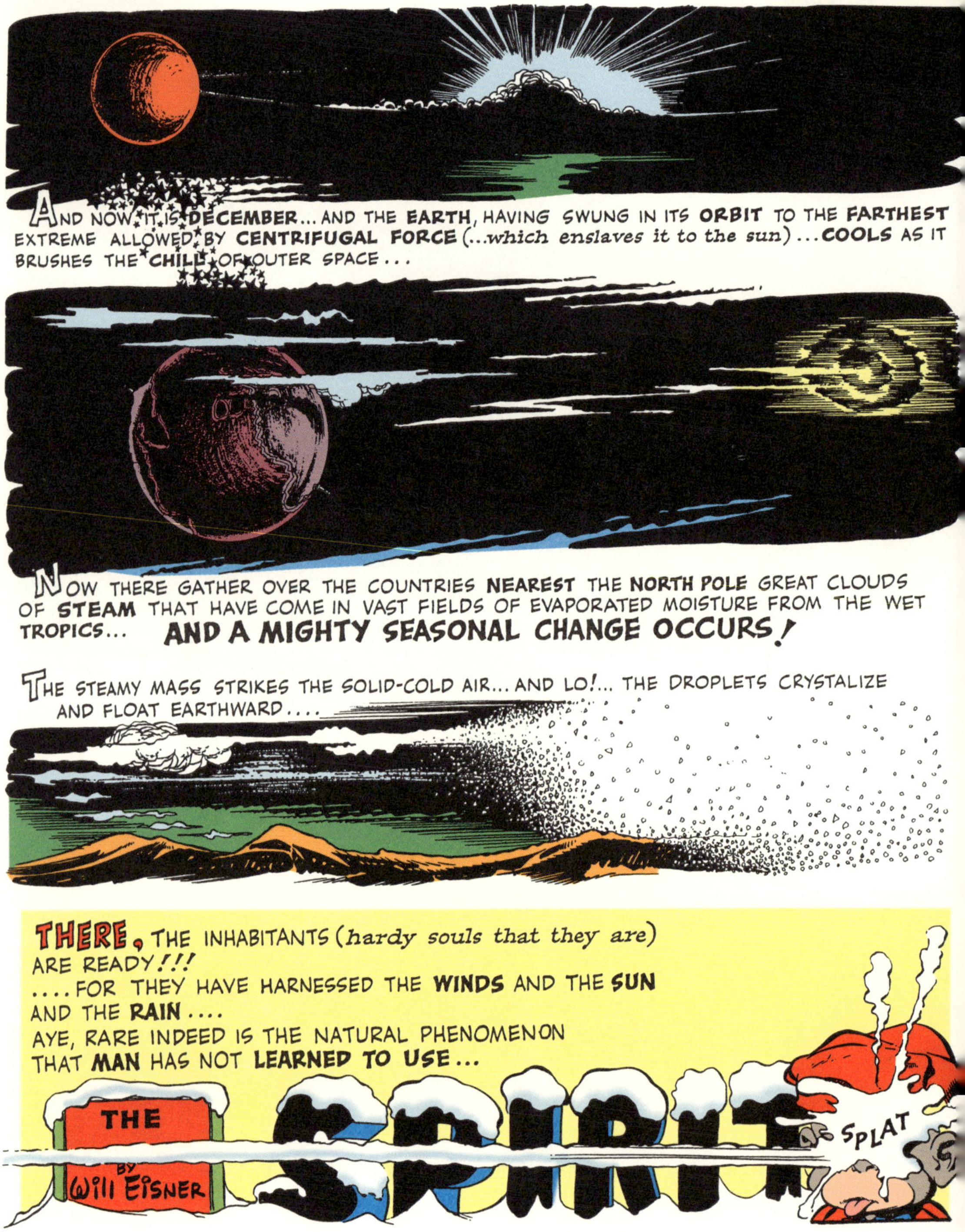

AND NOW IT IS DECEMBER... AND THE EARTH, HAVING SWUNG IN ITS ORBIT TO THE FARTHEST EXTREME ALLOWED BY CENTRIFUGAL FORCE (...which enslaves it to the sun)...COOLS AS IT BRUSHES THE CHILL OF OUTER SPACE...
NOW THERE GATHER OVER THE COUNTRIES NEAREST THE NORTH POLE GREAT CLOUDS OF STEAM THAT HAVE COME IN VAST FIELDS OF EVAPORATED MOISTURE FROM THE WET TROPICS... AND A MIGHTY SEASONAL CHANGE OCCURS!
THE STEAMY MASS STRIKES THE SOLID-COLD AIR... AND LO!... THE DROPLETS CRYSTALIZE AND FLOAT EARTHWARD....
THERE, THE INHABITANTS (hardy souls that they are) ARE READY!!! ....FOR THEY HAVE HARNESSED THE WINDS AND THE SUN AND THE RAIN.... AYE, RARE INDEED IS THE NATURAL PHENOMENON THAT MAN HAS NOT LEARNED TO USE...
THE
BY Will Eisner
SPIRIT
SPLAT

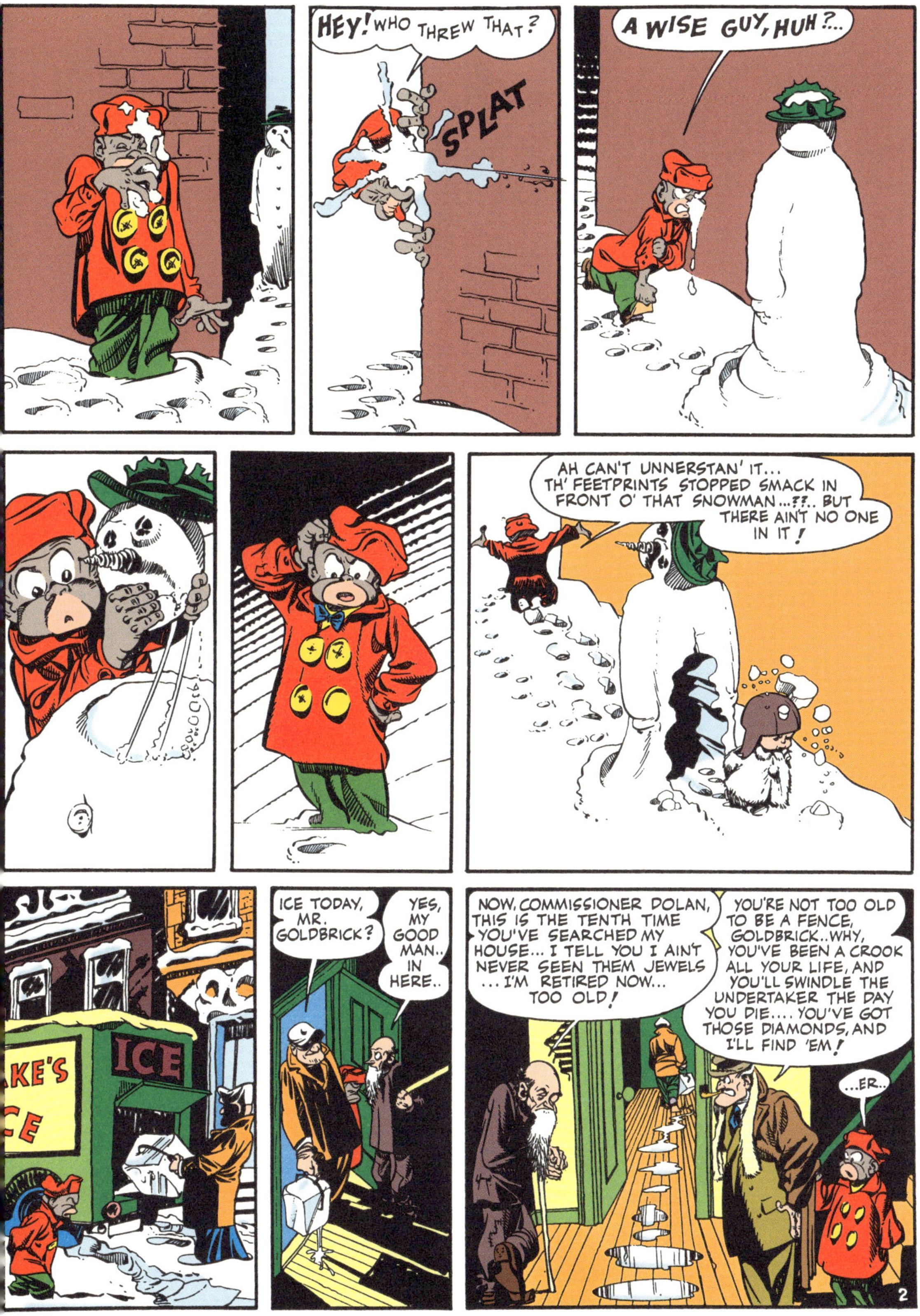
HEY! WHO THREW THAT?
SPLAT
A WISE GUY, HUH?..
AH CAN'T UNNERSTAN' IT... TH' FEETPRINTS STOPPED SMACK IN FRONT O' THAT SNOWMAN...??.. BUT THERE AIN'T NO ONE IN IT!
ICE
ICE TODAY, MR. GOLDBRICK?
YES, MY GOOD MAN.. IN HERE..
NOW, COMMISSIONER DOLAN, THIS IS THE TENTH TIME YOU'VE SEARCHED MY HOUSE... I TELL YOU I AIN'T NEVER SEEN THEM JEWELS ... I'M RETIRED NOW... TOO OLD!
YOU'RE NOT TOO OLD TO BE A FENCE, GOLDBRICK..WHY, YOU'VE BEEN A CROOK ALL YOUR LIFE, AND YOU'LL SWINDLE THE UNDERTAKER THE DAY YOU DIE.... YOU'VE GOT THOSE DIAMONDS, AND I'LL FIND 'EM!
...ER..
2

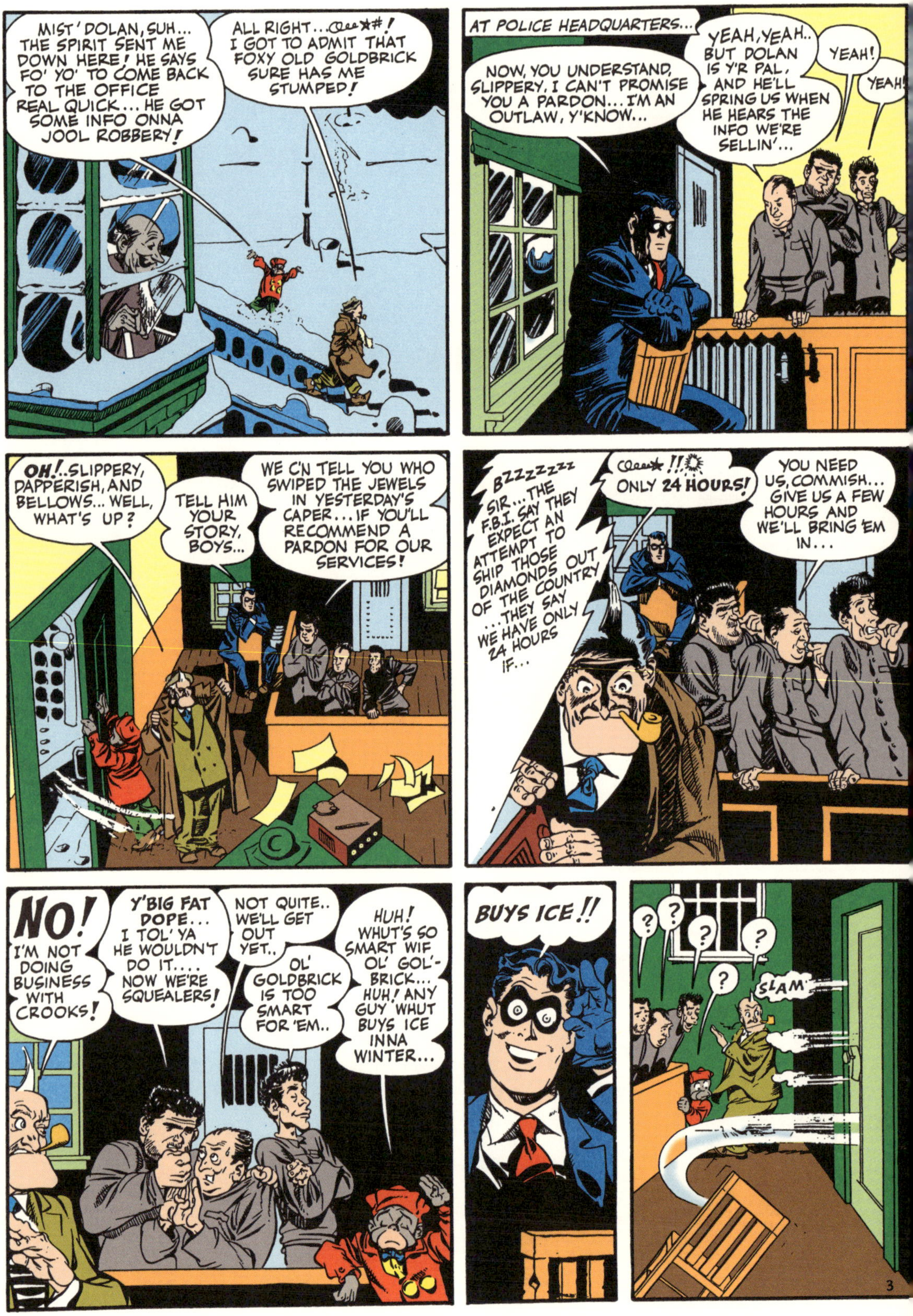
MIST' DOLAN, SUH... THE SPIRIT SENT ME DOWN HERE! HE SAYS FO' YO' TO COME BACK TO THE OFFICE REAL QUICK... HE GOT SOME INFO ONNA JOOL ROBBERY!
ALL RIGHT... I GOT TO ADMIT THAT FOXY OLD GOLDBRICK SURE HAS ME STUMPED!
AT POLICE HEADQUARTERS...
NOW, YOU UNDERSTAND, SLIPPERY, I CAN'T PROMISE YOU A PARDON... I'M AN OUTLAW, Y'KNOW...
YEAH, YEAH.. BUT DOLAN IS Y'R PAL, AND HE'LL SPRING US WHEN HE HEARS THE INFO WE'RE SELLIN'...
YEAH!
YEAH!
OH!..SLIPPERY, DAPPERISH, AND BELLOWS... WELL, WHAT'S UP?
TELL HIM YOUR STORY, BOYS...
WE C'N TELL YOU WHO SWIPED THE JEWELS IN YESTERDAY'S CAPER... IF YOU'LL RECOMMEND A PARDON FOR OUR SERVICES!
BZZZZZZZ
SIR... THE F.B.I. SAY THEY EXPECT AN ATTEMPT TO SHIP THOSE DIAMONDS OUT OF THE COUNTRY ...THEY SAY WE HAVE ONLY 24 HOURS IF...
ONLY 24 HOURS!
YOU NEED US, COMMISH... GIVE US A FEW HOURS AND WE'LL BRING 'EM IN...
NO! I'M NOT DOING BUSINESS WITH CROOKS!
Y'BIG FAT DOPE... I TOL' YA HE WOULDN'T DO IT.... NOW WE'RE SQUEALERS!
NOT QUITE.. WE'LL GET OUT YET..
OL' GOLDBRICK IS TOO SMART FOR 'EM..
HUH! WHUT'S SO SMART WIF OL' GOL'-BRICK... HUH! ANY GUY WHUT BUYS ICE INNA WINTER...
BUYS ICE!!
?
?
?
?
?
SLAM
3

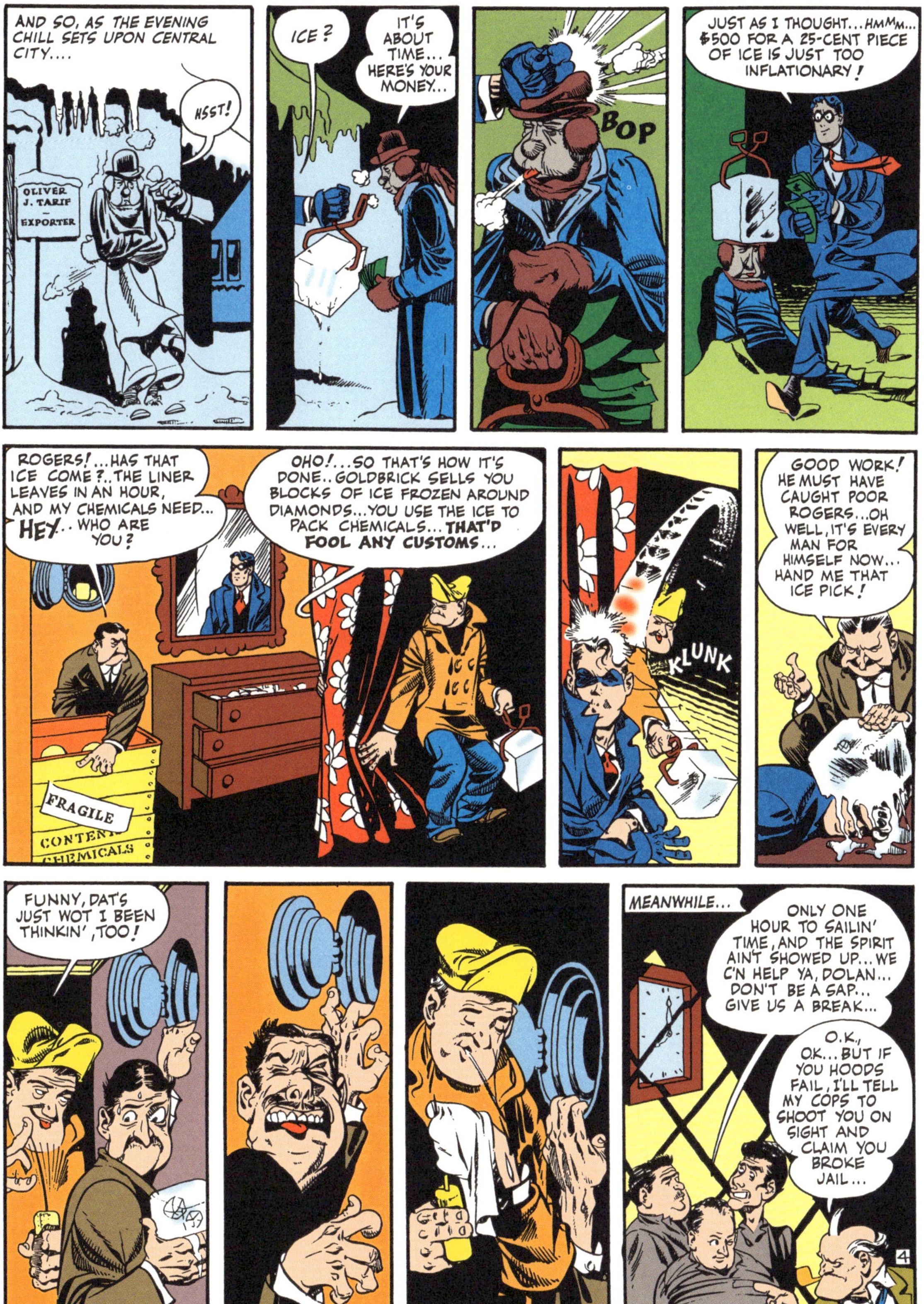

AND SO, AS THE EVENING CHILL SETS UPON CENTRAL CITY....
HSST!
OLIVER J. TARIF EXPORTER
ICE ?
IT'S ABOUT TIME... HERE'S YOUR MONEY...
BOP
JUST AS I THOUGHT... HMMM... $500 FOR A 25-CENT PIECE OF ICE IS JUST TOO INFLATIONARY!
ROGERS!... HAS THAT ICE COME?.. THE LINER LEAVES IN AN HOUR, AND MY CHEMICALS NEED... HEY.. WHO ARE YOU?
OHO!... SO THAT'S HOW IT'S DONE.. GOLDBRICK SELLS YOU BLOCKS OF ICE FROZEN AROUND DIAMONDS... YOU USE THE ICE TO PACK CHEMICALS... THAT'D FOOL ANY CUSTOMS...
FRAGILE
KLUNK
GOOD WORK! HE MUST HAVE CAUGHT POOR ROGERS... OH WELL, IT'S EVERY MAN FOR HIMSELF NOW... HAND ME THAT ICE PICK!
FUNNY, DAT'S JUST WOT I BEEN THINKIN', TOO!
MEANWHILE...
ONLY ONE HOUR TO SAILIN' TIME, AND THE SPIRIT AIN'T SHOWED UP... WE C'N HELP YA, DOLAN... DON'T BE A SAP... GIVE US A BREAK...
O.K., OK... BUT IF YOU HOODS FAIL, I'LL TELL MY COPS TO SHOOT YOU ON SIGHT AND CLAIM YOU BROKE JAIL...
4

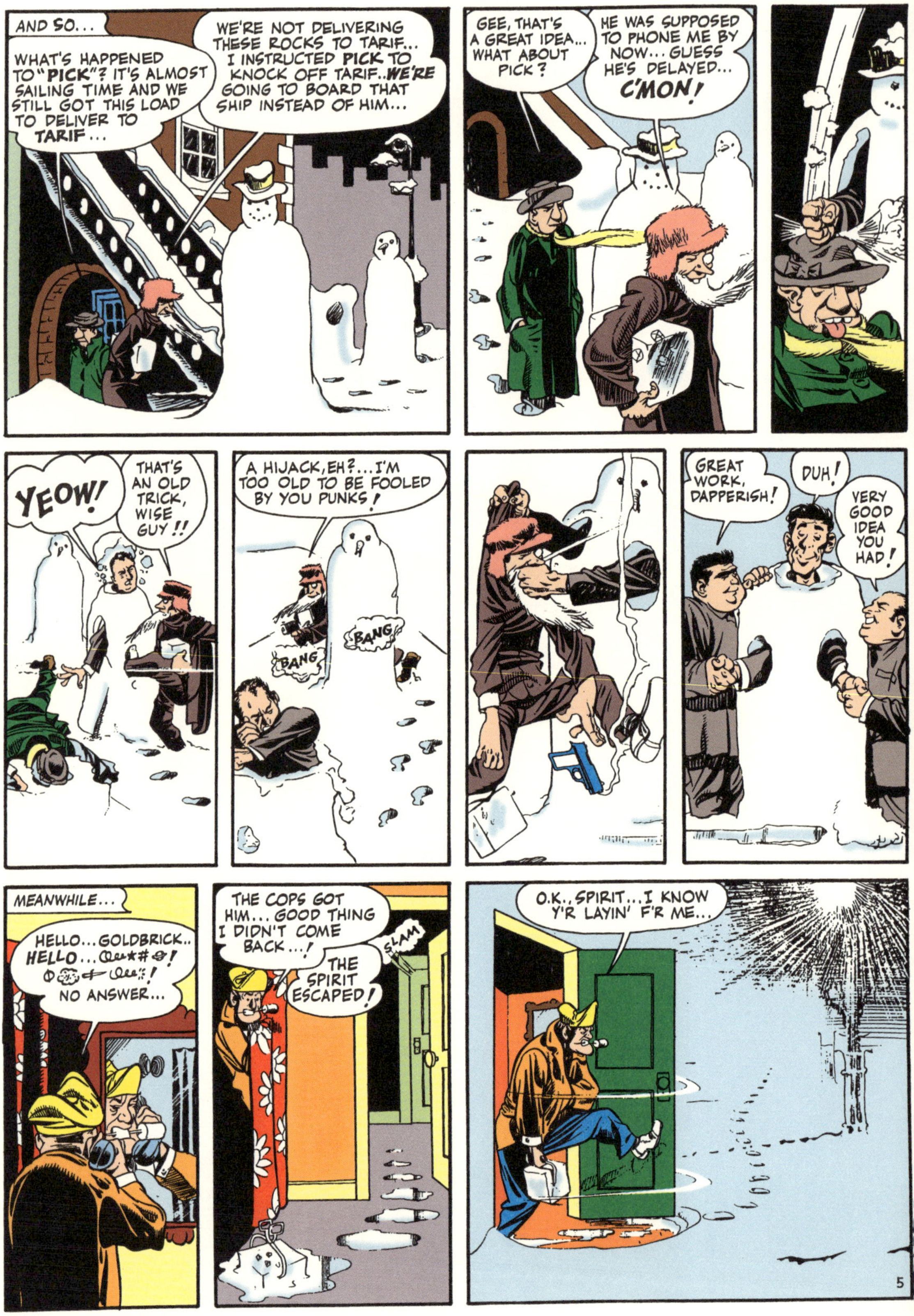
AND SO...
WHAT'S HAPPENED TO "PICK"? IT'S ALMOST SAILING TIME AND WE STILL GOT THIS LOAD TO DELIVER TO TARIF...
WE'RE NOT DELIVERING THESE ROCKS TO TARIF... I INSTRUCTED PICK TO KNOCK OFF TARIF.. WE'RE GOING TO BOARD THAT SHIP INSTEAD OF HIM...
GEE, THAT'S A GREAT IDEA... WHAT ABOUT PICK?
HE WAS SUPPOSED TO PHONE ME BY NOW... GUESS HE'S DELAYED... C'MON!
YEOW!
THAT'S AN OLD TRICK, WISE GUY!!
A HIJACK, EH?... I'M TOO OLD TO BE FOOLED BY YOU PUNKS!
BANG
BANG
GREAT WORK, DAPPERISH!
DUH!
VERY GOOD IDEA YOU HAD!
MEANWHILE...
HELLO... GOLDBRICK.. HELLO...
NO ANSWER...
THE COPS GOT HIM... GOOD THING I DIDN'T COME BACK...!
THE SPIRIT ESCAPED!
SLAM
O.K., SPIRIT... I KNOW Y'R LAYIN' F'R ME...
5

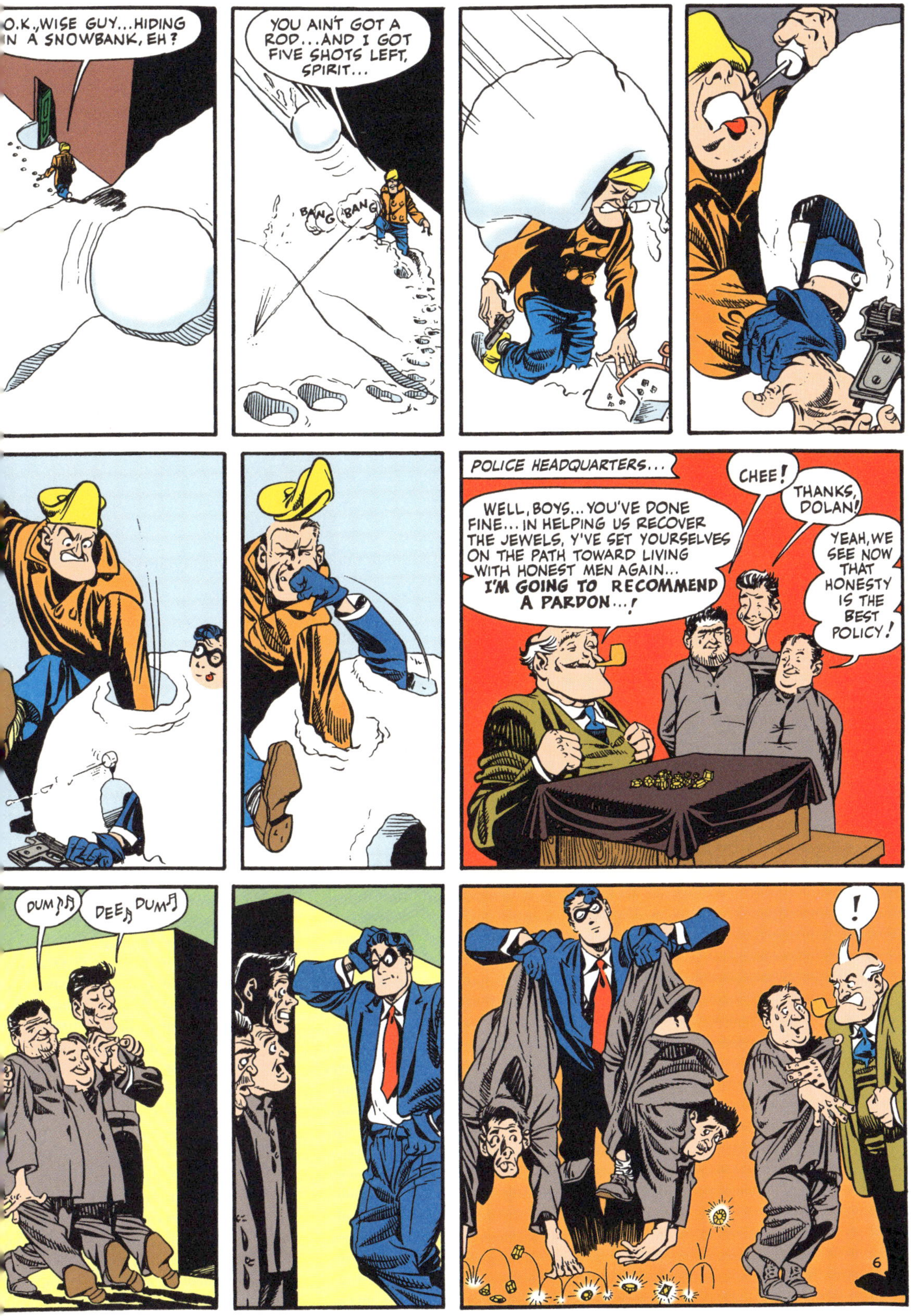
O.K., WISE GUY... HIDING IN A SNOWBANK, EH?
YOU AIN'T GOT A ROD... AND I GOT FIVE SHOTS LEFT, SPIRIT...
BANG
BANG
POLICE HEADQUARTERS...
WELL, BOYS... YOU'VE DONE FINE... IN HELPING US RECOVER THE JEWELS, Y'VE SET YOURSELVES ON THE PATH TOWARD LIVING WITH HONEST MEN AGAIN... I'M GOING TO RECOMMEND A PARDON...!
CHEE!
THANKS, DOLAN!
YEAH, WE SEE NOW THAT HONESTY IS THE BEST POLICY!
DUM
DEE DUM
!
6

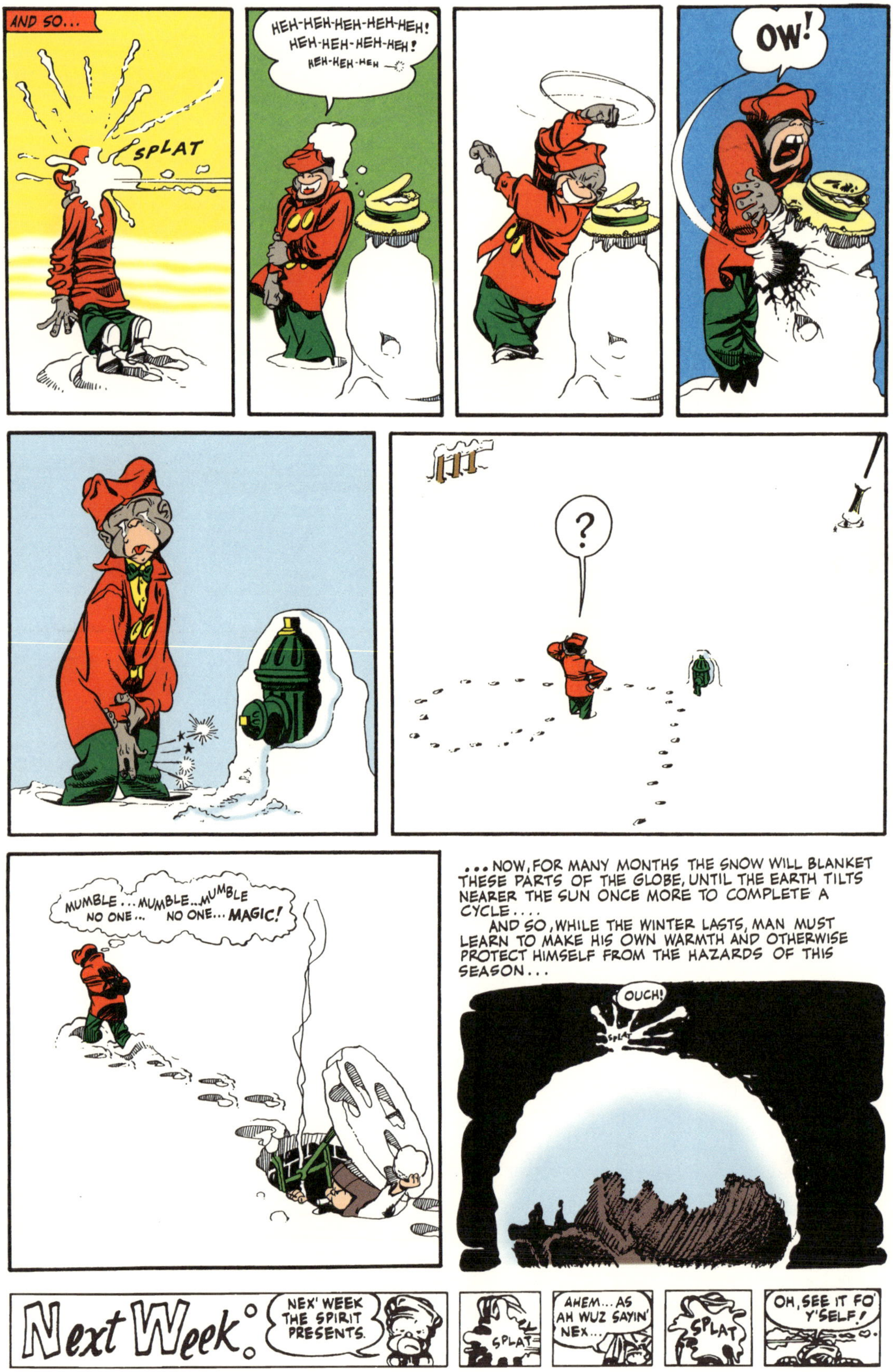
AND SO...
SPLAT
HEH-HEH-HEH-HEH-HEH!
HEH-HEH-HEH-HEH!
HEH-HEH-HEH
OW!
?
MUMBLE...MUMBLE...MUMBLE
NO ONE... NO ONE... MAGIC!
...NOW, FOR MANY MONTHS THE SNOW WILL BLANKET THESE PARTS OF THE GLOBE, UNTIL THE EARTH TILTS NEARER THE SUN ONCE MORE TO COMPLETE A CYCLE....
AND SO, WHILE THE WINTER LASTS, MAN MUST LEARN TO MAKE HIS OWN WARMTH AND OTHERWISE PROTECT HIMSELF FROM THE HAZARDS OF THIS SEASON...
OUCH!
SPLAT
Next Week:
NEX' WEEK THE SPIRIT PRESENTS.
SPLAT
AHEM...AS AH WUZ SAYIN' NEX...
SPLAT
OH, SEE IT FO' Y'SELF!

COMIC BOOK SECTION

THE CHRISTMAS SPIRIT OF 1947: JOY

ACTION Mystery ADVENTURE

December 21 1947

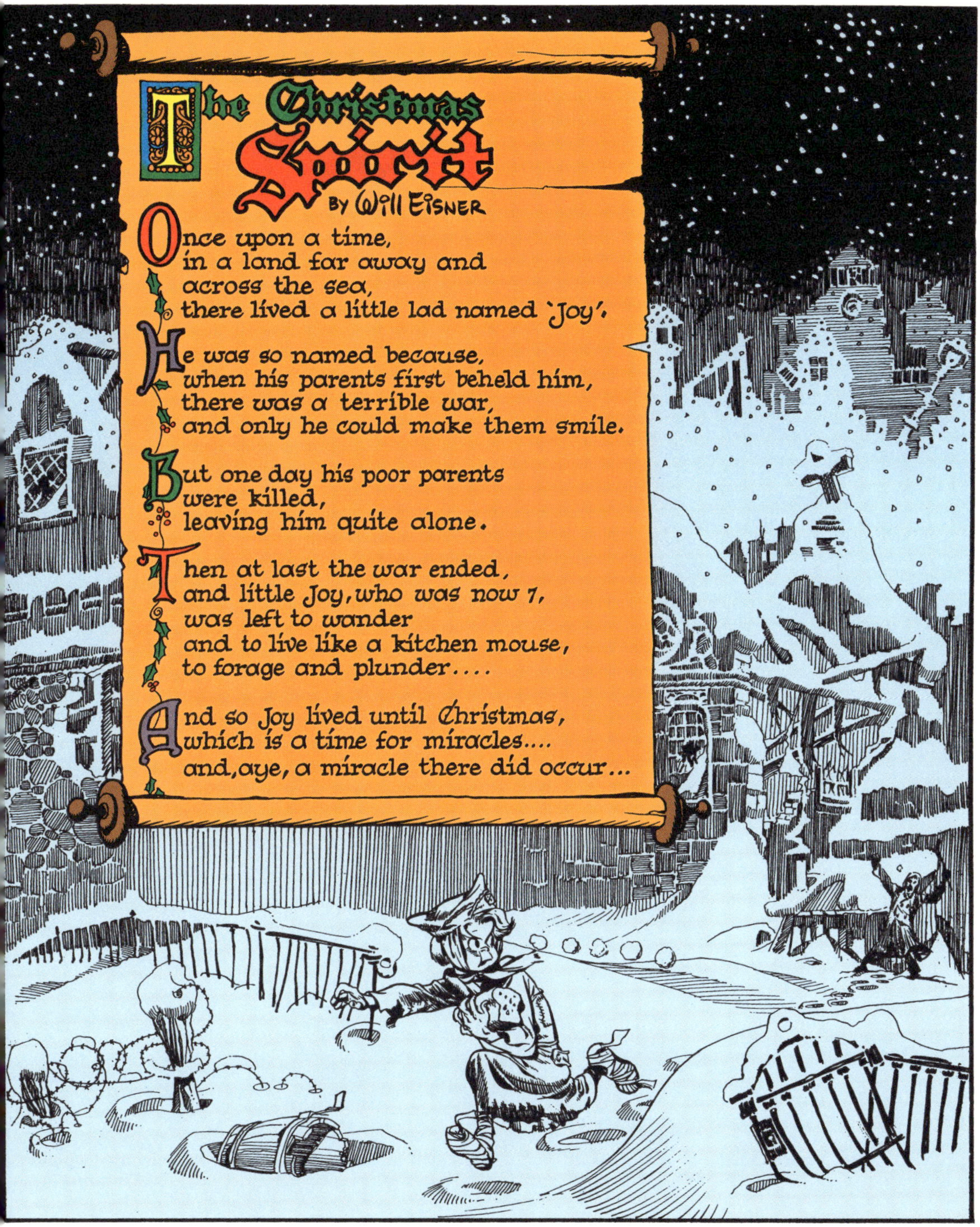
The Christmas Spirit
By Will Eisner
Once upon a time,
in a land far away and
across the sea,
there lived a little lad named 'Joy'.
He was so named because,
when his parents first beheld him,
there was a terrible war,
and only he could make them smile.
But one day his poor parents
were killed,
leaving him quite alone.
Then at last the war ended,
and little Joy, who was now 7,
was left to wander
and to live like a kitchen mouse,
to forage and plunder....
And so Joy lived until Christmas,
which is a time for miracles....
and, aye, a miracle there did occur...

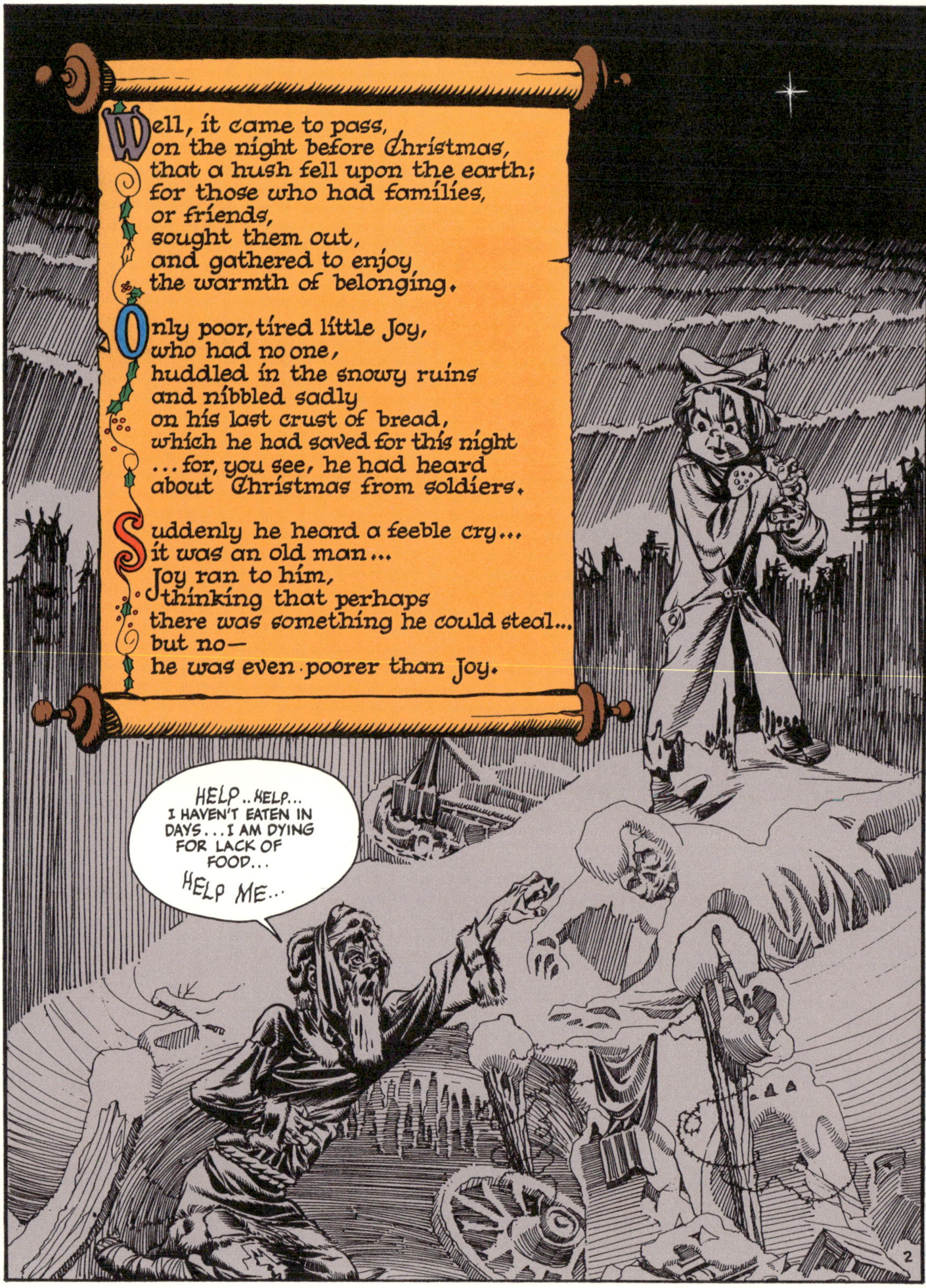
Well, it came to pass,
on the night before Christmas,
that a hush fell upon the earth;
for those who had families,
or friends,
sought them out,
and gathered to enjoy
the warmth of belonging.
Only poor, tired little Joy,
who had no one,
huddled in the snowy ruins
and nibbled sadly
on his last crust of bread,
which he had saved for this night
... for, you see, he had heard
about Christmas from soldiers.
Suddenly he heard a feeble cry...
it was an old man...
Joy ran to him,
thinking that perhaps
there was something he could steal...
but no—
he was even poorer than Joy.
HELP.. HELP... I HAVEN'T EATEN IN DAYS... I AM DYING FOR LACK OF FOOD... HELP ME...
2

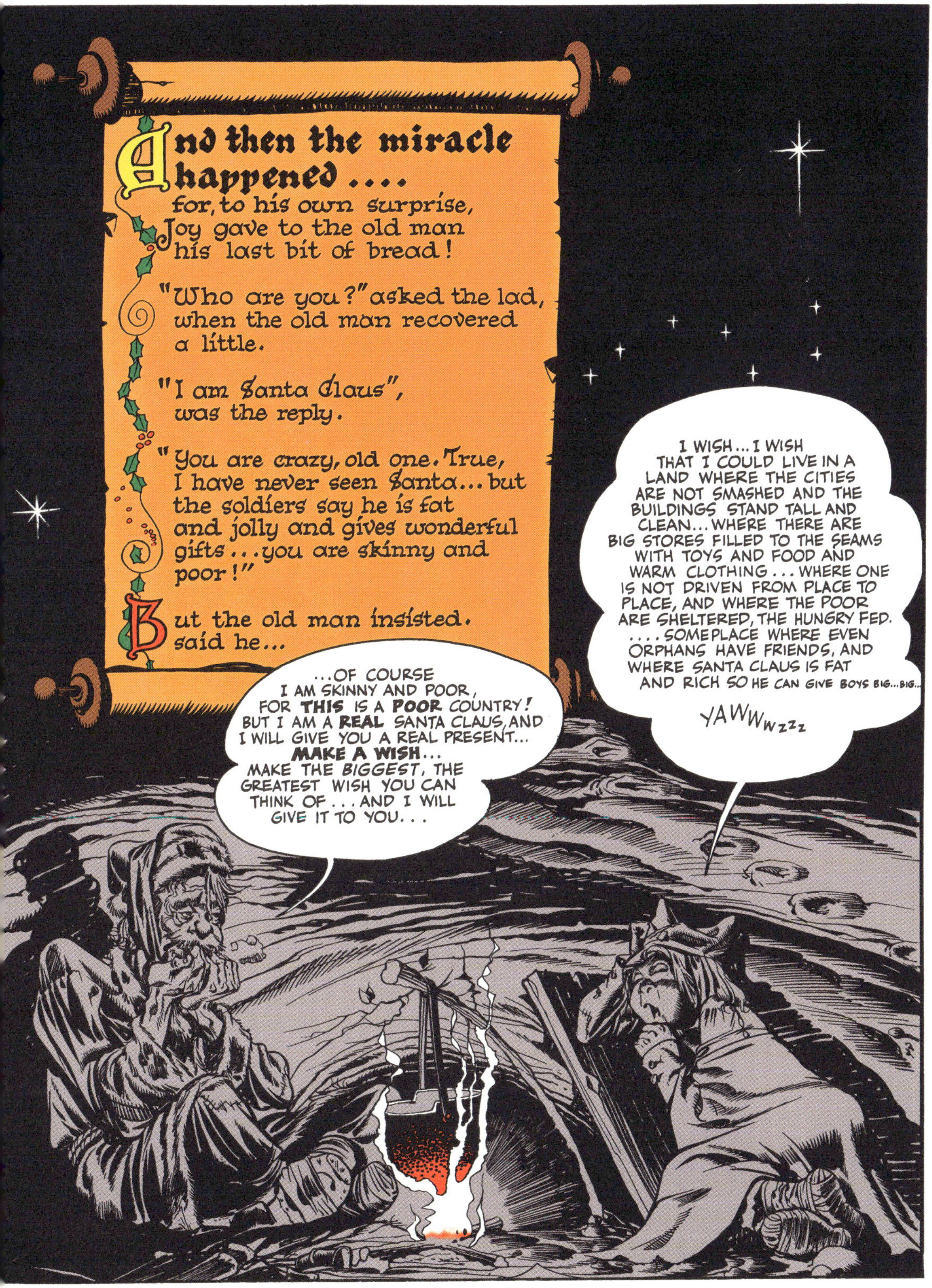
And then the miracle happened ....
for, to his own surprise, Joy gave to the old man his last bit of bread!
"Who are you?" asked the lad, when the old man recovered a little.
"I am Santa Claus", was the reply.
"You are crazy, old one. True, I have never seen Santa... but the soldiers say he is fat and jolly and gives wonderful gifts ...you are skinny and poor!"
But the old man insisted. said he...
...OF COURSE I AM SKINNY AND POOR, FOR THIS IS A POOR COUNTRY! BUT I AM A REAL SANTA CLAUS, AND I WILL GIVE YOU A REAL PRESENT... MAKE A WISH... MAKE THE BIGGEST, THE GREATEST WISH YOU CAN THINK OF... AND I WILL GIVE IT TO YOU...
I WISH... I WISH THAT I COULD LIVE IN A LAND WHERE THE CITIES ARE NOT SMASHED AND THE BUILDINGS STAND TALL AND CLEAN... WHERE THERE ARE BIG STORES FILLED TO THE SEAMS WITH TOYS AND FOOD AND WARM CLOTHING... WHERE ONE IS NOT DRIVEN FROM PLACE TO PLACE, AND WHERE THE POOR ARE SHELTERED, THE HUNGRY FED. ....SOMEPLACE WHERE EVEN ORPHANS HAVE FRIENDS, AND WHERE SANTA CLAUS IS FAT AND RICH SO HE CAN GIVE BOYS BIG...BIG...
YAWWWzzz

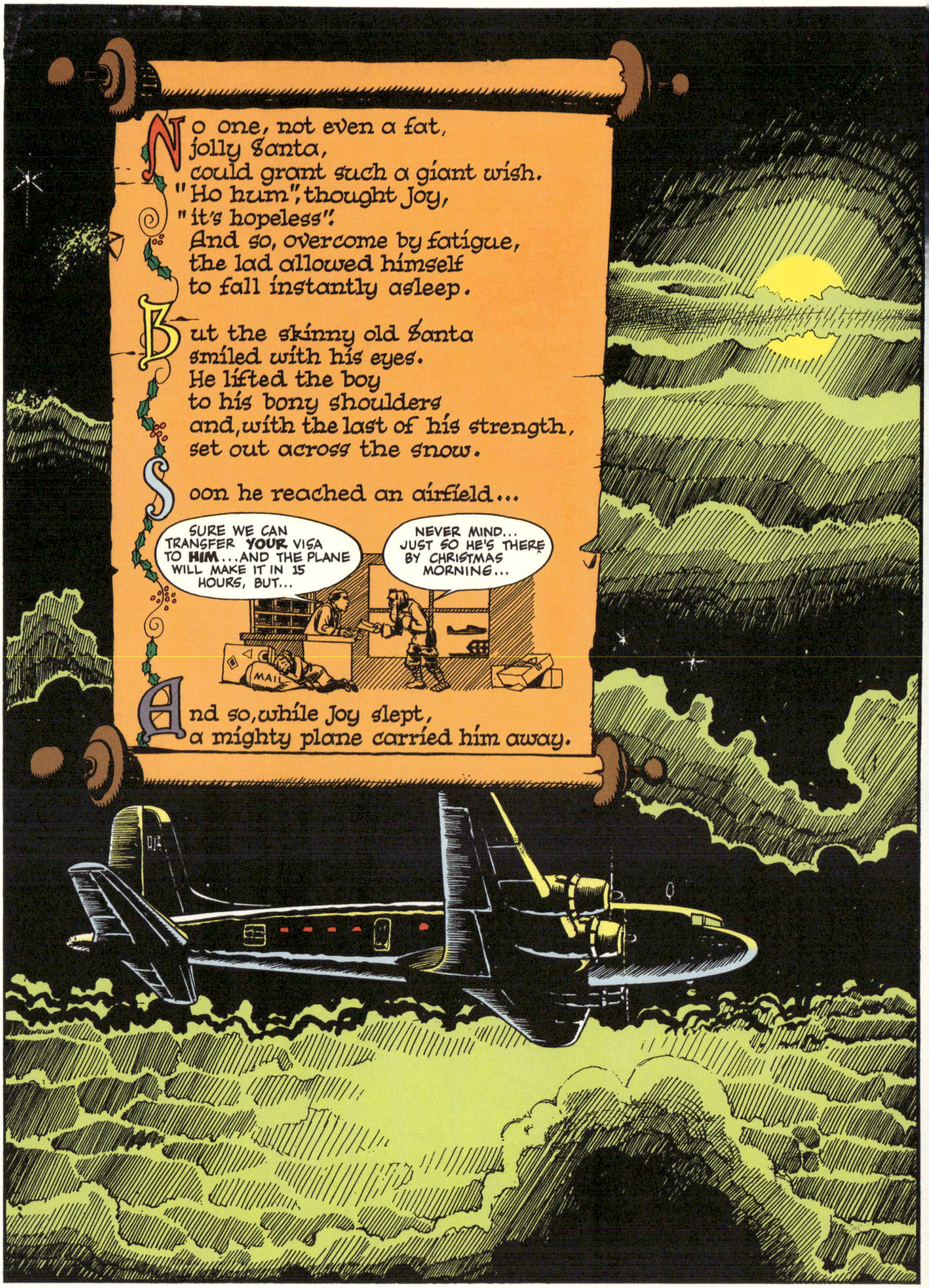

No one, not even a fat, jolly Santa, could grant such a giant wish. "Ho hum", thought Joy, "it's hopeless". And so, overcome by fatigue, the lad allowed himself to fall instantly asleep.
But the skinny old Santa smiled with his eyes. He lifted the boy to his bony shoulders and, with the last of his strength, set out across the snow.
Soon he reached an airfield...
SURE WE CAN TRANSFER YOUR VISA TO HIM...AND THE PLANE WILL MAKE IT IN 15 HOURS, BUT...
NEVER MIND... JUST SO HE'S THERE BY CHRISTMAS MORNING...
MAIL
And so, while Joy slept, a mighty plane carried him away.

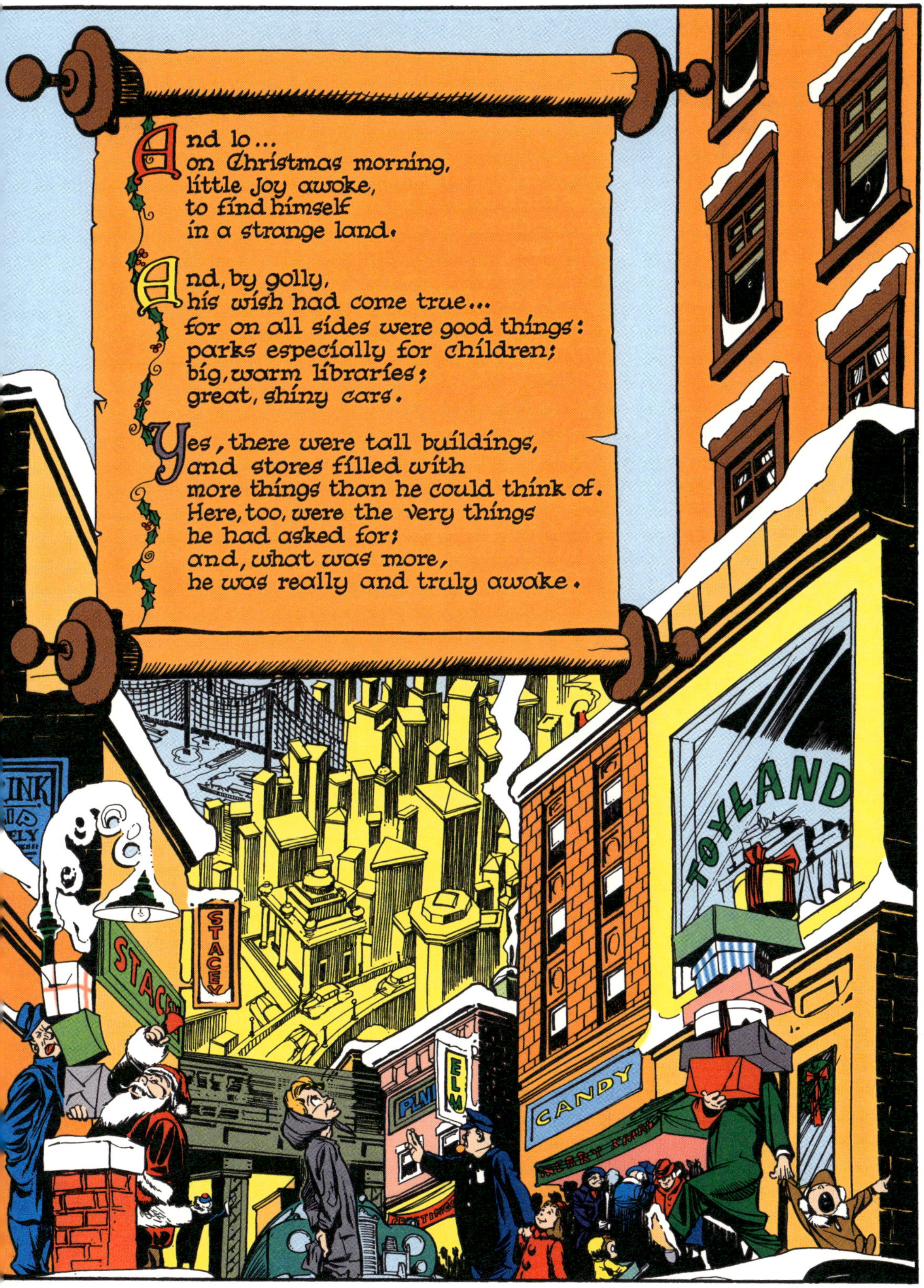
And lo...
on Christmas morning,
little Joy awoke,
to find himself
in a strange land.
And, by golly,
his wish had come true...
for on all sides were good things:
parks especially for children;
big, warm libraries;
great, shiny cars.
Yes, there were tall buildings,
and stores filled with
more things than he could think of.
Here, too, were the very things
he had asked for;
and, what was more,
he was really and truly awake.
STACEY
STACEY
TOYLAND
CANDY
ELM

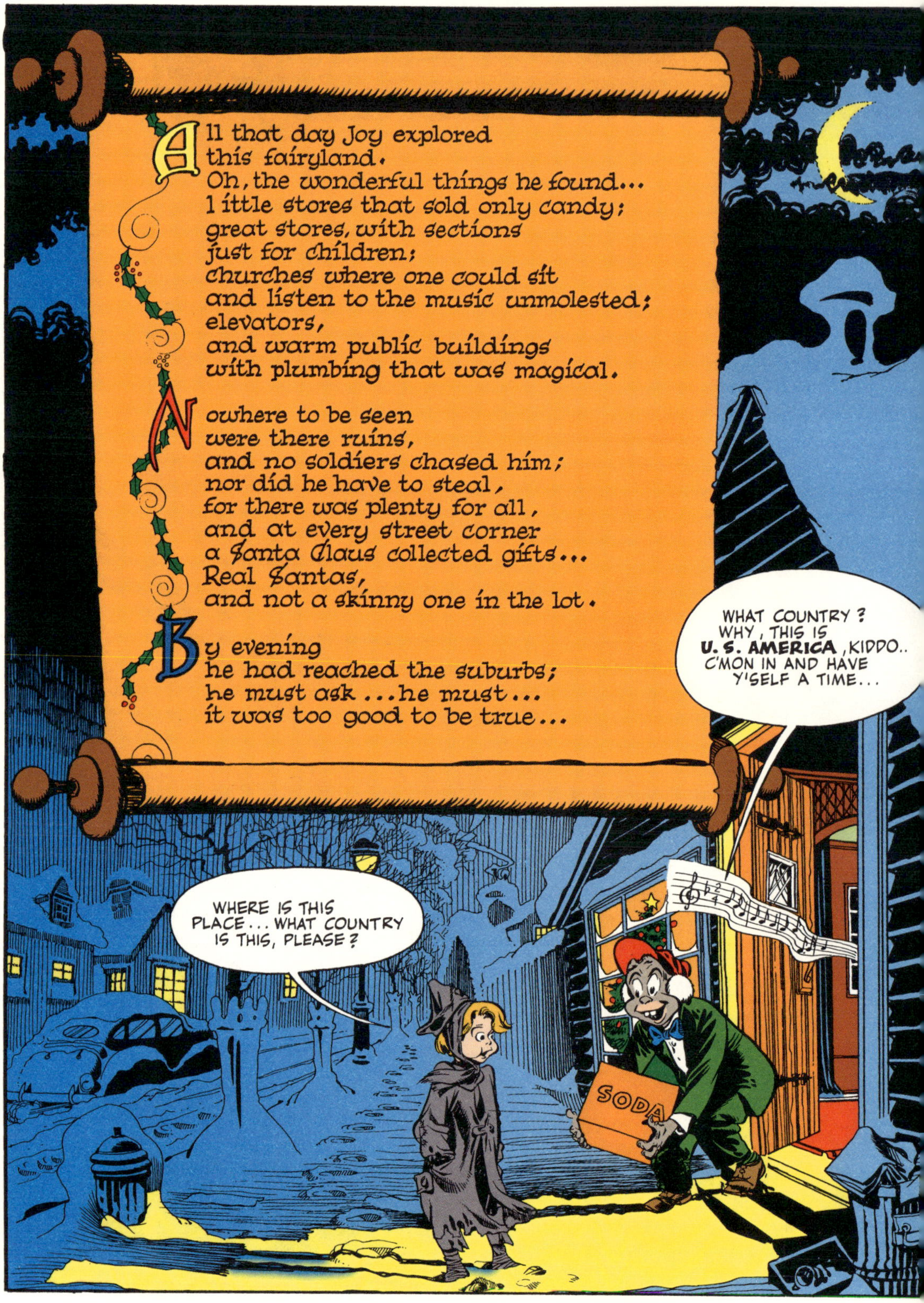
All that day Joy explored
this fairyland.
Oh, the wonderful things he found...
little stores that sold only candy;
great stores, with sections
just for children;
churches where one could sit
and listen to the music unmolested;
elevators,
and warm public buildings
with plumbing that was magical.
Nowhere to be seen
were there ruins,
and no soldiers chased him;
nor did he have to steal,
for there was plenty for all,
and at every street corner
a Santa Claus collected gifts...
Real Santas,
and not a skinny one in the lot.
By evening
he had reached the suburbs;
he must ask...he must...
it was too good to be true...
WHERE IS THIS PLACE... WHAT COUNTRY IS THIS, PLEASE?
WHAT COUNTRY? WHY, THIS IS U.S. AMERICA, KIDDO.. C'MON IN AND HAVE Y'SELF A TIME...
SODA

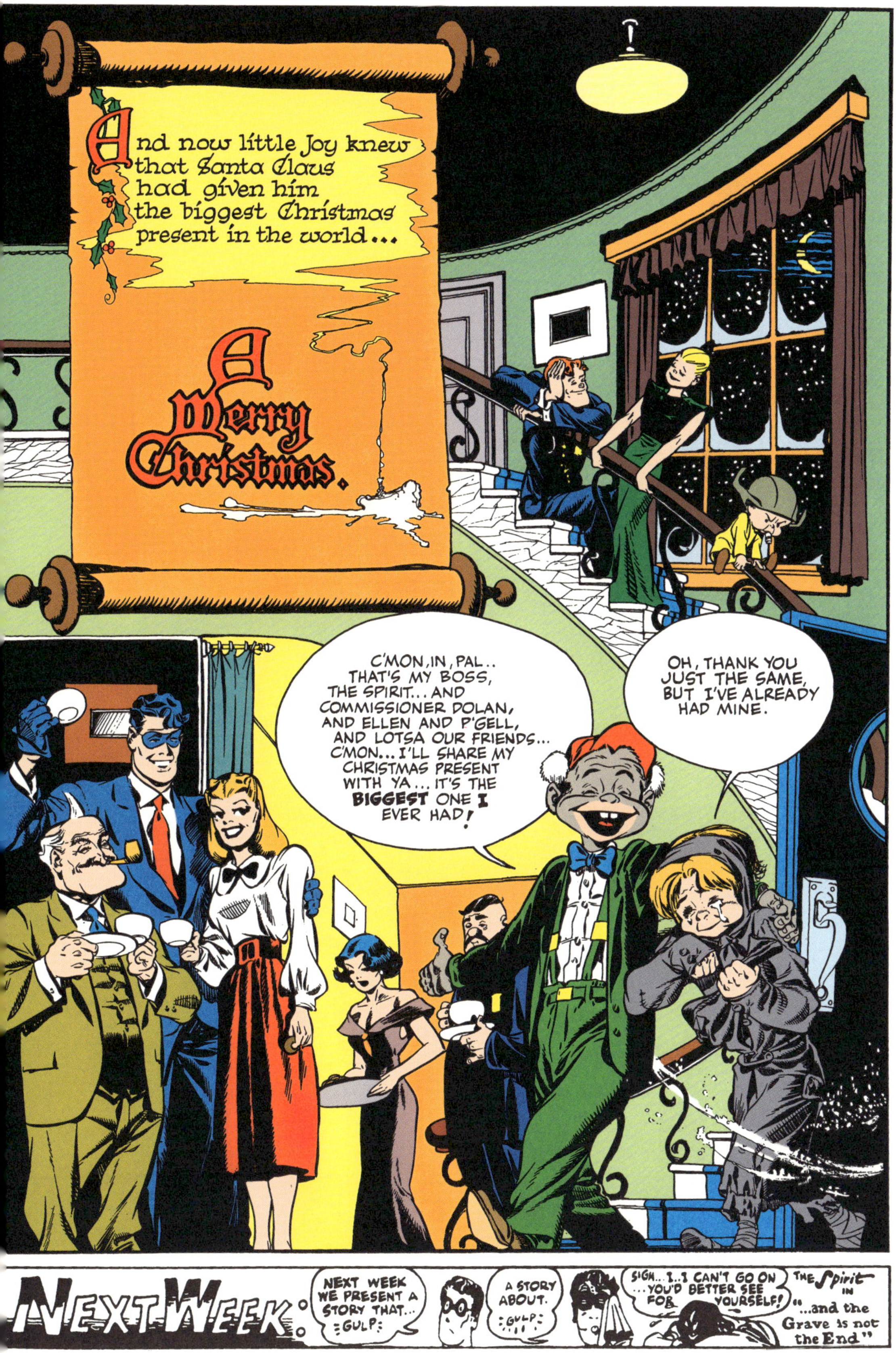
And now little Joy knew that Santa Claus had given him the biggest Christmas present in the world...
A Merry Christmas.
C'MON, IN, PAL.. THAT'S MY BOSS, THE SPIRIT... AND COMMISSIONER DOLAN, AND ELLEN AND P'GELL, AND LOTSA OUR FRIENDS... C'MON... I'LL SHARE MY CHRISTMAS PRESENT WITH YA... IT'S THE BIGGEST ONE I EVER HAD!
OH, THANK YOU JUST THE SAME, BUT I'VE ALREADY HAD MINE.
NEXT WEEK
NEXT WEEK WE PRESENT A STORY THAT... GULP
A STORY ABOUT. GULP
SIGH... I..I CAN'T GO ON ...YOU'D BETTER SEE FOR YOURSELF!
THE Spirit IN "...and the Grave is not the End"

UMBRELLA HANDLES

December 28 1947

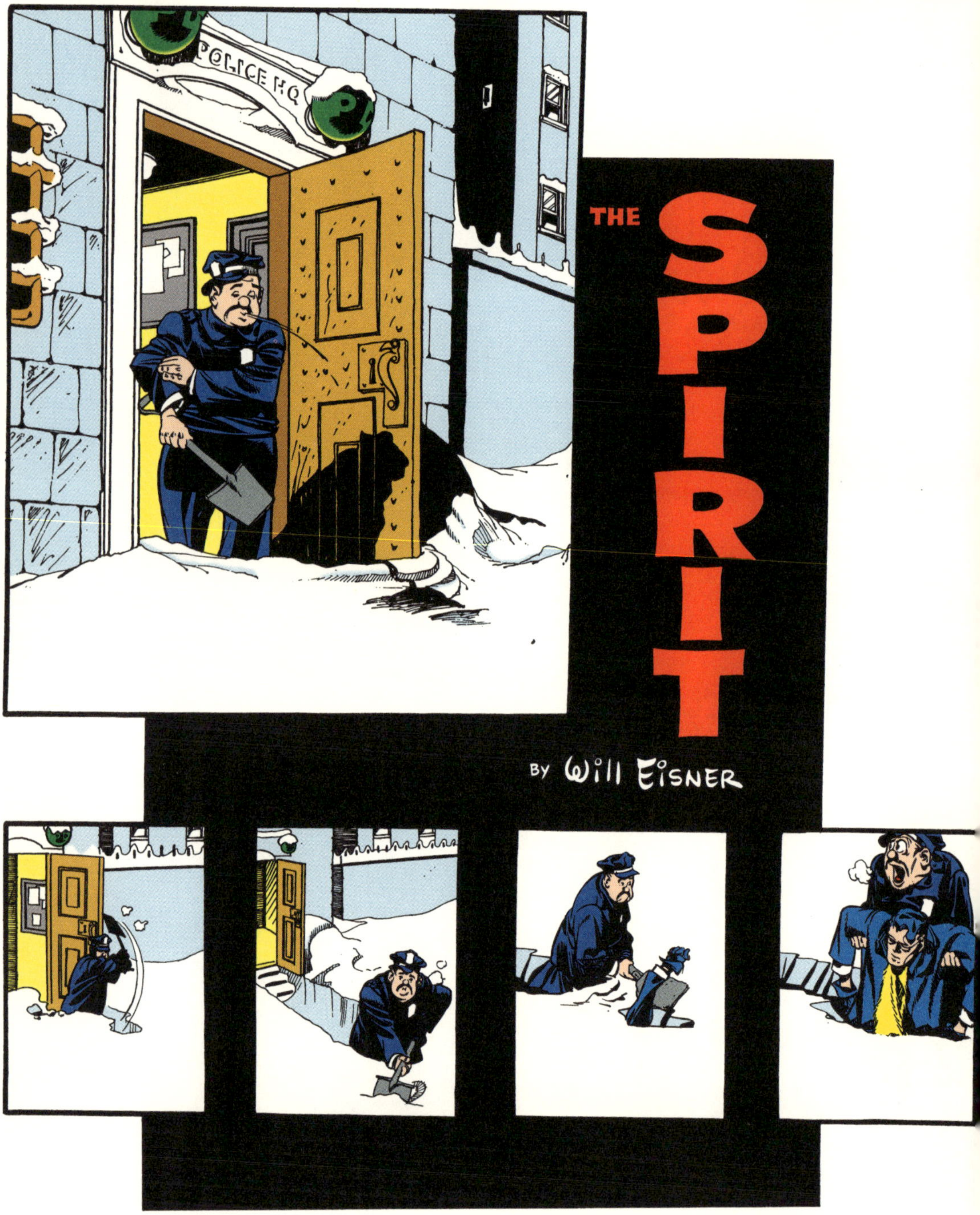
POLICE HQ
THE SPIRIT
BY Will Eisner

...OOH! SPIRIT, DARLING... YOU MUST HAVE BEEN LYING UNDER THE SNOW UNCONSCIOUS FOR HOURS!
WILL HE BE ALL RIGHT, DOC?
SURE!..THIS IS NOTHING COMPARED WITH SOME OF THE OTHER TIMES I'VE PATCHED HIM UP... MERELY A BRAIN CONCUSSION!
MEANWHILE... LET US LOOK IN UPON TWO PARTNERS IN CRIME, WHO PAUSE IN THE DAILY STRUGGLE TO MAKE A BUCK...
YOU ARE STUPID, STUPID!
BUT I TOLD YOU, I HIT THE SPIRIT ON THE NOGGIN WHEN I FOUN' OUT HE WUZ FOLLEYIN' ME... HE MUST BE DEAD BY NOW!
BUT ALWAYS THERE IS THAT DOUBT... NOW, WHAT ABOUT THOSE SURPLUS ARMY UMBRELLAS?
SURE... IT WUZ EASY... I EVEN GOT THE COPS T'HELP ME... DOLAN GIMME A LETTER TO W.A.A... SAID I WANTED TO GO STRAIGHT! ...CHUCKLE
I HOPE MY NAME, BARON VON SHLÖZZ, NEVER ENTERED THE TRANSACTION...
U.S. ARMY SURP
NAAAA... THEY WERE SO GLAD TO GET RID OF THEM UMBRELLAS THAT THEY GIMME THE STUFF ON THE FOIST BID!
FINE! NOW YOU CAN START REMOVING THE HANDLES OF ALL THESE UMBRELLAS...
THAT WAS SURE CLEVER, HIDING THEM JOOLS IN THE HANDLES OF U.S. ARMY UMBRELLAS!
BACK AT POLICE HEADQUARTERS, IN THE EMERGENCY WARD...
UGH..
MIST' SPIRIT, YO...
SHH... COME WITH ME...
AH DON'T LIKE THIS!
AH DOME WIKE FISS!
SHH!
2

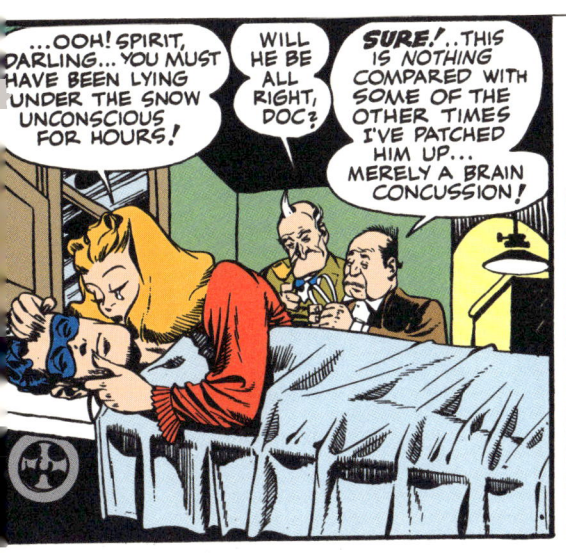

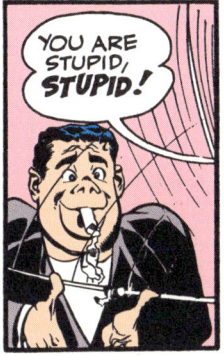

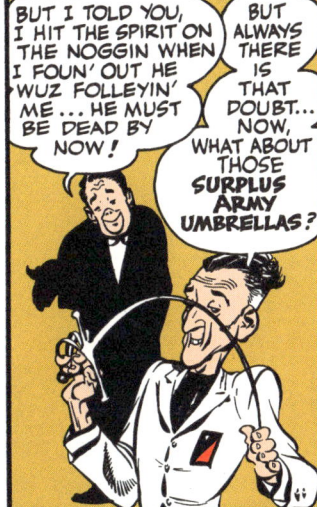

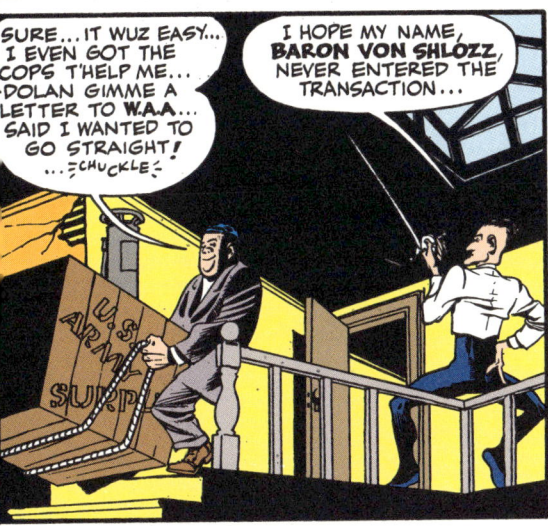

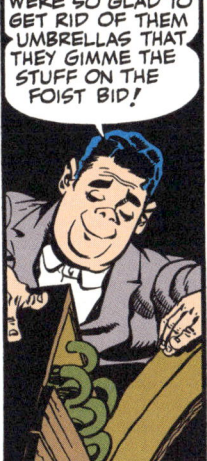

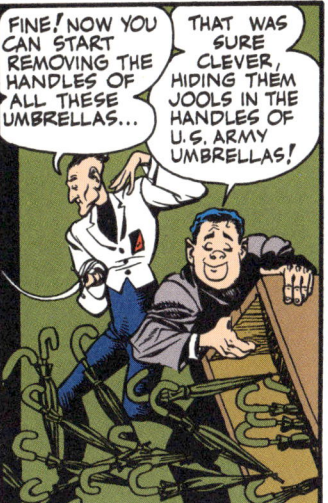

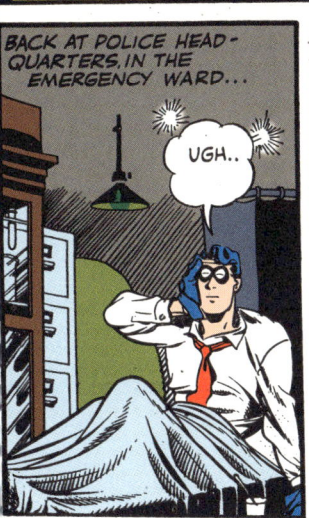

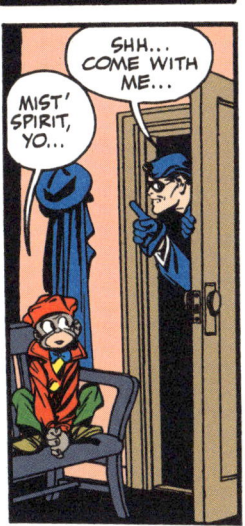

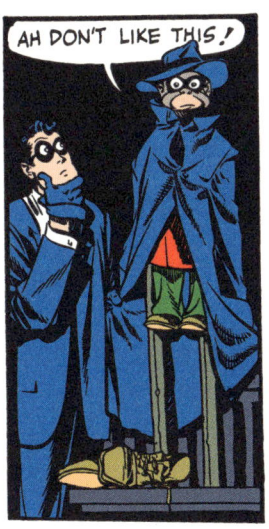

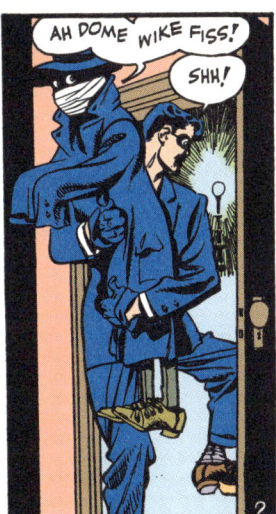

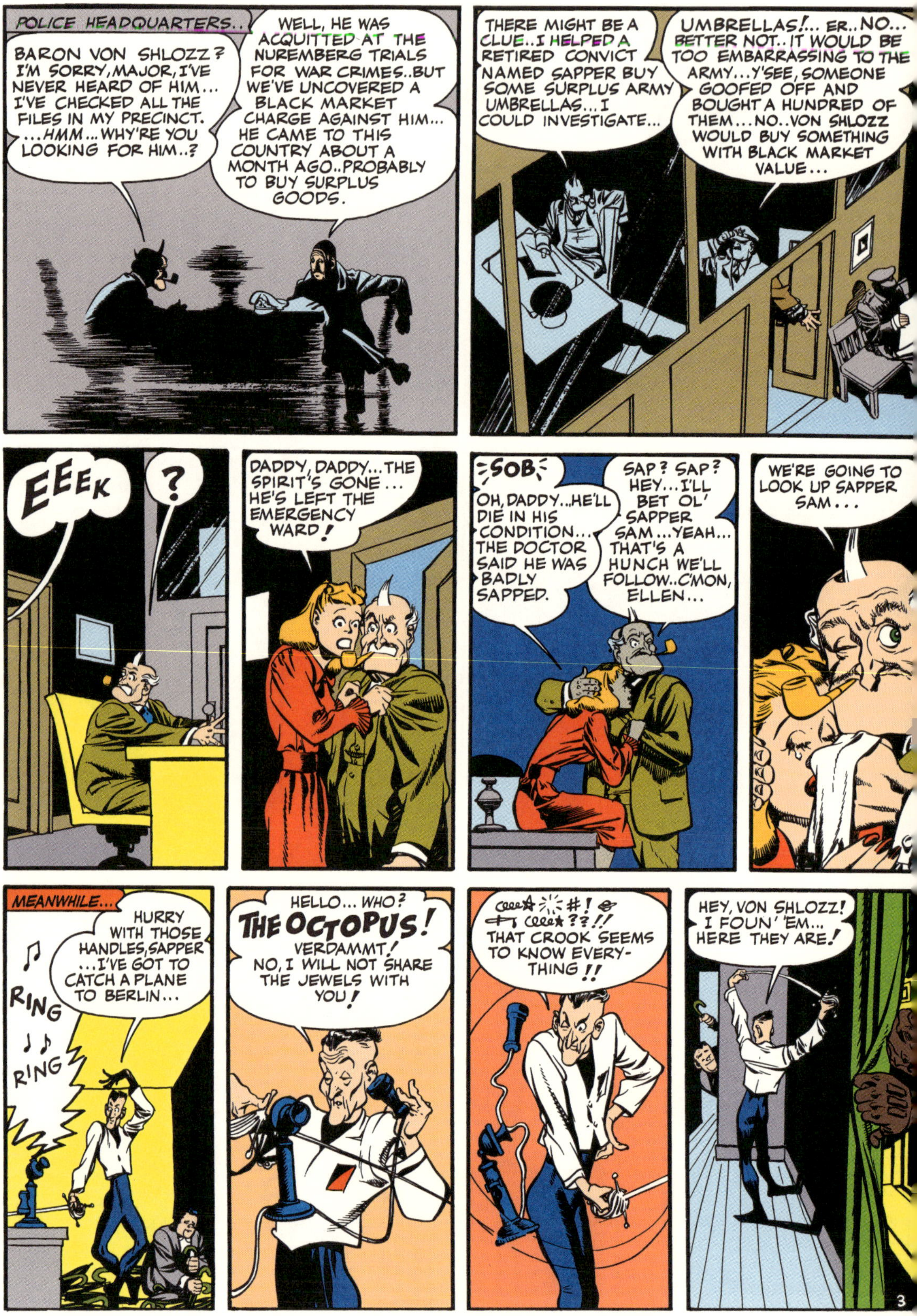
POLICE HEADQUARTERS..
BARON VON SHLOZZ? I'M SORRY, MAJOR, I'VE NEVER HEARD OF HIM... I'VE CHECKED ALL THE FILES IN MY PRECINCT. ...HMM... WHY'RE YOU LOOKING FOR HIM..?
WELL, HE WAS ACQUITTED AT THE NUREMBERG TRIALS FOR WAR CRIMES..BUT WE'VE UNCOVERED A BLACK MARKET CHARGE AGAINST HIM... HE CAME TO THIS COUNTRY ABOUT A MONTH AGO..PROBABLY TO BUY SURPLUS GOODS.
THERE MIGHT BE A CLUE..I HELPED A RETIRED CONVICT NAMED SAPPER BUY SOME SURPLUS ARMY UMBRELLAS...I COULD INVESTIGATE...
UMBRELLAS!... ER..NO... BETTER NOT.. IT WOULD BE TOO EMBARRASSING TO THE ARMY...Y'SEE, SOMEONE GOOFED OFF AND BOUGHT A HUNDRED OF THEM...NO..VON SHLOZZ WOULD BUY SOMETHING WITH BLACK MARKET VALUE...
EEEK
?
DADDY, DADDY...THE SPIRIT'S GONE... HE'S LEFT THE EMERGENCY WARD!
SOB
OH, DADDY...HE'LL DIE IN HIS CONDITION... THE DOCTOR SAID HE WAS BADLY SAPPED.
SAP? SAP? HEY...I'LL BET OL' SAPPER SAM...YEAH... THAT'S A HUNCH WE'LL FOLLOW..C'MON, ELLEN...
WE'RE GOING TO LOOK UP SAPPER SAM...
MEANWHILE...
RING
RING
HURRY WITH THOSE HANDLES, SAPPER ...I'VE GOT TO CATCH A PLANE TO BERLIN...
HELLO... WHO? THE OCTOPUS! VERDAMMT! NO, I WILL NOT SHARE THE JEWELS WITH YOU!
THAT CROOK SEEMS TO KNOW EVERY-THING!!
HEY, VON SHLOZZ! I FOUN' 'EM... HERE THEY ARE!
3

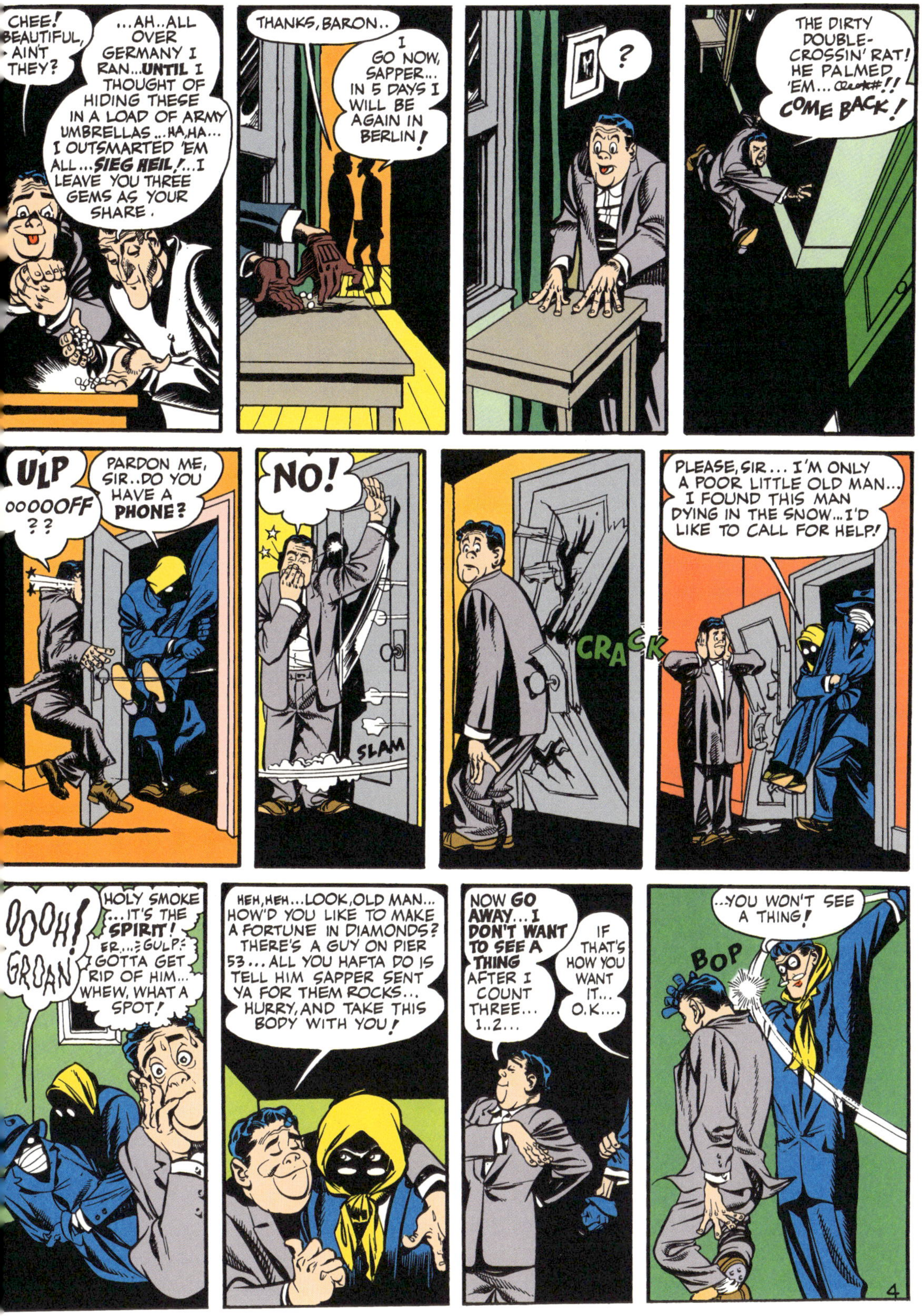
CHEE! BEAUTIFUL, AIN'T THEY?
...AH..ALL OVER GERMANY I RAN...UNTIL I THOUGHT OF HIDING THESE IN A LOAD OF ARMY UMBRELLAS...HA,HA... I OUTSMARTED 'EM ALL...SIEG HEIL!...I LEAVE YOU THREE GEMS AS YOUR SHARE.
THANKS, BARON..
I GO NOW, SAPPER... IN 5 DAYS I WILL BE AGAIN IN BERLIN!
?
THE DIRTY DOUBLE-CROSSIN' RAT! HE PALMED 'EM...
COME BACK!
ULP
OOOOOFF ??
PARDON ME, SIR..DO YOU HAVE A PHONE?
NO!
SLAM
CRACK
PLEASE, SIR... I'M ONLY A POOR LITTLE OLD MAN... I FOUND THIS MAN DYING IN THE SNOW...I'D LIKE TO CALL FOR HELP!
OOOH! GROAN
HOLY SMOKE ...IT'S THE SPIRIT! ER...GULP! GOTTA GET RID OF HIM... WHEW, WHAT A SPOT!
HEH,HEH...LOOK,OLD MAN... HOW'D YOU LIKE TO MAKE A FORTUNE IN DIAMONDS? THERE'S A GUY ON PIER 53...ALL YOU HAFTA DO IS TELL HIM SAPPER SENT YA FOR THEM ROCKS... HURRY, AND TAKE THIS BODY WITH YOU!
NOW GO AWAY...I DON'T WANT TO SEE A THING AFTER I COUNT THREE... 1..2...
IF THAT'S HOW YOU WANT IT... O.K....
...YOU WON'T SEE A THING!
BOP
4

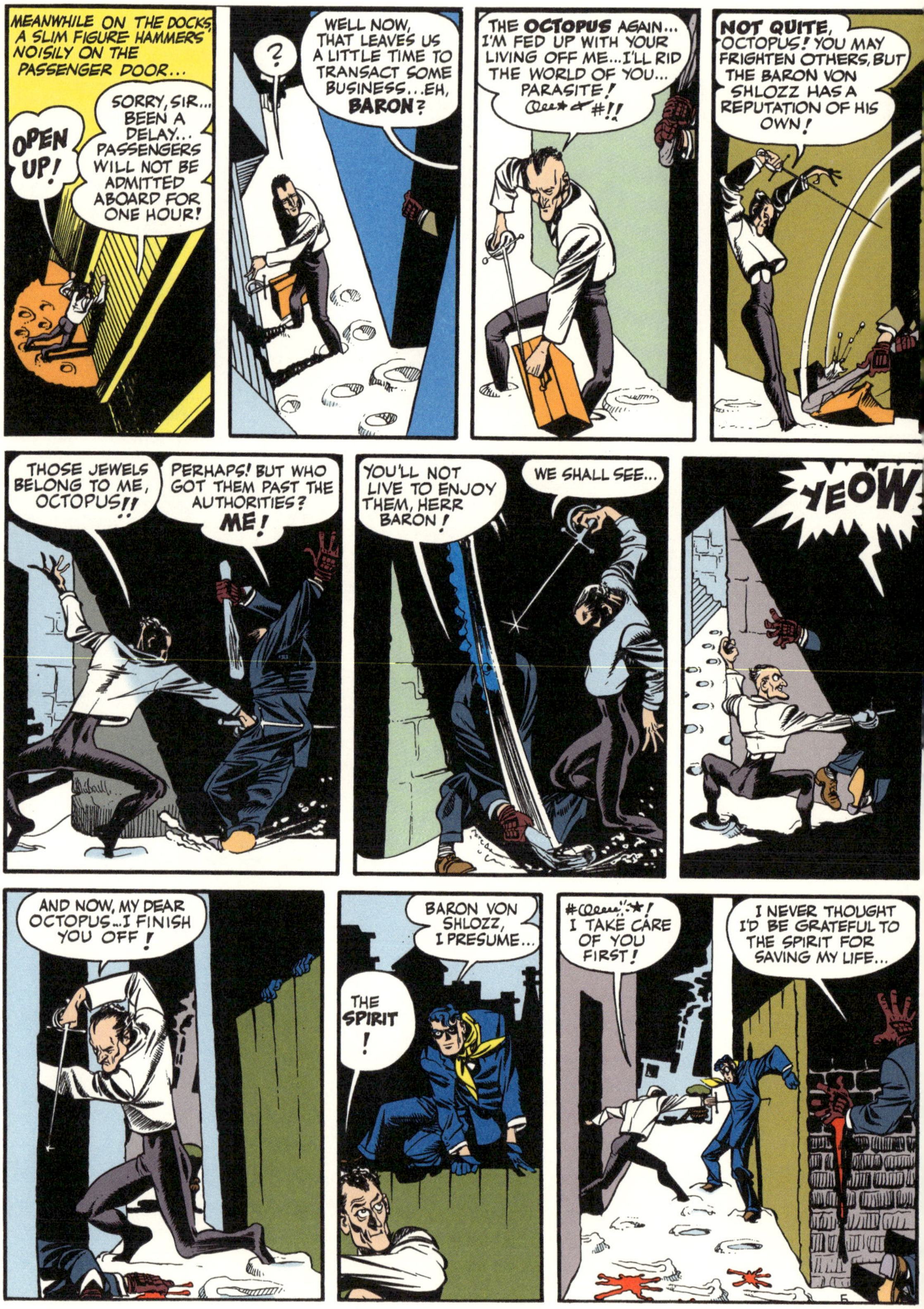
MEANWHILE ON THE DOCKS, A SLIM FIGURE HAMMERS NOISILY ON THE PASSENGER DOOR...
OPEN UP!
SORRY, SIR... BEEN A DELAY... PASSENGERS WILL NOT BE ADMITTED ABOARD FOR ONE HOUR!
?
WELL NOW, THAT LEAVES US A LITTLE TIME TO TRANSACT SOME BUSINESS...EH, BARON?
THE OCTOPUS AGAIN... I'M FED UP WITH YOUR LIVING OFF ME...I'LL RID THE WORLD OF YOU... PARASITE!
#!!
NOT QUITE, OCTOPUS! YOU MAY FRIGHTEN OTHERS, BUT THE BARON VON SHLOZZ HAS A REPUTATION OF HIS OWN!
THOSE JEWELS BELONG TO ME, OCTOPUS!!
PERHAPS! BUT WHO GOT THEM PAST THE AUTHORITIES? ME!
YOU'LL NOT LIVE TO ENJOY THEM, HERR BARON!
WE SHALL SEE...
YEOW
AND NOW, MY DEAR OCTOPUS...I FINISH YOU OFF!
BARON VON SHLOZZ, I PRESUME...
THE SPIRIT!
I TAKE CARE OF YOU FIRST!
I NEVER THOUGHT I'D BE GRATEFUL TO THE SPIRIT FOR SAVING MY LIFE...

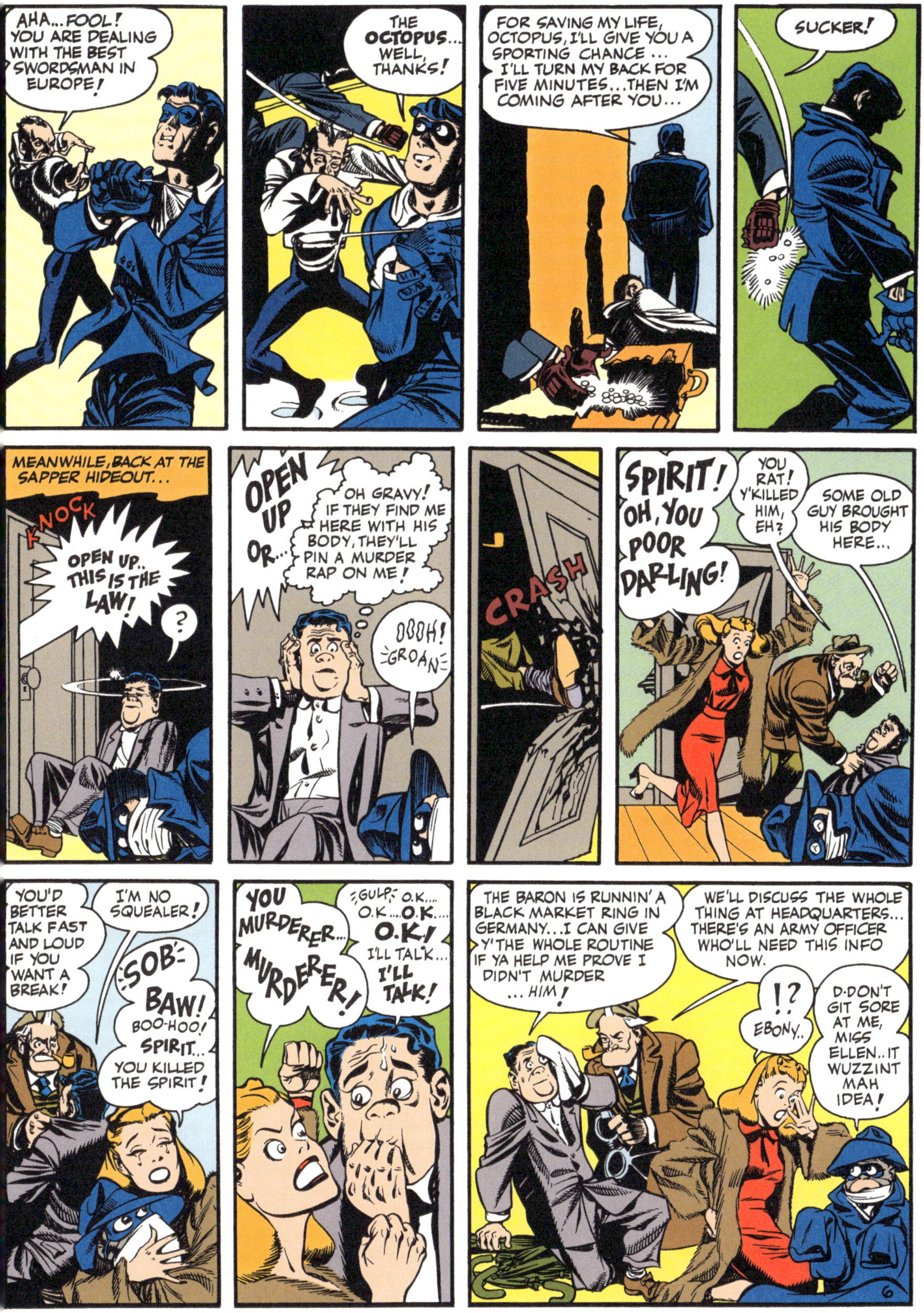
AHA...FOOL! YOU ARE DEALING WITH THE BEST SWORDSMAN IN EUROPE!
THE OCTOPUS... WELL, THANKS!
FOR SAVING MY LIFE, OCTOPUS, I'LL GIVE YOU A SPORTING CHANCE... I'LL TURN MY BACK FOR FIVE MINUTES...THEN I'M COMING AFTER YOU...
SUCKER!
MEANWHILE, BACK AT THE SAPPER HIDEOUT...
KNOCK
OPEN UP.. THIS IS THE LAW!
?
OPEN UP OR...
OH GRAVY! IF THEY FIND ME HERE WITH HIS BODY, THEY'LL PIN A MURDER RAP ON ME!
OOOH! GROAN
CRASH
SPIRIT! OH, YOU POOR DARLING!
YOU RAT! Y'KILLED HIM, EH?
SOME OLD GUY BROUGHT HIS BODY HERE...
YOU'D BETTER TALK FAST AND LOUD IF YOU WANT A BREAK!
I'M NO SQUEALER!
SOB BAW! BOO-HOO! SPIRIT... YOU KILLED THE SPIRIT!
YOU MURDERER... MURDERER!
GULP O.K.... O.K....O.K.... O.K.! I'LL TALK... I'LL TALK!
THE BARON IS RUNNIN' A BLACK MARKET RING IN GERMANY...I CAN GIVE Y'THE WHOLE ROUTINE IF YA HELP ME PROVE I DIDN'T MURDER ... HIM!
WE'LL DISCUSS THE WHOLE THING AT HEADQUARTERS... THERE'S AN ARMY OFFICER WHO'LL NEED THIS INFO NOW.
!? EBONY..
D-DON'T GIT SORE AT ME, MISS ELLEN..IT WUZZINT MAH IDEA!
6

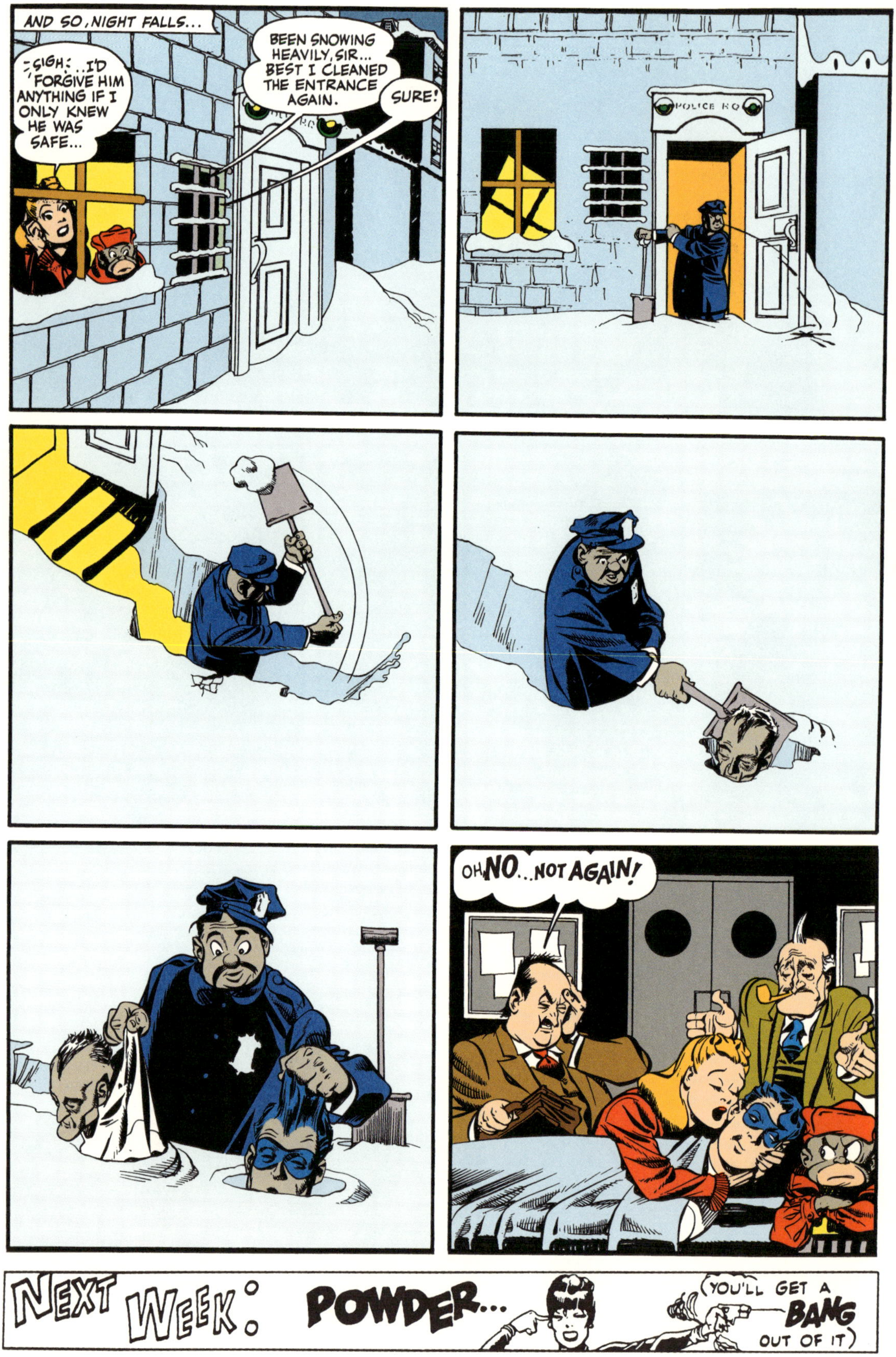
AND SO, NIGHT FALLS...
SIGH ..I'D FORGIVE HIM ANYTHING IF I ONLY KNEW HE WAS SAFE...
BEEN SNOWING HEAVILY, SIR... BEST I CLEANED THE ENTRANCE AGAIN.
SURE!
POLICE HQ
OH, NO... NOT AGAIN!
NEXT WEEK: POWDER... (YOU'LL GET A BANG OUT OF IT)

THE WILL EISNER LIBRARY

The Building
City People Notebook
A Contract With God
The Dreamer
Dropsie Avenue: The Neighborhood
Family Matter
Invisible People
A Life Force
Life on Another Planet
Minor Miracles
The Name of the Game
New York, the Big City
To the Heart of the Storm
Will Eisner Reader

WILL EISNER'S THE SPIRIT ARCHIVES

Will Eisner's The Spirit collected in chronological order in full-color, hardcover editions.

SPIRIT DARLING.. I'VE ALWAYS ADMIRED THE STRONG PRIMITIVE MAN...PULEEZE!

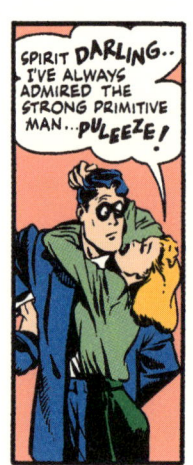

The Will Eisner Companion: The Pioneering Spirit of the Father of the Graphic Novel
by N. C. Christopher Couch and Stephen Weiner

THE DC ARCHIVE EDITIONS

Re-presenting historic comics characters and their stories as they were originally seen.

ALL STAR COMICS ARCHIVES
Volumes 1 - 10
(Featuring the adventures of the JUSTICE SOCIETY OF AMERICA)

BATMAN ARCHIVES
Volumes 1 - 5
(The Dark Knight's early adventures from DETECTIVE COMICS)

BATMAN: THE DARK KNIGHT ARCHIVES
Volumes 1 - 4
(The Dark Knight's early adventures from BATMAN)

BATMAN IN WORLD'S FINEST ARCHIVES
Volumes 1 - 2
(The adventures of Batman and Robin from WORLD'S FINEST COMICS)

THE BLACK CANARY ARCHIVES
Volume 1
(The Golden and Silver Age adventures of the Blonde Bombshell from FLASH COMICS and more)

GOLDEN AGE GREEN LANTERN ARCHIVES
Volumes 1 - 2
(The adventures of Alan Scott, the original Emerald Gladiator, from ALL-AMERICAN COMICS and the GREEN LANTERN quarterly)

THE GOLDEN AGE SANDMAN ARCHIVES
Volume 1
(The adventures of Wesley Todds from ADVENTURE COMICS)

GOLDEN AGE STARMAN ARCHIVES
Volume 1
(The Man of Night's earliest adventures from ADVENTURE COMICS)

PLASTIC MAN ARCHIVES
Volumes 1 - 5
(Jack Cole's classic stories from POLICE COMICS)

THE SHAZAM! ARCHIVES
Volumes 1 - 4
(Captain Marvel's adventures from WHIZ COMICS, CAPTAIN MARVEL ADVENTURES and SPECIAL EDITION COMICS)

THE GOLDEN AGE SPECTRE ARCHIVES
Volume 1
(The earliest adventures of the Spirit of Vengeance from MORE FUN COMICS)

SUPERMAN ARCHIVES
Volumes 1 - 6
(The Man of Steel's early adventures from SUPERMAN)

SUPERMAN IN WORLD'S FINEST ARCHIVES
Volume 1
(The Man of Steel's early adventures from ACTION COMICS)

SUPERMAN: THE ACTION COMICS ARCHIVES
Volumes 1 - 3
(The Man of Steel's early adventures from ACTION COMICS)

WONDER WOMAN ARCHIVES
Volumes 1 - 4
(The Amazing Amazon's adventures from SENSATION COMICS and WONDER WOMAN)

WORLD'S FINEST COMICS ARCHIVES
Volumes 1 - 2
The original team-up tales starring Batman, Superman and Robin)